AN INTRODUCTION TO
SOCIOLOGY

Sara Miller McCune founded SAGE Publishing in 1965 to support the dissemination of usable knowledge and educate a global community. SAGE publishes more than 1000 journals and over 800 new books each year, spanning a wide range of subject areas. Our growing selection of library products includes archives, data, case studies and video. SAGE remains majority owned by our founder and after her lifetime will become owned by a charitable trust that secures the company's continued independence.

Los Angeles | London | New Delhi | Singapore | Washington DC | Melbourne

AN INTRODUCTION TO
SOCIOLOGY

Edited by

KARIM MURJI, SARAH NEAL & JOHN SOLOMOS

Los Angeles | London | New Delhi
Singapore | Washington DC | Melbourne

Los Angeles | London | New Delhi
Singapore | Washington DC | Melbourne

SAGE Publications Ltd
1 Oliver's Yard
55 City Road
London EC1Y 1SP

SAGE Publications Inc.
2455 Teller Road
Thousand Oaks, California 91320

SAGE Publications India Pvt Ltd
B 1/I 1 Mohan Cooperative Industrial Area
Mathura Road
New Delhi 110 044

SAGE Publications Asia-Pacific Pte Ltd
3 Church Street
#10-04 Samsung Hub
Singapore 049483

Editor: Natalie Aguilera
Assistant editor: Ozlem Merakli
Assistant editor, digital: Katherine Payne
Production editor: Katherine Haw
Copyeditor: Fern Bryant
Proofreader: Sharon Cawood
Indexer: Elizabeth Ball
Marketing manager: George Kimble
Cover design: Francis Kenney
Typeset by: C&M Digitals (P) Ltd, Chennai, India
Printed in the UK

© Chapter 1 Karim Murji, Sarah Neal and John Solomos 2022
© Chapter 2 Noortje Marres 2022
© Chapter 3 Kate Burningham 2022
© Chapter 4 Eamonn Carrabine 2022
© Chapter 5 John Scott 2022
© Chapter 6 Manuela Boatcă 2022
© Chapter 7 Daniel Chernilo and Kieran Durkin 2022
© Chapter 8 Simon Susen 2022
© Chapter 9 Stella Chatzitheochari 2022
© Chapter 10 Cath Lambert 2022
© Chapter 11 Wendy Bottero 2022
© Chapter 12 Kath Woodward and Sophie Woodward 2022
© Chapter 13 Tina G. Patel 2022
© Chapter 14 Anna Wanka 2022
© Chapter 15 Rosalind Edwards 2022
© Chapter 16 Katherine Twamley and Julia Carter 2022
© Chapter 17 Lynne Pettinger 2022
© Chapter 18 Sarah Cant 2022
© Chapter 19 Nasima Hassan 2022
© Chapter 20 Adam Possamai and Kathleen Openshaw 2022
© Chapter 21 David Wright 2022
© Chapter 22 Christian Olsson 2022
© Chapter 23 Ros Williams 2022
© Chapter 24 Anna Gawlewicz 2022
© Chapter 25 Nick Crossley 2022
© Chapter 26 William Outhwaite 2022
© Chapter 27 Paul Jones 2022
© Chapter 28 Karim Murji, Sarah Neal and John Solomos 2022

Apart from any fair dealing for the purposes of research, private study, or criticism or review, as permitted under the Copyright, Designs and Patents Act, 1988, this publication may not be reproduced, stored or transmitted in any form, or by any means, without the prior permission in writing of the publisher, or in the case of reprographic reproduction, in accordance with the terms of licences issued by the Copyright Licensing Agency. Enquiries concerning reproduction outside those terms should be sent to the publisher.

Library of Congress Control Number: 2021947538

British Library Cataloguing in Publication data

A catalogue record for this book is available from the British Library

ISBN 978-1-5264-9280-7
ISBN 978-1-5264-9279-1 (pbk)

At SAGE we take sustainability seriously. Most of our products are printed in the UK using responsibly sourced papers and boards. When we print overseas we ensure sustainable papers are used as measured by the PREPS grading system. We undertake an annual audit to monitor our sustainability.

TABLE OF CONTENTS

List of Figures and Tables	viii
About the Editors	ix
About the Contributors	x
Thanks from the Publishers	xv
Discover the Online Resources	xvi
Preface	xvii

PART 1: THINKING SOCIOLOGICALLY — 1

Introduction to Part 1 — 2

1. Approaching Sociology — 5
   Karim Murji, Sarah Neal and John Solomos

2. What is Sociological about the Digital Society? — 18
   Noortje Marres

3. What is Sociological about the Environment? — 37
   Kate Burningham

4. What is Sociological about Crime? — 54
   Eamonn Carrabine

5. What is Society? — 75
   John Scott

6. Sociology of an Interconnected World — 89
   Manuela Boatcă

PART 2: THEORIES AND METHODS — 103

Introduction to Part 2 — 104

7. Classical Sociologies — 107
   Daniel Chernilo and Kieran Durkin

TABLE OF CONTENTS

8	Contemporary Social Theory *Simon Susen*	121
9	Beyond the Qualitative/Quantitative Divide *Stella Chatzitheochari*	142
10	Visual and Digital Methods of Research *Cath Lambert*	156

PART 3: INEQUALITIES AND IDENTITIES — 173

Introduction to Part 3 — 174

11	Class *Wendy Bottero*	177
12	Gender *Kath Woodward and Sophie Woodward*	196
13	Race *Tina G. Patel*	212
14	Age *Anna Wanka*	225

PART 4: CONNECTING THE PERSONAL AND THE SOCIAL — 241

Introduction to Part 4 — 242

15	Families and Households *Rosalind Edwards*	245
16	Intimacies and Relationships *Katherine Twamley and Julia Carter*	262
17	Work *Lynne Pettinger*	279
18	Health *Sarah Cant*	293
19	Education *Nasima Hassan*	310
20	Religion *Adam Possamai and Kathleen Openshaw*	325

TABLE OF CONTENTS

PART 5: SOCIOLOGICAL FRONTIERS — 341

Introduction to Part 5 — 342

21. Cultures and Consumption — 345
    David Wright

22. War and Violence — 360
    Christian Olsson

23. Science and Technology — 377
    Ros Williams

24. Migrations — 391
    Anna Gawlewicz

25. Social Movements — 409
    Nick Crossley

PART 6: WHAT IS SOCIOLOGY USEFUL FOR? — 425

Introduction to Part 6 — 426

26. Sociology as a Science — 429
    William Outhwaite

27. Public Sociology? — 443
    Paul Jones

28. Using Sociology — 457
    Karim Murji, Sarah Neal and John Solomos

Glossary — 469

Index — 490

LIST OF FIGURES AND TABLES

Image 3.1	The Message of Individual Responsibility for a Sustainable Future	48
Table 4.1	Merton's Individual Responses to Anomie	57
Table 4.2	Theoretical Reincarnations	64
Figure 4.1	Postmodern Urbanism	66
Figure 24.1	Cities with the Largest Foreign-Born Population Share	399

ABOUT THE EDITORS

Karim Murji is Professor of Social Policy at the University of West London. His research and publications cover areas such as racism, race equality and social policy, migration, and policing. With John Solomos and others, he is currently working on an ESRC-funded project on the Open City, which investigates how the city accommodates new forms of urban life, through the social reconfiguration of its spaces and places, and looks at the ways urban government at the city-wide and borough scales reflect, promote or limit the idea of the open city, using London as a case study. With Sarah Neal he is the Editor of *Current Sociology*, and they were previously the editors of *Sociology*.

Sarah Neal is Professor of Sociology in the Department of Sociological Studies at the University of Sheffield, UK. Sarah researches social relations and interactions in the fields of ethnicity, multiculture, community, belonging and place. Her publications include work on neighbours, friendships, social participation and the lived experiences of multiculture in both urban and rural contexts. She was a member of the editorial team (with Karim Murji) of *Sociology* (2013–17) and she is a co-editor (with Karim Murji) of *Current Sociology* and a member of the editorial board of *Ethnic and Racial Studies*.

John Solomos is Professor of Sociology at the University of Warwick. He has researched and written widely on the history and contemporary forms of race and ethnic relations in Britain, theories of race and racism, the politics of race, equal opportunity policies, multiculturalism and social policy, race and football, and racist movements and ideas. He is currently working on an ESRC-funded project on the Open City, which is investigating how London accommodates new forms of urban life, through the social reconfiguration of its spaces and places, and looks at the ways urban government at the city-wide and borough scales reflects, promotes or limits the idea of the open city. He is Editor-in-Chief of the international journal *Ethnic and Racial Studies*.

ABOUT THE CONTRIBUTORS

Manuela Boatcă is Professor of Sociology and Head of School of the Global Studies Programme at the University of Freiburg, Germany. She has published widely on world-systems analysis, decolonial perspectives on global inequalities, gender and citizenship in modernity/coloniality, and the geopolitics of knowledge in Eastern Europe, Latin America, and the Caribbean. She has a degree in English and German languages and literatures and a PhD in sociology. Her book *Creolizing the Modern: Transylvania Across Empires*, co-authored with literary scholar Anca Parvulescu (Washington University in St. Louis, USA), is forthcoming in English, German, and Romanian in 2022.

Wendy Bottero is Reader in Sociology at the University of Manchester. She researches and teaches in the areas of stratification and inequality, social mobility and class reproduction; and how social ties, interactions and identities are bound up with social divisions. She has a particular interest in subjective inequality and how ordinary people perceive, make sense of and respond to social inequalities.

Kate Burningham is Professor of Sociology in the Department of Sociology and the Centre for Environment and Sustainability at the University of Surrey. Kate's research focuses on issues of environment and sustainability, with a particular interest in the social construction of environmental problems, public environmental knowledge, environmental inequalities and sustainable lifestyles. Kate is currently Deputy Director of the ESRC-funded Centre for Understanding Sustainable Prosperity (CUSP) and has previously also conducted research for The Joseph Rowntree Foundation, The Environment Agency, Defra and the Scottish Government. She teaches undergraduates and postgraduate modules on Sociology of the Environment, Sociology of Consumption and Research Methods, and has supervised numerous PhD projects.

Sarah Cant is a Principal Lecturer and Medical Sociologist at Canterbury Christ Church University. Combined with her long-standing interest in complementary medicine, Sarah has undertaken research focused on the mental health of undergraduates, and this extends to a wider examination of the changing landscape of higher education. Her commitment to understanding and tackling social exclusion and health inequality is linked to a study on social polarization in the seaside town of Margate. Developing from her support for local sociology schoolteachers and students, Sarah has undertaken research examining the status of sociology and is developing new school-based resources that showcase the value of the discipline.

Eamonn Carrabine is a Professor of Sociology at the University of Essex, where his research interests lie in the fields of criminology, cultural studies and sociology more generally. He recently held a Leverhulme Trust Major Research Fellowship to research his project 'The Iconography of Punishment: From Renaissance to Modernity', which will be published as a book. He currently serves as Editor-in-Chief on the *British Journal of Criminology*, and co-edits the Palgrave Macmillan Crime, Media and Culture book series.

Julia Carter is a Senior Lecturer in Sociology at the University of the West of England, Bristol. Julia has published widely in the field of family research, focusing on couple relationships, inequalities and family practices. Her previous research projects have involved studying marriage, living apart together relationships, weddings and inequalities and, more recently, different-sex civil partnerships. She is particularly interested in how tradition and morality continue to operate within families and couple relationships, despite significant changes in the structure of intimacy. Her book *Reinventing Couples: Tradition, Agency and Bricolage* (with co-author Simon Duncan) was published in 2018; and in 2020 her co-edited collection (with Lorena Arocha) *Romantic Relationships in a Time of 'Cold Intimacies'* was published, both by Palgrave Macmillan.

Stella Chatzitheochari is Associate Professor of Sociology at the University of Warwick. Stella has published widely on various topics surrounding everyday life and time allocation, and has been previously involved in the survey design and implementation of large-scale time-use surveys. Another strand of her research focuses on inequalities experienced by disabled children and young people. She is currently Principal Investigator of a Leverhulme Research Project Grant on *Educational Pathways and Work Outcomes of Disabled Young People in England* (2020–23). Stella has a long-standing interest in making research methods accessible to undergraduate students through embedded learning strategies.

Daniel Chernilo is a Professor of Sociology in the School of Government at Universidad Adolfo Ibáñez in Santiago, Chile, and a Visiting Professor of Social and Political Thought at Loughborough University in the UK. His books include *A Social Theory of the Nation-State* (Routledge, 2007), *The Natural Law Foundations of Modern Social Theory* (CUP, 2013) and *Debating Humanity: Towards a Philosophical Sociology* (CUP, 2017).

Nick Crossley is a Professor of Sociology and co-founder/co-director of the Mitchell Centre for Social Network Analysis at the University of Manchester. He has published on a wide range of topics including music sociology, social theory, embodiment and social movements. In his most recent work, he sought to develop and advocate a relational approach to music sociology, building upon his own earlier work on relational sociology.

Kieran Durkin is currently Marie Skłodowska-Curie Global Fellow at the University of York and former Visiting Scholar at the University of California, Santa Barbara, where he has been studying the Marxist humanist tradition. He is interested in re-appraising the position of humanism relative to the dominant ideological positions in the humanities and social sciences, and in re-appropriating a critical, radical humanism for the theoretical and practical tasks of the future.

Rosalind Edwards is Professor of Sociology in the Department of Sociology, Social Policy and Criminology at the University of Southampton. She is an elected Fellow of the Academy of Social Sciences and a founding and co-editor of the *International Journal of Social Research Methodology*. Ros's substantive area of interest is families. She runs an undergraduate option on families as well as postgraduate modules on social theory and on qualitative methods. She has researched and published widely on family policies and family lives, nationally and internationally. At the moment, she is leading a project looking at parents' views on identifying particular families for service intervention by joining up and analysing data about them from different sources.

ABOUT THE CONTRIBUTORS

Anna Gawlewicz is Lecturer in Public Policy and Research Methods at the University of Glasgow. Anna has published on international migration and social diversity and, as well as teaching on undergraduate and postgraduate courses on migration and social policy, she has contributed to many research projects exploring Central and Eastern European migration to the UK, including in the context of Brexit and the COVID-19 pandemic. Anna has a PhD in human geography and extensive postdoctoral research experience. She is currently engaged in policy-strategic research investigating the impacts of COVID-19 on migrant essential workers in the UK.

Nasima Hassan works in teacher education and research at Star Academies. She has worked in strategic leadership in higher education, teaching at undergraduate and postgraduate level and supporting student volunteer experiences in sustainable education overseas. She has worked extensively in South Africa, India and, more recently, with UNHCR in Malaysia, supporting teacher education. Her research interests include postcolonial theory and representation. Her current project aims to re-write the narratives of British Muslim women as teachers of science and change-makers.

Paul Jones is Senior Lecturer in Sociology at the University of Liverpool. Paul runs modules on sociological theory, urban sociology, and visual methods, as well as one on 'Architecture and Power'. This last module fits squarely with his research, which often involves the sociological study of architecture, analysing the relationships between buildings and social life.

Cath Lambert is Associate Professor of Sociology at the University of Warwick. She teaches and researches in the areas of sociology of education, and gender and sexuality. Her most recent research focuses on the development and use of 'live' and creative sociological methods, and her work involves close collaboration with creative practitioners.

Noortje Marres is Professor in the Centre for Interdisciplinary Methodologies at the University of Warwick. Her work contributes to the interdisciplinary field of Science, Technology and Society, and she has played a leading role in the development of the emerging field of Digital Sociology. Noortje has published widely on new forms of participation in technological societies, such as sustainable living experiments, and she has contributed to the development of social research methodologies, in particular digital methods of issue mapping. She is currently PI on the international research project Shaping AI, which investigates artificial intelligence as a socio-technical phenomenon. She is the author of *Digital Sociology* (Polity, 2017).

Christian Olsson is Associate Professor in Political Science at Université libre de Bruxelles (Free University of Brussels, ULB) in Belgium, where he teaches international relations, international security and methodology courses, among others. He is director of ULB's REPI research centre (Recherche et études en politique internationale) in international politics and affiliated to its observatory of the Arab and Muslim worlds (OMAM). His current research and publications focus on non-state-armed groups and political violence in the Middle East, from a historical-sociological perspective, the privatization of security and Western military interventions in the region (Iraq, Libya, and also Afghanistan).

Kathleen Openshaw is a Lecturer in the School of Social Sciences at Western Sydney University where she also graduated with a PhD. Kathleen's main research interests are Pentecostalisms from the Global South, local lived migrant religious expressions of globalized Pentecostalisms and material religion. Her PhD research was an ethnography of the Brazilian megachurch, The Universal Church of the Kingdom of God

ABOUT THE CONTRIBUTORS

(UCKG), in Australia. Kathleen is currently a member of the research team for an Australian Research Council Discovery Project, 'The African Diaspora and Christianity in Australia'.

William Outhwaite studied at the universities of Oxford and Sussex and taught at Sussex and at Newcastle University, where he is Emeritus Professor of Sociology. He now lives near Oxford. William has published widely on the philosophy of science and social theory, especially the critical theory of the Frankfurt School. He has also worked substantially on contemporary Europe, comparing social structures and political systems across the sub-continent. His most recent work has been on large regions within Europe such as the Baltic and Danube areas. He is a fellow of the UK's Academy of Social Sciences.

Tina G. Patel is a Senior Lecturer in Criminology at the University of Salford, UK. Tina gained her PhD in Sociology from the University of Sheffield in 2004, following which she began a career in academia. In 2013, Tina was awarded the status of Senior Fellow for the Higher Education Academy and focused on undertaking teaching within the disciplines of Sociology and Critical Criminology. Tina has also undertaken various research work within these disciplines and has presented work and published papers on 'race'/ethnicity, post-race racism, identity, and experiences of crime and victimization within minority populations. Tina is currently working on several projects which examine patterns of continued racism in what is often referred to as a post-race society.

Lynne Pettinger is an Associate Professor in Sociology at the University of Warwick. Lynne has published widely on the nature of contemporary work and employment, including on service work, green work, technology and work, and work in the informal sector. She teaches on undergraduate and postgraduate modules in economic sociology.

Adam Possamai is Deputy Dean and Professor in Sociology in the School of Social Sciences at Western Sydney University. He is the (co)author and (co)editor of more than 20 books and special issues, and close to 100 referred articles and book chapters. He is a former President of the International Sociological Association's Committee 22 on the Sociology of Religion and of the Australian Association for the Study of Religions.

John Scott is Emeritus Professor at the University of Plymouth and has previously taught at the universities of Strathclyde, Leicester, and Essex. His research interests have covered social class and power, economic organization, historical studies of sociology, social networks, and social theory. He is a Fellow of the British Academy, a Fellow of the Academy of Social Sciences, and has been awarded a CBE for Services to the Social Sciences, the Distinguished Services to British Sociology Award of the British Sociological Association, and Honorary Doctorates from the University of Essex and the University of Edinburgh. He continues his research as a visiting professor at Essex and Exeter universities.

Simon Susen is Professor of Sociology at City, University of London. Before joining City in 2011, he held lectureships at Birkbeck, University of London (2010–11), Newcastle University (2008–10), and Goldsmiths, University of London (2007–8). He received his PhD from the University of Cambridge in 2007. Prior to that, he studied sociology, politics, and philosophy at a range of international universities and research centres – including the University of Cambridge, the University of Edinburgh, the Colegio de México, the Facultad Latinoamericana de Ciencias Sociales in Mexico City, and the École des Hautes Études en Sciences Sociales in Paris. He is Associate Member of the Bauman Institute and, together with Bryan S. Turner, Editor of the *Journal of Classical Sociology*.

Katherine Twamley is Associate Professor of Sociology and Programme Director for the BSc Sociology programme at the Social Research Institute, University College London. Her research has been funded by the ESRC, the British Academy and the Leverhulme Trust, amongst other funding bodies, and focuses on love and intimacy, gender, and family, with a geographical focus on the UK and India. Katherine is particularly interested in longitudinal and comparative research, to understand how time and context shape experience and meaning. She currently leads a consortium of studies across ten countries, exploring family life during COVID-19.

Anna Wanka is a Sociologist and Critical Gerontologist interested in the social construction of age. She currently works as a Postdoctoral Researcher in the Research Training Group 'Doing Transitions' at Goethe University, Frankfurt am Main, and the University of Stuttgart, Germany. Her areas of expertise comprise the social practices of doing age, life course transitions/retirement and the re/production of social inequalities across the life course, ageing and technologies, age-friendly cities and communities (including the COVID-19 pandemic), ageing migrants, and mixed-methods research.

Ros Williams is a Lecturer in Digital Media and Society at the University of Sheffield. She received her PhD in Sociology from the University of York in 2016. Ros's research explores the intersection of health, race, and digital media, and she is particularly interested in racialized health inequalities. She is currently a Wellcome Trust Research Fellow, studying how racially minoritized stem cell donors are recruited through the use of social media.

Kath Woodward is Emeritus Professor of Sociology at the Open University where she has taught and published a wide range of multimedia teaching and learning materials in sociology, women's studies and interdisciplinary social science. Her research focuses upon feminist theories and critical engagement with the politics of difference and sexualized and racialized social inequalities, especially in the empirical field of sport where she has published widely in sporting embodied practices, in boxing in particular.

Sophie Woodward is a Professor of Sociology at the University of Manchester. Sophie carries out research into materiality, fashion, consumption, feminist theory and everyday life. She has an ongoing interest in creative methods and material methods and is co-investigator for the National Centre for Research Methods (NCRM). She is currently carrying out research into 'dormant things' – things people keep but that they are no longer using, stored in the hidden spaces of the home such as attics, wardrobes and cupboards.

David Wright is an Associate Professor in the Centre for Cultural and Media Policy Studies at the University of Warwick. He has published widely on issues relating to cultural consumption, taste, popular culture, cultural policy and cultural work.

THANKS FROM THE PUBLISHERS

The publisher would like to thank all of the lecturers who spoke to us and helped to review this book's content to ensure it is as useful as possible:

Ciaran Acton, Ulster University

Patrick Baert, University of Cambridge

Adam Burgess, University of Kent

Chris Cameron, University of Huddersfield

Michael Dunning, University of Leicester

Beatriz Carrillo Garcia, University of Sydney

Izabela Handzlik, INTO Newcastle University

Katy Harsant, University of Warwick

Janice McLaughlin, Newcastle University

Donncha Marron, Abertay University

Lucy Mayblin, University of Sheffield

David Mellor, University of South Wales

Richard Mole, University College London

Natalie Pitimson, University of Brighton

Naomi Rudoe, University of Westminster

Thomas Sealy, University of Bristol

Marta Trzebiatowska, University of Aberdeen

Sivamohan Valluvan, University of Warwick

Robin West, London Metropolitan University

The publisher would also like to extend a special thanks to Adele Mason-Bertrand for her enormous contribution in creating the online resources that accompany this book.

DISCOVER THIS TEXTBOOK'S ONLINE RESOURCES!

Designed to support you through every step of the research process, *An Introduction to Sociology* offers a range of online resources to help support your learning. Find them at: **https://study.sagepub.com/murji**

Videos offer valuable insights from a range of sociology experts. You can also test your knowledge by considering and answering critical thinking questions related to each of the videos.

Annotated SAGE Journal Articles reinforce key concepts discussed in the book, showing you how they are applied in the real world.

For Lecturers

Visit **https://study.sagepub.com/murji** to access the following resources available to support you in your teaching:

Testbank: Test your students' understanding and help them prepare for assessments with this collection of multiple-choice questions.

Essay Questions: Use these essay questions to help consolidate student learning or to test your students' understanding.

Video Guide: Includes discussion questions related to each video to help you use the videos in teaching and seminars.

PREFACE

Karim Murji, Sarah Neal and John Solomos

In working on *An Introduction to Sociology* we had two key objectives in mind. First, we wanted to curate a book that could help inspire students to appreciate the richness of sociology as a discipline and provide them with an overview of key theories, concepts and sub-fields at the beginning of their sociological journey. Second, we sought to bring together a group of authors who could write the individual chapters in an accessible style, drawing on their knowledge of specific areas of sociology as well as the discipline as a whole. We hope that as you go through the various parts of the final product of these efforts you will appreciate the value of this approach. You will find that this is an interesting time to be starting your sociological journey. We are living through a time when there are important transformations going on in the world around us, as evidenced by economic and social transformations on a global scale, mass movement of refugees and migrants, social movements engaged in struggles for social justice and equality, the COVID-19 pandemic, and ongoing debates about changes in political institutions and civil society. At a juncture such as this, sociology will enable you to gain the conceptual and empirical tools that will help you to make sense of these transformations and to think about alternatives that may help to improve the situation we face in a wide range of societies across the globe. It will also enable you to think critically about key issues in contemporary society and to address important questions about the likely course of social and cultural change in the period ahead.

As with all major books of this kind, we have inevitably benefitted from the encouragement and support of a wide range of people. First of all, we are grateful to Natalie Aguilera from SAGE for suggesting to us that a book of this kind was needed in order to provide students with an accessible and up-to-date overview of sociology as an evolving and rapidly changing discipline. Throughout the process of developing the book, we worked closely with Nina Smith and then Sunita Patel at SAGE. Along the way, the drafts of chapters have received helpful comments from a wide range of external readers, and we are grateful to all of them for helping to develop the content of individual chapters, and to improve the pedagogic tools that they use to help students to engage with the issues that they cover. We also thank Adele Mason-Bertrand for her work on the online resources. Most importantly, of course, we are grateful to all the authors of individual chapters who have agreed to contribute to the book and who have responded to various requests for re-drafting with understanding and grace in difficult times. This book would not have been possible without their unstinting efforts and we very much see this volume as a collaborative effort to provide students with an accessible introductory text. We are also grateful to our institutions for providing us with working environments that allowed us to carve out a space to work on this project. Our experiences of working in a range of different university departments has enabled us to gain much from our efforts to teach sociology to different generations of students, and this has fed into the thinking that has helped to structure this volume.

As you go through the various parts of *An Introduction to Sociology*, we encourage you to explore both the arguments outlined in each of the chapters and the additional material that is suggested by authors in the 28 chapters that form the substantive content of the book.

PART 1
THINKING SOCIOLOGICALLY

PART 1 THINKING SOCIOLOGICALLY

Introduction to Part 1

The six chapters in this part are all framed around the overarching theme of thinking sociologically. As we argue in Chapter 1, we felt it best to begin with some concrete examples of how sociologists have used their conceptual and methodological tools to address key issues in contemporary societies. This is because we see sociology as a discipline that is constantly being made and re-made and not fixed in terms of its basic starting points and conceptual frames.

Chapter 2, by Noortje Marres, begins this part of the book by focusing on the ways in which sociology has analysed the emergence and development of what is termed digital society. This is a relatively new area of research and scholarship but, as Marres' account highlights, it is likely that it will have an important impact not so much on sociology as on related disciplines in the social sciences and humanities. As you read her chapter, you will see that she emphasizes the ways in which digital society gives rise to new forms of discrimination, the platformization of society, and changes in ways of knowing social life (you may also find it useful here to look at Chapter 10 by Lambert, Chapter 23 by Williams and Chapter 25 by Crossley). In addition, she outlines the concepts and methods that sociologists have developed in order to make sense of the important issues that have been raised by the digital transformations of society.

Chapter 3, by Kate Burningham, is concerned with the question of what is sociological about the environment. Studies of environmental sociology, including climate change, have been an important feature of sociological research and analysis in recent years, and Burningham provides an account that argues both for the centrality of environmental issues to sociology and the importance of sociological analysis of environmental issues. In developing her analysis, Burningham outlines some of the main contributions that sociology has made to the understanding of environmental issues and the impact that this has had on our understanding of society more generally. Given current debates about the environment and climate change, this chapter will help you to engage more deeply with an area that is likely to help shape both national and global policy agendas.

This is followed in Chapter 4 by Eamonn Carrabine's exploration of what is sociological about crime. In recent times, the study of crime, and criminology more broadly, has become an important component of the work of many sociology departments. It is therefore likely that you will come across questions about crime and related issues as you progress through your studies. This chapter frames crime not as a singular phenomenon, but rather argues that it is important to situate our understandings of crime and policies to deal with it within a broader social context. Carrabine's account also explores the ways that sociologists have advanced our understanding of crime as a complex social phenomenon.

From these three chapters, we move on to two chapters that have a broader analytical frame and seek to engage you with questions about what we mean by the notion of society and how we conceptualize both the historical and contemporary interconnections between societies.

Chapter 5, by John Scott, addresses a question that is in many ways at the heart of the study of sociology, namely: what is society? As Scott argues, this is not a new question and has been at the heart of the discipline since its emergence as a distinctive field of scholarship and research. Indeed, it is also a question that is addressed in a number of other disciplines in the social sciences and humanities, including philosophy. But, as Scott argues, the study of sociology needs to constantly engage with the question of how we define society. His account of this question should allow you to think more broadly about what sociologists mean when they refer to the idea of society (see also Chapter 26 by Outhwaite). You will note that it is also a theme that is explored throughout the various chapters of the book.

PART 1 THINKING SOCIOLOGICALLY

The final chapter in this part of the book, Chapter 6, is by Manuela Boatcă. She begins her chapter by outlining the way that sociology can help us to make sense of the global interconnections that have helped to shape and re-shape the modern world. In doing so, she argues that although much attention today is on cross-border migration, such movements and global interconnections are not in themselves new. She highlights this point through reference to the range of ways that our modern world has been shaped by the role of global interconnections over a number of centuries. Her chapter emphasizes in particular the role of European expansion into the Americas, intercontinental migration, the so-called triangular trade that forcefully displaced people enslaved in Africa to the Americas and exported the products of enslaved labour to Europe for several centuries, and the ensuing unequal economic exchange between world regions that has forged transregional connections. We hope that Boatcă's chapter will help you to think differently about the origins of modern societies and the global connections that made them possible.

Having explored key aspects of what it means to think sociologically, we move on in Part 2 to four chapters that explore the relationship between theories and methods in sociology.

Key Questions

- How have sociologists helped to analyse the development of digital society?
- In what ways can sociology contribute to the analysis of environmental change?
- What are the key features of sociological accounts of the role of crime in society?
- How can thinking sociologically about the notion of society help us to analyse the world around us?
- Boatcă argues that cross-border migrations and global interconnections are not a new phenomenon. How does this argument help us to make sense of the forces that have shaped modern societies?

APPROACHING SOCIOLOGY

Karim Murji, Sarah Neal and John Solomos

LEARNING OBJECTIVES

- To engage with what it means to think sociologically.
- To recognize the relevance and importance of sociology for understanding the contemporary world.
- To recognize the scale and scope of sociology.
- To reflect on universalism and marginalization within sociology.
- To understand how to navigate the various sections of this book and appreciate how they contribute to your sociological journey.

 Framing Questions

1. What is sociology?
2. What does it mean to think sociologically about the world?
3. What is the value of sociology?
4. How is sociology being challenged and how is it changing?

PART 1 THINKING SOCIOLOGICALLY

Approaching Sociology

Welcome to *An Introduction to Sociology*. In this book we have brought together a wide range of leading sociologists working across different **theoretical** and **empirical** approaches in **sociology**, and sometimes interdisciplinary frames, in order to provide you with an overview of key facets of the discipline and the way it has evolved and is developing. Each individual chapter can be read on its own, but we very much hope that you will see the value of using the book as a whole as a point of reference as you approach either general introductory sociology modules or more specialized modules that form part of your sociological education. This opening chapter aims to orient you to some of the key themes and contents of this book, as well as highlighting some issues for you to reflect on and think about. This includes reflecting on the structure of the book as a whole, and why it contains the chapters and topics that are here. Looking at the contents and coverage will, we hope, help inspire you to read further, and to think about the scale and scope of sociology. It may also prompt you to think about what is not here or what could have been included, and what you would have liked to read about too. This emphasizes that, first, one sociology book cannot cover every aspect of the discipline and, second, that the reach of sociology is vast and almost any topic or issue could come within its gaze.

As an introductory text, this book aims to provide you with a range of topics that you might expect to see in a sociology book, along with a few that you might be surprised to see. Indeed, this tension between and cutting across what may be *familiar* and what may be *strange* is one of the things that sociology is especially valuable for. The idea of sociology as a tool or an approach to defamiliarize the familiar and, conversely, to familiarize the unfamiliar is one of the ideas associated with the sociologist Zygmunt Bauman (1925–2017). Bauman (Bauman and May, 2019) points to the ways in which a sociological lens or perspective enables us to question the things that are taken for granted and appear ordinary, and to recognize the ways in which our everyday lives are shaped by social forces – and becoming knowledgeable about those things could lead to other ways of thinking about how social life should or could be.

If you look across a shelf in a bookshop or at an online catalogue of sociology books, you will see that there are any number of texts that introduce sociology. The surfeit of books and online materials is a sign that at school and university levels sociology is a highly popular subject. Yet while these sources all cover some of the same ground, they also all differ in smaller and bigger ways. In other words, a textbook in sociology is not like a textbook in, say, biology or maths, where there is a core corpus of material that students are supposed to know. That sociology is not like biology or chemistry is sometimes treated as a weakness of the discipline, and of the social sciences, compared to the natural sciences in general.

However, could it be a strength? The critics of sociology tend to treat its openness as a sign that *anything goes* and there are no widely agreed rules. However, approaching sociology as a dynamic or *living* discipline marked by diversity – and, yes, it is true, some lack of consensus – does not mean that it does not operate by the standards of good social science – including a concern with systematic procedures for gathering, assessing and evaluating empirical evidence; drawing on theories to contextualize data and advance understanding about the nature and direction of social changes in the world around us; and engaging with new and emergent social issues that are helping to shape contemporary societies. As the various contributions to this volume emphasize, the search for systematic theories and methods is an important facet of sociological research.

Introductory sociology texts often begin with or place great emphasis on telling students what sociology is; and this is also often tied up with some kind of account of the origins of sociology. As the editors of this book, we do not find this helpful and can illustrate the reason why through a couple of examples.

First, we draw on one of the sociologists who has most shaped the discipline in recent times, namely Pierre Bourdieu (1930–2002). Near the beginning of a documentary film that was made about Bourdieu and his work, *Sociology as a Martial Art* (2001), we see Bourdieu being interviewed in a radio show. This starts with him being presented with a definition of sociology as 'the scientific study of social phenomena among human beings'. Having written that down, Bourdieu, one of the most eminent sociologists of the 20th century, disarmingly responds, 'I doubt if anyone understood that. I certainly didn't!' So, if you ever felt unsure about the meanings of definitions of sociology, you are in very good company. (You can find this extract in a shorter segment on YouTube). Thus, a key part of this book and your wider sociological education will involve you in being introduced to a broad range of conceptual frameworks and empirical research about what sociology is.

It is worth adding what Bourdieu went on to say, after saying he didn't understand the definition he was presented with:

Like so many dictionary definitions, it's a tautology, it says the same thing twice. I'll try to explain it a bit better.

Like all scientists, the sociologist attempts to establish laws, to grasp regularities, recurrent ways of being and to define their principle. Why do people do the things they do? Why, for example, do teachers' children do better at school than working class children? By 'why', I mean 'how is it that…'? How is it that it happens like that in society and not otherwise?

By responding like this, Bourdieu usefully highlights the way in which sociology does not begin from assumptions about the way society works, even if it poses conceptual questions about the social phenomena that need to be understood and analysed.

Second, it is important to note that even the most basic definitions of sociology as the study of society, or how society is organized, lead to more questions than the definition itself assists us with. For example, what is meant by society? What does it include, and what does it exclude in the ways this term is used? These are questions which are asked by sociologists all the time, particularly as they seek to research and understand the relationship between specific social institutions and the wider society. You can explore the question of what sociologists mean by the notion of society by looking at discussion of this issue in Chapters 5 and 6 in this book, by John Scott and Manuela Boatcă. It is also addressed in Chapter 26, by William Outhwaite.

— Pause for Thought —

There is a lot to reflect on even in Bourdieu's short statement about sociology. So, we suggest you take a pause here and think through some of the definitions of sociology that you have come across and make some notes about what you think of these, including their strengths and limitations.

Sociology's Story

This book has the aim of guiding you through your sociological education, taking a view of sociology that positions it in a global, rather than simply a national, context. As Bhambra and Holmwood (2021), Steinmetz (2013) and Go (2016) among others argue, the history and practice of sociology might look substantially different if more sociology took this wider global view. This perspective tends to undermine the resort to or discussions of 'British society', as if the nation-**state** provides or defines the **boundaries** of a society. This way of thinking, about what a society is, is not necessarily inscribed in the term itself, as Scott argues in Chapter 5 of this book, but it has become deep-seated enough to become part of the problem of what has been called '**methodological** nationalism' (Beck, 2007). The limits of what is called the 'container model' of society have become increasingly clear. While it has become common to highlight processes of **globalization** and transnationalism, as well as ideas such as **network** societies and flows across national boundaries, the problem of thinking of society as equalling a nation-state has a longer span than the globalisation thesis imagines (Giddens, 2003). As Boatcă shows in Chapter 5 of this book, imperial trade and the **age** of empires made the world much more interconnected than has sometimes been recognised in sociology.

The approach, we are suggesting, has a further consequence for conventional accounts of sociology's story of itself. Usually, students are told that sociology emerged in Europe towards the end of the 19th century and its origins are linked to changes such as **modernity,** industrialization, and urbanization, as well as the rationalism of the Enlightenment and the rise of scientific **methods** that eventually contributed to the idea of sociology as a 'science of society'. Integral to these accounts, then, is also the idea of August Comte (1798–1857) as one of the 'founding fathers', as he is credited with coming up with the word 'sociology' itself. Yet as Ellwood (1902) pointed out over a century ago, Comte is only the founder of a new science if it is understood in quite a specific way – as a method of understanding social phenomena using quantitative measures and based on a view that the social world is essentially the same as the physical world. So, it is more accurate to say that Comte and others created the *discipline* of sociology in its modern form (although there is an ongoing tension between more 'scientific' and more 'literary and humanities' views of sociology), yet the idea of studying social phenomena systematically and rationally is much older than that. Indeed, Ellwood's (1902) article suggested the ancient Greek philosopher Aristotle (384–322 BC) as the first sociologist. Likewise, there are reasonable claims that well before Comte and well beyond Europe (Barnes, 1917), something that looked like sociological thinking was in the work of the Arabic scholar Ibn Khaldun (1332–1406), or the Chinese historian Ma Duanlin (1245–1322). References here to articles from 1902 and 1917 serve as a reminder that debates about the origins of sociology are not new. In a similar light, discussions of the so-called 'founding fathers' of sociology are also not something that started recently. There are names you may now rarely come across in a sociology book – such as Montesquieu, Pareto and Tocqueville – who were viewed as exemplary sociologists before and in the same time as Comte (Aron, 1968; Little, 2012).

A search for 'true' origins and 'real' sociologists is both less useful and less interesting than a sense that sociology is a lively and reflexive discipline that asks questions about itself as well as the world which it seeks to understand and account for. It is important to note, for example, that in relation to reflecting on its own story and practice, the search for the foundations of sociology in the work of particular, usually European, thinkers has tended to be selective and to underplay the work of scholars whose work has not been narrated traditionally as part of the origins of the discipline of sociology. A striking example of this till quite recently is the relative neglect of the work of black and minority sociologists within the foundational stories of sociology. As the sociologist Aldon Morris has argued, a particular gap or failure in this regard is the **role** of W.E.B. Du Bois (1868–1963) in accounts of the origins of sociology (Morris, 2015). Du Bois was a key figure in early efforts to make sense of the role of slavery, racial segregation and **racism** in shaping the modern world. He founded the Atlanta School of sociology that set a template for sociological practice well before the more renowned Chicago School. Yet is only in recent years that his contribution to sociological research has begun to be acknowledged and reflected in the curriculum that is taught to students at all stages of their studies.

Divergent Views and Perspectives

We see *An Introduction to Sociology* as an invitation to you to engage critically with what it means to *think sociologically* about the world around you. This is why we begin the volume with three chapters that are framed around the question of 'what is sociological?' about digital society, the environment and crime. Rather than begin with abstracted discussions about what sociology is, or perhaps should be, we felt it is important for you to see how sociologists have grappled with these issues and developed both theoretical concepts and empirical research tools in order to develop a better understanding of these social phenomena. Given this starting point, we have structured *An Introduction to Sociology* in such a way that it takes you through the various ways in which sociology can help you to think about and analyse the social world around us. Just the size of this book, with its 28 chapters each focused on sociology's approaches to different and diverse facets of the social world, gives an immediate indication of the exciting scale and scope of the discipline.

But as editors of this volume, we also felt it important to encourage you to explore divergent views and perspectives. Our aim has been to curate a book that highlights both the richness and the diversity of sociology as it is evolving in and responding to contemporary social environments. In order to achieve this overarching objective, we encouraged the authors of individual chapters both to engage with different theories and perspectives and to use pedagogical tools that highlight the range of approaches to particular topics and issues. So, as you go through the various chapters do try to make use of those pedagogical tools and use them as a way to develop conversations with both your lecturers and fellow students as you grapple with the concepts and empirical research evidence that is contained in them.

Earlier, we highlighted the importance that Bourdieu placed on the need to know 'Why do people do the things they do?'. But it is also worth noting the British Sociological Association definition of sociology, which defines it as 'the study of how society is organised and how we experience life'. The emphasis that the BSA definition gives to sociology paying attention to the lived experience is important and is a theme that threads through many of the chapters in the book (see, for example, Anna Gawlewicz's chapter on Migration). The ability to recognize and understand the dynamic interconnections between wider social forces and everyday and emotional personal lives is one of the things that makes sociology valuable. Sociology is particularly well placed in being able to effectively examine and to seek to understand the dynamic nature of social relations. Its ability to translate between abstract social forces and lived experience gives sociology its wider utility – not only in terms of offering ways of describing, understanding and analysing social worlds but also in terms of offering ideas and concepts that are relevant and relatable to everyday life.

It is also important to note that it is particularly striking how sociological ideas and concepts have percolated beyond the confines of sociology as such. The sociologist John Holmwood (2010) has described sociology as an 'exporter discipline', by which he means that sociology's concepts and methodologies have been influential in the ways other – interdisciplinary and more applied – academic disciplines, including education, social policy and business studies, think and work. But what is perhaps even more notable is how sociology has, perhaps more than any other academic discipline, been able to export concepts and terminologies into everyday thinking and language – for example, such terms as 'gentrification', '**moral panics'**, 'superdiversity' and '**social capital'** have emerged from sociology and have all found frequent and commonplace usage way beyond academic research and academic communities. Other terms such as 'gender', 'community' and 'social class', which are familiar in everyday language, are also central to sociological investigation to the extent that sociological insights are often taken for granted in their normal usage (see, for example, the chapters by Sophie Woodward and Kath Woodward and Wendy Bottero in Part 3 of this book).

As a way of illustrating this point, it may be useful to refer you to a research project that involved one of us, namely Sarah Neal. It was focused on exploring the role of everyday social relationships.

The first project focused on exploring social relationships in contexts of urban multiculture (Neal et al., 2018). During the course of this research, Neal and her colleagues found that the participants in the project spoke extensively and regularly in interviews with the research team about the effects of 'gentrification' in their everyday lives and how the increasing growth of an affluent middle class was changing what had been the poorer, and very working class, areas of London in which they lived. While 'gentrification' was a concept developed by the sociologist Ruth Glass (1964) in the early 1960s to describe and capture these residential social class shifts and the social consequences of them – including the **displacement** of poorer residents (Butler et al., 2013; Lees et al., 2008) – it has, like some of the other concepts listed above, since become a part of the everyday vernacular as well as a widespread urban transformation.

Sociologists are at the forefront of emerging bodies of scholarship and research that seek to give substance to the claim made by Sztompka that contemporary sociological research addresses the importance of everyday life:

What really occurs in human society, at the level between structures and actions, where the constraints of structures and the dynamics of actions produce the real, experienced and observable social events, the social-individual praxis making up everyday life […] which is neither completely determined nor completely free. (Sztompka, 2008: 25)

An important theme that recurs through many of the chapters in this book is the need for sociology to address more fully the complex relationships between the social world and the personal fields of social life. This was a central theme in C. Wright Mills' (1916–62) invitation to engage with how the **sociological imagination** could help us to make sense of the complex connections that exist between 'the personal trouble of milieu' and 'the public issues of **social structure'** (Mills, 1959: 14).

Sociology has always been a discipline which has been driven by its ambitions to develop theories of society and social relationships and interactions, but has been committed to theory building though empirical approaches and engagement with social worlds and the **social practices** that shape these worlds. This means that social research methods are a key part of sociological work. The research methods that are used by sociologists to generate data to inform and develop **social theory** have themselves been developing and diversifying. Whereas large-scale, quantitative survey data were once the more dominant form of data and evidence used for sociological analysis – for example, while W.E.B. Du Bois did use interviews his studies of poverty in Philadelphia relied on large-scale survey data of neighbourhoods, and Durkheim's suicide study was based on official statistics and demographic data – since the 1970s, when feminist (Butler, 1990; Crenshaw, 1989; Haraway, 1991; hooks, 1981), anti-racist and postcolonial (Gilroy, 2004; Hall, 1988; Hall et al., 1978; Spivak, 1988, 2008; West, 1993) critiques began to reshape sociology's 'world view', there has been a clear shift towards sociologists using **mixed methods** and qualitative research approaches in empirical studies of the social world, as Stella Chatzitheochari in Chapter 9 and Cath Lambert in Chapter 10 explore in Part 2 of this book.

Social research methods in sociology tend to now focus on the relationship between how sociologists conduct research and the relationship between researchers and those involved as participants in research and to place value on lived social experience. Reflecting these concerns, contemporary sociologists often use an ever-widening creative and diverse range of interpretative methods and data sources. These can range from diaries, letters, magazines, biographies, timelines, social maps and digital text and online interactions (see Noortje Marres' chapter in Part 1) to dialogue generated though objects, things, photographs, images, activities and walking practices to develop dialogue and research relationships and generate empirical data. You will find examples of this variety of approaches for identifying, generating and reflecting on sociological data sources in many of the chapters in the book, as well as being the focus of Chapters 9 and 10.

Sociology at Different Scales

You will see as you go through the various parts of this book that an important aspect of your sociological education is to understand the key theories and methods that sociology uses, what sociological research involves, the origins of sociology and its development, and the rich variety of sub-fields that have emerged in more recent times. But we also hope that as you work through the various **substantive** parts that make up this book, you will see that an important feature of sociology is that it is always evolving and developing new conceptual and methodological tools that help us to recognize and examine the ongoing social changes in the world around us. Part of the strength of sociology is that it has been able to constantly adapt to the need to address the emergence of new social phenomena.

But sociology also faces important challenges about how to stay relevant and be able to contribute to the understanding of social shifts (such as gentrification and globalization) and social shocks (such as Brexit) and what have been termed 'wicked problems' (Rittel and Webber, 1973). These 'wicked problems' refer to large-scale, persistent, complex, multidimensional, and interconnected social and cultural problems which have what Rittel and Webber call a 'no stopping rule' and 'multiple explanations'. Some of these, such as the COVID-19 **pandemic**, were largely unforeseen by sociologists (Connell, 2020), although a number of others, such as social inequalities, health and poverty, crime, violence and **conflict**, racism and sexism, have been at the heart of much recent sociological scholarship (see Sarah Cant's chapter on health, Eamon Carabine's chapter on crime, Christian Olsson's chapter on war and violence, and Tina Patel's chapter on race in Parts 1 and 2). Others, such as the environment and climate change, are now emergent concerns on sociological agendas (see Kate Burningham's chapter in Part 1). Equally important for sociology, as the chapters by Nick Crossley, Rosalind Edwards, Katherine Twamley and Julia Carter explain, are those other social phenomena that shape political and personal lives, social relations and interactions from human mobilities and social movements to families, intimacies, affects and emotions, bodies, identifications, solidarities and diversities, **age**, generation and the **life course**, through to materialities and the senses as well as science, **technologies** and digitalized social lives. All of these are expanding sociology's focus and scope (and are explored in depth in Parts 1, 3 and 4 of this book). Sociology's capacity to be relevant and relatable has increasingly led to questions and debates about the role of sociology (and sociologists) in the social world.

The ways in which sociology might have social value and contribute ideas and insights to wider publics is explored further by Paul Jones in Chapter 27 in the final section of the book.

One example of the way in which sociology engages with contemporary and immediate issues relates to the issue of Brexit – the decision of the UK government following the 2016 referendum to leave the European Union. Although much has been written about this issue from a range of disciplinary perspectives over the past few years, it is possible to identify a body of research that can be positioned under the broad label of a 'sociology of Brexit'. That research has highlighted a number of issues that may help us understand public support for Brexit, including processes of **deindustrialization**, the phenomenon of the 'left-behind' in some regions of the UK, race, **immigration**, nationalism, integration and multiculturalism (Favell and Barbulescu, 2018; Virdee and McGeever, 2018). Some sociologists have highlighted the role of immigration as being central to the success of the Brexit campaign. New patterns of migration and settlement, although largely from within Europe, came to symbolize concerns about the impact of immigration on sovereignty, national and cultural identity and on housing and health services (Patel and Connelly, 2019; Rogaly, 2019, 2020; Shilliam, 2020; Virdee and McGeever, 2018). Other researchers have suggested the need to link Brexit to an even broader set of issues. For example, Valluvan and Kalra (2019) argue that Brexit delivered a mainstreaming of 'little Englander' forms of nationalism and 'signalled one significant instantiation of a successful new nationalist political programme that hinges substantially on the ostensible problems of immigration, multiculturalism, and ethnic diversity more broadly'. Yet others have suggested that Brexit can only be fully understood through the optics of **colonialism** and racist melancholia (Back, 2021; Bhambra, 2017).

It is also important to note that in some accounts Brexit in the UK is seen as part of a wider phenomenon, namely a global populist nationalism that is explicitly focused on opposition to immigration and multiculturalism. A number of Global North and South countries have seen the emergence of anti-**migrant** and nationalist political parties and movements that espouse a mixture of xenophobia, white nationalism and opposition to immigration. The political impact of Donald Trump in the US in 2016, Victor Orban in Hungary, and Jair Bolsonaro in Brazil are seen as different facets of the same broad phenomenon (Geary et al., 2020).

Whatever the merits of these different efforts to make sense of and develop sociological accounts of Brexit, perhaps the key point arising from this example is to draw attention to the strength of sociology for the ways in which it is able to address new issues through a range of different methodological and conceptual frames. In the case of Brexit, sociologists were at the forefront of discussions about the wider social and political factors that helped to shape the conditions that eventually led to Brexit, both in explaining the vote and reflecting what it had to tell us about wider social relations and political attitudes and in what Maskovsky and Bjork-James (2020) call the growth of 'angry politics' across the UK and more globally.

Another good example of the ways in which sociology is able to respond to new challenges and issues came to the fore as we were completing the editing of this volume, namely the coronavirus pandemic. During much of 2020 and 2021, the whole of the world was in the midst of the coronavirus pandemic, with many societies having gone through various forms of lockdown in efforts to control the spread of the virus on a global scale. We shall return to a more detailed discussion of the pandemic in the Conclusion but suffice it to say here that what is already clear and without doubt is that the impact of the pandemic is as much about the social world as it is about medical responses and the biological world of viruses. Illustrative of this is the way in which our micro everyday social worlds have been profoundly affected as our mobilities, interactions and contacts are governed and regulated in new and extensive ways. The pandemic has put governments and states very directly and explicitly into everyday personal lives, and at the same time it has also illuminated and exposed entrenched social divisions and social inequalities.

Yet, it is also important to acknowledge that an important feature of contemporary sociologies is that they have been able to broaden their field of vision, both from a theoretical and an empirical angle, to address issues that have broadened to boundaries of sociological research as well as engaging with wider interdisciplinary research agendas. As we noted above, sociology needs to stay current even as sociological research has to grapple with the challenges of always working a little behind 'real time'.

Critical Self-reflection

However, even as sociology has sought to tackle new and emergent issues and open up insights into new forms of social interaction, and social phenomena, it is also important to acknowledge that it has been challenged and pushed to critically reflect on itself and the ways in which sociology as a discipline has reinforced and reproduced relationships of power and subjugation. Some of this pressure for critical self-reflection has come through the recognition (referred to in the first section of this chapter) that sociology's universalizing tendencies often resulted in the social experiences and phenomena of Europe and North America being used and presented as global rather than particular. This is a point made by Manuela Boatcă when she argues that 'in most sociological accounts, the "Europe" hailed as a standard of civilization, modernity, development, **capitalism** or human rights was poorly or not at all defined' (Boatcă, 2021: 390). This Eurocentric and universalizing process has been 'doubled down on', first, by simultaneously marginalizing other sociological voices within those geographies – the empirical and theoretical work of female and/or social theorists of colour. We discussed W.E.B. Du Bois and his sociological work earlier but there are many other postcolonial and/or feminist scholars, who were often also activists, journalists and creative writers, such as C.L.R. James (1901–89), Claudia Jones (1915–64) and Audre Lorde (1934–92), who have been largely excluded, invisibilized or neglected in the discipline – and, second, by ignoring the work of sociologists and social theorists outside of these geographies in what we might broadly categorize as the Global South. The consequence of this for sociology (along with a range of other academic disciplines) has meant that 'subjects of Western scholarship are enduringly pale, male (and often stale); where people of colour do appear they are all too often tokenistically represented, spoken on behalf of or reduced to objects of scholarship' (Bhambra, 2014: 6).

At the same time as these ongoing debates within sociology about the failures of the discipline to address key issues about power and knowledge, we have also seen a number of external pressures come to the fore in recent years. The emergence of social movements like Black Lives Matter and student-led protest campaigns such as 'Why is My Professor not Black, Why is My Curriculum White' has contributed to a range of recent debates about decolonizing universities (Bhambra et al., 2018; Santos, 2014), problematizing the whiteness of academic communities (Bhopal, 2018) and addressing higher education race inequalities (Alexander, 2018; Boliver, 2016). Such pressures have led to intense debate within sociology about the under-representation of black and ethnic minority students and academics, the differential degree outcomes of black and ethnic minority students, the urgencies of decolonizing academic curriculum generally and, as we noted earlier, for sociology itself to address its own marginalizations and the ways in which social theory has been too often taught from white and male perspectives (see above; these higher education concerns are discussed further by Nasima Hassan in Chapter 19). All these conversations highlight the challenge of developing a more inclusive and diverse sociology where sociologists of colour are both visible and proportionately represented.

It is interesting to note, for example, that a 2020 British Sociological Association survey of sociology in the UK found that when it came to the issue of bringing questions about race and **ethnicity** into the curriculum, the response across departments and the discipline as a whole was very mixed. It also found that while 24.5% of undergraduate sociology students are from black or minority ethnic groups, only 14.3% of sociology academics are from these groups. And in terms of senior academic status, only 9.8% of the total number of sociology professors are from black and minority ethnic groups (Joseph-Salisbury et al., 2020). The report concluded that although sociology has been at the heart of contemporary debates about social inequality, there was a need for the discipline to address questions of inequalities in access to the profession and the make-up of the curriculum.

These debates illuminate the ways in which, although sociology provides insights about social inequalities and divisions in society generally, it itself can be seen as being shaped by these very same patterns of inequality that it aims to understand, analyse and problematize.

Using the Book

Having outlined some of the key overarching themes that frame this book, we want to conclude this chapter by suggesting some ways in which you could use the book as a whole as you progress through your studies.

The first point we want to emphasize here is that sociology is characterized by different approaches and voices. As the various contributors to this volume make clear, there is a range of both conceptual and empirically-focused perspectives within sociology. In this sense, you may find it useful to think of a point made by Nicholas Gane and Les Back in their assessment of C. Wright Mills:

For Mills, sociology is a navigation device. It is a set of competences and a way of holding to the world that is to provide clues about how to defend oneself against its whims and mystifications. It is to do so by instilling a particular quality of mind – a sociological imagination – which makes the unfamiliar more familiar and treats the familiar as a source of astonishment. (Gane and Back, 2013: 405)

As you begin your sociological journey, you may find it useful to bear in mind this point about sociology being a 'navigation device'. It is also important for you to think about how sociology can help you both to better understand the social world around us and give you the tools you need to engage in conversations about how to identify and understand social interactions, relationships and institutions, on the one hand, and engage in discussions about how to change society and tackle social inequalities, on the other. For this reason, we have included a number of chapters in this book that will help you think about the uses of sociology in looking at the world around you, as well as the role that sociological research plays in addressing how societies can address the challenges that they face in the contemporary environment.

Unlike many introductory sociology texts which tend to be either single or multi-authored, *An Introduction to Sociology* brings together 28 chapters written by sociologists who have made expert contributions in developing their particular fields, and each of these invite you to explore how sociological research has addressed key areas of social life and, in doing so, has helped to transform how we see the world around us. Each of the chapters has been crafted by sociologists who have extensive and specialist knowledge of the issues covered, and they are organized in such a way that they allow you to explore the specific issues dealt with and to engage with key questions. To help you engage more fully with the key ideas and concepts, each chapter also includes discussion points that allow you to consider specific concepts and ideas in relation to particular events or issues.

We hope you will enjoy the various journeys that are at the heart of the book and that take you through key facets of studying sociology today. Rather than assuming that there is just one way to begin your sociological education, we have structured this book in a way that provides you with an opportunity to engage with different approaches to the study of society. This is because it is important to begin to understand that sociology is a very diverse discipline and is composed of different schools of thought and methodological approaches. *An Introduction to Sociology* aims to engage you with the key ideas, issues, research agendas and questions that are part of what studying sociology at university involves. The underlying aim of the volume is to help you engage more fully with what studying sociology is by introducing you, in an accessible and relatable way, to sociological accounts of the world. A key aim which threads through all parts of the book is to encourage you to debate the practical relevance, public value and political significance of sociology.

REVIEW QUESTIONS

1. What do you understand by the idea of *thinking sociologically*?
2. In what ways is sociology as a discipline evolving and changing?
3. What do you understand by the 'value of sociology'?
4. Why is it important that sociology examines itself in relation to the social world?

REFERENCES

Alexander, C. (2018) Breaking black: The death of ethnic and racial studies in Britain. *Ethnic and Racial Studies* 41(6): 1034–54.
Aron, R. (1968) *Main Currents in Sociological Thought. Vol. 1, Montesquieu, Comte, Marx, Tocqueville, the Sociologists and the Revolution of 1848*. Harmondsworth: Penguin.
Back, L. (2021) Hope's work. *Antipode* 53(1): 3–20.
Barnes, H.E. (1917) Sociology before Comte: A summary of doctrines and an introduction to the literature. *American Journal of Sociology* 23(2): 174–247.
Bauman, Z. and May, T. (2019) *Thinking Sociologically*. Oxford: John Wiley.
Beck, U. (2007) The cosmopolitan condition: Why methodological nationalism fails. *Theory, Culture & Society* 24(7–8): 286–90.
Bhambra, G.K. (2014) *Connected Sociologies*. London: Bloomsbury.
Bhambra, G.K. (2017) Brexit, Trump, and 'methodological whiteness': On the misrecognition of race and class. *British Journal of Sociology* 68(S1): S214–S232.
Bhambra, G.K. and Holmwood, J. (2021) *Colonialism and Modern Social Theory*. Cambridge: Polity Press.

Bhambra, G.K., Gebrial, D. and Nişancıoğlu, K. (eds) (2018) *Decolonising the University*. London: Pluto Press.
Bhopal, K. (2018) *White Privilege: The Myth of a Post-racial Society*. Bristol: Policy Press.
Boatcă, M. (2021) Thinking Europe otherwise: Lessons from the Caribbean. *Current Sociology* 69(3): 389–414.
Boliver, V. (2016) Exploring ethnic inequalities in admission to Russell Group universities. *Sociology* 50(2): 247–266.
Butler, J. (1990) *Gender Trouble: Feminism and the Subversion of Identity*. New York: Routledge.
Butler, T., Hamnett, C. and Ramsden, M.J. (2013) Gentrification, education and exclusionary displacement in East London. *International Journal of Urban and Regional Research* 37(2): 556–75.
Connell, R. (2020) COVID-19/Sociology. *Journal of Sociology* 56(4): 745–51.
Crenshaw, K.W. (1989) Demarginalizing the intersection of race and sex: Black feminist critique of antidiscrimination doctrine, feminist theory and antiracist politics. *University of Chicago Legal Forum* 1989(1): 139–68.
Ellwood, C.A. (1902) Aristotle as a sociologist. *Annals of the American Academy of Political and Social Science* 19(2): 63–74.
Favell, A. and Barbulescu, R. (2018) Brexit, 'immigration' and anti-discrimination. In P. Diamond, P. Nedergaard and B. Rosamond (eds) *The Routledge Handbook of the Politics of Brexit*. London: Routledge, pp. 118–33.
Gane, N. and Back, L. (2013) C. Wright Mills 50 years on: The promise and craft of sociology revisited. *Theory, Culture & Society* 29(7–8): 399–421.
Geary, D., Schofield, C. and Sutton, J. (eds) (2020) *Global White Nationalism: From Apartheid to Trump*. Manchester: Manchester University Press.
Giddens, A. (2003) *Runaway World: How Globalisation is Reshaping our Lives*, 2nd edn. New York: Routledge.
Gilroy, P. (2004) *After Empire: Melancholia or Convivial Culture?* London: Routledge.
Glass, R. (ed.) (1964) *London: Aspects of Change*. London: MacGibbon & Kee.
Go, J. (2016) *Postcolonial Thought and Social Theory*. New York: Oxford University Press.
Hall, S. (1988) New ethnicities. In K. Mercer (ed.) *Black Film/British Cinema*. London: Institute of Contemporary Arts, pp. 27–31.
Hall, S., Critcher, C., Jefferson, T., Clarke, J. and Roberts, B. (1978) *Policing the Crisis: Mugging, the State, and Law and Order*. London: Macmillan.
Haraway, D.J. (1991) *Simians, Cyborgs, and Women: The Reinvention of Nature*. New York: Routledge.
Holmwood, J. (2010) Sociology's misfortune: Disciplines, interdisciplinarity and the impact of audit culture. *British Journal of Sociology* 61(4): 639–58.
hooks, b. (1981) *Ain't I a Woman? Black Women and Feminism*. Boston: South End Press.
Joseph-Salisbury, R., Ashe, S.D., Alexander, C. and Campion, K. (2020) *Race and Ethnicity in British Sociology*. Durham, NC: British Sociological Association.
Lees, L., Slater, T. and Wyly, E. (2008) *Gentrification*. New York: Routledge.
Little, D. (2012) *Raymond Aron as a historian of sociology*. Available at: https://understandingsociety.blogspot.com/2012/12/raymond-aron-as-historian-of-sociology.html (last accessed March 2021).
Maskovsky, J. and Bjork-James, S. (eds) (2020) *Beyond Populism: Angry Politics and the Twilight of Neoliberalism*. Morgantown: West Virginia University Press.
Mills, C.W. (1959) *The Sociological Imagination*. New York: Oxford University Press.
Morris, A.D. (2015) *The Scholar Denied: W.E.B. Du Bois and the Birth of Modern Sociology*. Oakland, CA: University of California Press.
Neal, S., Bennett, K., Cochrane, A. and Mohan, G. (2018) *Lived Experiences of Multiculture: The New Social and Spatial Relations of Diversity*. London: Routledge.

Patel, T.G. and Connelly, L. (2019) 'Post-race' racisms in the narratives of 'Brexit' voters. *Sociological Review* 67(5): 968–84.

Rittel, H.W.J. and Webber, M.M. (1973) Dilemmas in a general theory of planning. *Policy Sciences* 4(2): 155–69.

Rogaly, B. (2019) Brexit writings and the war of position over migration, 'race' and class. *Environment and Planning C: Politics and Space* 37(1): 28–40.

Rogaly, B. (2020) *Stories from a Migrant City: Living and Working Together in the Shadow of Brexit*. Manchester: Manchester University Press.

Santos, B.D.S. (2014) *Epistemologies of the South: Justice Against Epistemicide*. Boulder, CO: Paradigm.

Shilliam, R. (2020) Redeeming the 'ordinary working class'. *Current Sociology* 68(2): 223–40.

Spivak, G.C. (1988) *In Other Worlds: Essays in Cultural Politics*. London: Routledge.

Spivak, G.C. (2008) *Outside in the Teaching Machine*. New York: Routledge.

Steinmetz, G. (ed.) (2013) *Sociology and Empire: The Imperial Entanglements of a Discipline*. Durham, NC: Duke University Press.

Sztompka, P. (2008) The focus on everyday life: A new turn in sociology. *European Review* 16(1): 23–37.

Valluvan, S. and Kalra, V.S. (2019) Racial nationalisms: Brexit, borders and little Englander contradictions. *Ethnic and Racial Studies* 42(14): 2393–2412.

Virdee, S. and McGeever, B. (2018) Racism, crisis, Brexit. *Ethnic and Racial Studies* 41(10): 1802–19.

West, C. (1993) *Race Matters*. Boston: Beacon Press.

WHAT IS SOCIOLOGICAL ABOUT THE DIGITAL SOCIETY?

Noortje Marres

LEARNING OBJECTIVES

- To learn to describe defining transformations of digital societies and grasp the relevance of sociological ideas to understanding these transformations.
- To gain knowledge of key concepts, methods and insights in the emerging field of digital sociology.
- To understand that fundamental relations between society, technology and knowledge are changing in a digital society.
- To learn about the potential of digital research practices to develop engaged ways of combining knowing and doing – representation and intervention – in society.

 Framing Questions

1. Digital technology gives rise to new forms of discrimination. Why is it too simplistic to attribute these harmful effects to technology itself?

WHAT IS SOCIOLOGICAL ABOUT THE DIGITAL SOCIETY?

2. Arguably, the rise of online platforms is leading to a 'platformization' of society. What are the key features of this process?
3. One important difference between digital and other technological societies is that digital technologies operate directly on social categories. Can you give an example to clarify how this works?
4. Sociologists have developed engaged approaches to knowing society with digital technologies. What distinguishes these approaches?

Introduction

In the summer of 2020, thousands of UK students took to the streets to protest against the computer-generated A-level exam results they had just received. Because of the COVID pandemic, no A-level exams took place that year, and after the government decided exam results were to be determined by algorithm, many received grades that were lower than anticipated. Instead of relying on the predicted marks already submitted by teachers, the government's algorithm determined scores on the basis not only of pupils' past performance, but also that of the school they attended. As a consequence, nearly 40% of students saw their expected grade reduced, and students from **state** schools in poorer neighbourhoods were significantly over-represented in this group, resulting in widespread criticism that the government's computational methodology was biased against young people from disadvantaged backgrounds (Pagnamenta, 2020; Satariano, 2020). The many student-led protests across the UK highlighted this bias, featuring slogans like 'judge potential not post code' (Clayton and Kleinman, 2020) and 'your algorithm doesn't know me' (Quinn and Adams, 2020).

The UK exams algorithm fiasco of 2020 provided a stark example of digital transformation of society to which sociologists have drawn attention over the last few decades: the digitalization of society is enabling new ways of knowing and intervening in society, which transform relations between knowledge, technology and power. In this chapter you will learn to think sociologically about such defining transformations of the digital society, focusing on the following changes in particular: the rise of new forms of discrimination, the platformization of society, and shifting arrangements for knowing and doing – representation and intervention – in a digital society. The chapter will show why it is not enough to consider features of digital technologies themselves if we are to understand these defining transformations of society: they arise from interactions between technology, people, organizations and data. You will learn about the contributions that sociology makes to understanding digital societies, and to connecting social analysis with social change: adopting a sociological approach makes possible engaged ways of knowing society with digital technologies. Sociological analysis does not just provide knowledge *of* society but enables responsive approaches to knowing and intervening in social life *with* social actors.

Digital Forms of Discrimination

Over the last few decades, sociologists have investigated the uptake of computational instruments like the UK exams algorithm in different sectors, from policing to education and culture, and its consequences for society. These studies have shown that as organizations increasingly rely on computational systems to deliver their services, new technological forms of discrimination are introduced into social life. Today, any type of organization, from a bank to a restaurant, is likely to rely on some form of digital data analytics, as they analyse customer data and other sources of information to derive actionable insights, such as calculating credit scores in order to make a mortgage offer (Poon, 2007), or analysing 'customer variables' to determine the personalized price of an airline ticket, and so on. As a consequence of these practices, people with particular attributes – like the postal code area they live in, as in the above example, or their **age** or ethnic background – are being singled out for advantageous or disadvantageous, and sometimes harmful, treatment. (The categories of age and ethnic background are also discussed in Chapters 13 and 14.) In a well-known case, a digital recommendation system that was used in US Courts to advise judges about the likelihood that a defendant would commit further crimes after their release from prison was shown to be biased against black people. White convicts with a similar criminal record received comparatively lower recidivism scores than their black counterparts (Angwin et al., 2016). Crucially, these types of computational bias usually arise without those affected having any direct knowledge of this, while at the same time they may have all too concrete effects on their lives. They have also given rise to intense debate about how computational forms of discrimination come about, and what should be done to address them (Selbst et al., 2019).

The Politics of Technology in a Digital Society

The insight that technology isn't always neutral and may be biased against particular social groups is not new. In a digital society, however, technological discrimination appears to be increasingly widespread, and it may also, sociologists have argued, be taking on new forms. Long before the advent of scoring by algorithm, sociologists of technology studied what they called the politics of technology (this topic is also covered in Chapter 22). They showed that a diverse range of supposedly neutral **technologies**, from road systems to dietary labels, discriminate against particular groups of people. One infamous example is the introduction, in the middle of the 20th century, of low bridges on Long Island in New York, as a consequence of which buses could no longer access the island. This prevented bus users, who were more often poor and black, from visiting Long Island's sandy beaches, while richer, and often whiter, car owners continued to do so (Winner, 1980).

2.1 Key Case

Star

Another well-known study focuses on the introduction of a new type of nutritional labelling on food products in the 1980s. This made it possible for consumers to calculate their calorie intake, but it did not help people with allergies or illnesses like diabetes to find out whether the food in question would be safe for them to eat (Star, 1991). Social studies of technical systems like roads and food labelling showed that the technologies in question are not neutral but have normative effects: their introduction into social life affects different categories of people differently, empowering and benefitting some while disempowering and harming others (such as dieters vs diabetics). They also have wider effects on society: once implemented, technological systems may help to establish certain practices as normal (such as dieting) or desirable (car ownership, as in the case of the Long Island bridges discussed above), while rendering others more difficult, unattractive or impossible.

The proliferation of digital technologies across social life from the 1990s onwards, from the web to smartphone apps, has given rise to new everyday practices, power asymmetries and social problems. The **digitalization of society** is a multi-faceted process, as different technologies, from search engines to computational navigation systems, play many different roles in the restructuring of social life (Sassen, 2002), as will be discussed in more detail below. However, the rise to prominence of so-called big data analytics is often singled out as playing a key **role** in the rise of new forms of discrimination in a digital society (Bigo et al., 2019). Taking advantage of the abundant data made available by digital devices in use across society, from web-browsing histories to credit card transaction records and GPS-based location data that is captured via smartphones, tech companies have developed sophisticated computational systems to collect, store and 'mine' this data and thus to monitor, understand and act on user behaviour (Kennedy and Moss, 2015). To add another example to those listed above, health insurance companies today use so-called red-flagging algorithms: they rely on computational data analytics to detect potentially fraudulent insurance claims, a practice which results in people being denied coverage or in the rejection of health benefit claims, often with the individuals in question having no way of knowing the cause of the denial of service (Eubanks, 2018).

Social studies of the role of data analytics in society show that particular social groups are disproportionately affected by their uptake. Those without stable jobs or homes are more often targeted by red-flagging algorithms used in insurance and monitoring for governmental purposes such as the provision of social benefits. In the United Kingdom, new online 'subprime' lenders like Wonga specifically target potential customers with low credit scores. As they rely on social media data and other sources of personal data to create these credit scores, it is especially less well-off social media users who are affected by the uptake of big data analytics by consumer debt providers like Wonga. Joe Deville (2016) has highlighted how big data has enabled the use of digital devices as 'captation devices' by companies like Wonga: big data analytics makes possible micro-targeted communications with potential clients, using personalized messages to lure vulnerable people into relations of financial obligation that it can seem impossible to get out of. Virginia Eubanks argues that the increasing use of data analytics in both the public and commercial sectors is giving rise to a 'digital poor house', a computational equivalent of the buildings constructed in the 19th century to govern the poor, and where the containment of the **population** in buildings made possible the observation and control of behaviour. Today, Eubanks argues, these architectures consist not only of brick-and-mortar but equally of data, algorithms, digital apps and online interfaces.

How Do Big Data Analytics Discriminate? The Cases of Insurance and Policing

What is distinctive about the forms of discrimination, and wider power asymmetries, that new computational techniques for knowing and governing populations give rise to in a digital society? To answer this question, sociologists argue that we should investigate not just the technical features of digital systems themselves, but also how these systems align with, exacerbate and/or transform forms of discrimination that already exist in society.

Alberto Cevolini and Elena Esposito (2020) have described how this works in the insurance sector. Here, the calculation of price has always been discriminatory in a narrow sense: particular social groups (for example, young male drivers) have had to pay more for their car insurance than others (say, older women) for a long time already, as insurance companies rely on the statistical analysis of risk to calculate the probability of accidents occurring for different segments of populations. However, today so-called 'predictive' data analytics is used to determine risk, and this is changing the ways in which price discrimination works in this sector. As long as insurance companies relied on probabilistic statistics to determine risk, the price of insurance (premiums) depended on *which population segment one belonged to* (with different segments defined in terms of fixed attributes such as age, gender, and education). However, computational data analytics makes it possible to predict risks on the basis of much more fine-grained categorizations of social groupings: by mining data as diverse as social media data, credit scores, behavioural data collected using smart watches or black boxes installed in people's cars, computational **methods** are today used to define new risk categories through social data analysis. Factors such as 'driving an orange car' or 'buying expensive spa treatments', it turns out, can serve as reliable indicators of risk, according to the new big data methodologies that are sometimes referred to as 'personalised insurance' (Cevolini and Esposito, 2020).

Further insight into how the dynamics of discrimination may be changing in an age of computational analytics can be found in Sarah Brayne's (2017) study of the use of data surveillance in neighbourhood policing. Brayne studied the use of Predpol, a predictive policing tool marketed by the software company Palantir, by the Los Angeles Police Department (LAPD). Some of the ways in which big data analytics gives rise to discrimination, her study makes clear, can be identified by examining the software itself. Predpol analyses location-based crime data to identify the 'hottest' individuals in a given neighbourhood, which can then be used to focus policing resources, an approach praised by the LAPD as 'the most efficient way to reduce crime' (Brayne, 2017). But in Predpol's methodology, prior 'police contact' is one factor that increases an individual's 'hotness' or risk score, marking this individual out as being more likely to commit a crime. This means that being suspected by the police – on whatever ground – leads to an individual being categorized as potentially dangerous, a cycle of escalating suspicion in which the prejudice of policemen and women are all too likely to play a role.

Furthermore, we would fail to understand the role of Predpol in discrimination if we only consider the methods built into this technological system: we also need to consider its role in policing practice and examine the effects of 'technology in use' (Suchman, 2007).

Brayne's fieldwork study, based on observations of policing on the street and interviews with police officers, shows how LAPD police officers use Predpol intelligence in unanticipated ways, for example using Predpol location-based information to address people in the street by their first name: 'so maybe it's put in his mind, "Oh, they're on to me, they know who I am"' (Brayne, 2017: 989). In describing how big data analytics is used by the LAPD in practice, Brayne shows that Predpol's discriminatory effects derive at least in part from the ways in which it aggravates biases already present in the policing technique of stop-and-search. Long before the introduction of Predpol, stop-and-search patterns were already unequally distributed across race, class and neighbourhood. And well before Predpol, the interpellation of individuals in the street by using their first names featured among policing methods. Indeed, Predpol relies on data gathered through previous stop-and-search interventions to enable policemen and women to identify suspicious individuals by name. In this way, this digital system does not simply cause discriminatory practices. Rather, its use by the LAPD amplifies and aggravates the discriminatory effects already present in existing policing arrangements.

It's Not Just the Technology, Stupid: Interactions Between Technology, Data and Society

Sociological studies of the use of computational analytics by the police and insurance companies help to identify the forms of discrimination enabled by data technologies in a digital society. They also make it clear that these forms cannot be adequately understood if we consider only the technical features of digital data systems themselves. Rather, the uptake of data analytics in specific sectors and practices transforms the dynamics of discrimination already present – or latent – in existing arrangements in society, arrangements on which the very functioning of digital systems often relies. In other words, in a digital society discrimination arises from social-technical arrangements: from interactions between technology, organizations, data, practices and people. In this fundamental respect, the effects of big data technologies on society are not so different from the politics of technology studied by sociologists of technology from the 1980s onwards.

But the politics of data technologies are distinctive in a number of ways. A key aspect of data analytics is that it facilitates interventions targeted at individuals. The new types of digital, networked environments for social life – social media, smartphone apps, CCTV cameras and data sensors in the built environment – generate masses of granular data pertaining to specific events, locations, individuals and behaviours. This in turn makes it possible for organizations to assign individuals to more fine-grained analytic categories, and on this basis target interventions at these individuals. This not only enables 'personalization' – treatment tailored to individual characteristics – but also new forms of discriminatory interventions, such as the red-flagging in insurance of customers with certain attributes. In other words, computational analytics makes possible the individuation of discrimination, as specific persons like 'Johnny' are singled out by software as suspicious.

However, sociological studies like Brayne's demonstrate that even if intervention is targeted at individuals, this does not mean that in a digital society discrimination lacks a social dimension – to the contrary. And this is for two reasons. First, even as big data methodologies enable forms of categorization and targeting that pertain to individuals, these processes still involve the creation of social groupings – the identification of shared attributes (Lury and Day, 2019). Second, as noted, because big data analytics are often used as part of existing practices and arrangements that involve categorizing individuals in groups based on the analysis of populations, they are especially prone to extend already existing patterns of discrimination. They frequently end up disadvantaging groups who share particular attributes, such as spending power, literacy, **ethnicity**, gender, location or class, and are likely to aggravate existing social asymmetries.

Expand Your Knowledge

- Brayne, S. (2017) Big data surveillance: The case of policing. *American Sociological Review* 82(5): 977–1008.
- Cevolini, A. and Esposito, E. (2020) From pool to profile: Social consequences of algorithmic prediction in insurance. *Big Data & Society* 7(2). DOI: 10.1177/2053951720939228.

Platform Societies? Digital Transformations of Everyday Life, Societal Arrangements, and Intimate Relations

To understand digital transformations of society, we should not only investigate the effects that particular technologies, such as 'big data analytics', have on specific institutions or social groups, important though this is. We should also examine how digital innovation affects, disrupts and transforms wider arrangements in everyday life: the economy, the public sphere and culture. The rise of **online platforms** has been a key focus of sociological research in this respect. Over the last two decades or so, a broad range of socio-economic arrangements, from retail to transport and entertainment, has been transposed onto online settings, with tech companies offering a plethora of user-friendly apps and services that make it possible to do anything from grocery shopping to watching a film and hailing a taxi via a smartphone or desktop computer. Large commercial platforms like Facebook and Amazon are the most well-known, but there is also a growing number of locally operating digital services, such as Nextdoor, a smartphone app for neighbourhoods, which enables sharing of local news, furniture for sale, gossip, and so on. The latter community-oriented services build on earlier volunteer-led, not-for-profit initiatives which were developed in the 1990s, such as freecycle. org, a website for the community-based exchange of goods. However, as today's large online platforms operate at scale, it has become indisputably clear that digitization transforms wider societal, economic and political arrangements.

The Platformization of Society

Platforms can be briefly defined as 'programmable digital infrastructures controlled by platform operators [...] which curate the interactions of [...] a variety of users' (Grabher and König, 2020). Their rise has enabled the development of new **forms of exchange** between organizations, individuals and places, and new forms of value extraction from these forms of exchange, which are often to the advantage and profit of the companies that own platforms. This development is sometimes referred to as the 'platformization' of society (Van Dijck et al., 2018). This process of platformization entails several interlocking transformations of existing activities, relations and arrangements in society.

First, the insertion of digital networked technologies into everyday life makes possible the transposition of key components of socio-economic activities into online settings, something which more often than not, results in changes in the types of actors involved in these activities, and the division of roles between them. For example, after the introduction of car-hailing apps, taxi drivers who used to be employed by a local car service were more likely to work as independent 'contractors' for a California-registered tech company, and as a consequence the number of local services has plummeted (McGregor et al., 2015). Second, in one and the same go, everyday socio-economic activities such as taking a taxi become the object of new forms of data capture, performance management and value extraction by tech companies. Driving for – and with – a car-hailing service like Uber means becoming the subject of data-driven evaluation, as both drivers and passengers are monitored and analysed, receiving scores on this basis. This use of performance analytics is key to the business model of 'on demand' mobility, enabling new economic forms of organization such as dynamic pricing. It also lends credibility to the investment proposition that platform-based services provide new ways of optimizing and valorising mobility. And it leads to the offloading of labour and costs onto other actors: in the platform economy, services are treated like software, with the 'hardware' of owning a car, not to mention maintaining the street environment, being left to drivers and other actors in society (Törnberg and Uitermark, 2020).

The uptake of online platforms across the economy and society has multi-faceted consequences for many different aspects of social life, which are currently being documented by sociologists. Take the case of the global platform Airbnb, which has changed tourism, real estate markets, the aesthetics of the home, as well as wider relations between the public and the private in our societies. As a growing number of home-owners rent out rooms via this platform across the world, this has contributed to a significant rise in rent in many cities, pricing out local communities. And, as photos of people's homes are now routinely posted on the web, private places are turned into public showcases in a new way, and something called the 'Airbnb aesthetic' has emerged, as the homes on **display** on this site, in cities from Budapest to Chicago, begin to look more and more the same (Bialski, 2017). This is also to say that a defining feature of the platformization of society is that it presents a cross-cutting phenomenon. Far from presenting a technological transformation primarily, the rise of digital platforms affects the economy, society, culture and public life all at once. Accordingly, a **sociology** of platformization cannot concern itself only with the relations between technology and society but must be ready to engage with all aspects of society, and sociology.

Infrastructuralization of the Digital Society?

Following the rise of platforms, governments, the public sector, and companies formerly belonging to the public sector, such as privatized utility companies, increasingly rely on online platforms for the delivery of essential services. As a consequence, digital services are becoming indispensable to the conduct of everyday life, a development that has been referred to as the **'infrastructuralization'** of the internet (Plantin et al., 2018). In an earlier period, that of the 1990s and the early 2000s, the Internet was primarily associated with the rise of participatory culture, enabling everyday people to take on a more active role in culture, politics and economy, and to assume the new, hybrid role of what has been called the prod-user (part-user and part-producer of cultural goods) (Beer and Burrows, 2007). By contrast, today's platforms are a lot more like electricity and transport systems, such as trains: it is exceedingly difficult to go about social life without using the internet, and more and more governments leave citizens no other viable way to conduct essential activities like paying for parking, applying for a residence permit, or submitting a gas meter reading. While platformization of societies involved the transposition of an ever-widening range of everyday activities onto digital settings, today internet-based systems are becoming critical to participation in and the functioning of society. Take the case of WeChat in China, a WhatsApp-like system which is heavily controlled by the Chinese government and also includes an app for making payments: as one user observed, the only way to sign up to the local football club is now via WeChat (Plantin and De Seta, 2019).

As digital arrangements acquire the status of infrastructure in our societies, they enable a succession of seemingly un-ending further transformations, from the **datafication** of social life – whereby more and more practices involve data generation, analysis and feedback (Van Dijck, 2014) – to the rise of 'sensing' societies (Gabrys, 2014), with digital sensors today being used to monitor anything from forests to air quality, the performance of buildings or your very own sleeping patterns (Neff and Nafus, 2016). It remains to be seen how enduring these digital arrangements will prove to be. Indeed, some digital innovations end up demonstrating the limits of digitalization, as in the case of COVID-19 tracking and tracing apps and other apps, the uptake of many of which has been highly limited, casting doubt on the idea of the 'appification' of governance, let alone society (Dieter et al., 2019).

The consequences of the digitalization society are thus varied and multi-faceted. But most sociologists are in agreement that digital transformations are affecting the organization of society on a fundamental level. One important aspect of this is what used to called the 'digital divide' (Selwyn, 2004): the emerging divisions in society between Internet users and non-users, and the social exclusion of those who lack access to increasingly common Internet-based services. With the infrastructuralization of the internet, the threat of digital innovation to **social cohesion** acquires a logistical dimension: as the infrastructuralization of the internet is actively pursued by governments, the ideal of universal coverage is falling victim to myriads of technical, material and organizational challenges – programmes of digitization are undertaken without credible guarantees that provisions will be accessible to all citizens. In countries like the UK at least, there is a close connection between the rise of the platform society and the dismantling of the welfare state.

'Friends': The Digital Remediation of Social Forms

Besides transforming socio-economic activities and wider societal provisions, digital innovation affects social life in a third fundamental way. One of the distinctive features of digital societies, as compared to the technological societies of other eras, is that digital technologies operate directly on the very forms of social life, such as what it means to be 'friends'. Sociologists have argued that what counts as a friend in today's society is transformed by popular social media like Facebook (Beer, 2017; Bucher, 2013). The algorithms that suggest friends to Facebook users implement a very particular definition of friendship: the most well-known of these algorithms is called People You May Know (PYMK) and is based on the assumption that you are likely to want to be friends with a friend of a friend. It is based on the idea of 'homophily', the idea that people will want to engage with people who like similar things as they do. Social and cultural theorists have criticized this conception of friendship, as '[t]he friend of friend approach represents a "subtle form of limiting access to *difference*"' (Chun, 2018).

The concept of re-mediation has been put forward to highlight that, in a digital society, social phenomena such as friendship do not just play out between people. As digital technologies increasingly serve as media of social life, social activities such as reading a message from an acquaintance become mediated – even 'formatted' – through digital devices, such as the 'friend' or 'like' button. And as practices such as 'liking' come to be inscribed into social life, they may also start to inflect shared understandings, such as what it means to be part of a community. As David Beer (2008) explains: 'as [social networking sites] become mundane, the version of friendship they offer begins to remediate and shape understandings of friendship more generally'.

As already suggested above, these **entanglements** of technology and society are also changing relations between society and economy. Platformization may lead to the economization of social life, as platforms fold more and more everyday activities, and actors, into economic logics of exchange, value extraction, performance management and optimization. However, in the current context in which global tech corporations dominate both the Internet and the global economy, it is easy to forget that digitalization equally makes possible the 'socialization' of economy: even as social activities – like staying over with an acquaintance in a different city – become re-formatted as participation in the platform economy (Airbnb), the opposite is also happening. Take the rise of co-work spaces in neighbourhoods, where the economic activity of work becomes re-formatted as a form of community participation. To understand these varied effects, sociologists are today studying the 'inter-articulation' of economy and social life, the ways in which activities that used to be considered as belonging to separate 'domains' of society become more closely interrelated through technology (Marres, 2017).

These dynamics are affecting not just friendship but many social phenomena, including reputation. For centuries, sociologists have studied how the structure of societies and social groups depends on the ways in which social status is gained and lost within them. In today's society, online platforms attempt to capture dynamics of reputation through technologies of rankings and scoring, such as the star system used by the travel site TripAdvisor, with the aim of deploying these reputational markers to valuate and organise services (Scott and Orlikowski, 2012). This has multi-faceted consequences, not least for *work* in the platform economy. As platform rankings and ratings increasingly serve as stand-ins for reputation, engagement with platforms has become practically *compulsory* in certain sectors such as freelance creative work (see Gandini (2016) on the reputation economy). Furthermore, as reputation gets re-mediated as a metric (stars and rankings), this also turns the social category of 'reputation' into something more akin to a technical artefact or a navigational system, something we can use to orient ourselves in the world (Esposito and Stark, 2019).

Expand Your Knowledge

- Plantin, J.C. and De Seta, G. (2019) WeChat as infrastructure: The techno-nationalist shaping of Chinese digital platforms. *Chinese Journal of Communication* 12(3): 257–73.
- Van Dijck, J., Poell, T. and De Waal, M. (2018) *The Platform Society: Public Values in a Connective World*. Oxford: Oxford University Press.

Thinking Sociologically About the Digital: Changing Relations Between Technology, Society, and Knowledge

How, then, to think sociologically about digital societies? While the previous sections discussed sociological contributions to our **empirical** understanding of defining digital transformations of contemporary societies, this section will offer a more general discussion of what is distinctive about sociological understandings of the digital. To this end, I will review three different sociological approaches: (1) the contextual perspective, which examines the development and use of digital technology in practice; (2) the interactive perspective, which analyses wider processes of interaction and 'interactivity' between technology, knowledge and society; and (3) the **methodological** perspective which seeks to understand transformations of ways of knowing and intervening in digital societies. Below, I will discuss the differences between these perspectives, but at the outset it is important to emphasise the fundamental commitment that they have in common. Today, virtually all social studies of digital technologies start from the insight that social transformations associated with digital innovation cannot be adequately understood by considering only the features of technologies themselves. To understand digital transformations, we must investigate **socio-technical arrangements** in society: the systems, organizations, practices and events that define digital societies are neither purely technical nor solely human but arise from and consist of interactions and associations between technologies and people.

Contextualizing the Digital: The Social Shaping of Technology

One tried-and-tested solution to the challenge of how to investigate, and demonstrate, the social dimensions of technological innovation is to conduct fieldwork studies of 'technology in use'. This approach was developed in the 1980s as a general methodology in the social study of technologies (MacKenzie and Wajcman, 1999), but it has been productively applied in the study of digital technology also, as in Brayne's (2017) study of the use of big data analytics in policing, discussed above. A related approach is comparative analysis, which offers a way to examine whether and how the same technology produces different effects on social life in different settings. Adopting the latter approach, Angela Christin (2018) has examined the introduction of metrics in newsrooms in two different news organizations, one in New York and one in Paris, showing that the uptake of metrics has very different consequences in these different organisations: 'At the U.S. site, editors make significant decisions based on metrics, but staff journalists are relatively unconcerned by them. At the French site, however, editors are conflicted about metrics, but staff writers fixate on them' (Christin, 2018: 1382).

Studies like Christin's can help to counter '**technological determinism**', the widespread tendency to understand technology as the principal engine of social change. Technological determinism can be defined in terms of a simple conceptual schema, with an arrow running from technology to society, but not the other way around: following this schema, digital transformations are explained by describing how technology as an active **force** impacts on a largely passive society. Studies of digital technology in context have shown time and again that this schema is too simplistic and indeed false: it is through their active uptake in **social practice** – something which tends to entail transformations of the technologies in question – that technologies acquire the capacity to change society (Wajcman, 2015; Woolgar, 2002).

Digital Sociology: Interactivity Between Technologies, People and Ideas

Some sociologists have argued that in order to understand digital transformations of society, we need to complement, elaborate and move beyond the core concept of the 'social shaping' of technology. They argue that in digital societies, it is becoming less and less plausible to assume that the 'social contexts' in which technologies are introduced – such as news organizations – are somehow 'given' in society. Today, digital innovation is transforming the very settings, environments and types of organizations in which social life unfolds (Marres, 2017). Social media, like Twitter and Facebook, technologically re-mediate existing forms of communication and interaction – the news report, the chat – and the way they combine different social forms in networked, data-intensive settings is giving rise to new types of social environments, like co-work spaces. For this reason, digital sociologists argue that to understand digital transformations we must adopt a more symmetrical perspective on society and technology: we should analyse not just the digital shaping of society, or the social shaping of the digital, but interactions between technology, forms of organizations, people, and much else besides, in socio-technical assemblages.

In making this proposal, digital sociology invokes classic sociological concepts. Take the well-known proposition put forward by Dorothy and William Thomas (1928), which states that 'when men define situations as real, they are real in their consequences'. A similar idea was put forward by sociologists like Howard Becker and Stanley Cohen in the 1960s and 1970s, as they drew attention to '**labelling** effects': putting people into categories can profoundly affect them – for instance, when young people were referred to in newspapers as 'gang members' this had profound consequences for the youth in question, in terms of how society perceived them, their self-understanding and the courses of action open to them. In the 1980s and 1990s, sociologists of technology such as Susan Leigh Star showed that, in technological societies, such interactive dynamics of labelling, by which placing people into certain categories affects how they are perceived, defined and treated, does not only unfold between people and ideas but notably involves technological agents of categorization. As discussed above, Leigh Star (1991) showed how, in a technological society, ideas gain power when they become materialized in technological devices and infrastructures, and interact with **social practices** in that way. For Star, this is key to 'the politics of technology': as technologies become embedded in social practices, categories materialized in technology, such as that of 'the healthy diet', can become inscribed into social practices in imperceptible ways, which can affect people profoundly: they may, for instance, feel ashamed for being allergic. It is these socio-technical dynamics of labelling that I refer to as 'interactivity' between technology, society and ideas, and which acquire new importance in a digital society.

In a digital society, dynamics of interactivity between categories, technologies and social practices may be taking on new forms, in the following two ways. First, in a digital society, dynamics of interactivity operate on distinctively social ideas, such as 'friendship' and 'reputation'. Second, in a digital society, interactivity gains a participatory dimension, as digital technologies make possible new forms of feedback between technology, data analysis and social practices (Lury and Day, 2019).

2.1 Key Case

Tay the Chatbot

The case of the racist chatbot, Tay, can serve as a helpful reminder of how the dynamics of socio-technical interactivity work in a digital society. Tay was released by Microsoft to showcase the potential applications of intelligent chatbots in the new 'service economy', but after little more than 24 hours the bot was found to be spewing racist abuse on the internet. It was subsequently declared that 'Twitter' or – in a different version of this story – the alt-right platform 4Chan had *taught* Tay to be racist by manipulating the machine-learning algorithm that was central to its functioning. However, tracing back Tay's racist behaviour to the extreme communities on the Internet that fed Tay racist expressions does not tell the whole story (Neff and Nagy, 2016). As Sanjay Sharma (forthcoming) argues, this case makes it clear that **racism** in a digital society remains misunderstood as long as we seek to trace back its effects to either social forces or to how the technology works. Digital racism arises from interactivity between social communities, ideas and digital technologies: digital artefacts like Tay make possible the amplification of racist ideas proliferating in society, while social communities amplify the racist ideas proliferating in digital platforms.

Methodological Transformations of Society, Technology and Knowledge

A third and last perspective on the digital society highlights that digital innovation has given rise to new ways of knowing and intervening in society. In a well-known early contribution to **digital sociology**, Mike Savage and Roger Burrows (2007) argued that the rise of computational analytics entails a shift in the methods for social research that prevail in society: in the second half of the 20th century, methods like survey analysis and focus groups dominated scientific, industry and governmental research on society, but in the 21st century, computational forms of social data analysis like network mapping and topic modelling are becoming influential in each of these sectors. This shift entails changes on many levels, including in the type of experts that contribute to making knowledge about society, which today includes many more computational scientists and physicists than before (Halford and Savage, 2017). Furthermore, these new ways of knowing do not just affect how prevailing social phenomena are represented, they also make possible new forms of intervention in social life, as demonstrated by the social studies of big data analytics in insurance and policing, discussed above. To understand these shifts in forms of representation and intervention in a digital society, sociologists have adopted a methodological perspective: their work details the methods, techniques and assumptions that underpin digital ways of knowing and intervening in society, and investigates whether and how these methods, techniques and assumptions may end up organizing relations between society, technology and knowledge in distinctive ways.

This methodological perspective has brought into view the following shifts in ways of knowing and intervening in a digital society. Before the rise of the Internet, a prevalent methodology for the representation of populations in science, government and industry was sample survey analysis: here, society is defined as a fixed statistical object (the population), which is measured against a grid of stable categories defined by variables such as age, gender, income level and educational attainment. Today, however, digital infrastructures make possible a different, more dynamic, way of knowing society. Instead of measuring society against pre-determined variables that define the population in terms of fixed attributes such as age, income, ethnicity, education and so on ('the population as aggregate'), today's data scientists 'seek to detect signals, behaviours, actions, performances' (Cardon, 2016: 49). Digital analytics enable the detection of new, fine-grained categories in data, and this makes it possible to analyse 'dynamic assemblages', ever-changing groupings who share some transient socio-material attributes (likes cats, lives in London, etc.), but not others (Lury and Day, 2019). Crucially, the composition of dynamic assemblages may change as a consequence of feedback in digital communications systems (for example, reading blogposts about trees has turned me into a buyer of a breathable raincoat, placing me in the environmental category). Carolin Gerlitz and Celia Lury (2014) refer to these shifting socio-cultural groupings as 'participatory assemblages', highlighting that the formation of user groupings is not just an artefact of data analysis but is equally informed by continuous user participation (recursive feedback).

Sociological studies of digital societies thus offer contextual, interactivist and methodological analyses of their defining transformations. But how can thinking sociologically about society make a difference to society? Answering this question, Jesse Daniels and Karen Gregory (2016) propose that digital sociology helps us understand technological innovation 'as an area of social formation and conflict'. Digital sociology researches practices and processes involving digital technology as a site of social change. We have seen in this chapter that, in contemporary digital societies, this involves a very broad range of phenomena, from the rise of the reputation economy to self-tracking and digital racism. That is also to say that while digital sociologists tend to reject the understanding of digital technology as the 'engine of change' as misguided – because it leads us to wrongly disregard the active roles played by social actors, practices and structures in processes of social change involving technology – many *do* affirm the close connections between digital innovation and social change. The digital, and 'tech' more widely, present a privileged site of transformation in contemporary societies. Arguably, this is a fortiori the case for *digital* technologies, as many of these technologies are specifically designed to operate on social phenomena, as we saw above. Digital sociology is then concerned with digital arrangements as critical sites in contemporary society, settings where deep-rooted societal structures, relations and tensions are undergoing transformation and, potentially, rendered contestable and negotiable.

Expand Your Knowledge

- Christin, A. (2018) Counting clicks: Quantification and variation in web journalism in the United States and France. *American Journal of Sociology* 123(5): 1382–1415.
- Lury, C. and Day, S. (2019) Algorithmic personalization as a mode of individuation. *Theory, Culture & Society* 36(2): 17–37.

Digital Methods: Developing Engaged Ways of Knowing Society

Understanding digital innovation as a critical site of social change, digital sociologists have explored different ways for digital sociology to actively engage with socio-technical processes of transformation in a digital society. They do so in diverse ways, including by developing our understanding of key digital transformations, as discussed in the previous sections. However, digital sociologists have also taken up digital methods to develop more responsive ways of knowing – and engaging with – society. (The topic of digital methods is also discussed in Chapters 9 and 10.)

Over the last decade or so, sociologists have taken up digital tools for data capture, analysis and visualization to conduct sociological research (Edwards et al., 2013). In doing so, sociologists are re-purposing research methods and techniques that are used across fields, from computer science to data journalism and social media studies, for sociological research. What is distinctive about this research, I want to propose here, is that sociologists are using digital methods to develop engaged ways of knowing society, and this in a number of ways.

First, sociologists have shown that digital methods can be used to surface critical phenomena in society and elucidate social problems which are difficult to capture by other means. Sharma and Brooker (2016) have used hashtag analysis to surface everyday racism in social media. Conducting an in-depth analysis of tweets that include hashtags like #notracist on Twitter, Sharma and Brooker (2016) show how racism denial and obfuscation are used as strategies in racist discourse on Twitter. Importantly, in demonstrating this, the authors also show how Twitter analysis can be used to surface *latent* social phenomena. 'Racism denial' is not a topic on Twitter: the users of the '#notracist' hashtag usually do not mention one another, and tweets involving this hashtag are rarely retweeted. (This topic of 'racism denial' is also covered further in Chapter 12.) Yet, by using hashtags to delineate a data set of all tweets using this expression, we can arrive at a composite view of seemingly individual, unconnected expressions. In this way, Sharma and Brooker are able to surface racism as a digital assemblage: a distributed phenomenon 'constituted by the informational logics of hashtags, software interfaces and algorithms, networked relations, racial dis/ordering, and meanings and affect' (Sharma and Brooker, 2016: 470). Their study surfaced a socio-technical phenomenon which otherwise would have remained latent, implicit and invisible, and unavailable for critical reflection and engagement.

Second, digital sociologists are using digital methods to develop more participatory ways of knowing society. Gregory and Maldonado (2020) designed a study of 'work in the **gig economy**' which involved Deliveroo delivery riders as active research participants. The researchers invited delivery drivers to contribute to their study in two ways: first, using smartphone apps and customized mapping software, delivery riders were invited to collect, share and discuss locative data showing their delivery routes through Edinburgh during one night in October 2016. Second, after visualizing the app data, the researchers invited delivery drivers to offer their interpretations of riding patterns. In this way, Gregory and her colleagues deployed data maps as devices of 'elicitation', inviting riders to name and make explicit aspects of their daily rides that cannot be gleaned from the maps without this. While some of the study's insights derived solely from data analysis – such as the finding that Deliveroo 'increases bike traffic on key roads and puts pressure on already busy streets' – in other cases, findings drew directly on the riders' interpretations, such as the insight that female riders placed value on familiarity with the neighbourhoods in which they worked, something which could account for their presence in less central parts of the city. In studies like Gregory's, digital sociologists take advantage of the interactive affordances of digital technology to actively engage everyday actors in the analysis of social life and the articulation of social problems which touch directly on their lives.

Finally, digital sociologists are using digital methods to develop different ways of intervening in social life, or more precisely, of combining representation and intervention in creative ways (Marres, 2017). Lonneke van der Velden and Joe Deville (Deville and Van der Velden, 2015; Van der Velden, 2014) developed a digital method for making 'data veillance' publicly visible. To do this, they used a tool, Ghostery, which was originally created by civic tech developers to 'show you the invisible web': when visiting a web page, the Ghostery browser plug-in shows you which companies have embedded scripts in that page to collect data about you. As an activist tool, Ghostery was designed to increase *individual* awareness of online surveillance. Re-purposing this tool for social research, Van der Velden and Deville transformed Ghostery into a digital method that can make visible how surveillance operates on the *collective* level. By amalgamating Ghostery data, their study showed how websites of specific organizations, ranging from the Dutch government to consumer credit lenders, use data to trace particular sets of users and to act upon them. In doing so, this study showed the potential for digital sociology to conduct engaged research in a third way: by engaging with activists and working with activist tools, sociologists can help to create publicly relevant knowledge of how digital arrangements, such as dataveillance, are transforming society, and in this case, the relations between citizens and the state, and between consumers and commercial organizations. (The subject of the public role of sociology is covered further in Chapter 13.)

Efforts to develop engaged ways of knowing society with digital methods are still underway, and we have seen that they raise complex questions about the changing role of social research, and the representation of society, in a digital age. In this respect, one further contribution of sociology, as compared to other fields using digital methods, is that digital sociologists engage with a fundamental challenge in digital social research: the double importance of the digital in knowing society. For digital sociology, the digital presents both a phenomenon in society (a topic), and also a method, a way of knowing society with the digital (Marres, 2017). This 'doubling' of object and method has long been a familiar trope in sociology, well before the advent of the digital. For example, sociologists study how knowledge is used in society, but at the same time sociologists themselves are creators of knowledge. It is often said that this 'double' engagement defines sociology as a reflexive form of knowledge (Beck et al., 1994). However, when it comes to digital sociology, which is concerned with technology, society and knowledge, we can draw a slightly different conclusion. As digital sociology attends to the connections between digital innovation, societal change and ways of knowing society, it raises the question: what alternative, even new, ways of connecting knowledge, technology and social change are made possible by digital innovation? In digital sociology, the doubling of method and object invites not only **reflexivity** but also experimentation: the development of engaged forms of social enquiry (Marres, 2017).

WHAT IS SOCIOLOGICAL ABOUT THE DIGITAL SOCIETY?

Expand Your Knowledge

- Deville, J. and Van der Velden, L. (2015) Seeing the invisible algorithm. In *Algorithmic Life: Calculative Devices in the Age of Big Data*. London: Routledge, pp. 87–106.
- Sharma, S. and Brooker, P (2016) #notracist: Exploring racism denial talk on Twitter. In *Digital Sociologies*. Bristol: Policy Press, pp. 463–85.

CHAPTER SUMMARY

This chapter provides an overview of defining transformations of digital societies: new forms of discrimination, the platformization of society and the rise of new ways of knowing society. To understand these transformations, sociological studies show, it is not enough to examine the features of digital technologies themselves: digital transformations of society arise from interactions between social practices, technologies, data and wider societal arrangements. To understand these interactions, sociologists have developed different approaches: contextual studies which examine technology in use, studies of wider socio-technical assemblages, and methodological analyses, which investigate emerging data-intensive ways of knowing and intervening in society. Each of these approaches elucidates digital innovation as a critical site of social change in contemporary society. However, sociologists do not only describe and reflect on digital transformations, they also use digital methods to develop more interactive ways of knowing – and engaging with – society.

REVIEW QUESTIONS

1. Digital technologies give rise to new forms of discrimination. What is special about digital technologies as compared to other technologies in this respect?
2. Sociologists have argued that digital systems have acquired the status of infrastructure in contemporary society. How does this affect relations between citizens and the state?
3. New computational technologies of big data analytics make it possible for organizations to target *individuals*. Sociologists have argued that this does not make these technologies any less 'social'. Why not?
4. Sociologists have put forward the concept of 'labelling' to understand how ideas gain power in society. Can you give an example of a process of labelling involving digital technologies? How does this exemplify the power of ideas, and of technology, in a digital society?
5. To have less oppressive technology, it is not enough to change technology – it equally requires changes in society. Why?
6. Many digital sociologists use digital methods of data capture, analysis and visualization in their research. This has led some to argue that we need to move beyond the *observation* of social life and develop more engaged styles of research. What is meant by this, and what is it about the digital that makes this possible?

> ### Go Further
>
> #### Books
>
> - Lupton, D. (2015) *Digital Sociology*. London: Routledge.
> - Marres, N. (2017) *Digital Sociology: The Reinvention of Social Research*. Cambridge: Polity.
> - Neff, G. and Nafus, D. (2016) *Self-tracking*. Cambridge, MA: MIT Press.
>
> #### Journal Articles
>
> - Esposito, E. and Stark, D. (2019) What's observed in a rating? Rankings as orientation in the face of uncertainty. *Theory, Culture & Society* 36(4): 3–26.
> - Kennedy, H. and Moss, G. (2015) Known or knowing publics? Social media data mining and the question of public agency. *Big Data & Society* 2(2): 2053951715611145.
> - Selbst, A.D., Boyd, D., Friedler, S.A., Venkatasubramanian, S. and Vertesi, J. (2019) Fairness and abstraction in sociotechnical systems. In *Proceedings of the Conference on Fairness, Accountability, and Transparency* (pp. 59–68).

REFERENCES

Angwin, A., Larson, J., Mattu, S. and Kirchner, L. (2016) Machine bias. *ProPublica*, 23 May. Available at: www.propublica.org/article/machine-bias-risk-assessments-in-criminal-sentencing (last accessed 30 May 2021).

Beck, U., Giddens, A. and Lash, S. (1994) *Reflexive Modernization: Politics, Tradition and Aesthetics in the Modern Social Order*. Stanford, CA: Stanford University Press.

Beer, D. (2008) Social network(ing) sites … revisiting the story so far: A response to Danah Boyd and Nicole Ellison. *Journal of Computer-Mediated Communication* 13(2): 516–29.

Beer, D. (2017) The social power of algorithms. *Information, Communication and Society* 20(1). DOI: 10.1080/1369118X.2016.1216147.

Beer, D. and Burrows, R. (2007) Sociology and, of and in Web 2.0: Some initial considerations. *Sociological Research Online* 12(5): 67–79.

Bialski, P. (2017) Home for hire: How the sharing economy commoditises our private sphere. In A. Ince and S.M. Hall (eds) *Sharing Economies in Times of Crisis*. London: Routledge, pp. 83–95.

Bigo, D., Isin, E. and Ruppert, E. (2019) *Data Politics: Worlds, Subjects, Rights*. London: Routledge.

Brayne, S. (2017) Big data surveillance: The case of policing. *American Sociological Review* 82(5): 977–1008.

Bucher, T. (2013) The friendship assemblage: Investigating programmed sociality on Facebook. *Television & New Media* 14(6): 479–93.

Cardon, D. (2016) Deconstructing the algorithm: Four types of digital calculations. In J. Roberge (ed.) *Algorithmic Cultures*. London: Routledge.

Cevolini, A. and Esposito, E. (2020) From pool to profile: Social consequences of algorithmic prediction in insurance. *Big Data & Society* 7(2). DOI: 10.1177/2053951720939228.

Christin, A. (2018) Counting clicks: Quantification and variation in web journalism in the United States and France. *American Journal of Sociology* 123(5): 1382–1415.

Chun, W. (2018) Queerying homophily. In C. Apprich, F. Cramer, W. Hui Kyong Chun and H. Steyerl (eds) *Pattern Discrimination*. Lüneburg: Meson Press.

Clayton, J. and Kleinman, Z. (2020) The algorithms that make big decisions about your life. *BBC News*, 17 August. Available at: www.bbc.co.uk/news/technology-53806038 (last accessed 30 May 2021).

Daniels, J. and Gregory, K. (eds) (2016) *Digital Sociologies*. Bristol: Policy Press.

Deville, J. (2016) Debtor publics: Tracking the participatory politics of consumer credit. *Consumption Markets & Culture* 19(1): 38–55.

Deville, J. and Van der Velden, L. (2015) Seeing the invisible algorithm: The practical politics of tracking the credit trackers. In L. Amoore and V. Piotukh (eds) *Algorithmic Life: Calculative Devices in the Age of Big Data*. London: Routledge, pp. 101–20.

Dieter, M., Gerlitz, C., Helmond, A. and Tkacz, N. (2019) Multi-situated app studies: Methods and propositions. *Social Media + Society* 5(2): 1–15.

Edwards, A., Housley, W., Williams, M., Sloan, L. and Williams, M. (2013) Digital social research, social media and the sociological imagination: Surrogacy, augmentation and re-orientation. *International Journal of Social Research Methodology* 16(3): 245–60.

Esposito, E. and Stark, D. (2019) What's observed in a rating? Rankings as orientation in the face of uncertainty. *Theory, Culture & Society* 36(4): 3–26.

Eubanks, V. (2018) *Automating Inequality: How High-Tech Tools Profile, Police, and Punish the Poor*. New York: St. Martin's Press.

Gabrys, J. (2014) Programming environments: Environmentality and citizen sensing in the smart city. *Environment and Planning D: Society and Space* 32(1): 30–48.

Gandini, A. (2016) *The Reputation Economy: Understanding Knowledge Work in Digital Society*. London: Springer.

Gerlitz, C. and Lury, C. (2014) Social media and self-evaluating assemblages: On numbers, orderings and values. *Distinktion: Scandinavian Journal of Social Theory* 15(2): 174–88.

Grabher, G. and König, J. (2020) Disruption, embedded: A Polanyian framing of the platform economy. *Sociologica* 14(1): 95–118.

Gregory, K. and Maldonado, M.P. (2020) Delivering Edinburgh: Uncovering the digital geography of platform labour in the city. *Information, Communication & Society* 23(8): 1187–1202.

Halford, S. and Savage, M. (2017) Speaking sociologically with big data: Symphonic social science and the future for big data research. *Sociology* 51(6): 1132–48.

Kennedy, H. and Moss, G. (2015) Known or knowing publics? Social media data mining and the question of public agency. *Big Data & Society* 2(2). DOI: 0.1177/2053951715611145.

Lury, C. and Day, S. (2019) Algorithmic personalization as a mode of individuation. *Theory, Culture & Society* 36(2): 17–37.

MacKenzie, D. and Wajcman, J. (1999) *The Social Shaping of Technology*. Milton Keynes: Open University Press.

Marres, N. (2017) *Digital Sociology: The Reinvention of Social Research*. Cambridge: Polity.

McGregor, M., Brown, B. and Glöss, M. (2015) Disrupting the cab: Uber, ridesharing and the taxi industry. *Journal of Peer Production* 6.

Neff, G. and Nafus, D. (2016) *Self-Tracking*. Cambridge, MA: MIT Press.

Neff, G. and Nagy, P. (2016) Talking to bots: Symbiotic agency and the case of Tay. *International Journal of Communication* 10: 4915–31.

Pagnamenta, R. (2020) The A-levels fiasco has revealed the socially toxic consequences of algorithmic bias. *The Telegraph*, 17 August. Available at: www.telegraph.co.uk/technology/2020/08/17/a-levels-fiasco-has-revealed-socially-toxic-consequences-algorithmic (last accessed 30 May 2021).

Plantin, J.C. and De Seta, G. (2019) WeChat as infrastructure: The techno-nationalist shaping of Chinese digital platforms. *Chinese Journal of Communication* 12(3): 257–73.

Plantin, J.C., Lagoze, C., Edwards, P.N. and Sandvig, C. (2018) Infrastructure studies meet platform studies in the age of Google and Facebook. *New Media & Society* 20(1): 293–310.

Poon, M. (2007) Scorecards as devices for consumer credit: The case of Fair, Isaac & Company Incorporated. *The Sociological Review* 55(2_suppl): 284–306.

Quinn, B. and Adams, R. (2020) England exams row timeline: Was Ofqual warned of algorithm bias? *The Guardian*, 20 August. Available at: www.theguardian.com/education/2020/aug/20/england-exams-row-timeline-was-ofqual-warned-of-algorithm-bias (last accessed 30 May 2021).

Sassen, S. (2002) Towards a sociology of information technology. *Current Sociology* 50(3): 365–88.

Satariano, A. (2020) British grading debacle shows pitfalls of automating government. *The New York Times*, 20 August. Available at: www.nytimes.com/2020/08/20/world/europe/uk-england-grading-algorithm.html (last accessed 30 May 2021).

Savage, M. and Burrows, R. (2007) The coming crisis of empirical sociology. *Sociology* 41(5): 885–99.

Scott, S.V. and Orlikowski, W.J. (2012) Reconfiguring relations of accountability: Materialization of social media in the travel sector. *Accounting, Organizations and Society* 37(1): 26–40.

Selbst, A.D., Boyd, D., Friedler, S.A., Venkatasubramanian, S. and Vertesi, J. (2019) *Fairness and abstraction in sociotechnical systems*. In: Proceedings of the Conference on Fairness, Accountability, and Transparency, January (pp. 59–68).

Selwyn, N. (2004) Reconsidering political and popular understandings of the digital divide. *New Media & Society* 6(3): 341–62.

Sharma, S. (forthcoming) *Digital Ecologies of Racism*. Lanham, MD: Rowman & Littlefield.

Sharma, S. and Brooker, P. (2016) #notracist: Exploring racism denial talk on Twitter. In J. Daniels, K. Gregory and T.M. Cottom (eds) *Digital Sociologies*. Bristol: Policy Press, pp. 463–85.

Star, S.L. (1991) Power, technology and the phenomenology of conventions: On being allergic to onions. In J. Law (ed.) *A Sociology of Monsters*. London: Routledge, pp. 26–56.

Suchman, L. (2007) *Human-Machine Reconfigurations: Plans and Situated Actions*. Cambridge: Cambridge University Press.

Thomas, W.I. and Thomas, D.S. (1928) *The Child in America: Behavior Problems and Programs*. New York: Knopf.

Törnberg, P. and Uitermark, J. (2020) Complex control and the governmentality of digital platforms. *Frontiers in Sustainable Cities* 2(6). DOI: 10.3389/frsc.2020.00006.

Van der Velden, L. (2014) The third party diary: Tracking the trackers on Dutch governmental websites. NECSUS. *European Journal of Media Studies* 3(1): 195–217.

Van Dijck, J. (2014) Datafication, dataism and dataveillance: Big Data between scientific paradigm and ideology. *Surveillance & Society* 12(2): 197–208.

Van Dijck, J., Poell, T. and De Waal, M. (2018) *The Platform Society: Public Values in a Connective World*. Oxford: Oxford University Press.

Wajcman, J. (2015) *Pressed for Time: The Acceleration of Life in Digital Capitalism*. Chicago: University of Chicago Press.

Winner, L. (1980) Do artifacts have politics? *Daedalus* 109(1): 121–36.

Woolgar, S. (2002) Five rules of virtuality. In S. Woolgar (ed.) *Virtual Society: Technology, Cyberbole, Reality*. Oxford: Oxford University Press, pp. 1–22.

WHAT IS SOCIOLOGICAL ABOUT THE ENVIRONMENT?

Kate Burningham

LEARNING OBJECTIVES

- To understand the centrality of environmental issues to sociology and the importance of sociological analysis of environmental issues.
- To enable critical engagement with debates about the social causes, consequences and unequal experience of environmental problems.
- To understand the variety of ways in which social change is necessary for moving towards a more sustainable future.

 Framing Questions

1. Why should sociologists be interested in environmental issues?
2. In what ways are environmental problems socially caused and socially constructed?
3. How are issues of social inequality relevant for understanding the impact of environmental problems?
4. What kinds of social change are needed for moves towards a more sustainable society?

PART 1 THINKING SOCIOLOGICALLY

Introduction

Many introductory sociology textbooks do not include a chapter on the environment. Yet it is well established that climate change has social or 'anthropogenic' causes and that environmental problems have a range of social impacts and are the topic for widespread social concern and action.

This chapter will help you develop an appreciation of what is sociological about the environment and the importance of including consideration of environmental issues in the study of contemporary society.

Sociological discussions of environmental issues often revolve around:

- Debates about the relationship between nature and society; whether the environment is an appropriate topic for sociology and, if so, how it should be conceptualized.
- Discussions of the underlying social causes of environmental problems.
- A focus on the unequal distribution and experience of environmental problems and risks.
- Discussions of environmental concern and action and what kinds of social change might be needed for moving towards a more sustainable society.

This chapter will introduce you to debates and research in these four key areas. It does not cover all sociological research on environmental issues but aims to convince you that the environment is a topic worthy of sociological attention and inspire you to find out more.

Mapping the Terrain

Sociology is about understanding contemporary society, and trying to do this without engaging with environmental issues ignores some of the most significant contemporary challenges and concerns.

Most explanations of why the environment has been absent from sociological attention trace this to the work of Durkheim. Durkheim was determined to establish sociology as a science in its own right, with a subject matter separate from that of any of the other sciences. This led him to emphasize the distinction of the social from the natural world and to insist that sociological explanations of 'social facts' must only consider other social facts, not factors which might be considered 'natural' or 'environmental'. Durkheim's legacy thus resulted in a taboo within the discipline against studying the interactions between social and natural or environmental factors. (The work of Durkheim is discussed further in Chapters 4 and 7.)

It was not until the late 20th century that the absence of serious consideration of environmental issues within sociology began to be challenged. Initial debates in the US focused on the character of the discipline. In a series of papers, Catton and Dunlap (see Dunlap, 2002, for an overview and references to this work) suggested that sociology had developed as an anthropocentric discipline which regarded humans and social life as able to be understood as entirely separate from the rest of nature and exempt from ecological limits. This profoundly un-ecological perspective needed to change to enable sociologists to explore interactions between society and the natural environment. For Catton and Dunlap, this amounted to a fundamental rethinking of the discipline's boundaries. One of the key debates in early sociological work on the environment revolved around how the discipline should approach environmental issues – did sociology need to fundamentally change to allow consideration of the interactions between natural and social factors, or could existing disciplinary concepts and theories be applied in a new focus on environmental topics?

WHAT IS SOCIOLOGICAL ABOUT THE ENVIRONMENT?

As with other areas of sociological inquiry, the substantive focus of sociological research on environmental issues has largely tracked broader societal concerns and priorities (Dunlap et al., 2002). Early sociological attention was often motivated by concerns about resource scarcity in the context of the oil crisis or focused on understanding the recent emergence of environmental groups and green parties, while by the 21st century attention had begun to focus on climate change and the related topics of energy use and sustainable consumption. Sociological research across diverse environmental topics has taken many forms. A strong strand of theoretical work has developed, both critically examining the applicability of existing perspectives for providing insights on environmental and sustainability issues, and developing new frameworks for thinking about society and nature interactions in more integrated ways. Alongside this, empirical studies have provided both quantitative and qualitative analysis of the environmental impacts, perspectives, priorities and practices of individuals, communities, governments and organizations.

When sociologists engage with environmental issues, their research questions are informed by established disciplinary concerns with social causes and consequences, social structures, social action, social practice, social change, social inequalities and social constructions. Thus, although their topic is 'environmental' and may involve the integration of findings and concepts from other disciplines, their analysis is thoroughly sociological. In this chapter, we will look in detail at how some of these sociological concepts have been employed to shed new light on environmental issues.

This chapter is divided into four sections, each of which provides an answer to the question 'what is sociological about the environment?' I argue that society and nature are interconnected and socially constructed, that environmental problems have systemic social causes, that environmental problems are unequally experienced and that social change is necessary to move towards sustainability.

Society and Nature: Interconnected and Socially Constructed

Environmental **sociology** involves recognition of the fact that physical environments can influence (and in turn be influenced by) human societies and behaviour. Dunlap and Catton argued that acknowledging and studying the connections between the natural and social worlds required a reshaping of the discipline's **boundaries**, so that 'natural' as well as **'social facts'** could be legitimately included in any analysis. While it may seem common sense to consider how social and natural factors interact, this move is highly challenging for sociologists.

As indicated above, Durkheim's insistence that only 'social facts' comprise the proper subject matter for sociology has made sociologists reluctant to engage with environment and nature. Another significant factor is the concern to avoid allegations of biological determinism. For instance, in Nazi Germany biological explanations were drawn on to legitimize the extermination of Jewish people, and they continue to be used by some to justify racial and class inequalities. It is not surprising, then, that for sociologists even to raise the question of what part natural factors may play in explaining social processes has been to 'run the risk of being tainted with an abhorrent political philosophy' (Newby, 1991: 7).

A sociologist who has taken up the challenge of theorizing the interactions between society and nature is Dickens (1992). For Dickens, considering the physical environment and society as if they are separate fails to recognize their profound interconnections; humans are 'natural' in important ways and nature has been increasingly 'humanized'. For instance, human settlements and farming shape landscapes, farm animals are selectively bred for certain characteristics and plants are modified by selective breeding and genetic modification. Dickens conceives of society and nature as in an ongoing dialectical relationship in which change in one results in change in the other. Human beings continually interact with and mediate nature's powers and properties (for example, through agriculture, land clearance, gardening, and conservation activities); as a result, some species flourish, others are constrained, and new species may be brought into being. The way in which people work on and change nature then has effects for them too. Writing in the 1990s, Dickens focused on the recent example of BSE (bovine spongiform encephalopathy), a brain disease which resulted from particular intensive farming practices. Cows developed the disease as a result of being fed BSE-infected offal (sheep's brains) and, in turn, people eating infected meat were at risk of developing Creutzfeldt-Jakob disease.

Pause for Thought

There are lots of other examples of human interactions with nature resulting in negative (environmental and) social impacts.
Do some online searches to explore the following questions:

- How might the destruction of animals' natural habitats be linked to the spread of COVID-19?
- How is eating meat related to climate change?
- What are the impacts of the use of pesticides on agricultural land for animal and insect life – and why does that matter for human beings?

Dickens concludes that to develop holistic understandings of the interconnections between nature and society, we need to challenge the idea of natural science for 'nature' and social science for people and society and instead combine different types of knowledge about the world.

Both Dickens' 'green **social theory**' and Dunlap and Catton's 'environmental sociology' can be characterized as **realist** perspectives. They both start from an acceptance of the independent reality and power of environmental phenomena and are clear that sociology has a role to play in understanding and responding to environmental problems. A rather different orientation to 'nature' and to environmental problems is offered by a **social constructionist** perspective.

Social constructionist approaches to environmental problems focus on understanding how and why particular issues come to be classified as 'natural' or 'environmental', considered problematic and rise to societal attention. Spector and Kitsuse suggest that sociologists interested in social or environmental problems should concentrate on the 'emergence, nature and maintenance of claims making and responding activities' (1977: 76). By this they mean the activities of making claims, complaints or demands for change, whether by making speeches, writing to the press, tweeting or blogging, forming a group, publishing material, holding demonstrations or boycotting a product. All of those who involve themselves in these activities participate in the process of defining environmental problems – they draw attention to the existence of a problem and seek to get it into the public eye.

The applicability of a social constructionist perspective to environmental problems is clear. It encourages sociologists to ask questions about how problems are being framed and why and how particular framings of them come to prominence at a particular time. For instance, Yearley focuses on the detail of how models and projections about climate change are constructed, applied and understood. He is clear that:

This is not to say that they are fictions, mere conventions or conclusions arrived at in tendentious ways […] But there are social scientifically interesting questions about the precise ways in which such knowledge has been **socially constructed**. (Yearley, 2009: 392–3)

Drawing on case studies of a range of environmental problems, Hannigan suggests that six factors for 'the successful construction of an environmental problem' can be identified (2006: 78). These are:

1. Scientific authority for and validation of claims.
2. Existence of popularisers who can bridge environmentalism and science.
3. Media attention in which the problem is framed as novel and important.
4. Dramatization of the problem in symbolic and visual terms.
5. Economic incentives for taking positive action.
6. Recruitment of an institutional sponsor who can ensure both legitimacy and continuity.

3.1 Key Case

The Problem of Plastic Waste

In 2017 the problem of plastic waste seemed to burst into public consciousness. The BBC documentary *Blue Planet*, fronted by Sir David Attenborough, broadcast footage of identifiable single-use plastic items such as straws, cotton buds and bottles in the stomachs of sea birds and a turtle caught in a plastic sack. The programme's message was widely taken up in news media which reproduced images of endangered marine life. Existing environmental campaigns about plastics were revitalized and new ones emerged. In response to a surge of public concern and demand for action, politicians and business leaders rushed to respond to the issue. The UK Government committed to phase out disposable packaging by 2042, many shops and organizations took steps to reduce or ban the use of single-use plastic and sales of reusable cups and bottles soared.

Environmental scientists and campaigners were surprised by the rapid rise of the problem. The level of plastic waste in the oceans had been recognized as problematic for decades without such attention, and surely climate change was a much more pressing problem? Some commentators suggested that plastic waste had been embraced as it offered an environmental issue which was much easier to respond to than climate change – something which businesses and individuals felt able to do something about. For politicians too, perhaps it provided an opportunity to be seen to be taking pro-environmental action. The response to plastic waste can be viewed positively as demonstrating growing public awareness of the impact of consumer lifestyles on the natural world, and as evidence of how quickly action can be taken, or more negatively as a 'convenient distraction' from the more profound challenge of climate change (Stafford and Jones, 2019).

 Pause for Thought

- Does the problem of plastic waste have all of the six factors which Hannigan identifies as essential for the 'successful construction' of an environmental problem?

- Hannigan suggests that economic incentives for action are essential for the success of environmental problems. What other kinds of interests might also motivate government, business and individual claims and action?

It is not only environmental problems but nature itself which may be treated as socially constructed. We have already seen Dickens' argument that what we consider to be 'natural' has been shaped by human activity but, furthermore, what we describe as 'natural' or part of 'nature' and what that implies is culturally specific, change over time and has distinct implications.

The social constructionist focus on claims has led realist environmental sociologists to suggest the perspective denies the 'reality' and independent existence of nature. Social constructionists respond that most of their studies explicitly acknowledge the existence of the problems (for example, see Yearley's insistence above that he is not suggesting that claims about climate change are 'fictions'). Their sociological research questions are not about the existence or severity of environmental problems but rather about how and by whom the reality of the problem is constructed and contested, and how different versions of that reality are used and responded to (Burningham and Cooper, 1999).

Debate about the relative merits of realist and constructionist perspectives for understanding environmental issues was fierce in the late 1990s. In a desire to move beyond this 'entrenched battle', Irwin (2013 [2001]: 162), developed a more nuanced perspective, building on aspects of **actor-network theory**. Drawing on Latour's work, he suggests that phenomena such as climate change, the hole in the ozone layer, BSE, and genetically modified organisms (GMOs) mix social and natural factors together so much that the categories of 'social' and 'natural' become meaningless. Rather than being either social or natural phenomena, they are 'hybrids'. Irwin suggests that the very categories of the natural and the social are 'actively generated co-constructions' (2013 [2001]: 173) and argues that sociologists should examine how the categories of both 'social' and 'natural' are constructed and deployed within specific cultural, institutional and ecological settings.

In this section, we've considered sociological debates about the relationship between society and nature, drawing attention to the importance of studying both profound interconnections between, and social constructions of, both. While informed by very different **theoretical** perspectives, and leading to distinct research questions, Dickens' emphasis on the profound interconnections between nature and society resonates with Irwin's discussion of 'hybrid' phenomena. We conclude with Irwin that 'theoretical pluralism and open-mindedness' (2013 [2001]: 162) are to be encouraged in the sociological study of environmental issues.

Environmental Problems Have Social Causes

In the previous section, we explored debates about the relationship between society and the environment. It is widely accepted that environmental problems are caused by human activity and have consequences for people as well as for nature. Sociologists are interested in unpacking both the characteristics of the **social systems** which underlie environmental issues and understanding the ways in which social groups and social life are affected by environmental risks and problems.

Human impacts on the environment are often understood at the level of individual behaviour: what we eat; how we get about; what we buy; how we heat our homes; how much waste we produce – all have environmental impacts. Rather than focusing on individual factors which shape behaviour, however, sociologists seek to understand the causes of environmental problems more systemically.

A body of research has developed in recent years which explores how everyday **social practices** have become more resource intensive – and thus environmentally damaging – over time. Social practice approaches focus on shared ways of doing everyday things within society – for instance, eating, washing, and travelling – and draw attention to the social understandings and the technological infrastructures which normalize and 'lock in' particular ways of doing things. For instance, a study by Hand et al. (2005) explores the increasing popularity of showering at least daily in the UK. This is an environmentally significant practice both in terms of water use and the energy required to heat water. The study highlights how technological developments, changing cultural ideas about the body and the self, and the prioritization of convenience have all contributed to shape what has become a widely shared, taken-for-granted practice.

Much of the sociological work which explores the social causes of environmental problems focuses more broadly on systems of production and consumption. In an early analysis, Schnaiberg (1980) emphasized the negative environmental and social consequences of the 'treadmill of production' in industrial societies. He describes the effect of industrial production on the physical environment as a series of withdrawals of natural resources and additions such as pollution. In industrial capitalist societies, the continual drive to increase production has negative effects on the environment, increasing the level and kind of withdrawals and additions. While the treadmill of production exists in all industrialized societies, Schnaiberg suggests that it is particularly characteristic of capitalist societies, as 'the basic social force driving the treadmill is the inherent nature of competition and concentration of capital' (1980: 230).

Schnaiberg's critique is echoed in contemporary discussions about the limitations of relying on economic growth (usually measured by GDP) as the key indicator of how well a country is doing. Jackson (2017) writes that the continual throughput of consumer goods necessary for economic growth threatens the resource and environmental conditions on which any meaningful 'prosperity' depends. Recent decades have witnessed a progressive decline in environmental quality across the world, particularly in relation to climate change, biodiversity loss and deforestation. While increases in GDP are highly correlated with increases in wellbeing in the poorest countries, the impacts are less pronounced in richer countries in the Global North, with life expectancy, infant mortality, participation in education and even life satisfaction all showing diminishing returns as incomes rise (Jackson, 2017). At the same time, inequalities within and between nations have deepened, with income and wealth increasingly concentrated at the top. Thus, the underlying economic system which shapes systems of production and consumption is identified as playing a fundamental role in causing both environmental and social problems.

For Beck (1992), the understanding that environmental risks are socially caused heralds a whole new social era. Writing in the 1990s, he suggested that industrial societies were becoming risk societies, characterized by anxiety about environmental risks and a questioning of **development**. More recently, geologists have heralded the emergence of a whole new geological **age**, the **Anthropocene**, in which the scale and pace of human activity now equal that of geological forces in shaping global environmental change. Moore (2017) argues that a more appropriate term would be the 'Capitalocene', drawing attention specifically to the impact of capitalist economies rather than to 'human' or 'industrial' activity in general terms.

Capitalism is not undermining itself by the proletariat becoming revolutionary, as Marx and Engels suggested, but by over-exploiting the resources on which it relies (Urry, 2010). Responsibility for this environmental damage is not equally distributed. Research indicates that richer people with bigger houses, more cars, more consumption of goods and more frequent overseas holidays have higher '**carbon footprints**' (Druckman and Jackson, 2009). Urry (2010) and Sayer (2015) draw particular attention to the 'excess consumption' of the 'super rich' for driving high greenhouse gas emission levels:

Their consumption is excessive and wasteful and diverts resources away from the needy and deserving. Their carbon footprints are grotesquely inflated and they may have an interest in continued fossil fuel production threatening the planet. (Sayer, 2015: 2)

This section has illustrated that debates about the underlying social causes of environmental problems permeate environmental sociology, with authors variously focusing on aspects of social practices, industrial production, consumption, capitalism and systemic economic factors.

Expand Your Knowledge

- To learn more about the global causes and consequences of environmental problems, and the implications for sociology, read: Lidskog, R. and Lockie, S. (2020) Globalizing environmental sociology. In K. Legun, J. Keller, M. Bell and M. Carolan (eds) *The Cambridge Handbook of Environmental Sociology: Volume 2*. Cambridge: Cambridge University Press, pp. 30–46.

Environmental Problems Are Unequally Distributed and Experienced

Environmental change is often presented as an issue which affects everyone, but the likelihood of being affected by environmental risks and hazards is unequally socially distributed. As Ageyman and Evans (2004) point out, globally and nationally environmental problems impact disproportionately upon the poor, but most environmental pollution and degradation are caused by the actions of the more affluent. Poverty often intersects with other elements of environmental disadvantage, for instance disabled people, members of minority ethnic groups, women and older people are disproportionately likely to be poor.

The existence of environmental inequality was highlighted first in relation to the location of hazardous sites in the United States. A grassroots '**environmental justice**' movement formed, protesting about the disproportionate location of toxic facilities and waste sites in poor black and Latino neighbourhoods. This inequality can be understood with reference to three factors (Harlan et al., 2015): economically, hazardous faculties tend to be located in sites where land is cheap, which is often also where poorer communities can afford to live; socio-politically, poorer communities have limited resources to successfully campaign against the siting of facilities, making it easier for developers to site them in their neighbourhoods; and, finally, historic racial discrimination in the United States has resulted in distinct patterns of residential segregation, limiting the capacity of people of colour to choose where to live. The environmental justice movement framed the issue as an extension of the civil rights agenda. The movement ultimately led to the signing of an Executive Order requiring federal regulatory agencies to make achieving environmental justice part of their mission. Thus, 'environmental justice' is both a vocabulary for grassroots mobilization and a policy principle (Ageyman and Evans, 2004).

Since its emergence in the United States, the concept of environmental justice (see Walker, 2012) has subsequently broadened to consider multiple dimensions of disadvantage and a broader range of environmental 'bads' and 'goods', both internationally and within other countries.

Taking the issue of climate change first, stark international inequalities are evident: 'Most basically, the world's most marginalised people are suffering worst and first from the rise in climate related disasters' (Harlan et al., 2015: 128).

This issue is increasingly framed as one of climate injustice, with those in the poorest countries worst affected by a crisis largely caused by emissions from the consumption activities of richer ones. MacGregor (2009) argues for the need for sociological research on the environment to also include gender analysis. She points particularly to the distinct ways in which women are likely to be adversely impacted by climate change in the Global South, both because they are more likely to be poor and 'because their everyday provisioning work will be made more difficult due to climate change-related impacts such as drought (e.g. walking further for clean water and firewood, spending more time growing food for **household** consumption)' (2009: 135). Similar patterns of inequality are evident in relation to a range of other environmental issues, with poorer countries (and the poorest within them) bearing the brunt of dirty, dangerous and environmentally damaging extraction, production and processing of resources while consumption benefits accrue elsewhere.

--- Expand Your Knowledge ---

- To learn more about the variety of ways in which a consideration of gender is important for understanding environmental issues, read: MacGregor, S. (2009) A stranger silence still: The need for feminist social research on climate change. *The Sociological Review* 57(2_suppl): 124–40.

While the environmental justice movement in the US drew attention to disproportionate environmental impacts along lines of race and **ethnicity**, in the UK the focus has largely been on class-based inequalities. This is largely because of different patterns of geographical settlement and political context in the two countries, and because of the historic lack of a civil rights movement in the UK (see Walker, 2012). Ground-breaking research was published by Friends of the Earth, who found that almost two-thirds of the most polluting industrial facilities were located in areas of below-average income. The authors claimed:

This is a clear cut case of environmental injustice in which poorer people are subjected to greater risks and impacts of pollution, and have less control over their environment, while the benefits of the industrial activity largely accrue elsewhere. (Mclaren et al., 1999: 2)

Exposure to air pollution from roads is also unequal; areas of the greatest poverty tend also to be areas which have the greatest concentration of roads yet the lowest levels of car ownership. Exposure to air pollution compounds other social inequalities in health, being linked to the likelihood of deaths from lung cancer, COVID-19 and other respiratory diseases.

Environmental inequalities do not only exist in relation to the likelihood of exposure to hazards but also in terms of differential levels of vulnerability in the event and its aftermath. For instance, considerable research has been carried out in relation to vulnerability to flooding. Poorer people are likely to be more vulnerable to the impacts of flooding as they are less likely to be aware of flood risks, more likely to live in housing which is particularly badly affected and less likely to have insurance to cover any losses. The physical and psychological health impacts of flooding also vary with pre-existing health status, which is often worse in deprived neighbourhoods. Here too, women and members of minority ethnic groups often bear particular impacts (see Walker and Burningham, 2011).

Many of the observations about unequal vulnerability to flooding also apply to other environmental risks associated with climate change, such as heatwaves. Those with existing respiratory or heart conditions and the very old and very young are most vulnerable to heatwaves. However, other factors such as the quality of housing and the built environment, local urban geography, income, employment and tenure type may all also influence an individual's exposure and sensitivity to high temperatures, as well as their ability to respond to conditions to avoid heat stress. Many of the factors tend to overlap, so that people on low incomes who live in high-rise social housing in central urban areas without access to green spaces, for example, may be particularly vulnerable to high temperatures (Harlan et al., 2015).

So, poorer people are likely to be disproportionately exposed to and vulnerable to environmental 'bads' such as pollution and flooding. They are also less likely to have sufficient access to the environmental 'goods' (e.g. clean air, healthy food, energy, green spaces) necessary for good health and quality of life. For instance, in England, single-parent households, unemployed people and those living in privately rented property are most likely to be fuel poor, paying above-average household fuel bills and having a disposable income left after paying for housing and fuel costs which is below the poverty line. Another environmental 'good' which seems to be unequally enjoyed is access to and use of green spaces, which is increasingly recognized as being important for health and psychological wellbeing. Research in both the UK (Roe et al., 2016) and the US (Dai, 2011) indicates that members of minority ethnic groups are less likely to have access to or regularly use green spaces.

Thus, it is clear that both between and within countries there are a range of both environmental 'bads' and 'goods' which are unequally distributed along existing lines of social inequality and difference. This is an issue which is the focus of campaigns by both local and global activist and environmental movements. There is a tendency to talk of climate change and other environmental threats in a universalizing way, as problems for all of the globe, for which we are all responsible; however, some are more responsible than others and some are more at risk.

3.2 Key Case

Fast Fashion

The availability of cheap clothing is a clear benefit for consumers in the Global North; however, its production comes at a considerable cost for the environment and for people in the Global South involved in its production.

In 2019 the UK Government's Environmental Audit Committee examined the issue. It concluded:

fast fashion has made it affordable for everyone to experience the pleasure of style, design and the latest trends … [but] the way we make, use and throwaway our clothes is unsustainable. Textile production contributes more to climate change than international aviation and shipping combined, consumes lake-sized volumes of fresh water and creates chemical and plastic pollution. Synthetic fibres are being found in the deep sea, in Arctic sea ice, in fish and shellfish. Our biggest retailers have 'chased the cheap needle around the planet', commissioning production in countries with low pay, little trade union representation and weak environmental protection. In many countries, poverty pay and conditions are standard for garment workers, most of whom are women. We are also concerned about the use of child labour, prison labour, forced labour and bonded labour in factories and the garment supply chain. Fast fashion's overproduction and overconsumption of clothing is based on the globalisation of indifference towards these manual workers. (House of Commons Environmental Audit Committee (2019) Fixing fashion: Clothing consumption and sustainability. London: House of Commons. Available at: https://publications.parliament.uk/pa/cm201719/cmselect/cmenvaud/1952/1952.pdf (last accessed 30 May 2021))

 — Pause for Thought

- What dimensions of social inequality are evident in the impact of fast fashion?
- What kinds of changes might be needed to respond to the environmental and social impacts of fast fashion, and where does responsibility for change lie?

Moving Towards Sustainability Requires Social Change

The concept of sustainability encompasses environmental, economic and social elements. It is not simply about mitigating and adapting to environmental problems, but also about ensuring economically secure and socially just societies which can deliver quality of life for present and future generations. I argued above that environmental problems have social causes, being bound up with systems of production and consumption. Clearly, then, changes to these systems are required if we are to move towards a more sustainable future.

Reducing greenhouse gas emissions is a pressing international priority. How these emissions are calculated has important implications for understanding where change is necessary, as Tim Jackson, Professor of Sustainable Development at the University of Surrey, explains:

Hear from the Expert

Every signatory to the UN Framework Convention on Climate Change (FCCC) must report national emissions of greenhouse gases – the gases that cause climate change – on a 'territorial basis'. This means that all emissions of carbon dioxide (for instance) from industry, government, households and transport activities within the country are calculated and reported annually to the FCCC. There are a couple of big problems with this 'territorial account'; it doesn't include 'international emissions' associated with aviation and shipping (for instance), or the carbon associated with making goods which are imported from outside the country. These omissions have led to calls for the 'carbon footprint' to be calculated on a 'consumption basis'. This would mean counting all of the carbon emissions associated with providing the goods and services consumed by everyone in the country – even if some of these emissions take place outside the country. This reveals that the carbon footprint of developed countries is typically higher than the emissions reported to the FCCC, because richer countries import so many goods from poorer ones. In the UK, the consumption-based account is almost 70% higher than the territorial account; and while the

(Continued)

> territorial emissions have been falling quite sharply over the last couple of decades as we focus on reducing carbon within the country, the 'carbon footprint' is declining much less rapidly. Another advantage of the 'carbon footprint' approach is that it's possible to see more clearly which bits of our lives are particularly 'carbon-intensive'. Flying is a very carbon-intensive way to travel. So is car-driving. Taken together, travel emissions in the UK constitute around one fifth of the carbon footprint. Food is also surprisingly carbon-intensive, though eating meat is much more carbon-intensive than being vegetarian. Eating less meat and driving and flying less are amongst the many actions individuals can take to reduce their impact on the planet. (Jackson, 2017)

Focusing on **consumption-based emissions** in this way highlights the connections between ordinary patterns of consumption and carbon emissions, and places the responsibility for carbon emissions with those countries enjoying the benefits of consumption. Changing entrenched, 'normal' patterns of travel and diet within countries requires attention to the social **norms** and physical infrastructures which sustain certain ways of doing things and constrain others.

However, rather than focusing on the challenges and opportunities for such social change, government and NGO campaigns often emphasize the responsibility of individuals to change aspects of their own lives – to drive less, fly less, eat less meat and turn their thermostats down. A very strong sense of individual responsibility is conveyed; it's up to each of us to change our own lifestyle in order to work towards a more sustainable future – the planet is literally in the hands of individuals in these campaigns:

Image 3.1 The Message of Individual Responsibility for a Sustainable Future

Credit: European Commission, *You Control Climate Change: An Awareness Raising Campaign of the European Commission* (2006–7). Reproduced under the Creative Commons Attribution 4.0 International (CC BY 4.0) licence. https://creativecommons.org/licenses/by/4.0/

In a study of green consumers, Connolly and Prothero (2008) understand the appeal of such narratives of individual responsibility through the theoretical lens of reflexive modernization, in particular its relevance to issues of self-identity. They argue that, as a result of globalization, people feel more interconnected with distant environments and people. At the same time, increasing **individualization** means that consumption becomes fundamental to the construction of self-identity. In combination, Connolly and Prothero suggest that these processes result in a situation where people feel that global issues are not only directly significant to them, but that through individual acts of consumption their personal decisions can contribute to a global influence. The focus on individualized responsibility also needs to be understood within the broader context of political ideologies of **neoliberalism**.

While changes in everyday consumption are critical, a focus on *individual* lifestyle change is problematic for a number of reasons. **Empirical** research with those trying to live more sustainably finds that compromise, inconsistency and feelings of confusion and guilt are common (Connolly and Prothero, 2008).

> ### Student Voices
>
> #### Students' Reflections on Sustainable Consumption
>
> I asked some students about their everyday experiences of sustainable consumption and their responses indicate that while they might want to consume sustainably, this is often challenged by other everyday priorities and pressures:
>
> At any point I could be trying to get on top of a number of things, be it setting a work timetable, making time for my partner and friends, or trying to manage my diet. I consume bottled water; it's something I don't feel good about, and something I periodically try to change. But in amongst all the things I'm trying to work through, drinking bottled water becomes a concession I make with myself. (Tom)
>
> As a young person I believe our generation feels pressure to consume sustainably more than any other, whether this be in the form of fashion, food or transport. On social media we are bombarded with posts showing plastic in the ocean or new sustainable brands all with 'affordable' prices. Despite wanting to consume sustainably, as a student with a part time job it can be hard to consume in the most sustainable way, because often it is the most expensive. As a result, we find ourselves in a constant battle between making sustainable choices and staying out of our overdrafts. (Eleanor)
>
> I find it difficult to consume sustainably sometimes because sustainable options are not always easily accessible. For example, sustainable fashion is often only sold online and at much higher prices than fast fashion. Charity shops can be a good option, but it can be hard to find specific pieces or items that fit you right. (Olivia)

The students' responses in the box above draw attention to the way in which issues of time, money, and accessibility often shape decisions about what to buy – or not buy – and the sense of dilemma they face in reconciling their desire to 'do the right thing' with the everyday hurdles in their way. Sustainable consumption is not only about buying – or not buying – specific products though; it is also about making changes to everyday practices of diet, travel and energy use. In all of these domains, issues of expense may come into play along with the fact that infrastructures may not support the uptake of less environmentally damaging practices. For instance, public transport may not be available and insulating your home or changing your home energy source may not be possible for those in rented accommodation or certain types of housing. Further, many 'choices' are not entirely individual but are made in the context of relationships and the competing priorities and needs of other household members. Maniates (2001) argues that individualizing responsibility for sustainable consumption deflects attention from the systemic changes needed and encourages people to think about their capacity for action only in terms of limited consumer decisions rather than the potential of collective citizen action to press for more fundamental institutional change (the role of social movements is covered further in Chapter 25).

Recognition of the extent to which more sustainable living will require infrastructural and cultural change is central to social practice approaches to consumption. The practice approach shifts the question from 'how do we change individuals' behaviour to be more sustainable?' to 'how do we shift everyday practices to be more sustainable?'. Reshaping these practices does not rely on changing individuals' attitudes and behaviours but by shifts occurring in the elements of practice – the cultural understandings, social meanings, **technologies** and infrastructures which support and facilitate particular resource-intensive modes of practice (Shove et al., 2012).

If industrial production, capitalism, consumerism or an economy based on growth are identified as the underlying causes of environmental problems, then fundamental social and economic transformation is necessary. Jackson (2017) suggests that moving towards a more sustainable society requires abandoning the preoccupation with economic growth to enable a more equal society in which people are able to live well within **ecological limits**. This might include changes in models of business ownership, shorter working hours, increased localization and a reprioritization of government spending towards:

investments in things that we value most: fine education, arts, healthcare, childcare and elderly services, public infrastructure, renewable energy, and community development. (Vergragt, 2013: 124)

While the scale of social change desired and identified as necessary here may seem 'unrealistic' (Geels et al., 2015), Levitas (2013) urges sociologists to engage with such utopian visions of the kind of society we want.

Whether authors identify individual behaviour change, changes in social practices or changes in the economic basis of society as necessary, all agree that widespread social change is necessary to respond to current environmental problems and future risks. Although the approaches outlined differ in focus and scale, in practice elements of them may be used in combination.

CHAPTER SUMMARY

- In this chapter, I have argued that the environment is an important area of sociological study because:
    - There are profound interconnections between society and nature.
    - Environmental problems are socially constructed.
    - Environmental problems have social causes.
    - Environmental impacts are unequally experienced.
    - Social change at all levels is necessary to respond to contemporary environmental challenges.
- This chapter is by no means a comprehensive overview of all of the exciting work which sociologists are carrying out in this important area. Sociological work on environmental issues is not confined within a distinct disciplinary sub-field. For instance, sociologists of consumption research sustainable consumption, sociologists of media and communication explore media framings of environmental stories and digital environmental activism, and sociologists of social movements study environmental organizations and activism. (The topics of consumption, social movements and media are covered further in Chapters 2, 21 and 25.)

WHAT IS SOCIOLOGICAL ABOUT THE ENVIRONMENT?

REVIEW QUESTIONS

1. How are society and nature interconnected?
2. What are some of the social causes of environmental problems?
3. What does it mean to describe environmental problems as being socially constructed?
4. In what ways are environmental impacts unequally experienced?
5. What kinds of social change might be necessary to respond to environmental problems?

Go Further

Books

- Dunlap, R.E. and Brulle, R.J. (eds) (2015) *Climate Change and Society: Sociological Perspectives*. Oxford: Oxford University Press.

A thorough and detailed presentation of sociological analyses of crucial aspects of climate change, including consumption, inequality and social movements.

- Sutton, P. (2017) *Nature, Environment and Society*. London: Macmillan International Higher Education.

An accessible overview of key issues for sociologists in engaging with issues of nature and environment and a critical review of the most significant debates in environmental sociology.

- Walker, G. (2012) *Environmental Justice: Concepts, Evidence and Politics*. London: Routledge.

A wide-ranging analysis of international research on environmental justice, exploring the diversity of ways in which environment and social difference are intertwined.

Journal Articles

- Pellow, D.N. and Nyseth Brehm, H. (2013) An environmental sociology for the twenty-first century. *Annual Review of Sociology* 39: 229–50.

A useful review of the origins and development of environmental sociology and key perspectives in the field, with a focus on issues of inequality.

- Mol, A.P. (2006) From environmental sociologies to environmental sociology? A comparison of US and European environmental sociology. *Organization & Environment* 19(1): 5–27.

An interesting overview and explanation of differences in theoretical perspective and emerging areas of consensus between sociologists studying environmental issues in America and Europe.

- Shove, E. (2010) Beyond the ABC: Climate change policy and theories of social change. *Environment and Planning A* 42(6): 1273–85.

An influential and provocative paper which argues for the potential for social science to make a much more extensive contribution to the challenges of climate change.

(Continued)

> ### Websites
>
> - www.britsoc.co.uk/groups/study-groups/climate-change-study-group
>
> The British Sociological Association has an active Climate Change study group. Its website provides information about events, links to prize-winning research papers and a series of blogs.
>
> - https://drrobertbullard.com
>
> Bob Bullard is both a sociologist and a key figure in the American Environmental Justice movement. His website has information about events, links to press articles and video interviews and a series of blogs.
>
> - https://friendsoftheearth.uk
> - www.greenpeace.org.uk
> - https://extinctionrebellion.uk
> - www.wwf.org.uk
>
> Environmental organizations often have good websites. You could use these to explore how particular environmental issues are being constructed by different groups and to understand more about campaigning strategies.

REFERENCES

Ageyman, J. and Evans, B. (2004) 'Just sustainability': The emerging discourse of environmental justice in Britain? *The Geographical Journal* 170(2): 155–64.

Beck, U. (1992) *Risk Society: Towards a New Modernity*. London: Sage.

Burningham, K. and Cooper, G. (1999) Being constructive: Social constructionism and the environment. *Sociology* 33(2): 297–316.

Connolly, J. and Prothero, A. (2008) Green consumption: Life-politics, risk and contradictions. *Journal of Consumer Culture* 8(1): 117–45.

Dai, D. (2011) Racial/ethnic and socioeconomic disparities in urban green space accessibility: Where to intervene? *Landscape and Urban Planning* 102(4): 234–44.

Dickens, P. (1992) *Society and Nature: Towards a Green Social Theory*. London: Harvester Wheatsheaf.

Druckman, A. and Jackson, T. (2009) The carbon footprint of UK households 1990–2004: A socio-economically disaggregated, quasi-multi-regional input–output model. *Ecological Economics* 68(7): 2066–77.

Dunlap, R.E. (2002) Environmental sociology: A personal perspective on its first quarter century. *Organization & Environment* 15(1): 10–29.

Dunlap, R., Michelson, W. and Stalker, G. (2002) Environmental sociology: An introduction. In R. Dunlap and W. Michelson (eds) *Handbook of Environmental Sociology*. Westport, CT: Greenwood Press, Ch. 1.

Geels, F.W., McMeekin, A., Mylan, J. and Southerton, D. (2015) A critical appraisal of sustainable consumption and production research: The reformist, revolutionary and reconfiguration positions. *Global Environmental Change* 34: 1–12.

Hand, M., Shove, E. and Southerton, D. (2005) Explaining showering: A discussion of the material, conventional, and temporal dimensions of practice. *Sociological Research Online* 10(2).

Hannigan, J. (2006) *Environmental Sociology*, 2nd edition. London: Routledge.

Harlan, S.L., Pellow, D.N., Roberts, J.T., Bell, S.E., Holt, W.G. and Nagel, J. (2015) Climate justice and inequality. In R. Dunlap and R. Brulle (eds) *Climate Change and Society: Sociological Perspectives*. New York: Oxford University Press, pp. 127–63.

Irwin, A. (2013 [2001]) *Sociology and the Environment: A Critical Introduction to Society, Nature and Knowledge*. London: John Wiley & Sons.

Jackson, T. (2017) *Prosperity without Growth: Foundations for the Economy of Tomorrow*. London: Routledge.

Levitas, R. (2013) *Utopia as Method: The Imaginary Reconstitution of Society*. London: Springer.

MacGregor, S. (2009) A stranger silence still: The need for feminist social research on climate change. *The Sociological Review* 57(2_suppl): 124–40.

McLaren, D., Cottray, O., Taylor, M., Pipes, S. and Bullock, S. (1999) *Pollution Injustice: The Geographic Relation Between Household Income and Polluting Factories*. A Report for Friends of the Earth.

Maniates, M. (2001) Individualization: Plant a tree, buy a bike, save the world? *Global Environmental Politics* 1(3): 31–52.

Moore, J.W. (2017) The Capitalocene, Part I: On the nature and origins of our ecological crisis. *The Journal of Peasant Studies* 44(3): 594–630.

Newby, H. (1991) *One World, Two Cultures: Sociology and the Environment*. A lecture given to mark the 40th Anniversary of the founding of the British Sociological Association, February 1991.

Roe, J., Aspinall, P.A. and Ward Thompson, C. (2016) Understanding relationships between health, ethnicity, place and the role of urban green space in deprived urban communities. *International Journal of Environmental Research and Public Health* 13(7): 681.

Sayer, A. (2015) *Why We Can't Afford the Rich*. Bristol: Policy Press.

Schnaiberg, A. (1980) *The Environment: From Surplus to Scarcity*. New York: Oxford University Press.

Shove, E., Pantzar, M. and Watson, M. (2012) *The Dynamics of Social Practice: Everyday Life and How It Changes*. London: Sage.

Spector, M. and Kitsuse, J. (1977) *Constructing Social Problems*. New York: Aldine de Gruyter.

Stafford, R. and Jones, P.J. (2019) Viewpoint – Ocean plastic pollution: A convenient but distracting truth? *Marine Policy* 103: 187–91.

Urry, J. (2010) Consuming the planet to excess. *Theory, Culture & Society* 27(2–3): 191–212.

Vergragt, P.J. (2013) A possible way out of the combined economic-sustainability crisis. *Environmental Innovation and Societal Transitions* 6: 123–25.

Walker, G. (2012) *Environmental Justice: Concepts, Evidence and Politics*. London: Routledge.

Walker, G. and Burningham, K. (2011) Flood risk, vulnerability and environmental justice: Evidence and evaluation of inequality in a UK context. *Critical Social Policy* 31(2): 216–40.

Yearley, S. (2009) Sociology and climate change after Kyoto: What roles for social science in understanding climate change? *Current Sociology* 57(3): 389–405.

WHAT IS SOCIOLOGICAL ABOUT CRIME?

Eamonn Carrabine

LEARNING OBJECTIVES

- To understand the key sociological perspectives on crime and how they have developed over time.
- To enable critical reflection on the differences between them and grasp some of the ongoing controversies in the field.
- To become aware of the leading figures and schools of thought in this area of sociology in order to be a confident and critical student of their ideas.
- To locate analyses of crime in broader sociological debates.
- To be able to scrutinize broader criminological 'texts' (such as film, TV, press, internet) and make sense of them through the theories discussed.

 Framing Questions

1. In what ways, if any, is crime normal?
2. Is deviance still a useful concept?
3. What are the relationships between crime and place?

WHAT IS SOCIOLOGICAL ABOUT CRIME?

4. How do classical ideas impact on more contemporary approaches?
5. Why do men commit more crime than women?

Introduction

The question of crime is one that has the capacity to stretch the sociological imagination endlessly. Crime is a widely used word, a central theme in popular culture and a crucial dynamic shaping the political landscape. Yet, for all the seeming simplicity, there lies considerable complexity and controversy at the heart of the concept of crime. The term 'crime' appears in public debate and popular culture as if it is straightforward and obvious what it means, but the concept has many meanings and is rooted in certain social processes that have powerful ramifications.

Mapping the Terrain

Crime is always socially defined. Inevitably, this proposition provokes debate, and several competing approaches have been identified, ranging from a 'legal-consensus' definition through to one that is best understood as both 'critical' and 'utopian' (Greer and Hagan, 2001: 208–13). The differences can be summarized as follows:

- The *legal consensus* insists that a crime is whatever the state has legitimately sought to ban. In other words, the criminal law specifies those acts that constitute a crime. As such, the study of crime should be restricted to those convicted in the courts and sanctioned by the criminal justice system.
- A *socio-legal* perspective broadens the conception of crime to recognize that social harms arise from both criminal offences (such as physical assault) and civil offences (such as unscrupulous business practices). Extending the field of study in this way suggests that crimes of the powerful should attract our attention.
- The *cross-cultural* approach maintains that violations of 'conduct norms', rather than legally defined crime, is a more appropriate basis from which to develop meaningful analysis. The suggestion that some conduct norms are universal and do not vary across different cultures has not been taken very far, but the question of cultural relativism remains an important issue.
- The *labelling* perspective emphasizes that certain behaviours are not recognized as criminal unless there is a social response that labels the activity as criminal. Here the significance of the ways in which categories are constructed through the course of interactions between the self and others is highlighted.
- Taking *human rights* seriously involves a dramatic shift in focus to include social systems and social relations that inflict injury. According to this view, a crime is committed whenever a human right is violated, irrespective of the legality or otherwise of the action. It expands the definition of crime to include oppressive practices of imperialism, racism, sexism and class-based forms of exploitation.
- Finally, the *utopian conflict* approach is one conveying the range of 'new criminologies' associated with the various directions critical work has taken since the 1970s. But for all their differences (and there are many), they all share a focus on power relations and the forces curtailing the diversity of human experience.

In this chapter, we will not delve deeply into each of these positions, nor will we arrive at a single shared definition of crime; rather, you will learn the important differences between them and understand how sociologists have advanced our thinking on such matters. We begin by reviewing some of the classic statements in the field – starting with the seemingly puzzling view that crime is a normal and necessary feature of social life – before considering more contemporary studies that take this sociological insight as a point of departure for the study of deviance.

Crime as Normal

Émile Durkheim (1858–1917) is regarded as one of the 'founding fathers' of **sociology**. He was a French social theorist who, more than any other, placed crime, law and punishment at the centre of the sociological enterprise. It was in his *Rules of Sociological Method* that Durkheim (1966 [1895]: 65) claimed that 'crime is normal', as there 'is no society that is not confronted with the problem of criminality'. Even a society composed only of saints will eventually criminalize some actions or attitudes. Moreover, crime performs a 'necessary' and 'integrative part in all healthy societies', suggesting there is nothing abnormal or pathological about **deviance**. Since there is no society where individuals do not differ from collective **norms**, it is also inevitable that there will be those who appear with a 'criminal character'. This criminal character is not the consequence of intrinsic criminogenic personality traits, though some may well be mad or bad, but results from the importance attributed to these 'divergences' by the 'collective conscience' (1966 [1895]: 70).

Durkheim is clearly arguing that deviance is as much the creation of social perceptions as of an objective reality, and this heralds a decisive break with the understanding of deviation as statistically normal toward one which recognizes cultural differences. The basic view of deviance is essentially statistical, defining as deviant anything that departs too much from the average. To be left-handed or redheaded, according to this reckoning, is deviant because most people are right-handed and brunette. As such, the statistical view simplifies the problem by ignoring the many questions of value and moral disapproval that arise in discussions of the concept (see also Becker, 1963: 4–5). The lasting significance of Durkheim's argument lies in his insistence that crime is a fundamentally social phenomenon, rejecting the prevailing tendency to reduce explanations of it to the level of individual psychology or biology. This sociological approach can be seen in his influential concept of **anomie**, which continues to inform understandings of crime and deviance. (The topic of sociological conceptions of society is covered further in Chapters 5, 7 and 8.)

4.1 Key Case

Suicide

This is most fully developed in Durkheim's (2002 [1897]) classic study, *Suicide*, which demonstrated the power of sociological analysis by showing how such an apparently individualistic decision (to take one's own life) could be explained by social forces. In Durkheim's analysis, variations in suicide rates among Protestant and Catholic countries could be explained by differences in the levels of social *integration* and *regulation* they displayed. *Integration* he defined through the strength of attachment a person has to social groups, which he measured on a scale from 'egoism' to 'altruism'. *Regulation* refers to the ways group norms control individual desires, which he measured on a different scale – from 'anomie' to 'fatalism'. All four ('egoism', 'altruism', 'anomie', and 'fatalism') led to distinctive types of suicide.

Durkheim's ideas were developed by Robert Merton, especially in an early essay on 'Social Structure and Anomie' (Merton, 1938). It became one of the most important essays in American sociology, not least because it highlighted how deviance and crime were rooted in the class structure of society. Merton's 'strain theory' of criminal behaviour emphasized the importance of 'structural frustration' in the specific context of American culture between the wars. For Merton, the defining characteristic of the post-Depression 1930s was the malaise produced by the tension between the American Dream (based on an egalitarian **ideology** that anyone can make it, with enough hard work) and the actual reality of extreme economic inequality – where there are only limited legitimate opportunities for achieving the kind of material success that is so culturally exalted.

Merton's central claim is that the gulf between culture (the values placed on symbols of success, which are inevitably monetary) and structure (only a few had the means to acquire such prosperity) gives rise to a 'malintegration' at the core of American society (Merton, 1938: 673). In developing his argument, Merton reworks the concept of anomie, to describe various forms of deviant conduct generated in the United States. Merton described four very different individual responses to such structural strain: 'innovation', 'ritualism', 'retreatism' and 'rebellion' – each depending on the wider context (see Table 4.1). Merton was keenly aware of the power of advertising and the **role** of **conspicuous consumption** in sustaining an intense, competitive pressure on people to keep acquiring status symbols.

Amongst sociologists, the piece was widely accepted and highly regarded, yet from the 1960s it began to be criticized as part of a broader movement against the sociology of deviance. Yet the idea that there is a structural tension produced by market inequalities and the failure of apparently **meritocratic** systems to deliver **social mobility** and social status remains an important one, as can be seen in more recent attempts to develop a 'general strain theory' (Agnew, 1999).

	Culture goals	**Institutionalized means**
Conformity	+	+
Innovation	+	-
Ritualism	-	+
Retreatism	-	-
Rebellion	+/-	+/-

Table 4.1   Merton's Individual Responses to Anomie

Source: adapted from Merton (1938: 676)

The Chicago School

The Durkheimian legacy has been especially pronounced across the Atlantic. North American sociology emerged out of a large and diverse assortment of non-academic reform organizations and philanthropic movements seeking to reduce '**dependency**' while advancing 'progressive' causes in the late 19th and early 20th centuries. In this initial phase of the discipline's development an uneasy mix of Christian evangelicalism, social Darwinism and eugenic thought was drawn upon. One of the significant achievements of what came to be known as the 'Chicago School' of sociology lay in rejecting these early ideas and then dominating the field for the first four decades of the 20th century, playing a pivotal **role** in professionalizing and institutionalizing the fledgling discipline. Indeed, it is the sheer diversity and vitality of studies produced by the

Chicagoans that command attention. They include investigations of migration patterns, racial **conflict**, organized crime, prostitution, real-estate offices, ghettos, local newspapers, motion pictures, hobos, dance halls, intermarriage, the central business district, hotel life, mental illness, chain stores, high society, vice districts, juvenile delinquency, mass transit systems and much more besides. It is hard to disagree with the view that Chicago in the 1920s is the most studied city of all time.

Chicago itself was an extraordinary city. It was a modern metropolis exploding with new populations, producing a kaleidoscope of differing social worlds, fuelled by mass migration from all over Europe and the southern states of America. It had grown from a small town of just a few hundred people in the 1830s to over three million in the 1930s and became the second largest industrial metropolis in the country. This phenomenal growth brought with it all the signs of **modernity** – from skyscrapers, dance crazes, movies and cars through to alcoholism, bootlegging, crime, prostitution and all the grim realities of urban poverty. It is no surprise then that the study of urbanism is indelibly associated with the Chicago sociologists.

Robert Park, who led the department of sociology through its heyday, had previously been a newspaper journalist and encouraged his students and colleagues to 'tell it like it is' through fieldwork 'out there' on the streets (cited in Sumner, 1994: 42).

From Park's (1915) defining statement on 'The City', the Chicagoans understood the city as an ordered mosaic of distinctive regions, including industrial districts, ethnic enclaves and criminal areas. These so-called natural areas evolved in relation to one another to form an **urban ecology**. Research on juvenile delinquency revealed how certain parts of the city were more crime prone, irrespective of which ethnic group lived there, and that as these groups moved to other areas their crime rates decreased (Shaw and McKay, 1931). This important finding challenged the then dominant psychological explanations of deviance, which held that crime resulted from individual pathologies and personality defects. The conclusion that slums had their own **social structure**s and cultural norms, which gave deviant lifestyles **validity** and normalized criminal activity in gangs, was seen as a response to the more general **social disorganization** accompanying rapid urban growth.

Park (1925) insisted that delinquency resulted from the breakdown of neighbourhood cohesion and the inability of community organizations to integrate adolescents into the wider social order. These Durkheimian themes were developed in a number of studies exploring transitional areas, where these problems were especially pronounced. Frederick Thrasher's (1927) study of *The Gang* maintained they originated in small, informal play groups, with an internal structure and shared traditions passed on from one generation of boys to the next. Conflict with other gangs and adults was only one type of activity associated with the gangs; they were also athletic clubs and secret societies, as well as having links with local politics and organized crime.

The idea that delinquency was the outcome of ordinary interactions, passed on in particular learning situations and rationalized criminal conduct, was initially proposed by Edwin Sutherland in 1924 in his theory of '**differential association**', which highlighted how deviant values are culturally transmitted in social groups. In the decades that followed, he and his students forcefully developed the theory and extended it to 'white-collar crime', revealing how business practices could generate violations of trust and be found in every occupation. His 'discovery' of 'white-collar crime' (a term he coined) was part of a broader ambition to develop a 'general' theory of crime, insisting that criminal behaviour did not just arise among the poor and disadvantaged, but was to be found across the social structure and in the highest reaches of society (Sutherland, 1940).

4.2 Key Case

Delinquent Boys

One key intervention in these debates is in Albert Cohen's (1955) study of *Delinquent Boys*, which has deservedly become a classic. He maintained that all three of the leading sociological theories of juvenile delinquency had failed to adequately address its causes and had used concepts in largely circular fashion. In his reckoning, the Chicago School had over-emphasized the social disorganization found in zones of transition, where these areas were not so nearly deprived of community spirit as some had imagined. Merton was criticized for his instrumental understanding of deviant behaviour as a way of achieving culturally approved goals. Instead, Cohen (1955: 35–6) argued that not all crime was committed in pursuit of wealth; many delinquent gangs engaged in violence simply for 'the hell of it', so the motivations were primarily expressive.

Likewise, Sutherland's theory of differential association had taken the existence of gangs for granted, ignoring why some juveniles join and others do not and failing to explain their origins – where they come from, why gang members do what they do, and why gangs persist in some places but not others. Cohen answered these questions through the concept of subculture, insisting that the social world of the juvenile delinquent provides an alternative means of acquiring recognition and respect among disadvantaged youth.

Subcultural Theory

Although the term **subculture** was initially coined by anthropologists, it has been extensively used by sociologists on a range of topics, including delinquency in the 1950s, education in the 1960s and style in the 1970s. The initial sociological definitions regarded subcultures as subdivisions of a national culture. This emphasis on the difference between a particular social group and a larger collectivity continues in later developments of the concept. In this sense, culture is understood as a 'whole way of life' and includes the 'maps of meaning' that give shape to how the world is experienced and understood. The prefix 'sub' draws attention to the ways that the groups studied tend to be subordinate, subversive or subterranean and are thereby viewed as beneath, but still within, a dominant or mainstream culture. Consequently, sociologists have not simply studied how subcultures are censured by the majority, but they have also examined the ways subculture members perceive their difference and can challenge the status quo by developing alternative lifestyles in opposition to the wider culture.

Contemporary critics have complained that subcultural theory relies on problematic binaries such as authentic–manufactured, resistance–incorporation, subordinate and dominant, which simplify the complexities of social practice. For instance, there are conflicts within subcultures and the differences are best understood as taste distinctions rather than forms of resistance. Some now argue that society has fragmented to the extent that we live in 'post-subculture' times, implying that the concept has outlived its usefulness and is unable to grasp contemporary cultural formations. In response, terms like 'carnival', 'tribe', 'scene' and 'lifestyle' have been advanced to deal with the problems associated with subcultural theory. The suggestion is that these are better equipped to capture the proliferation, fragmentation and individualized character of contemporary youth cultures. Few deny that the existing concept has limits, yet it is too soon to conclude that the idea has run its course. Subcultural theory and research have waxed and waned over the decades, but they are again experiencing a renaissance in recent approaches to 'deviant leisure' (see Raymen and Smith, 2019).

Expand Your Knowledge

- To learn more about the breadth of subcultural research, see Ken Gelder's (2005) edited collection, *The Subcultures Reader*. London: Routledge.
- A more recent, critical assessment of subcultural theory is contained in Shane Blackman's (2014) Subculture theory: An historical and contemporary assessment of the concept for understanding deviance. *Deviant Behavior* 35: 496–512.

Radical Directions

At the same time as this subcultural **tradition** was evolving, a second approach was also developing – later described as 'neo-Chicagoan' and associated with a new, younger group of scholars who settled in the city in the late 1940s and early 1950s. They revived a commitment to immersive **empirical** research, in an effort to understand how social realities are constructed through meaningful interactions with others. The leading representatives include Howard Becker, Erving Goffman and Joseph Gusfield, among others, who reworked the path opened up by George Herbert Mead a generation earlier. Mead had pioneered a distinctive type of social psychology at Chicago in the 1920s, called '**symbolic interactionism**' by his students, which emphasized process and interpersonal relations. He insisted that society and the self were mutually dependent and the product of dynamic, human-generated meanings and interconnected experiences. These insights formed the basis of a perspective that would provide a challenge to the orthodoxies then dominant in sociology, so that by the 1960s interactionist studies of deviance and social control were profoundly reshaping the field.

The central idea unsettling orthodox thinking was that deviance is not a property of the act committed but is rather a category constructed in the course of interaction between the self and others. Howard Becker's (1963: 9) famous studies of *Outsiders* popularized this approach by describing how deviance is a process created through the 'application by others of rules and sanctions to an "offender"'. This **labelling** process, as it soon became known, was by no means inevitable or irreversible, as Edwin Lemert's (1951, 1967) influential distinction between 'primary' and 'secondary' deviation emphasized. Secondary deviation is more than simply a response to passing episodes of primary deviance. It is meant to describe the ways in which societal reaction (through **stigma**, punishment, myth and so on) can shape crime or deviance by obliging offenders to re-organize their self-identity in accordance with the public symbols, designations and interpretations of their conduct.

The 1960s was a watershed decade. It was an era when all kinds of established authority came to be challenged: from popular culture to civil rights, revolutionary upheaval was in the air and academic disciplines too experienced profound changes. British sociologists began to study such topics as drug taking, sexual proclivities, youth cultures and mental illness, and they found themselves 'doubly marginalized' (Downes, 1988: 46) by both their own discipline and orthodox criminology. The National Deviancy Conference (NDC) was formed (see Knowledge Check below) in 1968, when revolutionary uprisings and street demonstrations helped forge a cultural utopian optimism among radical political movements. From the outset, the group was a dynamic mix of anarchists, interactionists, Marxists and phenomenologists committed to transforming the field of criminology from a science of social control into a struggle for social justice. Indeed, many would define themselves as anti-criminologists, so strong was the opposition to the establishment orthodoxy.

─────── Knowledge Check ───────

The National Deviancy Conference

The National Deviancy Conference (NDC) was established in the late 1960s as a reaction against mainstream British criminology. According to one of the key figures, it was conceived as follows:

In the middle of the 1960s, there were a number of young sociologists in Britain attracted to the then wholly American field in the sociology of deviance [...] Official criminology was regarded with attitudes ranging from ideological condemnation to a certain measure of boredom. But being a sociologist – often isolated in a small department – was not enough to get away from criminology; some sort of separate subculture had to be carved out within the sociological world. So, ostensibly for these reasons (though this account sounds suspiciously like colour-supplement history), seven of us met in 1968, fittingly enough in Cambridge in the middle of an Institute of Criminology conference opened by the Home Secretary. We decided to form a group to provide some sort of intellectual support for one another and to cope with collective problems of identity. (Cohen, 1988b [1981]: 80)

Although there was no shared view of what it was for, it was very clear what it was against.

The initial aim was to establish a forum that would not only include academics but also activists involved in militant social work, radical prisoners' groups, the anti-psychiatry movement and campaigners against **state** violence. Soon conflict and division would characterize the group as tensions rose over the different directions critical work should take – but not before the approaches pioneered at the NDC became established and institutionalized themselves. By the time of the last conference in 1979 they had fractured along the same rifts of sociology more generally, acrimoniously disputing the merits of the Marxist, feminist and Foucauldian approaches then dominant.

───────────────────────────────

Among the rich diversity of approaches, theories and **methods** developed in and around the NDC, the strand focusing on youth and class has proved to be especially influential. In both Stan Cohen (2002 [1972]) and Jock Young's (1971) work, there was an emphasis on the much publicized conflicts between youth subcultures and Establishment forces in the 1960s. Both were early formulators of the concept of **moral panic**. In Cohen's study, the notion of deviancy amplification is used to explain how the petty delinquencies of rival groups of mods and rockers at seaside resorts were blown up into serious threats to law and order. Likewise, Young's (1971) account of drug taking in bohemian London details how the mass media transformed marijuana use into a social problem through lurid and sensationalist depictions of hippie lifestyles. There is a strong Durkheimian theme here, in that the **boundaries** of normality and order are reinforced through the condemnation of the deviant, but what Cohen (2002 [1972]) and Young (1971) were both emphasizing was that this process only occurred in modernity through a considerable distortion of reality.

It would be Stuart Hall and his colleagues at the Birmingham Centre for Contemporary Cultural Studies who went on to explain how the process of defining a social group as deviant was a result of political struggle and ideological **coding**. The collection *Resistance through Rituals* (Hall and Jefferson, 1975) brought together papers stressing the creativity of subcultures, as opposed to the wooden determinism of earlier American theorization, in a sophisticated understanding of class conflict. Here, postwar youth cultures are seen as collective responses to the material conditions and problems the young, especially those from the working class, negotiate in their lived social realities of structural disadvantage.

These, and other themes, are later developed in *Policing the Crisis* (Hall et al., 1978), which is perhaps the landmark text of the Centre and imaginatively combines deviancy theory with Marxist analysis. The book sets out to examine 'why and how the themes of *race, crime* and *youth* – condensed into the image of "mugging" – come to serve as the articulator of the crisis, as its ideological conductor' (Hall et al., 1978: viii, emphasis in original). It demonstrates how the police, media and judiciary interact to produce ideological closure around the issue, leading black youth to be cast as the folk devil in police and media portrayals of the archetypal mugger – a scapegoat for all social anxieties produced by the changes to an affluent but destabilized society.

Fault Lines

Critics from all sides were quick to highlight the flaws involved in these radical directions. A bitter divide would come to split the Left during the 1980s and much of the 1990s along an 'idealist-**realist**' polarity. Left realists claimed a renewed commitment to social democratic principles and emphasized the need to take crime seriously. They insisted that the left idealists regarded 'the war against crime as a sidetrack from the class struggle, at best an illusion invented to sell news, at worst an attempt to make the poor scapegoats by blaming their brutalizing circumstances on themselves' (Lea and Young, 1984: 1). Left **realism** was seen as a 'Labour party criminology, produced by socialists moving from sectarian left groupings into the central political arena' (Cohen, 1988a [1981]: 22). It advocated reformist, not revolutionary, change and was committed to improving social relations in the inner-city.

Other work developed the insights from *Policing the Crisis* to reveal and challenge the intertwining of popular **racism** with notions of black criminality. Paul Gilroy (1987: 113) went on to describe how the rule of law and the maintenance of public order mobilized racist common sense to maintain support for a state in crisis, and criticized left realists for their 'capitulation to the weight of racist logic' despite all the 'polite social democratic rhetoric'. The study of 'race' and crime has a long and troubling history, but there have been efforts to confront problematic assumptions in the field over the last couple of decades (see Phillips and Webster, 2014, and Parmar et al., 2020 for a recent overview). Nevertheless, divisions remain between the different strands of critical criminology, and further radical understandings of crime and punishment soon challenged the NDC approaches.

Among the most damaging was the almost complete absence of women from the field, and a lack of any structural analysis of the consequences of male domination. Instead, as one critic put it, concepts 'of "man" were to the fore, and NDC portraits of soccer hooligans, "paki-bashers" and industrial saboteurs as proto-political deviants did nothing to dissipate a sense that the masculine was a privileged concern within even a radical sociology of deviance' (Sumner, 1994: 287). The beginning of feminist scholarship in British criminology is usually dated from the publication of Carol Smart's (1976) *Women, Crime and Criminology*, which documented how women had largely been neglected by the 'malestream' and the small amount of research that had been carried out on female offenders either reinforced sexual stereotypes or was outright misogynist.

It has become conventional now to describe the impact of feminist scholarship in criminology in a number of distinct phases and different approaches, yet there is much evidence to suggest that feminist perspectives still lie outside mainstream criminology. On Ngaire Naffine's (1997) reckoning, criminology remains a male-dominated discipline, largely involving academic men studying criminal men. Attention has shifted to address the multiple inequalities that structure identities and shape action. Initially associated with the struggles of black women in the civil rights movement in the US, the **theoretical** approach has come to be termed '**intersectionality**' (Crenshaw, 1991), which highlights the interlocking influences of class, gender, race and other forms of difference such as **age**, dis/ability, sexuality and so forth. They are analytically distinct, but concretely and historically they are inseparable (see Henne and Troshynski, 2013, for a discussion of these ideas in criminology).

The final fault line exposed in the radical turn lay in the impact of the French philosopher Michel Foucault's poststructuralist deconstruction of the entire criminological enterprise. By the time Foucault (1991 [1975]) had published his major work on *Discipline and Punish*, he was already a well-known intellectual, and the book is much more than a history of punishment, not least since he makes a broader argument about the disciplinary character of modern society. From the late 1970s onwards, there has been much debate over Foucault's ideas on the significance of surveillance for patterns of social control and 'penality' (Cohen, 1985; Garland, 1985; Garland and Young, 1983).

Other developments include the rapid expansion of electronic, information and visual **technologies**, all of which greatly enhance the surveillance capacities of the state. (Digital technologies are covered further in Chapters 2 and 23.) At the same time, a number of authors were drawn to Foucault's later writing on 'governmentality' to influentially describe a 'new penology' (Feeley and Simon, 1992) transforming criminal justice and the very nature of democracy. More recent interventions have argued that 'Big Data' rather than 'Big Brother' best describes contemporary patterns of surveillance, where surveillance is not only done to us but is also something we do routinely in everyday life – by clicking websites, texting messages and posting on social media (Lyon, 2018). Today's cultures of surveillance are inseparable from the data exhaust pouring from the myriad of digital technologies citizens now use.

It would be misleading to give the impression that all the changes described above are bound up with the NDC, even though it can rightly claim to have considerable impact in British sociology. Indeed, one of the consequences of the recent expansion of criminology as an academic discipline has been the proliferation of seemingly new theories of criminality. As Table 4.2 suggests, often these new approaches are revisiting older sociological ideas, which underlines why it is so important to understand the theoretical foundations on which they are based. To take some examples, we have seen how Merton's (1938) classic essay on 'Social Structure and Anomie' has been more recently reworked in Agnew's (1999) 'General Strain Theory', while the subcultural **tradition** has been revived in Presdee's (2000) account of the spectacular 'carnival of crime' and has been given fresh impetus in studies of 'deviant leisure' (Raymen and Smith, 2019).

Unlike traditional theories of crime, control theorists do not set out to explain why people commit crime but rather why they do *not* – so that early **control theory** sought to identify those sources of restraint against deviant impulses. Such insights can be seen at work in routine activity theory, which considers how changes in crime rate trends are produced through one of two mechanisms: (1) changes in the routine activities of people; and (2) the presence of more suitable targets. Here we can see the importance of understanding the spatial component of crime patterns, which was at the heart of the Chicago School and the more general understanding of the **social disorganization** accompanying rapid urban growth in certain neighbourhoods. These ideas also underpin recent studies of community **collective efficacy** – defined by the willingness of residents to exercise informal social control, driven by a mix of solidarity, trust and mutual support of one another, to prevent crime. It was found that a sense of **social cohesion** among neighbours, combined with their desire to intervene on behalf of the common good, is linked to reduced violence (Sampson, 2012).

Classic Term	New Term
Anomie	General Strain Theory
Control Theory	Routine Activities Theory
Deviant Careers	Lifecourse Criminology
Differential Association	Social Learning
Labelling	Edgework
Moral Panic	Risk Society
Social Disorganization	Collective Efficacy
Social Pathology	Medicalization
Subculture	Carnival of Crime

Table 4.2 Theoretical Reincarnations

Source: Adapted from Anderson (2014: xix)

Republished with permission of University of California Press from Andersson, Ruben, *Illegality, Inc: Clandestine Migration and the Business of Bordering Europe*, published by University of California Press, 2014. Permission conveyed through Copyright Clearance Center, Inc.

Taken together, all these theoretical developments make a compelling argument for the difference that place makes. In the next section, I will look in more detail at how current polarizing tendencies are built into the social and spatial divisions that define urban forms, and then we turn to the migrations of the rich and poor to make sense of illicit mobility.

Divided Cities

The relationships between crime and place have long animated the **sociological imagination**. From Victorian explorations of urban squalor in London, through the moral mapping of modernity in Chicago, to recent excavations of postmodernity in fortress Los Angeles, it is clear that the city has preoccupied thinking about crime. Going further back in time, the idea of an 'underworld' has been a persistent trope in popular culture and often depicted as a shadowy, deviant space of collaboration where sophisticated outlaw networks extend over many localities to form 'criminal areas'. Then as now, mobility is key. Indeed, it was the nomadic rootlessness of vagabonds and rogues that enabled some to prosper amid the growing social complexities of urban life in the 16th century.

Some insist that cities are now 'quartered' (Marcuse, 1989), suggesting that while they have always been divided the origins of contemporary urban divisions are different from and more destructive than those of the past. In this view cities are increasingly fragmented and chaotic, yet underlying the disarray there are patterns. Quartered cities are intricately linked and differentiated by walls or fortification. Several types of city can be identified: the residential, gentrified, suburban, tenement and abandoned city, while the economic city is further divided into the controlling city, advanced services, direct production, unskilled work and informal, and the residual city. Consequently, 'we may almost describe many of our contemporary cities as entirely fragmented, composed only of a collection of separate areas of concentration of different people all desiring to stay apart from all others' (Marcuse, 2000: 272). These ideas are taken further in Mike Davis' (1992, 1999) extraordinary analyses of the emergence of the 'fortress city' in Los Angeles.

The key theme that runs through his work is the increasing militarization of urban space and the defence of luxury lifestyles through private policing, state-of-the-art electronic surveillance and the destruction of public space. The driving **force** behind this militarization and segregation is fear in the imaginations of the middle classes. Although there have been dramatic increases in street violence, these are contained in ethnic and class enclaves, which serve to justify and reinforce urban apartheid in the ghettoes and barrios of North American cities, and Los Angeles is at the cutting edge of these transformations. The physical form of the city is divided into fortified cells of affluence and places of terror where the police wage war on the criminalized poor. Others too have found in Los Angeles a paradigm of the postmodern metropolis and one to be contrasted with Chicago as the epitome of the modern city organized around a single centre, whereas Los Angles is disorganized around a collage of many suburban nuclei:

The consequent urban aggregate is characterized by acute fragmentation and specialization – a partitioned gaming board subject to perverse laws and peculiarly discrete, disjointed urban outcomes. Given the pervasive presence of crime, corruption, and violence in the global city (not to mention geopolitical transitions, as nation-states gave way to micro-nationalisms and **transnational** criminal organizations), the city as gaming board seems an especially appropriate twenty-first century successor to the concentrically ringed city of the early twentieth. (Dear, 2005: 25)

This idea of city as gaming board can be seen most readily in Figure 4.1. Although the trend toward fortification and sequestration is most pronounced in the United States, it is a process that can be found in more or less brutal form in cities around the world.

In Britain, dystopian images of the city have tended to concentrate on the demonization of social housing. Council estates perform an ideologically important role as a signifier and marker of 'problem' people and places (Johnston and Mooney, 2007; McKenzie, 2014). In many of these estates across Britain, and also more broadly in Europe, there were and are heavy concentrations of unemployment and poverty that are 'without historical precedent in any "developed" society', and parallel processes of 'pauperization, evacuation and dereliction have been in full flow in the United States' since the early 1980s (Taylor, 1999: 115). This is not to imply that forms of marginality in Europe are exactly following the black American ghetto experience, rather that social and spatial exclusion on either side of the Atlantic shares some significant features. Indeed, Loic Wacquant (2007) has coined the term 'territorial stigmatization' to describe the symbolic and material assaults on the most disadvantaged and outcast. As he put it, in 'every metropolis of the First World, one or more towns, districts or concentrations of public housing are publicly known and recognized as those urban hellholes in which violence, vice, and dereliction are the order of things' (Wacquant, 2007: 67). These widely despised, blemished places are largely the product of state policies and are bound up with the condition of 'advanced marginality' resulting from uneven development in capitalist economies and neoliberal governance, where the formation of an enduring 'precariat' is one of the defining features of the post-industrial landscape.

PART 1 THINKING SOCIOLOGICALLY

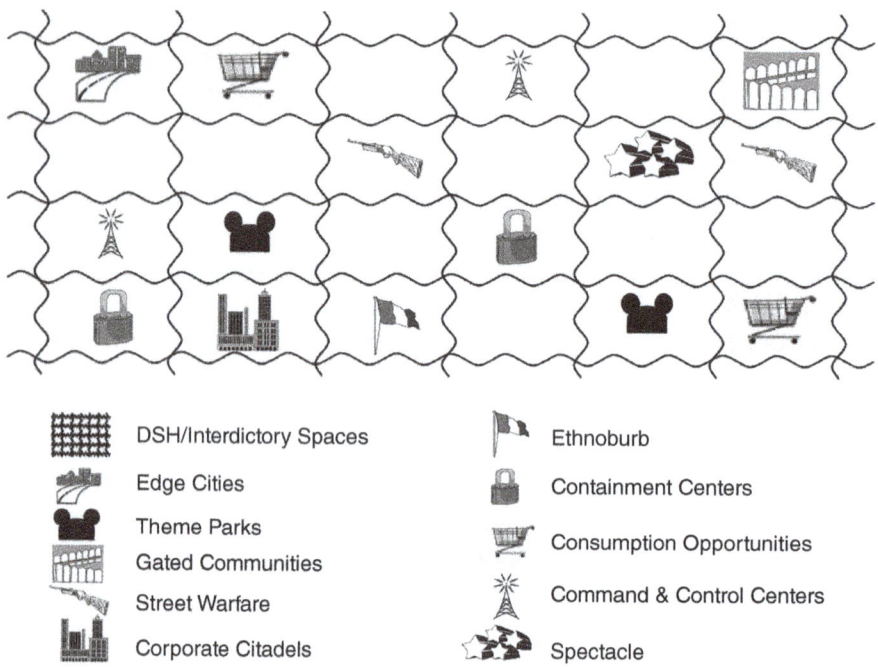

Figure 4.1   Postmodern Urbanism

Source: Dear (2005: 25) Reproduced with permission of John Wiley & Sons.

The distinctions drawn between 'problem' places and populations and supposedly 'normal' ones are inflected with classed assumptions about poor communities. For instance, social housing tenants are often criticized for lacking 'aspiration and enterprise', yet they are also defined 'as "victims" of the Keynesian welfare state in general and of social housing in particular' as the tenancies themselves are held 'responsible for tenants' lack of mobility, tying residents into the bounded space of the "welfare ghetto", unable to leave' (Hancock and Mooney, 2013: 54). Of course, life in council estates is considerably more complex and textured than these accounts allow, where networks of 'being and belonging' generate important ways of 'getting by' in disadvantaged neighbourhoods, which have been subjected to economic hardship, poor housing and territorial stigma for generations (McKenzie, 2014).

Excluded from regular, paid work, survival in the post-industrial milieu is found in 'individual strategies of "self-provisioning", "shadow work" and unreported employment, underground commerce, criminal activities and quasi-institutionalized "hustling"', each of 'which do little to alleviate precariousness' since the informal economy reinforces, rather than reduces, structural inequalities (Wacquant, 2007: 71). As Dick Hobbs (1988: 8) noted in his ethnography of London's East End, the **population** was constantly switching between legal and illegal entrepreneurial activities: 'everyone was "at it" and some were "at it" more than most'. The region is a distinct one in the capital, with its own inimitable and individualistic culture built up over centuries, to the extent that it had long been defined as a 'deviant area'. Yet as Hobbs (1988: 108) maintains, it was market forces that 'created the East End, and its culture is a cumulative response to the problems created by those forces'. Throughout his work, Hobbs emphasizes how crime is an integral, everyday feature of urban life, and in doing so reveals the close ties between 'underworld' culture and 'upperworld' institutions.

 —— Pause for Thought ——

There are lots of other examples of close ties between underworld and upper worlds. Do some online searches to explore the following questions:

- How is the illicit cash from the street transformed through digital transactions on the legal, electronic financial markets?
- How is fake fashion related to the legal economy?
- Counterfeiting is hard to detect, yet many seem to like having a 'designer label', even though they know it is fake. Why is this?

The influential sociologist Zygmunt Bauman (1998: 6) has argued that our postmodern, **consumer society** is a stratified one; like every other known society it is organized by social divisions, yet today the dynamic along which those 'high up' and 'low down' are charted is through their degree of mobility – their freedom to choose where to be. Bauman situates these inequalities in terms of two 'postmodern types': the welcome tourist (which includes business entrepreneurs along with holidaymakers) and the unwelcome vagabond, arguing that 'the vagabonds are the waste of the world which has dedicated itself to tourist services' (Bauman, 1998: 92). While 'tourists' have the potential to invigorate local economies through investment or consumption, vagabonds are regarded as a fiscal liability. Moreover, in the liquid world of late modernity, 'tourists' are financially independent and have the capacity to voluntarily leave, while with 'vagabonds', particularly **asylum seeker**s, the concern is that they are wanting to stay and make demands on the state (Weber and Bowling, 2008), issues to which we now turn. (The idea of consumer society is covered further in Chapter 21.)

Illicit Mobilities

The concept of 'crimmigration' refers to the interlinking of crime control with **immigration** control. It represents the distinct laws and legal processes that states employ as a means of exerting control in an increasingly global, mobile society. As US legal scholar Juliet Stumpf (2013: 59) explains, the integration of immigration and criminal spheres 'tends to generate more severe outcomes, limit procedural protections, and encourage enforcement and adjudication processes that segregate non-citizens'. Yet what is emerging is not only differential treatment but an independent, specialized penal system – what is best described as a 'crimmigration control system' – and has given rise to the distinct field of border criminology in an effort to understand the creeping criminalization of migration (Bosworth, 2014).

Jeff Ferrell (2018) has sought to capture the shifting dynamics of such illicit mobility, describing how ongoing civil and transnational warfare continues to generate spiralling **refugee** populations. The 'Hear from the Expert' feature below gives a sense of his argument.

PART 1 THINKING SOCIOLOGICALLY

> ### Hear from the Expert
>
> Repressive governmental regimes engage in the forced expulsion of dissidents and minority groups. Within China, across Europe, and around the globe, economic migrants wander in search of work, or are simply moved en masse from one work locale to another as economic demands change and dictate. In the United Kingdom, Europe and the United States, the corporate criminality of the past decade's mortgage/banking crisis, the ongoing destruction of low-cost housing as part of urban redevelopment schemes, and the proliferation of part-time and low-wage service work all conspire to preclude certainties at home, shelter, or destination. Moving from house to house or country to country, sleeping in cars or temporary encampments, haunting streets and train stations, those cut loose from certainty and stability find themselves caught up in the world of illicit mobility. (Ferrell, 2018: 6)
>
> Republished with permission of University of California Press from Ferrell, Jeff, *Drift: Illicit Mobility and Uncertain Knowledge*, published by University of California Press, 2018. Permission conveyed through Copyright Clearance Center, Inc.

It must always be remembered that the very term 'illegal immigrant' is a derogatory one, implying that migrants are criminal, when in fact they have usually only committed an administrative infraction.

The considerable movement of people crossing borders since the 1990s has hastened since the collapse of the Soviet Union, the expansion of the EU and wars in the Middle East and elsewhere. In his ethnography of clandestine migration routes from Africa to Europe, Ruben Andersson (2014: 14) makes it clear there is an extensive industry built on subterranean movement, where the 'people smugglers' widely dubbed "mafias"' are 'nowhere near as organized as such a term implies – yet their trade, which grows alongside tougher controls, generates revenues estimated in the billions'. The term industry is used to emphasize how **migrant** illegality is processed and produced in several distinct, geographically dispersed domains that ultimately render the business profitable. At the same time, a vast security industry has been created around their clandestine movements, tightening border controls and preventing illegal entry (see below).

> ### Border Security
>
> The border security industry has long been a feature of the United States. When President Clinton launched Operation Gatekeeper in 1994 along the US–Mexico border, it doubled the number of patrols and fortified the controls using the latest military hardware and infrastructure. The ineffectiveness of border militarization realized by it did little to deter future bipartisan efforts to build more physical barriers and increase the use of deterrents along the border. In 2006, the Secure Fence Act was passed with broad bipartisan support, authorizing the construction of additional fencing as well as the expansion of advanced technology to police the border, including drones, cameras and satellites. Many key Democrats in the Senate (including several who publicly opposed President Trump's efforts to build the infamous 'wall') voted in favour of the measure, including Hillary Clinton, Dianne Feinstein, Joe Biden and Barack Obama. Ironically, the Secure Fence Act of 2006 was cited in the first paragraph of Trump's executive order as rationale for his executive authority to order the wall's construction, under the heading 'Border Security and Immigration Enforcement Improvements', in 2017.

> It is also important to note that Operation Gatekeeper forced migrants away from the relatively safe coastal areas into the mountains and deserts straddling San Diego. An estimated 1,600 migrants died in the first four years of the initiative, perishing either in the cold of the mountains or the heat of the desert (Webber, 2004: 137). Fifteen years later, the death count stood at well over 5,000 and humanitarian activists have highlighted the systematic human rights violations that directly result from this policy (Cubbison, 2010). In 'Fortress Europe', the borderlands are today described as extremely conflicted, 'where the objectives of protecting state security clash with the needs of vulnerable groups in precarious life situations' (Aas and Grundhus, 2015: 2). Here, there is a fraught and unruly set of relationships between policing and human rights at these key sites of global inequality. As such, the many serious harms generated in these spaces returns us to important conceptual questions on what is 'crime' and whether certain activities of states and corporations should be addressed in sociological criminology. (The question of immigration and borders is covered further in Chapter 24.)

Expand Your Knowledge

- See the 'border criminologies' website at www.law.ox.ac.uk/research-subject-groups/centre-criminology/centreborder-criminologies (Border Criminologies, Oxford Law Faculty) to better understand the effects of border control and explore alternatives.
- To learn more about the complexities of policing borders, read Ana Aliverti's (2020) Benevolent policing? Vulnerability and the moral pains of border controls. *British Journal of Criminology* 60(5): 1075-1135.

Yet, we also live in a world where power and wealth move ever farther out of sight and beyond the reach of law. In his account of the 'offshore' practices of the rich and super-rich, John Urry (2014a) reveals how their geographical mobility is at the heart of mammoth inequalities, which are sustained by a vast system of secrecy that damages not only democracy but the very future of the planet. There is not one secret world but many: the offshoring of manufacturing work, of waste, especially e-waste, of energy, of torture, of leisure and pleasure, of CO_2 emissions and of taxation. Water is fundamental to these offshore worlds:

> Seven billion humans are crowded onto one-quarter of the earth's surface. Almost all the ocean world is out of sight. The oceans contain many unregulated 'treasure islands'; ships sail oceans flying flags of convenience, with conditions of work driven to the bottom; many poor migrants lose their lives in oceans; oceans are a global rubbish dump with the 'Great Pacific Garbage Patch' twice the size of France. The sea is a neoliberal paradise for the rich class, a vision of the world almost without government, taxes and laws, and where only the powerful ships and their companies survive, with the rest often literally sinking to the bottom. It is a frontier-land but where the frontier covers most of the earth's surface. The outlaw sea also subjects humans to heightened unruliness: more intense storms, hurricanes, tsunamis, rising sea levels and flooding.
> (Urry, 2014b: 2)

In this account, offshoring is not only incompatible with democracy but it is inherently challenging for social science, as these practices are now how wealth and power operate. It is also the case that the very wealthy have largely evaded sociological scrutiny, and we will need new methods to grasp the processes by which these financial elites secure their mobility (Savage, 2014).

PART 1 THINKING SOCIOLOGICALLY

CHAPTER SUMMARY

- Identified competing definitions of crime.
- Charted the European origins of deviance.
- Examined the Chicago School legacy.
- Discussed the fragmentation and proliferation of theories since the 1970s.
- Highlighted the relationships between crime and place in contemporary cities.
- Explored the concept of crimmigration and the consequences of illicit mobility.

REVIEW QUESTIONS

1. How is crime socially defined?

In your answer, think through the different approaches and the contradictions between them, ranging from a 'legal-consensus' definition through to 'critical' and 'utopian' positions. In particular, pay attention to how crime is an essentially contested concept, with multiple (and sometimes contradictory) dimensions.

2. In what ways, if any, is crime normal?

Here the starting point for your answer should be with the sociologist Émile Durkheim, who made the striking claim that 'crime is normal' at the end of the 19th century. Examine why he felt that crime was a necessary feature of every society, performing a socially integrative function, and then explore how these ideas were influentially developed by Robert K. Merton in the United States.

3. Has the concept of subculture outlived its usefulness?

Although the question is suggesting that the concept has run its course, remember it is a question, and in your answer be sure to set out what was distinctive about the subcultural tradition, as well as the many critical objections to it. If you wish to argue that it still retains a usefulness, then the recent scholarship on deviant leisure will be helpful here.

4. What are the relationships between crime and place?

Emphasize that they are many and varied. The idea of an 'underworld' has long been a persistent feature in popular culture and it is often depicted as a shadowy, deviant space of collaboration where sophisticated outlaw networks extend over many localities to form 'criminal areas'. You should also discuss the legacy of the Chicago School and the geographies of exclusion in contemporary, postmodern cities.

5. Identify, illustrate and critically discuss the key features of crimmigration control systems.

Begin by defining the concept of crimmigration. Explain how it refers to the interlinking of crime control with immigration control, representing the distinct laws and legal processes that states employ as a means of exerting control in an increasingly global, mobile world. Illustrate, through examples, how what is emerging is not only differential treatment but also an independent, specialized penal system and the creeping criminalization of migration.

Go Further

Books

- Brisman, A., Carrabine, E. and South, N. (eds) (2017) *The Routledge Companion to Criminological Theory and Concepts*. London: Routledge.

An introductory collection, containing over 100 short and accessible essays, many written by the leading scholars in the field.

- Carrabine, E. (2017) *Crime and Social Theory*. London: Palgrave.

This book develops many of the ideas presented here, exploring the rapid growth of criminology in recent years and arguing for a renewed engagement with social theory.

- Downes, D., Rock, P. and McLaughlin, E. (2016) *Understanding Deviance*. Oxford: Oxford University Press.

In many respects, this is the classic introduction to the field. That the book is now in its seventh edition is testimony to the enduring quality of the writing.

- Liebling, A., Maruna, S. and McAra, L. (eds) (2017) *Oxford Handbook of Criminology*. Oxford: Oxford University Press.

Another classic book, now in its sixth edition, containing extensive essays on a diverse set of topics, it remains the most authoritative statement on the discipline – especially for those students looking for a deeper dive into key topics.

- McLaughlin, E. and Muncie, J. (eds) (2019) *The SAGE Dictionary of Criminology*. London: Sage.

The fourth edition of this popular dictionary makes it the essential reference work for students and the entries cover the discipline in exemplary fashion.

- Newburn, T. (2017) *Criminology*. London: Routledge.

This book has quickly established itself as a leading introduction to the discipline. Encyclopaedic in range, it is accessibly written and enlivened with examples.

Websites

- www.crimeandjustice.org.uk

The Centre for Crime and Justice Studies has an excellent website with up-to-date analysis, evidence and reports.

- https://thebscblog.wordpress.com

The British Society of Criminology hosts a regular blog that covers a wide range of issues in a lively fashion.

- https://global.oup.com/uk/orc/criminology/hale3e/student/weblinks/general

Oxford University Press has collated an excellent set of links to general criminology websites (such as the American Society of Criminology and other national organizations, as well as more eclectic sources).

References

Aas, F. and Grundhus, H. (2015) Policing humanitarian borderlands: Frontex, human rights and the precariousness of life. *British Journal of Criminology* 55(1): 1–18.

Agnew, R. (1999) A general strain theory of community differences in crime rates. *Journal of Research in Crime and Delinquency* 36(2): 123–55.

Anderson, T. (2014) Preface. In T. Anderson (ed.) *Understanding Deviance*. London: Routledge, pp. xvii–xx.

Andersson, R. (2014) *Illegality, Inc: Clandestine Migration and the Business of Bordering Europe*. Berkeley, CA: University of California Press.

Bauman, Z. (1998) *Globalization: The Human Consequences*. Cambridge: Polity Press.

Becker, H. (1963) *Outsiders*. New York: Free Press.

Bosworth, M. (2014) *Inside Immigrant Detention*. Oxford: Oxford University Press.

Cohen, A. (1955) *Delinquent Boys: The Culture of the Gang*. New York: Free Press.

Cohen, S. (2002 [1972]) *Folk-Devils and Moral Panics: The Creation of the Mods and Rockers*. London: Routledge.

Cohen, S. (1988a [1981]) Against criminology. In S. Cohen (ed.) *Against Criminology*. Oxford: Transaction Books, pp. 8–34.

Cohen, S. (1988b [1981]) Footprints in the sand: A further report on criminology and the sociology of deviance in Britain. In S. Cohen (ed.) *Against Criminology*. Oxford: Transaction Books, pp. 67–94.

Cohen, S. (1985) *Visions of Social Control*. Cambridge: Polity.

Crenshaw, K. (1991) Mapping the margins: Intersectionality, identity politics and violence against women of color. *Stanford Law Review* 43: 1241–99.

Cubbison, G. (2010) Operation Gatekeeper, 15 years later. Available at: www.nbcsandiego.com/news/politics/Operation-Gatekeeper-at-15--62939412.html (last accessed 14 March 2016).

Davis, M. (1992) *City of Quartz: Excavating the Future in Los Angeles*. London: Verso.

Davis, M. (1999) *Ecology of Fear: Los Angeles and the Imagination of Disaster*. New York: Vintage.

Dear, M. (2005) Los Angeles and the Chicago School: An invitation to a debate. *City & Community* 1(1): 5–32.

Downes, D. (1988) The sociology of crime and social control in Britain, 1960–1987. In P. Rock (ed.) *A History of British Criminology*. Oxford: Clarendon Press.

Durkheim, É. (1966 [1895]) *Rules of Sociological Method*. New York: Free Press.

Durkheim, É. (2002 [1897]) *Suicide*. London: Routledge.

Feeley, M. and Simon, J. (1992) The new penology: Notes on the emerging strategy of corrections and its implications. *Criminology* 30(4): 449–74.

Ferrell, J. (2018) *Drift: Illicit Mobility and Uncertain Knowledge*. New York: New York University Press.

Foucault, M. (1991 [1975]) *Discipline and Punish: The Birth of the Prison*. London: Penguin.

Garland, D. (1985) *Punishment and Welfare*. Aldershot: Gower.

Garland, D. and Young, P. (eds) (1983) *The Power to Punish*. Aldershot: Ashgate.

Gilroy, P. (1987) *There Ain't No Black in the Union Jack: The Cultural Politics of Nation and Race*. London: Unwin Hyman.

Greer, S. and Hagan, J. (2001) Crime as disrepute. In S. Henry and M.M. Lanier (eds) *What Is Crime? Controversies Over the Nature of Crime and What to Do about It*. New York: Rowman & Littlefield, pp. 207–27.

Hall, S. and Jefferson, T. (eds) (1975) *Resistance through Rituals*. London: Hutchinson.

Hall, S., Critcher, C., Jefferson, T., Clarke, J. and Roberts, B. (1978) *Policing the Crisis: Mugging, the State and Law and Order*. London: Macmillan.

Hancock, L. and Mooney, G. (2013) 'Welfare ghettos' and the 'broken society': Territorial stigmatization in the contemporary UK. *Housing, Theory and Society* 30(1): 46–64.

Henne, K. and Troshynski, E. (2013) Mapping the margins of intersectionality: Criminological possibilities in a transnational world. *Theoretical Criminology* 17(4): 455–73.

Hobbs, D. (1988) *Doing the Business*. Oxford: Oxford University Press.

Johnston, C. and Mooney, G. (2007) 'Problem' people, 'problem' places? New Labour and council estates. In R. Atkinson and G. Helms (eds) *Securing an Urban Renaissance: Crime, Community, and British Urban Policy*. Bristol: Policy Press.

Lea, J. and Young, J. (1984) *What Is to Be Done about Law and Order?* London: Pluto Press.

Lemert, E. (1951) *Social Pathology*. New York: McGraw-Hill.

Lemert, E. (1967) *Human Deviance, Social Problems and Social Control*. Englewood Cliffs, NJ: Prentice Hall.

Lyon, D. (2018) *The Culture of Surveillance*. Cambridge: Polity.

Marcuse, P. (1989) Dual city: A muddy metaphor for a quartered city. *International Journal of Urban and Regional Research* 13(4): 697–708.

Marcuse, P. (2000) Cities in quarters. In G. Bridges and S. Watson (eds) *Companion to the City*. Oxford: Blackwell.

McKenzie, L. (2014) *Getting By: Estates, Class and Culture in Austerity Britain*. Bristol: Policy Press.

Merton, R.K. (1938) Social structure and anomie. *American Sociological Review* 3(5): 672–82.

Naffine, N. (1997) *Feminism and Criminology*. Cambridge: Polity.

Park, R. (1915) The city: Suggestions for the investigation of human behaviour in the city environment. *American Journal of Sociology* 36(3): 577–612.

Park, R. (1925) Community organization and juvenile delinquency. In R. Park and E. Burgess (eds) *The City*. Chicago, IL: University of Chicago Press.

Parmar, A., Earle, R. and Phillips, C. (2020) Race matters in criminology: Introduction to the Special Issue. *Theoretical Criminology*, 24(3): 421–26.

Phillips, C. and Webster, C. (eds) (2014) *New Directions in Race, Ethnicity and Crime*. London: Routledge.

Presdee, M. (2000) *Cultural Criminology and the Carnival of Crime*. London: Routledge.

Raymen, T. and Smith, O. (eds) (2019) *Deviant Leisure: Criminological Perspectives on Leisure and Harm*. London: Palgrave.

Sampson, R. (2012) *Great American City: Chicago and the Enduring Neighborhood Effect*. Chicago: University of Chicago Press.

Savage, M. (2014) Piketty's challenge for sociology. *British Journal of Sociology* 65(4): 591–606.

Shaw, C.R. and McKay, H.D. (1931) *Social Factors in Juvenile Delinquency, Vol. 2: Report on the Causes of Crime*. Washington, DC: US Government Printing Office, National Commission on Law Observance and Enforcement.

Smart, C. (1976) *Women, Crime and Criminology*. London: Routledge & Kegan Paul.

Stumpf, J. (2013) The process is the punishment in crimmigration law. In K. Aas and M. Bosworth (eds) *The Borders of Punishment*. Oxford: Oxford University Press, pp. 58–75.

Sumner, C. (1994) *The Sociology of Deviance: An Obituary*. Milton Keynes: Open University Press.

Sutherland, E. (1940) White-collar criminality. *American Sociological Review* 5(1): 1–12.

Taylor, I. (1999) *Crime in Context*. Cambridge: Polity.

Thrasher, F. (1927) *The Gang: A Study of 1,313 Gangs in Chicago*. Chicago: University of Chicago Press.

Urry, J. (2014a) *Offshoring*. Cambridge: Polity.

Urry, J. (2014b) The migration of the rich. In B. Anderson and M. Keith (eds) *Migration: A COMPAS Anthology*. Oxford. Available at: www.compas.ox.ac.uk/wp-content/uploads/COMPAS-Anthology.pdf (last accessed 30 May 2021).

Wacquant, L. (2007) Territorial stigmatization and the age of advanced marginality. *Thesis Eleven* 91: 66–77.

Webber, F. (2004) The war on migration. In P. Hillyard, Pantazis, C., Tombs, S. and Gordon, D. (eds) *Beyond Criminology: Taking Harm Seriously*. London: Pluto Press, pp. 133–55.

Weber, L. and Bowling, B. (2008) Valiant beggars and global vagabonds: Select, eject, immobilize. *Theoretical Criminology* 12(3): 355–75.

Young, J. (1971) *The Drugtakers*. London: Paladin.

WHAT IS SOCIETY?
John Scott

LEARNING OBJECTIVES

- To examine contending views on the nature of society.
- To understand the importance of seeing societies as social systems with distinct subsystems.
- To learn how to see the structure of a society as a social fact and to see individual agency and social structure as interdependent.
- To appreciate the importance of concepts of norm, institution, and role, including their contribution to our sense of identity.
- To begin to examine the relationships between subsystems, stratification, and conflict.

Framing Questions

1. Where is British society? We cannot see it, so can it really exist?
2. Does the idea of sociology itself make any sense?
3. What is society?

PART 1 THINKING SOCIOLOGICALLY

Introduction

Sociology is often said – even by sociologists themselves – to be 'the study of society'. This is generally taken to mean studying a national society: 'British society', 'American society', or 'French society', for example. Increasingly, in an era when 'globalization' is on everyone's lips, it might be taken to mean 'European society' or even 'international society'. The problem with defining the subject in this way is that it is not at all clear what kind of object such a society is. Where, for example, *is* British society? We cannot see it, so can it really exist? If it doesn't exist, then what do sociologists *really* study?

This question has been central to libertarian political writers, for whom a society is seen as a collection of individuals and nothing more. Conservative advocates of 'one nation' may refer to 'the country' and 'the nation', as their preferred euphemisms for 'society', but see these as comprising only individual families, groups, and communities. During the 2020 coronavirus crisis, Prime Minister Boris Johnson argued that social interaction had to be limited, on a temporary basis, for the benefit of 'the whole society', which he saw as a collection of healthy individual citizens. His predecessor, Theresa May, had recognized such social interaction as being central to what she called 'the shared society', but saw this simply as the social bonds that individuals sustained in their everyday lives. Her predecessor, David Cameron, spoke of the 'big society', by which he meant the voluntary activities undertaken by individuals as members of community groups. This view that there is nothing more to society than individuals and their interactions had its recent foundations in the claim of former Conservative Prime Minister Margaret Thatcher that 'There is no such thing as society. There are individual men and women and their families'. She held that a society is not an abstract entity but merely 'a living state of individuals, families, neighbours and voluntary associations'.

These arguments all make the point that social and economic life has to be seen in individualistic terms. Societies don't 'do' anything and have no 'needs': they consist simply of individual people interacting with each other. If the word 'society', then, implies some kind of collective or extra-individual phenomenon, and if these conservative and libertarian views are correct in dismissing this as nonsense, then the whole idea of sociology as the study of society must be misguided. In fact, the Conservative government of the 1980s was responsible for financial cuts and policy changes in education that were directed, disproportionately, at school, college, and university provision in sociology.

We sociologists have, for the most part, rejected such criticisms – they would seem to do us out of a job – yet there is a nagging feeling that they might have some validity. If we can't point to an observable 'thing' existing beyond individuals, shouldn't we stop talking about and trying to analyse 'society'? Does the idea of sociology itself make any sense? If we reject the idea of collective entities that exist separately from individuals, can we, nevertheless, identify a social reality that has the capacity to influence the actions of those individuals? I think we can. So, what is society? Let's try to find out. (This question is also discussed in Chapters 7 and 8.)

Mapping the Terrain

Questions about the nature of 'society' are not new but have a long history within philosophy and within sociology itself. The earliest, and simplest, form in which they were discussed was by Greek philosophers in terms of the relationship between the individual and society or '*polis*', understood as separate and distinct entities. As political philosophy developed, this came to be seen in terms of an opposition between individualism and collectivism as two ways of living a human life. The liberal idea of the free individual inspires opposition to the collectivism that seeks to repress and control individual freedom in the name of the abstract entity 'society', making this word a mask for totalitarian state control over individuals.

In philosophy of science, this was generalized into a question of the opposition between 'atomism' and 'holism', between an emphasis on isolated units or atoms and an emphasis on social 'wholes' that have powers that are separate and distinct from those of their various 'parts'. As the philosophical debate was formed into methodological arguments for the social sciences, it was subtly transformed. Attempting to avoid the larger metaphysical questions about the ultimate nature of reality, it was argued that social science had to make a choice between analysing social life *as if* it were the simple result of individual actions ('methodological individualism') or the result of autonomous collective influences ('methodological collectivism').

Classical sociology in the late 19th and early 20th centuries was – like the other social sciences of politics, economics, and law – divided between protagonists of these two methodological positions. The key figure arguing for a methodological collectivist position was the French sociologist Emile Durkheim, while a methodological individualist position was set out by the German sociologist Max Weber. (The development of classical sociology is discussed further in Chapter 7.)

Durkheim set out his position in his book *The Rules of the Sociological Method* (Durkheim, 1895), where he argued that all social phenomena must be explained by forces operating at the social level and not in terms of individual psychological or biological factors. These forces are distinct 'social facts' that together constitute society. A society therefore comprises a population that is held together by a *conscience collective*, a system of ideas and social meanings that belong, collectively, to the individual members of the society. These ideas – termed 'collective representations' – form the shared culture of a population. They exist 'externally' to the individual members of the population and 'constrain' their actions. This argument led many critics to claim that Durkheim saw societies as collective entities, as a kind of collective mind floating around like an invisible cloud or mist that influences the way that individuals think and feel. Durkheim, then, was seen as making a particularly strong collectivist or holist statement about society.

Max Weber was the principal exponent of the alternative view. Strongly influenced by the individualism of economic theory, Weber held that social phenomena such as the state, bureaucratic organizations, churches, and nations should not be abstracted and reified, made into 'things' that exist in their own right (Weber, 1904). While individuals may form subjective ideas concerning such things, they exist only as these subjective ideas and as more or less permanent and recurrent complexes of individual actions guided by these subjective ideas. Sociology, Weber argued, must see the conflicting and cooperative actions of individuals as the building blocks of the complex societies.

The third of the founding figures in classical sociology – Karl Marx – was not aligned with either position. His view of society combined an awareness of both individual actions and complex structures. Individuals involved in production and exchange activities, Marx argued, 'objectify' their ideas in complex and conflictual relations of exploitation, relations that set them apart and 'alienated' from each other. These relations – the relations of production – comprise an economic structure that provides the individuals with greater or lesser opportunities for action. Actions are, then, constrained by relations that operate 'behind the backs' of the individuals and of which they may be unaware or misinformed. Their 'false consciousness' is an ideological representation of the economic structure and informs the actions through which they build a political and legal 'superstructure' (Marx, 1859). A society, then, for Marx, is both the product of individual action and a determinant of it.

Marx did not, however, clarify exactly how this comes about, and the view that there is an opposition between the individual and society persisted. However, the view that Durkheim and Weber held opposed and irreconcilable positions is an overstatement: Durkheim did not see the *conscience collective* as a 'mind' but as a system of communication, a mental system; and Weber did not rule out any consideration of social structures. Nevertheless, the supposed opposition has been an influential view and is found today in the much discussed opposition between the interactionism of Erving Goffman (1959) and the structuralism of Claude Lévi-Strauss (1949). Anthony Giddens (1976) has presented this as a fundamental 'dualism' between agency and structure.

 Pause for Thought

How do today's politicians view 'society', and how does it figure in their rhetoric? Explore this through an online search for speeches by the various party leaders:

- How often does each use the word society and its alternatives (nation, Britain, etc.)?
- How do they vary in what they mean by the term?
- Can you identify any individualistic and collectivist views?

How, then, is **sociology** to use a valid concept of 'society'? I will develop the idea that a society is a system of related elements that hang together as a more or less integrated structure. In order to understand this, we must first see how it is possible to overcome the supposed opposition of the individual and society.

Individual Action and Social Structure

A society comprises a **population**, an aggregate of individuals living in a particular place or involved in some activity. Those individuals must adapt to the environment in which they live, but they also influence each other through their communication with each other, and it is through this communication that they also produce the cultural ideas and meanings that Durkheim called the *conscience collective* and which they learn through their socialization. Socialized individuals, then, act on the basis of the very ideas that they have produced.

These mechanisms have been explored in studies of language. Contemporary linguistics regard language as a Durkheimian social fact. The vocabulary and grammar of a language are collective phenomena; they are properties of a 'speaking mass', a population of communicating individuals. Each individual speaks to others using words and rules of grammar that are stored in their individual minds. The words and rules are not, however, private and unique to the individual. They have been learned during their socialization and are similarly held in the minds of all other members of the population. Unless language is shared, mutual understanding is impossible. Because it is shared, it is possible to say that a person is using a word or forming a sentence that is 'incorrect': such an individual is deviating from rules and ideas that have a reality independently of him or her. If anyone were to claim that 'There is no such thing as language. There are individual words and sentences', we would immediately see the illogicality of the claim. The language exists in the words and sentences, but it is its independence from each individual that makes the effective use of words and sentences possible.

 Pause for Thought

- Why do some people say it is wrong to use a split infinitive ('to boldly go') or to begin a sentence with 'So'?
- Can there be any absolute standards about what is 'right' and what is 'wrong' in language?
- Is there any source of authority in matters of grammar?
- What does it mean when people say that English is a 'living language'?

WHAT IS SOCIETY?

External Constraint and Individual Creativity

It was a recognition of this that allowed Giddens to claim that the dualism or opposition of agency and structure had been resolved. A society, he argued, is a collection of organized actions and recurrent relations among a population of communicating individuals. Just as the words spoken by a population of individuals are organized by its grammar, so the thoughts, feelings, and actions of a population are organized by its **social structure**. A society is organized as a system of action by this social structure. Giddens goes on to show that, of course, the social structure is reproduced and transformed only through the actions of the individuals, as the grammar of the language is reproduced and transformed only through the speech of individuals. However, those actions are organized by the very structure that they reproduce and transform, as, again, the words of a language are organized by the very grammar that they reproduce and transform.

The speech recorded in the novels of Jane Austen in the 18th century is very different from that reported for the 20th century by an author such as J.K. Rowling. Both are organized by the grammatical rules of the English language, yet these rules seem to be different in the two periods. The grammar has been transformed through changes in the speech patterns of people over that 200-year period. In the same way, the social manners of Elizabeth Bennett are very different from those of Hermione Granger, yet both are (fictional) members of an English society that has been transformed through the actions of numerous individuals over that same period.

 Pause for Thought

Children always used to write – or be made to write – 'thank you' letters to relatives who gave them gifts for festivals such as Christmas and their birthdays. Are children today expected to do this? Why is that?

A society, then, can legitimately be seen as an external and constraining social fact, as Durkheim and the structuralists have argued. Yet it is also something that exists only in so far as individuals form and use ideas about it and act upon those ideas, as Weber and the interactionists have argued.

Such societies are quite diverse. A society can be understood as a population located in a particular environment, engaging in actions that are organized by a social structure, and so constitutes a **social system** of interdependent actions. A society can comprise a geographically bounded population, organized as a nation, a region, or a town or village, but it can also be a more extended population formed through the connections of national societies into international or **transnational** ones. Societies may also exist, however, without geographical **boundaries** in a population linked through their involvement in particular activities: a church, a trade union, a **family**, a **state**, and a political party are all societies in this broad sense, though they are often referred to simply as 'associations' or 'groups'. Such societies are rarely completely enclosed and self-sustaining. They typically overlap and connect through the involvements that their members have in a variety of different associations or groups.

 Pause for Thought

What societies in this broad sense are you a member of? How do they relate to your membership, as a citizen, of British society?

Culture and Social Structure

A society, as a system of actions and relations undertaken by a population of individuals, exists within a physical environment but is also culturally formed. It is the culture that gives those actions and relations the structure through which they are organized into an enduring form. As Durkheim recognized, culture exists as a *conscience collective* that must be understood as a collective mental system, not as a substantial collective 'mind'. How exactly is this to be understood?

A culture comprises the totality of ideas, feelings and values held in individual minds and that are communicated from one individual to another in their speech, their self-presentations, and all other forms of intentional and unintentional communication. Individuals learn these social meanings through their socialization, through observation and inference from the actions of others, from reading books or digital messages written by others, and so come to internalize them as their own. The social meanings, then, are shared by the members of a society.

In this sense, culture is an abstraction. It is a word that stands for the various meanings to which individuals subscribe and form a common pool of ideas, values, and ways of feeling. It is the commonality that gives people's actions and relations a degree of similarity. Although it is an abstraction, in the same sense that the vocabulary of a language is an abstraction, it has a reality that each individual recognizes in seeing it as both external and constraining. Just as the speaker of a particular language must use its vocabulary and grammar if he or she is to be understood by other speakers of that language, so must shared cultural meanings be employed by all who are members of the same society. Thus, Durkheim showed that goods and services can be bought and sold within a particular population only if they recognize the same objects as money and share ideas about its value and acceptability. If I buy or sell in Britain I must use pounds sterling, in the US I must use American dollars, and Japanese yen are not recognized as acceptable currency in France. (The topic of culture is discussed further in Chapter 21.)

 Pause for Thought

Why are shopkeepers willing to accept bits of paper and metal in exchange for the goods they have for sale? Why are they equally willing to give up their goods when a person waves their phone in front of a till?

It is the sharedness of meanings that makes culture a reality rather than a mere abstraction. Its reality is sustained by the 'flow' of ideas, values, and feelings from one individual to another in their communication and forms of interpersonal influence. Meanings are in constant circulation, allowing each individual to recognize their commonality. So, while meanings are dispersed in the minds of individuals, they are sustained and transformed through a constant flow of communication. Culture is, then, totally different from the mind or consciousness of an individual, but it is apparent only in individual minds. It is the characteristics of externality and constraint that allow us, methodologically, to treat it as a 'thing', a social fact.

Norms, Institutions, and Roles

Through communication with each other, individuals build up particular kinds of social meanings concerning their behaviour and the behaviour of others towards them and that become a part of their culture.

WHAT IS SOCIETY?

These are behavioural expectations: beliefs about how others are likely to respond to their behaviour and so how they themselves ought to behave if they are to elicit certain kinds of response. These expectations are built up as '**norms**'. These are assumptions about how they and others will 'normally' behave and that may come to be regarded as rules of behaviour that generate social order. These normative expectations may be implicit or unconscious – as is typically the case with the rules of grammar – but they may also be explicitly codified and taken as maxims or principles of action. A society is most orderly when norms have been 'instituted', explicitly recognized and sanctioned through the application of rewards and punishments geared towards normative conformity. When instituted, they acquire a 'moral' character, and Durkheim described the normative order of a society as a moral order. The most explicit codified norms are the laws that comprise a legal order.

Clusters of related norms that have been instituted are '**social institutions**'. These may often concern small-scale and limited aspects of social life. This is the case with the norms governing 'small talk' and conversational turn-taking or the **institution** of 'queuing' in certain societies. Institutions may also, however, regulate broad areas of social activity, as in the case of the institutions of marriage and parenthood that regulate family life. Each area of social life is regulated by a complex combination of institutions and uninstitutionalized norms, as well as by established habits and transient expectations. It is, however, the institutions that define the broad features of a particular cluster of activities.

Institutions have their effects on thoughts, feelings and actions by defining, implicitly or explicitly, the various categories or positions that individuals can occupy relative to each other. Individuals do not encounter and interact with each other as 'individuals' but always as occupants of culturally defined categories or positions that specify how they are expected to behave towards each other. Ways of behaving are not innate or genetically determined but involve learning about the ways that others expect one to behave. Once learned, these expectations are formed into a taken-for-granted pattern of action – a **role** – that can be performed in appropriate encounters. Thus, an institution of parenthood may define roles of father, mother, son, daughter, brother, sister, and through connected institutions of marriage may involve such further roles as husband, wife, grandparent, uncle, cousin, and so on.

Specialized ways of behaving are identified through particular labels that become the bases of individual identities. Thus, individuals act as mothers, shop assistants, teachers, priests, government ministers, doctors, and as black British, gay, working class, male, shy, sick, and so on, each person occupying a multiplicity of such roles. Roles and their associated identities are the bases of social differences and diversity. An individual's various roles reflect the interconnections of norms and institutions and involve the '**intersectionality**' of identity (Hill Collins, 2019).

 Pause for Thought

Make a list of the roles that you occupy and have performed over the course of the last few weeks:

- Have you been aware of any role conflict?
- Which of these roles do you feel to be an important part of your identity?
- How do you manage your multiple identities?

Roles are learned through socialization. This begins in childhood when individuals learn about their language and their immediate social world of mother, father, siblings, and other kin, and it continues through life as they acquire a more detailed understanding of how the wider society works. Individuals always act towards each other in the role which they have been assigned or taken on within an institution and so will be expected to enact specific rights, duties, and responsibilities. Occupants of roles, therefore, are involved in specific relations with each other: parents and children are involved in relations of socialization, shopkeepers and their customers are involved in relations of buying and selling and so on. Roles are not, of course, simply fixed and given ways of acting. They are actively and continually defined and redefined by the individual members of a society, each member making his or her own roles through enacting them creatively in their everyday performances.

Structure and Embodiment

A society, then, comprises a diverse combination of norms and institutions that define a plurality of roles and identities. While some theorists have emphasized normative consensus and institutional coherence, it is rarely, if ever, the case that institutions will hang together seamlessly like the parts of a jigsaw puzzle. A lack of normative consistency means that role behaviours may come into **conflict**. A woman who is both a mother and an employee, for example, may experience contradictory role expectations that put a strain on her ability to perform either role as expected (Myrdal and Klein, 1956). Where there is a lack of institutional coherence, the actual social relations of a society – its relational structure – will not correspond directly to its ideal institutional structure. A social structure, then, has to be seen as comprising both a culturally defined and sanctioned institutional structure *and* a relational structure, these two aspects of structure being more or less incongruent with each other and each being subject to forces that reduce the integration or coherence of the overall social structure.

The structure of a society, then, is both institutional and relational, but it is also more than this. Individuals do not typically act through conscious deliberation on the rules that they are expected to follow or through a direct calculation of the advantages and disadvantages of their particular relations, though this does, of course, occur. More typically, they act on the basis of habits and dispositions that have been built up over time through their socialization. These habits of thought, feeling, and action allow them to behave smoothly in their role relations and without conscious thought and deliberation.

Pause for Thought

Think about a recent visit to a shop to browse its stock or to make a purchase:

- Did you have to think about how to behave towards a shop assistant or to mentally rehearse your behaviour?
- Why was this?

The example of language is, again, instructive. When a person speaks to another, he or she does not consciously think about the correct selection of words or how to apply a particular grammatical rule of tense, plurality, and so on. No one routinely calculates the use of adjectives, nouns, and adverbs, or the correct word order to indicate the possessive case. People simply speak. They are able to do this because, in learning a language, they have inferred the rules, which have then been encoded in their minds as mental dispositions. Exactly the same is the case with other norms of behaviour. Through observation of their parents, a child learns what is involved in the roles of mother, father, child, etc., but not as explicit rules to be consciously followed in everyday life. This may sometimes happen, of course, but more typically role expectations are learned as habits and dispositions that guide behaviour unconsciously and may be quite difficult to put into words. Consider the case of learning to ride a bicycle. A person will observe other cyclists, may receive some general instruction, and may eventually learn the need to correctly position their centre of gravity in order to remain upright. They can successfully ride a bicycle when these have become habitual, but they do not need to 'follow' the rules they have learned, and they may be completely unable to formulate the principles of mechanical equilibrium that they exhibit in riding it.

In all these ways, normative expectations are embodied in the mind and body of the individual, forming what Pierre Bourdieu (1972) refers to as the 'habitus'. It is the habitus that underpins the everyday routines in which we all engage and through which social order is generated. Social structure, then, is institutional, relational, and embodied (López and Scott, 2000).

Societies as Social Systems

Attempts to analyse societies and to construct models of them have typically used the concept of a social system to grasp the ways in which they operate. The idea of a system is relatively recent and early sociologists referred, instead, to a 'social organism'. They were not trying to make simplistic comparisons between societies and organic bodies but were suggesting that sociology could learn a lot from the methodology that had successfully been used in biology to study animal and human organisms.

In biology, it was seen that a body consists of a number of different organs: heart, lungs, kidneys, liver, etc. Each organ has a distinct '**function**' and they depend on each other for the import of the resources – blood, oxygen, enzymes, etc. – that they require in order to perform their function. The lungs acquire oxygen from the air, taken in through breathing, and transfer this to the blood that flows into the heart, which then pumps oxygenated blood through the arteries to supply other organs. The veins return the depleted blood to the lungs and heart for recirculation. A body, therefore, consists of a set of interdependent parts that function together to maintain the organism as a living thing.

What Herbert Spencer (1873–93) and others claimed was that a society could be seen, by analogy, as a collection of interdependent parts (its institutions, roles, and constituent groups and associations) that function together to maintain the society as a thriving and developing thing. This was the origin of the sociological approach termed '**functionalism**'. An over-enthusiastic use of this approach could easily imply that the various parts of a society always work together and that societies are, therefore, perfectly integrated units, and this view was often found in the writings of many – but not all – American 'structural functionalists' of the 1960s. More sophisticated uses, however, recognized that societies did not work in this way and that social organisms were far more complex than biological organisms.

System, Structure, and Change

Developments within biology introduced the idea of the organism as a 'system' and so stimulated what came to be called general system theory. Ideas from system theory allowed **functionalist** approaches in sociology to be put on a new basis by recognizing that there are a whole range of systems, of which the social system is one particular type and the animal organism is another, distinct type. The key thinker in developing the idea of a social system was Talcott Parsons (1966, 1971), who devised a sophisticated model of societies as social systems. Parsons was, unfortunately, a poor writer and his work is difficult to understand, but he helped to establish a powerful approach to sociological analysis that has been much extended by other writers (Buckley, 1967).

In system theory, a 'function' is a causal influence from one part of the system to another. A social system is a set of parts or components that are causally interconnected through more or less stable links that ensure an ongoing flow of material resources (or 'energy') and symbolic information, or 'rules' in the terminology of Giddens. Thus, speech is a combination of a physical sound with a symbolic meaning, and money is a combination of a physical base (metal, paper, or electronic) with a trusted symbolic 'promise'. Individuals respond to the flow of energy and information and shape their actions accordingly.

When the relations among the parts are stable, there is no tendency to change, but when deviation occurs, the system is likely to change as agents respond to these deviations. Circular and reciprocal influences result in 'feedback' – the provision of information that results in a tendency for agents to alter their behaviour – and this may reduce or increase any tendency for the system to change. For example, the initial response of one actor may lead to a change in behaviour in another, and this changed behaviour may make the initial response more likely to be repeated. This may, in turn, reinforce the tendency to change, and so on in a process of 'amplification'.

An example might be a response from the mass media to an increase in illegal drug taking that creates a **moral panic** that leads to public pressure to clamp down on the availability of drugs. Greater difficulty in finding a supply of drugs may open up opportunities for criminal gangs to supply the drugs and so lead to a greater problem of illegal drug use (Young, 1971). Processes of amplification and reduction, through vicious and virtuous feedback circles, occur at different points in the social system. The complex interplay of different circular processes and their ramifications ensure that the process of system change is unpredictable.

System Integration and Social Integration

A key issue in the analysis of a social system is its degree of integration as a system. This integration involves two aspects (Lockwood, 1964). 'Social integration' is the degree of consistency that exists in the actions of individuals and collectivities as they enact their roles. It refers to the degree of consensus or conflict in a society. 'System integration', on the other hand, is the overall functional coherence of the system itself and refers to the relative **autonomy**, coordination, or contradiction that exists among the institutional and relational parts. In a fully stable social system, there would be consensual social integration and coordinated system integration, but actual social systems show more complex patterns and there can be varying degrees of overall coherence and stability.

Pause for Thought

How useful do you think it is to think about societies in such general and abstract terms? Why do sociologists think that general theory is so important?

Many recent writers have sought to avoid the conservative implications of system theory and have rejected the use of the terminology of societies as systems as a way of understanding functional connections. They have instead talked about societies as loose 'assemblies' or 'archipelagos' in which pluralistic and diverse parts have considerable autonomy and systemic processes are more protracted (Foucault, 1975; Latour, 2005). Others have recognized this diversity and plurality but have argued that new forms of system theory that focus on the complexity of social life can provide a useful extension to the basic system model (Byrne, 1998; Urry, 2003).

Elements of a Social Structure

In his key work on the structure of a social system, Talcott Parsons (1951) established the basic outlines for a social system consisting of various parts. While individuals are the ultimate constituents of social systems, they are not its parts. The parts of a social system are positions or roles, various clusters of roles (the groups and association that he refers to as 'collectivities'), complexes of relations among roles and collectivities, and the clusters of norms ('institutions') that define roles and relations.

Where these institutions, roles, and collectivities are specialized in relation to a particular type of activity, they may form larger parts of the system that Parsons referred to as 'subsystems'. Thus, roles, collectivities, relations, and norms that are specialized around the production, distribution, and consumption of goods and services may comprise an economic subsystem, while those specialized around reproduction, socialization and the regulation of families may comprise a kinship subsystem. A society as a social system comprises a number of such subsystems. The task of the sociologist is to look at the interrelations through which they are connected. These connections are the 'functional' contributions, positive and negative, that each part makes to others.

Stratification and Power

The connections between the subsystems involve the flow of information and resources, and the balance that exists in the flow determines the overall level of system integration. Parsons held that there are four functional subsystems, concerned with economic, political, communal, and value conservation, and saw the flow of resources and information as tying them into a social system with varying degrees of integration. Marx, too, adopted a system model of society, seeing societies as formed into a 'base' and a 'superstructure'. The base is a subsystem of economic relations through which capital flows in monetary circuits, while the superstructure is a subsystem of political and ideological relations through which ideas and values flow and so shape the consciousness of individuals. For Marx, 'contradictions' within the economic base are the basis of the social conflicts that lay behind political struggles and ideological differences. This two-subsystem model has more recently been recast by Habermas (1981) as a differentiation between a 'steering' subsystem of economic and political relations and a 'sociocultural' subsystem of ideas and values that shape consciousness and everyday life.

The flow of information and resources through a system involves a distribution characterized by varying forms and levels of inequality. The unequal distribution of wealth and productive resources between roles and collectivities has been seen as the basis of 'class' relations. These were most systematically studied by Marx, who argued that all societies beyond the simplest are characterized by a class conflict over resources driven by the contradictory relations of production that are central to the economic subsystem. The flow of information, on the other hand, has been seen by Weber and by Parsons as being central to cultural and ideological activity and as resulting in inequalities of prestige that define 'status' relations. Class and status relations are 'power' relations that coexist in any society and that together comprise its system of 'stratification'.

Stratification typically occurs within national societies, though recent research on globalization has shown that the formation of international systems of societies has resulted in transnational processes of social stratification. System inequalities between developed and less-developed societies within the first, second, and third worlds, or between the Global North and the Global South, have been seen as forming social conflicts between an emergent global capitalist class and a global proletariat (Bauman, 2000; Sklair, 2001). (The issue of class is explored further in Chapter 11.)

 Pause for Thought

- What are the most important resources in British society?
- What institutions, norms, and laws govern their distribution?

Look online for evidence on the distribution of these resources to various categories of individuals:

- What does this evidence tell you about the stratification of British society?
- Can you find similar evidence on inequalities between nations?

CHAPTER SUMMARY

- Political and philosophical opposition to collectivism is associated with an ambivalence towards the idea of society and, quite often, opposition to sociology as the study of society.
- Sociologists have tended towards either a holistic or an individualistic view of society. There have been a number of theorists who have tried to overcome this supposed opposition of structure and agency.
- Societies range from small groups and associations, through regional and national populations, to global patterns of association.
- The structure of a society is a pattern of norms and relations that individuals regard as being external and constraining over them but that is held only in individual minds and actions.
- Societies can best be understood as systems that contain subsystems that are often contradictory or antagonistic in their operation.

WHAT IS SOCIETY?

REVIEW QUESTIONS

1. How would you answer a lay person who told you that there is no such thing as society?
2. What did Durkheim mean by 'social fact'? Discuss two or three examples of what he had in mind.
3. Is it useful to see language as a model for other forms of social interaction and social structure?
4. What objections might be raised against the idea of society as a social system? How valid do you think these objections are?
5. What are the main problems in identifying particular subsystems as fundamental or the base of a whole society?

Go Further

Books

- Frisby, D. and Sayer, D. (1986) *Society*. London: Routledge.

This is an intriguing attempt to combine varying views of society, especially those in the classic tradition of sociology, and to relate them to contemporary concerns.

- Goffman, E. (1959) *The Presentation of Self in Everyday Life*. Harmondsworth: Penguin.

A classic statement of a view of society focused on individuals and their agency. The book develops an idea of creative role playing and performance.

- Scott, J. (2020) *The Emerald Guide to Talcott Parsons*. Bingley: Emerald Publishing.

A simple but comprehensive introduction to Talcott Parsons and his understanding of the social system and its subsystems.

Journal Articles

- Carastaltis, A. (2014) The concept of intersectionality in feminist theory. *Philosophy Compass* 9(5).

This article provides an explanation, with specific reference to feminist theory, of the concept of intersectionality. Try to think through its wider implications for questions of identity.

- Emerson, J. (1970) Behaviour in private places: Sustaining definitions of reality in gynaecological examinations. *Recent Sociology, Number 2*, edited by H-P Dreitzel. New York: Macmillan.

This article is an important and influential application of the role concept to medical encounters. Its argument also makes an important contribution to the sociology of the body.

- Mouzelis, N. (1997) Social and system integration: Lockwood, Habermas, Giddens. *Sociology* 31(1).

A well-argued contribution to discussion of the work of three major theorists who have tried to extend and develop the idea of a system theory of society.

REFERENCES

Bauman, Z. (2000) *Liquid Modernity*. Cambridge: Polity Press.
Bourdieu, P. (1977 [1972]) *Outline of a Theory of Practice*. Cambridge: Cambridge University Press.
Buckley, W. (1967) *Sociology and Modern Systems Theory*. Englewood Cliffs, NJ: Prentice-Hall.
Byrne, D.S. (1998) *Complexity Theory and the Social Sciences*. London: Routledge.
Durkheim, E. (1982 [1895]) *The Rules of the Sociological Method*. London: Macmillan.
Foucault, M. (1977 [1975]) *Discipline and Punish*. London: Allen Lane.
Giddens, A. (1976) *New Rules of Sociological Method*. London: Hutchinson.
Goffman, E. (1969 [1959]) *The Presentation of Self in Everyday Life*. Harmondsworth: Penguin.
Habermas, J. (1987 [1981]) *The Theory of Communicative Action, Volume Two: The Critique of Functionalist Reason*. London: Heinemann.
Hill Collins, P. (2019) *Intersectionality as Critical Social Theory*. Durham, NC: Duke University Press.
Latour, B. (2005) *Reassembling the Social*. Oxford: Oxford University Press.
Lévi-Strauss, C. (1969 [1949]) *The Elementary Structures of Kinship*. Boston: Beacon Press.
Lockwood, D. (1964) Social integration and system integration. In G.K. Zollschan and W. Hirsch (eds) *Explorations in Social Change*. London: Routledge & Kegan Paul.
López, J. and Scott, J. (2000) *Social Structure*. Buckingham: Open University Press.
Marx, K. (1964 [1859]) Preface to a Contribution to the Critique of Political Economy. In K. Marx and F. Engels (eds) *Werke, Volume 13*. Berlin: Dietz Verlag.
Myrdal, A. and Klein, V. (1956) *Women's Two Roles: Home and Work*. London: Routledge & Kegan Paul.
Parsons, T. (1951) *The Social System*. New York: Free Press.
Parsons, T. (1966) *Societies: Evolutionary and Comparative Perspectives*. Englewood Cliffs, NJ: Prentice-Hall.
Parsons, T. (1971) *The System of Modern Societies*. Englewood Cliffs, NJ: Prentice-Hall.
Sklair, L. (2001) *The Transnational Capitalist Class*. Oxford: Blackwell.
Spencer, H. (1873–93) *Principles of Sociology, Three Volumes*. London: Williams and Norgate.
Urry, J. (2003) *Global Complexity*. Cambridge: Polity Press.
Weber, M. (1949 [1904]) 'Objectivity' in social science and social policy. In M. Weber (ed.) *The Methodology of the Social Sciences*. New York: Free Press.
Young, J. (1971) *The Drugtakers*. London: McGibbon and Kee.

SOCIOLOGY OF AN INTERCONNECTED WORLD

Manuela Boatcă

LEARNING OBJECTIVES

- To look for connections between countries and regions often discussed separately.
- To understand modernity in a global context.
- To place connections between social groups, states and regions in historical perspective.
- To question the newness of worldwide interconnections and rethink the scope of globalization.

 Framing Questions

1. Is globalization new?
2. How are world regions and states interconnected?
3. How can sociology account for complex connections between social groups, countries and regions?

PART 1 THINKING SOCIOLOGICALLY

Introduction

This chapter will teach you to view interconnections as constitutive of the world in which we live. We will examine key sociological aspects in which interconnections have played an important role in the past centuries and will then point to continuities in these interconnections up to this day. Some of them, such as globalization or migration across borders, easily come to mind when we think of connections. Others, such as development and underdevelopment or modernity (in the singular or the plural), are more abstract notions that have, however, sparked long and heated debates. These are only a few instances of a larger set of phenomena and processes to which interconnections between world regions apply.

Sociological approaches to interconnections frequently deal with:

- The widespread assumption that sociology is the study of national societies, even if the processes and phenomena being studied take place at a more local (e.g. only in Sussex) or at a supranational level (e.g. throughout the EU) – conflating society with the nation-state has been criticized as the 'container model' of sociology or as 'methodological nationalism'.
- The patterns that the study of interconnections allows us to detect both across the world and in historical perspective – think of the transcontinental migration between Europe, Africa and the Americas since the 16th century, the international division of labour between regions specializing in agriculture or industry, or the role of early transnational enterprises in the emergence of capitalism. Such examples show that these processes or institutions are not entirely new.
- What connections between countries or regions mean for the possibility of comparing them – comparison usually presupposes that the compared cases are *independent* of each other, or unrelated. How does our perception of their differences and similarities change if we view them instead as *interdependent*, that is, entangled or interconnected?

We will examine the sociological concepts at stake in these debates and get a sense of a sociology of the interconnected world by asking for how long some of its key dimensions such as *transnational migration*, *global capitalism*, and *modernity* have been around and how widespread they have been since.

Expand Your Knowledge

In his 1961 book *The Wretched of the Earth*, Martinican philosopher and psychiatrist Frantz Fanon addressed interconnections otherwise barely acknowledged at the time when he wrote: 'Europe is literally the creation of the Third World'. In the 1980s, the Sri Lankan-born director of the London Institute for Race Relations, Ambalavaner Sivanandan, summarized the situation of the increasing number of people migrating from Asia, Africa, and Latin America to Western Europe and the United States with the phrase: 'We are here because you were there'. This expression has since been used by numerous activists protesting migration regulations in wealthy Western countries. What is the common denominator of the two statements made at different times and in different contexts? Today, as in 1961, the island of Martinique in the Caribbean is an overseas territory of France and, as such, part of the French Republic. Sri Lanka, a British crown colony from 1815 until 1948, is among several countries in south and south-west Asia from which large numbers of labour migrants leave in search of better incomes and access to resources lacking in their home countries. Fanon and Sivanandan were therefore both addressing present-day conditions in Europe in relation to the region's history of colonialism. They viewed colonization as having enriched European states through the extraction of resources from the colonies and at the same time as having led to the displacement of labour migrants from regions impoverished through European colonial rule. They thus pointed to the important insight that systematic migration between world regions is a very old phenomenon.

Mapping the Terrain

If you treat 'British society', 'Indian society' or 'South African society' as if all the information you needed to explain their functioning were contained within their borders, you end up studying social contexts that appear independent of each other – but they are not. This is the container model of society (this topic is also covered in Chapter 5). Sociological approaches to an interconnected world, as the name suggests, focus instead on how today's national societies and their present borders are the result of colonial conquest, negotiations, resistance to occupation, economic subordination to a foreign power, as well as large-scale migration and refugee movements.

Central to an interconnected approach is therefore the issue of the proper unit of analysis. This refers both to the boundaries of interconnections and the scale at which they are most adequately captured. That means that, if you want to find out what the adequate unit of analysis is for the phenomenon you want to study, you need to ask whether nation-states, regions within a country, large cities, world regions, or instead the world as a whole are the units that contain the sum of social relations to be analysed. If you want to discuss the UK state school curriculum, you need to take into account both local council level and the nation-state level at which decisions about state-funded schools are taken; if you want to study global financial flows, you have to consider the City of London, but should not ignore New York City, Shanghai, Tokyo, and Singapore.

Yet what is it that keeps the world interconnected? The question is older than the institutionalization of sociology as a discipline. Scholars who engaged systematically with the interconnected world have answered it by focusing on issues such as the international division of labour under capitalism, development and underdevelopment, the transformation of the world-economy, and transnational social mobility.

In *The Communist Manifesto* of 1848, Marx and Engels attributed Europe's rapidly developing trade, navigation and industry to the colonial expansion into the Americas and to the growing commercial exchange between Europe and Asia, made possible by the extraction of gold and silver from Europe's American colonies. For Marx and Engels, it was due to these increasing global interconnections that self-sufficient feudal societies in Europe, which primarily catered to local needs, were transformed into capitalist ones, increasingly embedded in a worldwide interdependent network. Looking at the impact of the same phenomenon – colonial conquest – but from the perspective of the colonized rather than that of the conquerors, Guyanese scholar and activist Walter Rodney pointed to the impact that the European trade in enslaved people had on the development of the African continent. Forcibly displacing more than 12 million people from their homeland over a period of four centuries stunted population growth, destroyed the local industry and thwarted local and regional trade in Africa. German feminist scholar Maria Mies pointed out that the imposition of Western family and marriage norms disrupted local family relations and gender arrangements.

 Pause for Thought

- Try to explain the last sentence in this quote by adding a couple of sentences after it:

'Latin America, China, and Africa. From all these continents, under whose eyes Europe today raises up her tower of opulence, there has flowed out for centuries towards that same Europe diamonds and oil, silk and cotton, wood and exotic products. Europe is literally the creation of the Third World.' (Fanon, 1961 : 41)

Is Globalization New?

The term is some 30 years old, but the phenomena it describes go back several centuries. For instance: today's **transnational** migration, the process through which people work and live in and feel connected to more than one **state**, is often hailed as a decades-old trend related to **globalization** and as a new means of global **social mobility**, especially for business and academic elites. However, cross-border movements and global interconnections are not new. At least since the European expansion into the Americas in the 16th century, intercontinental migration, the so-called triangular trade that forcefully displaced people enslaved in Africa to the Americas and exported sugar, coffee, or cotton – products of enslaved labour – to Europe for several centuries, has forged transregional connections. The unequal economic exchange between world regions was one of the long-term consequences of these interconnections, but they decisively shaped all of the social contexts and states involved on the political, cultural, religious, and demographic level as well. Yet none of the territories impacted by these processes were nation-states at the time. We should therefore speak of trans-border or trans-regional connections and reserve the term 'transnational' for the aftermath of nation-state formation. Sociology has addressed such interconnections for a long time and from different theoretical perspectives, yet a focus on interconnections has tended to remain marginal to most sociological approaches and under-represented in sociology textbooks. A **sociology** that systematically takes our interconnected world into account offers the tools to identify and link similar processes, such as different instances of transnational labour migration, both across different moments in time and across world regions. It also allows us to uncover patterns and causal relations between seemingly disconnected phenomena, such as distant colonial rule and present-day industrialization levels.

The Emergence of a Sociology of an Interconnected World

At the beginning of the 20th century, scholars discussing the integration of Europe's East into a world market for agricultural products were among the first to address the unequal **division of labour** among world regions. In his 1910 book *Neoserfdom: An Economic-Sociological Study of Our Agrarian Problem*, Russian-Romanian socialist Constantin Dobrogeanu-Gherea addressed two main consequences of incorporating the Romanian principalities Moldavia and Wallachia into the 'great world division of labor' (1910: 32): first, the transformation of the subsistence economy, that is, agricultural production for the peasants' own use, into a money economy linked to international trade; and, second, the gradual disappearance of the peasant handicraft industry in the face of competition from cheap industrial products from the West. Gherea was thus one of the first theorists to argue, in 1910, that traditional modes of production in 'backward' countries, such as a peasant workforce performing coerced labour, interacted with **capitalism** to form a unique combination. In the decades after Gherea's book appeared, European, Latin American, and African scholars kept pointing to similar instances in which capitalism utilized precapitalist labour forms in unique ways.

For Latin American theorists of **dependency** in the 1960s, too, capitalism represented an asymmetrical power relation controlled by the developed, industrialized West, which functioned as the centre of the system, and the underdeveloped, agricultural Third World, economically exploited by the **centre** and making up the system's **periphery** (Cardoso and Faletto, 1979). In their view, **development** and **underdevelopment** were not different 'stages' in a continuum leading up to modern developed economies, but, like centre and periphery, interdependent economic structures co-existing in time and mutually reinforcing each other. The dependency theorists' point of departure was the fact that the international division of labour between centres and peripheries had been established with the European colonial expansion in the 16th century. In time, it had gradually reorganized the economies of the colonies according to the needs of the European colonial centres so as to ensure the extraction of cheap raw materials in exchange for expensive industrial goods. They therefore viewed the 'development of underdevelopment' (Frank, 1966) as the process actively and systematically producing 'backwardness' in the world's peripheries by draining their resources and using them towards the industrial development of the centres. In their view, Latin America's underdevelopment was not due to the region's 'semifeudal' or 'pre-capitalist' character. Instead, it was a result of its incorporation into the global capitalist system as an area reduced to the production of raw materials such as silver and gold and staple foods such as sugar and coffee under coerced labour such as slavery or indentureship since colonial times (Frank, 1967). Importantly, dependency theorists stressed that theirs was a 'Third World perspective' on development. As such, it was meant to challenge the 'First World perspective' dominant at the time and best represented by the modernization school, funded by the US government and advocating a Western model of development for the entire world.

Rather than in terms of one's theoretical standpoint, proponents of the **world-systems approach** addressed interconnections in terms of the unit of analysis and suggested that incorporating them was an issue of methodology. At the congress of the German Sociological Association in 1984, Immanuel Wallerstein argued against the assumption that each society corresponds to a nation-state and that nation-states are the necessary and sufficient unit of analysis of social processes. In order to make that point, he used the examples of Germany and Puerto Rico. At the time, and throughout most of the Cold War, Germany was divided into two states: the Federal Republic in the West and the state socialist Democratic Republic in the East. Moreover, during Nazi rule, Austria had been briefly incorporated into Germany. The German case illustrated that a society can be made up of two or even three states. The Puerto Rican case stood in turn for a society which had, since the 16th century, never corresponded to an independent, sovereign state, but had instead gone through several forms of colonial rule. Society, Wallerstein cautioned, was primarily a rhetorical construct, not an adequate unit of sociological analysis, comparison, and measurement. Instead, for world-systems analysts, the unit of analysis for patterns of capitalist development and processes of class formation was the **historical system** corresponding to the **modern capitalist world-economy**.

Before its emergence in the 16th century, historical systems had a single division of labour, which linked various areas through economic exchange, as well as a common political structure (world-empires would be such systems). In turn, a world-economy, such as the one that took shape as a consequence of Europe's colonial expansion at the end of the 15th century, is politically fragmented into (nation-)states, so the accumulated surplus can only be redistributed unequally through the market. That makes a world-economy's mode of production necessarily a capitalist one. Drawing on the analyses of Romania's peripheralization and on the relational notions of (under)development and centre-periphery from Latin American dependency theories, Immanuel Wallerstein viewed 'relations of production' as a feature of the entire European-led world-economy that emerged in the 16th century (Wallerstein, 1974). It was therefore this entire world-economy – not only the industrialized states within it – that operated according to a capitalist logic.

The defining feature of the capitalist mode of production was therefore not **free labour**, as most theorists of capitalism had maintained until then. This view, Wallerstein pointed out, was based on an overgeneralization of Marx's analysis of British industrialization, which was, however, one of the very few cases to which this definition applied. At the global level, free labourers working for wages in the enterprises of free producers represent a tiny minority. Most of the world's workers producing surplus value for a global capitalist market did so for a long time as enslaved plantation labourers, enserfed peasants, or in other unfree forms of labour instead. If we take the entire world-economy, rather than individual nation-states, as the unit of analysis of capitalist labour relations, all of these examples will no longer appear as exceptions to the rule of free wage labour under capitalism, or as the residue of premodern times such as feudalism, but as typical of capitalism.

The **methodological** shift from particular nation-states to the world-economy allows us to view precisely the *mixture* of free and unfree forms of labour control, instead of free labour alone, as constituting the essence of capitalism: free labour in the system's core or industrialized countries, coerced labour in its periphery, or the largely agricultural economies, and a mix of them in the system's semiperipheral areas situated in-between centre and periphery (Komlosy, 2018; Wallerstein, 1974: 127). To sum up: in the capitalist world-economy that emerged with the establishment of Europe's overseas colonies in the 16th century, slavery, serfdom, sharecropping, and tenancy were equally capitalist modes of labour control: they all employed labour-power as a commodity, as did industrial wage labour. This shift of focus also helps unpack what may seem contradictory combinations: capitalists who held enslaved people on Caribbean plantations or 20th-century serf labour alongside industrial labour in Europe's East. From a world-systems perspective, such mixtures of labour forms are 'not exceptions to be explained away but patterns to be analysed' (Wallerstein, 2000: 143). They are interconnected forms of various relations of production within a global capitalist system.

 —— Pause for Thought ——

- Can you think of examples of unfree or coerced labour in today's world?
- What connects these different types of labour?
- Are unfree labour forms today different from those of past centuries? If so, how?

Shifting the unit of analysis from the nation-state to the world as a whole immediately impacts our notion of society. The dominant concept of society, Wallerstein maintained, is 'fundamentally wrong' (Wallerstein, 2000) because it freezes fluid social phenomena into a rhetorical construct and thus reduces the interconnected social reality of world regions to the fiction of independent societies considered autonomous units that transform and develop on their own. This was an unpopular opinion that never became sociological common sense, since it seemed to question the very basis of sociology, which has long relied upon the concept of 'society'. In other words, most sociologists wanted to keep studying 'society'. Rather than dismissing sociology's main object of study, Wallerstein pointed out that, by focusing on artificially separated units, sociologists are missing the interconnections that characterize our current historical system and that straddle state borders. Decades later, discussions of **globalization** have finally brought interregional connections and dependencies to the forefront of sociological debate.

SOCIOLOGY OF AN INTERCONNECTED WORLD

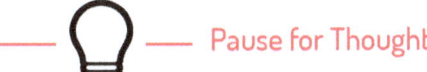 Pause for Thought

- What similarities do you find between the sociological concerns in the quotes below? Pay attention to the different times in which they were first formulated.

[...] the social system in which we all operate is for the first time in human history a single unit in which the entire game is resumed in the internal relationships to be found within the capitalist world-economy: of core to periphery, of bourgeois to proletarian, of hegemonic culture to cultures of resistance, of dominant strata with their demand for universalistic individual measurement to institutionally oppressed racial and ethnic strata. (Wallerstein, 2000: 107)

[...] the concept of globalization has involved the simultaneity and interpenetration of what are conventionally called the global and the local, or – in a more abstract vein – the universal and the particular. (Robertson, 1992: 30)

[...] global risks are per se unequally distributed. They unfold in different ways in every concrete formation, mediated by different historical backgrounds, cultural and political patterns. In the so-called periphery, world risk society appears not as an endogenous process, which can be fought by means of autonomous national decision-making, but rather as an exogenous process that is propelled by decisions made in other countries, especially in the so-called centre. (Beck, 2010: 265)

Feminist theorists of the Bielefeld school of development sociology applied the same methodological shift from the national to the world-economy in order to reframe the understanding of women's labour and the nuclear **family** (this topic is also covered in Chapters 12 and 15). Drawing on **empirical** work in India and Mexico as well as on World Bank data, Claudia von Werlhof, Maria Mies and Veronika Bennholdt-Thomsen (1988) showed that the rise of the nuclear family as a norm in Western Europe occurred in parallel to the classification of subsistence labour outside Europe as a 'backward' and 'underdeveloped' labour form. This devaluation of subsistence production outside Europe made it possible to view all female housework as 'non-work' and to define women into the norm of non-wage work altogether. The naturalization of women, as well as that of peasants and slaves in the colonies, many of whom performed subsistence work alongside women, occurred in parallel with two significant processes in the industrial centres: on the one hand, the rise of the norm of the bourgeois housewife, whose housework was accordingly not considered work; and on the other hand, the proletarianization of male workers, whose wage work became the only legitimate form of work under capitalism. Both developments were conceived as dimensions of a larger civilizing process (Mies, 1996; Von Werlhof et al., 1988). What Maria Mies described as 'the double-faced process of colonization and housewifisation' (1996: 97) therefore did not necessarily take place in two different locations, the colonial zone on the one hand and the colonizing centre on the other. Rather, the emergence of bourgeois marriage and family as protected institutions was causally linked to the disruption of clan and family relations of the 'natives' in colonial areas (Boatcă, 2016).

Modernity(ies) – One or Many?

Interconnections became central to approaches centred on sociology's core concept of **modernity** towards the end of the 20th century. Latin American scholars drew on dependency theories, **world-systems analysis**, and Chicana feminism in order to link the rise of the modern world, of modernity more generally, to the European colonial expansion into the Americas and to the emergence of **coloniality**. You can think of coloniality as a set of political, economic, and sociocultural hierarchies between colonizers and colonized that emerged with the conquest of the Americas in the 16th century and thus as capitalist modernity's 'dark side'. Coloniality differs from premodern forms of colonial rule by translating the administrative hierarchies imposed through colonization into a racial/ethnic division of labour. At the same time, coloniality is more encompassing than modern European **colonialism** alone, in that it includes both the racial/ethnic hierarchies between groups of people and the **international division of labour** between world regions produced during colonialism, all of which endure after the colonies' independence (Mignolo, 2000; Quijano, 2000). The juxtaposition of both notions in the composite term 'modernity/coloniality' is meant to convey the mutual constitution and inseparability of modern and colonial aspects of the social world, or of the modern/colonial world-system.

Multiple modernities theorists took a different approach. For them, the units of analysis of a sociology of modernity are the civilizations centred around the world's major religions. They conceived of Western modernity as first and foremost a cultural programme developed in Christian European civilization and including institutional patterns, self-conceptions, and forms of collective consciousness, as well as the Western political order. In their view, this cultural programme had first been radically transformed with the expansion of modernity in the Americas, and later in Asia and Africa, where they produced multiple institutional and ideological patterns (Eisenstadt, 2003). Central to the multiple modernities approach is the primacy of Western modernity as a reference point for continuity as well as discontinuity in the emergence of further cultural programmes. The multiple modernities were therefore expected to eventually decouple from the European prototype and become independent.

According to Shmuel Eisenstadt, the confrontation with Western Europe played an important part in the development of multiple modernities elsewhere, as did colonialism and **imperialism** as vehicles of such confrontation. These processes appeared, however, as a logical consequence of Western economic and military superiority. Shalini Randeria has therefore suggested taking a relational perspective on modernities, which foregrounds processes of interaction and intermixture (Randeria, 2006). She builds her approach of 'entangled histories of uneven modernities' on the work of Nicholas Dirks and Bernard Cohn on British colonialism in India, who had stressed that 'colonial conquest was not just the result of the power of superior arms, military organization, or economic wealth' (Dirks, 2001: ix), but also a cultural project of control. From this perspective, cultural forms in societies classified as 'traditional' in the wake of their colonization had in fact been reconstructed and transformed through colonial rule and according to its purposes. They were thus actively produced as traditional in contradistinction to a Western colonial understanding of the 'modern'. What instead appeared as 'modern' administrative practices – think of urban planning measures, the emergence of the census as a form of **population** control, or medical experiments – had first been attempted in Europe's colonies. It is only when the results of such measures and experiments were exported back to the metropole that they were considered 'modern' achievements particular to Western civilization.

The perspective of entangled modernities thus underscores the fact that Europe's colonies were not only recipients of impulses of the cultural programme of European modernity, but also laboratories of a global, colonial modernity. Through the notion of 'entangled histories of uneven modernities', Randeria proposes thinking of metropoles and colonies jointly, departing from their mutual dependence and **entanglement** and analysing them as a transnational formation and unit, in which distinct forms and paths of modernity have crystallized during a common history (Randeria, 2006). The reconceptualization of modernity undertaken in the perspective of entangled modernities makes the history of (violent) interaction and exchange between regions of the world central to the construction of both the modern and the non-modern. By viewing Western and non-Western modernities as constituted in and through interaction, this perspective foregrounds the cultural dimension of social processes in a non-**Eurocentric** fashion, that is, without recourse to the norm of European civilization or the primacy of the Western cultural programme. At the same time, such an approach explicitly points to the empirical and theoretical consequences of the shift of focus from the uniqueness of Western modernity to the interconnections characteristic of global modernity.

For sociology as a discipline, this shift of focus entails two caveats: on the one hand, sociological theory can no longer build on generalizations made on the basis of a narrow range of societies that the same theory declares to have been unique and exceptional – Western European ones; rather, it needs to engage with and theoretically incorporate the experiences of non-Western societies in terms of their historical, cultural and socio-structural specificities so that the entanglement of colonial and postcolonial modernization in the peripheries with modernization in the metropoles becomes visible as a central component of global modernization. On the other hand, Europe's modernization cannot be analysed only against the background of different phases of capitalist development, but must also consider colonial and imperial rule as constitutive of European modernity and incorporate the various configurations of modernity in Europe as the result of the interdependencies established in this context (Randeria, 2006).

Interconnections and the Proper Unit of Analysis

In studies of global inequality, too, replacing nation-state centred 'container concepts' with transnational or cosmopolitan 'relational concepts' of space has featured prominently among the solutions for overcoming methodological nationalism proposed in the past two decades (Amelina et al., 2021). However, the rise of global inequality is frequently viewed as a new phenomenon that sets in with 20th-century globalization. The emphasis therefore lies on newness. As late as 2007, in an article titled 'Beyond Class and Nation: Reframing Social Inequalities in a Globalizing World', Ulrich Beck insisted that 'We are witnesses to the emergence of a new kind of capitalism, a new kind of internationality, new kinds of social inequalities, new kinds of nature, new kinds of subjectivity, new kinds of everyday co-existence with the excluded, indeed even a new kind of state organization, and it is precisely this kind of epochal transformation of meaning which sociologists must understand, research and explain' (Beck, 2007: 700).

Others have instead suggested that a relational perspective on inequality would not only provide more complex answers than the mere comparison of national inequality levels but would raise different questions altogether. Göran Therborn (2010) made this point with respect to the route on which plundered silver and gold were transported from the Americas to Europe during colonial times – the southwest-northeast diagonal across the Atlantic. Today, the same imaginary line connects the most unequal regions of the world in terms of income – Latin America and the Caribbean – with the most equal, the northwest of Europe. A sociology of inequalities and their global interconnections, Therborn stressed, should be able to explain the formation of these poles in a historical perspective and their reversal in a comparative perspective – rather than focus on inequality patterns characterizing relatively new nation-states. Shifting the unit of analysis from the nation-state to the world as a whole should therefore not only apply to the most recent present and be associated with 20th-century globalization, but also shed light on the interrelationships between regions both before and after the founding of the nation-state in a historical-comparative perspective.

PART 1 THINKING SOCIOLOGICALLY

 Pause for Thought

- Taking interconnections into account, how would you explain the 'reversal of fortune' that saw Latin America and the Caribbean as the resource-richest regions during colonial times become poor and rank among the most unequal parts of the world today?

> ### Student Quotes
>
> Focusing on just one country as a way of doing global research was beyond the limits of my understanding in the beginning, but now I think that even a short interview with a man selling sandwiches on the streets of Thailand can give a lot of clues about the current state of globalization. Therefore, I think one should not limit the levels and units of analysis for global social research. Individuals, countries, regions, areas or the world... If we ask the right questions, all of them can serve our purpose to create a global perspective.
>
> Sinan Gürcan, Freie Universität Berlin
>
> To view the world and the society we live in through a sociological lens focused on the historical context and the relationships between certain parts within this societies helped me tremendously to look behind easy explanations for all social phenomena. To learn how to examine the way we construct our specific forms of living and interacting with each other, be it on a small scale like the people in my direct environment or on a much larger like a global scale alerted me to the connections to our own past and to the relationships we have formed as people and as society to each other and how these connections inform our own way of living. And I see it as my duty as a future researcher in the field of sociology to open my eyes to these interconnections.
>
> Cindy Scholz, University of Freiburg

For Korzeniewicz and Moran (2009), transregional, transcontinental, and transnational inequalities represent the very premise upon which the functioning of the capitalist world-economy has been based since the 16th century, and which took a decisive turn in the 19th. Accordingly, global stratification results from the social positions allocated by nationality in a global country hierarchy.

As the gaps in average income between countries have been increasing alongside the global gap between the rich and the poor, international migration has become one of the most effective strategies of upward mobility (Korzeniewicz and Moran, 2009; Milanovic, 2016; Shachar, 2009). Accessing the territory and resources of a country richer than one's country of birth or residence offers immediate economic benefits to people from most parts of the world. Migration thus becomes a means of eluding the ascribed position derived from the national **citizenship** of a poor state – either legally, or, for those able and willing to risk undocumented or non-citizen status in a rich state, hazardously.

Another way of understanding the large disparities in income that transnational migration makes it possible to bridge, is to look at differences in urban wages across the world.

SOCIOLOGY OF AN INTERCONNECTED WORLD

6.1 Key Case

Wages across the world

For the past few decades, the Union Bank of Switzerland has collected wage data on its clients and their corresponding occupations. Korzeniewicz and Albrecht (2013) used this dataset to reconstruct average wages, benefits, working hours and vacation days for over a dozen occupational categories in more than 30 cities worldwide. Occupations ranged from male construction labourers to unskilled female factory workers, to bus drivers and primary school teachers, to managers and engineers. Surveyed cities were located in Latin America, Africa, Asia, the Middle East, as well as the United States, Western Europe, Canada, Japan, and Australia. The authors found that, from 1982 to 2009, the average hourly wage in New York, based on the surveyed occupations, was more than 10 times higher than in Mumbai. The gap between the two cities was so large that it dwarfed opportunities for mobility within the whole of India. In other words, the rise in income that a worker in Mumbai could derive either from an improvement of her level of education or from India's economic growth, pales in comparison to the upward mobility she could accomplish by migrating to New York City (Korzeniewicz and Albrecht, 2013). Large disparities were consistent across cities and occupations, such that, in 1982, engineers in Mumbai, Buenos Aires and Madrid were found to have lower wages than even building labourers in New York. As the authors note, the focus on global patterns of wage inequality provides striking insights into long-term patterns of social stratification.

In order to explain that being born in a very rich country equates with being better off than someone born in a very poor country at any point of income distribution, Branko Milanovic (2016) has recently coined the term 'citizenship premium'. Just by being born in the United States rather than in Congo, a person would multiply their income 93 times (Milanovic, 2016). Depending on where they are located and where they can migrate to, citizens of poor countries can thus double, triple or even increase their real income ten-fold by moving to a rich country. Yet access to international migration to a richer country is itself highly unequally distributed. Knowledge about possible travel routes and better economic prospects, transportation costs (whether legal or unauthorized), and travel expenses require considerable physical mobility as well as material and immaterial resources that are often unavailable to those willing to migrate. Moreover, most citizenships of poor countries offer very limited opportunities to travel or settle abroad because of strict visa regulations and the financial guarantees required for travel.

Legal scholar Dimitry Kochenov (2019) has drawn attention to the interconnections between migration, citizenship, and stark inequalities of life expectancy as well as access to basic goods across world regions and countries. He explains this in the 'Hear from the Expert' section below.

Hear from the Expert

Only a micropercentage of the world population swapping countries throughout their lifetime escapes the initial ascription of predetermined well-being or ruin. Even more: as a key instrument of the preservation of the global inequality, citizenship wields huge biopower by locking the

(Continued)

PART 1 THINKING SOCIOLOGICALLY

> world's poor in the places where their economic power is nil and life expectancy extremely short. In the crudest example, the chances of reaching the age of five are from twenty-five to fifty times higher among Finnish children than among Congolese children […] but the Finns also have a freedom to reside in dozens of other extremely rich, very high HDI countries, while the Congolese de facto cannot improve their lives via legal migration: their citizenship effectively locks them in. (Kochenov, 2019: 12)
>
> Dimitry Kochenov, *Citizenship*. Published by The MIT Press, Cambridge, MA. Copyright © 2019 Massachusetts Institute of Technology.

The material and immaterial resources needed for migration are much less available to the poorest strata, the lower-skilled, racialized people, and women (especially when accompanied by children), than to the middle and upper classes, the educated, the racially unmarked, and men able to travel alone. In addition, the limitation of women's rights, mobility and access to capital, which has historically made them more vulnerable to physical and sexual violence in Western societies (and all the more so in the context of colonialism and enslavement), continues to do so today. Currently, non-Western women and LGBTIQ+ people are the most vulnerable migrants (Boatcă and Roth, 2019). A sociology of an interconnected world therefore needs to take into account not only past and present interrelations between world regions, but also the intersecting axes of inequality across the globe (the concept of **intersectionality** is covered in Chapter 12).

CHAPTER SUMMARY

- The key dimensions of a sociology of interconnections are transnational migration, global capitalism, and modernity/coloniality.
- Sociology has for a long time focused on national structures as the sums of social relations to be analysed. The sociology of interconnections starts from questioning the assumption that the nation-state is the only adequate unit of analysis.
- Focusing on interconnections means dealing with phenomena and processes that straddle borders, such as transnational migration, or were responsible for drawing them, such as colonial and imperial rule.
- The international division of labour between centres and peripheries of global capitalism emerged with Europe's colonial expansion in the 16th century.
- Tradition and modernity are relational notions commonly defined in opposition to each other. When understood as entangled modernities or as modernity/coloniality, the history of interaction and exchange between world regions that co-produced the modern and non-modern becomes visible.

REVIEW QUESTIONS

1. What do you understand by a container model of society? Why should it be overcome?
2. How do we decide which unit of analysis is adequate for the phenomenon we study?

3. When did globalization start?
4. What did dependency theorists mean by the interdependent economic structures of centre and periphery?
5. What are interconnected forms of relations of production in global capitalism? Can you give examples?

Go Further

Books

- Frank, A.G. (1966) *The Development of Underdevelopment.* New York: Monthly Review Press.

The original formulation of the interconnection between the development of some regions at the expense of the underdevelopment of others in global capitalism.

- Komlosy, A. (2018) *Work: The Last 1,000 Years.* London: Verso.

A global and historical perspective on the coexistence of multiple forms of labour on the local and the world levels and their regional and large-scale interconnections.

- McMichael, P. and Weber, H. (2020) *Development and Social Change: A Global Perspective.* London: Sage.

Explains how development thinking and practice have shaped our world by introducing students to the four interconnected projects of colonialism, developmentalism, neoliberal globalization and sustainable development.

- Rodney, W. (2018 [1973]) *How Europe Underdeveloped Africa.* London: Verso.

A classic of the literature on development and underdevelopment, analysing Africa's contribution to developing Europe and Europe's role in underdeveloping Africa through enslavement and colonialism.

- Wallerstein, I. (2004) *World-Systems Analysis: An Introduction.* Durham, NC: Duke University Press.

Wallerstein explains the defining characteristics of world-systems analysis and describes the world-system as a social reality comprised of interconnected nations, firms, households, classes, and identity groups of all kinds.

- Young, R.C. (2021) *Postcolonialism: A Very Short Introduction,* 2nd edition. Oxford: Oxford University Press.

Presents current issues and the main economic, social, and political effects of colonialism and decolonization in an accessible way.

Website

The Transatlantic Slave Trade database: www.slavevoyages.org. This website offers an overview of the European trade in enslaved people in a series of maps and digital resources on the topic.

REFERENCES

Amelina, A., Boatcă, M., Bongaerts, G. and Weiß, A. (2021) Theorizing societalization across borders: Globality, transnationality, postcoloniality. *Current Sociology* 69(3): 303–15.

Beck, U. (2007) Beyond class and nation: Reframing social inequalities in a globalizing world. *The British Journal of Sociology* 58(4): 679–705.

Beck, U. (2010) The terrorist threat: World risk society revisited. In G. Ritzer and Z. Atalay (eds) *Readings in Globalization: Key Concepts and Major Debates*. Chichester: Wiley-Blackwell.

Boatcă, M. (2016) *Global Inequalities Beyond Occidentalism*. London: Routledge.

Boatcă, M. and Roth, J. (2019) Women on the fast track? Coloniality of citizenship and embodied social mobility. In S. Cohn and R.L. Blumberg (eds) *Gender and Development: The Economic Basis of Women's Power*. London: Sage.

Cardoso, F.H. and Faletto, E. (1979) *Dependency and Development in Latin America*. Berkeley, CA: University of California Press.

Dirks, N.B. (2001) *Castes of Mind: Colonialism and the Making of Modern India*. Princeton, NJ: Princeton University Press.

Dobrogeanu-Gherea, C. (1910) *Neoiobăgia: studiu economico-sociologic al problemei noastre agrare*. Bucharest: Socec.

Eisenstadt, S.N. (2003) *Comparative Civilizations and Multiple Modernities*. Leiden: Brill.

Fanon, F. (1961) *The Wretched of the Earth*, trans. C. Farrington. New York: Penguin Books.

Frank, A.G. (1966) *The Development of Underdevelopment*. New York: Monthly Review Press.

Frank, A.G. (1967) *Capitalism and Underdevelopment in Latin America*. New York: Monthly Review Press.

Kochenov, D. (2019) *Citizenship*. Cambridge, MA: MIT Press.

Komlosy, A. (2018) *Work: The Last 1,000 Years*. London: Verso Books.

Korzeniewicz, R.P. and Albrecht, S. (2013) Thinking globally about inequality and stratification: Wages across the world, 1982–2009. *International Journal of Comparative Sociology* 53(5–6): 419–43.

Korzeniewicz, R.P. and Moran, T.P. (2009) *Unveiling Inequality: A World-Historical Perspective*. New York: Russell Sage Foundation.

Mies, M. (1996) *Patriarchy and Accumulation on a World Scale*. London: Zed Books.

Mignolo, W.D. (2000) *Local Histories – Global Designs: Coloniality, Subaltern Knowledges, and Border Thinking (Princeton Studies in Culture, Power, History)*. Princeton, NJ: Princeton University Press.

Milanovic, B. (2016) Global inequality of opportunity: How much of our income is determined by where we live? *Review of Economics and Statistics* 97(2): 452–60.

Quijano, A. (2000) The coloniality of power and social classification. *Journal of World-Systems Research* 6(2): 342–86.

Randeria, S. (2006) Entangled histories: Civil society, caste solidarities and legal pluralism in post-colonial India. In J. Keane (ed.) *Civil Society: Berlin Perspectives*. New York: Berghahn Books, pp. 213–42.

Robertson, R. (1992) Glocalization: Time-space and homogeneity-heterogeneity. In M. Featherstone, S. Lash, and R. Robertson (eds) *Global Modernities*. London: Sage, pp. 25–44.

Shachar, A. (2009) *The Birthright Lottery: Citizenship and Global Inequality*. Cambridge, MA: Harvard University Press.

Therborn, G. (2010) *European Modernity and Beyond: The Trajectory of European Societies 1945–2000*. London: Sage.

Wallerstein, I.M. (1974) *The Modern World System, Vol. I: Capitalist Agriculture and the Origins of the European World-Economy in the Sixteenth Century*. New York: Academic Press.

Wallerstein, I.M. (ed.) (2000) *The Essential Wallerstein*. New York: New Press.

Von Werlhof, C., Mies, M. and Bennholdt-Thomsen, V. (1988) *Women, the Last Colony*. London: Zed Books.

PART 2

THEORIES AND METHODS

PART 2 THEORIES AND METHODS

Introduction to Part 2

This second part of *An Introduction to Sociology* builds on the issues you have covered in the first part and is concerned with the key theoretical and methodological tools that you will come across as you continue your sociological education. You will have seen already in the various chapters in Part 1 that an important feature of sociology as a discipline is the interplay between theory and methods in the development of sociological analysis. We have therefore brought together four chapters that are focused on providing you with overviews of key theories and methods you will encounter as you progress through your studies.

In Chapter 7, Daniel Chernilo and Kieran Durkin begin this part of the book by providing an overview of the development and growth of the field of classical sociological theory. Chernilo and Durkin focus particularly on the period between the 1850s and the 1920s, as it was during this period that we saw the emergence of sociology as a distinctive field of scholarship and research. They argue that what is now defined as classical sociology emerged through a range of diverse sources during this period and helped to establish the boundaries of the discipline of sociology as compared to other social sciences. But they also suggest that it is important to pay some attention to the core ideas and methods that helped to establish the uniqueness of sociology as a discipline.

Chapter 8, by Simon Susen, takes the analysis of theories a step further by looking at the development of the key dimensions of contemporary sociological theories. Susen's account argues that it is important to locate these theories against the social and historical context in which they emerge, identifying their principal contributions to human knowledge, and assessing their strengths and weaknesses. In his wide-ranging account, Susen emphasizes that a diversity of different approaches has been an important feature in contemporary sociological theorizing, and he seeks to highlight the value that can be added by approaching sociology through the lens of different paradigms and perspectives.

Taken together, these two chapters provide you with an overview of the evolution of sociological theories from the early history of the discipline to the present. You may find it useful to read these two chapters together and to think about what the differences and similarities are between classical and contemporary sociological theories.

Chapter 9, by Stella Chatzitheochari, moves the analysis a step further though a detailed exploration of key methodological traditions in sociology. Chatzitheochari suggests that it is important to simultaneously scrutinize both quantitative and qualitative research, and she highlights the similarities of these two methodological traditions. In so doing, she suggests that it is important to move away from long-standing views that treat the aims and idiosyncrasies of qualitative and quantitative methods as irreconcilable. In developing this account, Chatzitheochari argues that there is much to be gained from bringing quantitative and qualitative research methodologies into a closer dialogue.

Chapter 10, by Cath Lambert, completes this part of the book by providing an overview of the use of visual methods in sociological research. There has been a noticeable engagement with visual methods in contemporary sociological research and Lambert argues that it is important for sociologists to think sociologically about the selection, creation and interpretation of visual materials. She illustrates her account with examples of how the use of creative visual methods has enhanced the study of important sociological questions.

Having explored key aspects of sociological theories and methods in this part of the book, we shall move on in Part 3 to a detailed analysis of key facets of the role of inequalities and identities in contemporary societies.

PART 2 THEORIES AND METHODS

Key Questions

- In what ways can classical sociology help us to better understand contemporary social relations?
- How have contemporary sociological theories been seen as being influenced by social and political transformations?
- Explore the ways in which both quantitative and qualitative research methods can help us to develop our sociological imagination.
- How can the use of creative visual methods be an important tool in sociological research?

CLASSICAL SOCIOLOGIES

Daniel Chernilo and Kieran Durkin

LEARNING OBJECTIVES

- To outline the main developments in classical sociology.
- To comprehend the ways in which classical sociologists were responding to the societal developments of their time in new and radical ways.
- To understand why classical sociological theories are relevant and useful today.
- To comprehend how the classical sociologists tried to combine particular sociological analyses with global social trends.

 Framing Questions

1. Why did classical sociology develop in Europe between 1850 and 1920?
2. What is scientific about the ways the classical sociologists approached their studies?
3. In what ways can classical sociological theories help us to explain not only their world at that time but also the world as we see it today?
4. Can we speak, as the classical sociologists did, of particular case studies that have relevance to the world as a whole?

PART 2 THEORIES AND METHODS

Introduction

This chapter introduces you to the field of classical sociology. You will learn about the development of classical sociology between the 1850s and 1920s. You will see that classical sociological discussions tend to revolve around the following concerns:

- Making sense of a rapidly changing world that was being transformed in unprecedented ways, into what is known as the period of 'modernity'.
- Making sense of these changes in ways that looked at the collective, or *the social*, above and beyond the concern with the actions or motivations of individuals.
- Making sense of the modern world *as a single unit*, i.e. as a global world, so that while human populations are of course divided into nations, classes, and all kinds of social groupings, the possibility of understanding modern social change required a global perspective.
- Making the study of society more scientific and less speculative; a new *science* of society was needed in order to understand a world that was itself being radically and rapidly transformed.

This chapter will explore these concerns to guide you in your understanding of classical sociologies. The classical sociologists we discuss are many and varied, and do not form a single or unified movement. A detailed discussion of the theories of each individual classical theorist is not offered here; rather, we want to give you a sense of the *main trends* that made classical sociology possible and the ways these theories can be said to work together. By the end of the chapter, you will have a good grasp of the general development of classical sociology as a whole. This understanding will provide you with solid ground from which to embark upon your wider sociological journey.

Mapping the Terrain

The Idea of Classical Sociology

The field that we now know as classical sociology includes works by a wide range of scholars, academics, and public intellectuals, not all of whom saw themselves as sociologists, and whose writings were published, roughly, between the 1850s and the 1920s. Classical sociology has been traditionally associated with three main names – Karl Marx, Émile Durkheim, and Max Weber – and there are good reasons for this to have been the case: they represent distinct intellectual sensibilities, social backgrounds, and political views about what a new science for the study of society needed to do. But the list of writers to be included as classical sociologists has grown and now rightly includes many other figures, such as Frank Park, Herbert Spencer, Harriet Martineau, Charlotte Perkins Gilman, G.H. Mead, Georg Simmel, W.E.B. Du Bois, Karl Mannheim, and Frantz Fanon, among others. (The development of classical sociology is discussed further in Chapters 5 and 26.)

There is no single way in which classical sociologists structured their inquiries. But in retrospect we do know that they were interested in understanding the fast-paced social changes that were being witnessed in European societies (and beyond) at the time: the growth of cities; new forms of work and the new social inequalities between the extremely rich and the extremely poor that they generated; new forms of political democracy and struggles for a widening of civil and political rights; transatlantic commerce and financial transactions across the globe; technological transformations of unprecedented scale; new forms of identities and patterns of social interaction;

the supposed decline in the dominance of religious worldviews; and the evolution of moral and legal codes. These changes, often grouped together under the term 'modernity', marked out a new epoch in human history.

Classical sociologists were also unique insofar as they started making connections between areas of society that did not seem related at first sight: the relations between religious beliefs and economic behaviour; the unintended consequences of technological transformations in several domains of everyday life; the linkages between economic class, positions of status, and political affiliations, etc. Their explanations for these phenomena are exciting, original, and daring. Yet, from our current standpoint, they are far from flawless. For example, early sociologists tended to misrepresent some concerns that have become key for sociology in the present, such as questions of gender inequalities, racial discrimination, and the degradation of nature.

It would be wrong to suggest that there is a unifying programme that brings their writings together. If you were to look at definitions of key concepts from the period of classical sociology, for example, 'the state', you would find very different ideas expressed across their writings: a bureaucratic structure that claims the legitimate use of violence (Weber), an instrument of class domination at the service of the bourgeoisie (Marx) or an organization dedicated to enhancing social solidarity and recreating social bonds (Durkheim). Yet, in their different ways, they were all trying to lay the foundations for a new field of social enquiry, and their writings are filled with references to the need to discard old ideas about social life and to come up with new, alternative perspectives. Understanding new phenomena required new theories, concepts, and methods with which to study them. Indeed, the idea of *new beginnings* was central to the ways in which they envisaged their intellectual contributions.

Time was needed for the theories and methods of sociology to prove successful and for new journals, teaching jobs and university degrees to be established. It wasn't until the late 1930s that the American sociologist Talcott Parsons attempted to find a unifying thread between the works of classical sociologists in his book *The Structure of Social Action* (1967). The 1930s edition of Parsons' book was not particularly influential, but as sociology degrees grew exponentially in American universities in the 1960s, there was a new lease of life to Parsons' main thesis. (You will find more discussion about Parsons in Chapter 5.) An original science of social life proper had actually developed in the late 19th and early 20th centuries, whose task it was to bring together separate insights so that they could be applied systematically to different fields of society: from family to military life, from schools to the workplace. In other words, the *idea* of 'classical' sociology took root primarily as a teaching device that helped students make sense of a number of intellectual developments that seemed disconnected from each other. The terminology comes from the notion of 'classics' in literature and philosophy, for example works by Confucius, Plato, Aristotle, Ibn Khaldun, Shakespeare, or George Elliot. Classic texts are those that have achieved a certain *canonical status* because of their ability to be applied to different circumstances and because they have shaped a particular field of study. Within sociology, this is the case with key concepts such as 'capitalism', 'secularization', 'social differentiation', 'social structure', 'norms', 'roles', etc. (see the Glossary for an explanation of the preceding concepts and others used in this chapter).

 —— Pause for Thought ——

Note how classical sociology grew out of intense social changes and struggles that gave rise to what is collectively known as 'modernity'. Think about how sociology, as we know it today, has continued to develop following new but related forms of social change and struggle. Many of the problems of classical sociology became the starting points for developments in contemporary sociology, such as issues concerning globalization or the marginalized position of women and racialized groups.

Rapid Historical Change is *Social* Change

As we have mentioned, while classical sociologists had all sorts of different ideas, they tended to share a common view that the social world was changing rapidly, radically, and in an unprecedented way. It was changing rapidly because social transformations were gathering pace; radically because these changes were altering the core of the traditional foundations of society (think of Marx's famous dictum, in the *Communist Manifesto* (Marx and Engels, 2011 [1847]), that 'all that is solid melts into air'); and in unprecedented ways because they were convinced that the future of human societies was going to be unlike anything that had gone before. Classical sociologists looked mostly in awe, and on occasion also, as we will see, with some trepidation, at several social phenomena that are still significant in our contemporary world. Let us focus on four of them.

The Rise of Capitalism

A common feature among many classical sociologists was the attempt to understand the phenomenon of modern **capitalism** – a novel economic system characterized by the twin developments of '**free labour**' and a systematic pursuit of profit. The historical origins of capitalism go back to the 17th century and to how imperial expansions and property concentration allowed for a 'primitive' (meaning 'original') accumulation of capital. The closure of collective lands for general pasture, which took place in Britain, for instance, in the 18th century, meant the rise of a new class of disposed tenants and labourers, on the one hand, and the expansion of land as private property, on the other. Along with technological advancements in industry, it also heralded the rise of a new form of specialized **division of labour** (what we today know as the factory system of labour). Marx famously opposed what he saw as the dehumanization of this system as a form of '**alienation**' in which human individuals were controlled by the demand for profit and the mechanical properties of machines. For Emile Durkheim, this new **specialization** of economic functions had consequences for society as a whole, as it triggered new, more complex, forms of social integration based on professional affiliations. For Max Weber, capitalism was also explained in relation to the rise of a new kind of religious ethics, primarily within Protestant groups, that stopped treating commerce as a form of sin, as was historically the case.

In order to understand modern capitalism, classical sociologists also went deeper into a number of other issues. They sought to understand the **role** of money as a 'universal commodity' that can be exchanged for everything and yet has no value in itself; they looked for how **social differentiation** took place along class lines but also had an impact on culture and politics, as well as at the opposition of these classes; they looked at how international trade grew increasingly complex in terms of accounting, contracts and insurance; they wanted to understand how the expansion of modern cities changed people's conceptions of self and otherness; why and how newspapers grew and expanded in the ways that they did – not least in the rise of the novel marketplace of news. One key idea on which classical sociologists do tend to agree is the fact that while capitalism is primarily an economic system, it involves a radical reorganization of society as a whole. This was the first time in human history when the modern economy transformed all other domains of life and, because capitalism changes everything, its proper study required them to look at a wide range of other phenomena whose impact on the economy was anything but evident.

CLASSICAL SOCIOLOGIES

 — Pause for Thought

Think about how new and distinct capitalism was. Moving from a **social system** organized around the relationship between the feudal lord and serf, capitalism exploded these old ways and, along with technological developments made possible in the **Industrial Revolution**, created the basis for the world that we know today. From trains, to telephones, to factories, to alienation through labour, our present world an the extension of the changes brought into being under capitalism.

The Rise of the Modern State

Classical sociologists sought to understand both the rise and main features of the modern **state**, that is, the bundle of separate political institutions that govern daily life and that are characterized by bureaucratic organization and a claim to a monopoly in the use of physical violence. A modern state requires a new cadre of civil servants who are tasked with carrying out most of its functions – in the judiciary, the army and the police, the administration of its resources, and so on – and yet they are expected to remain politically neutral vis-à-vis elected officials. Indeed, modern states grew also as *fiscal* states, insofar as they required significant resources to fund this whole new range of social functions: there can be no modern state without increased forms of taxation.

Understanding the rise and main features of the modern state required classical sociologists to look in new ways at a number of issues that had so far been approached mostly by philosophers and historians. They noted the fact that the basis of legal codes changed, from a system of 'natural' to a system of 'positive' laws: that is, a system of law that is made by humans and not based on allegedly unchanging 'human nature'. They saw the rise of mass political parties with memberships that rose to hundreds of thousands, and how class became a key factor in this new kind of democratic politics. They studied the establishment of a sovereign parliament that was answerable to popular vote and meant that elected officials had to attend to public opinion as much, if not more, than they did to royals and courts. New military campaigns at home and abroad meant that colonial expansion, imperial wars, nationalism, and patriotism were all mashed up together when it came to fostering people's sense of loyalty towards state institutions. Classical sociologists highlighted the significance that ideas of national identity have for the **development** of modern states, but struggled to come to terms with more precise ways to account for their interrelations.

 — Pause for Thought

Think about the nature of the government you live under. How many aspects of your life are regulated by the laws of centralized governments? Think too of the nature of democracy and allegiance in our contemporary world: the ways in which democracy is often said to be under 'attack'. Think of the related revival of nationalism, from Brexit, to the rise of Donald Trump, to the role of leaders such as Modi in India, to Bolsonaro in Brazil, to Orban in Hungary.

Modern Science

Classical sociologists tended to align themselves with a progressive view about the benefits of modern science. They were hugely impressed by the sophistication and possibilities of the practical applications of the natural sciences, which they equated with the expansion of a more rationalistic and **empirical** method for looking at natural phenomena. (You will find more discussion about the **sociology** of science in Chapter 23.) Indeed, classical sociologists saw sociology itself as part of that movement, having a crucial contribution to make in both the diagnostics and remedies of social ills. For example, Émile Durkheim was famously interested in the role of crime and **deviance** for the normal functioning of society. He argued that, even in a society of saints, there would still be deviance because, counter-intuitively perhaps, deviance is crucial to affirming the **norms** of a particular society, to ensuring its cohesion as well as facilitating pressing forms of social change. As previously deviant behaviour becomes more accepted, then law and practices change as well. This is clearly what we observe in terms of attitudes and laws relating to homosexuality, for instance in the 20th and 21st centuries.

The dedication to science on the part of many of the classical sociologists springs from their relationship to the **European Enlightenment** and the role that science played in moving beyond philosophical and theological dogma. It is important to note that this reliance on science was not always conceived in the same way. Some classical sociologists, such as Auguste Comte, conceived of sociology as a science very much in the mould of the natural sciences. Other sociologists, such as Max Weber, had an understanding in which sociology, as a *human* science, was qualitatively distinct from the kind of inquiry found in physics or biology. Finally, many of the classical sociologists were heavily invested in the development of the modern university system that started to take shape by the late 19th century. They saw sociology as having a key contribution to make in the establishment of the modern university as an **institution** devoted to teaching and research. The foundation of sociology degrees at the time meant that universities could no longer remain places for the education of elites *only* in a traditional curriculum of law, philosophy, and theology. Universities would have to open themselves to other social groups (religious minorities, women, the lower classes) as well as to novel forms of knowledge.

 Pause for Thought

Think of what it means to call sociology a 'science'. Should sociologists be able to declare what is heathy and unhealthy in society? What happens when they do so? What happens when they refrain from doing so? Think too of sociology's place in the modern university, and why it might be separate from philosophy, history, psychology, and biology. Are there ever cases where it might make sense for sociology to make common cause with philosophy or psychology, for instance?

Social Differentiation

Most classical sociologists sought to understand novel processes of **social differentiation**; that is, the ways in which individuals or groups mark themselves out as different from other individuals or groups.

CLASSICAL SOCIOLOGIES

They understood this process as a powerful drive behind societies becoming more complex, uncertain and, indeed, more egalitarian. Societies were more complex because the specialization of economic functions led to the rise of a number of new groups that had different interests. For instance, early 'global cities' brought together peoples from different parts of the word: marketplaces where different needs and products met and changed hands, public spheres with a booming expansion of pubs, coffee houses, books, newspapers, magazines, mass demonstrations, theatres and sporting events – all of which contributed to exchanges of ideas, viewpoints and so much more.

The richness and excitement of modern society lies precisely in the fact that different groups are able to develop ideas and ideals that make sense to them rather than to society as a whole. In other words, there was greater recognition of the fact that the positions people occupy in society have a direct impact on the ways in which they comprehend society and their own positions within it. Conversely, it became apparent that society as a whole could not be represented from the standpoint of a single group – however powerful. Societies became more egalitarian through new processes of class struggle and the development of a wide range of interest groups. There was a growing sense that people could choose who they wanted to become, rather than being born into specific roles, classes, or religious groups – a process of emancipation that was also experienced as **anomie** and anxiety, prejudice, and misfortune.

A main innovation coming out of these classical works, therefore, is that social change could not be explained through the actions or motivations of particular individuals – not even as its aggregated result. A new notion of 'the collective' was needed to be able to capture the uniqueness and unpredictability of these processes, and this was precisely what the idea of *the social* allowed classical sociologists to do. This is why the idea of the social became common currency at the time, so that people speak about **social structure**s, *social* classes, **social action**, *social* reality, and so on, in a way that emphasizes its unique, novel, status. In what is arguably one of sociology's most famous formulations, Durkheim speaks of the social as a reality that is *sui generis*: a reality that is unique, unlike any other. He also speaks of the social as a realm of its own causation: that human life is conditioned by larger social and cultural forces, such as language, law, religious beliefs, or national histories, and so on. In short, humans inhabit a world that is linguistically articulated and subject to regulations; a world that can be changed but not at will; a world that exercises influence on our actions without the use of physical **force**. But if the social exists and is not just aggregated individual action: what *exactly* is it? There is no consensus here – neither back then nor now are we able to find a common notion of the social. Yet 'the social' remains the way in which sociologists refer to their own domain of study: those historical trends, patterns of interaction, collective representations, laws and institutions that describe the world around them.

 — Pause for Thought

Think of the ways in which concerns over groups recognizing themselves is still a major feature of our social world today: think of class and gender, but also race, sexuality, and identity in general. Can we say that this concern for social differentiation is changing? Can we think, for instance, of differentiations across these categories, i.e. to be a black, intersex, working-class man? What does this mean for the development of sociology and of society more generally?

PART 2 THEORIES AND METHODS

The Modern World is a Single Place

The question of whether classical sociologists sought to develop a parochial or nationalist outlook, or whether they were instead after a global or cosmopolitan perspective, has attracted a great deal of debate in recent decades. On the one hand, some argue that a main feature of classical sociology was the extent to which it interpreted as universal social trends and theories that were fundamentally European developments. The argument here is that this 'European' perspective on classical sociology contaminated it in a dual sense: it focused *exclusively* on what happened within Europe, to the expense of other parts of the world, and thus it systematically *disconnected* those European experiences from those taking place everywhere else. This is commonly referred to as the problem of **Eurocentrism**.

On the other hand, the globalist view of classical sociology argues that the social trends classical sociologists sought to understand were actually having an impact all across the globe. They were not immune to some shortcomings about how exactly we ought to understand this emergent global reality, but this was surely what they were trying to do. They did not speak about globalization in the way that we do in the present, but their **sociological imagination** was one that always kept global trends at the forefront. Crucially, they were perplexed by how socio-cultural diversity and ethical disagreements between human communities coexisted with global exchanges in ideas, technologies, commodities, and so on. The whole point of the new discipline of sociology was that it required a global orientation. Classical sociologists were thus very much aware that *the modern world is a single place*, even if their theories were often ethnocentrically framed to greater-or-lesser extents.

We can see this by looking at three different levels in which this globalist outlook finds expression within their works.

Conceptual

At the level of *concepts and theories*, classical sociologists sought to grasp emerging forms of 'sociality' in a universalistic fashion: their theories make sense because such key notions as 'the social' or 'society' referred to human affairs that are not restricted by their locale but, on the contrary, are global in their reach. There are ambiguities in the use of these concepts, however, and they reflect some real problems. Let's think, for instance, about the idea of society: at times it was meant to mark a political, geographical, or cultural unit, so that 'society' was in effect another way of talking about nation-states – thus the idea of 'national societies'. The idea of the *national* society emphasizes what constitutes a group of people so that it can claim a right to self-determination; it emphasizes the fact that nations are different from each other and that all peoples are to become nations in their own right.

Yet there was also a second use of the term 'society', which had to do with a more general conceptualization of modern social relations. This use of the idea of society presupposes that all human beings – from all cultures and corners of the world – are able to create and recreate society (though under conditions that are not of their own choosing). Indeed, the new science that the classical sociologists were about to establish was more a science of the social *in general* than the science of any particular national society. Thus, whereas Marx attributed to *labour* the key human capacity of transforming nature and in the process transforming human beings themselves, Weber stressed that *meaning* was involved in all kinds of social actions; Simmel's notion of **sociation** underlined the formative moment of interaction; and Durkheim conceived of **social facts** as external and exercising normative **coercion**. Even as we locate their reflections within the context of the rise of European nation-states, their point was, above all, that we now live in a world, literally the whole planet, which needs to be taken as a single place.

— Pause for Thought —

Think of any particular sociology statement. Does it refer to only one particular society, or part of that society? Or can the statement be applied beyond that particular society? For instance, the presence of capitalism today: does this mean that capitalism is a universal fact? What is the balance between the universal (something that applies the world over) and the particular (something that applies in only one specific time and place)?

Methodological

A second level of classical sociology's global outlook is *methodological*: the concepts being created by classical sociologists needed to be translated into workable procedures for empirical research. At first sight at least, there does not seem to be much in common between Weber's **typologies**, Marx's **dialectics**, and Durkheim's **positivism**. Whether their **methods** were more 'quantitative' or 'qualitative', 'explanatory' or based on 'meaning' and 'understanding', the key challenge was the possibility to *translate*, as it were, trends and processes between different contexts and settings. Nothing seemed to have mattered more to classical sociologists than this need for intercultural learning. This cross-cultural approach is fundamental to their methodologies. The critical impetus of Marx is missed if we argue that his explanation of the generation and appropriation of profit in capitalism holds true for Belgian but not for Venezuelan workers. Weber's repeated dictum that 'one need not to be Caesar in order to understand Caesar' is pointless if, because you were born, say, in Chile in the late 20th century, it is assumed that you will never be able to understand *sociologically* the nature of British rule in India or the rationale behind the suicide bombers in the Middle East. And despite a certain *naiveté* in his use of official statistics, there is clearly a resemblance between Durkheim's (2002 [1897]) methodological reflections on statistically construed comparisons between suicide rates and, say, guidelines on COVID-19 that are issued by the World Health Organization.

Our point here is neither to uncritically defend their proposals as flawless nor to honour their writings as sacred texts. These writers' own application of their procedures may be judged as inconsistent and the proposals themselves might not have lived up to their own high standards. But the opposite view, which wholly disregards their work purely because it is 'dated' and '**Eurocentric**', has its own problems. Similar to what we discussed at the conceptual level above, these procedures have had a lasting influence within sociology because of their universalistic and scientific orientation. These methodological procedures owed their **validity** to the fact that they had to account for cultural and historical diversity within some kind of more general, universalistic framework.

 Pause for Thought

Think about the nature of the methods of the classical sociologists and sociological approaches today. In what ways have they changed and in what ways have they stayed the same? Think of the dangers of an approach that focuses on Europe at the expense of the rest of the world. Think too of the extent to which your location as part of a particular culture might, or might not, erect barriers that might hamper your comprehension of different cultures or sub-cultures.

Normative

The third and final level of this universalistic orientation is *normative*; that is, a claim on how we, as agents, would like the world to be. Our argument here is that many classical sociologists came close to offering what we may refer to as a 'cosmopolitan programme', that is, the idea that all human beings are members of a single species. As you have seen, their idea of society was local in its origins, mostly national in organization through state action, and global in impact and reach – for instance, through the expansion of capitalism and international law. Perhaps best illustrated in the opening pages of Weber's work on the *The Protestant Ethic and the Spirit of Capitalism* (1958 [1905]), a key question that puzzled the classical sociologists was the extent to which a set of historical processes that were in clearest evidence in one part of the world (Western Europe) were able to have an impact all over the world. The simple but by no means trivial normative implication of this is that, despite all differences (and these differences are otherwise very important), humankind is ultimately one entity.

The idea of **modernity**'s global reach is underpinned by the assumption of a universalistic conception of humanity from which no one is in principle excluded. For classical **social theory**, the emergence of modern society is understood as humanity itself being able to forge its destiny at last – even if the emphasis on the colonial **coercion** of a vast part of the world population at the hands of Europe was largely lacking. Indeed, even if modernity is not conceptualized as humanity's conscious development, this idea of humanity now differs from previous notions of human nature because it is seen for the first time as an accomplishment of humanity's own social and political history. Classical sociologists advanced the view that, if the notion of a modern society was to make genuine sense, it could only do so as it progressively encompassed the whole globe and all human beings. This did not mean a one-size-fits-all approach to normative questions, as cultural, religious and indeed class differences all played a major role in the rise and development of modernity. But it did mean that universalistic ethical approaches – for instance, through the idea of universal human rights – touched on the core of what they were trying to say.

 Pause for Thought

What does it mean to think of the world as a single place inhabited by just one human genre? If we want to object that there are many different types of human genre, are we not guilty of slipping into Eurocentric and racialized modes of thinking? Try to think of the dangers of Eurocentric modes of thinking, but also keep in mind the dangers of denying the universality of the human. What position convinces you the most? Is there a way for us to reconcile the two?

Between Science and Philosophy

We have said that classical sociology emerged as part of a wider trend towards the institutionalization of several scientific disciplines within modern universities. Apart from history and philosophy, which were 'traditional' fields that were undergoing their own transformations, sociology was slowly accepted within universities as a field in its own right, from roughly the 1910s onwards. Indeed, sociologists took a keen interest in novel areas of scientific inquiry – such as psychology – as well as in developments within the natural sciences – most notably modern biology. This integration of sociology into the university curriculum meant that it needed to find legitimacy as an empirical discipline – that is, it needed to justify itself as a *science* that was able to produce new knowledge about the social world. 'Science' was undoubtedly a keyword for most classical sociologists. Although it could mean a number of different things, all of them were positive and forward looking, with a genuine desire for true, dispassionate, knowledge; the human ingenuity to develop novel, more **rational** methods to study all domains of life; and the practical conviction that advancing pure knowledge was always the best way to address and eventually solve concrete social problems.

A first way to carry out this scientific outlook was to look at the generalization of historical trends. In studying, for instance, the variation of suicide rates between different countries and religious affiliations, or the social organization of various professional groups, comparative and historical methodologies were being developed and applied more widely. Indeed, even as classical sociologists approached some well-rehearsed topics – such as the study of political revolutions or the history of commerce – these had to be studied through detailed historical and comparative research.

At the same time, for sociology to establish itself as a scientific field, it needed also to justify the originality and **autonomy** of its claim to knowledge of the social world. These justifications cannot be made through empirical findings alone; instead, they require further elaboration and reflection. In other words, the success of sociology as a new *science of social life* depended not only on its empirical contributions but also on the *philosophical grounds* on which it made those empirical claims. As you briefly saw in the previous section, this may explain the time and efforts that all classical sociologists devoted to writing about the methodological and **epistemological** presuppositions that supported their research: the rules of sociological method, the differentiation between (causal) explanation and (interpretative) understanding, the need for historical knowledge that can be generalized, the challenges of intercultural comparisons, the separation between facts (what 'is') and norms (what 'ought to be'). Their empirical science could and indeed *was* based on research that could be quantitative or qualitative, be based on original, first-hand data, or based on secondary information. It could be more or less politically oriented, more or less conceptually or historically driven. And while none of this translated into a unified intellectual programme, they all remained committed to the progressive drive of rigorous scientific work.

Scientific interests took the role of the leading partner in their work, while their philosophical writings played the role mostly of an underlabourer with responsibility for clearing the ground for science to do the 'real' work. This view has some unquestioned merits: on the one hand, this is how classical sociologists tended to see themselves *when writing as sociologists*; on the other, the successful continuation of sociology as an academic discipline in its own right did depend on its ability to do scientific research – and indeed doing so alongside other social and even natural sciences. But there is also something problematic in the view that science has unquestioned primacy over philosophy in the works of classical sociologists. However committed they were to the development of sociology as a science, this was never their *only* interest. All of them wrote about a variety of themes and contributed to a variety of fields. Their status as classical writers owes a great deal precisely to their ability to move beyond disciplinary **boundaries** and reach across several areas of study.

If we go deeper into what classical sociologists actually did, one of the main reasons that their work became classics was that they raised more general questions about the human condition. They wrote about power and domination, the flows and ebbs of rational and mythical beliefs, how people combine secrecy, competition and cooperation in their everyday interactions, the relationships between local norms, particular cultures, global trends and universal values: these are also some of the most perennial themes of philosophy. To put it differently, if philosophy is an expression of an existential condition of human beings who always pose questions for which there are no definitive answers, then sociology is a similar endeavour in relation to the *social* conditions under which all human life takes place. Philosophical questions about the ultimate nature of human life were surely not the explicit goal of their research – not least because it is a question that does not lend itself to the kind of empirical investigations they carried out. And yet this general quest for the prospects of human life under the challenging conditions posed by modern life remains a fundamental motive of their works. It is through a combination of scientific and philosophical questions that they were able to address some of the most fundamental questions: the interplay of material and ideal factors in social life, the relationships between social action and human fate, the disjuncture between existential concerns we all share as human beings and our particular socio-historical contexts.

We understand best what the classical sociologists were trying to do if we pay attention to the *relationships* between science and philosophy within their works. Rather than seeing them as standing in opposition – science is modern and empirically driven; philosophy is backward-looking and mostly deductive – classical sociologists saw that they needed to call upon the best of each **tradition** for their own work.

 Pause for Thought

If sociology grew out of philosophy, with elements of philosophy still contained in it, to what extent can we say that contemporary sociology retains a trace of these philosophical aspects today? What does it mean to say that something is philosophical versus scientific? Can there be a simple divide between the two? Can we speak, sociologically, about what it is to be human?

CHAPTER SUMMARY

- Classical sociology does not cohere on a single theme, approach, or method; instead, the multiplicity of their voices remains a major source for contemporary sociology.
- Classical sociologists were interested in the rapid and unprecedented social change the modern world was bringing about. They sought to understand the global reach of those economic, political, and social transformations.
- Classical sociologists were very much committed to a progressive view of science as playing a key contribution to the amelioration of social ills. Yet they did not have a unified idea of science.
- The value and contemporaneity of classical sociology is, and must continue to be, a subject of reflection and debate. We must read the classics rather than revere them, reflexively criticize them rather than merely

applaud or uncritically discard them. We should not search for unified theories that can be applied wholly or uncritically, nor do we need to agree with or seek to justify every single statement they produced.
- We remain truer to their legacy as we open up our sociological imagination to a variety of sources, to the questioning of apparently self-evident truths, to the self-critical attitude of challenging ourselves when seeking to understand others.

REVIEW QUESTIONS

1. What is 'modernity' and why was it central to the different approaches of classical sociologists?
2. What are the main areas classical sociologists focused on while characterizing modern society?
3. Why and how did classical sociologists look at the global dimensions of modernity?
4. What is 'scientific' about the concerns of the classical sociologists? Do you think that this focus is important in terms of making sense of contemporary social issues?
5. What is the relationship between sociology and philosophy in the classical sociologists? Is this a relationship that remains fruitful for sociologists today?

Go Further

Books

- Allan, K. (2010) *Explorations in Classical Sociological Theory: Seeing the Social World*, 2nd edition. London: Pine Forge Press.

Clear account of many of the main classical sociological thinkers, from Marx, Durkheim and Weber to Harriet Martineau, Charlotte Perkins Gilman and W.E.B. Du Bois.

- How, A. (2016) *Restoring the Classic in Sociology: Traditions, Texts and the Canon*. London: Palgrave Macmillan.

Offers an account of the notion of 'classicity' – what it is to be classic – in relation to sociology and to what it means to *think* what a tradition is.

- McIntosh, I. (ed.) (1997) *Classical Sociological Theory: A Reader*. Edinburgh: Edinburgh University Press.

Selections from the key works of Marx, Weber and Durkheim, including an introduction and guide to further reading.

(Continued)

Journal Articles

- Chernilo, D. (2007) A quest for universalism: Re-assessing the nature of classical social theory's cosmopolitanism. *European Journal of Social Theory* 10(1): 17–35.

Offers an explanation of classical sociologists' global orientation in both its scientific and philosophical registers.

- Levine, D.N. (2015) The variable status of the classics in differing narratives of the sociological tradition. *Journal of Classical Sociology* 15(4): 305–20.

Offers an account of different ideas of what makes classical sociology 'classical'.

- Turner, B.S. (2006) Classical sociology and cosmopolitanism: A critical defence of the social. *British Journal of Sociology* 57(1): 133–55.

Discusses the significance of classical sociology's idea of the social for contemporary society.

Websites

- www.thesociologicalreview.com/blog

An influential website dedicated to the advancement and study of sociology in everyday life

- http://thesociologistdc.com

A periodic magazine of public sociology for a general audience

- https://globaldialogue.isa-sociology.org

Offers a global sociological lens on contemporary world events, including interviews with noted international sociologists.

REFERENCES

Allan, K. (2010) *Explorations in Classical Sociological Theory: Seeing the Social World,* 2nd edition. London: Pine Forge Press.

Chernilo, D. (2007) A quest for universalism: Re-assessing the nature of classical social theory's cosmopolitanism. *European Journal of Social Theory* 10(1): 17–35.

Durkheim, E. (2002 [1897]) *Suicide: A Study in Sociology*. London: Routledge.

How, A. (2016) *Restoring the Classic in Sociology: Traditions, Texts and the Canon*. London: Palgrave Macmillan.

Levine, D.N. (2015) The variable status of the classics in differing narratives of the sociological tradition. *Journal of Classical Sociology* 15(4): 305–20.

Marx, K. and Engels, F. (2011 [1847]) *The Communist Manifesto*. New York: Penguin Books.

McIntosh, I. (ed.) (1997) *Classical Sociological Theory: A Reader*. Edinburgh: Edinburgh University Press.

Parsons, T. (1967) *The Structure of Social Action, Vol. 1: Marshall, Pareto, Durkheim*. New York: Free Press.

Turner, B.S. (2006) Classical sociology and cosmopolitanism: A critical defence of the social. *British Journal of Sociology* 57(1): 133–55.

Weber, M. (1958 [1905]) *The Protestant Ethic and the Spirit of Capitalism*. New York: Scribner.

CONTEMPORARY SOCIAL THEORY

Simon Susen

LEARNING OBJECTIVES

- To provide you with a brief introduction to key issues and major currents in contemporary social theory.
- To introduce you to a range of debates and controversies in late-20th and early-21st century social theory.
- To demonstrate the relevance of social theory to studying the constitution, functioning, and development of social reality.
- To enhance your understanding of the connections between empirical, methodological, epistemological, terminological, and theoretical concerns in contemporary sociology.
- To reflect upon the main challenges faced by social theorists in the early 21st century.

Framing Questions

1. What is social theory?
2. Why should we bother with social theory?
3. What is the place of social theory in contemporary sociology?
4. What are the main challenges faced by social theorists in the 21st century?

PART 2 THEORIES AND METHODS

Introduction

This chapter aims to provide you with a brief introduction to contemporary social theory. To this end, the chapter is divided into seven parts. In the first part, you will learn about the *concept* of social theory. This part argues that, while the history of social theory is inextricably linked to the rise of modernity, in the early 21st century its status vis-à-vis the social sciences has been called into question. In the second part, you will find out about the *relevance* of social theory, notably in terms of the central place it occupies in the contemporary social sciences. In the third part, you will be invited to grapple with the *knowledge-seeking spirit* of social theory, which, as you will see, obliges us to examine the epistemic differences between 'ordinary' and 'scientific' ways of engaging with the world. In the fourth part, you will be made aware of *key dimensions* that should be taken into account when studying social theories – notably their historical situatedness, their principal contributions to human knowledge, and their strengths and weaknesses. In the fifth part, you will acquire some basic insights into the *scope* of social theory, including the distinction between 'classical' and 'contemporary' approaches. In the sixth part, you will be presented with an overview of different *versions* of social theory, recognizing that its contemporary variants are far more diversified than their classical predecessors. In the seventh part, you will benefit from a synopsis of noteworthy *trends and developments* in contemporary social theory, emphasizing its heterogeneous nature and pluralistic outlook.

The Concept of Social Theory

You may have asked yourself what **social theory** actually is. You may find the following shorthand definition useful: *in the most general sense, social theory is the attempt to provide a conceptually informed – and, in many cases, empirically substantiated – framework designed to (1) describe, (2) analyse, (3) interpret, (4) explain, and (5) assess the constitution, functioning, and development of social reality, or particular aspects of social reality, in a more or less systematic fashion* (see Susen, 2015a: 5; cf. Susen, 2020a: 313–14).

Historically, the emergence of social theory cannot be dissociated from the rise of modernity. To be precise, social theory is both a product and a carrier of modernity. As a product of modernity, it is an epistemic endeavour exploring the numerous structural transformations that have led to the consolidation of modern *formations* of society. As a carrier of modernity, it is a discursive vehicle contributing to critical debates on modern *conceptions* of society. In other words, social theory is an integral component of both the *real* and the *representational* constitution of the modern world (see Susen, 2015a: 5).

By definition, social theory is characterized by a 'general concern with the nature of the social in modern society' (Turner, 1996: 1). Its *raison d'être* is to grasp the complexity of the social in its key dimensions (cf. Susen, 2016c):

- *actions and behaviours* (what people do), *beliefs and ideologies* (what people think), and *traditions and institutions* (how people's performative and cognitive ways of engaging with the world result in relatively solidified forms of sociality);
- *objectivity* ('the' world of facts), *normativity* ('our' world of conventions, habits, and customs), and *subjectivity* ('my' world of experiences, feelings, thoughts, and perceptions);
- *foundational* elements (which – in terms of their specificity – are indispensable to the emergence of social order), *contingent* elements (which are potentially significant for, but – in terms of their specificity – not indispensable to, the emergence of social order), and *ephemeral* elements (which are relatively short-lived and – in terms of their specificity – largely irrelevant to the emergence of social order).

Social theory plays a pivotal role in equipping social scientists (especially sociologists) with useful conceptual frameworks, capable of strengthening their understanding of empirical data. It is no accident, then, that both classical and contemporary versions of social theory continue to occupy a central place in social research (Appelrouth and Edles, 2011 [2006]; Baert and Silva, 2010 [1998]; Calhoun et al., 2012a [2002], 2012b [2002]; Delanty, 2017; Inglis and Thorpe, 2019 [2012]; Ritzer and Stepnisky, 2014 [1988], 2018 [2003]); Susen, 2015a, 2020a, 2020b). And yet, the question of what social theory can (or cannot) achieve is a major source of dispute. Traditionally, social theory has been associated with the task of delivering reliable conceptual tools for (1) describing, (2) analysing, (3) interpreting, (4) explaining, and (5) assessing the constitution, functioning, and development of social reality, or particular aspects of social reality. On this account, it is committed to examining the social practices, structures, and arrangements by which human forms of life are not only constructed and sustained but also, potentially, reconstructed and transformed.

In recent decades, however, social theory has undergone a 'legitimacy crisis', in the sense that 'a deep uncertainty about the development of modern society' (Turner, 1996: 5) has been accompanied by a decline in confidence in the epistemic authority of the humanities and social sciences. Consequently, 'the status of social theory vis-à-vis the social sciences has [...] become increasingly uncertain and needs to be reassessed' (Baert and Silva, 2010 [1998]: 285). This is not to suggest that social theory is now widely regarded as an entirely pointless undertaking. This is to recognize, however, that more and more contemporary social theorists have abandoned the notion that their mission is to engage in conceptual 'system building', epitomized in the defence of '**metanarratives**':

A metanarrative is a set of more or less logically interconnected assumptions made in order to provide a coherent and comprehensive account of the underlying mechanisms that shape, or are supposed to shape, both the constitution and the development of human existence in a fundamental way. (Susen, 2015a: 140, emphasis in original.)

From a historical point of view, five types of metanarrative have been remarkably influential (see Susen, 2015a: 140–3; cf. Susen, 2020a: 12, 35, 49n113, 158, 173, 292, 331n19):

1. *political metanarratives* (such as anarchism, communism, socialism, liberalism, conservatism, and fascism as well as nationalism, feminism, and environmentalism);
2. *philosophical metanarratives* (which are frequently conceived of in terms of diametrically opposed epistemic frameworks – such as idealism vs. materialism, constructivism vs. realism, interpretivism vs. positivism, subjectivism vs. objectivism, relativism vs. absolutism, particularism vs. universalism, utilitarianism vs. deontologism, contextualism vs. foundationalism, or voluntarism vs. determinism);
3. *religious metanarratives* (for instance, faith-based interpretations of existence in general and history in particular – notably within Christianity, Judaism, Hinduism, Islam, and Buddhism);
4. *economic metanarratives* (which are commonly conceptualized in terms of diametrically opposed economic models – such as capitalism vs. socialism, monetarism vs. fiscalism, or laissez-faire liberalism vs. Keynesian interventionism);
5. *cultural metanarratives* (as illustrated in the anthropological classification of human forms of life in terms of definitional antinomies such as 'premodern' vs. 'modern', 'primitive' vs. 'complex', 'undeveloped' vs. 'developed', 'tight' vs. 'loose', 'horizontally structured' vs. 'vertically structured', 'control-based' vs. 'freedom-based', or 'collectivist' vs. 'individualist').

PART 2 THEORIES AND METHODS

In recent decades, social theorists have engaged in the critique of metanarratives, shedding light on their substantial (and, on several levels, detrimental) impact on human history and reminding us that '[g]reat crimes often start from great ideas' (Bauman, 1997: 5). Expressing their 'incredulity toward metanarratives' (Lyotard, 1984 [1979]: xxiii, xxiv; cf. Susen, 2015a: esp. Ch. 4), social scientists are required to be attentive to the historical specificities of social constellations, which – because they are relationally constructed and, thus, spatiotemporally variable – are irreducible to the deceptive certainties provided by 'catch-all' theoretical frameworks. This takes us to the relevance of social theory to inquiries in the social sciences, which is the focus of the next section.

 — Pause for Thought

What is social theory?

- Why should we bother with social theory?

Try to think of some examples that illustrate the importance of the central points made in this section. Please reflect on their relevance to your own life and, when doing so, try to answer the following questions:

1.
   - What are the main forms of *action* and *behaviour* you perform on a daily basis?
   - What are your main *beliefs*? Are these beliefs part of a *belief system*? If so, do you subscribe to an *ideology* or, indeed, to several *ideologies*?
   - What are the main *traditions* and *institutions* that shape your life? Can you imagine life without traditions and institutions? Give reasons for your answer.
2.
   - Consider the concepts of 'time' and 'space'. What is *objective*, what is *normative*, and what is *subjective* about 'time' and 'space'?
   - Ask yourself the same question in relation to key sociological variables – such as 'class', 'ethnicity', 'gender', 'age', and '(dis)ability'. In other words, to what extent are these sociological variables *objective*, *normative*, and/or *subjective*?
3.
   - Consider the following social fields: the economic field, the political field, the cultural field, the linguistic field, the artistic field, the religious field, the sexual field, the judicial field, the scientific field, the technological field, the military field, the journalistic field, the field of social media, the field of fashion, and the field of sport. Which of these fields do you regard as *foundational*, which ones do you regard as *contingent*, and which ones do you regard as *ephemeral*?
4.
   - Reflect on the previous list of *metanarratives*. Which of these metanarratives are (still) important in the 21st century? Are any of these (or other) metanarratives important to you on a personal level? If so, why?

——— Expand Your Knowledge ———

To learn more about *the concept of social theory*, you may consult the following sources:

- Inglis, D. and Thorpe, C. (2019 [2012]) *An Invitation to Social Theory*, 2nd edition. Cambridge: Polity.
- Susen, S. (2015) *The 'Postmodern Turn' in the Social Sciences*. Basingstoke: Palgrave Macmillan (esp. pp. 1–39, 140–3).

CONTEMPORARY SOCIAL THEORY

The Relevance of Social Theory

In one way or another, most forms of social-scientific research involve a combination of (1) **empirical**, (2) **methodological**, (3) **epistemological,** (4) **terminological,** and (5) **theoretical** dimensions. (The role of scientific research is explored further in Chapters 9, 10 and 26.)

1. At the *empirical* level, social scientists deal with real-world problems and phenomena. For the right or the wrong reasons, these are often characterized in terms of sociological dichotomies, such as the following: material vs. symbolic, structural vs. agential, stable vs. volatile, objective vs. subjective, factual vs. value-laden, micro vs. macro, local vs. global, private vs. public, normal vs. deviant, cultural vs. natural, active vs. passive, conscious vs. unconscious – to mention only a few.
2. At the *methodological* level, social scientists grapple with the question of how social reality can and/or should be studied. For instance, some researchers rely solely on primary data, some resort exclusively to secondary data, and others draw on both primary and secondary data. Some researchers prefer quantitative approaches, some favour qualitative approaches, and others employ mixed-method strategies, combining different – but arguably complementary – modes of gathering information.
3. At the *epistemological* level, social scientists subscribe to particular conceptions of knowledge, regardless of whether they do so consciously or unconsciously. Paradigmatic dichotomies – such as **positivism** vs. **interpretivism**, materialism vs. idealism, **realism** vs. constructivism, objectivism vs. subjectivism, determinism vs. voluntarism, collectivism vs. individualism, inductivism vs. deductivism – reflect crucial intellectual divisions in the social sciences, all of which are, to a greater or lesser extent, informed by philosophical assumptions about the nature of being, knowledge, and logic.
4. At the *terminological* level, social scientists employ specific words, expressions, and labels to capture the phenomena they study. Indeed, different traditions of thought (which may be defined in disciplinary, ideological, and/or cultural terms) generate different vocabularies, which their users tend to take for granted. Yet, these vocabularies – which, effectively, serve as conceptual toolboxes – are constantly being reinvented, permitting researchers to account for behavioural, ideological, and institutional changes taking place in society.
5. At the *theoretical* level, social scientists endeavour to provide conceptually informed – and, in many cases, empirically substantiated – frameworks designed to (a) describe, (b) analyse, (c) interpret, (d) explain, and (e) assess the constitution, functioning, and **development** of social reality, or particular aspects of social reality, in a more or less systematic fashion. Without these frameworks, there would be no point in gathering and processing empirical data, creating and applying sophisticated methodologies, generating and distributing authoritative knowledge, or inventing and reinventing useful terminological devices.

The aforementioned dimensions, which are intimately interrelated, are integral elements of social-scientific research. One may wish to focus on class, **ethnicity**, gender, **age**, (dis)ability, or any other key sociological **variable**. (These topics are covered further in Chapters 11, 12, 13 and 14.) It is hard to say anything authoritative about their stratifying influence, however, unless one's approach is empirically substantiated, methodologically rigorous, epistemologically reflexive, terminologically precise, and theoretically informed. Social research without **social theory** would be tantamount to a pre-scientific venture, lacking any serious ambition to grasp the complexities of social reality by uncovering its underlying constituents. Most forms of social-scientific research involve a combination of (1) empirical, (2) methodological, (3) epistemological, (4) terminological, and (5) theoretical dimensions. At the same time, they depend on five vital modes of engaging with the world in an epistemically oriented – that is, knowledge-seeking – manner: (1) description, (2) analysis, (3) interpretation, (4) explanation, and (5) evaluation. As shall be elucidated in the following section, this multilayered epistemic orientation is reflected in the knowledge-seeking spirit of social theory.

— Pause for Thought —

Think of a topic in which you are particularly interested. Let us assume you decide to study this topic from a social-scientific perspective:

- What are the main (1) *empirical*, (2) *methodological*, (3) *epistemological*, (4) *terminological*, and (5) *theoretical* dimensions that you would have to take into account when studying your topic?
- To what extent does your theoretical perspective *influence* the way you (1) *describe*, (2) *analyse*, (3) *interpret*, (4) *explain*, and (5) *assess* the key aspects of your topic?

———— Expand Your Knowledge ————

To learn more about *the relevance of social theory*, you may consult the following sources:

- Baert, P. and Silva, F. C. da (2010 [1998]) *Social Theory in the Twentieth Century and Beyond*, 2nd edition. Cambridge: Polity.
- Inglis, D. and Thorpe, C. (2019 [2012]) *An Invitation to Social Theory*, 2nd edition. Cambridge: Polity.

The Knowledge-Seeking Spirit of Social Theory

There would be no point in pursuing social science if, as researchers, we did not aspire to go beyond – and, hence, to challenge – the epistemic realm of everyday preconceptions. In order to undertake this 'epistemological break' (Bourdieu, 1999: 334–5; Bourdieu and Eagleton, 1992: 117; Robbins, 1998; Susen, 2007: 135–7, 261–2; Susen, 2016a: 62–6; 2016b: 217), we need to draw a distinction between **ordinary knowledge** (generated and used by laypersons) and **scientific knowledge** (produced and employed by researchers and experts). Considering the distinction between 'ordinary knowledge' and 'scientific knowledge', we are confronted with three main options:

- *Option 1:* The former is superior to the latter, because it is based on the 'genuine' (individual and/or collective) experiences of human actors in 'real life'. On this view, the former provides a degree of perspectival authenticity that the latter, due to its socially detached constitution, fails to embrace, let alone to convey.

- *Option 2:* The latter is superior to the former, because it is – at once – empirically substantiated, methodologically rigorous, epistemologically reflexive, terminologically precise, and theoretically informed. On this view, the latter guarantees a degree of epistemic certainty that the former, owing to its inevitable reliance on everyday preconceptions, fails to strive for, let alone to achieve.
- *Option 3:* Little is to be gained from constructing a rigid epistemic hierarchy between the former and the latter. Although 'ordinary knowledge' and 'scientific knowledge' are qualitatively different, they reflect equally legitimate types of epistemic engagement with the world. Rather than opposing 'ordinary' and 'scientific' ways of attributing meaning to and acting upon reality, we should seek to cross-fertilize these – arguably complementary – modes of relating to the world. As *laypersons*, we can navigate our everyday lives *and* – whether we do so consciously or unconsciously – draw on scientifically established insights. As *experts*, we can study objective, normative, and/or subjective aspects of the world *and* take ordinary people – including their conceptions, as well as their misconceptions, of reality – seriously.

Without developing *theories* about the constitution, functioning, and development of social reality, or of particular aspects of social reality, it is difficult, if not impossible, to engage with the world in an enlightening manner (cf. Swedberg, 2016). Social theory, in this sense, can be regarded as a systematic attempt to make sense of reality in a simultaneously (1) descriptive, (2) analytic, (3) interpretive, (4) explanatory, and (5) evaluative fashion. Rather than simply *describing* the surface level of social phenomena, social theorists take on the challenge of *analysing, interpreting, explaining,* and *making value judgements* about their underlying constitution and (actual or potential) development. To be clear, this is not to posit that social reality (either as a whole or in its multiple parts) is coherently structured. This is to contend, however, that the constitution, functioning, and development of social reality, or particular aspects of social reality, can be *more or less* (1) adequately described, (2) systematically analysed, (3) insightfully interpreted, (4) convincingly explained, and (5) critically assessed by virtue of robust (that is, empirically substantiated, methodologically rigorous, epistemologically reflexive and terminologically precise) theoretical frameworks. In the next section, we shall consider some of the key dimensions that should be taken into account when researching these frameworks.

Pause for Thought

- What are the main similarities between *ordinary knowledge* and *scientific knowledge*?
- What are the main differences between *ordinary knowledge* and *scientific knowledge*?
- To what extent are the boundaries between *ordinary knowledge* and *scientific knowledge* blurred?
- What role does *ordinary knowledge* play in your everyday life?
- What role does *scientific knowledge* play in your everyday life?
- Are *ordinary knowledge* and *scientific knowledge* (1) equally important, (2) equally insightful, (3) equally biased, (4) equally interest-laden, and (5) equally power-laden? Give reasons for your answer.
- What is the role of *reason* and *rationality* in generating different types of knowledge?
- What is the role of *affect* and *emotion* in generating different types of knowledge?
- What is the difference between *knowledge* and *opinion*?

Expand Your Knowledge

To learn more about *the knowledge-seeking spirit of social theory*, you may consult the following sources:

- Bourdieu, P. and Eagleton, T. (1992) Doxa and common life. *New Left Review* 191: 111–21.
- Susen, S. (2007) *The Foundations of the Social: Between Critical Theory and Reflexive Sociology*. Oxford: Bardwell Press (Ch. 5, esp. pp. 133–7).

Key Dimensions of Social Theory

When examining the works produced by social theorists, it is useful to focus on three dimensions: (1) historical context, (2) central issues and contributions, and (3) strengths and weaknesses. Thus, we are confronted with the threefold challenge of (1) shedding light on the *historical circumstances* in which particular paradigmatic approaches have emerged and developed, (2) explaining the essential *issues* at stake in specific intellectual traditions as well as the principal *contributions* made by different scholars, and (3) drawing attention to the most significant *strengths and weaknesses* of rival conceptual frameworks (see Susen, 2013: 81).

This tripartite approach enables us to pursue the following objectives:

1. To grasp the historical conditions under which particular social theories emerged, as well as the biographical trajectories of those who developed them;
2. To identify the central themes covered, issues discussed, and contributions made by particular social theories, while uncovering their underlying assumptions;
3. To offer balanced accounts of particular social theories – not only by scrutinizing their respective strengths and weaknesses, but also by assessing their relevance and usefulness for the study of specific elements of human forms of life.

Having taken into consideration the aforementioned dimensions, it is possible to evaluate whether or not a particular social theory succeeds in (1) describing, (2) analysing, (3) interpreting, (4) explaining, and (5) assessing the constitution, functioning, and development of social reality, or particular aspects of social reality, in a convincing manner. Arguably, this judgement call depends on the extent to which the approach in question makes significant claims whose epistemic **validity** is substantiated by empirical evidence, sustained by methodological rigour, informed by epistemological **reflexivity**, sharpened by **terminological** precision, and conducive to conceptual innovation.

In order to pursue the aforementioned objectives, it is important to draw on both **primary sources** and **secondary sources**. Primary sources are texts produced by major scholars, whose contributions are typically examined and discussed by commentators in the secondary literature. Secondary sources usually involve systematic descriptions, analyses, interpretations, explanations, and evaluations of primary sources. Primary sources are often more difficult to comprehend than secondary sources – especially if they were produced in a different historical context and/or written in a different language, but also if they are marked by a high degree of conceptual abstraction. Secondary sources may be useful not only in terms of making primary sources more accessible, but also, crucially, in terms of permitting readers to familiarize themselves with key debates and controversies surrounding the works of prominent thinkers. Having considered key dimensions of social theory, let us turn to reflecting on the scope of its main intellectual and thematic developments.

 **Pause for Thought**

- Pick a particular social theorist and reflect on their work in terms of (1) *historical context*, (2) *central issues and contributions*, as well as (3) *strengths and weaknesses*.
- Why is it difficult, if not impossible, to examine level '2' (*central issues and contributions*) without knowledge of level '1' (*historical context*)?
- Why is it difficult, if not impossible, to discuss level '3' (*strengths and weaknesses*) without knowledge of level '2' (*central issues and contributions*) and, arguably, at least some knowledge of level '1' (*historical context*)?
- Why is it important to cover *both primary and secondary sources* when exploring the contributions made by seminal social theorists?

Expand Your Knowledge

To learn more about *key dimensions of social theory*, you may consult the following sources:

- Baert, P. and Silva, F.C. da (2010 [1998]) *Social Theory in the Twentieth Century and Beyond*, 2nd edition. Cambridge: Polity.
- Susen, S. (2013) Comments on Patrick Baert and Filipe Carreira da Silva's *Social Theory in the Twentieth Century and Beyond* – Towards a 'Hermeneutics-Inspired Pragmatism'? *Distinktion: Scandinavian Journal of Social Theory* 14(1): 80–101.

The Scope of Social Theory

It is common to draw a distinction between **'classical' and 'contemporary' social theory**. Although the **boundaries** between the two are often blurred, they can be distinguished as follows: the former generally refers to influential social theories developed in the 19th and early 20th centuries, whereas the latter usually designates social theories developed from the mid-20th century onwards.

Arguably, the three most influential *classical social theorists* are Karl Marx (1818–83), Émile Durkheim (1858–1917), and Max Weber (1864–1920). Notwithstanding the question of whether or not they deserve to be regarded as the 'founding figures' of **sociology**, the far-reaching significance of their legacy is undeniable. Among other scholars who, owing to their lasting impact on the discipline, are frequently considered 'classical sociologists' are intellectual pioneers such as Auguste Comte (1798–1857), W.E.B. Du Bois (1868–1963), Norbert Elias (1897–1990), Harriet Martineau (1802–76), George Herbert Mead (1863–1931), Vilfredo Pareto (1848–1923), Georg Simmel (1858–1918), Herbert Spencer (1820–1903), and Gabriel Tarde (1843–1904).

With regard to the intellectual landscape formed by *contemporary social theorists*, the picture is more complex and, arguably, far more diverse. Among the most prominent thinkers who fall into this category are the following:

Theodor W. Adorno (1903–69), Jeffrey C. Alexander (1947–), Margaret S. Archer (1943–), Jean Baudrillard (1929–2007), Zygmunt Bauman (1925–2017), Ulrich Beck (1944–2015), Luc Boltanski (1940–), Pierre

Bourdieu (1930–2002), Judith Butler (1956–), Craig Calhoun (1952–), Manuel Castells (1942–), Randall Collins (1941–), Ralf Dahrendorf (1929–2009), Donatella della Porta (1956–), Paul DiMaggio (1951–), Shmuel Noah Eisenstadt (1923–2010), Michel Foucault (1926–84), Nancy Fraser (1947–), Anthony Giddens (1938–), Erving Goffman (1922–82), Jürgen Habermas (1929–), Stuart Hall (1932–2014), Sandra Harding (1935–), Axel Honneth (1949–), Hans Joas (1948–), Krishan Kumar (1942–), Bruno Latour (1947–), Henri Lefebvre (1901–91), Niklas Luhmann (1927–98), Steven Lukes (1941–), Jean-François Lyotard (1924–98), Michael Mann (1942–), Karl Mannheim (1893–1947), Robert Merton (1910–2003), Talcott Parsons (1902–79), Hartmut Rosa (1965–), Nikolas Rose (1947–), Edward Said (1935–2003), Saskia Sassen (1947–), Richard Sennett (1943–), Charles Taylor (1931–), Alain Touraine, (1925–), and Bryan S. Turner (1945–).

Despite significant differences between these (and other) scholars, most classical and contemporary social theorists share several key concerns. Let us mention just two of them:

1. They share a deep concern with the extent to which *relations of power and domination* shape the constitution of human forms of life (Clegg and Haugaard, 2009; Susen, 2014a, 2015a: esp. 117–18, 2018). Different social theorists emphasize different types of power: social power, cultural power, economic power, political power, judicial power, sexual power, physical power, mental power, military power, technological power, ideological power, religious power, scientific power, epistemic power, or noumenal power – to mention only a few. Moreover, they often attach dichotomous meanings to the concept of power, notably 'soft power' vs. 'hard power', 'power to' vs. 'power over', and 'power for' vs. 'power against'. 'Optimistic' social theorists tend to assume that it is possible to subvert, if not to eradicate, relations of power and domination. Their 'pessimistic' (or, arguably, 'realistic') counterparts, on the other hand, tend to maintain that relations of power and domination represent an inevitable part of social life. According to the former, the construction of emancipatory forms of life is both viable and desirable. According to the latter, the pursuit of human emancipation is a futile endeavour to the degree that 'the will to power', which manifests itself in the construction of systems of domination, is an anthropological constant – that is, an essential element of the human condition.
2. They share a deep concern with the *historical* constitution of social reality. On this view, it is crucial to examine the past, in order to obtain an accurate understanding of the present and/or to speculate, in an informed way, about the future. Put differently, in one way or another, most social theorists take, so to speak, 'the long view': they reject 'presentist' accounts of social reality (which aim to explain particular aspects of the present without taking the trouble to study their past) as short-sighted and reductive. It is far from clear, however, to what extent a 'strong consciousness of historical complexity' (Inglis, 2014: 100) is gradually being undermined (and replaced) by the increasing popularity of 'presentist' accounts of social reality. Part of this apparent paradigm shift is a collectively shared preoccupation – if not obsession – with '*the new*', rather than a sustained engagement with the degree to which the present is profoundly shaped by behavioural, ideological, and institutional patterns transmitted from the past.

 —— Pause for Thought ——

- Should we draw a *distinction between 'classical' and 'contemporary' social theory*? Give reasons for your answer.
- Why are most social theorists interested in *relations of power and domination*?
- Why are most social theorists interested in *the historical constitution of social reality*?

- Is a social theory that ignores (1) *relations of power and domination* and (2) *the historical constitution of social reality* a contradiction in terms? Why (not)?

Expand Your Knowledge

To learn more about *the scope of social theory*, you may consult the following sources:

- Appelrouth, S. and Edles, L.D. (eds) (2011 [2006]) *Sociological Theory in the Contemporary Era: Text and Readings*, 2nd edition. Thousand Oaks, CA: Pine Forge.
- Ritzer, G. and Stepnisky, J. (2018 [2003]) *Contemporary Sociological Theory and Its Classical Roots: The Basics*, 5th edition. London: Sage.

Versions of Social Theory

When teaching social theory at university level, one is inevitably confronted with the following two questions: Where should we start? Where should we end? In this respect, it is common to draw the aforementioned distinction between 'classical' and 'contemporary' social theory. In one way or another, most – if not all – versions of the latter will draw on the works produced by the founding figures of the former. In other words, it is difficult to grasp the key trends, developments, and controversies in contemporary social theory without a solid, or at least a basic, understanding of its classical predecessors.

Within contemporary social theory, one finds a large variety of rival approaches, which converge and diverge to different degrees and on different levels. In fact, given the multiplicity of social theories that have emerged ever since sociology came into existence, it is hard to do justice to all of them in an introductory chapter. It *is* possible, however, to categorize at least the most influential currents of thought that have shaped, and continue to shape, the development of social theory.

Classical Social Theory

Three main 'classical' traditions of social theory have emerged out of early-modern sociology. These approaches are also discussed in Chapters 5, 7 and 26:

- *Marxist* social theory, associated with 'historical-materialist sociology';
- *Durkheimian* social theory, associated with '**functionalist** sociology';
- *Weberian* social theory, associated with 'interpretive sociology'.

Marxist and *Durkheimian* approaches tend to be linked to *social holism*, in the sense that they conceive of the constitution, functioning, and development of **social practices,** structures, and arrangements in terms of a 'social whole'. On this view, social forces operate 'behind people's backs', influencing – if not determining – the interplay of relationally interconnected actions and constellations.

Weberian approaches tend to be linked to *methodological individualism*, in the sense that they seek to comprehend the constitution, functioning, and development of social practices, structures, and arrangements by considering 'individual actors' as the ontological foundations of society and the epistemological starting point of social inquiry. On this account, human beings are capable of drawing on different (notably practical, theoretical, formal, and **substantive**) types of rationality, permitting them to make reason-guided decisions and, by implication, to shape the course of history.

The epistemic spirit of *Marxist* and *Durkheimian* approaches is pervaded by the **paradigm** of *explanation* [*Erklären*], suggesting that it is the mission of social scientists to shed light on the underlying structural forces whose determining power escapes people's common-sense perceptions of the world. By contrast, the epistemic spirit of *Weberian* approaches is permeated by the paradigm of *understanding* [*Verstehen*], positing that social scientists need to engage with actors' ordinary ways of interpreting reality, since the human world is a universe of meaning-laden practices.

Contemporary Social Theory

Directly or indirectly influenced by these 'classical' traditions of thought, numerous currents of contemporary social theory have emerged. These can be categorized according to different criteria. Among the most influential branches of contemporary social thought are the following:

- *'early' functionalism* (Émile Durkheim, Bronisław Malinowski, Alfred Reginald Radcliffe-Brown, Herbert Spencer) and *neofunctionalism / systems theory* (Jeffrey Alexander, Niklas Luhmann, Robert Merton, Talcott Parsons);
- *linguistic structuralism* (Ferdinand de Saussure), *anthropological structuralism* (Claude Lévi-Strauss), *sociological / genetic structuralism* (Pierre Bourdieu), and *poststructuralism* (Roland Barthes, Jean Baudrillard, Judith Butler, Gilles Deleuze, Jacques Derrida, Michel Foucault, Julia Kristeva);
- *philosophical and sociological pragmatism* (Patrick Baert, Luc Boltanski, Hans Joas, Joseph Margolis, Louis Quéré, Richard Rorty, Cédric Terzi);
- *critical theory, both 'within and beyond' the Frankfurt School* (Theodor W. Adorno, Hannah Arendt, Walter Benjamin, Jürgen Habermas, Axel Honneth, Max Horkheimer, Herbert Marcuse; and – more recently – Robin Celikates, Rainer Forst, Rahel Jaeggi, Hartmut Rosa, Martin Saar, Simon Susen);
- *micro-sociology and the sociology of everyday life* (Herbert George Blumer, Randall Collins, Harold Garfinkel, Erving Goffman, Russell Hardin, George Herbert Mead)
- **conflict** *theories* (Randall Collins, Lewis Coser, Ralf Dahrendorf, Gene Sharp);
- **rational** *choice theories, game theories, social exchange theories, and neo-institutionalist approaches* (Gary S. Becker, Peter M. Blau, Paul DiMaggio, Jon Elster, Richard Marc Emerson, Martin Hollis, George C. Homans, Harold H. Kelley, David M. Kreps, John W. Thibaut, Walter W. Powell);
- *social theories of* **modernity** */ modernities* (Shmuel Noah Eisenstadt, Gerard Delanty, Anthony Giddens, Krishan Kumar, Michael Mann, William Outhwaite, Theda Skocpol, Charles Tilly, Bryan S. Turner, Peter Wagner);
- *social theories of late modernity, second modernity, and reflexive modernity* (Ulrich Beck, Anthony Giddens, Christoph Lau);
- *social theories of postmodernity / postmodern social theories* (Perry Anderson, Jean Baudrillard, Zygmunt Bauman, Manuel Castells, Luce Irigaray, Fredric Jameson, Douglas Kellner, Scott Lash, Jean-François

Lyotard, Michel Maffesoli, Linda J. Nicholson, Saskia Sassen, Steven Seidman, Richard Sennett, Simon Susen, Keith Tester, John Urry, Gianni Vattimo, Robert Venturi, Wolfgang Welsch, Iris Marion Young, Slavoj Žižek);

- *social theories of **globalization*** (Martin Albrow, Zygmunt Bauman, Ulrich Beck, Manuel Castells, Donatella della Porta, Shmuel Noah Eisenstadt, Mike Featherstone, Anthony Giddens, David Held, Paul Hirst, Robert J. Holton, Ankie Hoogvelt, Elizabeth King, Scott Lash, Charles Lemert, Michael Mann, Marjorie Mayo, Anthony G. McGrew, Lydia Morris, Jan Nederveen Pieterse, George Ritzer, Roland Robertson, Chris Rumford, Saskia Sassen, Leslie Sklair, Grahame Thompson, Bryan S. Turner, Linda Weiss);
- *social theories of **cosmopolitanism*** (Anthony Appiah, Daniele Archibugi, Ulrich Beck, Seyla Benhabib, Carol A. Breckenridge, Craig Calhoun, Roland Dannreuther, Gerard Delanty, Robert Fine, Jürgen Habermas, David Held, Kimberly Hutchings, Chris Rumford, Bryan S. Turner);
- *social theories of space* (David Harvey, Henri Lefebvre, Doreen Massey, Saskia Sassen, Edward Soja, Nigel Thrift, John Urry);
- *social theories of gender / feminism* (Lisa Adkins, Judith Butler, Raewyn Connell, Nancy Fraser, Lynn Hankinson-Nelson, Donna J. Haraway, Sandra Harding, Luce Irigaray, Linda Nicholson, Beverley Skeggs, Sylvia Walby, Iris Marion Young);
- *social theories of class and stratification* (Daniel Bell, Pierre Bourdieu, Richard Breen, Rosemary Crompton, Gøsta Esping-Andersen, John Goldthorpe, Mike Savage, Erik Olin Wright);
- *social theories of 'race' and ethnicity* (Michael Banton, Eduardo Bonilla-Silva, Patricia Hill Collins, Denise Ferreira da Silva, Paul Gilroy, Stuart Hall, Richard Jenkins, Tariq Modood, John Rex, John Solomos, Cornel West, William Julius Wilson);
- *post- and decolonial theories* (Homi K. Bhabha, Gurminder Bhambra, Raewyn Connell, Julian Go, Boaventura de Sousa Santos, Aníbal Quijano, María Lugones, Walter Mignolo, Edward Said, Gayatri Spivak);
- *social theories of power and domination* (Pierre Bourdieu, Judith Butler, Craig Calhoun, Randall Collins, Raewyn Connell, Ralf Dahrendorf, Michel Foucault, Nancy Fraser, Stuart Hall, Sandra Harding, David Harvey, Mark Haugaard, Barry Hindess, Steven Lukes, Michael Mann, Gianfranco Poggi, Nikolas Rose, Martin Saar, John Scott, Gayatri Spivak, Simon Susen);
- ***science and technology studies / actor-network theories*** (Karen Barad, Wiebe Bijker, Michel Callon, Andrew Feenberg, Steve Fuller, Donna Haraway, Sandra Harding, Donald Angus MacKenzie, Bruno Latour, Bernard Stiegler, Langdon Winner, Steve Woolgar).

Having identified some of the most influential branches of contemporary social thought, let us consider some key trends and developments that have marked, and continue to mark, social theory in the 21st century.

 **Pause for Thought**

- What are the advantages and disadvantages of *categorizing* influential currents of thought?
- What are the main similarities and differences between *Marxist*, *Durkheimian*, and *Weberian* approaches in the social sciences?
- Are all *'contemporary'* social theories simply *a series of footnotes to their 'classical' predecessors*? Give reasons for your answer.
- Which contemporary social theories (and theorists) do you find particularly interesting? If possible, try to figure out *why* you find some contemporary social theories (and theorists) more interesting than others.

Expand Your Knowledge

To learn more about *versions of social theory*, you may consult the following sources:

- Calhoun, C., Gerteis, J., Moody, J., Pfaff, S., and Virk, I. (eds) (2012 [2002]) *Classical Sociological Theory*, 3rd edition. Oxford: Wiley-Blackwell.
- Calhoun, C., Gerteis, J., Moody, J., Pfaff, S., and Virk, I. (eds) (2012 [2002]) *Contemporary Sociological Theory*, 3rd edition. Chichester: John Wiley & Sons.

Trends and Developments in Social Theory

As indicated above, contemporary social theory is marked by a large variety of rival approaches. Despite the substantial differences between these perspectives, it is possible to identify a number of trends and developments in contemporary social theory (see Susen, 2015a: 6–11; cf. Susen, 2020a).

1. Increasingly, social theory is regarded as an *interdisciplinary* endeavour. The 'advocacy of social theory' (Seidman, 1994b: 119), which is inspired by the 'critique of sociological theory' (p. 119), is based on a commitment to interdisciplinary research. When communicating across disciplinary boundaries, it becomes clear that a lot is to be gained from cross-fertilizing the knowledge generated within different realms of inquiry. A commitment to interdisciplinary research – cutting across traditional epistemic boundaries within and between the humanities, the social sciences, and the natural sciences – is motivated by the conviction that there is no analytic approach that can claim to capture the entire complexity of human reality.
2. Increasingly, social theory is regarded as a *foundationless* endeavour. More and more researchers in the social sciences take the view that 'the quest for foundations and for a totalizing theory of society' (Seidman, 1994b: 119) is not only pointless, but also potentially dangerous (cf. Baert, 2005: 126–45, 146–69; Baert and Silva, 2010 [1998]: 285–307). In the face of inescapable sociocultural diversity, it seems impossible to provide context-transcending standards of epistemic validity. In a world characterized by multiplicity and heterogeneity, the system-building task of grasping the complexity of society by virtue of 'grand theories' (cf. Skinner, 1985) and 'big-picture ideologies' (cf. Susen, 2014b) appears to have lost credibility.
3. Increasingly, social theory is regarded as a *directionless* endeavour. In this context, 'directionless' does not signify 'meaningless', 'pointless', or 'clueless'. Rather, it indicates that we, as critical researchers, should resist the temptation to invent conceptual apparatuses that lead to the 'false closure' (Seidman, 1994b: 120) of theoretical frameworks, preventing us from 'prying open present and future social possibilities' (p. 120) and from 'detecting fluidity and porousness' (p. 120), rather than discovering determinacy and eternity, in the daily construction of human reality. A social theory without guarantees 'carries no promise of liberation [...], of a society free of domination' (pp. 119–20), thereby rejecting the teleological spirit underlying some classical accounts of human emancipation (cf. Susen, 2015b).
4. Increasingly, social theory is regarded as a *public* endeavour. As such, it cannot make any major claims about the constitution of society without engaging with the everyday processes that shape the development of reality. It will lose its wider 'social and intellectual importance' (Seidman, 1994b: 119) if 'it is disengaged from the conflicts and public debates' (p. 119) taking place on a daily basis. The 'plea

for a "public sociology", which uses expert knowledge to promote debate with and amongst various non-academic publics' (Baert and Silva, 2010 [1998]: 302), is aimed at recognizing the following: to the extent that sociological analysis 'has turned inward and is largely self-referential' (Seidman, 1994b: 119), it runs the risk of degrading itself to an elitist language game, whose autopoietic conceptual frameworks are disconnected from everyday concerns and experiences. Not only do we need to avoid a scenario in which '[s]ociological theory [...] is produced and consumed almost exclusively by sociological theorists' (p. 119), and not only do we need to discard mainstream notions of 'professional sociology' and 'policy sociology' (see Baert and Silva, 2010 [1998]: 302), but, moreover, we need to take on the challenge of *cross-fertilizing academic and non-academic discourses*. This can be achieved by doing away with the traditional **division of labour** between the 'scientific enlighteners', who direct and control their epistemic inferiors 'from above', and the 'ordinary to-be-enlightened', who follow and obey their epistemic superiors 'from below'.

5. Increasingly, social theory is regarded as a *situationist* endeavour. Owing to its interest in the spatio-temporal specificities of locally experienced realities, it 'speaks the language of particularity' (Seidman, 1994b: 121), rather than obeying the logic of the search for lawfulness and universality. In this sense, it is driven by 'the more modest aspiration of a relentless defence of immediate, local pleasures and struggles for justice' (Seidman, 1994b: 120, quotation modified), instead of aiming 'to uncover a logic of society' (p. 120), 'to discover the one true vocabulary that mirrors the social universe' (p. 120), and 'to find a universal language, a conceptual casuistry that can assess the truth of all social languages' (p. 121) and thereby 'articulate humanity's universal condition' (p. 121). If we abandon the futile project of defining 'our principal task as providing foundations for sociology' (p. 122), as 'giving ultimate reasons' (p. 122), and as delivering 'a universal epistemic rationale that provides objective, value-neutral standards' (p. 122), then we are in a position to recognize that the complexity of materially and symbolically differentiated realities cannot be captured in terms of the context-transcending frameworks and principles of grand sociological theories.

6. Increasingly, social theory is regarded as a *pragmatic* endeavour. This tendency 'suggests that the search for ultimate or universal grounds for our conceptual strategies should be abandoned in favour of local, pragmatic justifications' (Seidman, 1994b: 123, quotation modified). Such a pragmatist approach to social existence is interested in discursive processes accomplished by ordinary actors capable of mobilizing their cognitive resources in relationally constituted – and, hence, sociologically diverse – contexts. A 'pragmatic turn' (p. 125) in social theory has various significant advantages, notably that '[i]t expands the number of parties who may participate more or less as equals in a debate about society' (p. 125) and, therefore, permits us to do justice to the fact that human actors – that is, both experts *and* laypersons – are equipped with reflective, critical, and moral capacities (Blokker, 2011; Boltanski and Thévenot, 1999; Susen and Turner, 2014). In short, the 'pragmatic turn' in sociology draws attention not only to multiple ways in which *human practices* allow for the construction of social reality, but also to the pivotal role that *human capacities* play within performative processes.

7. Increasingly, social theory is regarded as an *ethno-conscious* endeavour. To be aware of the cultural specificity of one's epistemic claims to validity requires recognizing that the attempt to overcome ethnocentrism is fraught with difficulties. All modes of knowledge generation – irrespective of whether they are scientific or non-scientific, academic or non-academic, based on expertise or guided by common sense – represent *culturally specific* practices performed by spatiotemporally embedded entities. If we accept the sociocultural particularity underlying all epistemic claims to validity, then we are obliged to face up to the structuring power exercised by the ineluctable weight of historicity. To be ethno-conscious means to be aware of the fact that all modes of cognition – including the most reflexive ones – are influenced by context-dependent prejudices, preconceptions, and presuppositions.

8. Increasingly, social theory is regarded as a *socio-conscious* endeavour. As such, it insists not only upon the cultural specificity that shapes epistemic communities, but also, in a broader sense, upon the *relational contingency* underlying the seemingly most liberating forms of human agency (cf. Susen, 2020a: 10–11). Indeed, it is due to this relational contingency that the human condition is permeated by radical indeterminacy: highly differentiated societies produce intersectionally constituted actors expected to take on multiple roles, develop plural identities, and carry various coexisting – and, often, conflicting – selves within themselves. A socio-conscious perspective has major implications for our conception of knowledge: the question of whether we consider a statement right or wrong depends not only on *what* is being said, but also on *who* says it *when*, *where*, and *to whom*. For *objectivity* ('What?') is – inevitably – a matter of *social authority* ('Who?'), *spatiotemporal contextuality* ('Where and when?'), and *interactional relationality* ('To whom?'). The idea of abstract epistemic universality evaporates when confronted with the multi-layered constitution of normative – that is, value-laden, meaning-laden, perspective-laden, interest-laden, power-laden, and tension-laden – realities.

9. Increasingly, social theory is regarded as a *pluralist* endeavour. Highly differentiated societies are centreless formations in the sense that they lack a structural, ideological, or behavioural epicentre from which all institutions, discourses, and practices derive and upon which peripheral areas of interaction, or derivative forms of existence, are parasitical. In the global jungle of flows, networks, and diversified local events, the human actor is '*a self with multiple identities and group affiliations, which is entangled in heterogeneous struggles with multiple possibilities for empowerment*' (Seidman, 1994b: 136, emphasis added). Given both the real and the representational complexity of materially and symbolically differentiated societies, we need to abandon the modern project of developing big-picture ideologies and to face up to the existence of situation-laden normativities created in response to relationally constituted realities. In the global **network** society, there is no such thing as an overriding agenda that can justifiably declare to possess a normative monopoly in the landscape of decentred and diversified subjectivities.

10. Increasingly, social theory is regarded as a *historicist* endeavour. One of the main limitations of classical sociological thought, undermining its applicability to the study of highly differentiated forms of sociality, is its 'quest for foundations' (Seidman, 1994b: 119, 127; cf. Seidman, 1994a: 12), which is expressed in 'the project of creating a *general theory*' (Seidman, 1994b: 127, emphasis added), understood as 'an overarching totalizing conceptual framework that would be true for *all times* and *all places*' (p. 127, emphasis added). In this respect, three issues are particularly worth mentioning:

    a. *Ethnocentrism*: '*Human history* in these modernist tales really meant *Western history*' (Seidman, 1994b: 129, emphasis added; cf. Bhambra, 2014; Connell, 2007; Spivak, 1988, 1990). Their capacity to conceal 'the mark of their own national origin' (Seidman, 1994b: 129) permits them to present their explanatory insights into social developments 'as if their particular pattern were of world-historical importance' (p. 130, quotation modified).

    b. *Evolutionism*: In classical sociological thought, '[n]on-Western societies [are] relegated to a marginal position in past, present, and future history' (Seidman, 1994b: 129; Bhambra, 2014; Connell, 2007; Spivak, 1988, 1990). Following this modernist logic, historical events and trends can be measured against the teleological benchmark of 'progress' (cf. Allen, 2016), which can be defined in numerous – notably, social, cultural, political, economic, technological, scientific, religious, demographic, and civilizational – terms. 'The *grand narratives of industrialization, modernization, secularization, democratization*, these sweeping stories that *presume to uncover a uniform social process* in a multitude of different societies […] should be abandoned' (Seidman, 1994b: 130, emphasis added).

c. *Dichotomism*: Teleological metanarratives are 'stories with [...] simplistic binary schemes' (Seidman, 1994b: 130), such as *Thesis* vs. *Antithesis* (Georg W.F. Hegel), *Gemeinschaft* vs. *Gesellschaft* (Ferdinand Tönnies), *Kapitalismus* vs. *Sozialismus/Kommunismus* (Karl Marx), *Wertrationalität* vs. *Zweckrationalität* (Max Weber), or *solidarité mécanique* vs. *solidarité organique* (Émile Durkheim) – to mention only a few examples (cf. Seidman, 1994b: 130; see also Jenks, 1998). Universalist evolutionary and binary categories artificially homogenize the heterogeneously constituted constellations of historical realities. If, however, we acknowledge the sociohistorical specificity underlying all epistemic claims to validity, then we are obliged to expose the spatiotemporal relativity permeating the symbolic authority asserted by universalist accounts of history.

In short, it appears that most social theorists in the 21st century, irrespective of the significant differences that may exist between them, have abandoned the ambitious pursuit of providing 'catch-all' conceptual frameworks, designed to offer once-and-for-all explanations of both the agential and the structural forces shaping society. Social theory is not dead, but its contemporary versions tend to be far less interested in uncovering the alleged determinacy of social reality than its classical variants.

Finally, it is worth pointing out that, in the early 21st century, social theorists face major challenges. These comprise a range of issues: social, cultural, political, economic, technological, military, epistemic, scientific, philosophical, religious, organizational, demographic, and environmental – to mention only the most salient ones. It is one thing to diagnose the various problems with which humanity is confronted in the 21st century; it is quite another to come up with viable solutions. Social theory has played, and will continue to play, a pivotal role in the battle of ideas for building a global society capable of determining its own destiny in a way that addresses the interests shared by all, rather than just some, members of humanity.

— **Pause for Thought** —

- What are the main trends and developments that have shaped social theory in the late 20th and early 21st centuries?
- What, if anything, do these trends and developments tell us about the constitution of contemporary societies?
- Which of these trends and developments do you consider particularly important?
- Can you think of any significant trends and developments (in society in general and in the social sciences in particular) that are *not* included, but – in your view – *should* be included, in the above account?

— **Expand Your Knowledge** —

To learn more about *trends and developments in contemporary social theory*, you may consult the following sources:

- Inglis, D. and Thorpe, C. (2019 [2012]) *An Invitation to Social Theory*, 2nd edition. Cambridge: Polity.
- Susen, S. (2020) *Sociology in the Twenty-First Century: Key Trends, Debates, and Challenges.* Basingstoke: Palgrave Macmillan.

PART 2 THEORIES AND METHODS

CHAPTER SUMMARY

This chapter has provided a brief introduction to contemporary social theory. To this end, it has covered a number of central issues that need to be addressed when grappling with the task of studying, or indeed producing, theoretical frameworks in the social sciences in general and in sociology in particular. The main points made in this chapter can be summarized as follows:

- Social theory may be defined as the attempt to provide a conceptually informed – and, in many cases, empirically substantiated – framework designed to (1) describe, (2) analyse, (3) interpret, (4) explain, and (5) assess the constitution, functioning, and development of social reality, or particular aspects of social reality, in a more or less systematic fashion.
- Most forms of social-scientific research involve a combination of (1) empirical, (2) methodological, (3) epistemological, (4) terminological, and (5) theoretical dimensions. At the same time, they depend on five vital modes of engaging with the world in an epistemically oriented – that is, knowledge-seeking – manner: (1) description, (2) analysis, (3) interpretation, (4) explanation, and (5) evaluation. Social theory permits us to make sense of their interconnectedness.
- Since, as critical researchers, we are expected to go beyond the epistemic realm of everyday preconceptions, we need to draw a distinction between *ordinary knowledge* (generated and used by laypersons) and *scientific knowledge* (produced and employed by researchers and experts).
- When studying the works produced by social theorists, we need to consider their historical situatedness, their principal contributions to human knowledge, and their strengths and weaknesses.
- Notwithstanding the large variety of 'classical' and 'contemporary' social theories, most – albeit not all – of them share a concern with (1) relations of power and domination as well as (2) the historical constitution of social reality.
- Directly or indirectly influenced by 'classical' traditions of thought, diverse currents of contemporary social theory have emerged over the past century, exploring key issues arising from the development of modern societies.
- Most social theorists in the 21st century have abandoned the ambitious pursuit of providing 'catch-all' conceptual frameworks, designed to offer once-and-for-all explanations of both the agential and the structural forces shaping society.

REVIEW QUESTIONS

1. What is social theory? In your answer, think about how it can be defined.
2. Why should we bother with social theory? In your answer, reflect on its main purpose and why it is important.
3. What is the place of social theory in contemporary sociology? In your answer, discuss its role in sociology and, more broadly, in the social sciences.
4. What are the main challenges faced by social theorists in the 21st century? In your answer, examine the extent to which these challenges reflect some of the principal problems with which humanity is confronted in the 21st century.

Go Further

Books

- Baert, P. and Silva, F.C. da (2010 [1998]) *Social Theory in the Twentieth Century and Beyond,* 2nd edition. Cambridge: Polity.

This book offers an easy-to-read but provocative account of the development of social theory, covering a range of key figures and influential schools of thought.

- Inglis, D. and Thorpe, C. (2019 [2012]) *An Invitation to Social Theory,* 2nd edition. Cambridge: Polity.

Wide-ranging in scope and coverage, this book provides a concise, jargon-free, and thought-provoking introduction to social theory.

- Ritzer, G. and Stepnisky, J. (2018 [2003]) *Contemporary Sociological Theory and Its Classical Roots: The Basics,* 5th edition. London: Sage.

This volume comprises a useful survey of sociology's major theorists and theoretical approaches, covering the works of both classical and contemporary figures.

Journal Articles

- Delanty, G. (2017) The *European Journal of Social Theory* at twenty years. *European Journal of Social Theory* 20(1): 4–8.

This introduction to the 20th anniversary of the *European Journal of Social Theory* offers an opportunity to reflect on the current position of social theory in light of the past two decades, but with a view to the future.

- Susen, S. (2020) The resonance of resonance: Critical theory as a sociology of world-relations? *International Journal of Politics, Culture, and Society* 33(3): 309–44.

This article explores recent developments in critical social theory, focusing on the work of the German sociologist Hartmut Rosa. It provides an example of a social theory that claims that one central paradigm (in this case, 'resonance') can be considered 'a meta-criterion of the good life' – that is, a criterion by means of which it is possible to assess the quality of a particular set of social arrangements.

- Swedberg, R. (2016) Before theory comes theorizing or how to make social science more interesting. *The British Journal of Sociology* 67(1): 5–22.

The basic argument in this article is that, in the present context, sociology and social science more generally are severely hampered by the lack of attention being paid to theory. It suggests that one way to redress the current imbalance between 'methods' and 'theory' in the social sciences is to pay more attention to *theorizing* – that is, to the actual process that precedes the final formulation of a theory.

(Continued)

> ### Websites
>
> - https://socialtheoryapplied.com
>
> This website provides an online space with useful ideas and resources on the numerous ways in which social theory can be applied to the study of central areas of social life.
>
> - https://globalsocialtheory.org
>
> Divided into three broad categories (that is, 'concepts', 'thinkers', and 'topics'), this website contains valuable resources for anyone interested in global social theory.
>
> - www.bbc.co.uk/programmes/b006qy05/episodes/downloads
>
> This website offers a range of (BBC) 'Thinking Allowed' episodes, most of which draw on, and further develop, social theories in a critical, creative, and dialogical fashion.

REFERENCES

Allen, A. (2016) *The End of Progress: Decolonizing the Normative Foundations of Critical Theory*. New York: Columbia University Press.

Appelrouth, S. and Edles, L.D. (eds) (2011 [2006]) *Sociological Theory in the Contemporary Era: Text and Readings*, 2nd edition. Thousand Oaks, CA: Pine Forge.

Baert, P. (2005) *Philosophy of the Social Sciences: Towards Pragmatism*. Cambridge: Polity.

Baert, P. and Silva, F.C. da (2010 [1998]) *Social Theory in the Twentieth Century and Beyond*, 2nd edition. Cambridge: Polity.

Bauman, Z. (1997) *Postmodernity and its Discontents*. Cambridge: Polity.

Bhambra, G.K. (2014) *Connected Sociologies*. London: Bloomsbury Academic.

Blokker, P. (2011) Pragmatic sociology: Theoretical evolvement and empirical application. *European Journal of Social Theory* 14(3): 251–61.

Boltanski, L. and Thévenot, L. (1999) The sociology of critical capacity. *European Journal of Social Theory* 2(3): 359–77.

Bourdieu, P. (1999) Scattered remarks. *European Journal of Social Theory* 2(3): 333–40.

Bourdieu, P. and Eagleton, T. (1992) Doxa and common life. *New Left Review* 191: 111–21.

Calhoun, C., Gerteis, J., Moody, J., Pfaff, S. and Virk, I. (2012a [2002]) *Contemporary Sociological Theory*, 3rd edition. Chichester: John Wiley & Sons.

Calhoun, C., Gerteis, J., Moody, J., Pfaff, S. and Virk, I. (eds) (2012b [2002]) *Classical Sociological Theory*, 3rd edition. Oxford: Wiley-Blackwell.

Clegg, S. and Haugaard, M. (eds) (2009) *The SAGE Handbook of Power*. London: Sage.

Connell, R. (2007) *Southern Theory: The Global Dynamics of Knowledge in Social Science*. Cambridge: Polity.

Delanty, G. (2017) The *European Journal of Social Theory* at twenty years. *European Journal of Social Theory* 20(1): 4–8.

Inglis, D. (2014) What is worth defending in sociology today? Presentism, historical vision and the uses of sociology. *Cultural Sociology* 8(1): 99–118.

Inglis, D. and Thorpe, C. (2019 [2012]) *An Invitation to Social Theory*, 2nd edition. Cambridge: Polity.

Jenks, C. (ed.) (1998) *Core Sociological Dichotomies*. London: Sage.

Lyotard, J.-F. (1984 [1979]) *The Postmodern Condition: A Report on Knowledge*. Trans. G. Bennington and B. Massumi, foreword by F. Jameson. Manchester: Manchester University Press.

Ritzer, G. and Stepnisky, J. (eds) (2014 [1988]) *Sociological Theory*, 9th edition. Maidenhead: McGraw-Hill Higher Education.

Ritzer, G. and Stepnisky, J. (2018 [2003]) *Contemporary Sociological Theory and Its Classical Roots: The Basics*, 5th edition. London: Sage.

Robbins, D. (1998) The need for an epistemological 'break'. In M. Grenfell and D. James (eds) *Bourdieu and Education: Acts of Practical Theory*. London: Falmer Press, pp. 27–51.

Seidman, S. (1994a) Introduction. In S. Seidman (ed.) *The Postmodern Turn: New Perspectives on Social Theory*. Cambridge: Cambridge University Press, pp. 1–23.

Seidman, S. (1994b) The end of sociological theory. In S. Seidman (ed.) *The Postmodern Turn: New Perspectives on Social Theory*. Cambridge: Cambridge University Press, pp. 119–39.

Skinner, Q. (ed.) (1985) *The Return of Grand Theory in the Human Sciences*. Cambridge: Cambridge University Press.

Spivak, G.C. (1988) Can the subaltern speak? In C. Nelson and L. Grossberg (eds) *Marxism and the Interpretation of Culture*. Basingstoke: Macmillan Education, pp. 271–313.

Spivak, G.C. (1990) *The Post-Colonial Critic: Interviews, Strategies, Dialogues*, ed. S. Harasym. London: Routledge.

Susen, S. (2007) *The Foundations of the Social: Between Critical Theory and Reflexive Sociology*. Oxford: Bardwell Press.

Susen, S. (2013) Comments on Patrick Baert and Filipe Carreira da Silva's *Social Theory in the Twentieth Century and Beyond* – Towards a 'Hermeneutics-Inspired Pragmatism'? *Distinktion: Scandinavian Journal of Social Theory* 14(1): 80–101.

Susen, S. (2014a) 15 theses on power. *Philosophy and Society* 25(3): 7–28.

Susen, S. (2014b) Luc Boltanski: His life and work – An overview. In S. Susen and B.S. Turner (eds) *The Spirit of Luc Boltanski: Essays on the 'Pragmatic Sociology of Critique'*. London: Anthem Press, pp. 3–28.

Susen, S. (2015a) *The 'Postmodern Turn' in the Social Sciences*. Basingstoke: Palgrave Macmillan.

Susen, S. (2015b) Emancipation. In M.T. Gibbons, D. Coole, E. Ellis and K. Ferguson (eds) *The Encyclopedia of Political Thought*, Vol. 3. Chichester: Wiley-Blackwell, pp. 1024–38.

Susen, S. (2016a) The sociological challenge of reflexivity in Bourdieusian thought. In D. Robbins (ed.) *The Anthem Companion to Pierre Bourdieu*. London: Anthem Press, pp. 49–93.

Susen, S. (2016b) Towards a critical sociology of dominant ideologies: An unexpected reunion between Pierre Bourdieu and Luc Boltanski. *Cultural Sociology* 10(2): 195–246.

Susen, S. (2016c) Scattered remarks on the concept of engagement: A socio-philosophical approach. *Philosophy and Society* 27(2): 459–63.

Susen, S. (2018) The seductive force of 'noumenal power': A new path (or impasse) for critical theory? *Journal of Political Power* 11(1): 4–45.

Susen, S. (2020a) *Sociology in the Twenty-First Century: Key Trends, Debates, and Challenges*. Basingstoke: Palgrave Macmillan.

Susen, S. (2020b) The resonance of resonance: Critical theory as a sociology of world-relations? *International Journal of Politics, Culture, and Society* 33(3): 309–44.

Susen, S. and Turner, B.S. (eds) (2014) *The Spirit of Luc Boltanski: Essays on the 'Pragmatic Sociology of Critique'*. London: Anthem Press.

Swedberg, R. (2016) Before theory comes theorizing or how to make social science more interesting. *The British Journal of Sociology* 67(1): 5–22.

Turner, B.S. (1996) Introduction. In B.S. Turner (ed.) *The Blackwell Companion to Social Theory*. Oxford: Blackwell, pp. 1–18.

BEYOND THE QUALITATIVE/QUANTITATIVE DIVIDE

Stella Chatzitheochari

LEARNING OBJECTIVES

- To grasp the main principles of research design and appreciate their relevance for both qualitative and quantitative research projects.
- To understand the centrality of the research question for research design.
- To appreciate the importance of methodological pluralism for sociology.

Framing Questions

1. How do sociologists choose their research methods?
2. What are the main principles of research design? How are they applied in quantitative and qualitative research?
3. Why is engagement with both qualitative and quantitative research crucial for sociological understanding?

BEYOND THE QUALITATIVE/QUANTITATIVE DIVIDE

Introduction

The aim of this chapter is to introduce you to some key concepts for sociological research. You will discover the main principles of research design and see how these are applied in different research projects. By simultaneously scrutinizing quantitative and qualitative research, this chapter aims to highlight the similarities of these two methodological traditions. In so doing, it moves away from long-standing views that treat the aims and idiosyncrasies of qualitative and quantitative methods as irreconcilable. The goal is to help you develop a well-rounded understanding of methodological considerations that are relevant for all types of sociological research, and to encourage critical engagement with existing empirical evidence irrespective of its methodological nature.

The chapter starts with a background section on the long-standing qualitative–quantitative debate in British sociology, calling into question some simplistic dichotomies often used to describe the underpinnings and aims of the two methodological traditions. In this section, you will also read about some classic sociological studies that combined qualitative and quantitative methods. The main part of this chapter principally focuses on a broad sociological topic, namely the temporal dimensions of work and leisure. You will be introduced to some key empirical studies that have approached this topic using qualitative and quantitative methods. This discussion is accompanied by the introduction of some key methodological concepts and more detailed reflections on their relevance for qualitative and quantitative research. The aim is to highlight how quantitative and qualitative evidence often complement each other and how sociological understanding can benefit from embracing methodological pluralism.

Mapping the Terrain

It has been over 200 years since Henri Poincare, a French mathematician and philosopher of science, commented that 'The natural sciences talk about their results. The social sciences talk about their methods' (cited in Barnes, 2006: 2). Indeed, sociology entails that theoretical and philosophical reflection about the production of knowledge and findings of sociological research are viewed as inseparable from the **methods** used to produce them. However, what is troubling is that for the last 100 years these reflections have been largely dominated by the so-called qualitative–quantitative divide, which views **quantitative** and **qualitative methods** as two irreconcilable methodological **paradigms** of opposing aims and procedures. If you are currently studying for a Sociology degree in the UK, you are no doubt already aware of the **scientific paradigm** divide: it is reflected in the way your methodological training is provided in the classroom and in introductory textbooks, and it is more often than not reinforced by many of your lecturers too.

Let's now clarify what is commonly understood as quantitative and qualitative research in **sociology**. Quantitative research involves the collection and statistical analysis of information that can be numerically represented. Such information is usually collected by social surveys that use structured questionnaires. Quantitative data can also come from sources like the internet (e.g. Facebook), the census, and administrative records (e.g. national education records). In contrast, qualitative research involves the collection and analysis of detailed non-numerical data, typically focusing on a smaller number of subjects (e.g. individuals) than quantitative research. There are various qualitative research tools such as the in-depth interview and ethnography.

It is, however, important to note that it is not always possible to entirely delineate what research counts as quantitative or qualitative. (The question of social research methods is discussed further in Chapters 5, 7, 8 and 10.)

(Continued)

There are pieces of sociological research that collect information using **data collection instruments** traditionally viewed as belonging to the qualitative toolkit and then proceed to analyse this information numerically. One such example is the time-diary method, which is discussed in more detail in the main section of this chapter. Participants in time-diary studies fill in 24-hour diaries describing what they were doing in their own words, producing a rich account of their daily lives. These diary records are then **coded** and analysed quantitatively in order to identify regularities in the lifestyles of different social groups. This is just one example of a research method that blends techniques from the two **methodological** traditions. You will no doubt encounter many others during your studies.

Differences between quantitative and qualitative methodologies are often overemphasized in methodological training. **Epistemological** discussions often abound, with quantitative research branded as **positivist** and qualitative research branded as **interpretivist**. **Positivism** is a philosophical tradition postulating that social phenomena can be understood through objective scientific methods such as statistics. **Interpretivism** involves a contextual approach to knowledge, recognizing the contribution of the values of the researcher in the production of meaning during the research process. Although it is true that procedures of **statistical inference** follow standard scientific conventions, quantitative sociology makes use of measures that are usually the result of researchers' subjective judgements. It follows that the idea of two diametrically opposed epistemological standpoints within **empirical** sociology cannot be upheld (Onwuegbuzie and Leech, 2005).

Another common distinction is that quantitative research is employed to answer *what* questions, whereas qualitative research focuses on the *how* and *why*. There is no doubt that one of the strengths of qualitative research is its potential to reveal the **mechanisms** behind empirical regularities highlighted by quantitative research. For example, quantitative analyses from several countries have consistently shown that working-class children have lower educational aspirations than middle-class children, even when they attain similarly well at school. Quantitative analyses cannot explain why this happens. The reasons behind this pattern can only be revealed by intensive qualitative observations exploring the formation of educational aspirations within the home and the classroom. However, such qualitative findings can then inform quantitative data collection that collects information on **variables** that tap into the underlying processes found to suppress working-class children's aspirations. Statistical analyses of such data can then quantify the relative influence of different processes. In this sense, then, quantitative research also goes beyond that which questions and contributes to explanatory accounts within sociology.

Some classic sociological studies have successfully combined methods from the two methodological traditions to provide answers to key sociological questions. Published in 1974, Mark Granovetter's landmark study *Getting A Job: A Study of Contacts and Careers* is one such example. For this study, Granovetter interviewed a sample of around 100 US workers in Newton, Massachusetts, to explore the factors that were influential for their recent job changes. Having gained a better understanding of the processes at play, he then designed a social survey that was administered to a larger number of workers. This **mixed-methods research design** allowed him to demonstrate that 'it is not what you know but who you know that gets you a job', highlighting the importance of social networks and 'weak ties' for the reproduction of social inequality (Granovetter, 2018).

Another example of a mixed-methods research design comes from Doug McAdam's *Freedom Summer* (1988). An event of major importance for the Civil Rights Movement, Freedom Summer was a volunteer campaign aimed at increasing the number of registered black voters in Mississippi in 1964. Freedom Summer became a case study for McAdam, who was interested to understand the drivers of high-risk activism. This was achieved by comparing those volunteers who turned up to join the Mississippi project and those who had originally applied but were 'no shows'. The project drew on volunteers' original applications, and also gathered primary data by employing questionnaires and in-depth interviews with volunteers and 'no shows'.

Data analysis provided insights surrounding the importance of different factors such as biographical constraints, organizational affiliations, and attitudinal factors. (The role of social movements is discussed further in Chapter 25.)

These are just two examples that have successfully blended qualitative and quantitative methods to arrive at a better understanding of the social world. I hasten to note, however, that these examples are not meant to suggest that mixed-methods research designs are superior to exclusively qualitative or quantitative research designs. It is the **research question** that should be dictating which methods are employed in a research project. For example, a statistical analysis is adequate if the aim is to document educational attainment gaps in the UK. Similarly, in-depth interviews suffice to explore the various processes through which experiences of discrimination among disabled young people can be translated into social disadvantage, especially when taking into account that such processes are very difficult to capture in a social survey context.

It is of course likely that you will find yourself more drawn to either qualitative or quantitative research early on during your studies. It is relatively common for the rich accounts generated by ethnographies and in-depth interviews to capture the interest of sociology students in the UK. This is partly due to the sheer volume of qualitative research that far outweighs quantitative research in UK sociology (this is not the case in other countries like the US, where sociology has a very strong quantitative research tradition). Still, one should always keep in mind that sociology cannot fulfil its role without a systematic examination of large-scale evidence surrounding different dimensions of social change and social inequality. For example, studying experiences of poverty without considering its prevalence and its distribution in society or the ways it has been understood and measured by different governments is not likely to generate a well-rounded understanding nor lead to policy-relevant insights. Similarly, the quest to make inequalities visible in the public realm requires measurement and identification and is a prerequisite for social change. For this reason, this chapter aims to foster your ability to critically engage with research from both methodological traditions and to demonstrate the importance of methodological pluralism for sociological understanding.

Student Voices

'My undergraduate degree consists of several qualitative and quantitative methods modules. Some of my professors argue in favour of the consistent use of a single research methodology. During my studies, I have come to realize that this attitude is not helpful and that different methodological approaches work together to advance sociological knowledge. I see this when researching empirical literature for my substantive modules. For my final year dissertation project, I am conducting a quantitative analysis on the family factors that contribute to adolescent obesity in the UK. My analysis shows that children in single parent households are more likely to be obese than those in two parent households. Qualitative studies have allowed me to understand this finding by pointing me to the different mechanisms through which this association comes into place, that is, the lack of time and money experienced by single parents and the ways it influences their children's eating and exercise habits.'

Understanding Principles of Research Design

This section focuses on a topic of sociological significance, namely the temporal dimensions of work and leisure. Through a critical discussion of research that has explored different aspects of this broad topic, you will learn about key methodological principles that influence decisions about data collection, analysis, and interpretation in quantitative and qualitative social research.

A Research Problem

It is funny to think that back in the 1960s several sociologists were predicting a 'leisure revolution' driven by economic progress and technological **automation** in the workplace and the **household**. Contrary to this optimism, the last few decades have witnessed increasing concerns about the spread of 'time famine' in Western societies. A quick Google search will inform you that American and British workers are too busy to take breaks, go to the doctor, or have lunch. Actually, if you think about it, it is really quite common for British people to simply say they are busy when asked how they are. Several long-running social surveys that are repeated at regular intervals (e.g. every 5 or 10 years) have been asking respondents how rushed they feel, which is considered a good indicator of experiences of 'hurriedness' and stress. Analyses of such questions confirm that a substantially larger proportion of working people today report that they *always* feel rushed compared to the 1960s. How would you explain this? Naturally, your first thought may be that today's workers are probably working longer hours than their grandparents did. This leads to the formulation of a clearly defined research question, namely whether working hours in the Western nations have increased over time.

Evaluating Measures in Quantitative Research: Validity and Reliability

A particularly influential study with regard to this topic was Juliet Schor's *The Overworked American: The Unexpected Decline of Leisure*, originally published in 1991 when concerns about the time famine and work–life balance were beginning to grow (Schor, 2008). As suggested by the title of the book, the study provided evidence that working hours in the US had grown substantially since the 1960s. In order to provide an answer about the trend in working hours, Schor conducted **secondary data analysis** of Current Population Surveys from the 1960s onwards. Information about working hours in these surveys was collected with the use of a question that asked respondents how many hours they worked last week. While this may seem unproblematic at first glance, there are in fact many shortcomings in this measure of working time.

To start with, not everyone interprets 'work' in the same way. While one respondent may choose to include commuting time or lunch breaks in their calculation, another may choose not to. Another shortcoming relates to recall difficulties. This is especially relevant for the growing segment of workers who do not have a fixed 9 to 5 Monday–Friday work schedule. Adding different 'episodes' of work is a difficult calculation to perform within a few seconds. Finally, this question is also prone to **social desirability**. This term refers to the tendency of respondents to portray themselves in a socially desirable manner in a survey context. It has been claimed that busyness has become the new 'badge of honour' in contemporary societies (Gershuny, 2005). It would therefore be sensible to expect that some respondents may provide somewhat exaggerated estimates of their working week to conform to societal **norms** and expectations about working time. These propositions have all been confirmed by methodological research (Robinson and Godbey, 2010). This suggests that the working time measure used in social surveys like the ones analysed by Schor have low **validity** and **reliability**.

Validity focuses on whether a measure employed in a study is a true measure of the concept or the property it claims to capture. Simply looking at a survey question and considering whether it makes sense is the first step to assess validity. You can then specifically focus on whether a measure captures all facets of the concept of interest, also known as content validity. For example, a measure of paid work may be worded in such a way that results in not capturing work conducted from home, an admittedly important element of working life today. Reliability refers to the consistency of a measure. A reliable measure should yield the same result in a repeat study, assuming that the property has not changed for respondents (i.e. their work patterns have remained the same). Hence, the above-mentioned measure of working time does not score well on the reliability criterion. Validity and reliability are two very important indicators of data quality for quantitative research. There are many tests that quantitative researchers can perform to assess whether their employed measures satisfy different validity and reliability criteria.

It seems a good idea to now turn our attention to an alternative way of obtaining a reliable and valid working time measure. Time-diary surveys are specifically designed to obtain estimates of time spent in different activities. Rather than relying on conventional questionnaires, such studies ask respondents to fill in a 24-hour diary in their own words, recording what they did for every 10-minute slot. The diary contains separate columns where the respondent can report who they were with, whether they were doing anything else at the same time, and where they were. A comprehensive and contextual account of respondents' everyday lives is thus obtained, offering many analytical possibilities to the researcher. Respondents' own descriptions are then coded into activity categories. With regard to paid work, this coding would allow the researcher to identify time spent commuting or time on lunch breaks and analyse a paid work measure that has consistent content across all respondents. Methodological studies have shown that the time-diary method obtains the most reliable and accurate measures of time spent in different activities (Robinson and Godbey, 2010). This is because the grid format facilitates memory and minimizes social desirability. Indeed, estimates of paid work from time diaries are generally lower than those obtained from questionnaires. In conducting secondary analysis of paid work estimates from time-diary surveys collected from the 1960s onwards, Robinson and Godbey (2010) arrived at a very different conclusion about working time. They actually found that working time in the US had been decreasing. Americans had more leisure time than their grandparents, so why were they feeling more rushed?

Media often cite statistics about social issues such as attitudes towards refugees, Islamophobia, or sexual harassment. Have you ever wondered what measures have been used to capture these? Try to think of survey questions that can tap into some concepts that interest you. Can you identify any threats to the validity of the items you constructed?

Validity and Qualitative Research

You may now be wondering how we can assess validity and reliability in qualitative research. Whether these two concepts are applicable to qualitative research has been a subject of fervent debate. One the one hand, some scholars have claimed that validity and reliability are two inherently positivist principles that cannot be applied to qualitative methodology given its interpretivist foundations. On the other hand, a growing number of methodologists have acknowledged the need for equivalent criteria that allow an assessment of the level of trustworthiness and credibility of observations and inferences made by qualitative researchers.

Imagine that you decide to approach the topic of working time from a different perspective, that is, by conducting participant observation of a contemporary workplace characterized by the so-called 'long hours culture'. You approach a consulting firm in London and succeed in gaining consent from employees to begin your observations. Your observations could be potentially influenced by the **Hawthorne effect**: consultants may alter their working time and schedules simply because they are aware that they are being watched. They may work less than they usually do to signal that they have healthy working patterns or work more to ensure they fit the image of the 'ideal worker' with high levels of job commitment. How would you decide which of their behaviours are artefacts of your methodological approach? Some other important considerations relate to your analysis and interpretation of your observations. How would you decide which workplace dynamics and behavioural patterns of the consultants are of interest and therefore central to your **theoretical** interpretations? How would you ensure that your interpretations are not influenced by your prior ideas about the topic or your subjective views about the sector?

Methodological literature explores these issues at length, proposing a wide range of techniques that can be used during the qualitative research process in order to increase validity. It is impossible to cover these in detail in this introductory chapter (but see Expand your knowledge and Exercise sections below). This is because such assessments in qualitative research encapsulate a much wider range of issues to consider. Stages of the qualitative research process (data collection, analysis, interpretation) are not discrete and cannot be scrutinized in a stand-alone fashion as in quantitative research. To put it simply, it is not possible to merely assess a researcher's qualitative observations in a similar way to how we assessed working time measures. This is because the way observations are conducted is heavily influenced by the researcher's various interpretations during the research process – so we need to scrutinize the legitimacy of the interpretations at the same time too.

Still, it is very important to emphasize the importance of **transparency**, a crucial principle of research design directly linked with credibility and legitimacy that has not been consistently adhered to in public reports of qualitative research. Any empirical study should provide adequate details on how the research was conducted and how it arrived at its conclusions. The level of detail should be such that it allows the study to be **replicated** irrespective of its methodological nature. It goes without saying that the task of documentation is invariably more complex and sensitive in projects using methods like ethnography. However, it is a necessary one to ensure minimum standards of academic integrity and scientific rigour in the field. To further consider this issue, you may want to read Howard Becker's (1958) classic text on the importance of documentation and transparency for participant observation.

Expand Your Knowledge

- To learn more about validity in qualitative research, read Onwuebguzie and Leech (2007) Validity and qualitative research: An oxymoron? *Quality and Quantity* 41: 233–49.
- To appreciate the importance of transparency in ethnography, read about the case of *On the Run* by Alice Goffman at https://slate.com/news-and-politics/2015/06/alice-goffmans-on-the-run-is-the-sociologist-to-blame-for-the-inconsistencies-in-her-book.html

Sampling and Representativeness in Quantitative Research

So how did Robinson and Godbey (2010) explain the increase in feelings of 'hurriedness'? Having established that the average working time had decreased overall, the researchers examined whether the distribution of working time had changed. They found that, towards the end of the 20th century, highly educated US workers were working longer hours than any other socio-economic group. This was not the case a few decades earlier when the rich and the educated enjoyed more leisurely lifestyles. This finding makes sense. Higher professional occupations have now moved away from clock-based Fordist employment models to more 'flexible' and task-based conceptions of working time, often associated with long hours and overwork. Building on this finding, Robinson and Godbey (2010) claimed that media stories surrounding time pressure were solely reflective of this time-poor/cash-rich group (which also controls the media), and that other US workers were not facing particularly pronounced time pressures.

While I think that this is a relatively sensible argument to make, it is not my intention to assess the researchers' explanation here. Rather, I would like to use this analysis as an opportunity to outline the main issues surrounding **representativeness** in quantitative research. Social surveys like the Current Population Survey and the Time Use Survey are administered using random **sampling** procedures that ensure they are representative of a wider **population** of interest. The population of interest in such social surveys varies. For example, it may be adults of working age or anyone over the age of 16 in the US. Sampling is a procedure undertaken in both qualitative and quantitative research. This is simply because we cannot study everyone. What is unique about sampling in quantitative research is that it is collected in such a way that it allows the researcher to make **statistical inference**s about the population of interest simply by analysing the sample. So, given that the Time Use Survey made use of appropriate sampling procedures that ensured representativeness, Robinson and Godbey (2010) could consider their analyses of US workers as being representative of the entire US workforce.

It is, however, important to note that *representativeness* is not a given, even when the appropriate procedures have been followed. It is not uncommon for those who were selected to participate in a survey to refuse to respond or for interviewers to be unable to find them. If responders are substantially different from non-responders, then **non-response bias** may threaten the **external validity** of a study. Time diaries are particularly burdensome to fill in. It would be reasonable to hypothesize that those who are the busiest are the least likely to complete a time diary. If this were true, any secondary analysis of the Time Use Survey could severely underestimate working time and distort comparisons between different groups like the ones conducted by Robinson and Godbey (2010). Methodological research on different time-diary surveys has consistently shown that the 'busyness hypothesis' cannot be confirmed. However, the main lesson from this discussion is that, when engaging with quantitative research, it is important to make note of whether the researcher has discussed patterns of non-response in their data and whether they have considered how these may be influencing their inferences. This relates to the practice of transparency that was discussed in the previous section.

Sampling and External Validity in Qualitative Research

Qualitative research has limited external validity, in the sense that its findings are rarely generalizable to a wider universe or population. Rather, its findings can only be generalizable to a broader set of theoretical propositions, which can be termed as analytical generalizability. This does not mean that choosing a sample is a simple task. Sample size is a key consideration for qualitative researchers too. However, there are no hard and fast rules about how many interviews or cases are needed. The answer to 'how many' is 'it depends'. There are qualitative research projects that solely focus on one case and others that gather over 100 interviews in order to answer their research questions. Determining how many interviews or cases are needed is an iterative process that is related to **saturation**. This is a key concept for qualitative research, referring to the point where additional data collection does not add any new theoretical insights.

My graduate dissertation project sought to understand why elderly people in Greece had been so active in a series of nationwide protests organized by the Orthodox Greek Church, aiming to block the introduction of a new identity card document that would omit the mention of citizens' religious affiliation (the so-called 'identity card crisis'). I visited many churches in my hometown and managed to recruit participants from different socio-economic backgrounds – although it had been some years since the protests had taken place, older churchgoers were all very keen to talk about the issue. The first weeks of fieldwork were full of surprises, with each interview revealing something unexpected. After a while, I had interviewed 35 participants and I had identified two different types of elderly protesters: those for whom participation was simply a result of political opposition to the government and those who resonated with the Church's nationalistic discourse and conspiracy theories. I continued interviewing but it was clear that the same patterns and themes were repeated in the new interviews. Not only did my interviewees consistently fit one of these two profiles but they were also providing me with similar narratives about the formation of their national and political identities. Taking into account time and financial constraints, I considered saturation had been reached and completed my fieldwork.

Expand Your Knowledge

- To learn more about saturation and sample size in qualitative research, see S. Baker and R. Edwards (2012) *How Many Qualitative Interviews Is Enough?* National Centre for Research Methods Review Paper. This is an excellent read that includes reflections from renowned methodologists and early career researchers working on a wide range of qualitative research projects.

Although representativeness is not a concern for qualitative research, I would argue that it is still extremely important for researchers to reflect on how their findings would change if they included other cases or subjects in their study. Such reflection is an essential part of theory-building processes that are central for qualitative research. Imagine that your study of the London consulting firm found that long days at work were not in fact associated with objectively heavy workloads but, rather, with consultants' perception that they were required to be constantly present in the firm. Your theoretical propositions would need to consider a number of issues, such as whether other consulting firms have different workplace culture and performance expectations – would your results be different if you had conducted your observations at a different firm?

9.1 Key Case

The Second Shift by Arlie Hochschild and Anne Machung

A comparison group can be very helpful too. A landmark study in the area of work and leisure was *The Second Shift* by Arlie Hochschild and Anne Machung (2012), first published in 1989. The research consisted of intensive observations and interviews with approximately 50 couples recruited through a Fortune 500 company. Findings from the study suggested that the increasing participation of women in the labour market was not accompanied by a more equitable gender division of domestic work and childcare within the home. That is, working mothers continued to conduct most of the domestic work at home, resulting in a gender leisure gap that was associated with work–family conflict. The research also highlighted the influence of gender ideologies in couples' experiences. As mentioned by the researchers, their comparison group were couples from the same geographical area that were characterized by more flexible work schedules and more liberal ideologies, resulting in more equitable gender roles within the household. Such analytic comparisons between different samples are key for theoretical reasoning and for assessing the transferability of qualitative findings in different contexts.

Pause for Thought

This section has introduced you to some of the main principles of research design and discussed how these are applied in qualitative and quantitative research projects. Despite their differences, both methodological traditions collect information in a systematic manner in order to make inferences about the social world. Both are also concerned with maximizing the rigour of their data collection and analysis procedures. Perhaps it has also become obvious that all research designs are imperfect. To a large extent, the craft of social research is essentially one of reflection on the ways different shortcomings affect our inferences.

Research on Women's Time: A Case Study on the Importance of Methodological Pluralism

The last section of this chapter focuses on gender inequalities in free time, a topic that has occupied a central place in feminist approaches to justice and equity (Fraser, 2014). Empirical research on gendered temporal inequalities is discussed to demonstrate that engagement with findings from both methodological traditions can be instrumental for advancing **scientific knowledge** and producing policy-relevant research. Aside from emphasizing the importance of methodological pluralism, this section will also help you consolidate knowledge on principles of research design acquired in the previous section.

Qualitative studies like *The Second Shift* showed that women continue to do the lion's share of domestic work and childcare, resulting in a significant leisure gap between spouses. Such studies clearly demonstrate that we need broader conceptualizations of work than those employed by Schor (2008) and Robinson and Godbey (2010), whose analyses had only focused on paid work (this topic is also covered in Chapter 17).

Indeed, it makes sense that to understand the distribution of free time in society we need to study paid as well as unpaid work, as both types of work constrain free time availability.

Quantitative research has the potential to make different dimensions of structural inequality visible, which is the first step for any social change. However, the measurement of domestic work and childcare is particularly difficult. Many of the points presented above to explain shortcomings of paid work estimates apply here too. In addition to these, it is sensible to hypothesize that there may be gender differences in the ways domestic work and childcare related questions are answered. On the one hand, social desirability may be at play for men, who may seek to portray themselves as active fathers given contemporary parenting ideologies about engaged fatherhood, thus exaggerating the time they spend in domestic work and childcare. On the other hand, women may be prone to underestimating theirs, given that some routine activities like minding children do not seem to have clear boundaries and may appear 'natural' to them. Such measurement difficulties have meant that women's domestic contributions had remained largely invisible and were not systematically considered in quantitative analyses of gender inequalities.

The time diary was subsequently recognized as the most efficient data collection instrument for obtaining accurate estimates of daily life activities, and there was great hope that it could act as a feminist tool that would help to finally fully document the magnitude of unpaid work inequalities (Bryson, 2007). It was a surprise – and a disappointment – that analyses of time diaries kept showing that men and women now spend the same time in total (paid and unpaid) work (Robinson and Godbey, 2010), leading to claims about an ongoing 'gender convergence'. This was in direct opposition with the findings of feminist qualitative research that suggested that the concept of free time is simply not applicable to mothers and that women's work in the home never ends.

You may already be thinking that simply focusing on the duration of paid and unpaid work time is not sufficient to capture the various leisure constraints people experience. Indeed, this is what explains the stark disagreement between the findings of quantitative and qualitative research on the topic. Qualitative accounts show that women's leisure time is regularly interrupted by childcare that often takes place alongside home leisure activities. For example, a woman reading a book or watching TV at home may need to regularly interrupt her activity in order to engage in routine childcare tasks, whilst being at home during her free time may actually be the result of the need to mind her children. This suggests that women's free time is of lower quality than that of men. It follows that a singular focus on the quantity of free time constitutes poor **operationalization** of what is a multi-dimensional concept.

Insights from qualitative research have influenced subsequent quantitative analyses of time diaries that moved beyond the exclusive focus on duration. These analyses demonstrated novel aspects of free time disadvantage that had not been captured by earlier quantitative research. By scrutinizing a wide range of dimensions such as fragmentation and contamination of free time, researchers demonstrated that women have lower quality and quantity leisure time than men (Bittman and Wajcman, 2000; Chatzitheochari and Arber, 2012). Such studies confirmed that the findings of small-scale studies like *The Second Shift* were generalizable across different groups, making different aspects of gendered temporal inequalities visible in the public realm.

This brief example nicely demonstrates the merits of engaging with research, irrespective of its methodological nature. In this case, it was the theoretical propositions of qualitative research surrounding women's free time experiences that influenced the way quantitative researchers operationalized temporal disadvantage. The construction of gender-sensitive and theoretically-grounded measures of temporal inequality would not have been possible without the insights produced by qualitative research. This is just one among many examples that add considerable weight to arguments in favour of methodological pluralism and pragmatic approaches to social research methods.

Expand Your Knowledge

How Might Sociologists Study the Impact of Mobile Devices on Daily Life?

It is tempting to partly attribute increasing levels of stress and anxiety to the widespread diffusion of internet-enabled mobile devices. Mobile technologies have radically changed the way we live our lives. They allow us to conduct work from home and to share information with our colleagues at unprecedented speed, essentially blurring the boundaries between domains of 'work' and 'leisure'. Indeed, it has been argued that being always 'on call' is what makes today's workforce anxious. But there are also broader concerns about the influence of mobile devices on our lives. We are all aware of the tremendous opportunities that mobile technologies and the internet offer us: we can make new friends who share similar interests, use apps to optimally use public transport or find a date for the weekend, access information on pretty much anything we can imagine, have more things to do while at home – the list goes on and on. Still, not a day goes by without us reading about the effects of so-called 'screen time' on children's health and development and on family and societal wellbeing. (The topic of digital sociology is discussed further in Chapter 2.)

How might we explore the extent to which mobile devices such as smartphones are embedded in our lives? This is a key question that poses unique methodological challenges but is nonetheless an important one to answer, considering sociology's aim is to document social change (and it is difficult to think of a more radical change in everyday life in the last few decades). Before you delve further into the existing literature, think of some different research designs that could be employed to answer this question. You may want to specifically focus on the nature of smartphone use – how similar is this activity to other daily activities like childcare or exercise? Consider both quantitative and qualitative approaches and identify the pros and cons of each approach. To conclude your research, read: K.N. Hampton (2017) Studying the digital: Directions and challenges for digital methods. *Annual Review of Sociology* 43: 167–88.

CHAPTER SUMMARY

- Qualitative and quantitative evidence complement each other; therefore, methodological pluralism is important for advancing sociological understanding.
- The differences between qualitative and quantitative methodologies are regularly overemphasized.
- Both quantitative and qualitative research adhere to key principles of research design.
- The methodological knowledge acquired in this chapter will enable you to start critically engaging with existing research using a wide range of methods, further contributing to the development of a pragmatic approach towards methodological choices in social research.

REVIEW QUESTIONS

1. What is sampling? How does it differ in quantitative and qualitative research designs?
2. What is validity and reliability? Are these concepts relevant for qualitative research?
3. What are the key methodological considerations when designing a study?

Go Further

Books

- Brannen, J. (2017) *Mixing Methods: Qualitative and Quantitative Research*. London: Routledge.

This volume includes contributions from several renowned methodologists on how qualitative and quantitative methods can be combined.

- Bryman, A. (2015) *Social Research Methods*. Oxford: Oxford University Press.

This is a classic introductory textbook that takes you through all stages of the research process.

- De Vries, R. (2018) *Critical Statistics: Seeing Beyond the Headlines*. Basingstoke: Macmillan International Higher Education.

This is a very accessible and fun-to-read textbook for those of you who are somewhat fearful of quantitative methods terms like the ones discussed in this chapter.

Journal Articles

- Oakley, A. (1999) Paradigm wars: Some thoughts on a personal and public trajectory. *International Journal of Social Research Methodology* 2(3): 247–54.

This article provides an honest account of the different factors that have contributed to the methodological divide in sociology.

- Onwuegbuzie, A.J. and Leech, N.L. (2005) On becoming a pragmatic researcher: The importance of combining quantitative and qualitative research methodologies. *International Journal of Social Research Methodology* 8(5): 375–87.

This article provides an excellent discussion on the misconceptions surrounding the differences between quantitative and qualitative methodologies, and nicely highlights the importance of pragmatism in social research.

- Schwemmer, C. and Wieczorek, O. (2020) The methodological divide of sociology: Evidence from two decades of journal publications. *Sociology* 54(1): 3–21.

This is a recent study that empirically examines the extent to which the demarcation between the two methodological traditions remains prevalent today.

Websites

- www.youtube.com/user/NCRMUK/videos

The National Centre for Research Methods offers several videos on methodologies and research methods.

- https://methods.sagepub.com

The SAGE methods website includes research tools, guides, and case studies from real research.

- www.youtube.com/channel/UCmK1mj5dCq0XuCWI7DVKx2w/featured

The Pioneers of Social Research Youtube Channel of the UK Data Service includes interviews from renowned sociologists on research methods and how they used them in landmark sociological projects.

REFERENCES

Barnes, J.A. (2006) *Models and Interpretations: Selected Essays*. Cambridge: University of Cambridge Press.

Becker, H.S. (1958) Problems of inference and proof in participant observation. *American Sociological Review* 23(6): 652–60.

Bittman, M. and Wajcman, J. (2000) The rush hour: The character of leisure time and gender equity. *Social Forces* 79(1): 165–89.

Bryson, V. (2007) *Gender and the Politics of Time: Feminist Theory and Contemporary Debates*. Bristol: Policy Press.

Chatzitheochari, S. and Arber, S. (2012) Class, gender, and time poverty: A time-use analysis of British workers' free time resources. *British Journal of Sociology* 63(3): 451–71.

Fraser, N. (2014) *Justice Interruptus: Critical Reflections on the 'Postsocialist' Condition*. London: Routledge.

Gershuny, J. (2005) Busyness as the badge of honor for the new superordinate working class. *Social Research* 72(2): 287–314.

Granovetter, M. (2018) *Getting a Job: A Study of Contacts and Careers*. Chicago: University of Chicago Press.

Hochschild, A. and Machung, A. (2012) *The Second Shift: Working Families and the Revolution at Home*. New York: Penguin.

McAdam, D. (1988) *Freedom Summer*. Oxford: Oxford University Press.

Onwuegbuzie, A.J. and Leech, N.L. (2005) On becoming a pragmatic researcher: The importance of combining quantitative and qualitative research methodologies. *International Journal of Social Research Methodology* 8(5): 375–87.

Robinson, J. and Godbey, G. (2010) *Time for Life: The Surprising Ways Americans Use Their Time*. University Park, PA: Penn State Press.

Schor, J. (2008) *The Overworked American: The Unexpected Decline of Leisure*. New York: Basic Books.

VISUAL AND DIGITAL METHODS OF RESEARCH

Cath Lambert

LEARNING OBJECTIVES

- To introduce visual sociology as an approach to studying sociology: how are visual materials produced and interpreted from a sociological perspective?
- To present the key methods used within visual sociology.
- To evaluate critically the benefits and challenges of using these methods from a sociological perspective.
- To understand the key developments in visual methods including a shift to incorporate digital media and culture.
- To consider the ethical implications of visual research.

Framing Questions

1. What can sociologists learn from using a visual approach that other methods might not enable?
2. What kinds of social issues and situations might lend themselves to a visual approach? Why?
3. What specific (practical, ethical) issues need to be considered when using visual methods for sociological research?

Introduction

In this chapter, you are encouraged to think sociologically about the selection, creation and interpretation of visual materials. Visual sociology can be regarded as a sub-discipline of qualitative sociology, but it also overlaps with the broader interdisciplinary field of visual methods. It is becoming more and more common for sociologists to make use of visual methods, either as part of a mixed methods approach or as a methodological strategy in its own right. Whilst visual sociology is established as a field of study, it is a rapidly changing field, not least because of the growth of digital technologies and the increasing importance of visual media in contemporary culture.

These developments offer many possibilities to us as sociological researchers but also bring practical, intellectual and ethical challenges. This chapter helps you to consider the possibilities and the challenges, locating questions about the visual in the context of what has already been considered in previous chapters around sociological theory and method. The discussion begins by tracing the many possible roots of visual sociology in order to demonstrate its interdisciplinary and multi-media character. This mapping of the field demonstrates what the study and use of visual media and methods bring to sociological enquiry. In the latter part of the chapter, you will be introduced to recent research in the area of digital and online visual methods before finishing with reflections on issues of power and ethics inherent in all research practice but presenting particular possibilities and challenges in relation to visual methods.

Mapping the Terrain

What is Visual Sociology?

In attempting to define a field of study, it is common to provide an account of its emergence. However, it is difficult to know where to begin a history of visual sociology. We could start with the photo-journalism of Jacob Riis, documenting New York slums in the 1890s; or with the visual ethnography of Balinese culture produced by anthropologists Margaret Mead and Gregory Bateman in the 1940s (see Harper, 2012); or maybe with photographs taken by the sociologist Pierre Bourdieu in colonized Algeria between 1958 and 1961 (see Back, 2009). We could look to the 1960s, when amidst the social and political turmoil and activist spirit of the decade, new methodological strategies and approaches were sought and tried out. Or we could begin our story in 1981 when the International Visual Studies Association (ISVA) was founded, followed a few years later by their own academic journal, *Visual Sociology* – now *Visual Studies*. There are some good studies paying closer attention to all these heritages (see Harper, 2012, and further reading in the Go Further section), but the fact that there are so many possible origins to the current field of visual sociology demonstrates its roots in different disciplines (anthropology/film/art and design/cultural studies/geography) and diverse media (photography/film/drawings/graphicillustration/maps). Such an eclectic genealogy shapes contemporary visual sociology in important ways.

The first publication to claim the title *Visual Sociology* is the relatively recent 2012 book by Douglas Harper. Harper frames this book as a response to the provocative call by Howard Becker in 1995 to 'make sociology visual'. Let's pause for a moment to ask *What might it mean to make sociology visual? What is at stake?*

The world [that] is seen, photographed, drawn or otherwise represented visually is different than the world that is represented through words and numbers ... visual sociology leads to new understandings

(Continued)

and insights because it connects to different realities than do conventional empirical research methods. (Harper, 2012: 4)

This quote is indicative of the significant claims made for the potential of using the visual as a sociological resource. Sociologists interested in this approach suggest that visual data brings something new and different to our investigations as well as distinctive ways to look at the social world. Furthermore, visual sociology, it is suggested, can connect to different realities than other methods. Clearly, visual methods deserve our critical attention.

Over the years, visual sociology has adapted and expanded as the mechanical means of production and circulation have developed. Where once a small number of people had access to the technologies to take, produce and publish still and moving images, now, across the world, many of us have such devices in our pockets in the form of smartphones, giving us the ability to not only take pictures and films but also to easily edit and share them. This widening of digital access has massively expanded the field of visual sociology. At the same time, visual media increasingly saturate our social interactions.

Methodological Considerations

Before we consider what visual **methods** might look like and what they might enable us to do, we need to look at the **methodological** presumptions underpinning such methods. Like any methods, if we select and deploy visual research strategies, it reflects our understandings of the social world and the kinds of investigations we wish to undertake. Visual methods share many features with qualitative **sociology** more broadly, paying attention to the ways in which people as individuals or communities live, experience, interpret, understand and communicate their social realities. In common with qualitative research endeavours, attention is paid to matters of **reliability** (would the research produce the same findings if done again?) and **validity** (is it 'true'?). Even more so than other **qualitative methods**, visual approaches can be controversial as they present a high degree of subjective interpretation, ambiguity of meaning and the 'mess' in social science research. As Harper (2012: 4) puts it, 'seeing is very complicated', and what we see and how we see it depends to a large extent on the viewer, their social position and viewpoint based on their own (intersectional) experiences and identities. This subjective positioning affects the production of visual images as well as your reception to them. Seeing involves selecting, abstracting and interpreting. When you look at a visual image, what do you see and what do you not see? How do you make sense of what you see? To what extent do you believe the image to represent 'reality'? You will be asked to consider these questions in relation to some examples in the next section. Of course, as with all research methodologies, these processes are political and ethical. They are infused with issues of power. A critical consideration of the political and ethical implications of visual research weaves throughout the following discussion.

Expand Your Knowledge

- If you want to find out more about visual methodologies, check out: Rose, G. (2012) *Visual Methodologies: An Introduction to Researching with Visual Materials*. London: Sage.

VISUAL AND DIGITAL METHODS OF RESEARCH

Visual Methods

You will now be introduced to some of the different ways in which sociologists use visual media as part of their research methods. The four approaches covered in this section are: (1) the use of existing images as evidence; (2) using pictures to prompt memory; (3) integrating visual media into interviews; and (4) producing visual and audio-visual diaries. These areas do not by any means capture the wide range of possible visual methods, but they provide you with an introduction to some of the most common methods that have been developed over time and written about in the visual sociology literature.

Using Existing Images as Data

Sociologists can learn a great deal by looking at historical or contemporary images as evidence. The sources for such images include archives and print and digital media. In Carol Wolkowitz's (2006) research on bodies at work, she uses historical images representing the embodied labour of working-class women and girls in the Victorian era. Through these photographs and accompanying documentation, we can learn a lot about the social **role** of domestic servants and the ways in which their 'dirty' labour contributed to the making of the gendered and racialized social order at this time. Other good examples of historical photographic analysis can be found in research undertaken in the sociology of education. The study of photographs can be a way of looking closely and critically at everyday cultures of schooling. Visual resources enable us to better access and record observable information which is crucial to understanding the everyday realities of school life. The use of photographs – whether historical or recent – as evidence, leads us to ask how we select and make sense of the images. Sociological analyses of formal photographs of school classes show these are not random but highly structured according to conventions of representation. We can look at the body language of children and teachers photographed and examine visual clues such as arrangements of bodies and what people are wearing, as indicators of social status, poverty or wealth. Catherine Burke and Helena Ribeiro de Castro (2007: 214) examine the use of school photographs in relation to representations of schoolchildren. They note that:

A powerful symbol of modern schooling, the school photograph, once taken, is assembled in school albums held by institutions and families as valuable material histories of school the world over.

Perhaps you can visualize your own or a member of your **family**'s school photographs. If you can, most likely the image presents orderly rows of children, organized by height and/or gender, perhaps wearing uniform, facing forward and framed at the sides by their teacher/s. These examples might make you wonder how it is that certain images come to be produced and reproduced over time and place, and how we come to see and understand these images.

 Pause for Thought

- What do we see in an image and how do we make sense of it?

PART 2 THEORIES AND METHODS

Hear from the Expert

The very commonality and seeming universality of the image of 'the school' and 'the teacher' should raise questions. We recognize the setting, the pose, the expressions all over the world. How did that happen? If a 19th-century school scene in Bermuda or Japan seems familiar to Americans over 100 years later, we might wonder why. Why are these scenes so familiar, so seemingly universal? Are the common structures the result of colonialism and the dominance of Western practices? Or are we, as products of those same practices, merely seeing what we have been taught to see? The very universality of these images can raise provocative questions about what we see and how we see it. (Rousmaniere, 2001: 110)

Kate Rousmaniere (2001) Questioning the visual in the history of education. *History of Education*, 30(2): 109–116. Reprinted by permission of the publisher (Taylor & Francis Ltd, http://www.tandfonline.com.)

As well as attending to what we *can* see in pictures, we also need to think about what we do *not* see. We can gain a great deal from a critical focus on what and who is *not* photographed. The fact that many people find themselves un-represented in history, or only partially represented in very limiting and often problematic ways, is a stark reminder of the powerful work of representation and the ways that certain people, communities and practices can be make invisible and written out of history. What gets 'left out' of photographic representation?

Hear from the Expert

Many things [in the online archives of school photographs] were not photographed. I found, for instance, no views of teacher unions or organizing activities, no photographs of school boards or teacher meetings where the central decisions shaping schooling were made. There were no photographs of conflicts and tensions in schools – between teachers and students, among students, between school boards and communities – no pictures of discipline and punishment, no photographs of boredom. And even if such photos did emerge, they would not solve the central problem of the photograph; photography is powerless to represent some things. (Margolis, 1999: 34)

Margolis, E. (1999) Class Pictures: Representations of Race, Gender and Ability in a Century of School Photography. *Visual Studies* 14(1): 7–38. Reprinted by permission of the publisher (Taylor & Francis Ltd, http://www.tandfonline.com).

The very nature of photography as a medium disrupts the possibility of asserting a final and single Truth ... the temporal disjuncture between the moment when a photograph was taken and

> subsequent moments when it is viewed, entails recognition of, at the very least, two different points of view: that of the photographer and that of the viewer … The question is not 'who is right' but, rather, how might each point of view tell us something different or feel compelled to keep certain things 'off screen'. In addition, the way that the photograph mediates our distance from the past invokes uncertainty about what it is possible to know from the images. As such, the photograph evades the closure of complete(d) knowledge. As viewers, if we cannot be certain about what happened in the past, then neither can the photographer be certain about how her or his photographs will be read in the future. (Kuhn and McAllister, 2006: 15)

Thinking about what we see and how we see it – and what we don't see – prompts us to be critical and reflexive about our sociological use of visual resources. As you will see in the following discussion, researchers can also make use of visual methods to address some of the missing knowledges and make hidden knowledges more visible.

Using Visual Materials to Prompt Memory

Visual resources have a powerful role in assisting memory. Sometimes researchers will use visual materials to prompt their memory in the same way they make notes in a research diary. In ethnographic settings, researchers might make a drawing or use a camera to help them later recall how things look and feel, to document aesthetic and affective aspects of the setting that might be difficult, if not impossible, to put into words. This strategy is doubtless becoming more common as people use the cameras on their smartphones to quickly capture scenes they wish to recall at a later stage.

That photographs can be powerful triggers for remembering gives them a central role in sociological research. Looking at photographs can lead to vivid testimonies. You might be able to relate this to your own experiences of looking at photographs from your childhood or listening to an elderly friend or relative tell stories from the past prompted by a picture. The act of remembering can be emotional and physical. John Berger (in Harper, 2002: 13) talks about how 'the thrill found in a photograph comes from the onrush of memory'. Harper (2002: 22–3) suggests that photographical images 'mine deeper shafts into a different part of human consciousness than do words-alone interviews'. Photographs invite storytelling and might enable deeper and richer engagement with people and their memories and recollections. The fact that photography can have this effect makes it particularly useful for many **empirical** areas of investigation: sociological work around family or childhood, for example. Penny Tinkler (2008: 255) suggests that 'Important aspects of childhood, belonging and memory, are often experienced and/or expressed in part through photographs and photography'. One of the articles suggested in further reading at the end of this chapter presents recent empirical research by Tinkler (2020) on the mnemonic potential of photographs documenting life in north-west England in the 1960s and '70s. As storytelling is a feature of other qualitative methods, such as oral history or life-story interviews, visual resources such as photographs are often incorporated into these methods.

Using Photos in Interviews: Photo-elicitation

When photographs are used within the context of an interview in order to provoke or elicit memory and stories, it is known as photo-interviewing or **photo-elicitation**. The photographs might be already in existence, such as old family photographs or resources taken from an archive, or they might be images which have been produced by the participant for the purposes of the interview. The images can create a shared resource for the interviewer and interviewee to refer to, helping to develop rapport between them and leading to greater depth and detail of response than just a spoken-word interview. Such a method can be very useful when working with children and young people: both young people and researchers are used to talking about photographs of friends and family, and referring to a shared image helps researchers listen to and understand children's viewpoints and social worlds. In relation to family photos, there are familiar formats and tropes reproduced over time and place (as we saw with the school photographs) which provide common points of recognition and shared value and meaning even between, potentially, people with very different life experiences. Children, perhaps more than many research respondents, might struggle with the language to explain and describe complex social realities: photographs enable social realities, identities, experiences and emotions to be conveyed. As Marisol Clark-Ibáñez (2007: 171) puts it, the photos 'generate responses beyond the language based conventional interview protocols'. A good example of the use of photo-elicitation is a study conducted by Analía Meo.

10.1 Key Case

Analía Meo's use of Visual Methods with Young People

Meo (2010) used photo-elicitation as part of an ethnography exploring social inequalities and secondary schooling in Buenos Aires in Argentina. She worked closely with young people to try to understand their day-to-day experiences of social class, noting that 'talking about students' photos was a useful way to unpack their ways of classifying others and themselves, and their class and gendered practices in different fields such as family, education, labor market, and leisure' (Meo, 2010: 152). After the study, Meo (2010: 155) compared photo-elicitation and spoken-word interviews with the same group of young people in order to establish the advantages and disadvantages of using photographs in this way, and found that 'photo-interviews were richer than traditional interviews':

In both interviews I gathered similar information about topics such as housing, occupation of students' family members, family relations, neighbourhood, friendship groups, young people's subcultures, schooling, and gender relations. From my initial comparison of both types of interviews, I argue that photo-interviews were richer than traditional interviews. I identify seven major advantages of photo-interviews over traditional oral interviews: (a) they elicited longer and more enjoyable interviews; (b) they enhanced the participation and control of interviewees; (c) [they allowed] the gathering of richer data about similar topics; (d) they reinforced what was already stated in the traditional interview; (e) they offered a closer look at what and whom participants considered important; (f) they allowed the emergence of unexpected topics; and (g) they enabled making sense of some data, which otherwise would have been difficult to interpret. (Meo, 2010: 155)

There were also some disadvantages. These related to the practical demands of photo-elicitation, the increased time it took, and ensuring photographs could be clearly linked to the person speaking in the transcription. Gaining consent was more complicated and time-consuming, and there were greater challenges to archiving and analysing visual images alongside text-based sources such as interview transcripts and documents. Some of Meo's problems stemmed from the fact that her research training had not prepared her for undertaking visual methods. Hopefully, the growth of visual methods within sociological research as well as the growth of teaching courses and materials relating to visual sociology (see Harper, 2012: Ch. 10) mean today's researchers – such as you – will be better prepared for utilizing visual methods.

....

The images Meo's young participants produced were very different from the 'formal' school ones we talked about earlier. Handing the camera over to participants led to different aspects of schooling and schoolchildren's lives being represented. Similarly, in Louisa Allen's (2017) research with young women and men in schools in Australia, she discovered the potential of photographs to make visible what is often hidden or invisible. In order to access 'unofficial' aspects of schooling, Allen (2017) gave students a disposable camera each in order to take photos of how they learnt about sexuality at school, over a period of seven days. These **'photo-diaries'** were then used as the basis for photo-elicitation interviews. The photographs the young women took revealed what Allen, drawing on the work of Michelle Fine, referred to as the 'missing discourse of female desire'. Rather than desire being 'missing' from school settings, a view held by much of the critical literature on schooling and sexuality, Allen (2017) found that desire was very much evident in the images the young people took. She suggests that the photographs make desire 'visible and tangible in a way that conventional talk-based methods find more difficult. Desire is materialized here through image, via the use of visual methods … photo-methods enable female desire to literally be "seen" through young women's own eyes via the camera lens' (2017: 69).

Photo and Video-diaries

Keeping a visual diary deserves some attention as a method in its own right. Diaries, whether produced by the researcher as part of their fieldwork reflections or by participants asked to document specific things about their lives, have long had an important role in ethnographic enquiry. They can be incredibly useful research tools for gaining a sense of people's routine, perhaps everyday, activities and for capturing experiences over a period of time. They are seen as a good way to enable participants to take some control of the research process. We are all familiar with the idea of a text-based diary. Among Elizabeth Chaplin's (2004: 44) many visual projects was one in which she maintained a daily photographic diary over 15 years, noting that 'Keeping a daily photographic diary … makes you look at life around you differently from how you would if you weren't keeping the diary'. This simple statement goes to the heart of sociological enquiry, for sociologists are concerned with looking at life 'differently', more deeply and from different perspectives. The ordinariness of everyday life is captured well by such methods. These may be things that are considered *too* ordinary to be of interest to a researcher, so they never get mentioned. Ordinary moments are captured, 'frozen', and their significance heightened by being fixed as an image and subject to attention (Chaplin, 2004: 35). However, capturing the 'ordinary' does not make it any more 'true' or less **socially constructed** than any other image. Even banal and seemingly insignificant details which a participant photographs are chosen for a reason.

Other research possibilities emerge with the use of video-diaries. Videos can bring visual material together with dialogue, enabling participants to explain and demonstrate how what is documented relates to the construction and narrativization of their identities. Such approaches have been facilitated by the availability of digital **technologies**.

——————— Expand Your Knowledge ———————

- If you are interested in exploring further, a good example of audio-visual research methods in action is: Bates, C. (2013) Video diaries: Audio-visual research methods and the elusive body. *Visual Studies* 28(1): 29–37.

Digital Visual Methods

The massive growth and increased availability of digital technologies have not only had a dramatic impact on who can create, edit and publish visual materials but have also affected the ways in which we relate to visual images in knowledge terms. So far in this chapter, we have seen how visual media can be approached sociologically as a subject of study, as well as being used as a research method. The same is true of the internet, which is of sociological interest in itself and also provides researchers with ways to engage with information and with research participants. Because of limited space here, we are not going to consider the significant and growing field of **digital sociology**: instead, you will be introduced to some key examples where digital methods are used in ways that expand and develop the field of visual sociology.

 ——— Pause for Thought ———————

- Can we just add digital media to our existing visual research practices?

Hear from the Expert

Multimedia in visual sociology is more than a discussion of the impact of digital technologies on mass culture. Since the 1990s, visual sociologists ... have begun to use multimedia to study the world and to present their work. Multimedia first appeared as an adjunct for texts, adding data, visuals or other information; adding *more* rather than something *new* ... to a standard book. That has slowly given way to new forms of imagining and imaging the world. (Harper, 2012: 142)

Videos that circulate on the internet have inscriptions (titles, comments, tags, rankings) that the producers explore and exploit, and which transform the audiovisual experience in shaping the materiality of the visual object itself. The internet and its particular technologies [such as YouTube] ... mediate the production of the visual object, the kind of content recorded, the circulation of the image and its consumption. When internet practices and infrastructures mediate the visual object in this way, all the dimensions of the visual analysis must be rethought. (Ardévol, 2012: 81–2)

As you can see from these examples, our use of digital media brings new methodological challenges. Although the status of a photograph as 'evidence' of reality and able to represent 'truth' about the social world has always been contested in visual sociology, it is the advent of digital production that shakes **realist** suppositions as we become more aware of the ways in which images are produced, manipulated and circulated. In the 'selfie' era, it seems common sense to acknowledge that we perform our identities in part through visual representations of ourselves and others via social media. This is particularly true of younger adults and teenagers, making it no surprise that one key area of sociological study around the use of digital images relates to work with young people. Tinkler (2008: 259) suggests that:

Photographic practices can serve three main identity purposes: the production of statements of identity; experimentation and play with identities; and the deconstruction of identity. An important historical change that seems to have occurred in young people's photographic practices is the increased range of identity purposes that they now serve.

When was the last time you sent a photograph or video via text on social media? What did you intend for that image to convey? Maybe you sent the image to accompany or illustrate text or maybe you just sent the photograph on its own? The use of photo messages (for example, used extensively on platforms such as Snapchat or Instagram) emphasizes the visual image as a means of connection between people, making visual images central to contemporary practices of friendship. Particularly amongst young people, digitally produced images are also central to the 'experimentation and play' with identities that Tinkler (2008) refers to. Digital photographic technologies such as smartphones enable people to construct, deconstruct, represent and perform their identities in multiple ways that sociological researchers are keen to understand more about.

10.2 Key Case

Kathryn M. Orzech et al.

A study by Kathryn M. Orzech and her colleagues (2017) compared the practices of taking and sharing digital photographs between young adults leaving secondary school and older adults retiring from employed labour. They found that:

[For the group of young adults] the co-created nature of online identity (or identities) was an accepted norm ... They also recognised that online identity was an edited (not necessarily accurate) version of self ... The crafting of this edited identity was guided by a digital social norm involving a balance between accuracy and approval-seeking, posting pictures of oneself and one's activities that would be 'liked' by friends on social media.

[...]

Retirees treated digitally mediated photo sharing as an extension of their previous behaviour – sharing *physically* printed photos. They did not feel obliged to share online or co-create identity in the way young adults did. (Orzech et al., 2017: 323, original emphasis)

A further change to our social and research practices is brought about by the temporalities of the digital world. Digital technologies add *immediacy* to our social interactions: our phones pinging in our pockets demand our attention and we can communicate across the world in seconds. This means that developing tools for 'real-time' investigation is key to sociology's capacity to respond quickly to lived experiences as they unfold, bringing a liveliness to sociological investigation through methodological innovation and experimentation. As Les Back and Nirmal Puwar (2012: 7) write: 'The tools and devices for research craft are being extended by digital culture in a hyper-connected world, affording new possibilities to re-imagine observation and the generation of alternative forms of research data'. They also caution against being 'enchanted' by digital opportunities: it is vital that as sociologists we attend to the methodological values and concerns of any research project. Back and Puwar (2012) call for a more 'artful and crafty' approach to sociological investigation. This involves collaborations with other disciplines and practices to widen sociological repertoires for understanding the world. Such collaboration has been a feature of visual sociology since its inception, working with mechanical and conceptual resources from photography, documentary makers and artists. The challenges and new possibilities of digital media and culture help to explain the increased popularity of visual methods in contemporary sociology as researchers grapple to make sense of and bring about social change in an increasingly interconnected, complex world. In the final part of this section, we consider what methodological developments are emerging, reimagining visual methods as an integral part of 'live' and sensory sociological practices.

 **Pause for Thought**

- Technologies are constantly changing: what does the future hold for visual sociological methods?

Hear from the Expert

Live Sociological Methods

The first principle of live sociology is an attention to how a wider range of the senses changes the quality of data and makes other kinds of critical imagination possible. How quickly we want to say 'observation' when describing social research. In itself the notion automatically privileges the eye … The challenge for the future is how to develop, based on an equality of the senses, attentiveness to the multiple registers of life. (Back, 2012: 29)

Live sociology involves developing the methodological opportunities offered by digital culture *and* expanding the forms and modes telling sociology through collaborating with artists, designers, musicians and film-makers and incorporating new modes and styles of sociological representation. The use of digital devices … offers the opportunity to augment sociological attentiveness and develop mobile methods that also enable the production of empirical data simultaneously from a plurality of vantages. (Back, 2012: 34)

Sarah Wilson's (2016) study of young people with experience of living in a social care setting rather than with their biological family, provides a great example of **multi-sensory methods**, including digital visual media. Her methods involved doing two interviews with the young people: in preparation for the interviews, they were given a 'script' of instructions which involved them taking photographs of their favourite and least favourite spaces and of objects that were significant to them. They were also asked to record sounds they liked, including a music track. In the second interview, they identified music tracks with messages for others and drew their ideal or current living space. Some participants were involved in the creation of films and music to disseminate the project.

We can't predict the future, but these quotes and the example above point to developments in sociological method that have emerged as important in recent years and look likely to demand more attention in the near future. In a nutshell, they involve using and being aware of all our senses alongside the visual and making imaginative and critical use of digital and creative cultural resources. As you can see, there are many exciting possibilities emerging for sociologists who engage with visual, digital and live methods. These new methods also bring new challenges, the most urgent of which are ethical. Our final section of this chapter considers in more detail these ethical challenges and responses to them, as well as possibilities for good ethical practice opened up by utilizing these methods.

Ethical Considerations

You will not be surprised to learn that the ethical challenges and possibilities of working with digital and non-digital visual media constitute a field of study in their own right. As we have seen, photographs can have powerful effects and questions of who is represented, and in what ways, who is viewing the image and with what purpose, are also questions about power. Wolkowitz (2006: 36) reminds us that 'understanding the power relations of representation has to include the study of social institutions within which photographs are made, chosen, edited, printed, circulated and experienced by viewers'. It is also vital that researchers using visual methods think about their own positioning in terms of power, as this power shapes research relationships and the kinds of knowledge that are produced.

Ethical issues which are routinely considered in sociological research, such as confidentiality and informed consent, present additional challenges in relation to visual media, and in response to this, specific guidelines have been developed for working with visual methods (see Papademas, 2009). These challenges relate to both ensuring that participants are offered appropriate protection from harm and that their privacy is respected, as well as ensuring that visual research is not unduly hampered by ethical procedures and requirements which are often imposed by institutional ethics committees. Let's take a look at issues of confidentiality and consent in relation to visual methods.

Confidentiality

Ensuring confidentiality in sociological research usually entails only sharing data in limited and careful ways and hiding or changing participants' names or other identifying features to ensure that they remain anonymous even after data and analysis are made public. It can sometimes be difficult, if not impossible, to preserve the anonymity of people in images. Faces can be blurred to disguise identities, but that can sometimes get in the way of the powerful effects of the image that we considered earlier. And faces are of course not the only clues to identity: clothes, accessories and environmental clues could reveal a person's identity even if their face were hidden. Sometimes people want credit and recognition rather than to be anonymized. Researchers have to make decisions in their selection and production of visual images that best protect participants, and honour their informed wishes, ranging from blurring faces to taking photographs without people in them. These decisions depend on the context of the research and the uses to which the visual media are being put.

Consent

Gaining informed consent is key to open and honest research relationships, no matter what method is being used. Accessible participant information and consent forms can be adapted to include the use of visual methods, ensuring that images are not taken or reproduced without clear permission from research participants. Of course, it is not always so straightforward: consent can be given without researchers fully knowing if participants understand the intent or reach of the research; some participants, such as children or vulnerable adults, might not fully understand the implications of their consenting; it might not be possible to identify everybody visible in a photograph or film; and consent might be clearly given for some aspects of a project (for example, to take photographs) but not so clearly articulated for others (for example, to reproduce it in a book years later). Rather than assuming informed consent is simply a box we can tick and move on from, the most ethically sound position is to recognize the complexity of gaining consent and to work closely, carefully and collaboratively with participants and with the visual data itself in order to make the best judgements possible.

Digital Ethics

Digital technologies add new ethical challenges. Think about the ways in which you and others around you produce and share digital images. The kinds of images produced – not least the ubiquitous 'selfie' – and the almost instantaneous platforms for circulating, communicating with and commenting on such images, provide practical and ethical conundrums for researchers that are not always adequately addressed by traditional research ethics guidelines. Dedicated resources for engaging digital methods have been produced (see BSA, 2017) but part of the methodological innovation and experimentation covered in the discussion of **live sociology** is ethical.

Ethical Opportunities?

It is important not to see ethical research requirements as problems to be overcome. Good ethical processes produce better, more accountable research data and there are many ways in which visual methods offer ethical opportunities. Earlier in this chapter, you were encouraged to imagine or recall the vivid stories that

VISUAL AND DIGITAL METHODS OF RESEARCH

can flow from looking at an old photograph: such methods can make visual research encounters enjoyable, and participatory visual methods can give participants more control of the research process, as we saw in the examples of photo-elicitation interviews carried out with young people by Meo (2010) and Allen (2017), and the mixed sensory methods in Wilson's (2016) study. No methods take power inequalities out of research encounters, but visual methods, including digital visual methods, can offer different possibilities for making research more democratic and inclusive.

CHAPTER SUMMARY

- Visual sociology is a fast-changing, exciting field of theory, method and practice. It is interdisciplinary, with origins in photography and anthropology; current practice often involves collaborations with art and technology as digital media and culture increasingly shape our social interactions.
- Visual methods and approaches bring many benefits to sociological research, including the power of photographs to prompt memory and elicit storytelling, and the potential of photographic methods to access and represent different realities and perspectives than more traditional methods.
- Although many of the ethical questions raised by using visual methods overlap with other qualitative research in sociology, visual and digital approaches bring new challenges and possibilities, putting questions of ethics at the heart of new developments in visual method.
- Current and future developments for sociological method include paying attention to visuality alongside *all* the senses – making sociology 'live' and 'sensory'.

REVIEW QUESTIONS

1. What makes sociology 'visual'?
2. What kinds of visual methods do sociologists commonly use?
3. What are the key advantages and disadvantages of using visual methods?
4. What kinds of changes have digital technologies meant for visual sociology?
5. What kinds of ethical challenges and possibilities do visual methods entail?

Go Further

Books

- Back, L. (2007) *The Art of Listening*. London: Bloomsbury.

A readable, important book that incorporates rich examples of visual methods together with aural and sensory approaches to introduce the idea of live sociology.

(Continued)

- Margolis, E. and Pauwels, L. (2011) (eds) *The SAGE Handbook of Visual Research Methods*. London: Sage.

This chunky book offers lots of chapters by different authors, including many key researchers in visual methods, ranging across conceptual, practical and ethical issues and providing examples and perspectives from different disciplines.

- Pink, S. (ed.) (2012) *Advances in Visual Methodology*. London: Sage.

As the title suggests, this edited book advances and expands the field of visual methods with a focus on new theoretical and methodological approaches and the intersections of visual research and digital media.

Journal Articles

- Martiniello, M. (2017) Visual sociology approaches in migration, ethnic and racial studies. *Ethnic and Racial Studies* 40(8): 1184–90.

This short article addresses how visual methods add value to research in the areas of migration, ethnicity and race, providing a useful overview of visual methods before providing some historical and contemporary examples.

- Mizen, P. and Ofosu-Kusi, Y. (2010) Unofficial truth and everyday insight: 'Voice' and visual research with Accra's poor children. *Visual Studies* 25(3): 255–67.

This article draws on photographs and spoken accounts of children who live and work on the streets of Accra, Ghana, to show how photos can assist our knowledge and understanding of others' everyday realities.

- Tinkler, P. (2020) Intimate relationships with Shirley Baker's photos of Manchester and Salford: The mnemonic potential of documentary photos. *Visual Studies*, online 13 November: 1–17.

This readable article shows the powerful ways in which documentary photographs prompt people to remember and 're-enact' their belonging in a particular time and place as well as helping them narrate their stories.

Websites

- https://visualsociology.org

Home of the International Visual Sociology Association, with links to lots of historical and new resources.

- www.thesociologicalreview.com/introduction-may-digital-theme-visual-sociology

An exploration of contemporary visual sociology through images, blogs, book reviews, links to academic articles and more.

- https://photovoice.org

A UK-based charity using ethical photography and community participation in projects all over the world with the aim of bringing about positive social change.

REFERENCES

Allen, L. (2017) *Schooling Sexual Cultures: Visual Research and Sexuality Education*. London: Routledge.

Ardévol, E. (2012) Virtual/visual ethnography: Methodological crossroads at the intersection of visual and internet research. In S. Pink (ed.) *Advances in Visual Methodology*. London: Sage, pp. 74–94.

Back, L. (2009) Portrayal and betrayal: Bourdieu, photography and sociological life. *The Sociological Review* 57(3): 471–90.

Back, L. (2012) Live sociology: Social research and its futures. In L. Back and N. Puwar (eds) *Live Methods*. Oxford: Blackwell, pp. 18–39.

Back, L. and Puwar, N. (2012) A manifesto for live methods: Provocations and capacities. In L. Back and N. Puwar (eds) *Live Methods*. Oxford: Blackwell, pp. 6–17.

British Sociological Society (BSA) (2017) Ethical Guidelines and Collated Resources for Digital Research: Statement of Ethical Practice Annexe (to BSA Statement of Ethical Practice). Available at: www.britsoc.co.uk/media/24309/bsa_statement_of_ethical_practice_annexe.pdf (last accessed 30 May 2021).

Burke, C. and Ribeiro de Castro, H. (2007) The school photograph: Portraiture and the art of assembling the body of the schoolchild. *History of Education* 36(2): 213–26.

Chaplin, E. (2004) My visual diary. In C. Knowles and P. Sweetman (eds) *Picturing the Social Landscape*. London: Routledge, pp. 35–48.

Clark-Ibáñez, M. (2007) Inner city children in sharp focus: Sociology of childhood and photo-elicitation interviews. In G. Stanczak (ed.) *Visual Research Methods: Image, Society and Representation*. London: Sage, pp. 167–96.

Harper, D. (2002) Talking about pictures: A case for photo elicitation. *Visual Studies* 17(1): 13–26.

Harper, D. (2012) *Visual Sociology*. London: Routledge.

Kuhn, A. and McAllister, K.E. (2006) Locating memory: An introduction. In A. Kuhn and K.E. McAllister (eds) *Locating Memory: Photographic Acts*. Oxford: Berghahn Books, pp. 1–20.

Margolis, E. (1999) Class pictures: Representations of race, gender and ability in a century of school photography. *Visual Studies* 14(1): 7–38.

Meo, A. (2010) Picturing students' habitus: The advantages and limitations of photo-elicitation interviewing in a qualitative study in the city of Buenos Aires. *International Journal of Qualitative Methods* 9(2): 149–71.

Orzech, K.M., Moncur, W., Durrant, A., James, S. and Collomosse, J. (2017) Digital photographic practices as expressions of personhood and identity: Variations across school leavers and recent retirees. *Visual Studies* 32(4): 313–28.

Papademas, D. (2009) International Visual Sociological Association (IVSA) Code of Research Ethics and Guidelines. *Visual Studies* 24(3): 250–57. Available at: https://visualsociology.org/wp-content/uploads/IVSA-Ethics-and-Guidelines.pdf

Rousmaniere, K. (2001) Questioning the visual in the history of education. *History of Education* 30(2): 109–16.

Tinkler, P. (2008) A fragmented picture: Reflections on the photographic practices of young people. *Visual Studies* 23(3): 255–66.

Tinkler, P. (2020) Intimate relationships with Shirley Baker's photos of Manchester and Salford: The mnemonic potential of documentary photos. *Visual Studies*. DOI: 10.1080/1472586X.2020.1837004.

Wilson, S. (2016) Digital technologies, children and young people's relationships and self-care. *Children's Geographies* 14(3): 282–94.

Wolkowitz, C. (2006) *Bodies at Work*. London: Sage.

PART 3

INEQUALITIES AND IDENTITIES

PART 3 INEQUALITIES AND IDENTITIES

Introduction to Part 3

The four chapters in this part of the book develop two of the key themes that have preoccupied sociological debate and research. In particular, in the late 20th century and in the early decades of this century we have seen a significant increase in sociological analysis of identities and their intersections with widening social inequalities. Importantly, as the chapters in this part of the book show, social inequalities and social (and embodied) identities are relational. By this we mean that patterns of inequality and the processes and experiences of inequality are driven, shaped and marked by such social categories as class, gender, race and age (as well as sexual orientation, dis/ability, cis/trans status, citizenship status). We can understand social inequalities and social identities not as separate from each other but rather as continually intersecting, overlapping and interacting. The various and dynamic ways in which inequalities and identities are related – for example, through reproducing, reinforcing or resisting social divisions – are explored in the following chapters.

In Chapter 11, Wendy Bottero opens up the debate about the relationship between inequalities and identities through an analysis of social class in which race and gender are central. A key concern in the chapter is to think about how class-based inequalities can be understood and the ways in which they work in people's lives. As part of this, the chapter explores social class in terms of unequal access to resources but stresses that the social, emotional and embodied consequences of class-based inequalities, for example health, security, senses of agency, are also very much part of the lived experience of class inequalities (see also Chapters 17 and 18 on work and health). Bottero emphasizes the ways in which class inequalities have increased since the 1970s, despite rising affluence, and have become ever more polarized with the emergence of the superrich elites and the intensification of precarity. The chapter also stresses the ways in which class inequalities 'endure' – they are not passing 'moments' but last across lifetimes and generations. As you will see, the chapter brings to our attention the importance of recognizing class divisions as having a global as well as national scale, and shows how the stark patterns of global inequality are shaped by postcolonial relationships.

Gender is the focus of Chapter 12 by Kath Woodward and Sophie Woodward. This chapter introduces the dynamic debates in sociology around gender and sex, what these mean and why they matter as a lens for understanding social relations and inequalities. The chapter outlines the challenges that have been made to the binary division of gender and sex, and emphasizes the diversity of gender and sex and the fluidity of gendered lives and identities (see also Chapter 15 on families and households and Chapter 16 on intimacies and sexualities). The chapter argues against a position of biological essentialism, and, while it explores the ways in which gender and sex are culturally and socially located, Kath Woodward and Sophie Woodward also discuss how sex/gender is embodied. To help make these debates less abstract, the chapter looks at sport and in particular focuses on Serena Williams to show how sex/gender is intersected by race and class. The chapter highlights patterns of gender inequalities though data from large-scale global and national surveys as well as smaller qualitative studies. It also shows how feminist approaches to social research methods have changed research methodology through its calls for reflexivity and the recognition of identities and the importance of listening to lived experience in research processes (see also Chapter 9 on research methods).

Chapter 13 by Tina Patel examines how race, racism and racialization work as sites of identity and resistance – the Civil Rights, Black Power and Black Lives Matter protest movements, for example – and as a sites of power and subjugation. It traces the evolvement of sociological thinking on race and processes of racialization through Critical Race Theory, social constructionism, cultural theory, black feminism and intersectionality. The chapter emphasizes the importance of understanding race situationally and in relation

PART 3 INEQUALITIES AND IDENTITIES

to context. It illustrates this through its discussion of xeno-racism, which emphasizes how migration and religion – anti-migrant hostilities and Islamophobia – are types of racism (see also Chapter 20 on religion and Chapter 24 on migration, which both examine these developments). This emphasis on context and how the meanings of race and the processes of racialization are not fixed shows how we need to understand race in anti-essentialist ways. In the chapter we see that racism is not reducible to individualized prejudice but is a structural force systematically shaping cultural norms and institutional processes within societies. The chapter shows how racism works in a variety of ways and at different scales: coded and explicit, extreme (e.g. race hate) but also normative and everyday.

The final chapter in Part 3 takes a sociological approach to the analysis of age. Chapter 14 by Anna Wanka argues that age affects the social world and how people are perceived. There is an emphasis on age and the life course (by which Anna Wanka means the 'whole sequence of the stages of life') being more than physical and biological – they are also social and cultural. Societies tend to be fixed in a range of age-arranged ways that shape social inequalities as well as identities and personhood. The chapter highlights how these inequalities can obviously be seen in the differences between life expectancy rates in poorer and richer (national and global) geographies (see also Chapter 18 on health), but shows how, even in poor areas, there are increases in longevity with all populations living longer. The chapter goes on to focus on the diversity of the category 'older adults', the global demographic shift towards older age and the social implications of this. Outlining the key conceptual debates for understanding processes of ageing, the chapter details the ways in which inequalities are age patterned, with ageism being a widespread discriminatory experience.

We have highlighted examples where the chapters each connect with other chapters in the book, but what you will find is that the themes and debates explored in these four chapters resonate widely and are revisited across the book.

Key Questions

- Why are class inequalities increasing?
- What does gender diversity mean?
- Intersectionality has been a central contribution of black feminism. How would you define intersectionality?
- How does sociology change understandings of age?

CLASS
Wendy Bottero

LEARNING OBJECTIVES

- To understand competing theoretical accounts of class and how they locate class inequalities within long-term structural shifts in societies.
- To understand how affluence and individualization affect class advantage and the visibility of class inequalities.
- To understand how increased inequalities in income and wealth and the rise of the super-rich have reshaped class relations.
- To recognize how changing class relations are bound up in global, postcolonial inequalities.
- To recognize how ordinary people perceive and understand the class inequalities around them.

Framing Questions

1. What is class inequality?
2. How are class relations changing?
3. What affects the visibility of class inequality?

PART 3 INEQUALITIES AND IDENTITIES

Introduction

'Class' is about *relative* inequality and is an inherently comparative and relational concept. Class inequality is not just about your level of poverty or deprivation, or what goods, status or rights you have, but what you have *compared to others*. Whether we see this in terms of money, property, occupational position, cultural assets, or power and influence, the significance of class resources is in how they give those who possess them greater control over the external forces which affect us all.

This chapter examines how class analysis has shown how such inequalities endure – over lifetimes, between generations or across periods of long-term social change. It considers how very stark class inequalities have re-emerged in many countries in the last 40 years, with the rise of a super-rich elite reshaping class relations in ways which have important consequences for everyone in society, not just the rich or poor. We will look at how national class inequalities must be understood within broader global inequalities and postcolonial power relations. And we will consider to what extent people recognize the scale of the class inequalities they experience.

Mapping the Terrain

There is disagreement about how best to understand what class inequality is and how it works. Goran Therborn (2013) identifies different aspects to inequality, arguing that we experience *vital inequality*, through unequal bodily life-chances (for example, life expectancy, illnesses); *existential inequality*, through the unequal allocation of autonomy, rights and freedom (political rights, civil liberties); and *resource inequality*, through unequal opportunities to act (via uneven access to income, wealth or education). Most sociological discussions of class have tended to focus on the unequal distribution of resources. But Therborn argues that to focus just on resource inequality and 'the arrival of the first pay cheque' means 'disregarding the fact that by then many bodies have been buried, and many lives have been stunted for ever by humiliations and degradations' (2013: 49). To understand class inequalities we must address not just the unequal distribution of resources (crucial though these are), but also inequalities in health and wellbeing, safety and security, and control, autonomy and dignity.

There are several competing approaches to understanding class relations. One approach sees class inequality as the main economic dimension of society; however, alternative approaches identify other sources of inequality structuring society (such as gender or race), with class relations just one dimension of influence, whilst more recent accounts place greater significance on cultural assets in shaping class relations. Sociological accounts of class emerged from 19th-century theories of the rise of 'modernity', or industrial capitalism, though with a decidedly Eurocentric focus. The most famous of these theories, by Karl Marx (1818–83) and Max Weber (1864–1920), still influence contemporary class analysis.

As Chapter 7 explores, Marx argued that in a capitalist society our economic relations shape our social interests, and so the members of different classes have opposed interests and an antagonistic relationship. This is because, in order to ensure high profits, the capitalist must force workers' wages down to the lowest possible level. Marx believed this process would make capitalist exploitation increasingly stark and visible, provoking the working class to become a revolutionary 'class-for-itself'. However, during the greater part of the 20th century, capitalist societies in the Global North experienced rising affluence rather than pauperization, and when revolutionary class consciousness emerged it did so in a very intermittent fashion. This cast doubt on Marx's *economic* account of social relations (1990). An alternative approach, by Weber (1978), identified additional sources of power (status group membership or party affiliation) which cross-cut economic class interests and provide alternative social identities and group affiliation. For Weber, since economic location (and its associated life chances) represents only one factor among many affecting our social consciousness and identity, we cannot predict that *class* consciousness (or action) will emerge from a common class situation – this is only one possible contingency. These accounts remain important influences on contemporary theories of class. However, contemporary theories must grapple with how class inequalities have survived the shift to postindustrial societies.

Since Marx and Weber, one important strand of sociological class analysis has looked to the labour market, and to production relations, as the key arena of class inequality (Erikson and Goldthorpe, 1993). This approach categorizes people according to the production and market relations of different *occupations*, examining how these place people in relations of control or subordination with others in different classes. This unites the Marxist emphasis on economic structure with the Weberian emphasis on the multiple influences on life chances, investigating the *extent* to which occupational class influences life chances, identity and action. This strand of class analysis has produced extensive cross-national programmes of survey research which show that how we make a living (and the economic resources and opportunities this brings) affects almost every aspect of our lives. To take just a few examples, class inequalities strongly influence our material life chances, shaping – amongst other things – our life expectancy, our risk of serious illness or disability, our chances of educational success, the quality of our house and neighbourhood, and our risk of falling victim to crime. And class inequalities in one generation bleed over into the next, with our class position influencing the prospects of our children, shaping children's chances of low birth weight and infant mortality, their risk of ill health and disability, and their success in school and in the labour market.

Yet, despite the enduring impact of class position on life chances, rising affluence in many countries makes some question whether class remains important in postindustrial societies. During the 1980s and 1990s, there was a strong reaction – amongst both politicians and some sociologists – against the relevance of class as a concept for explaining social relations in postindustrial societies. This was not because economic inequality had declined – the period actually marked the start of a dramatic increase in income and wealth inequalities – but because postindustrial transformations had resulted in a process of *individualization* undermining 'class' as a collective, communal feature of social life. The coming of a 'late' phase of modernity restructured economies in the Global North away from the manual sector towards the service sector, and with the expansion of educational and labour-market opportunities, and the rising significance of affluent, consumption-based lifestyles, some argued that postindustrial societies had become more individualistic, more differentiated, and more meritocratic, all of which undermined the social significance of class inequalities.

For sociologists who research class inequalities, these arguments are deeply flawed. Lifestyles *are* individualized and highly differentiated, but as the next section shows, they remain systematically related to class inequalities. However, in the attempt to explore how class inequalities endure within long-term social change, a 'cultural turn' to class analysis, influenced by Pierre Bourdieu (1930–2002), has argued that we need to significantly rethink how 'class' operates.

The Persistence of Class Inequalities Within Long-term Structural Change

A central achievement of class analysis has been to show how class inequalities not only survive but thrive when societies become more affluent, with those from higher-class backgrounds able to maintain their relative advantage even when opportunities for all improve. For much of the 20th century, many societies in the Global North experienced affluence and expanding opportunities, which meant that many individuals saw their position improve compared to earlier generations. But class inequalities endured within these changes. Whilst working-class individuals took advantage of expanding opportunities to improve their social position, the middle-class has also seized the advantage, and at the same rate, so relative differences between class groups stayed the same (Bukodi and Goldthorpe, 2018; Erikson and Goldthorpe, 1993).

When there is upward mobility, the relative chances of children from different class backgrounds gaining access to high-level positions remain sharply unequal. Only 10% of those from working-class backgrounds make it into Britain's higher managerial or professional occupations (compared to 33% in the workforce overall), with access particularly restricted in areas such as medicine, law and journalism (Friedman and Laurison, 2019). We cannot rely on **meritocratic** explanations of this because class background strongly shapes chances of success, even for the most high-achieving. Meritocracy is the idea that rewards reflect people's ability and effort. Meritocracy (and **social mobility**) are seen by many politicians as the best solution to class inequalities. But meritocratic explanations overstate the individual components of inequality, whilst greatly underestimating the structural components (such as inheritance, unequal educational opportunity, the changing structure of job opportunities, or discrimination) of how people get on.

11.1 Key Case

Friedman and Laurison

Friedman and Laurison's (2019) British research on class advantage shows that when those from working-class backgrounds do make it into elite occupations (such as medicine, law and journalism), they still earn on average £6,400 less per annum than colleagues from middle-class backgrounds (even with exactly the same level of education). Even when we compare those with the most prestigious level of education – attending Oxbridge – working-class individuals earned £5,000 less per annum than their middle-class peers (Friedman and Laurison, 2019).

Friedman and Laurison's work shows that career progression in sectors such as television, accountancy, architecture and acting never rests solely on the hard work of individuals but also depends on resources and support from others. This can be from the 'bank of mum and dad', who provide financial support for low or unpaid internships which provide a crucial 'foot in the door', or it can come from the senior figures whose sponsorship helps juniors to progress, but who are more likely to favour those with the right 'fit' from similar (middle) class backgrounds. But either way, those from middle-class backgrounds have a huge competitive advantage.

- Why do you think that senior figures in elite professions are more likely to favour juniors from similar (middle) class backgrounds?
- How might race and gender also be factors here?

Class theorists reject the claim that affluence, social change and **individualization** undermine the relevance of 'class', arguing that class inequalities continue to be reproduced *through* affluence and mass consumption and exist *within* processes of individualization, as these shifts open up new arenas for class competition and disadvantage (Savage, 2000; Skeggs, 2004). With the rise of knowledge-based economies, access to educational credentials and cultural knowledge is increasingly vital to maintaining or improving social position, with education and cultural knowledge assets much like property or income. Because of this, some accounts have increasingly looked to the role of cultural and educational resources (as well as economic 'capital') in placing people in the class structure and in reproducing class inequalities, with investment in education and cultural knowledge a key strategy in class competition.

Such approaches see 'class' operating in the varying ability of individuals to draw on *different kinds* of resources or 'capitals'. Bourdieu (1984) distinguishes four main types: economic capital (wealth, income); **cultural capital** (cultural knowledge, educational credentials); **social capital** (social connections, patronage); and symbolic capital (symbolic legitimation). Symbolic capital is the power that emerges from the symbolic recognition of other resources (i.e. from the acceptance of certain types of resources as being of greater value than others). For Bourdieu, the reason educational credentials are such significant assets in postindustrial societies is the result of social struggles in which middle-class groups with a vested interest in education have been able to establish qualifications as being increasingly valuable and necessary in social life. Here, class inequality is not just a question of uneven access to valued resources but also the struggles between people to establish *their* resources as the ones that are recognized and socially valued.

Cultural class analysis focuses on how class inequalities exist in processes of individualized hierarchical differentiation, with people using different valued resources in competitive strategies to advance or maintain their social position (Savage, 2000). This individualized form of class struggle is seen as more pernicious than older collective forms: because it is less visible and often works to legitimate inequality. A great deal of policy and public discourse now represent structural inequality as a question of individual success or failure, and this placing of the responsibility for unequal outcomes on the individual (the 'individualization of inequality') not only legitimizes inequality but also heightens class anxieties and competition, and provides increased sanction for class contempt (Skeggs, 2004).

What does all this mean for people's consciousness of their own class situation, or their perceptions of wider class inequalities? Writing from a Bourdieusian perspective, Savage (2000) has pointed to evidence that people are uncomfortable with class labels (such as 'working class' or 'middle class') and are often reluctant to spontaneously self-identify as belonging to a social class category. He argues that this suggests Britain is no longer a 'class-conscious society' in the sense that class is 'seen as embodying membership of collective groups' (Savage, 2000: 40). So despite the enduring structural importance of class to people's lives, Savage suggests that there is a 'paradox of class', in that this structural importance 'appears not to be recognised by the people themselves. Culturally, class does not appear to be a self-conscious principle of social identity' (Savage, 2000: xii). The reason for this, Savage argues, is that people often experience 'class' in a tacit but morally charged way that is hard to speak about, with class 'encoded in people's sense of self-worth and in their attitudes to and awareness of others', making it difficult for class distinctions to be 'explicitly named and identified' (Savage, 2000: 107).

Others, however, writing from a neo-Weberian perspective, argue that class identity is still alive and well (in Britain at least) (Evans and Mellon, 2016). Certainly, when prompted in surveys, most people in Britain claim a class identity – and it is often a working-class one. Working-class occupations amount to only about a quarter of the **population** in Britain but, when asked to express a class identity in the British Social Attitudes Survey, 60% of people still claim to be 'working class' (Evans and Mellon, 2016).

The proportion of people claiming a working-class identity has hardly changed in Britain over the last 30 years, and even more strikingly, around half of people in *middle-class jobs* (jobs classified as managerial or professional) also claim to be working class (Evans and Mellon, 2016). One reason is that many of those in middle-class jobs who see themselves working class come disproportionately from working-class backgrounds, so it is clear that **family** background matters to people's sense of class identity. But personal class identity is also linked to how people perceive wider class inequalities. Those who describe society as being polarized by sharp class inequalities – seeing a division between a large disadvantaged group and a small privileged elite – are much more likely to see themselves as being working class (Evans and Mellon, 2016). Evans and Mellon conclude from this that not only is class identity alive and well in Britain, but also that a majority of people appear to perceive very significant class divisions and **boundaries** in British society.

There are other disagreements with cultural class analysis. Some criticize cultural class analysis for overstating the significance of cultural resources in class processes. For those who continue to see 'class' in economic terms, whilst cultural assets may be significant in *allocating* people to employment positions, the class *locations* themselves are still largely generated by economic processes. This is disputed by cultural class theorists, who insist that struggles over both cultural and economic resources shape the class structure (Savage et al., 2015). But the debate over employment relations versus cultural resources often misses a bigger question – the question of wealth and property ownership and its effect on societies. Critics argue that by shifting the emphasis from political economy to the labour market, and by focusing on the cultural dimension of class relations, practically all forms of class analysis missed the most striking feature of changing inequality in the last 40 years – soaring wealth inequalities and the rise of the super-rich.

The rise of super-rich elites is significant not just because of their enormous power and influence, but also because the steep inequality they represent seems to have a negative impact on everyone in a society, and not just the disadvantaged. For Mike Savage, the stark gap between the super-rich and the rest of society represents an important shift in class relations: 'The old class war may be over; the new politics of class is just beginning. The widening fracture between the wealthy elite and the rest is a huge threat to our social fabric' (Savage, 2015: np). In recent debates, the most high-profile interventions have come from researchers working in **epidemiology**, social geography or economics, whose focus is often more on income and wealth than class relations (Dorling, 2017; Milanović, 2016; Piketty, 2014, 2020; Wilkinson and Pickett, 2010, 2018). But whilst they may not always draw on class categories, these interventions reveal dramatic shifts in class processes across the globe. However, these shifts also raise the question of how national class inequalities are shaped by global inequalities, and the racialized nature of class processes.

Virdee (2019) argues that class analysts have often shown a 'wilful indifference' to the intersections of race and class, failing to recognize the role racialized inequalities and **imperialism** have played in producing class relations. Some trace this neglect back to the **Eurocentric** understanding of **modernity** which has influenced and limited sociological accounts of class, by neglecting the significance of **racism** and imperialism to the formation of capitalist modernity (Bhambra, 2007). From this perspective, **colonialism** (and the dispossession and enslavement of people from the non-European world) was central to the constitution and rapid growth of industrial **capitalism** and created the starkly unequal global balance of power and the deeply racialized class relations which exist today.

CLASS

The Rise of the Rich and Global Inequalities

Many countries have experienced a dramatic and sustained increase in inequalities in income and wealth since the 1970s. For some analysts, this means class struggle is now (or, perhaps, is now again) fundamentally a question of the super-rich versus the rest of society, in ways which are entangled with stark *global* inequalities. Both the rise of the rich and the scale of global inequalities show the significance of class power.

 Pause for Thought

The scale of inequality today is staggering. In America, for example, just three men hold more wealth ($357 billion) than the bottom 50% of the US population (160 million people) whilst 20% of US households have zero or negative net worth (Collins and Hoxie, 2017: 1). If we consider income, in 2018, the top decile (the upper 10% of income earners) took the lion's share of overall income: the top 10% received 34% of overall income in Europe, 41% in China, 46% in Russia, 48% in the United States, 54% in sub-Saharan Africa, 55% in India, 56% in Brazil and 64% in the Middle East (Piketty, 2020). Given the richest can 'offshore' their income and wealth to avoid tax, these official figures likely significantly understate economic inequalities.

- How aware are you of the scale of economic inequality?

Rising economic inequality is not the inevitable outcome of global economic forces or technological change, because in some countries it has been stable or even fallen. Regions which have experienced the same exposure to globalization and new **technologies** have experienced sharp differences in inequality over time. For example, in America the income share of the bottom 50% collapsed from 20% to 10% from 1980 to 2016, whereas in Europe it declined slightly from 24% to 22% (Alvaredo et al., 2018). And taking a longer timeframe, income and wealth inequality actually fell substantially in most countries during the first three-quarters of the 20th century (Piketty, 2014). Such variation shows that national institutions, politics and policies (such as **redistributive taxation**; investment in public services, education and welfare; regulation of employment, a living wage and strong trade unions) have substantial impacts on inequality.

However, these inequality-busting policies have been under attack since the 1970s. Many see this as both the cause and consequence of the rise of the super-rich. The extraordinary wealth of the super-rich is hard to grasp. In 2019, the activist organization Oxfam pointed out that the world's billionaires, just 2153 people, held more wealth than 4.6 billion people combined (Oxfam, 2020). The richest 0.1% of the world's population own 20% of the wealth in the world, whilst the richest 1% own 50% (Piketty, 2014: 692). Analysts warn such stark inequality is a danger to political equality, with the super-rich not only holding more political power but using it to sway policy to advance their own sectional interests. The impact of big money on the political system can be seen in the fact that wealthy individuals and corporations have seen their tax bill slashed since the 1970s. In rich countries, the average top rate of personal income tax fell from 62% in 1970 to 38% in 2013, whilst globally only 4 cents in every dollar of tax revenue comes from taxes on wealth; in countries like Brazil and the UK, the poorest 10% now pay a higher proportion of their incomes in tax than the richest 10% (Oxfam, 2019).

Since the 1970s, there has been widespread adoption of a range of neoliberal policies, including deregulation of markets, increasing restrictions on trade unions, **financialization** (the increasing significance of financial services and shareholder value in the economy), more regressive taxation and retrenchment of the welfare **state**. These policies have facilitated the rise of super-rich corporations and individuals. Simultaneously, the emergence of sub-contracting, the casualization of labour and the rise of the gig economy have increased work insecurity whilst forcing more of the risks and costs of employment onto workers. For Piketty (2014), the rise or fall of inequality depends on who holds the most power over policies on taxation, wages and workers' rights. Since the 1970s, the balance of class power has increasingly shifted to the rich. In 2011, the billionaire Warren Buffett pointed out that he paid less income tax (he meant a lower rate of tax) than his receptionist or cleaner, and in 2006 he reportedly said: 'There's class warfare, all right. But it's my class, the rich class, that's making war, and we're winning' (Stein, 2006).

— Pause for Thought

- Why should we care about high economic inequality and the rise of the super-rich?

Some argue that class inequality does not matter if it accompanies economic growth which raises living standards. This kind of argument suggests that inequality is necessary for competition and growth, and that the benefits that come from economic growth and rising living standards outweigh the negative aspects of inequality. The idea here is that inequality is associated with increasing the size of the pie – if everyone gets more pie, who cares how much bigger other people's slice might be? Others see poverty, rather than class inequality, as the real problem, arguing that if inequality accompanies growth which reduces poverty levels then inequality can actually be positive. However, there are good reasons why we might be concerned about steep inequality and the rise of the super-rich, even in the context of improving standards of living and poverty reduction, because critics warn that economic inequality is now so stark that it is producing significant social harm for all of us – not just the poor and disadvantaged.

The focus of recent debates has been on the negative consequences of rising class inequality for *everyone* in a society, from top to bottom: negatively affecting our shared social lives through its disruptive impact on growth, educational performance, social mobility, social stability and cohesion, and the environment, as well as political accountability. Epidemiological research (Wilkinson and Pickett, 2010, 2018) suggests that all members of a society – not just the poor or working-class – are adversely affected if they live in a country with very high inequality (even if that country is a rich one), because high inequality damages the fabric of society and increases status anxiety and insecurity for all. From this perspective, the health and wellbeing of populations is related less to how wealthy a society is than to how equally income and wealth are distributed amongst the population. More egalitarian societies – with narrower income or wealth distributions – have better health outcomes than countries with greater inequality.

Health inequalities demonstrate the relational aspects of class inequality, whose damaging effects endure the transition to more affluent societies and cannot just be explained by poverty or material deprivation. Health differences occur between class groups who are clearly not deprived, with health inequalities at every level of the class structure. Because class position continues to be important for health, even when a society's living standards are high, it has been argued that it is not just the absolute level of our material resources that affects our health but also our position relative to others. For Wilkinson and Pickett (2010), a sense of relative deprivation (not just less income, but also less respect, dignity and **autonomy** than others) is translated 'inside' the body into stress and poorer health but is also translated 'outside' to society via anti-social behaviour and reduced trust and **social cohesion**. Countries with higher levels of inequality have higher levels of crime, stress and mental illness, even when we control for the wealth of a country. And Wilkinson and Pickett (2018) argue that because the increasing gap between rich and poor increases status anxiety, it also results in a stronger emphasis on wasteful **conspicuous consumerism** which degrades the environment.

Very high levels of inequality are certainly linked to overconsumption and climate change (Dorling, 2017). The richest 10% in the world are responsible for 49% of the total global carbon dioxide emissions, whereas the poorest 50% are only responsible for 10% (Dorling, 2017). This is partly a question of absolute poverty and wealth: richer countries have more consumption-oriented economies. But it is also a question of relative inequality within rich countries. The breakdown of CO_2 emissions by income group within richer countries shows that it is the environmental footprint of the richest 10% which disproportionately accounts for carbon dioxide emissions in those countries and raises the average level of pollution in them (Dorling, 2017).

There is also evidence that very high levels of class inequality can actually hurt economic performance. The Organisation for Economic Cooperation and Development (the OECD) argues that, on average, high levels of inequality in a country lead to periods of lower, and less stable, economic growth in the future. Long-term economic growth has been achieved by countries with both high and low inequality (Therborn, 2013), but OECD (2019) research indicates that high inequality has put a significant brake on long-term economic growth in the Global North, because the incomes of the bottom 40% have remained stagnant, curbing opportunities for lower and middle-lower income groups. There have not been fair shares or **equal opportunities** in the growth that has occurred, with little 'trickle down' of wealth. Levels of social mobility are also negatively associated with rising inequality – the more unequal the country, the less social mobility there is in it (Dorling, 2017). One reason rising inequality stifles upward social mobility is because countries with greater income inequality are also countries where a greater fraction of class advantage is passed on from parents to children. Far from stimulating (fair) competition and opportunity, high levels of inequality seem to undermine it.

Much of the discussion in this section focuses on class inequalities within nations. However, critics point out that the renewed concern about inequality and the rise of the rich only emerged when inequality rose in the *Global North*, whilst the mainstream analysis of social class has often neglected the enormous socio-economic inequalities between countries in the **Global North and Global South** (Bashi Treitler and Boatcă, 2016). From this perspective, we must reconnect the analysis of class inequalities *within* nations to *global* inequalities, and the dynamics of global power relations.

Connecting Class Inequalities to Global Inequalities and Global Power Relations

Global inequality is even more dramatic than class inequalities within nations. This is partly a question of the rise of the super-rich. The wealthiest 1% in the world not only owns more wealth than the remaining 99% of the world's population, they own more than twice as much wealth as 6.9 billion people, whilst the world's 26 richest individuals collectively held the same amount of total wealth as the world's poorest 50%, i.e. 3.8 billion people (Oxfam, 2020). The economist Branko Milanović (2016) argues that the most decisive question for people's life chances is not their class but the wealth of their country, with 50 to 60% of the income differences between individuals in the world due simply to the mean income differences between the countries where people live. The very poorest people in the United States have an income level equal to that of the middle-class in China or the upper-middle-class in India (Milanović, 2016). Analysis of global inequality shows very stark inequalities and also the existence of a 'global elite' which includes people from countries in the Global South, such as China, India and Nigeria, as well as from the Global North.

 — Pause for Thought

- Can we justify increasing inequality within nations if it helps reduce poverty and inequality globally?

Some people argue that higher national inequalities – particularly in the Global North – may be the price to bear for the greater globalization of economic competition if it reduces global inequality and poverty in the Global South. Certainly, on some measures global inequality has declined in recent decades, as some poorer countries have caught up with richer ones, although measures of global inequality are strongly affected by the rapid economic growth of two very large countries, China and India (Hickel, 2017; Milanović, 2016). Their rapid economic growth led to significant poverty reduction in these two countries, and because they are relatively poor and very large, their improving living standards have had an impact on global inequality measures. Some see these shifts as a potential justification for national inequalities, arguing that the globalization which has increased inequality within many countries in the world has also lifted millions out of poverty globally, and improved general standards of living.

Large-scale poverty reduction in the Global South is a vitally important positive trend. But critics of rising inequality within nations argue that it is simply not true that such inequality is the price we have to pay to lift the global poor out of poverty. Cross-national analysis (Alvaredo et al., 2018) indicates that countries that experienced steeper increases in inequality were *not* better at lifting the incomes of their poorest citizens than more egalitarian ones. And whilst we can see improvements in standards of living in some poorer countries, enormously stark inequalities remain between the Global North and the Global South.

The 2018 World Inequality Report (Alvaredo et al., 2018) argues that between 1980 and 2016, global inequality actually increased, despite strong growth in 'emerging markets' (such as China). Again, we see a familiar pattern of enduring relative inequality, because while some poorer countries have become more affluent, richer countries have also moved forward and at a much faster rate. Per capita income has increased in the Global South, but the Global North has captured the vast majority of new income generated by global growth since 1960. From 1980 to 2016, the poorest 50% of humanity only captured 12 cents in every dollar of global income growth, whilst the top 1% captured 27 cents of every dollar (Alvaredo et al., 2018). The inequality gap between the Global North and South remains stark: in 2015, Europe and North America had 84% of the world's wealth in per-capita terms, while the rest of the world had only 16%, and the income gap between the average person in the North and the average person in the South has nearly quadrupled in size (Hickel, 2017).

CLASS

> ### Hear from the Expert
>
> Jason Hickel argues that we cannot justify rising inequality on the basis that it reduces the gap between the Global North and South, because the gap has actually increased. Since 1960, the gap between the per-capita GDP of the US and Latin America has grown by 206%; the gap between the US and south-Saharan Africa has grown by 207%; the gap between the US and the Middle East and North Africa has grown by 155%; and the gap between the US and South Asia has grown by 196% (Hickel, 2017: 2217). Hickel argues that to understand this we must consider the geopolitical relations which connect countries. The fortunes of rich and poor countries are not unrelated phenomena but inherently connected, historically through the violently coercive depredations of colonialism and imperialism, and later, in the **postcolonial** era, from the very unequal power relations which have allowed countries in the Global North (and particularly America) to sway global economic and trade policy to their advantage, through their domination of key organizations like the World Bank, the International Monetary Fund and the World Trade Organization. For Hickel (2017: 2209), the inequality between the Global North and the Global South is a relational phenomenon, the product of a very uneven balance of global power. A failure to recognize this 'depoliticises inequality' and 'erases the geopolitical relationships – and the class relationships – that we know to be central to structuring patterns of distribution in the global economy' (Hickel, 2017: 2211, 2213).

Class inequality is very stark and increasing globally and within many nations. But to what extent do people recognize the scale of class inequalities? Various theories predict high and rising class inequality *should* have important political outcomes, creating pressures for redistribution or even inciting revolution, but most studies show a weak relationship between levels of inequality and grievance or political discontent. Views on inequality are generally better related to people's – often inaccurate – *perceptions* of inequality. This is partly a question of how living within a structure of class inequality itself shapes what people come to see of it. But if people systematically misperceive class inequality, increasing inequality may not lead to greater pressures for equality and redistribution. So it is important to explore what shapes everyday 'views' on inequality if we want to explain levels of discontent and protest to it.

Perceptions of Inequality

Research on subjective inequality is often focused on the Global North or on class subjectivities within specific countries, with a marked lack of work on everyday understandings of global inequalities. Within this national focus, all versions of class analysis have struggled with how the experience of class inequality translates into everyday understandings of it. The consensus is that the relationship is far from straightforward, not least because 'class' means different things to different people.

 Pause for Thought

One study of ordinary people (Payne and Grew, 2005: 903) found they interpreted the concept of 'class' in at least 14 different ways (including lifestyle, housing, aspirations, education, aristocracy, the upper class, superiority and deference, money, income, job types, inequality, capitalism and the class system).

- What do you think of when you hear the term 'class'?

People's views on class inequality are complex and depend not only on what levels of inequality they perceive and how much they regard as acceptable, but also on whether they think it has been fairly generated. Ordinary people's understandings of inequality are both complex and sometimes counter-intuitive, with research showing that people in more unequal countries often show *greater* tolerance for inequality, and that sharp increases in inequality are sometimes associated with declining support for redistribution, and more negative views about the poor. As a result, people's subjective grasp of class inequalities has been identified as problematic, restricted or 'paradoxical' in a range of work.

Many analysts assume ordinary people *should be* concerned about class inequality and are troubled when they sometimes seem less concerned than expected. The widespread compliance of people in the face of stark inequality, with less dissent or **conflict** than analysts expect, is seen as a key factor explaining the persistence of class inequality. In fact, high inequality in a society (where elites exert a strong influence on politics) can create greater political disengagement, particularly among the less advantaged. It is well known that poorer people are less likely to vote, but increasing inequality in a country sharpens this trend, increasing political disengagement especially for those on low incomes, partly because they feel politicians represent elites, not ordinary workers (Bottero, 2019). But does class inequality create other kinds of discontent?

One often expressed concern is that increasing class inequality will not just result in disengagement from formal politics, but also that the disenfranchised will be drawn into extremist and de-stabilizing 'populist' movements.

11.2 Key Case

How is Class Inequality Related to Populism in the USA?

The US presidential election of Donald Trump has been popularly characterized as a reaction against rising inequality, in which a working-class 'left behind' by **deindustrialization** turned to populist parties as part of an anti-establishment rejection of 'politics as usual'. However, the election of Trump was in fact more strongly affected by the status anxieties of the relatively better-off (Bhambra, 2017). In America, economic hardship was not significantly related to voters switching to Trump. Instead, voting for Trump was much more connected with *racial* divisions related to middle-class white Americans' sense of a threat to their dominant group status (Mutz, 2018), with voters' racism correlated more closely with support for Trump than their economic dissatisfaction (Schaffner et al., 2018). White Americans voting for Trump felt a loss of privilege compared to African Americans and experienced this as a threat (Bhambra, 2017) because of a long-held expectation that their whiteness *should* bring them a relative advantage over African Americans, as part of the 'psychological wages of whiteness' (Du Bois, 1935).

- How are perceptions of class inequality affected by the *kinds* of social comparisons that shape people's sense of relative deprivation or relative advantage?

....

More generally, the assumption that '**populism**' is a working-class phenomenon that manifests in times of economic crisis or hardship is flawed. Mols and Jetten's (2017) analysis of long-term voter patterns in Europe (France, Germany, Denmark, Sweden, The Netherlands, Austria, Switzerland and the United Kingdom) shows no correlation between economic conditions and populist anti-establishment voting, with populist parties often remarkably successful in times of economic growth and prosperity. Populist parties do attract support from working-class voters experiencing hardship, but they also attract significant support from middle-class voters with above-average wealth and income. Mols and Jetten argue that in Europe, the evidence suggests that support for populist parties among the better-off increases with their *status anxiety* – the more they feel a sense of entitlement and fear they might lose their relative advantage over other groups.

One reason why levels of objective inequality do not straightforwardly produce discontent is that people's sense of inequality is related to how their expectations and assessments of injustice emerge from comparisons between reference groups. People feel relatively deprived if they think their situation is worse than others they identify and compare themselves with, that is, via comparison to groups they think *should* be in the same (or a worse) situation. The significance of frames of reference means we must consider how and why people develop their view of broader social circumstances. People most often develop their sense of class inequality in relation to their own practical concerns, so they are generally more aware of, and more concerned by, 'local' inequalities in their own lives and immediate milieu (Bottero, 2019). But '**reference group effects**' can cause people to misjudge inequality and their own relative class position, with people often underestimating levels of inequality and having a poor sense of their own place in the distribution of incomes.

People typically establish their relative class position by comparing themselves to people in their everyday lives, so that they base their sense of class inequality on their immediate milieu. However, inequality is baked into such social arrangements, with workplaces, neighbourhoods and personal networks strongly 'sorted' by class. Because inequality structures everyday lives, such comparisons are usually to people in *similar* class positions, so the truncated nature of 'reference-group' comparisons restricts perceptions of the wider scale of inequality.

 Pause for Thought

- Think of the people in your everyday life, in your neighbourhood, school, and your family and friends: to what extent are they from similar social class backgrounds as you? Are there many people from very different social backgrounds?
- How do you think your social situation and relationships affect your awareness of class inequality?

PART 3 INEQUALITIES AND IDENTITIES

For some analysts, the restricted nature of our 'reference groups' explains not only the relative lack of discontent about class inequality but also why people in more unequal societies are *more likely* to 'underestimate the extent of inequality and the role of structural advantages or barriers that help or hurt them' (Mijs, 2019: 7). Widening class inequality makes reference group comparisons *more restricted* because growing inequality has a segregative effect, creating greater social and spatial distance between the wealthy and the poor who increasingly live separate lives with limited interaction (2019: 6). For Mijs, this explains why people in highly unequal societies are more likely to believe their society is **meritocratic**, with inequality creating the social conditions for its legitimation.

People's perceptions of class inequality are also affected by political discourses and media debates which affect not just the visibility but also the legitimacy of inequality. Here the argument is that understandings of inequality are not just restricted but also systematically distorted as part of the symbolic legitimation of class inequalities. For example, in Britain, political and media debates have presented an increasingly negative view of the poor as lazy 'scroungers', hardening attitudes to welfare recipients and legitimizing cuts to welfare (Jensen and Tyler, 2015). Various theories argue that class inequality is legitimated through processes which misrepresent or mask its real nature.

One prominent legitimating **ideology** is the belief – widespread in media and politics – that inequality is the product of meritocratic processes. Questions of fairness and opportunity are very significant when people assess class inequality. However, the idea of meritocracy both naturalizes inequality (with class inequality seen as the result of unequal abilities) and legitimates it (where, if inequality reflects effort, it is seen as deserved). For class analysts (Littler, 2017), meritocracy is a distorting and legitimating 'myth' of how people are rewarded, because the focus on merit greatly overestimates the impact of individual ability or effort on class outcomes, whilst ignoring how the structure of opportunities strongly influences chances of success.

For Mijs (2019), the key 'paradox' of inequality is that rising class inequality has not fuelled growing popular concern about it, with those living in more unequal societies showing no greater concern than those in more egalitarian societies. As Mijs notes, explanations for this paradox – in which it is argued that people are unaware of the true extent of inequality, or else that people associate increasing inequality with fair meritocratic processes – are all explanations founded on how living within a structure of inequality itself shapes what people come to see and think about it. And because people are generally more aware of – and more exercised by – 'local' inequalities in their own lives and social contexts, this means they develop their sense of wider class inequality in relation to their practical concerns and local contexts of activity, which can limit their grasp of the scale and causes of class inequality.

 — Pause for Thought

Times of crisis and social disruption sometimes reveal the stark nature of class advantage and inequality. In the COVID-19 pandemic, for example, those in lower social classes (and people of colour, showing the **entanglement** of class and racial inequalities) have been much more likely (seven times more) to lose their job (Joyce and Xu, 2020), but when they are still employed they are less able to work from home, increasing their risk of infection. The pandemic also reveals the perversity in how we value people within class structures. The designation of many of those in precarious, low-paid and 'low-skilled' jobs as 'key workers' – who must still perform their work despite quarantine because it is vital to the basic functioning of society – shows the true value of the bus drivers, cleaners, supermarket workers and carers upon whom we all depend, a value far from their 'market' worth.

- How has COVID-19 influenced your viewpoint on inequality? What social conditions might make class inequalities *more* visible to people?

Whilst people do underestimate class inequality, we should not overstate the significance of this. For research also shows that most people *are* concerned about high inequality and would like to live in a more egalitarian society. As McCall argues, people's awareness of inequality is 'accurate and critical enough' (2013: 167) and their preferred level of inequality is so low it would require a substantial reorganization of society. However, while people do care about class inequality and would prefer a more equitable society, their concerns and point of view are strongly shaped by how inequality affects their own daily lives and opportunities, and those of the people around them, which may place constraints on struggles for greater equality.

--- Expand Your Knowledge ---

- To learn more about how people's position within a structure of inequality shapes what they can see of it, read Jonathan Mijs on how rising inequality creates the social conditions for its own legitimation: Mijs, J. (2019) The paradox of inequality: Income inequality and belief in meritocracy go hand in hand. *Socio-Economic Review*. Available at: https://static1.squarespace.com/static/55e8aafee4b011f0abb1b06d/t/5c483fe7c74c5023692e12de/1548238828312/Mijs.+2019.+Paradox+of+Inequality.pdf
- To get a comprehensive perspective on global patterns of inequality and trends in inequality over time, read: Alvaredo, F., Chancel, L., Piketty, T., Saez, E. and Zucman, G. (2018) *The World Inequality Report 2018*. Available at: https://en.unesco.org/inclusivepolicylab/sites/default/files/publication/document/2018/7/wir2018-full-report-english.pdf

CHAPTER SUMMARY

- Class is a question of inequality: about the uneven resources, status, opportunities or rights which affect people's chances in life. Fundamentally relational, class is a question of relative advantage and of how some people have *more* – more opportunities, more resources, more power or status – whilst others have *less*.
- Class inequality is never just a question of economic distribution but always entails relations of power and subordination, and unequal respect, autonomy and accountability.
- Sociological work on class has established the continuing relevance of class – in social life and in sociological analysis – in the face of major socio-economic transformations.
- In demonstrating that class inequalities show remarkable continuity, analysts have made significant changes in how 'class' processes are understood.

- Class inequalities cannot be understood solely as a question of national divisions but must be seen in the wider context of the rising power of a global super-rich as well as stark postcolonial global inequalities.
- There remains a question of just how visible wider class inequalities are to ordinary people, because while most people do express concern about high and rising inequality, they are generally more aware of, and more concerned by, how unequal relations affect their own immediate situation and concerns.

REVIEW QUESTIONS

- Why is a sociological understanding of class inequalities important?
- How and why have theoretical perspectives on class inequalities shifted over time?
- What are the main impacts of rising class inequality which have led researchers to suggest that high class inequality has adverse effects for *everyone* in a society (not just the poor)?
- How are national class inequalities connected to global inequalities?
- What are the main factors that can limit our perception of the nature of class inequality?

Go Further

Books

- Bhattacharyya, G. (2017) *Rethinking Racial Capitalism*. London: Rowman & Littlefield.

A reappraisal of the history of capitalism which examines how racial division and expropriation were central to capitalist development and still shape it today.

- Friedman, S. and Laurison, D. (2019) *The Class Ceiling: Why It Pays to Be Privileged*. Bristol: Policy Press.

Friedman and Laurison explore in detail the factors which explain the 'class pay gap' in elite professions, unpacking the complex barriers that face the upwardly mobile.

- Wilkinson, R. and Pickett, K. (2018) *The Inner Level*. London: Penguin.

Wilkinson and Pickett's book argues that economic inequality negatively affects *everyone* in a society, showing that less-equal societies fare worse than more equal ones across a range of indicators (crime, educational performance, social trust, life expectancy, etc.). They explore the reasons for this by considering how high inequality societies create status pressures affecting people's self-esteem, stress, rates of anxiety and depression.

Journal Articles

- Bhambra, G. (2017) Brexit, Trump, and 'methodological whiteness': On the misrecognition of race and class. *The British Journal of Sociology* 68(S1): S214–32.

Bhambra critically analyses accounts which explain populist movements as the backlash of a 'left behind' white working class. She shows that populism is less about class inequality and more about racial divisions and politics, and she explores the rhetoric that reshapes white majority political action as the action of a more narrowly defined white working class.

- Hickel, J. (2017) Is global inequality getting better or worse? A critique of the World Bank's convergence narrative. *Third World Quarterly* 38(10): 2208–22.

Hickel critically examines the widespread belief that there has been a convergence in global income inequality since 1960. He argues that the idea of convergence relies on a misleading presentation of the data, failing to acknowledge rising absolute inequality and ignoring the divergence between geopolitical regions. By looking instead at the gap between the core and periphery of the world system, he argues that global inequality has tripled since 1960.

- Mijs, J. (2019) The paradox of inequality: Income inequality and belief in meritocracy go hand in hand. *Socio-Economic Review*. Available at: https://static1.squarespace.com/static/55e8aafee4b011f0abb1b06d/t/5c483fe7c74c5023692e12de/1548238828312/Mijs.+2019.+Paradox+of+Inequality.pdf

Mijs explores the reasons for the 'paradox of inequality', namely that increasing inequalities in a society do not lead to increased popular concern about it, whilst people who grew up in societies with rising levels of inequality believe more strongly in meritocracy. He argues that income inequality creates greater spatial and social distance between the wealthy and the poor, which insulates people from seeing the full extent of it. People underestimate the structural forces that create inequality because they are increasingly unable to see it from their isolated position within their segregated society.

Websites

- The Compare Your Income tool – www.compareyourincome.org

Where do you or your family stand in the distribution of incomes? This tool allows you to compare your income with the rest of the population, so that you can find out how many households are better or worse off than yours.

- The Dollar Street Project – www.gapminder.org/category/dollarstreet

Provides a window into the lived experience of inequality, by presenting images and information on the everyday lives of people around the world arranged by income level.

- The World Inequality Database – https://wid.world

The most extensive available database on the current status and historical evolution of the world distribution of income and wealth, both within countries and between countries.

REFERENCES

Alvaredo, F., Chancel, L., Piketty, T., Saez, E. and Zucman, G. (eds) (2018) *The World Inequality Report 2018*. Available at: https://wir2018.wid.world/files/download/wir2018-full-report-english.pdf (last accessed 30 May 2021).

Bashi Treitler, V. and Boatcă, M. (2016) Dynamics of inequalities in a global perspective: An introduction. *Current Sociology* 64(2): 159–71.

Bhambra, G. (2007) *Rethinking Modernity*. Basingstoke: Palgrave.

Bhambra, G. (2017) Brexit, Trump, and 'methodological whiteness': On the misrecognition of race and class. *The British Journal of Sociology* 68(S1): S214–32.

Bottero, W. (2019) *A Sense of Inequality*. London: Rowman and Littlefield.

Bourdieu, P. (1984) *Distinction: A Social Critique of the Judgement of Taste*. London: Routledge.

Buffett, W. (2011) Stop coddling the rich. *New York Times*, 15 August. Available at: www.nytimes.com/2011/08/15/opinion/stop-coddling-the-super-rich.html (last accessed 2 April 2020).

Bukodi, E. and Goldthorpe, J. (2018) *Social Mobility and Education in Britain*. Cambridge: Cambridge University Press.

Collins, C. and Hoxie, J. (2017) *Billionaire Bonanza: The Forbes 400 and the Rest of Us*. Washington, DC: Institute of Policy Studies. Available at: https://inequality.org/wp-content/uploads/2017/11/BILLIONAIRE-BONANZA-2017-Embargoed.pdf (last accessed 15 April 2018).

Dorling, D. (2017) *The Equality Effect: Improving Life for Everyone*. London: New Internationalist.

Du Bois, W.E.B. (1935) *Black Reconstruction*. New York: Harcourt, Brace.

Erikson, R. and Goldthorpe, J. (1993) *The Constant Flux: The Study of Social Mobility in Industrial Societies*. Oxford: Clarendon Press.

Evans, G. and Mellon, J. (2016) Social class: Identity, awareness and political attitudes: Why are we still working class? *British Social Attitudes* 33: 1–19.

Friedman, S. and Laurison, D. (2019) *The Class Ceiling: Why It Pays to Be Privileged*. Bristol: Policy Press.

Hickel, J. (2017) Is global inequality getting better or worse? A critique of the World Bank's convergence narrative. *Third World Quarterly* 38(10): 2208–22.

Jensen, T. and Tyler, I. (2015) Benefits broods: The cultural and political crafting of anti-welfare commonsense. *Critical Social Policy* 35(4): 470–91.

Joyce, R. and Xu, X. (2020) *Sector Shutdowns during the Coronavirus Crisis: Which workers are most exposed?* IFS Briefing Note BN278, Institute of Fiscal Studies. Available at: www.ifs.org.uk/uploads/BN278-Sector-shutdowns-during-the-coronavirus-crisis.pdf (last accessed 15 April 2020).

Littler, J. (2017) *Against Meritocracy*. London: Routledge.

Marx, K. (1990) *Capital*. London: Penguin Classics.

McCall, L. (2013) *The Undeserving Rich*. Cambridge: Cambridge University Press.

Mijs, J. (2019) The paradox of inequality: Income inequality and belief in meritocracy go hand in hand. *Socio-Economic Review*. Published online first at: https://static1.squarespace.com/static/55e8aafee4b011f0abb1b06d/t/5c483fe7c74c5023692e12de/1548238828312/Mijs.+2019.+Paradox+of+Inequality.pdf (last accessed 5 April 2019).

Milanović, B. (2016) *Global Inequality*. Cambridge, MA: Harvard University Press.

Mols, F. and Jetten, J. (2017) *The Wealth Paradox*. Cambridge: Cambridge University Press.

Mutz, D. (2018) Status threat, not economic hardship, explains the 2016 presidential vote. *PNAS* 11(44): E4330–E4339.

OECD (2019) *Under Pressure: The Squeezed Middle-Class*. Paris: OECD Publishing. Available at: https://doi.org/10.1787/689afed1-en (last accessed 15 April 2019).

Oxfam (2019) *Public Good or Private Wealth*. Oxfam Briefing Paper. Available at: https://oxfamilibrary.openrepository.com/bitstream/handle/10546/620599/bp-public-good-or-private-wealth-210119-en.pdf (last accessed 5 April 2019).

Oxfam (2020) *Time to Care*. Oxfam Briefing Paper. Available at: https://oxfamilibrary.openrepository.com/bitstream/handle/10546/620928/bp-time-to-care-inequality-200120-en.pdf (last accessed 15 April 2020).

Payne, G. and Grew, C. (2005) Unpacking 'class ambivalence': Some conceptual and methodological issues in accessing class cultures. *Sociology* 39(5): 893–910.

Piketty, T. (2014) *Capital in the Twenty-first Century*. Cambridge MA: Harvard University Press.

Piketty, T. (2020) *Capitalism and Ideology*. Cambridge, MA: Harvard University Press.

Savage, M. (2015) The 'class ceiling' and the new class war. *The Guardian*, 22 October. Available at: www.theguardian.com/books/2015/oct/22/new-class-war-politics-class-just-beginning (last accessed 15 April 2020).

Savage, M. (2000) *Class Analysis and Social Transformation*. Buckingham: Open University Press.

Savage, M., Cunningham, N., Devine, F., Friedman, S., Laurison, D., McKenzie, L., Miles, A., Snee, H. and Wakeling, P. (2015) *Social Class in the 21st Century*. London: Pelican.

Schaffner, B., MacWilliams, M. and Nteta, T. (2018) Explaining white polarization in the 2016 vote for president: The sobering role of racism and sexism. *Political Science Quarterly* 33(1): 9–34.

Skeggs, B. (2004) *Class, Self, Culture*. London: Routledge.

Stein, B. (2006) In class warfare, guess which class is winning? *New York Times*, 26 November. Available at: www.nytimes.com/2006/11/26/business/yourmoney/26every.html (last accessed 2 April 2020).

Therborn, G. (2013) *The Killing Fields of Inequality*. Cambridge: Polity Press.

Virdee, S. (2019) Racialized capitalism: An account of its contested origins and consolidation. *The Sociological Review* 67(1): 3–27.

Weber, M. (1978) *Economy and Society*, ed. G. Roth and C. Wittich. Berkeley, CA: University of California Press.

Wilkinson, R. and Pickett, K. (2010) *The Spirit Level*. London: Penguin.

Wilkinson, R. and Pickett, K. (2018) *The Inner Level*. London: Penguin.

GENDER

Kath Woodward and Sophie Woodward

LEARNING OBJECTIVES

- To understand what is meant by the term gender and the role gender plays in making and remaking social relations and divisions.
- To show how gender connects to other social relations, such as class, race and ethnicity.
- To look at some of the links between gender as an empirical description of societies and gender as an explanatory concept.

 Framing Questions

1. Why and how does gender matter?
2. What are sex and gender and how are they connected?
3. *How* do we know about sex and gender?
4. What do sociological analyses contribute to the study of gender?
5. What is the relationship between gender and other social relations and inequalities?

GENDER

Introduction

This chapter outlines some of the developments in the sociological understanding of gender as a useful concept for explaining social relations and inequalities over time and in different places. Gender studies is an important, fast-changing area of sociological inquiry, which strongly relates to other sociological concerns and theoretical frameworks explored in this book. Sex and gender are features of the classification of animate creatures, including human beings and all known societies. You will be familiar with the terms sex and gender as they are part of everyday language, but are sex and gender the same thing or do they mean something different but connected? We will address these questions in this chapter as well as how gender relates to other social relations, such as class and race. (Questions about gender also feature in Chapters 15, 16, 17 and 18.)

We write this chapter as sociologists, which means that we ask questions which are relevant to daily life and experiences. Think about your everyday life. How often are you asked to state your gender? Why do you think it is important to know what sex you are when you apply for a driving licence, insurance or welfare benefits? There are some occasions where this information may seem especially relevant, such as in some health care. For example, COVID-19 impacts more upon men than women (Global Health, 2020), which demands explanation for further research and treatment. In everyday life, sex or gender may seem self-evident to many people but sociologists question the taken-for-granted and ask: how is gender decided? Why are such divisions deemed so important? The sociology of gender involves mapping out and documenting how people experience gender and gendered divisions, as well as providing explanations for these divisions and experiences. This chapter therefore introduces you to how we develop knowledge of gender as well as to theories of gender, which offer ways of making sense of gender.

Gender is complex and contested, which, in the tradition of sociology, presents us with arguments and disputes and raises different questions. This chapter will therefore start by mapping the terrain to familiarize you with where the sociology of gender comes from. We then move on to discuss the relationship between sex and gender as well as get you thinking about how gender and sex relate to other social differences. The chapter then focuses on thinking about where our understanding and knowledge of gender come from – big data and statistics are often used to paint pictures of gender inequality and we explore how these are useful, as well as what their limitations are, by considering research which uses qualitative data that centres people's experiences and stories of gender and inequalities. Once you are familiar with the key terms and debates around sex and gender, we will look at two different examples to demonstrate how a sociological critique of gender works, focusing on: how gender is lived and how we might explain gender as a form of social organization. The first area is sport, which is almost always divided into male and female competitions and serious gender inequalities, often with different rules for men's and women's competitions and a history of excluding women. Ruling bodies of sport have claimed certainty about who is a woman and who is a man through gender verification testing. Sport is governed by rules that sociologists argue are the everyday interactions of social life. The second case study looks at the socialization of children and examples of raising a child in a gender-neutral way and what we can learn about gender from exploring challenges to traditional, gendered child rearing.

Mapping the Terrain

Gender has not always been a key focus of sociology. The 'founding fathers' of the discipline assumed that 'man' was the (gender-neutral) standard by which everyone was judged rather than being a male norm.

(Continued)

'Men', and more specifically 'man', stood for humanity, as evident in sociology texts with titles like 'man in society'. Terms such as 'mankind' and 'everyman' are still routinely used. 'Womankind' means people who are classified as women and not humanity. Even in the 21st century you will see and hear references to the characteristics, beliefs and practices of 'man'. How often have you heard 'woman' used to describe everyone that is male as well as female? Women per se have played little part in sociological inquiry. By the 1950s, it was argued that women were located within the private arena of the family, for example within functionalist sociological theories (for example Talcott Parsons (1937) and Robert K. Merton (1968), who developed Émile Durkheim's (1956) view of society as an organism with necessary and functional component parts), which saw women and men playing different social roles to facilitate the smooth running of society as a whole (see Chapter 15). Men were breadwinners, fulfilling instrumental roles, whereas women served in what were understood as expressive roles. Gender was social and cultural, but arose from sex, which was biological, with women largely being relegated to and dominated by a reproductive role, whether or not they actually had children.

Early sociological analyses of social relations assumed that:

1. Men stood for humanity and thus for women too.
2. Women, when identified as such, were seen as occupying largely domestic, caring roles. In many sociological texts in the 1950s and 1960s, the only time women were ever included was under the auspices of 'family'.

The rigidity of such views was challenged by feminist critics who argued that there is a distinction between sex and gender. For example, Ann Oakley (1972) argued that sex is biological and closely linked to bodies, especially reproductive capacities, whereas gender is a social and cultural construct seen in: the job you do, domestic and childcare responsibilities, the clothes you wear and the leisure activities you engage in, differing within and across societies. This approach provided ammunition for women coping with discrimination, such as being paid less than men for doing the same job and not having rights over their own bodies in terms of contraception or control over childbirth. This was in stark contrast to policies which reduced women to biology and suggested that the sexed body you have determines everything else, even how much you are paid. Oakley's approach stressed gender as a social institution and made a distinction between social and cultural practices which made and remade gendered identities and sexed bodies and the categories of sex. If gender was cultural, it could be changed.

Although this distinction has endured and still has considerable purchase, the idea that sex and gender can be separated, or that sex is biological and gender cultural, has been questioned. One of the most powerful and influential challenges comes from Judith Butler (1990), who argues that sex as well as gender is socially constructed through iterative acts: what we do and how we do it. Sex and gender are made through repeatedly performing those actions and bodily practices. We define sex from the moment of birth when the infant is accorded a sex based on external physical characteristics, which already carry a series of expectations about what is appropriate for either a female or a male person. The speech act of announcing 'it's a boy' or 'it's a girl' at birth establishes one of two possibilities and, having stated which one, the sex of the new person is made. This is not a one-off event but the beginning of an ongoing process wherein sex and gender are, in Butler's terms, performed, as a baby girl is given pink clothes, we talk to children and give toys differently, depending on perceived gender, etc. This repeats the message that this is a girl or boy and of how she or he is supposed to look, behave and act; this carries on throughout the life course.

If this is how the binary logic of man/women or boy/girl is created, then this is also how it can be subverted and undone. By changing practices (what we wear, how we walk, how we talk, what we do and what we value), the restrictions of sex as well as gender can be transformed. Subsequent developments of Butler's ideas and those of Michel Foucault, upon whose work Butler draws, have opened up new ways of re-thinking gender, including, for example, opening up a space for and instituting non-binary sex. This has impacted upon social policy in multiple ways, from equality legislation, like the UK 2010 Equalities Act, to LGBTQQI (lesbian, gay, bisexual, trans, queer, questioning, intersex) classifications and multiple gender identity options on Facebook (71 at the time of writing). It has also had a role to play in the creation of gender-neutral toilets, which have been a particularly welcome development for people who are non-binary (those who do not see themselves as exclusively male or female and, for example, may choose to be referred to by the pronouns they/them). Feminist research has questioned the 'naturalness' of gendered traits, with men and masculinities also becoming the focus of attention (Anderson and Magrath, 2019; Connell, 2005; Segal, 1990, 2007; Whitehead, 2002). Sex/gender may be a false dichotomy because the two are interrelated and in conversation much of the time, so thinking about sex and gender together, 'sexgender', might be a more useful description and a more productive way of understanding gender (Woodward, 2012).

Sex/Gender

Feminist sociologists put gender on the map first by drawing attention to what is socially specific and distinctive about women and their experience and, second, by researching women's social roles as well as embodied experience, which were often very different from men's. This was a key contribution of the second wave of feminism; the first wave of feminism is understood to be the fight for legal rights and especially women's suffrage (women having the right to vote) and the second wave, which was particularly active from the 1960s to the 1980s, brought together **theoretical** explanations and political activism to combat gender inequalities, showing that 'the personal is political'. Gender impacted upon all aspects of life from housework, contraception and childbirth to law, public life and war, and was worthy of serious research as well as political activism. These were radical suggestions at a time when humanity was coded male and the public arena was male. Women were relegated to the private sphere of domesticity and, by implication, as a result of the artificial separation of public and private spheres, the less important and less powerful half of the world. Feminist sociologists argued that women had been 'hidden from history' (Rowbotham, 1975) in public narratives and allocated seemingly insignificant private roles subsumed into **'family'**, where what women did was mostly taken for granted as 'natural', as if women were biologically programmed to do all the housework and childcare. Marxist feminists argued that women's reproductive labour was essential to the economy in spite of being marginalized and unrewarded within capitalist economies. Ann Oakley's seminal research on domestic labour, *The Sociology of Housework* (1974), detailed the significance of domestic labour and, in particular, its practice by women as everyday routine, as an important and highly relevant focus of sociological inquiry. Oakley's work is important because it puts the specificities of gender into critical sociological analysis through the use of substantial quantitative and qualitative research (the relationship between quantitative and qualitative research is discussed further in Chapter 9).

These feminist views were based on the idea that gender as a social and cultural construct which oppresses women cannot derive entirely from biological or anatomical features. Anthropological evidence of diversity both within societies and between different cultures across the globe supports the view that gender practices are culturally specific and changeable. So too is sex. Sex has been seen as a binary division between male and female, and yet this obscures the diversity within the category female and male. Sex might initially appear to be straightforward: anatomical, biological and genetic, defined by DNA. However, these multiple biological markers do not always coincide, as sex is in fact very complex. In addition, the wide-ranging, repeated, socially reinforced everyday practices of making and re-making gender also impact upon what we think of as sex (Butler, 1990). There is, however, a case for using the term sexgender in order to incorporate distinctive and influential anatomical, genetic and corporeal aspects of sex, and the cultural practices of 'gender as sex' and gender are powerfully interrelated. Sexgender includes culture and biology and shows how they can be inextricably interconnected. Using the concept sexgender means being attentive to the body you have and the shared culture in which you live, and paying attention to the words we use and classifications we have to describe gender identities. The physical body you have matters enormously and powerfully shapes who you are – for example, if you cannot have a baby and want one very much. Contraception for heterosexual people is dependent upon a sexed body, or needing to terminate an unwanted pregnancy, for whatever reason, is an embodied experience and responsibility. Bodies matter, but bodies do not entirely determine how people live their sex and gender. Sexgender is a way to navigate the complex, connected and at times contradictory relations between bodies and experiences. Saying sex is not straightforward does not come at the expense of denying the powerful ways in which sexual differences have been linked to and mark inequalities and experiences. An example of this is childbirth, which has been the basis of significant social inequalities. Maternal and infant morbidity and mortality are heavily dependent upon socio-economic factors. Pain and mortality are corporeal, although in every case the social and cultural meanings shape experience, and what is natural and what is social are deeply interconnected.

Sex and gender have intersected with different social forces, notably race and class, to shape the impact of COVID-19 in often complex ways. More women were diagnosed, possibly because more women are health workers than men, but – once infected – more men have died (Global Health, 2020). Bodies and what they can do are shaped by cultural practices, which include diet, exercise, and how you use your body, such as how you stand, walk and cross your legs. Think about it the next time you're on the underground or on a train, or maybe in a meeting or social gathering. How do men sit and how do women sit? How much space do they occupy? Men often sit with their legs wide apart and occupy a great deal of space, whereas women are expected to sit more primly with their knees together, keeping to their own seat space. As Iris Marion Young argues, girls learn to walk (and throw) in particular ways, so that they seem to be natural, as highlighted in the title of her influential work, 'Throwing Like a Girl' (Young, 1980).

Sexuality is sometimes included in discussions of gender. For example, within the recent classificatory systems of sexgender, such as LGBTQ (lesbian, gay, bi-sexual, trans, queer and others, such as questioning (Q) and intersex (I)), trans is grouped with the sexual orientations of lesbian and gay people. Intersex covers genetic and hormonal variations in determining gender, while trans includes how you see yourself. LGB are classified by the gender of the people to whom you are sexually attracted; in this case, there is a clear connection to gender as sexuality. However, the classification of trans, for example, pertains to gender and not sexuality.

Gender is the preferred term of sociologists and policymakers, used to describe the categories of women and men. Increasingly and more recently, gender includes identities involving the characteristics of both sexes and cannot be clearly put into one of two categories. Gender has been distinguished from sex, with gender denoting social and cultural attributes and sex being biological and physiological and characterized by greater certainty, which can be ascertained and measured. This separation has been challenged. Contemporary **sociology**

GENDER

accepts the interrelationships of sex and gender and uses gender to explore how and why gender as an expression of difference operates in particular societies, and accepts the inequality of such classifications, not least because the vast majority of societies are dominated by the male/female binary, with women having experienced social, political, cultural and economic deprivation and disadvantage in varying degrees.

— Pause for Thought —

Sex and gender as biology and culture elide. Can you think of examples in everyday life of when people determine how someone should behave or act according to their sexgender? It is often especially evident with children, when we react differently to lively behaviour from small boys than from girls. We may be more shocked by violence when perpetrated by women than by men. Can you think of times when 'it's only natural' is based on gender? Later in the chapter, we will look at two different areas – sport and the socialization of children – to explore the relations between bodies, culture, gender norms and practices in the formation of gender and the intersection of gender with other social inequalities and categorizations.

Evidence of Sexgender: Measuring Gender Inequalities

In the contemporary world especially, our understanding about how gender operates in social worlds derives from quantitative (often called 'big') data and qualitative research which provides knowledge about the lived experience of gender in everyday life in different societies and situations. As the United Nations (which now collects evidence about all aspects of gender relations) argues, 'in a digital age, social movements and policy priorities are increasingly shaped by the use of data to inform our daily decisions and help us connect with each other' (UN Data, 2019). The UN defines gender statistics as 'statistics that adequately reflect differences and inequalities in the situation of women and men in all areas of life' (UNSTATS, 2015). These align with sociologists' concerns with what the UN describes as 'differences in health, education, work, family life or general well-being'. The UN, like most sociologists and those who shape social policy, prefers the term 'gender', because of the associations of 'sex' with biological fixity and 'gender' with more fluid and malleable social and cultural practices. More recently, in the coronavirus **pandemic,** reproductive capacities have been underplayed and sex is defined in relation to risk of disease, hormonal and immunological responses and gender, following the UN definition in 2016, as what is expected, allowed and valued in a woman or a man, which is subject to change (Global Health, 2020).

Quantitative **empirical** evidence of gender in everyday life across the globe demonstrates the persistence of gender as a social **force** (UN Women, 2018). Data relating to sex provide part of the story and are very important in informing policy and practice. Including women's experience is relatively new in the collection and collation of such data, giving particular emphasis to differentials in pay and access to education (UN Women, 2018, 2019; UNSTATS, 2015). In the UK, the Office for National Statistics provides evidence, for example, of the gender pay gap, which meant that in the year to April 2019, pay was 8.9% higher for men (ONS, 2019), in spite of the UK having had equal pay since 1970. Such official statistics also cover attitudes to gendered social attitudes, such as responsibilities for housework, childcare and care of dependent family members, which remain disproportionately 'women's work' (ONS, 2019). Recent evidence covers the hitherto private arena of domesticity, including domestic violence, and women's health, such as health and the management of menstruation, in relation to human rights and economic deprivation and local cultural practices (UNPF, 2019).

UN statistics show that gender inequality is a major cause and effect of hunger and poverty worldwide, estimating that 60% of chronically hungry people are women (UN Women, 2019). Similarly, in education, women make up two-thirds of the world's 796 million illiterate people, and only 39% of rural girls go to secondary school compared with 45% of boys. Rates of illiteracy are especially high in some parts of the world; in Cambodia, 48% of rural women are illiterate compared to only 14% of men.

The stark inequities of these data demand explanation. Poverty and economic forces are clearly evident, but the question remains as to why, given very scarce resources, women, for example girls in education, are deemed less deserving than boys. Cultural practices offer some explanation, as does the feminist concept of **patriarchy** (Walby, 1991), which clearly operates in relation to economic forces. Patriarchy is the systemic, organized advantaging of older men over younger men and men who do not conform to a particular version of masculinity, and especially, men over women, in that men and masculinity are valued more than women and femininity. Patriarchy is a **social system** rather than just the practice of individuals. Recent developments (Gilligan and Snider, 2018) of the concept embrace more diversity than the idea as developed by radical feminists in the second wave suggest, but it remains useful for making sense of gender, especially through the intersection of different power axes, such as gender, race, class, **ethnicity**, location and disability.

Qualitative Data

Whereas **quantitative methods** are able to paint a broad picture of the scale of gendered inequalities, as well as the correlations between different factors, **qualitative methods** allow people's voices – particularly women's – to be heard and their experiences made visible. Qualitative methods such as conducting interviews through a feminist lens were a way to access women's experiences, many of which had been hitherto unheard within academic research. This was a way to question and to challenge the implicit maleness and whiteness of academic research (Hesse-Biber, 2007) as well as the presumed neutrality of statistics. Qualitative methods allow exploration of how gender is constituted and experienced in everyday life as well as on the macro scale of big data. Qualitative methods allow insight into lives which are both hidden from history and lived outside the spotlight of a public gaze. They can facilitate access to the relationship between inner worlds of feelings and emotions and outer worlds of cultural **norms**. People have strong personal investment in gender as part of their sense of who they are, which cannot be easily understood from large-scale, quantitative approaches, especially in terms of the contradictory feelings people have about gender identifications.

Feminist qualitative methods allow people's experiences of gendered inequalities to be centred and also entail a political commitment to letting those experiences be heard (Ramazanoglu and Holland, 2002). There are many different qualitative methods, but one of the most widely adopted ones in feminist empirical research is semi-structured interviews (Reinharz, 1992), as open-ended questions allow people to talk about their own stories and experiences. Researchers are encouraged in interviews – and all qualitative methods – to be reflexive, that is, to think about the influence they have had on the participant and the interview data that has been produced. One popular variant of the semi-structured interview in feminist research is the narrative approach. This method focuses on the 'how' and 'what' aspects of stories, allowing an understanding of particular events such as childbirth, or the telling of histories of sexual abuse (Fraser and MacDougall, 2017), to highlight the processes through which wider structural inequalities intersect with personal experiences. Gender is both a personal experience and an embodiment of wider structures, and so narrative **methods** and exploring the stories people tell is one way to understand how the personal is political – a key tension that feminist research explores.

Ethnographic methods are another well-used qualitative approach in feminist research. Participation and observation form the core of these methods, as researchers spend time with people to observe their practices as well as listen to what they say. Observing interactions can be a way to understand how gendered inequalities take place; observations can take place in public settings to highlight how gendered inequalities are part of the everyday world, or in private settings. Woodward (2007) shows how women balance social expectations and their own personal preferences and feelings about their bodies when they get dressed every day. Auto-ethnography is a form of ethnography on the self and can be a way to centre **reflexivity** of our experiences, in particular to reflect upon marginalized identities. For example, Crawley's (2012) autoethnographic work highlights the tensions and relations between being butch and being trans through how the body is experienced and is seen. The emphasis that qualitative methods places on depth and experience allows us to see the relations between multiple forms of oppression and inequalities and how these are negotiated. Skeggs' (1997) ethnographic research with working-class women highlighted how gender and class intersect in their experiences and subjectivities over time.

Expand Your Knowledge

Intersectionality has been developed as a theoretical base for understanding the cumulative nature of gendered inequalities as relational rather than additive – that is to say that different axes of power and social systems such as race, class and gender connect together rather than piling up one on top of another. Kimberlie Crenshaw's (1989) seminal work developed the concept to provide a lens through which to explore how power operates, and in particular in response to the homogeneity of 'woman' coded as white in some feminist schools of thought, to explain the oppression of African American women and how gender worked with race and class in their experience. Racism and patriarchy work together along with other forces and institutions in which inequalities are embedded, such as social class, sexual orientation, disability, regional location and religion.

Embodied Selves

In some of the distinctions that have been made between sex and gender, it is apparent that bodies and biology sometimes elide. Sex may seem to be about the body you have, especially its reproductive capacities and visible differences. Bodies are sexed, through chromosomes and hormones, cellular and bone structure, but they are also social. Bodies are not simply biological, nor are they fixed. Think of how much intervention there is, especially in the contemporary world with its body projects, enhancements and constant monitoring. Nutrition and exercise play key roles in shaping bodies – for example, athletes' bodies and those of people who engage in manual labour will be more muscular.

Bodies are not just biological subjects of the medical sciences: bodies and minds are interrelated and shape who we are, how we feel about ourselves and are always part of the world we live in. Bodies are also political because we define ourselves (and others define us) by our bodies. The body you have, especially if it is marked by visible difference, can challenge expected gender norms and affect how you are seen. Social movements are organized around people's feelings about how they can be defined by their bodies and by their efforts to use their bodies to make new selves and new identities. There is, however, considerable disagreement about the extent to which the physical, anatomical body each of us inhabits determines who we are and how far we can self-identify and adopt whatever identity we choose. This in part is determined by whether gender is viewed as fluid and cultural and sex as biological. Bodies and biology are not the same thing but they are always connected, just as sex and gender are interrelated and cannot be entirely disaggregated. Sometimes bodies and biology matter more than others, however.

Sport is one area of social life in which bodies are central and sexgender plays out in very particular ways. Sport also offers an example of the dilemmas faced when trying to fix gender identity and to limit gender to one of two categories.

Sex Gender Classification in Sport

Sport presents a useful site for looking at gender because it has always been marked by separate competitions for women and men, as well as the exclusion of women from many sports on the grounds of sex gender. For example, women were entirely excluded from the first modern Olympics in 1896 and only very gradually joined in through the 20th century; women's boxing was not included until 2012. Sport is governed by rules and regulatory bodies such as the International Olympic Committee, which has had to engage with changing sexual politics and address questions of gender.

Sport involves two sexes: most competitions are either for women or for men, with a few mixed events, but, on the whole, you have to be one or the other. Sometimes there has been doubt about the sex of women, the implication being that men would cheat and try to pass as women to gain advantage; no woman would ever pretend to be a man, because there would be no competitive benefit. Sport has a long history not only of empirical participation by men, who dominated most sports and competitions until well into the 20th century, but also because sport manifests a particular version of masculinity. This dominant or hegemonic masculinity (Connell, 2005) defines sporting success as competitive, strong, aggressive and powerful, all characteristic of a dominant masculinity. Masculinity is changing, even in sport, with wider inclusion of gay athletes and acknowledgement of men's vulnerabilities, including the incidence of eating disorders and mental health problems among elite male athletes.

Until 2016, sex or gender 'verification tests' were used in order to ascertain 'the truth' of sex, initially by humiliating checks of female athletes' bodies by panels of medical experts which were extended to include psychologists. Recent developments in gender politics and the growing visibility of trans athletes have effected changes. There has been a move from 'objective' testing informed by binary sex, which was subject to assessment by experts, to self-identification and a single criterion: testosterone (Trans, 2019). These debates have implications, first, for how sex and gender are defined and understood and, second, for the importance of women's bodies, for sexual politics and the politics of equality.

The International Olympic Committee (IOC) medical code, Chapter 3 (IOC, 2014), stated that all female competitors are subject to gender verification out of a concern about formerly male athletes participating in women's events. This might be expressed in terms of men's body size and particular musculature and strength, but although less stated, they have participated in men's competitions and benefitted from all the social and cultural advantages of men and masculinity in sport.

One of the few trans male athletes to speak out is Thomas Page McBee (2017). As a child, McBee suffered abuse at the hands of his father and as a poor black girl was grossly mistreated by him. Despite this negative experience of masculinity, he transitioned and came out as a man and became the first ever trans boxer to fight at Madison Square Garden. McBee critiques masculinity as a socio-cultural construct deeply embedded in male bodies and the embodied practices of boxing, and combines the personal and the social in more complex ways than the regulatory bodies of sport. In spite of his negative experiences of masculinity, McBee still felt powerfully and intensely that he was a man. There are other challenges to biological certainties. Self-identification might operate differently if, as in the case of many people, you have some **deviance** from the expected criteria of sexual difference as measured by DNA and hormones.

In August 2009, the black South African 800-metre athlete, Caster Semenya, was suspended from competition until a decision could be made about whether or not she was a woman and, thus, whether she could retain her medal and compete as a woman. The International Association of Athletic Federations (IAAF) instigated testing which ultimately allowed Semenya, who was classified as intersex because of her excessive production of testosterone, to continue to compete as a woman (Woodward, 2012).

Ten years later, the case was re-visited because the criteria had changed and all that mattered was testosterone. In 2019, testosterone levels were the key determinant of a person's ability to compete as a man or as a woman in a shift from the previous use of multiple criteria (the IAAF ruling). In May 2019, Semenya was told she must compete as a man or take oestrogen to reduce her naturally occurring testosterone levels to .5 to combat her hyperandrogenism (an excess of predominantly male hormones such as testosterone, in a female body). She was told this even though she has been female since birth and has only ever participated in women's events.

These debates are contentious and sensitive, but they raise big questions – for example, how sex and gender should be distinguished and how gendered bodies and sexed lives interrelate. The IAAF ruling suggested that sex and gender can be reduced to testosterone levels; this marginalizes life and experience, which are the focus of sociological inquiry, and raises questions about the links between disciplinary fields. It is difficult in sport to be the sex you say you are if your body is classified and measured in reductive ways. In spite of her talent and success, Semenya, as a black athlete from a poor rural family, has not been able to challenge the dominant hierarchies of sport. Race and gender intersect with class privilege across the field of sport; in the following case study, we will address in more depth one of the core questions of this chapter: how does gender intersect with other axes of inequality? We do so through a case study of Serena Williams.

Expand Your Knowledge

- To understand debates within transgender issues within feminism, read: S. Hines (2020) Sex wars and (trans) gender panics: Identity and body politics in contemporary UK feminism. *The Sociological Review* 68(4): 699–717.
- To appreciate the wider context of a backlash against trans rights and the use of 'science', read: R. Pearce, S. Erikainen and B. Vincent (2020) TERF wars: An introduction. *The Sociological Review* 68(4): 677–98.

PART 3 INEQUALITIES AND IDENTITIES

12.1 Key Case

Serena Williams

When Serena Williams won her 21st tennis grand slam at Wimbledon in 2015, instead of focusing on her significant athletic achievement, journalists spoke mainly about her muscular body (Rothenberg, 2015). As a black woman in a mainly white sport, strongly associated with the privileged middle classes and aristocracy, Williams' performance and her athleticism are always framed by race and gender. Williams uses the fact that as a black, African American woman she does not conform to the white gendered norms of tennis to unsettle spectators and commentators by her unconventional clothing and unorthodox behaviour during matches which challenge cultural norms. Williams doesn't hit or serve 'like a girl' or conform to the white feminine norms of the tennis court.

Racialized narratives of popular discourse intersect with those of gender (the topic of race is discussed further in Chapter 13). Rather than performing femininity (Markula and Kennedy, 2012), Williams shapes her own practice and performance and challenges conventional norms of femininity. Bodily practices and training regimes are part of the performance of gender. As an elite athlete, Williams occupies a contradictory position. The very training regimes which render athletes docile also provide them with the means of succeeding and overcoming opposition and re-deploy disciplinary practices to their own ends. As Nancy Spencer argues, 'the most visible traces of scientific racism remain in the obsession with black athletic bodies and black athletes are supposed to have an almost "natural" physicality' (2004: 120), a view which nonetheless unsettles conventional gendered stories of femininity.

In September 2018, Williams called the umpire a liar and a thief when her opponent Naomi Osaka won the US Open final. Instead of adopting the more conventional, passive reaction associated with femininity, especially in tennis, she was politically assertive and accused the umpire of sexism and treating her unfairly as a woman. Noisy arguments and uproars in tennis are usually associated with men, but Williams has quite often included angry protest in her behaviour on court. She has certainly challenged the dress code. She has re-appropriated male behaviour to express her own outrage at how the women's game is marginalized and trivialized as if men's tennis is more serious and substantial than women's.

Pause for Thought

- How does Serena Williams resist and subvert the social norms of the traditional tennis culture?

Think particularly about the differences between her and the mostly white, conservative upper-class audience.

- How are race and gender made visible by Serena Williams?
- What assumptions are made about black athletes and how Serena Williams responds to these?

The example of sport shows how gender is regulated by official rules and institutions as well as cultural norms, and how people respond to these. It highlights the links between bodies, biology and social forces, especially the intersection of class, race and gender. The next example develops this relation between norms and everyday performances and practices.

GENDER

Raising Your Child Gender-Neutral

We have already introduced Butler's idea that gender is a performance that is repeated; this performance comes from how people are categorized and treated as well as how a person dresses, walks and behaves. So, clothing is bought for a girl such as a dress, and the girl, as she grows up, may continue to wear this type of clothing and learns through interacting with others how to become a girl. If practices make gender, then changing practices can also unmake gender. If gender is the source of inequalities, then changing these practices can also be a source of challenging these inequalities. One place where these ideas have been put into practice is in the area of how to bring up boys and girls. In May 2020, Elon Musk (CEO of Tesla) and Grimes (the singer) announced the birth of their first child, and that they would be bringing the child up gender-neutral. Raising your child gender-neutral has become more visible in the last few years, but rejecting gender norms for children has a longer history (such as within second-wave feminism; see Statham, 1986). Elon Musk's decision is mirrored in other celebrity examples, as well as those not in the spotlight.

One couple covered in the popular press is a particularly interesting example to think through. They are bringing up their child Anoush, who they refer to as 'they' rather than 'him' or 'her', as gender-neutral. Family members have not been told the sex the child has been classified as and Anoush is dressed in gender-neutral clothing. They do not want to impose a gender (as clothing, pronouns and naming are seen to do) but instead for the child to choose their own. The parents state that without being seen by others as a particular gender, they can 'grow into their own person' (Whitehead, 2019). The implication is that gender is a restriction and, being free from gender norms, the child will be able to develop their own identity. In this example, identity is seen to precede gender. They want the child to 'choose their gender' when they are old enough. Gender then is presumed to be a choice, although the **age** at which they see this as happening is unclear.

 Pause for Thought

- Think through the example of gender-neutral parenting – how is gender seen? As liberating or as restrictive?
- How does gender-neutral parenting reveal how gender is imposed and experienced through childhood? How can raising a child gender-neutral challenge the norms of gender?

We have already introduced Butler's theory of the performance of gender and how it is created through what people do. Butler also writes about how we are 'subjectivated' by gender, not just 'subjected' (Butler, 1993: 535), as it is also the space in which people may find their identity. Gender is a complex interrelationship between structures and societal expectations and how people identify and see themselves. Examples like this raise the question of how much – even as a child – people can live outside society. The world is heavily gendered, with expectations and interactions being framed through gender. An example like gender-neutral childhood opens up challenges to the gendering of children through a binary logic of boys (blue, cars) and girls (pink, dolls) but also raises many issues of its own.

CHAPTER SUMMARY

This chapter has traced some of the developments in sociological understanding of gender as a useful concept for explaining social relations and inequalities over time and in different places. Gender is an important, fast-changing area of sociological inquiry, which strongly relates to other sociological concerns and theoretical frameworks explored in this book.

- Gender is a social force, which interconnects to other social and political systems and structures, such as class, race and ethnicity.
- Many sociologists prefer the word gender to sex because it can accommodate diversity and the range of cross-cultural practices that are linked to gender.
- Gender is central to people's sense of who they are and thus a key element in identity politics; gender links the personal and the social.
- Sex and gender are closely interconnected and in many ways inextricable since sex as well as gender is socially constructed, making sex gender a useful way of talking about these social forces.
- Trans and queer theories offer a challenge to the narrow binary logic of gender as divided into male and female, and open up the possibilities of non-binary sex and greater fluidity in thinking about gendered bodies and gendered lives.
- Although you cannot simply explain gender by the body a person has, bodies are still central to sex and gender and people can feel that their gender has a complex relation to the body they have.
- Gender interrelates with other social forces and serves to discriminate against groups of people. The persistence of gender inequalities requires explanation and redress through political engagement.

REVIEW QUESTIONS

1. What is gender and what is sex?

    In your answer, try to think about how these definitions have changed over time. Draw from examples to think through how sex and gender are connected. In particular, think through what role culture has.

2. How does gender intersect with other social inequalities?

    As you think about answering this question, what are the inequalities that might be good to think with? Think about what these inequalities are and then how they intersect with gender. What does 'intersectionality' mean and how might this help you to answer this question?

3. What is the difference between qualitative and quantitative data generated on gender?

    Be clear about what the differences are between these two forms of data generation, and then think of the kinds of questions around gender that these methods can answer. You are not trying to see one as 'better' than the other but instead what kind of data around gender the different methods can allow insight into.

4. Why are bodies so important in sport, especially to understanding sex and gender?

    There are separate men's and women's events, but is this based entirely on fixed physical differences? You will need to think about how far bodies are anatomical and biological and the extent to which gendered bodies are socially and culturally defined. Recent new rules about classifying sex suggests that sex as well as gender can be changed and you can be the sex you want to be, even in sport.

Go Further

Books

- Connell, R.W. and Pearse, R. (2014) *Gender*. Oxford: Polity.

This is a clear introduction to the sociology of gender, which traces the historical development of the idea of gender and explores how gender inequalities have been made, with some recent examples and examples from across the globe.

- Mirza, H. and Joseph, C. (eds) (2012) *Black and Postcolonial Feminisms in New Times*. London: Routledge.

This is an edited collection of work on different examples of the intersection of gender, race and class in higher education, which is written by black and postcolonial feminist scholars. The book includes empirical evidence from education and the media with critiques written from postcolonial and anti-racist perspectives.

- Richardson, D. and Robinson, V. (2020) *Introducing Women's Studies,* 5th edition. London: Macmillan/Red Globe Press.

This is an up-to-date collection of wide-ranging accessible critical essays on what is important in contemporary gender studies, including clear summaries of well-illustrated theories.

Articles

- Beechey, V. (1979) On patriarchy. *Feminist Review* 3: 66–82. https://doi.org/10.1057/fr.1979.21

This article is useful as one of the first explanations of patriarchy which put the concept into academic, theoretical discourse as an explanatory concept. Patriarchy *explains* gender inequalities and doesn't just describe them.

- Collins, P.H. (2015) Intersectionality's definitional dilemmas. *Annual Review of Sociology* 41: 1–20.

Patricia Hill Collins has published extensively on the theorization of intersectionality to challenge the idea that oppressive forces like racism and patriarchy and class inequality add on; rather, they intersect. In this article, she problematizes the concept and argues that a major explanatory strength of intersectionality which brings together different forces like race, class, gender, sexuality, ethnicity, nation, and age is the way in which the concept focuses on power and inequality.

- Haraway, D.J. (1988) Situated knowledges: The science question in feminism and the privilege of partial perspective. *Feminist Studies* 14(30): 575–99.

Donna Haraway has been very influential and useful, especially for those working in gender studies, for her creative development of understanding how knowledge comes from different positions. This article shows how useful it is to ask questions about where knowledge comes from, who's making it and stating it, and how knowledge is produced.

(Continued)

PART 3 INEQUALITIES AND IDENTITIES

> ### Websites
>
> - https://repository.duke.edu/dc/wlmpc
>
> This Duke University website includes resources on the Women's Liberation Movement in the 1960s and 1970s in the United States specifically.
>
> - www.bl.uk/sisterhood#
>
> This British Library site includes oral histories of those in the Women's Liberation Movement in the 1970s and 1980s.
>
> - www.sistersuncut.org
>
> This is the website of the campaigning group Sisters Uncut, who take direct action for domestic violence services and is a good example of feminism in action.

REFERENCES

Anderson, E. and Magrath, R. (2019) *Men and Masculinities*. London: Routledge.
Butler, J. (1990) *Gender Trouble: Feminism and the Subversion of Identity*. London: Routledge.
Butler, J. (1993) *Bodies that Matter: On the Discursive Limits of Sex*. London: Routledge.
Connell, R.W. (2005) *Men and Masculinities*, 2nd edition. Cambridge: Polity.
Crawley, S. (2012) Autoethnography as feminist self-interview. In J. Gubrium, J. Holstein, A. Marvasti and K. McKinney (eds) *The SAGE Handbook of Interview Research*. London: Sage, pp. 143–60.
Crenshaw, K. (1989) Demarginalizing the intersection of race and sex: A black feminist critique of antidiscrimination doctrine – Feminist theory and antiracist politics. *University of Chicago Legal Forum* 1(1). Available at: http://chicagounbound.uchicago.edu/cgi/viewcontent.cgi?article=1052&context=uclf (last accessed 31 October 2019).
Durkheim, E. (1956) *Education and Sociology*. London: The Free Press.
Fraser, H. and MacDougall, C. (2017) Doing narrative feminist research: Intersections and challenges. *Qualitative Social Work* 16(2): 240–54.
Gilligan, C. and Snider, N. (2018) *Why Does Patriarchy Persist?* Cambridge: Polity Press.
Global Health (2020) Global Health 5050. Available at: https://globalhealth5050.org/covid19 (last accessed 19 October 2020).
Hesse-Biber, S. (2007) The practice of feminist in-depth interviewing. In S. Hesse-Biber and P. Leavy (eds) *Feminist Research Practice*. London: Sage, pp. 111–47.
IOC (2014) www.childabuseroyalcommission.gov.au/sites/default/files/AOC.0001.001.0001.pdf (last accessed 1 July 2021).
Markula, P. and Kennedy, E. (2012) *Women and Exercise: The Body, Health, and Consumerism*. New York: Routledge.
McBee, T.B. (2017) *Man Alive*. Edinburgh: Canongate Books.
Merton, R.K. (1968) *Social Theory and Social Structure*. New York: Macmillan.
Oakley, A. (1972) *Sex, Gender and Society*. London: Temple Smith.
Oakley, A. (1974) *The Sociology of Housework*. Bristol: Policy Press.

ONS (2019) Gender Pay Gap. Available at: https://amp.usatoday.com/amp/1242832002 (last accessed 31 October 2019).
Parsons, T. (1937) *The Structure of Social Action*. London: The Free Press.
Ramazanoglu, C. and Holland, J. (2002) *Feminist Methodology: Challenges and Choices*. London: Sage.
Reinharz, S. (1992) *Feminist Methods in Social Research*. Oxford: Oxford University Press.
Rothenberg, B. (2015) Tennis's top women balance body image with ambition. *New York Times*, 11 July. Available at: www.nytimes.com/2015/07/11/sports/tennis/tenniss-top-women-balance-body-image-with-quest-for-success.html (last accessed 7 September 2021).
Rowbotham, S. (1975) *Hidden from History: 300 Years of Women's Oppression*. London: Pluto Press.
Segal, L. (1990) *Slow Motion*. London: Virago.
Segal, L. (2007) *Slow Motion: Changing Masculinities, Changing Men*, 3rd edition. London: Palgrave Macmillan.
Skeggs, B. (1997) *Formations of Class and Gender: Becoming Respectable*. London: Sage.
Spencer, N.E. (2004) Sister act VI: Venus and Serena Williams at Indian Wells – 'Sincere fictions' and white racism. *Journal of Sport and Social Issues* 28: 115–35.
Statham, J. (1986) *Daughters and Sons: Experiences of Non-sexist Childraising*. New York: Basil Blackwell.
Trans (2019) www.bbc.com/sport/athletics/50049449.amp (last accessed 1 July 2021).
UN Data (2019) Available at: www.un.org/development/desa/en/news/statistics/better-data-more-gender-equality.html (last accessed 27 October 2019).
UNPF (2019) www.unfpa.org/resources/procurement-procedures (last accessed 1 July 2021).
UNSTATS (2015) Available at: https://unstats.un.org/unsd/demographic-social/gender/index.cshtml
https://unstats.un.org/unsd/GenderStatManual/What-are-gender-stats.ashx
UN Women (2018) Available at: www.unwomen.org/en/digital-library/publications/2018/1/gender-equality-and-big-data (last accessed 27 October 2019).
UN Women (2019) Available at: www.unwomen.org/en/news/in-focus/commission-on-the-status-of-women-2012/facts-and-figures (last accessed 31 October 2019).
Walby, S. (1991) *Theorizing Patriarchy*. Oxford: Blackwell.
Whitehead, J. (2019) Couple raise gender neutral baby. *The Independent*, 17 September. Available at: www.independent.co.uk/life-style/health-and-families/gender-neutral-baby-sex-gender-bias-boy-girl-clothing-a9108126.html (last accessed 30 May 2021).
Whitehead, S.M. (2002) *Men and Masculinities: Key Themes and New Directions*. Cambridge: Polity Press.
Woodward, K. (2012) *Sex, Power and the Games*. Basingstoke: Palgrave Macmillan.
Woodward, S. (2007) *Why Women Wear What They Wear*. London: Berg.
Young, I.M. (1980) Throwing like a girl. *Human Studies* 3: 137–56.

RACE

Tina G. Patel

LEARNING OBJECTIVES

- To outline how race is made significant.
- To understand the contribution of sociological analysis to race, racism, and identity in society.
- To examine the social utility of race and racialization.
- To provide an argument for the continued importance of sociological analysis into race matters.

 Framing Questions

1. How is race socially constructed?
2. What is the sociological commentary on race, racism, and identity?
3. What is racialization and why is it so powerful?
4. How can sociology best address race matters?

Introduction

This chapter aims to introduce you to some of the key sociological discussions around 'race', racism, and identity. Acknowledging the varied cultural and political contexts to how race is situated in countries whose racialized narratives and histories differ, this chapter will primarily focus on UK-based developments – occasionally referring to

RACE

other countries, such as the USA. The remit and readership of this chapter is such that this is considered a good place for you to start.

This chapter will encourage you to examine the concepts of race and racism, particularly their socially constructed nature – that is, how they are shaped by the social and economic structures within which human interaction takes place. There will be a focus on how race is both used as a tool of identification and a means by which power and control are exerted by some over others. In reading the chapter, you will understand the popularity of views on a hierarchy of races – even within the social sciences, and the contributions made by those critical race, anti-racist and social constructionist sociologists to challenge these views, as well as comment more widely on matters of race, identity and inequality. The chapter invites you to critically evaluate racialization processes and consider the value of continued sociological attention. Throughout the chapter, key sociological literature, theory, and empirical research will be covered.

A Note on Terminology

First, it is useful to have some clarification on use of terminology in this chapter. There has in recent times developed a somewhat fierce dispute over whether sociology should continue to use the term 'race' itself, suggesting that doing so gives weight to those who use it as a means of discrimination, exploitation, and abuse. What do you think about this view? Some therefore use the term in 'inverted commas', illustrating simultaneously its meaningful nature and its sociologically contested status. Some call for it to be removed altogether from sociological acknowledgement, opting instead for alternative and/or more representative terms which highlight the socially constructed nature of identity and culture – terms such as ethnicity.

In this chapter, the terms race and racialization are used as shorthand to refer to matters of race, racism, racialization, and identity development. Although not perfect, they are seen as sociologically fitting – acknowledging not only their socially constructed nature but also their use as a tool for exploitation and abuse. This author takes sole responsibility for the adoption of these terms in this chapter – they are not perfect and cause me much discomfort, professionally and personally, but this is a narrative that is beyond the scope of this chapter. For now, you should be able to appreciate that although there is no such thing as race, many behave as if it is real, and that has very real consequences. For this reason, this thing referred to as race should still be sociologically examined and challenged.

Student Voices

'The thing I found most challenging in the module [titled: Intersectionality and Crime], is how I needed to look at the ways in which groups are racialized, and then how this is used to determine who has advantages or disadvantages across their lives, in a whole range of different environments. It was hard to be honest and open about my place and yes, I guess my role in reaping the benefits of such racialization processes – even though I just didn't see my position as a white, male, heterosexual, and middle-class person as a privilege supported by all these various systems. That was really hard to openly acknowledge and unpick. But, by week 3 when I had done this, I felt I was really able to understand the ways in which critical sociology is important.'

Talking about race and related issues can be very difficult. It is uncomfortable and can leave you guilt-ridden to hear about what has been done in the name of race. But this discussion must be had. People experience abuse or death because of views about race, and it is our sociological duty to challenge these views, and to ask how and why these views persist in the powerful ways that they do. This is the importance of critical sociological work.

Mapping the Terrain

Making Race Significant

This section begins by providing you with a background to the scholarly work on race, including a note on some key theorists. During this time, both UK and US thought on the subject shared common ideas. The early commentary on race – a pre-text to what we would term 'classical' thought – can be traced back to the 16th century, where (white = good and black = evil) references to race were viewed in religious terms. Later, during the Enlightenment period (c.1720–1820), various disciplines, including biology, philosophy, history, economics, and political science, categorized humankind into typologies. Based on limited and poorly designed research, British Enlightenment thinkers such as Herbert Spencer (1864) argued that non-white European 'races' were biologically and genetically (read: naturally) inferior. Spencer and others argued that race needed to be understood by combining elements of science with revisionist theology. Race in this sense was used as a marker of identity to then categorize populations based on ideas about human potential, citizenship rights, and deviant tendencies. These ideas contributed to the use of race as a means of abuse, exploitation, and control – including the UK's practices of colonialism and empire building and the US's African slave trade.

Beyond the biological and genetic analysis, there emerged social scientific contributions to how the *idea* of race began. Here, at the start of the 20th century, American sociologist W.E.B. Du Bois offered a critical discussion of race and racialized identity in his ground-breaking *The Souls of Black Folk* (1903), where he sought to highlight the humanity and strength of black populations. Although basing his work on situations faced by black African Americans, the contributions of Du Bois were considered to be of global relevance, particularly for the Pan-Africanism movement. In seeking to understand the black African American experience further, Robert Park (1928) wrote on the complex social and cultural relations found within the urban areas of 1920s and 1930s America – what he called the 'race relations cycle' – which he used to explain the human ecology of black–white relations in the US.

During the 1960s, social science disciplines such as sociology gained momentum in their critical examination of race. This focused on addressing how race was being used as a mechanism for dividing populations according to problematic stereotypes and assumptions that were themselves based on crude characteristics and notions of un/desirability. In sociological terms, then, race is imagined. It is complex, multi-layered and, importantly, it is socially constructed. Racial meanings are 'found' and made significant. UK sociologist Michael Banton (1967) called this 'racialization'. That is making race significant in order to serve racist ends. In developing theorization of race and racism, John Rex (1970) argued that race is linked to marginalization, and constructed within the social and economic structures of a given context. Similarly, Robert Miles (1989) argued that racialization often occurred for the purpose of power, control, and exploitation, which led him to state that we should reject race and instead study how groups come to be racialized as races.

Within this framework, race is a non-essential category whose boundaries change across space, time, and context. This is a point emphasized in the 1990s' UK-based work of sociologist Tariq Modood (1994), who wrote about Islamophobia and critiqued the essentialist tendencies of previous race analysis that dominated the 1960s–80s UK and US. Modood highlighted how although Islamophobia constitutes a form of racism, it also transcends race to factor in important religious and cultural differences. There are 'multi-textured identities' and differences among black, Asian and minority ethnic (BAME) groups which inform experiences of discrimination, and Modood argues that the political and essentialist 'catch-all' conceptualization of a politicized black identity needed to be updated to acknowledge this.

Having provided you with an outline on how race was made significant, the next section gives you a more detailed discussion on the sociological contributions to critically understanding race, racism, and identity in society.

RACE

Understanding Race, Racism, and Identity in Society

The nature and content of race, **racism**, and identity has been subject to much sociological attention over the years. It can be claimed that not only is it one of the most covered subjects in **sociology** but also one that has attracted the most controversy. Earlier claims in the social sciences, including some quarters of sociology, supported views of distinct and separate races. These in effect created race and racial identity, which then created a hierarchical order and legitimized racist practices. This idea of race reinforced views of biological and genetic ordering. In other words, they supported the view that race is something that is natural and (thus, god-)given, and that all ensuing discriminatory actions are therefore justified, and a requirement for a successful society.

Although race need not imply racism, sociologically speaking, the two concepts are inextricably linked. Racism is more than **personal prejudice**. Racism is dis/advantage based on race, which is systematically supported by institutional and cultural power, for instance in their policies and procedures which actively enhance the chances of one group over another. Consider the work of Remi Joseph-Salisbury and Laura Connelly (2018) on powerful racial micro-aggressions within the education system (featured below).

Hear from the Expert

Dr Remi Joseph-Salisbury and Dr Laura Connelly's Research on Racism in Education

Joseph-Salisbury has studied the experiences of young BAME populations within the education system, and Connelly has looked more widely at the policing of vulnerable groups. Together they considered the experiences of racism within English schools in a powerful analysis of the simultaneous embeddedness and enactment of racialized social control within English secondary schools. Using a critical race framework, Joseph-Salisbury and Connelly (2018) focus on black hair as a key site of racialized social control, arguing that the routinized discipline of black hair is a method by which white supremacy becomes centralized – that is, the policing of black hair and the inevitable victimization of black youth permit whiteness to rest in its normative and powerful position. Joseph-Salisbury and Connelly argue that despite claims to be race-neutral and aligned with anti-discrimination/race equality legislation, schools are still able to perform racialized governance behind the **post-race** mask. Schools do this by referring to what they claim are non-racial rules/regulations, i.e. a school uniform policy that is standardized for all pupils, regardless of 'race', etc. Joseph-Salisbury and Connelly use the case study approach (specifically, the case of a 12th-year pupil at Fulham Boys School in England, who was placed in 'isolation', and later threatened with suspension, after the school deemed his dreadlocked hairstyle to be in breach of their uniform policy) to illustrate their argument. Indeed, since their article's publication, other cases from all over the world have emerged to validate their

(Continued)

> arguments around the policing of black hair. For example, consider the case in 2018 of a New Jersey (US) wrestling referee, who told one of the competing students (who identifies as 'multiracial') that due to competition rules (which later were identified as having been misinterpreted by the referee), he could not keep his dreadlocked hair and compete in the match, and moments later proceeded to cut the student's hair at the sidelines. In highlighting the importance of black hair as a site of positive identities (based on racial, ethnic, cultural, religious, and aesthetic self-expression) and where anti-racist resistance occurs, Joseph-Salisbury and Connelly's work makes a significant contribution to the sociological body of knowledge on the normativity and persistent nature of structured racism today. (The **role** of education in relation to race is discussed further in Chapter 19.)

Often, although not always, racism is experienced by non-white, non-European populations, or what is currently referred to in the UK as BAME groups. However, it is important to recognize that racism is complex, varied and at times appears contradictory. Racism can be perpetrated or experienced by any racial group against another (inter-level), as well as being perpetrated by a member within the same racial group (intra-level). For example, consider the practices of '**colourism**' (aka 'shadeism') within some Asian and African communities. In exploring the content of racism, Steve Garner (2010) usefully emphasizes the need for three elements to be incorporated into any definition of racism: first, that it has emerged from a 'historical power relationship' that has racialized groups; second, that it is 'a set of ideas' or an '**ideology** dividing the human race into distinct "races" with specific natural characteristics'; and finally, the idea that 'forms of discrimination' flow from racism. In this sense, racism is both a set of ideas and a set of practices (Garner, 2010: 11). Racism can be individual, collective (or, institutional), direct and indirect, as well as hidden or visible.

The governance of race relations has changed over time. For example, although never subject to legislative restrictions in the UK (unlike in the US, South Africa and (Nazi) Germany), interracial marriage has historically been subject to public hostility on the basis that children born of such unions would pose a threat to the success of the white majority **population**. More recently though, there seems to be a shift in such (informal) governance in somewhat seemingly positive ways – consider the British Royal **family** and Prince Harry's marriage in May 2018 to Meghan Markle (who is of black African American and white European American mixed heritage). However, it is argued that racism still continues today, not least illustrated with the very public racist harassment that has been directed at the afore-mentioned Duchess of Sussex.

At its most basic, race is still used to define, categorize, and hierarchically order population groups. From this, groups are assigned a position of privilege or disadvantage. This is the case despite the existence of equality and anti-discriminatory legislation, such as the UK's Race Relations Act (1965 – amended in 1968, repealed in 1976 and amended again in 2000), which was later replaced by the Equality Act (2010). The legislation is designed to prevent racial discrimination. However, the reality tells us that it continues to fail those who need its protection. Consider here the recent claims of racism within the medical services. For example, in late 2019, UK surgeon of more than 20 years Dr Radhakrishna Shanbhag made national headlines when he reported his disappointment and anger when a patient had

RACE

asked to have a white doctor instead of him. In a powerful interview, Dr Shanbhag demonstrated his commitment to the UK's National Health Service (NHS) but stated that the request and limited response of the NHS to such daily casual racism made him feel 'worthless'. Similarly, at the time of writing the COVID-19 **pandemic** (which is thought to have originated in Wuhan, China) had started to reveal the racist experiences of medical staff of East Asian heritage and/or appearance, who were being subjected to abuse by patients. Indeed, despite the popular claim of a post-race condition (Lee, 2013), racism thrives in contemporary society.

Pause for Thought

It is suggested that racism is a growing and more common occurrence today. Think about recent events and consider the following questions:

- How is racism popularized?
- Is racism today worse than it was in the past?
- Should we pay more attention to other types of discrimination?

Many **social constructionist** sociologists, especially those from critical race positions, contest the claim to a post-race condition, arguing instead that racism has developed into a 'newer' type of racism, 'xeno' in nature and marked out by cultural or national factors, but still underpinned by notions of race and hierarchy (Fekete, 2001; Sivanandan, 2006). In addition, the critical race position argues that racialized experiences are complex, multi-layered, myriad, and are based on the relationship between race and other social variables, for example gender, sexuality, and class, to name a few. Racism's newer/xeno and interconnected nature means that racism persists in even more normative and powerful ways than it has done in the past. For instance, consider the racialized framing of non-racial events, such as the 2012 case centring on the town of Rochdale, England, involving 47 young girls who were identified as victims of child sexual exploitation. The case, like any other child sexual exploitation case, was clearly about the dynamics of power, financial gains (through exploitation), violence, and gender. However, because this case involved white victims (whose victimhood is not denied) and 'brown-bodied' offenders who were either of British Pakistani or Afghan background, and of Muslim faith, the case was immediately framed as an 'Asian Other' problem – a new type of racial crime threat symptomatic of a supposed restrictive Asian culture and pent-up sexual frustration (Patel, 2017). As well as marginalizing the victims, the case presented *all* Asians (itself a broad racialized category) as sexual predators.

From a social constructionist approach, identity is considered to be something that is flexible, negotiated, and the outcome of various socio-political factors. Identity can be something that is assigned by oneself or others, pursued but never achieved, allocated but challenged, as well as created, dismantled, and recreated. In terms of race, identity has often been used to create 'othering' **boundaries** between 'them' and 'us'. As you have just seen, racial identity has often been used for detrimental purposes. However, there have been those instances where racial identity has been used to coordinate collective activism in order to achieve equality and/or justice. For instance, consider the case of the global Black Lives Matter movement.

13.1 Key Case

Social and Political Mobilization in the Black Lives Matter Movement

Research on racialized policing is plentiful (see Spencer et al., 2016), and there are numerous cases illustrating deaths arising from policing, for instance Eric Garner, Michael Brown, and Breonna Taylor in the US, and Jimmy Mubenga, Sarah Reed, and Sheku Bayoh in the UK. The Black Lives Matter (BLM) movement began in 2013, following the acquittal of George Zimmerman, who had shot and killed black African American teenager Trayvon Martin in February 2012. BLM advocate use of non-violent civil disobedience to protest police brutality against BAME citizens and the terrorizing of these citizens more widely in society. On 25 May 2020, a 46-year-old black African American male, George Floyd, was accosted by officers from the Minneapolis Police Department for allegedly attempting to pass a fake $20 bill in a grocery store. During Floyd's arrest, police officer Derek Chauvin was filmed restraining a handcuffed Floyd by kneeling on his neck continuously for approximately 8 minutes. Two other officers, J. Alexander Kueng and Thomas Lane, assisted the restraint, whilst a third, Tou Thao, prevented bystanders from intervening. Footage filmed by these bystanders and the police officers' own bodycam footage showed that Floyd had stated more than 20 times that he could not breathe, had called for his (dead) 'mama' and called out 'I'm going to die'. Two autopsies declared Floyd's death to be homicide, that is, the act of one human being killing another. Floyd's death increased support for the BLM movement and triggered global protests against police racism, brutality, and lack of accountability. The BLM movement highlighted and challenged the normality of white exceptionalism, especially within those spaces historically rooted in colonialism. In doing so, it echoed the work of social scientists such as those discussed in this chapter. (The role of social movements such as Black Lives Matter is discussed further in Chapter 25.)

Now that you have some knowledge of how race is made, and the impact of this, the next section will discuss the relationship between **racialization** and power.

The Social Utility of Race and Racialization

Modern sociological thinking has developed to examine more closely the subject of race, racism, and racial identity from a critical race position. Black feminism, critical whiteness studies, and cultural theory have all emerged from the critical race position. These approaches have highlighted the varied experiences of race, racism, and racial identity, at both individual and group levels, and the interconnected (or intersectional) relationship between race and other social variables, e.g. gender, sexuality, and class. **Theoretical** perspectives from this critical strand are discussed more fully in other parts of this chapter, but for now you are encouraged to explore the contribution of cultural theory and critical whiteness studies.

UK-based cultural theorists Paul Gilroy (1993) and Stuart Hall (1996) both wrote widely on developing an understanding of **racialization** and identity. Gilroy's analysis of African history and cultural construction challenges the idea of ethnic absolutism – that is, a reductive, essentialist understanding of ethnic and national difference, which he argues only serves to separate people and position them within distinctly different social and historical locations. Gilroy highlights the importance of 'double consciousness', and in focusing on populations of the Black Atlantic, i.e. those who suffered from the Atlantic slave trade, argued that they had now developed a relationship with both their land of birth and their European location. They developed a double consciousness and strove to be both black and European. In this sense, one's 'routes' as opposed to one's 'roots', were significant in cultural identity formation(s). Similarly, Hall (1996) argued that racial or what he termed 'cultural identity' is not a fixed, static entity. Rather, it is in a continuous state of transformation and a reflection of our historical and cultural position of the time. For Hall, although we *may* share similarities based on culture and history, we also have significant differences based on how we are positioned by, and indeed position ourselves within, narratives of the past. Cultural identity is not an essence but a positioning which exists through notions of similarity, but significantly also through difference and hybridity – the latter concept highlighting how BAME populations' identities are constantly hybridizing influences from country of heritage (in Africa), the legacy of colonization (in Europe) and more recent experiences from wherever in the world they are currently located. In combination, Gilroy (1993) and Hall (1996) examined the role and power of social institutions in the defining, presentation and control of BAME (or what they termed 'black') bodies within **postcolonial** societies in Europe and the US, and the varied diasporic identities and experiences of those with heritage in ex-colonial territories.

Relatedly, in focusing on the genealogy of race and a history of decolonization in Europe, Frantz Fanon illustrates how race is historically and culturally constructed within a specific political context. Fanon argues that colonial cultures created and legitimized a racialized economic structure, which normalized racialized economic hierarchies, as well as firmly establishing white supremacist systems of power (Fanon, 2004). These racial ideologies continue today, and one of the key contributions of critical whiteness studies is in identifying how 'whiteness' is 'a power relationship' based on the historical circumstances of its situated place. For instance, in places such as the UK and Europe more widely, as well as the US, 'whiteness' for BAME groups is a pervading threat of 'terror', given a history of the use of violence against indigenous populations and colonial subjects (Garner, 2010; hooks, 1992). Whiteness then is powerful, as it has a privileged position of in/visibility given its normalized and dominant position. A legacy of this in terms of racial identity, argues Fanon, is that there are instances where whiteness may be internalized and enacted by 'black subjects' in an attempt to reach a position that is closer to whiteness (advantage) and away from blackness (disadvantage), resulting in a split consciousness.

It was W.E.B. Du Bois (1903) who contributed significantly to our core understanding of identity and self-formation under racialized conditions. Du Bois developed the concept of 'double consciousness' in 'self' to highlight how there is a 'colour line' that creates a different process of self-formation for those groups who are subject to racializing, i.e. black African Americans. Du Bois argued that there were three elements of 'double consciousness'. First, there is 'the veil' (or 'colour line') that separates the races, which determines how the racialized subject and racializing subject each view and experience their social world. Second, there is the internal processing of the external gaze, which gives rise to 'the sense of twoness' where the racialized subject takes the position of two very different worlds (the black one and the white one). Third, there is 'second sight', which is the sense of always looking at one's self through the eyes of others. Considered today as a significant advance on the works of classical sociological theorists George Herbert Mead and Charles Horton Cooley, Du Bois' work at the time was largely ignored, unsurprisingly, some may argue, given the historical dominance of the white male middle-class presence in sociology.

A reading of this chapter so far permits you to be able to consider the argument that racialization serves to 'other' groups. It is used as a tool of power and control, meting out disadvantage to some and privilege to others. As Garner and Selod (2015: 14) note, despite some disagreement in sociology as to what 'racialization' is, 'the overwhelming area of agreement appears to be that racialization is something the powerful do to the less powerful'. Historically, racialization has used 'civilization racism' and 'institutional racism'. In brief, civilization racism refers to the idea that only certain cultures (read: races) are able to progress into a civilized society. Civilization and the claim 'to civilize' has been underpinned with **Eurocentric** and racist ideas about (white) Western progress over the (black) backward populations and, unsurprisingly, was used as a rationale to justify many population control and domination practices, such as the Stolen Generations – the children of Australian Aboriginal and Torres Strait Islander descent who were forcibly removed from their families by Australian government agencies and church missions between the early 1900s and mid-1970s and raised by white families in Australia, some of whom later moved to the UK and US. 'Institutional racism' was first applied and developed by founding members of the US Black Power Movement Stokely Carmichael (who later changed his name to Kwame Ture) and Charles Hamilton, who used the term to refer to the less overt, more subtle forms of racism that operate within society's structures and organizations – for example, the practice of 'redlining' in government home loans in the US which is disadvantageous to minorities (Dreier, 2015). Carmichael and Hamilton argued that institutional racism remains relatively hidden and normalized, meaning that it receives far less public condemnation yet is just as powerful as other (individual) forms of racism. What all these forms of racialization do is to reinforce crude ideas of BAME populations as being unable to be civil members of society.

More recently, sociologists in the UK such as Liz Fekete (2001) and Ambalavaner Sivanandan (2006), have started to discuss newer forms of less overt racism. They argue that racialization has been used to present seemingly non-racial/racist narratives, for instance in the form of '**xeno-racism**', which is a newer type of racism popularized in what is claimed to be post-race times. Xeno-racism expands the racism category by handing out a type of non-colour-coded racism. It is a racism typically aimed at **asylum seeker**s and migrants, even those who appear 'white', and passed off instead as xenophobia – the 'natural' fear of strangers (Sivanandan, 2006: 2). Because xeno-racism is embodied with narratives around nationality and cultural tension, a limit of available resources and services, environmental factors, crime and security and the economy, its nativist elements, i.e. the protection of 'our people', 'our culture', 'our race', ultimately become excuses for continuing to practise racism (Sivanandan, 2006: 2). Consider, for example, Donald J. Trump's 2016 election cycle for President of the US, which sloganized and popularized a call to 'Make America Great Again', and the UK's 'Take Back Control' slogan used in the Leave campaign during the 2016 European Union referendum. In both cases, these slogans could be seen as referring to economic desires. However, they relied heavily on nostalgia around empire (in the UK) and resentment of pre-Civil Rights advances (in the US). The racially coded elements of these slogans were therefore key to stoking hostility towards BAME populations considered a threat to the position of white authority. That is, they talked about racialized zones of inclusion and exclusion.

The Importance of Sociological Analysis in Race Matters

This section will discuss the contribution and significance of the critical approaches to the study of race, identity, and racialization that have developed in more recent times, highlighting in particular the work of black feminism and its conceptualization of '**intersectionality**'. The key concerns of this section are to examine why there is a continued need for such critical approaches and how they can meaningfully penetrate the 'normative whiteness' of both social interactions and the discipline of sociology itself.

RACE

Race is complex, varied, powerful and persistent. It is all of these things whilst at the same time being something that is not actually real. Society treats race as real, and consequently the experiences and life chances of population groups become significantly shaped by race and racialized processes. For sociologists then, race and racialization are important. They remain meaningful – not least analytically, in terms of identity, power relations, ideology, and discrimination. It is the essence and impact of the persistent nature of race and racialization that sociology should address.

 **Pause for Thought**

The value of sociological analysis is important and can contribute significantly to the study of racialization. In drawing on your reading to date, consider the following questions:

- What is the most important contribution sociology can make to the study of race, racism and racialization?
- Do you think sociological investigation into racialization should be the same across the world?
- Does sociology have a universally anti-racist focus?

Race, amongst the sociological community, is agreed to be a **socially constructed** concept, influenced by socio-political conditions of the time: race exists, despite not actually existing. Contributions made by critical race, anti-racist, and social constructionist approaches have been particularly valuable for the **development** of knowledge in this area, specifically critical whiteness studies. In addition, a significant contribution has also been made by black feminism and its conceptualization of 'intersectionality', which your attention will now be drawn to.

It is important to recognize that race and racialization processes vary, given that they are both relational and situational – in other words, fluid and continuously being (re)negotiated. This means that some are subjected to more 'rigorous' and harsher forms of racialization than others. There is a growing body of work that has highlighted this issue. For instance, in drawing on their **empirical** data – a series of 54 semi-structured interviews with Bosnian refugees, community leaders and activists, resettlement workers, and service providers (i.e. nurses, teachers, counsellors and social workers), collected between 2001 and 2003, Colic-Peisker (2005) highlights the fluid and (re)negotiated status of race (in terms of colourism) of Bosnian refugees in Australia, many of whom were Australia's preferred humanitarian immigrants given assumptions held about social-cohesion and resettlement potential, based on their 'Europeanness' and them being 'the right (skin) colour' (Colic-Peisker, 2005: 615). Similarly, in terms of gendered **Orientalism**, Vasquez's (2010) qualitative empirical study of 29 third-generation Mexican Americans highlights gendered racialization processes in a post-race era, specifically how '[w]omen are racialized through exoticization, whereas men are racialized as threats to safety' (Vasquez, 2010: 45).

Black feminism developed as a critique to mainstream (white) feminism, which it argued failed to consider the experiences and needs of black women, especially those from working class or economically deprived backgrounds. Do you think there is a need for different types of feminism, or are all women's causes universally shared? In highlighting the ethnocentric values of mainstream feminism, black feminism argued that there exist significant differences between women in terms of racialized processes. They have a qualitatively different experience from their white/black male and white female counterparts. Black women's experiences, they argued, are based around racist oppression and the struggle to survive and resist such oppression. In this sense, black women can (re)negotiate victim labels and develop in their place ones based on empowerment. Race and racism, then, is not just something to be added onto mainstream feminism, but black feminists argue that it is an important theoretical and social movement in its own right. Black feminism also highlights the gendered nature of differential treatment and/or outcomes to argue more specifically how one's social and political identities combine to create unique modes of discrimination – or intersectional experiences. This theoretical strand emphasizes the relevance of 'intersectionality'. Intersectionality is considered important in enabling sociology to understand the specific multi-layered and varied experiences of BAME groups. (Questions about intersectionality are explored further in Chapters 12, 14, 15 and 16.)

In drawing this chapter to a close, your attention will now be drawn to the potential impact of this sociological consideration for what is often referred to as real-world life matters – specifically, to enhance life chances/experiences and the pursuit of equality and anti-discrimination practices. Here, it is important we recognize that racialization also refers to a self-defining process whereby groups may use the process to racialize themselves in a particular way, in order to assert a positive identity and/or political strategy/organization (Garner and Selod, 2015: 14). In the real world then, it is a very important practice of collectively unifying to challenge discrimination. Consider, for instance, the Black Power movements of the UK and US emerging in the 1960s through to the more recent BLM movement (discussed earlier in this chapter). These movements, and others like them, are activist based which seek to campaign against systematic racism and structural violence by majoritizing and empowering discriminated groups. It is this 'activist' element, in addition to the theoretical one, that makes the sociological contribution to race analysis vital for the development and progression of human society.

CHAPTER SUMMARY

- Race is not a naturally occurring biological trait. It is a status emerging from a socially constructed process influenced by cultural, economic, historical, and political conditions.
- BAME people are persistently presented as biologically or culturally flawed, despite evidence to the contrary. This is used to justify socially- and culturally-based inequalities, such as those in education, employment, healthcare, and the criminal justice system.
- Sociology has historically been dominated by biological and social positivist ideas about race. Recently, these have been theoretically and empirically challenged by critical race, anti-racist and social constructionist sociologists, within black feminism, critical whiteness studies and cultural theory.
- Sociological work has contributed to understanding how race is used to self-identify and empower those in racially marginalized positions. The discipline has also contributed to equality and anti-discrimination legislation, both in its development and as a way of challenging inadequate measures.

REVIEW QUESTIONS

1. What is 'race'? How has it been used and what is its impact? In your answer, think about how race has been defined and who has played a lead role in this defining process.
2. How is context important to understanding race? In your answer, think about the contributions made by biological and social constructionist sociologists, and the period and/or context they were working in.

RACE

3. What is the value of sociology's contribution to the understanding of race, racism, and identity? In your answer, think about the work of critical sociological and anti-racist positions.
4. What is the future of race, both in society and sociology? In your answer, think about the methods for achieving a society free from racism and life-limiting racialized processes.

Go Further

To explore more of the ideas discussed in this chapter, there are a number of recommended sources.

Books

- Anthias, F. and Yuval-Davies, N. (1993) *Racialized Boundaries: Race, Nation, Gender, Colour and Class and the Anti-Racist Struggle.* London: Routledge.

This explores how and why sociology should develop an approach that considers the role of factors in addition to that of race.

- Garner, S. (2010) *Racisms: An Introduction.* London: Sage.

This is a good starting point on the journey of 'race' and racism within society and the discipline of sociology.

- Patel, T.G. (2017) *Race and Society.* London: Sage.

An authoritative yet accessible resource on key developments in 'race' and racialization, in relation to claims of a 'post-race' society.

Journal Articles

- Bonilla-Silva, E. (2017) What we were, what we are, and what we should be: The racial problem of American sociology. *Social Problems* 64: 179–87.

This develops the critical discussion of race, focusing on those areas where race is viewed as absent, such as within the discipline of sociology and in an era marked out as 'post-race'.

- Colic-Peisker, V. (2005) 'At least you're the right colour': Identity and social inclusion of Bosnian refugees in Australia. *Journal of Ethnic and Migration Studies* 31(4): 615–38.

This examines the issue of skin tone politics, alerting you to the varied processes of racialization.

- Meer, N. and Nayak, A. (2015) Race ends where? Race, racism and contemporary sociology. *Sociology* 49(6): 3–20.

This offers an introductory and critically reflective discussion on the journey of race within the discipline of sociology.

(Continued)

> **Websites**
>
> - www.irr.org.uk
>
> The Institute of Race Relations is a UK-based website that offers updated information on race-related research and analysis.
>
> - www.equalityhumanrights.com/en
>
> The Equality and Human Rights Commission is a UK-based website providing details of work that promotes equality and human rights ideals and laws.
>
> - https://blacklivesmatter.com
>
> The Black Lives Matter website outlines the work and activity of an international activist-based organization.

REFERENCES

Banton, M. (1967) *Race Relations*. London: Tavistock.

Colic-Peisker, V. (2005) 'At least you're the right colour': Identity and social inclusion of Bosnian refugees in Australia. *Journal of Ethnic and Migration Studies* 31(4): 615–38.

Dreier, P. (2015) Redlining cities: How banks color community development. *Challenge* 34(6): 15–23.

Du Bois, W.E.B. (1903) *The Souls of Black Folk: Essays and Sketches*. Chicago, IL: A.C. McClurg & Co.

Fanon, F. (2004) *Black Skin, White Masks*. New York: Grove Press.

Fekete, L. (2001) The emergence of xeno-racism. *Race and Class* 43(2): 23–40.

Garner, S. (2010) *Racisms: An Introduction*. London: Sage.

Garner, S. and Selod, S. (2015) The racialization of Muslims: Empirical studies of Islamophobia. *Critical Sociology* 41(1): 9–19.

Gilroy, P. (1993) *The Black Atlantic, Modernity and Double Consciousness*. London: Verso.

Hall, S. (1996) Cultural identity and diaspora. In P. Mongia (ed.) *Contemporary Postcolonial Theory: A Reader*. London: Arnold, pp. 110–21.

hooks, bell (1992) *Representing Whiteness in the Black Imagination*. London: Routledge.

Joseph-Salisbury, R. and Connelly, L. (2018) 'If your hair is relaxed, white people are relaxed. If your hair is nappy, they're not happy': Black hair as a site of 'post-racial' social control in English schools. *Social Sciences* 7(11): 219. DOI: 10.3390/socsci7110219.

Lee, C. (2013) Making race salient: Trayvon Martin and implicit bias in a not yet post-racial society. *GW Law School Public Law and Legal Theory Paper No. 2013-97*.

Miles, R. (1989) *Racism*. London: Routledge.

Modood, T. (1994) Political Blackness and British Asians. *Sociology* 28(4): 859–76.

Park, R. (1928) 'Human migration and the marginal man.' *American Journal of Sociology* 33(6): 881–93.

Patel, T.G. (2017) *Race and Society*. London: Sage.

Rex, J. (1970) *Race Relations in Sociological Theory*. London: Routledge and Kegan.

Sivanandan, A. (2006) Race, terror and civil society. *Race and Class* 47(1): 1–8.

Spencer, H. (1864) *The Principles of Biology*, 2 volumes. London: Williams and Norgate.

Spencer, K.B., Charbonneau, A.K. and Glaser, J. (2016) Implicit bias and policing. *Social and Personality Psychology Compass* 10(1): 50–63.

Vasquez, J.M. (2010) Blurred borders for some but not 'others': Racialization, 'flexible ethnicity', gender, and third-generation Mexican American identity. *Sociological Perspectives* 53(1): 45–71.

14

AGE
Anna Wanka

LEARNING OBJECTIVES

- To discuss sociological theories and concepts regarding social age and **aging**.
- To identify the practices through and domains in which age is socially constructed as a societally relevant category.
- To learn more about the differences among older adults – they are a heterogeneous group.
- To discuss and question age-based stereotypes, attitudes, and discriminatory behaviour towards older adults.

Framing Questions

1. What is age from a sociological perspective?
2. How is age socially constructed?
3. How can older adults be sociologically characterized?
4. What is **ageism**?

PART 3 INEQUALITIES AND IDENTITIES

Introduction

Have you ever waited for the green light when you wanted to cross the road just because there was a child beside you? Have you ever been asked for your ID when buying alcohol? Have you ever wondered if it was time to finish your degree and get a job? If you answered 'yes' to any of these questions, age plays a relevant role in your everyday life. But what is age from a sociological perspective?

The concept of age is highly relevant in contemporary Western societies as well as in various research disciplines, ranging from biology to psychology and sociology. Chronological age usually refers to one's date of birth; biological age assesses one's physical and functional status; psychological age refers to one's psychological development and maturity; and social age is defined as one's location within the life course and the respective social norms, values, and expectations that this location entails (Kohli, 2007). Sociology is predominantly concerned with the last definition. This means that, as sociologists, we ask when and how age becomes relevant as a social category, how this relevance is constructed, and how it contributes to social (in)equalities. This chapter introduces a sociological understanding of age with a focus on older age and the later stages of life. Specifically, it aims to elucidate that aging is not a natural biological process of decline but, largely, a social construct, and that older adults are not a homogeneous but in fact a very diverse social group.

To do so, we first lay out the basic principles of what it means to understand age as a socio-cultural construct. Subsequently, we focus on older age and the field of research that specializes in its analysis, gerontology, and present data and figures on what characterizes older adults as a social group. Finally, we discuss the social problem of ageism, i.e. age-based stereotypes, attitudes, and discriminatory behaviour towards older people.

Based on the author's area of expertise, this chapter is predominantly based on Western literature and perspectives on age and aging and is not necessarily indicative of a seemingly universal experience of aging – which does not exist, as such. If you want to learn more about aging research in different parts of the world, skim to the end of the chapter for journal recommendations.

Mapping the Terrain

When we talk about age, we must be careful with the terms we use. The most basic differentiation in the sociology of age refers to the difference between age, aging, life stages, and the life course.

- Age is a category of difference that can be quantified in a number. From a sociological perspective, it is a social construct that entails specific roles, expectations and practices. Whereas age is a static category, aging is the process of growing older. It refers to the social mobility between age categories.
- Life stages consolidate a sequence of age categories. Together, the sequence of life stages constitutes the life course. The life course is the societal equivalent of the aging process – it shapes ages and life stages with respective institutions (such as school or work), norms, expectations, roles and practices.

Life stages as we know them in modern European societies were 'invented' in different periods: childhood in the 18th century (Ariès, 1962), old age in the late 19th century (Kohli, 2007), adolescence in the early 20th century (Hall, 1904), and prolonged adolescence/adultescence in the late 20th century (Crawford, 2006). Accordingly, they are the product of the very specific period in history in which they emerged and became dominant. But why is it particularly important that sociologists study age today? There are at least two answers to this question: demographic change and social inequalities.

AGE

Demographic Change and Population Aging

We live in times of **demographic change** that are fundamentally transforming the **social structure** of our societies, and we need to study how these changes affect various realms of societies. How age is constructed and negotiated becomes particularly pressing against the backdrop of aging societies.

Demographic change refers to the change in **population** that results from low fertility and mortality, as well as increased life expectancy. Life expectancy at birth amounted to 70.8 years worldwide between 2010 and 2015, with continental differences ranging from 79.2 years in North America to 60.2 in Africa (however, life expectancy has begun to slightly decrease again in the US and Sweden). When talking about the growing number and percentage of older adults as compared to younger adults and children, some researchers also use the terms 'population aging' or 'aging societies'. The United Nations (UN) defines aging societies as having between 7% and 13% of citizens 65 years and older; aged societies have 14% to 20%, and super-aged societies have more than 20%. In 2018, eight of the 28 European countries (including Germany and Italy) as well as Japan were 'super-aged societies'. By 2050, persons aged 60 or over will outnumber adolescents and youth aged 10 to 24 (United Nations, Department of Economic and Social Affairs, 2017).

Age and Social Inequalities

Second, the sociological study of age is of crucial importance to understanding social inequalities, as 'chronological age is one of those key markers – like race and gender – that greatly influence how a person is treated' (Crawford, 2006: 27). This poses various threats to social equality and social inclusion. First, it results in what Riley et al. (1994) called an **age-segregated society**, in which different age groups are assigned specific roles, corresponding institutions (like school), and places. This form of society restricts other age groups' access to certain locations, limiting intergenerational relationships and fostering age-based stereotypes. This becomes, second, particularly problematic when people deviate from the age-based **norms** and roles assigned to them. The concept of **chrononormativity** (cf. Freeman, 2010) refers to this as a system of notions and ideals around proper timing that also entails sanctions for deviations – one can be deemed too young/too old, too early/too late, or too fast/too slow. At age 50, for example, people might be called 'too old' to have children, study, or play lead roles in movies. Deviations from such assessments are, then, sanctioned through different forms of social exclusion – for example, through regulations, like restricting access, or social stigmatization.

This means that today we live in societies in which increasing numbers of people are growing older, and these people are becoming more diverse, but the roles and responsibilities assigned to certain age limits don't change as quickly. Riley et al. (1994) call this phenomenon **'structural lag'**. But how do such assigned roles and responsibilities, as well as the resulting inequalities, emerge? How can we study them from a sociological perspective, and what can we do to overturn the structural lag? These are among the questions that this chapter aims to answer.

Student Voices

'When we first discussed this in class, I didn't think that we live in an age-segregated society, because older adults can go everywhere and do everything that they want. But then I thought about how many friends I have that are 15 years older or younger than me. My friends identify as different genders, they are from different social and cultural backgrounds, but I have no friends older or younger than me. And wouldn't it be strange to have a friend who is twice my age? So, I understood that's what age-segregation means – it's not about explicit rules, but implicit norms.'

Age as a Socio-cultural Construct

Most contemporary sociological research understands age and aging, **life stages** and the **life course** as socio-cultural constructs (cf. Krekula, 2010). But what does this mean? First and foremost, it means that (social) age is not naturally given but socially and culturally constructed (cf. Berger and Luckmann, 1991). Social constructivist approaches to age aim to emancipate it from biological and psychological 'naturalizations' of age categories by arguing that (social) age is **socially constructed** can can be transformed. Age as a social construct is not stable but results from historically, socially, and culturally contingent and dynamic practices and processes. Hence, social age has and is evolving historically and differs depending on the socio-cultural context. Meanings, norms and practices of age differ depending on country and 'culture' (Gullette, 2004). Even across Europe, survey data shows that assessments of 'young' and 'old' differ by up to 18 years (discussed in more detail below) (Abrams et al., 2011).

Various scholars have developed **theoretical** and **empirical** understandings of how 'age' is constituted as a societally relevant category in modern societies. Life stage-specific sub-disciplines, like childhood studies, critical adulthood studies, or critical and **cultural gerontology**, have developed differentiated constructivist perspectives on their particular life stage focus (cf. Katz, 2000; Twigg and Martin, 2015). But how exactly are age and life stages constructed? Sociologists of aging have formulated different answers to this question, depending on their ontological perspective.

Institutional approaches, like that of Martin Kohli (2007), describe the social construction and stabilization of age through social institutions, like work, **family** or retirement, and their respective organizations, policies and regulations, like the right to vote, marry or retire. These institutions provide individuals with orientation for their own biographical trajectories and decisions. For example, not finding a job after school might be interpreted as an individual failure, whereas retiring at the statutory retirement age might be considered well-deserved. Consequently, Kohli understands the standardized sequence of life stages that constitute our life courses, and their close ties to chronological age, as the fundamental socialization programme of our time.

Normative approaches emphasize the age norms that influence and are reproduced through institutional practice, and that materialize in attitudes towards 'age-appropriate' behaviour. Elizabeth Freeman (2010) has coined the term chrononormativity for these norms. Originally formulated in queer theory, her concept refers to the temporal schemes that 'may include (but are not exclusive to) ideas about the "right" time for particular life stages' (Riach et al., 2014: 1678), such as education, childbearing, or the 'right time' to retire.

Post-structural perspectives have criticized both institutional and normative approaches for being overly structuralist and deterministic, however. More recently, practice-theoretical 'un/doing' approaches have been adopted in studying the construction of age. Such approaches build upon concepts of (un)doing gender (cf. Butler, 2004) and (un)doing difference (cf. Hirschauer, 2017) and aim to deconstruct categories of social difference by examining the **social practice**s that make these differences relevant (doing) or irrelevant (undoing) in different contexts. Accounts of doing age often place great emphasis on the socio-materiality of age performances – bodies, spaces and things. From an (un)doing perspective, therefore, age can be understood as a practical accomplishment – not something people are or do, but something that is being done by a variety of actors (Hui et al., 2017). In her work on doing age codings, for example, Clary Krekula (2010) focuses on 'practices of distinction that are based on and preserve representations of actions, phenomena, and characteristics as associated with and applicable to demarcated ages' (p. 7). Such practices constitute age, age groups, life stages and, on a large scale, the life course itself.

However, many social constructivist approaches, as discussed above, tend to treat 'age' as a categorical difference, like race or gender, instead of a continuous process and dynamic marker of difference. People age continuously and hence 'change' their age much more frequently than they might change their gender, race or even socio-economic status. Duality of age as both a category of difference and a process, and hence the mobility between ages as most clearly exemplified in life-course transitions, is not yet sufficiently accounted for in the existing concepts (cf. Van Dyk, 2015).

Older Age as a Stage of Life

The previous section discussed age and aging as categories that are relevant across the life course. In this sense, a toddler is assigned an age as much as a centenarian is, and both are equally in the process of aging. However, very often when we talk about 'age' what we actually mean is 'older age', or the stage of later life. But what is 'older'?

With demographic change, age and aging have both gone through structural and cultural changes. Increased longevity, physical as well as cognitive health, and **socio-cultural changes** have resulted in a variety of lifestyles for those later in life. People live longer, and they stay physically and cognitively fit for a longer period of their lives. Headlines like '60 is the new 40' are, thus, not that wrong after all. These changes are reflected in the subjective perception of age. The gap between subjective age and calendrical age in terms of years becomes greater the older we get (cf. Weiss and Lang, 2012). Featherstone and Hepworth (2005) coined the term **'mask of aging'** for this phenomenon: older adults feel their 'true', youthful inner self being 'masked' by an aging body. The Baby Boomer generation in particular has pushed to increasingly reject old age. With the abandonment of traditional values and ways of living, they rejected traditional definitions of old age too (Gilleard, 2008; Featherstone and Hepworth, 2005). Hence, subjective age can differ greatly from calendric age.

Finally, we can see that the assessment of what 'old' and 'young' means in terms of calendric age differs significantly between different countries. In the European Social Survey 2008, respondents from all across Europe were asked at which ages they perceived 'young' and 'old age' to start. In Greece, people are believed to be 'young' until they reach the age of 52; in Norway, 'young' was only attributed to persons aged 34 or younger. Old age, on the other hand, was perceived to start at 68 in Greece but 55 in Turkey (Abrams et al., 2011).

 — Pause for Thought

- When does 'old age' start, and how can you tell? Does it start with a certain birthday, the greying of hair, retirement or a subjective feeling?

The study of older age, **gerontology**, has emerged against the backdrop of these changes. In a wider sense, the study of age is rooted in the medicalization of the aging body, which started in pre-modern times, and the creation of an elderly population through social surveys, like censuses, and institutions, like the pension system (cf. Katz, 1996; Kohli, 2007; Moreira, 2017). In a narrower sense, what we today consider **social**

gerontology emerged out of the political need to cope with demographic change and the potential shortage of 'younger' workers following the Second World War, when population aging was first framed as a 'social problem' (Vincent, 1996). Whereas gerontology per se refers to the multidisciplinary study of age and aging, including the work of medical, biological and economic researchers, social gerontology focuses on the social aspects of age and aging and includes social psychologists, sociologists, social workers and nursing studies. At the time of its emergence, the social sciences in the United States were dominated by **functionalist** accounts of society, and accordingly, the first social theories of age and aging were functionalist in character (Powell, 2001): disengagement theories (cf. Cumming and Henry, 1979) and activity theories (cf. Havighurst, 1961). Although both kinds of theory have undergone serious criticism and even been pronounced dead in gerontology multiple times, they are still heavily influential in gerontological thinking and policy responses to aging. For this reason, they are discussed in a nutshell below.

- Disengagement theories assume that later life is characterized by an overall disengagement from all social spheres. Society gradually releases a person from their social roles, and the individuals themselves give up these roles – they disengage from work when they (have to) retire, from their parenting **role** when their children move out, from sexuality and social networks, and from the public sphere altogether. Disengagement theories, thus, frame the later stage of life as a societally functional withdrawal with death as its end point (cf. Powell, 2001).
- Activity theories form the (not less normative) counterpart to disengagement theories. They suggest that older age is not necessarily related to loss and withdrawal but should be filled with new roles and activities to enhance health, wellbeing and life satisfaction. Activity theories have been further developed in concepts like successful aging (cf. Rowe and Kahn, 1987) or productive aging (Butler and Gleason, 1985).

— Pause for Thought —

- How do you personally think of older age? Is it a stage of life you are afraid of or look forward to?

Both disengagement and activity theories have been criticized for being overly functionalist, deterministic and normative, relying on and reinforcing deficient images of aging. This criticism is mainly formulated by critical and cultural gerontology.

Critical gerontology is the umbrella term for many sociologists of age and aging. It has evolved from social gerontology along two pathways. One embraced a political economy of aging framework that put structural relationships of power at the centre of analysis and was inspired by the classical critical theory of Adorno and Horkheimer and the political economy of **Marxism** and Neo-Marxism. The second stems from a humanistic (and interdisciplinary) orientation that would share some of the characteristics of today's cultural gerontology (see below).

Cultural gerontology has emerged as a new line of thinking within gerontology and is mainly concerned with the meanings, identities and lived experiences of later life. Compared to general **sociology**, which has witnessed a series of turns towards cultural theory since the 1970s, the cultural turn came relatively late to the study of aging. Central to cultural gerontology is its shift from structural to post-structural theories and its empirical emphasis on culture and consumption as crucial factors in the making of later life. Aside from sociology and social and cultural anthropology, it also involves the humanities.

Despite the emergence of critical and cultural gerontology, however, positivist, functionalist and normative approaches are still widespread in (mainstream) gerontology, and activity theories in particular have gained and maintained political popularity (cf. the European Year of Active Aging in 2012). These theories are attractive to policymakers as they suggest that activity and productivity are not matters of age, and older adults do not need to rely on the welfare **state** as long as they stay active and productive. In the wake of neoliberal politics and the increasing withdrawal of welfare in Western societies, activity theories form the basis for a self-responsibilization of older adults (Katz, 2000). Examples comprise health promotion and lifelong learning programmes, the political imperative to extend working lives, policies for 'aging in place', as well as lifestyle and activity regimes based on self-optimization techniques (Katz, 1996). With gerontology emerging as, and remaining, a highly applied field, it remains in 'danger of "selling its soul"' to such political and economic endeavours (Estes et al., 1992: 60).

——————— Expand Your Knowledge ———————

If you want to learn more about how the study of aging emerged as a research field, and the breadth of gerontological theories, read:

- Katz, S. (1996) *Disciplining Old Age: The Formation of Gerontological Knowledge.* Charlottesville, VA: University of Virginia Press.
- Moreira, T. (2017) *Science, Technology and the Aging Society.* Abingdon: Routledge.

Older Adults as a Social Group

One reason why gerontology has gained momentum as a field of research is the growing number of older adults, resulting from increased longevity and decreased mortality in later life. These developments have caused socio-structural and socio-cultural changes of the aging experience and impact the characteristics of older adults as a social group.

Socio-structural Changes

Increased longevity has resulted in a structural change of age and aging. This means that the socio-structural composition of the group of older adults is changing. Characteristics of this **development** are the growing number of very old adults over the age of 85 (as the fastest growing demographic group), the increase of centenarians (100+ years), or the feminization of old age, i.e. the increasing percentage of women compared to men due to the higher female life expectancy.

Socio-cultural Changes

Complementing structural change, old age has gone through socio-cultural changes. Diverse cultures of aging are emerging in today's societies, resulting in a wide array of lifestyles and milieus among older adults, as well as cultural representations of older adults (Gilleard and Higgs, 2000). In particular, increased longevity has led to the coexistence of different generations of older adults.

Basically, there are two contrasting images of aging that circulate in our societies: the poor, care-dependent elderly and the active, wealthy Baby Boomers. Neither is accurate and sufficient to alone describe the diverse group of older adults. But how can they be characterized?

1. Older adults are heterogeneous in terms of age. The label 'old' applies to a 65-year-old and a 95-year-old alike – whereas a 5-year-old and a 35-year-old would never be put in the same age category. Worldwide, only 2% of the female and 1% of the male population is over 80; however, in Europe, this percentage is nearly four times as high (World Bank, 2017). This group is the fastest growing demographic in Europe and the US.
2. Older adults are predominantly female, as women tend to live longer than men. Worldwide, life expectancy at birth amounted to 73.1 years for women and 68.6 years for men between 2010 and 2015. The difference in life expectancy between the sexes is highest in Europe (seven years). Thus, the older population is predominantly female.
3. Older adults are ethnically diverse. Two-thirds of the world's older population live in developing countries; this percentage is expected to increase to 80% by 2050.
4. Consequently, socio-economic status differs greatly among older adults. The poverty rate among persons aged 60 and older ranged from 2% in the Netherlands (2013) up to 80% in Zambia (2005). This is also due to the fact that, in 2010/12, nearly half of all people over pensionable age did not receive a pension. In most countries, the risk of poverty increases with age and is higher among women than men.
5. Older adults differ in regard to health and care-**dependency**. In 2016, healthy life expectancy amounted to 63.3 years in all OECD countries (Europe: 68.1). However, this does not mean that all older adults are seriously ill, frail or care-dependent. In the US, the chance of living in a nursing home or care facility amounts to about 15% for people 85 years and older, but only 1% for persons between the ages of 65 and 74. In Europe, OECD data suggests that the percentage of persons 65 and older who are institutionalized ranges from less than 2% in Italy or Poland to 8% in Sweden (OECD, 2012). (For a sociological perspective on health, see Chapter 18.)
6. Older adults differ in regard to the vibrancy of their social lives. The majority of older adults are not socially isolated and do not feel lonely. The majority of older adults have a strong family **network** and maintain social contacts beyond the **household**, too. In Europe, most older adults reside with their spouses, whereas in Asia, Africa, Latin America, and the Caribbean, over half of persons aged 60 or over co-reside with a child as well (UN, 2017). There are significant gender differences between European countries, and older women are more likely to live alone than older men. However, living alone does not equal social isolation. Based on data from the sixth wave of the Survey of Health, Aging and Retirement in Europe (SHARE), the average adult aged 60 and older maintains daily contact with more than one person (Fawaz and Mira, 2019). (For more on families and households, see Chapter 15.)
7. Older adults differ regarding the activities they engage in, ranging from paid employment to unpaid reproductive labour, like care-giving for children, grandchildren and parents (in-law), voluntary work or political participation, as well as leisure activities like physical exercise, lifelong learning, or the use of information and communication **technologies**. (For more details and country differences, see the online accessible Active Ageing Index (AAI)). Technology especially has become a vivid (and future) field of gerontological research, with the 'digital divide' concept underlining the differences in technology use between and within older generations (for a research overview, see Wanka and Gallistl, 2018). Older women and older persons of lower socio-economic status groups score lower than older men in all of these areas of activity, except for lifelong learning and care-giving activities. (The diversity of lifestyles is also covered in Chapter 21; the digital divide is further discussed in Chapter 2.)

8. Older adults differ in terms of personality traits, values, and preferences. Recent research findings suggest that personality traits show patterns of change across the life course and into later life (cf. Gouveia et al., 2015). The 2017 Survey for Health, Aging and Retirement in Europe (SHARE) was the first wave to collect the 'Big Five' personality traits (openness to experience, conscientiousness, extraversion, agreeableness and neuroticism). Controlling for the effects of the potentially confounding variables of gender, years of education, and country of residence, Erlich and Litwin (2019) show that there are significant differences in regard to these personality traits among older adults, with the 'oldest old' (older than 80 years) ranking highest in 'agreeableness' and lowest in 'openness'.

Aging researchers have tried to grasp the growing diversity of older adults conceptually in different ways. Neugarten (1974) made one of the first attempts by differentiating between the 'young old' (55 to 74 years) and the 'old old' (75+ years). Laslett (1989) further elaborated on that concept and proposed differentiating between a **third age** and **fourth age** in the second half of the life course. Empirical data, for example from the Berlin Aging Study (BASE), shows that the so-called 'third-agers' are physically and cognitively fit, socially integrated and highly active, whereas the fourth age is characterized by frailty, loss of **autonomy**, skills and resources, and social isolation (Baltes et al., 1999). Cultural gerontologists, on the contrary, argue that the fourth age is not a life stage but a social imaginary, comprising everything today's society detests about aging: decline, dementia and death (cf. Gilleard and Higgs, 2013).

Generational approaches have referred to Karl Mannheim (1928) and applied his conceptualization of generations to the 'Baby Boomers'. This high-birth-rate cohort, born after the Second World War, is of particular interest, as they are now entering the later stage of life. In Western Europe and the US, Baby Boomers grew up in economically and educationally privileged circumstances (as compared to former generations): they profited from the economic growth and educational expansion of the 1960s and 1970s and were the first generation to come of age in the rise of consumerism and mass media. But beyond belonging to the same birth cohort and, on average, a more privileged class than their parents, Baby Boomers also form a community with shared values and beliefs. As the founding fathers of the Cultural Revolution, they established liberal opinions in the fields of sexuality and partnership, education and politics. By abandoning traditional values and ways of living, they rejected traditional ways of aging too; they neither perceive themselves as nor want to be perceived as old people (Gilleard, 2008; Hepworth and Featherstone, 2005).

 — Pause for Thought

- How do you observe the aging of your grandparents and parents?
- Can you see generational differences in how they live their lives in older age?

However, structural and **socio-cultural changes of aging** have not only resulted in older adults living longer, being healthier and sharing more progressive values; they have also created a variety of new demands for age-related welfare services. For example, an increasing number of migrants and refugees are aging in their new home countries (cf. Torres, 2015), and an increasing number of persons identifying as lesbian, gay, bisexual, transgender, or queer (LGBTQ) are growing old (Ward et al., 2012). Furthermore, so-called 'new aging populations' – populations that have previously often not reached older age – are growing in Western societies.

They comprise persons with chronic illnesses, like HIV, persons with physical and mental disabilities, persons suffering from drug addictions, homeless older persons, and older adults with criminal backgrounds. This increasing diversification of older adults results in a variety of new challenges and demands for welfare states, social and health services and age-friendly communities, and provides new fields for aging research.

Ageism

Sociologists should study age because it helps us understand how social inequalities are (re-)produced. In the study of aging, the concept of ageism can be used to analyse age-based stereotypes, attitudes, and age-discriminatory behaviour. First introduced by Robert N. Butler in 1969, he called ageism 'the great sleeper in American life' – a societal challenge comparable to racism. In Butler's definition, ageism subsumes three aspects (Butler, 1980):

1. Prejudice against certain age groups, e.g. older adults or children, life stages, e.g. old age or childhood, or aging as a process,
2. discrimination against these age groups, and
3. institutionalized norms and strategies that support prejudice and discrimination.

The concept of ageism assumes that these three aspects mutually reinforce one another, and a vast body of research supports this assumption, even if the causal relationships are difficult to prove (cf. Voss et al., 2018). But which prejudices towards and stereotypes about older adults can result in age discrimination and social exclusion? Hockey and James (1993) argue that autonomy, self-determination, choice and rationality are traits mainly associated with middle age or adulthood. The current framing of childhood and old age, in contrast, is based upon the non-attribution of autonomy, self-determination and choice, or, more simply, the denial of full personhood (Blatterer, 2009). As Blatterer argues: 'adulthood is a metaphor for membership in society through the attainment of full personhood' (2009: 12). Dependency is one of the dividing lines between age-based ascriptions, 'making childhood and adulthood, immaturity and maturity, into political categories' (Sennett, 2004: 203). Adulthood is assigned more power than childhood or later life. Similar to gender studies, in which researchers analyse the construction of 'male' as the default or neutral category, whereas 'female' is the marked, notable 'other' (cf. Wilkinson, 1996), adulthood is framed as the 'unmarked' age category and childhood and old age as 'others' (cf. Krekula, 2010). (This topic is also covered in Chapter 12.)

14.1 Key Case

Emile Ratelband and the Question of Age Discrimination

In 2018, the ageism debate gained significant media attention through the case of Emile Ratelband, who wanted to legally change his age from 69 to 49, because he felt discriminated against due to his age. Even though this case was ridiculed in the media, the court ruling – dismissing his request – is very revealing in terms of the structuring function that age is assigned in today's Western societies, and the lack of a public discourse or movement around age. 'Rights and obligations are also attached to age … for example, the right to vote, the right to marry, the opportunity to drink alcohol and to drive a car […] Mr Ratelband is at liberty to feel 20 years younger than his real age and to act accordingly', but changing his age in legal documents would have 'undesirable legal and societal implications' and would cause 'all kinds of legal problems' by effectively erasing 20 years of events. In response to the question about why it is possible to legally change one's gender but not one's age, the court referenced the scale of the debate surrounding transgender issues, saying that the global movement had influenced the ruling. As Ratelband was the only person to have asked for their age to be changed, the two issues were not comparable. This ruling suggests that changing the law to allow a person to change their age would be difficult, but possible, if there was a (global) movement for cases like Emile Ratelband's.

Pause for Thought

- What do you think about the possibility of legally changing one's age? What arguments speak for and against it?

Within the past 50 years, many Western societies have established legal protections against age-based discrimination, such as the Discrimination in Employment Act, enacted in the US in 1967, or the 'Allgemeines Gleichbehandlungsgesetz', enacted in Germany in 2006, as well as EU legislation. These laws provide clear definitions of illegal age discrimination (e.g. age-dependent recruiting in the workplace), but do not cover all aspects of life, as the case of Emile Ratelband shows. Age discrimination legislation, moreover, can obviously not forbid age-based stereotypes, prejudices and *everyday ageism*. Survey data from the 2009 European Social Survey (ESS) or the 2012 Eurobarometer suggest that everyday ageism is even more widespread, but less visible, than sexism and racism. ESS data, comprising interviews with 55,000 people across 28 European countries, show that nearly half of all respondents think that age discrimination is a (very) serious problem in their country. More than a third report first-hand discrimination experiences – which is higher than on the grounds of gender or race – such as unfair treatment based on age, being shown a lack of respect because of their age, and/or being insulted, abused, or denied services on the grounds of age (Abrams et al., 2011). Most recently, the COVID **pandemic** has laid bare the rampant ageism that is still widespread in many societies, with older adults being homogeneously assigned to the 'at-risk group', publicly portrayed as being helpless, frail, and in need of protection, and the value of their lives being up for debate (for example, regarding age-based triage; Ayalon et al., 2021).

Hear from the Expert

Examples of ageism are widespread in our societies and touch upon many practical issues, from losing a job or being refused insurance because of your age to receiving lower quality medical service. During the COVID-19 pandemic, ageism has become particularly visible, with many countries discussing age-based triage or isolating people over 70. Like many minority groups, older adults have traditionally been excluded from clinical trials, and only a small part of the medical curriculum is devoted to age and aging, which leads to a lack of understanding of seemingly age-related health issues, says geriatrician Louise Aronson, who observes: 'That's ageism: dismissing an older person's concerns simply because the person is old. It happens all the time.'

PART 3 INEQUALITIES AND IDENTITIES

CHAPTER SUMMARY

- Most contemporary sociological research understands age as a socio-cultural construct, meaning that age is a social category that is assigned to people; that results from historically, socially and culturally contingent and dynamic practices and processes; and that can be changed.
- However, when we talk about age, we very often actually refer to the stage of later life. Demographic, socio-structural and socio-cultural changes have resulted in older adults becoming an increasingly diverse social group in terms of health, socio-economic status, gender (identity) and sexual orientation, ethnicity, social connectedness, leisure lifestyles and personality traits.
- Yet ageism, that is, age-based stereotypes, attitudes and discriminatory behaviour towards older adults, persists in society. Our lives are still largely age-segregated, and chronological age remains one key factor that influences how a person is perceived and treated. As critical sociologists, we should therefore study age because it helps us understand how social inequalities are (re-)produced.

REVIEW QUESTIONS

1. What does it mean to say age is a socio-cultural construct?
2. What changes has aging undergone?
3. How did the study of aging, i.e. gerontology, emerge?
4. What is ageism?

Go Further

Books

- Bengtson, V.L. and Settersten, R.A. (eds) (2016) *Handbook of Theories of Aging*. New York: Springer.

The *Handbook of Theories of Aging* contains a comprehensive collection of theoretical approaches to study aging, from biology to sociology, and new editions are published on a regular basis.

- Minkler, M. and Estes, C.L. (eds) (1999) *Critical Gerontology: Perspectives from Political and Moral Economy*. New York: Baywood.

This seminal work in critical gerontology explores the intersections of race, class, gender and aging in relation to a wide range of contemporary issues in gerontology.

- Twigg, J. and Martin, W. (eds) (2015) *Routledge Handbook of Cultural Gerontology*. London: Routledge.

This publication assembles current developments in aging research after the 'cultural turn' and discusses issues ranging from embodiment to identities, consumption, and leisure, as well as space and time.

Journal Articles

- Ekerdt, D. (1986) The busy ethic: Moral continuity between work and retirement. *The Gerontologist* 26(3): 239–44.

This gerontological classic discusses the phenomenon of a 'busy ethic' among retired adults as a means to defend retired people against judgements of senescence, and defines the retirement **role**.

- Gilleard, C. and Higgs, P. (2013) The fourth age and the concept of a 'social imaginary': A theoretical excursus. *Journal of Aging Studies* 27(4): 368–76.

Complementary to the 'busy ethic' (see above), this seminal paper explores the idea of a 'fourth age', a life stage purely characterized by deficits and decline, as a form of social imaginary in late modernity.

- Katz, S. (2000) Busy bodies. *Journal of Aging Studies* 14(2): 135–52.

With the increasing scientific and political popularity of old-age lifestyles based on activity, this paper examines the theoretical and practical aspects of activity in the gerontological field and considers 'active aging' in the wider political context of a neoliberal 'active society'.

Journal recommendations for global perspectives on age and aging:

- *Anthropology & Aging:* the official journal of the Association for Anthropology, Gerontology, and the Life Course (AAGE), dedicated to the exploration and understanding of aging within and across the diversity of human cultures. University Library System, University of Pittsburgh. Website: https://anthro-age.pitt.edu/ojs/index.php/anthro-age
- *Journal of Cross-Cultural Gerontology*: offers an international and interdisciplinary forum for discussions of the aging process and issues of the aged throughout the world. Springer Nature. Website: www.springer.com/journal/10823

Websites

- Aging Bites, YouTube channel of the British Society for Gerontology: www.youtube.com/user/AgingBites

The YouTube channel of the British Society for Gerontology (BSG) offers a series of short films about gerontological and aging issues.

- International Network for Critical Gerontology: https://criticalgerontology.com

This network aims to connect international scholars and graduate students from various disciplines and provides a space for dialogue about critical perspectives on the study of aging and late life.

- The Big Middle Podcast: Rethinking aging in a world obsessed with youth: http://susanflory.com

In this podcast, journalist Susan Flory discusses provocative questions around a longer, healthy midlife with experts from different fields in order to deconstruct stereotypes about age and aging.

REFERENCES

Abrams, D., Russell, P.S., Vauclair, C-M. and Swift, H.J. (2011) *Ageism in Europe: Findings from the European Social Survey*. London: Age UK.

Ariès, P. (1962) *Centuries of Childhood: A Social History of Family Life*. New York: Vintage Books.

Ayalon, L., Chasteen, A., Diehl, M., Levy, B. R., Neupert, S. D., Rothermund, K., Tesch-Römer, C. and Wahl, H.-W. (2021) Aging in times of the COVID-19 pandemic: Avoiding ageism and fostering intergenerational solidarity. *The Journals of Gerontology: Series B*, 76(2): e49–e52. https://doi.org/10.1093/geronb/gbaa051.

Baltes, P.B., Mayer, K.U. and Berlin-Brandenburgische Akademie der Wissenschaften (eds) (1999) *The Berlin Aging Study: Aging from 70 to 100*. Cambridge: Cambridge University Press.

Berger, P.L. and Luckmann, T. (1991) *The Social Construction of Reality: A Treatise in the Sociology of Knowledge*. Harmondsworth: Penguin.

Blatterer, H. (2009) *Coming of Age in Times of Uncertainty*. New York: Berghahn Books.

Butler, J. (2004) *Undoing Gender*. New York: Routledge.

Butler, R.N. (1980) Ageism: A foreword. *Journal of Social Issues* 36(2): 8–11. DOI: 10.1111/j.1540-4560.1980.tb02018.x.

Butler, R.N. and Gleason, H.P. (eds) (1985) *Productive Aging: Enhancing Vitality in Later Life*. New York: Springer.

Crawford, K. (2006) *Adult Themes: Rewriting the Rules of Adulthood*. Sydney: Pan Macmillan Australia.

Cumming, E. and Henry, W.E. (1979) *Growing Old*. New York: Arno Press.

Erlich, B. and Litwin, H. (2019) Personality, age and the well-being of older Europeans. In A. Börsch-Supan, J. Bristle, K. Andersen-Ranberg, A. Brugiavini, F. Jusot, H. Litwin and G. Weber (eds) *Health and Socio-economic Status over the Life Course*. Oldenbourg: De Gruyter, pp. 35–42.

Estes, C.L., Binney, E.A. and Culbertson, R.A. (1992) The gerontological imagination: Social influences on the development of gerontology, 1945–present. *The International Journal of Aging and Human Development* 35(1): 49–65. DOI: 10.2190/YWL3-WX80-UM2U-YEUN.

Fawaz, Y. and Mira, P. (2019) Bereavement, loneliness and health. In A. Börsch-Supan, J. Bristle, K. Andersen-Ranberg, A. Brugiavini, F. Jusot, H. Litwin and G. Weber (eds) *Health and Socio-economic Status over the Life Course*. London: Degruyter, pp. 259–66.

Featherstone, M. and Hepworth, M. (1991) The mask of ageing and the postmodern life course. In M. Featherstone, M. Hepworth and B. Turner, *The Body: Social Process and Cultural Theory*. London: Sage, pp. 371–89.

Featherstone, M. and Hepworth, M. (2005) Images of ageing: Cultural representations of later life. In M. Johnson (ed.) *The Cambridge Handbook of Age and Ageing*. Cambridge: Cambridge University Press, pp. 354–62.

Freeman, E. (2010) *Time Binds: Queer Temporalities, Queer Histories*. Durham, NC: Duke University Press.

Gilleard, C. (2008) The third age and the Baby Boomers: Two approaches to the social structuring of later life. *International Journal of Ageing and Later Life* 2(2): 13–30. DOI: 10.3384/ijal.1652-8670.072213.

Gilleard, C.J. and Higgs, P. (2000) *Cultures of Ageing: Self, Citizen, and the Body*. Harlow: Prentice Hall.

Gilleard, C.J. and Higgs, P. (2013) *Ageing, Corporeality and Embodiment*. London: Anthem Press.

Gouveia, V.V., Vione, K.C., Milfont, T.L. and Fischer, R. (2015) Patterns of value change during the life span: Some evidence from a functional approach to values. *Personality and Social Psychology Bulletin* 41(9): 1276–90. DOI: 10.1177/0146167215594189.

Gullette, M.M. (2004) *Aged by Culture*. Chicago: University of Chicago Press.

Hall, G.S. (1904) *Adolescence: Its Psychology and Its Relations to Physiology, Anthropology, Sociology, Sex, Crime, Religion, and Education (Vols. I & II)*. New York: D. Appleton & Co.

Havighurst, R.J. (1961) Successful aging. *The Gerontologist* 1(1): 8–13. DOI: 10.1093/geront/1.1.8.

Hirschauer, S. (2017) *Un/doing Differences: Praktiken der Humandifferenzierung (Erste Auflage)*. Weilerswist: Velbrück Wissenschaft.

Hockey, J.L. and James, A. (1993) *Growing Up and Growing Old: Ageing and Dependency in the Life Course*. London: Sage.

Hui, A., Schatzki, T.R. and Shove, E. (eds) (2017) *The Nexus of Practices: Connections, Constellations, Practitioners*. London: Routledge, Taylor & Francis.

Katz, S. (1996) *Disciplining Old Age: The Formation of Gerontological Knowledge*. Charlottesville, VA: University Press of Virginia.

Katz, S. (2000) Busy bodies: Activity, aging, and the management of everyday life. *Journal of Aging Studies* 14(2): 135–52. DOI: 10.1016/S0890-4065(00)80008-0.

Kohli, M. (2007) The institutionalization of the life course: Looking back to look ahead. *Research in Human Development* 4(3–4): 253–71. DOI: 10.1080/15427600701663122.

Krekula, C. (2010) Age coding: On age-based practices of distinction. *International Journal of Ageing and Later Life* 4(2): 7–31. DOI: 10.3384/ijal.1652-8670.09427.

Laslett, P. (1989) *A Fresh Map of Life: The Emergence of the Third Age*. London: Weidenfeld and Nicolson.

Mannheim, K. (1952 [1928]) The problem of generations. In P. Kecskemeti (ed.) *Mannheim: Essays*. London: Routledge, pp. 276–322.

Moreira, T. (2017) *Science, Technology and the Ageing Society*. Abingdon: Routledge.

Mortimer, J.T. and Moen, P. (2016) The changing social construction of age and the life course: Precarious identity and enactment of 'early' and 'encore' stages of adulthood. In M.J. Shanahan, J.T. Mortimer and M. Kirkpatrick Johnson (eds) *Handbook of the Life Course: Volume II*, pp. 111–29.

Neugarten, B.L. (1974) Age groups in American society and the rise of the young-old. *The ANNALS of the American Academy of Political and Social Science* 415(1): 187–98. DOI: 10.1177/000271627441500114.

OECD (2012) OECD *Health Data: Long-term care resources and utilisation*. Paris: Organisation for Economic Co-operation and Development (OECD). www.oecd-ilibrary.org/ content/data/data-00543-en (last accessed 12 February 2013).

Powell, J.L. (2001) Theorising social gerontology: The case of social philosophies of age. *The Internet Journal of Internal Medicine* 2(1). DOI: 10.5580/15d1.

Riach, K., Rumens, N. and Tyler, M. (2014) Un/doing chrononormativity: Negotiating ageing, gender and sexuality in organizational life. *Organization Studies* 35(11): 1677–98. DOI: 10.1177/0170840614550731.

Riley, M.W., Kahn, R.L. and Foner, A. (eds) (1994) *Age and Structural Lag: Society's Failure to Provide Meaningful Opportunities in Work, Family, and Leisure*. New York: Wiley.

Rowe, J. and Kahn, R. (1987) Human aging: Usual and successful. *Science* 237(4811): 143–9. DOI: 10.1126/science.3299702.

Sennett, R. (2004) *Respect in a World of Inequality*. New York: W.W. Norton.

Torres, S. (2015) Expanding the gerontological imagination on ethnicity: Conceptual and theoretical perspectives. *Ageing and Society* 35(5): 935–60. DOI: 10.1017/S0144686X14001330.

Twigg, J. and Martin, W. (eds) (2015) *Routledge Handbook of Cultural Gerontology*. London: Routledge.

United Nations, Department of Economic and Social Affairs, Population Division (2017) *World Population Ageing 2017: Highlights* (ST/ESA/SER.A/397).

Van Dyk, S. (2015) *Soziologie des Alters*. Bielefeld: transcript.

Vincent, J. (1996) Who's afraid of an ageing population? Nationalism, the free market, and the construction of old age as an issue. *Critical Social Policy* 16(47): 3–26. DOI: 10.1177/026101839601604701.

Voss, P., Bodner, E. and Rothermund, K. (2018) Ageism: The relationship between age stereotypes and age discrimination. In L. Ayalon and C. Tesch-Römer (eds) *Contemporary Perspectives on Ageism*. Berlin: Springer, pp. 11–31.

Wanka, A. and Gallistl, V. (2018) Doing age in a digitized world: A material praxeology of aging with technology. *Frontiers in Sociology* 3: 6. DOI: 10.3389/fsoc.2018.00006.

Ward, R., Rivers, I. and Sutherland, M. (eds) (2012) *Lesbian, Gay, Bisexual and Transgender Ageing: Biographical Approaches for Inclusive Care and Support*. London: Jessica Kingsley.

Weiss, D. and Lang, F. (2012) 'They' are old but 'I' feel younger: Age-group dissociation as a self-protective strategy in old age. *Psychology and Aging* 27: 153–63. DOI: 10.1037/a0024887.

Wilkinson, S. (1996) Making connections: *Feminism & Psychology* and the BPS 'Psychology of Women' Section. *Feminism & Psychology* 6(4): 477–80. DOI: 10.1177/0959353596064001.

World Bank (2017) https://data.worldbank.org (last accessed 28 October 2019).

PART 4

CONNECTING THE PERSONAL AND THE SOCIAL

PART 4 CONNECTING THE PERSONAL AND THE SOCIAL

Introduction to Part 4

In examining the relationship between personal life and the social world, the six chapters included in this part of the book demonstrate the ways in which sociology is able to offer insight across a range of social domains and across different macro (structural), meso (organizational) and micro (personal and everyday life) scales. Running through each of the six chapters is an emphasis on the ways in which these sites or domains are not separate silos but are interconnected and relational. In other words, they dynamically influence and shape each other. Family, work, health, education and religion have had a well-established presence in the discipline and have been a focus of much sociological analysis and debate (see Chapters 4 and 6, for example). However, the development of the sociology of personal life has placed a more recent emphasis on the need to acknowledge and examine how personal choice, the life course, bodies, materialities and home spaces, plural notions of families, networks and other close relationships intersect and impact wider social contexts. While they each have distinct areas of consideration, Chapters 14 to 19 all variously demonstrate the impossibility of separating out individual lives from what C. Wright Mills called 'public issues'.

In Chapter 14, Rosalind Edwards examines the meanings that have been attached to the family and the household, exploring who is included in these categories and the social consequences of this. The chapter explores how older understandings and definitions of family have shifted and expanded as part of wider social shifts. Late modernity has been identified as an era in which the family has declined but Edwards argues that what is more evident – and significant – is the increasing diversity and diversification of family forms. This can be seen, for example, in the increase in same-sex families, trans families, global families, blended (step) families, multi-generational and mixed race/multiracial families, but also in the idea of 'chosen families'. In this way friendships and social networks may generate a range of close relationships that take on familial roles in people's everyday lives. However, while sociology has repositioned thinking on families, the chapter argues that more fixed and narrow definitions of what families are have not disappeared, and shows how macro and meso forces (migrant legislation and social welfare policies, for example) continue to be based on (and reinforce) the norms of the 'traditional family'.

Chapter 15 continues to develop the debates about the diversity of families and emphasizes the significance of personal life in sociology. Focusing on intimate social relations and bringing together ideas of close relationships, social ties and the sociology of emotions, the chapter asks us to think about intimacy in ways that go beyond romantic heterosexual couple relationships and reposition intimacy as a much broader category which involves a variety of social relationships and interactions that are constantly re/shaped by social dynamics as well as cultural and geographical contexts. The chapter outlines the different approaches to theorizing intimacy and shows how we can (and need to) understand intimacy in relation to wider social structures and processes. In this way, Katherine Twamley and Julia Carter suture gender, intersectionality, digital societies and globalization into intimacy to show the changes as well as the continuities in our intimate lives.

Chapter 16 considers why we need to think about work sociologically. While the focus on work might seem to signal a shift away from the more micro social worlds discussed in Chapters 14 and 15, Lynne Pettinger reminds us in her chapter that sociology as a discipline allows us to link the global processes and dynamics of economies, industries, labour, markets and consumption with everyday lives, lived experience and our social identities. The chapter outlines the shifting sociological analysis of work in capitalist economies – for example, it looks at factories, Fordism, alienation, emotional work – and pushes us to think about what work actually is,

PART 4 CONNECTING THE PERSONAL AND THE SOCIAL

what it involves and the diverse and the hierarchical forms it takes, paid and unpaid, visible and invisible, valued and undervalued. The chapter uses denim jeans as a case study object through which to explore the global, interconnected processes and inequities of labour, production and consumption, and in doing so the chapter makes links to earlier chapters on social class (Chapter 10) and on the environment (Chapter 2) as it highlights the increasing precarities of employment and the environmental harms of work.

This emphasis on the precarities and the environmental harms resonate with Chapter 17's consideration of health as a sociological domain. In this chapter, Sarah Cant shows us why it is necessary to move away from narrow biomedical understandings of what (physical and mental) health is. The chapter details the ways in which it is possible to identify stark social patterns and inequalities in the experiences of health, illness, medicine, disease and treatment. While the COVID-19 health crisis exposed these in unprecedented ways, the chapter examines the long and persistent nature of health inequalities, detailing entrenched health divisions even in affluent societies like the UK which have free access to health services. Reviewing the ways in which these inequalities are global, gendered, classed and racialized and the ways in which particular groups are medicalized through race, gender and sexuality is a core theme of the chapter. In concluding with an overview of debates about agency and health – e.g. lay knowledge, alternative medicine and healing, health technologies and monitoring apps – the chapter emphasizes how sociological health perspectives powerfully connect macro social processes and outcomes with individual lives and bodies.

Like health and work, education is a social site which has particularly preoccupied sociology. Chapter 18 outlines and examines some of the key reasons for this. Drawing on a range of global and postcolonial debates, the chapter details the entangled and intersectional relationship between what happens in schools, different educational outcomes between different groups of pupils and wider social inequalities. The chapter also discusses alternative approaches to education and introduces inclusive cultural pedagogies which disrupt the hierarchies of the traditional teaching model and recentre pupils. While school-based education inequalities have long interested sociologists, Nasima Hassan invites us to think about education as a more multifaceted, 'holistic' life course set of institutions that can stretch from reception class through to continuing education in older age (see also Chapter 13). The chapter has a particular focus on higher education as a site of social ordering and racialized inequalities. It is only relatively recently that universities have become integral to the sociology of education and the chapter draws on a range of sources, including biographical accounts, to outline the range of decolonizing concerns about race and racism within higher education institutions (see also Chapter 12).

The final chapter in Part 4 considers what is sociological about religion. Chapter 19 explains that for sociologists the focus of inquiry is not the 'existence of god/s' but how, why, in what ways and with what consequences religion is socially meaningful as it shapes societies and personal lives. Like education, religion has a well-established presence in the development of sociology, and in this context Adam Possamai and Kathleen Openshaw outline how sociology has approached and studied religion and increases/declines in levels and forms of religiosity. They highlight the Western/Global North dominance of these approaches (for example, the work of Durkheim and Weber) and map the challenges of defining religion, the uneven rise of secularism as well as the increasing globalization of religion and the ways in which this reflects particular colonial histories and increasing levels of migration and mobility. In this way, the chapter shows how religion adapts and recalibrates itself in relation to social contexts. Demonstrating the dynamic and fluid relationship between abstract structures, social institutions and micro social life, the chapter concludes by considering how religion is lived (and thrives) in day-to-day life, independent of formal or official religious institutions.

PART 4 CONNECTING THE PERSONAL AND THE SOCIAL

Key Questions

- To what extent has sociology moved away from fixed and narrow definitions of what families are?
- How can we understand intimacy sociologically?
- How has the nature of work in capitalist economies evolved and changed?
- What factors explain inequalities in the experiences of health, illness, medicine, disease and treatment?
- What is the relationship between differential educational outcomes and wider social divisions?
- In what ways can we consider religion as a lived experience?

FAMILIES AND HOUSEHOLDS

Rosalind Edwards

LEARNING OBJECTIVES

- To understand the development of key sociological perspectives on families, households and close relationships.
- To apply theoretical and conceptual debates to aspects of contemporary family and household life.
- To enable critical engagement with the issues at stake in debates about family and household lives.
- To understand and evaluate arguments about family and household lifestyles and social change.

 Framing Questions

1. What are families and households?
2. Are families and households changing, and if so how and why?
3. Why do people behave the way that they do in their family and household lives?

PART 4 CONNECTING THE PERSONAL AND THE SOCIAL

Introduction

In this chapter, you will be able to develop your sociological understanding of families and households in contemporary society. We will look at key concepts and debates about what families and households are: ideas about transformations in family lifestyles and household relationships; perspectives on meanings and activities in family lives; and explanations for divisions of household labour and distribution of resources.

Sociological discussions of families and households often revolve around:

- what are called 'grand social theories' that explain how society works and families' part in this, particularly those which suggest that there has been a radical transformation in family life and relationship aspirations, either for good or for ill;
- a more specific 'interpretive' focus on family as an activity encompassing people's identifications, feelings, values, interactions, and the responsibilities that stem from them; and
- challenges to assumptions about social inequalities and family life, including the division of labour in families and households, and the implications of social divisions for how people live their family lives.

We will explore the sociological concepts that guide our understanding of families and households through looking at a set of connected topics, including: administrative statistics, family relationships and their dynamics, and daily living arrangements and decision-making.

Mapping the Terrain

Developments in the Sociological Study of Families and Households

Families are part of our common-sense understandings. We usually have our own families, and we see images of family in soaps and serials, political and celebrity news, our social media timelines, and so on. The families that we *live with* (our everyday experiences of family life) and ideas about the family that we *live by* (our idealized images of family) can be taken for granted (Gillis, 1997). Often, it is asserted that families today are not what they used to be – for good or for ill. Studying families and households from a sociological perspective opens up to question such easy assumptions about the nature of families and social shifts. The sociology of families and households helps us to analyse and think critically about our own and others' ideas about family and household trends and lives, and the wider implications for society.

Sociological concepts and discussions of households and family life revolve around the theme of social change. The dominant focus of these understandings shifts over time, to address prevalent family and household trends. Taking a brief overview of the dominant thrust of sociological conceptualizations of family and household life from the post-war period through to the early 21st century, there has been a gradual shift from a focus on structure and roles, to uncovering negotiation of responsibilities, towards understanding intimate quality and democratized relationships.

Preoccupations with structure, roles and household relations characterized sociological work on families in the post-Second World War period. There were concerns about the stability of marital status and family gender order. Functionalist ideas were influential. These theorized 'the family' as an institution that constituted one of the foundations of society. The nuclear family of male breadwinner and authority and female homemaker and caregiver was said to play a positive part in industrialized societies. It performed functions of the socialization of children and the stabilization of adult relationships that make social order possible (e.g. Parsons and Bales, 1955).

FAMILIES AND HOUSEHOLDS

15.1 Key Case

Post-war Shift

Post-war family studies, such as Michael Young and Peter Willmott's (1957) influential study of extended working-class family life in east London, identified the beginnings of a shift away from a delineated gendered household division of labour towards more home-centred 'companionate' and 'symmetrical' marital relations.

This was succeeded by a desire to take a more critical look at family and household divisions of labour, stimulated by second-wave feminist ideas. A classic example of such work is Ann Oakley's (1974) study of housewives' alienation, challenging assertions about incipient gender symmetry. In the following decades, family lives seemed to be in flux. A growing diversity of family structures (nuclear, step, extended, single parent, cohabiting, transnational, same-sex, and so on) seemed to signal an ebbing of previous norms governing family relationships and responsibilities. Many sociologists moved away from using the term 'the family', referring instead to 'families' to reflect this diversity (e.g. Bernardes, 1985). By the late 20th century, phenomenological analyses had placed an emphasis on meaning. The complex, contingent reality of family to its members became a significant feature of the sociological study of families and households. This work illuminated the interpersonal dynamics of family and household life, demonstrating how relationships are constructed and maintained through routine communication (e.g. Finch and Mason, 1993, discussed below).

Phenomenological investigation of the negotiation of family life transitioned to a concern with the quality of relationships as both a response to and feature of social change. This concern is shaped by one of the most influential 'grand' sociological theses: individualization. The process of individualization is said to have transformed family relationships. In place of prescriptive forms, they have become characterized by values of autonomy, equality, and communication – or at least a desire for these values (this topic is also covered in Chapter 16). Even if these notions have been challenged as the reality of family lives, individualization has formed an intellectual zeitgeist for family and household sociology.

Sociological theories about family and household shift in response to different social conditions, but they do not suddenly disappear as times change. Functionalism as a grand social theory explaining how society works has been robustly criticized, but some of its influences may be seen in sociological debates that are concerned with what family forms mean for society, and why people behave in the way that they do in households. Phenomenological approaches, with their focus on meanings and actions, remain important in studying the detail of family and household life. And the theory of individualization, with its assertion of freedom from standard family obligations, has been highly influential. These perspectives can all be seen in the elements of understanding families and households in contemporary society that are covered in the rest of this chapter.

Understanding Families and Households in Contemporary Society

Describing all the sociological concepts and approaches that can be applied to understanding families and households usually takes up a whole book. In this chapter, therefore, we will look at some of the prevalent ideas that provide a lens on contemporary **family** life. These cover different definitions of families and households, debates about transformations in family and **household** lifestyles, concepts we can use to focus on the detail of family life, and theories for understanding how and why household members divide their labour.

What Are Families and Households?

In everyday language, our understanding of 'families' and 'households' is often taken for granted. We do not have to explain what we mean when we use these terms, and we can take them to mean the same thing. But this sort of common use can hide a diversity of relationships and understandings between people. As sociological concepts, families and households mean quite different things.

Family usually refers to the bonds of blood, legal or intimate relationships that endure over time and across generations. But everyday life makes this more complex, and specifying who belongs to families is not straightforward because, as we will see, family can be just as much about meaning as it is about particular structures. Household commonly refers to a physical structure that houses or provides shelter for people and directs attention to practical resources in everyday living. A household can contain an individual, or it can contain a social group who sleep under the same roof and typically share a range of domestic activities, such as housework and meals. The people involved do not necessarily need to have any kinship link with each other, as in shared student rentals.

The sociological concept of **boundaries** can help in drawing attention to knotty questions around who is 'in' and who is 'out' in different definitions and understandings of families and households. Boundaries can include or exclude people in several ways. This can be in a spatial sense, as in who lives under the roof of a household; in a symbolic sense, as in who is considered a member of a family through kinship terminology (grandparent, aunt, brother, niece, etc.); and in a relational sense, through intimacies and interdependencies between people (siblings feeling deep attachment to each other, adult children caring for elderly parents). Who is considered inside and who is outside a family or household boundary can vary according to time and place, such as grandchildren being legally required to care for grandparents under Chinese law but not in the US (Silverstein and Xu, 2017), as well as who is doing the drawing and defining (McKie et al., 2005).

A focus on the permeation or coherence of boundaries highlights the way that official statistics in many Global North countries conflate family and household, idealizing the nuclear family of parents living together with their children as the baseline. In the UK, the Office for National Statistics uses the following definitions (www.ons.gov.uk):

A family is a married, civil partnered or cohabiting couple with or without children, or a lone parent, with at least one child, who live at the same address. Children may be dependent or non-dependent.
A household is one person living alone, or a group of people (not necessarily related) living at the same address who share cooking facilities and share a living room, sitting room or dining area. A household can consist of a single family, more than one family, or no families in the case of a group of unrelated people.

We can see that the boundary drawn around what is considered family for administrative statistical purposes is equated with household (the same address) but that while two adults do not need resident children to be a family, a lone parent does.

Where parents are separated or divorced, or as part of extended families, children may live in more than one household and different families. Children's and adult's considerations about who is 'their' family can be quite different from predefined categories. It may vary between family members in the same household, stretch outside a household boundary and shift across time and circumstances (e.g. Sweeting and Seaman, 2005). 'Community mothering' has long roots across black communities in Britain, the Caribbean and the US. Black women may take a collective responsibility for children, whether biologically related and co-resident or not, and 'family language' situates non-kin within the boundary of family (Reynolds, 2003). Pets can also be considered as family members (Charles and Davies, 2008). The sociological concepts of **families of choice** and **queer families**, emphasizing achieved (made) rather than ascribed (given) relationships (which we return to below), similarly reshape the conventional boundaries of who is considered family. Sociological interrogation of who is and is not family, and of whether or not this coincides with household co-residence, illuminates the complexities involved.

Hear from the Expert

Living Apart Together (LAT) Relationships

LAT refers to 'living apart together', where people are in a long-term partner relationship, and they and other people regard them as a couple, but they live separately for most of the time. They may be of the same sex as well as opposite sexes, they may or may not be married to each other, they may have joint children, and either partner may be living in a household containing other people. They may live nearby each other, or in different countries. As a category, LAT contains different sorts of relationship, with different needs and desires around personal autonomy, emotional management, couple intimacy, other family commitments, and how to respond to external circumstances (Duncan et al., 2013).

 —— Pause for Thought ——

- Where might the boundaries of family and household lie in the case of LAT (Living Apart Together) relationships, and from whose perspective?

As well as raising difficult questions about definitions, the sociological concepts of families and households each direct our attention to different sorts of issues. A focus on families places emphasis on relationships between generations across households as well as within them, while a focus on households puts more emphasis on domestic organization between people who are co-resident. Nonetheless, the concepts of family and household can merge into one another in **sociology** as much as they do in everyday life. Indeed, the majority of households contain family members who are living together, so questions of relationships and resources are often interlinked. These two issues, relationships and resources, will recur throughout the discussion in the rest of this chapter.

Expand Your Knowledge

- Dyer, H., Sinclair-Palm, J. and Yeo, M. (2020) Drawing queer and trans kinship with children: Affect, cohabitation and reciprocal care. *Review of Education, Pedagogy and Cultural Studies.* DOI: 10.1080/10714413.2020.1724764
- Pallotta-Chiarolli, M., Sheff, E. and Mountford, R. (2020) Polyamorous parenting in contemporary research: Developments and future directions. In A.E. Goldberg and K.R. Allen (eds) *LGBTQ-Parent Families: Innovations in Research and Implications for Practice.* Cham: Springer, pp. 171–83.

Ideas about Transformations in Family and Household Life

Statistics showing changes in household and family structures over time are often cited as evidence of radical transformations in our family and household relationships since the mid-20th century. Such changes include marriage at a later **age**, more cohabitation, and births outside marriage (Hunt, 2009). Just as the theory of **functionalism** exerted an influence over sociological work on families and households in the 1950s and '60s, **individualization** has been a hotly debated thesis in contemporary family studies.

The individualization thesis posits that family obligations and permanent ties have lost their relevance (this topic is also covered in Chapter 16). The thesis claims that the universal education, economic growth, comprehensive welfare **state** and freely available contraception that were embedded in state provision by the 1960s led to greater choice in the types of families that people can form and the sorts of lifestyles that they can live. This has led to a diversity of family forms.

Marriage, it is said, is no longer a necessary **institution** for sex, reproduction, or social status. People are rejecting hierarchical gender and generational relations. This means parent–child communication has become characterized by mutual respect and negotiation. The idea of families of choice, where people create their own families of chosen friends and (ex)lovers as well as selected kin (Weeks et al., 2001), is regarded as an exemplar of trends associated with individualization. **Same-sex relationships** are posed as being in the vanguard of experimenting with new forms of kinship, and the term queer families has been developed to describe a set of identities that represent family lifestyles that challenge traditional and heteronormative binaries (Fish and Russell, 2018). Marriage and family are said to have shifted from being a legal and social institution to being personal concerns about intimate relationships.

In sum, in the individualization thesis family is subject to broad processes of **detraditionalization**, where people are able to create their lives and relationships without reference to past orthodoxies, and relationships are subject to **democratization** in the values of **autonomy** and equality that guide them.

In some sociological views, individualization processes have opened up family lives in a positive way, other assessments are ambivalent, and for yet others such processes signal the rise of damaging self-absorption. An optimistic view of individualization and its implications for family relationships is evident in the work of Anthony Giddens (1992). Individuals have become 'disembedded' from traditional family roles, enabling them to seek out new life experiments involving democratic, autonomous, open and mutual relationships.

Other noted individualization theorists, such as Ulrich Beck and Elisabeth Beck-Gernsheim (1995), are more circumspect. For them, the high expectations about egalitarian and emotionally satisfying family relationships flounder in the reality of everyday life. They posit post-familial families, where people create families, leave them and then create other families in search of a fulfilling **intimacy** to ease their inner dissatisfaction.

In contrast to Giddens' stress on active and positive choice in family living, Beck and Beck-Gernsheim say people *must* (are forced to) choose. Children take on a new significance in this scenario, promising a profound and durable loving bond that contrasts with fragile adult intimate relationships.

Other assessments regard individualization as more akin to individualism, creating fractured families and selfish individuals. Children's wellbeing is said to be damaged by rejection of the married-parent nuclear family (Popenoe, 2017). Democratization results in a loss of control by parents over children, with harmful consequences for wider social order. It is claimed that the forces of detraditionalization promote choice at the expense of commitment to family and parenting. This has led to demoralization, resulting in **conflict**, unhappiness and family breakdown (Fevre, 2000).

Another sociological assessment of the individualization thesis is that it has been overemphasized and offers less understanding of contemporary family life than supposed. Lynn Jamieson (1998), for example, highlights continued systematic gender inequality that has implications for divisions of labour in the household. After reviewing the evidence, she finds little to support assertions that detraditionalization and democratization are the driving motifs of contemporary family relationships. Rather, studies point to the broad and contradictory complexity of intimacy and family life across time (Jamieson, 1998). Indeed, the practice of community mothering in black communities, mentioned in the section above, suggests such practices are as much long-standing as they are new life experiments.

Hear from the Expert

Perspectives on Same-sex Marriage

While the norms, values and practices of heterosexual marriages are often assumed to be socially 'given' along gendered lines, those linked to same-sex relationships are often assumed to be creatively 'made' in the absence of clear-cut gender differences. This is a crude take on relational agency and power that undermines developments in heterosexual and same-sex relationships, which are intrinsically interlinked. The fact is that social changes are reconfiguring marriage, heterosexuality, homosexuality and gender in situated ways on the ground, and legal developments in same-sex marriage are linked to these … It would be mistaken to see marriage as a static and omnipotent institution or to ignore that marriage continues to speak to relational ideals, imaginaries and practices in powerful ways … Notable findings from our research include the common belief among younger same-sex partners that gender and sexual inequalities in relationships have largely been overcome, and that couple-centred life remains the obvious and natural answer to life-political questions about how to live and relate. These beliefs partly influenced many partners' claims to have 'ordinary' marriages, which in turn were grounded in a conviction that contemporary heterosexual and same-sex relationships were much the same.

Heaphy, B., Smart, C. and Einarsdottir, A. (2013) *Same Sex Marriages: New Generations, New Relationships.* Basingstoke: Palgrave, pp. viii–ix and 5. Reproduced with permission of the Licensor through PLSclear.

(Continued)

PART 4 CONNECTING THE PERSONAL AND THE SOCIAL

> [Some] claim that same-sex marriage would be different from heterosexual marriage and as such would challenge its traditional heteronormative ideologies ... [But] the key criticisms made by second wave feminists related to not only the gendered division of labour and other unequal power relationships within individual marriages but also the privatization of reproduction and caretaking within the family. I argue that these concerns are no less relevant to contemporary marriage ... While same-sex marriage would be hugely significant in providing symbolic recognition that lesbians and gay men are fit to participate in the institution of marriage and family, a queer and feminist lens also highlights the privileging of the monogamous sexual relationship over other forms of family.
>
> Barker, N. (2012) *Not the Marrying Kind: A Feminist Critique of Same-Sex Marriage*.
> Basingstoke: Palgrave Macmillan, pp. 1, 3, 4 and 15.
> Reproduced with permission of the Licensor through PLSclear.

— Pause for Thought —

- Is same-sex marriage an example of individualization and creative new relationships, or of imitating a heterosexual institution and conventions?

— Expand Your Knowledge —

- Charsley, K., Bolognani, M., Ersanilli, E. and Spencer, S. (2020) Family relations: Extended family living, gender and 'traditionalism'. In *Marriage, Migration and Integration*. Cham: Palgrave Macmillan, Ch. 7, pp. 197–226.
- Morris, C. (2019) 'I wanted a happy ever after life': Love, romance and disappointment in heterosexual single mothers' intimacy scripts. In J. Carter and L. Arocha (eds) *Romantic Relationships in a Time of 'Cold Intimacies'*. Basingstoke: Palgrave Macmillan, pp. 261–83.

The individualization thesis has also been criticized for being an abstracted **social theory**, disengaged from people's everyday relations. In response, Carol Smart (2007) has developed the sociological concept of **'personal life'** in order to address these issues, as well as to acknowledge diversity in people's close and family relationships. Smart argues that the idea moves sociological thinking beyond the heteronormative and gender ideologies embedded in the term 'family', and the privileging of household arrangements associated with institutionalized biological kin or marriage. At the same time as the term 'personal life' rejects the individualization thesis, however, her argument that fluid reconfigurations of conventionally understood families need to be centred also builds on its ideas about detraditionalization.

The concept of 'personal life' proposed by Smart is an inherently relational view of people's lives. Personal life comprises connections to a range of significant others that shape people's sense of self, social and generational relationships. For Smart, the concept brings together sexuality, bodies, emotions, intimacy, memories and desires. Indeed, she argues for a shift away from use of the term 'family' in sociological work. Rather, it can be subordinated within the broader idea of 'personal life' as just one of many forms of intimate relationships in contemporary society.

The notion of 'personal life' has the merits of challenging assumptions of 'traditional' family that, for example, equate the term with household, and throwing the spotlight on the often fraught emotions in our intimate relationships. Whether or not it is able to replace or encompass the concept of family in sociological understandings, however, is subject to debate. There are conceptual and **empirical** issues related to family that are not captured by 'personal life'. Conceptually, the self is still pivotal in 'personal lives', even if relational, whereas family enables a focus on generational collectivities over time that would otherwise be lost (Edwards et al., 2012). Empirically, family still exercises influence as an institution, including through inheritance law whereby the state prioritizes particular generational biological and marital relations. The boundaries around particular sorts of families and households constructed by administrative statistics and social policies that we noted above, cannot be analysed through the lens of personal life (Edwards et al., 2012). In order to identify and analyse a sense of collective fusion beyond the self, or the **labelling** of boundaries between types of families and households, it is important to retain family and household as distinct sociological concepts.

Ideas about radical changes in family life shape political debates and are popular in media discussion, mainly in the form of claims about social breakdown. Sociological viewpoints are essential here, so that such ideas are opened up to scrutiny.

A Focus on Meanings and Actions in Family Life

A focus on transformations in family and household life has led to questions about how people live their relationships under such circumstances. Phenomenological and interpretive approaches draw attention to the way people's own family meanings are created through routine and mundane, as well as special, interactions and activities. From this perspective, family sociologists have identified 'negotiation' between family members, the active 'doing' of family, and members 'displaying' their family relationships to each other, as key motifs of fluid contemporary family lives.

The concept of **negotiation** draws attention to the interactions between family members about how to understand a situation and the course of action that emerges from these understandings. Negotiation as an aspect of family life is invoked in Peter Berger and Hansfried Kellner's (1964) classic sociological discussion of marital life in the mid-20th century US. They proposed that, through their everyday interactions, husbands and wives constantly construct, develop and reaffirm a taken-for-granted shared sense of a meaningful reality in their relationship, parenting and family life. The concept of negotiation has been developed analytically by Janet Finch and Jennifer Mason (1993) as part of their work on obligations between adult kin. They argue that, rather than being duty-bound by ascribed rules of relationships status – for example, adult children owing a duty of care to elderly parents – the nature of family members' responsibilities to each other (or not) is shaped by negotiated understandings and commitments worked out and accumulated over time.

Also rooted in the premise that the contemporary family is not a static structure, common household residence or institutionalized ties, the UK family sociologist David Morgan (e.g. 2011) developed the concept of '**family practices**'. Family practices draw attention to the 'doing' of family as an activity, rather than a form or an institution to which individuals belong. The concept is a major contribution to the field of family sociology and study of families because it highlights the need to define and understand families by what family members do, rather than only by co-residence, kinship and marriage. Morgan argues that because contemporary society is complex and fluid, family needs to be actively constructed by its members. It is the participation in family practices that produces family relationships and thus families. Family practices are broadly everything concerning relationships and activities that are to do with family matters:

- the perspectives of family members themselves as the actors, and also the evaluations of observers such as other family members, neighbours, social workers – and indeed the definitions of administrative statistics we looked at earlier in this chapter, as well as the interactions between these viewpoints;
- the sense of action rather than an object – family is something that people 'do' rather than something people 'are', like family get-togethers and outings or family arguments;
- the daily, mundane activities that are linked to wider systems of meaning about family in society, that locate unremarkable activities within wider social understandings of family life, such as everyday preparation of family meals, bathing the children, etc.;
- habit, regularity, ritual and repetition – for example, children's bedtime, family lunch on a Sunday, who sits where in the living room;
- fluid and open-ended – family practices relate to other values and practices, such as how people from particular ethnic, religious or social class groups live their family lives – for example, acting as a good oldest son in a Chinese family;
- forming a link between history and biography, with understandings of family relationships and the carrying out of activities being shaped both by a family member's biography and by social and historical context.

The concept of **display** is an extension of family practices, developed by Janet Finch (2007). She argues that family members need to 'display' as well as 'do' their family, and claims that relationships do not exist as family relationships unless they can be successfully displayed as such. Examples of how display may occur are through direct social interactions that demonstrate and affirm the quality of the familial relationships in question, and through the use of tools such as photos, keepsakes, family stories and domestic objects. As with ideas about negotiation and practices, Finch says that the reason people need to convey family relationships to each other through display is because today's families are fluid reconfigurations over time. This means that it is not immediately apparent what and who is 'my family' at any point. Family practices, doing family things, need to be recognized as associated with a familial relationship, which means they have to be linked to wider systems of meaning about family relationships and lives. Through display, people are seeking to show others 'this is my family and it works' in a way that will be recognized.

The need to display is the case for all contemporary families because it is now the quality of relationships that are regarded as important in families, not just biological and legal ties. But it is especially the case in circumstances where people live in relationships that they consider family but that do not align with conventional ideas of where a family is located or what it looks like, such as LATs (those living apart together), same-sex, and mixed-race relationships.

FAMILIES AND HOUSEHOLDS

Expand Your Knowledge

Mixed-race Families

Mixed-race families are a growing population in many countries. Research on parent couples from different racial and ethnic backgrounds shows that they need constantly to negotiate the differences between them to create a sense of belonging for their 'mixed' children. Some place a stress on encouraging children to think beyond racial and ethnic categories, others may encourage children to see themselves as a mix of backgrounds, while still others stress one aspect of a child's background. As well as negotiating different stances between themselves, such that they feel that their approach works for their family, parents may also have to negotiate their approaches around their children's physical appearance and, sometimes related to this, children's own identity and affiliation preferences. Differences between parents' and children's racial appearance can also mean questioning looks from passers-by when, say, a black father takes his 'white'-in-appearance mixed-race child to the park, or the stereotypical assumption is made by service providers that a white mother of a mixed-race child is a lone parent. Parents may also have to deal with other family members who may not approve of their partnering someone from a different racial or ethnic background, or how they bring up their children (Caballero et al., 2008).

 **Pause for Thought**

- What issues might parents who are from different racial or ethnic backgrounds with 'mixed-race' children face in negotiating, practising and displaying family?

It is through a phenomenological sociological lens that the routine microprocesses that underpin and enable us to live family lives become evident. The concepts of negotiation, family practices and display have been used to guide analysis in sociological research into a variety of aspects of family life. But the approach and its concepts can be subject to criticism because the focus is on people as active in their everyday interactions. The structures of power and inequalities between family members are set aside, as are the material and cultural implications of wider social divisions for people's abilities to negotiate, practise and display family.

Expand Your Knowledge

- Morgan, D.H.J. (2020) Family practices in time and space. *Gender, Place & Culture* 27(5): 733-43.
- Walsh, J., McNamee, S. and Seymour, J. (2019) Family display, family type, or community? Limitations in the application of a concept. *Families, Relationships and Societies*. www.ingentaconnect.com/content/tpp/frs/pre-prints/content-frsd1800057r3

Roles or Rationalities in Family and Household Behaviour?

A shift of emphasis from family to household draws our attention to inequalities in divisions of labour. Internationally, women still do more housework than men (Altintas and Sullivan, 2016) and are more likely to take on unpaid care roles. In same-sex households, domestic **division of labour** tends to be more equal, though this is not always the case (Rothblum, 2017). In this section, we consider some key sociological explanations for this situation.

One explanation for the gendered patterns of inequality in household labour is a structural version of **role theory** that has its roots in functionalism (Biddle, 1986). Role theory attempts to explain divisions of labour as people occupying particular family roles, whether ascribed or achieved, and conforming with wider social expectations of how they should behave in that role. For example, our implicit ideas about the gendered nature of different parenting roles is evident in the term 'role reversal', where mothers take on primary breadwinning and fathers primary caring roles. Or we may talk about fathers 'babysitting' their children if their female partner goes out, but we are unlikely to refer to mothers in this way. Sociological notions of 'role strain' and 'role conflict' also point to our gendered assumptions when they are referring to mothers attempting to balance family responsibilities and paid employment. In essence, role theory tries to link together the patterning of family members' behaviour, their social position, and collective conventions. But it has the drawback of smoothing over the variety of ways in which someone may perform a particular family role and the complexity of social expectations.

The notion of 'rationalities' attempts to explain how family members in particular roles decide what to do. **Rational choice theory** is an influential **theoretical** model that claims to be universally applicable, regardless of context, and has been used to explain gendered patterns of divisions of labour in family households. Notably, Gary Becker (1991) posited that family members make economically **rational** choices. When there are differences of skills between them in paid market work as against domestic labour, then it will be rational for whoever has the greater income-generating skills to devote more of their time to paid employment. In rational choice theory, the gendered division of labour is a result of individuals weighing up costs and benefits and taking the course of action that maximises benefits for the household. Rational choice theory has been subject to criticism, especially by feminists, because, for example, it is not really rational for women to specialize in domestic work when their relationship may end in separation or divorce. Further, rational choice theory assumes a collective household unit. The assumption that all household members will benefit and enjoy the same standard of living from the rational division of labour choice hides the differential access to material and other resources that women and children may have within family households (Daly et al., 2012).

Rational choice theory has also been criticized as making a 'rationality mistake' when it comes to household decisions. Rather than cost-benefit economic calculations and decisions, people exercise a moral rationality; they make a moral choice about what is 'the right thing to do'. These moral rationalities are gendered (Duncan and Edwards, 1999). Mothers may, for example, feel a moral obligation to provide full-time care for children, or prioritize paid employment as personal fulfilment, or regard being a good mother as being an employed mother. The concept of **gendered moral rationality** prioritizes the social as primary and economic interest as secondary. Moral rationalities are shaped by diverse understandings about the proper way to behave that are negotiated in the context of the **variable** social networks and cultural settings in which people live.

Despite its drawbacks, rational choice theory often guides social policymaking. It can be the framework adopted explicitly or implicitly in contemporary family policy initiatives to motivate people to act in particular ways (Himmelweit et al., 2013).

FAMILIES AND HOUSEHOLDS

Expand Your Knowledge: Benefits Policy

Universal Credit is a welfare benefit introduced by the UK Government in 2013, which combines a range of benefits (including in-work, unemployment, housing) into one system. Below are extracts from the Department for Work & Pensions leaflet, 'Universal Credit: Further Information for Families' (2019):

The Department for Work and Pensions classes a family as a single claimant or couple claimants who are responsible for one or more children or qualifying young persons (someone aged 16 to 19 and in full time non-advanced education or training) ... Universal Credit will help you combine work with being a parent and makes it easier to take part-time, flexible or temporary jobs ... Universal Credit makes it easier to start work if you're a parent, with increased help towards registered childcare costs ...

When you make a Universal Credit claim and have children, you will need to nominate a lead carer. If you are a lone parent, you will automatically be the lead carer ... What's expected of the lead carer in return for getting Universal Credit will be based on the age of the youngest child in the household. For example, if your child is under 1 you do not need to look for work to get Universal Credit ...

If you do not do what you've agreed to in your claimant commitment to find work – for example, if you fail to attend appointments or turn down job offers – you may receive a sanction. A sanction is a reduction in your benefit ...

You will receive one monthly University Credit payment. If you are claiming with a partner, this will cover both of you. This will be paid into a suitable account of your choice ...

www.gov.uk/government/publications/universal-credit-and-your-family-quick-guide/universal-credit-further-information-for-families

---
 ### Pause for Thought
---

- What might be the implications of ideas about roles and rationalities for government policies concerning work, welfare and families?

A sociological perspective on policies affecting families allows us to see inbuilt assumptions about family relationships and how household members should behave, such as underlying ideas about the gendered division of labour and breadwinning head of household, economic cost-benefit calculations as motivating family household members' behaviour, assumptions about shared resources within family households, and a lack of attention to moral rationalities.

Expand Your Knowledge

- Kaufman, G. and Grönlund, A. (2019) Displaying parenthood: (Un)doing gender – parental leave, daycare and working-time adjustments in Sweden and the UK. *Families, Relationships and Societies.* www.ingentaconnect.com/content/tpp/frs/pre-prints/content-frsd1800049r2.

- Perry-Jenkins, M. and Gerstel, N. (2020) Work and family in the second decade of the 21st century. *Journal of Marriage and Family* 82(1): 420–53.

CHAPTER SUMMARY

- Sociology helps us to think critically about our own and others' ideas about family and household trends and lives.
- Sociological theorizing about families has shifted from a focus on structure and roles, to uncovering negotiation of responsibilities, towards understanding the quality of democratized relationships.
- Sociological interrogation of who is and is not family and whether or not this coincides with household co-residence, illuminates the complexities involved.
- In some sociological views, individualization processes have opened up family lives in a positive way, other assessments are ambivalent, and for yet others such processes signal the rise of damaging self-absorption.
- A phenomenological approach identifies key motifs of contemporary family lives as negotiation between family members, practices that are the active 'doing' of family, and members displaying their family relationships to each other.
- Role theory and ideas about rational decision-making provide explanations for gendered and generational patterns of family and household inequalities in division of labour.

REVIEW QUESTIONS

1. Why is a sociological understanding of families and households important?
2. How and why have theoretical perspectives on families shifted over time?
3. What are the strengths and drawbacks of phenomenological understandings of family?
4. What features of family and household life does a focus on roles draw out?

Go Further

Books

- Dermott, E. and Seymour, J. (eds) (2011) *Displaying Families: A New Concept for the Sociology of Family Life*. Basingstoke: Palgrave Macmillan.

The concept of displaying families that was outlined in this chapter is applied across an interesting range of types of families and contexts in this collection of pieces, to show you the strengths and drawbacks of the concept of display for understanding contemporary family life.

- Goulbourne, H., Reynolds, T., Solomos, J. and Zontini, E. (2010) *Transnational Families: Ethnicities, Identities and Social Capital*. Abington: Routledge.

Flows of migration have meant that the boundaries of families discussed in this chapter can stretch not only across different households but across national boundaries too. This book about transnational family connections is an important demonstration of the ways that family is cross-cut with ethnic identities and material and social resources.

- Hall, S.M. (2019) *Everyday Life in Austerity: Family, Friends and Intimate Relations*. Basingstoke: Palgrave Macmillan.

Hall's book provides you with a gripping account of people's family lives and intimacy in times of austerity. It will demonstrate how these sociological concepts can reveal the solidarity, fragility, despair and creativity of everyday relationships in hard times.

Journal Articles

- Airey, L., Lain, D., Jandrić, J. and Loretto, W. (2020) A selfish generation? 'Baby boomers', values and the provision of childcare for grandchildren. *The Sociological Review*. DOI: 10.1177/0038026120916104.

This article relates to the discussion about individualization in this chapter. The authors explore whether or not members of the post-Second World War generation are selfish and reject family obligations, specifically in relation to grandparents looking after their grandchildren. The selfish stereotype doesn't hold up.

- Dyer, H., Sinclair-Palm, J. and Yeo, M. (2020) Drawing queer and trans kinship with children: Affect, cohabitation and reciprocal care. *Review of Education, Pedagogy and Cultural Studies*. DOI: 10.1080/10714413.2020.1724764.

How do children with queer and transsexual parents negotiate between their experiences of their own family and the mainstream images of family life that marginalize their families? This article provides more complexity to this chapter's discussion of boundaries and who is 'in' families for children in LGBTQ families, illustrated with children's drawings.

- Notten, N., Grunow, D. and Verbakel, E. (2017) Social policies and families in stress: Gender and educational differences in work–family conflict from a European perspective. *Social Indicators Research* 132: 1281–1305. DOI: 10.1007/s11205-016-1344-z.

Do different family policies make any difference to parents' experiences of work–family role conflict? This article takes your reading about role theory in this chapter further. It looks at the way that gender and education shape work–family tensions across European countries. It seems that highly-educated mothers experience the most conflict, regardless of the national family policies.

Websites

- www.bbc.co.uk/programmes/b09xkdhd

Listen to the BBC Radio 4 Thinking Allowed programme to hear: (i) Ann Oakley discussing her 1974 housework study and what's changed since then: www.bbc.co.uk/programmes/m0001jpz; and

(Continued)

(ii) about the contemporary lives of mixed-race families and transnational relationships, and issues in collecting official statistics.

- http://itunes.apple.com/itunes-u/theories-concepts-family/id380231496

To get a taste of debates in family sociology, listen to four British family sociologists discussing the merits and drawbacks of concepts.

- www.ons.gov.uk/peoplepopulationandcommunity/birthsdeathsandmarriages/families/publications

The UK Office for National Statistics issues regular bulletins on family and households, providing and explaining up-to-date statistics.

REFERENCES

Altintas, E. and Sullivan, O. (2016) Fifty years of change updated: Cross-national gender convergence in housework. *Demographic Research* 36(16): 455–70.

Beck, U. and Beck-Gernsheim, E. (1995) *The Normal Chaos of Love*. Cambridge: Polity Press.

Becker, G. (1991) *A Treatise on the Family*. Cambridge, MA: Harvard University Press.

Berger, P.L. and Kellner, H. (1964) Marriage and the construction of reality: An exercise in the microsociology of knowledge. *Diogenes* 46: 1–24.

Bernardes, J. (1985) Family ideology: Identification and exploration. *The Sociological Review* 33(2): 275–97.

Biddle, B.J. (1986) Recent developments in role theory. *Annual Review of Sociology* 12: 67–92.

Caballero, C., Edwards, R. and Puthussery, S. (2008) *Parenting 'Mixed' Children: Negotiating Difference and Belonging in Mixed Race, Ethnicity and Faith Families*. York: Joseph Rowntree Foundation.

Charles, N. and Davies, C.A. (2008) My family and other animals: Pets as kin. *Sociological Research Online* 13(5): 4.

Daly, M., Kelly, G., Dermott, E. and Pantazis, C. (2012) Intra-household poverty, PSEUK Conceptual Note No. 5. University of Bristol. Available at: www.poverty.ac.uk/sites/default/files/attachments/Conceptual%20note%20No.5%20-%20Intra%20Household%20Issues%20%28Daly%20et%20al%2C%20April%202012%29.pdf (last accessed 15 August 2019).

Duncan, S. and Edwards, R. (1999) *Lone Mothers, Paid Work and Gendered Moral Rationalities*. London: Macmillan.

Duncan, S., Carter, J., Phillips, M., Roseneil, S. and Stoilova, M. (2013) Why do people live apart together? *Families, Relationships and Societies* 2(3): 323–38.

Edwards, R., Gillies, V. and McCarthy, J.R. (2012) The politics of concepts: Family and its (putative?) replacements. *British Journal of Sociology* 63(4): 730–46.

Fevre, R. (2000) *The Demoralisation of Western Culture*. London: Continuum.

Finch, J. (2007) Displaying families. *Sociology* 41(1): 65–81.

Finch, J. and Mason, J. (1993) *Negotiating Family Responsibilities*. London: Routledge.

Fish, J.N. and Russell, S.T. (2018) Queering methodologies to understand queer families. *Family Relations: Interdisciplinary Journal of Applied Family Studies* 67(1): 12–25.

Giddens, A. (1992) *The Transformation of Intimacy: Sexuality, Love and Eroticism in Modern Societies*. Cambridge: Polity Press.

Gillis, J. (1997) *A World of Their Own Making: Myth, Ritual, and the Quest for Family Values*. Cambridge, MA: Harvard University Press.

Himmelweit, S., Santos, C., Savilla, A. and Sofer, C. (2013) Sharing of resources within the family and the economics of household decision-making. *Journal of Marriage and Family* 75(3): 625–39.

Hunt, S.A. (ed.) (2009) *Family Trends: British Families Since the 1950s*. London: Family and Parenting Institute.

Jamieson, L. (1998) *Intimacy: Personal Relationships in Modern Societies*. Cambridge: Polity Press.

McKie, L., Cunningham-Burley, S. and McKendrick, J. (2005) Families and relationships: Boundaries and bridges. In L. McKie and S. Cunningham-Burley (eds) *Families in Society: Boundaries and Relationships*. Bristol: Policy Press.

Morgan, D.H.J. (2011) *Rethinking Family Practices*. Basingstoke: Palgrave Macmillan.

Oakley, A. (1974) *The Sociology of Housework*. London: Martin Robertson.

Parsons, T. and Bales, R.E. (1955) *Family: Socialisation and Interaction Process*. New York: Free Press.

Popenoe, D. (2017) *War Over the Family*. Abingdon: Routledge.

Reynolds, T. (2003) Black to the community: Black community parenting in Britain. *Journal of Community, Work and Family* 6(1): 29–41.

Rothblum, E.D. (2017) Division of workforce and domestic labor among same sex couples. In R. Connelly and E. Kongar (eds) *Gender and Time Use in a Global Context: The Economics of Employment and Unpaid Labor*. New York: Palgrave Macmillan.

Silverstein, M. and Xu, L. (2017) Grandchildren as support and care providers to disabled older adults in China. *Population Horizons* 13(2): 63–73.

Smart, C. (2007) *Personal Life*. Cambridge: Polity Press.

Sweeting, H. and Seaman, P. (2005) Family within and beyond the household boundary: Children's constructions of who they live with. In L. McKie and S. Cunningham-Burley (eds) *Families in Society: Boundaries and Relationships*. Bristol: Policy Press.

Weeks, J., Donovan, C. and Heaphy, B. (2001) *Same Sex Intimacies: Families of Choice and Other Life Experiments*. London: Routledge.

Young, M. and Willmott, P. (1965 [1957]) *Family and Kinship in East London*. London: Routledge and Kegan Paul.

16

INTIMACIES AND RELATIONSHIPS

Katherine Twamley and Julia Carter

LEARNING OBJECTIVES

- To understand and evaluate arguments about intimacy and social change.
- To be familiar with and able to critically engage with debates about intimate relationships.
- To understand how the intersection of structure and agency shapes intimate relationships.

 Framing Questions

1. What do we mean by 'intimacy' and intimate relationships?
2. Are intimate relationships changing, and if so how and why?
3. How are experiences and meanings of love affected by the social context and circumstances in which individuals live?

Introduction

Intimacy, relationships and love are very important for sociological analysis, because they form a key part of most people's everyday lives and because knowing about these issues can tell us important information about wider social questions and changes. For example, whether people choose to marry or not may seem like a personal decision, but changes in marriage rates reflect wider social changes in the economy, policy, global movements and how people relate to one another generally.

Understandings of 'intimacy' in everyday talk are often associated with sexual behaviour or closeness, but when sociologists discuss intimacy we are referring to a much larger range of relationships. Lynn Jamieson defines intimacy as 'the quality of close connection between people and the process of building this quality', leading to 'a type of personal relationships that are subjectively experienced and may also be socially recognized as close' (2011: 1.1). These could be relationships which are formed within an understanding of 'family' or kin, or they may be formed with those who do not typically fall within an understanding of family, such as friends or lovers. Typically, sociologists use the term 'intimacy' or 'personal life' as one which is more inclusive of the various kinds of relationships which are important to individuals. A sociology of intimacy examines the varied understandings and practices associated with intimacy, as well as the interplay between intimate life and social organization. Scholarship from across the globe demonstrates how experiences and practices of intimacy and love differ across the cultural, socio-economic and political contexts in which individuals live.

In this chapter, you will learn about key sociological concepts and debates about intimacy; ideas about transformations in intimate relationships, both within Euro-American contexts and in the 'Global South' (i.e. low- and middle-income countries); the extent to which intimate relationships are experiencing both change and continuity in patterns of relating; how the political economy is theorized to relate to intimate relationships; and how state policies and changing cultural understandings of family and relationships have influenced the practices and experiences of intimacy.

Mapping the Terrain

Intimacy studies grew out of the sociology of family, in particular from a perception that studying families may exclude important close relationships that do not necessarily fall within common understandings of the 'family'. This was also at a time when sociology was moving away from a focus on structure as a defining element in family research, towards practices and interpretive meanings associated with different kinds of relationships. (This topic is also covered in Chapter 15.) Family and intimacy then often overlap, with intimacy frequently an assumed aspect of family life. Relatedly, how we understand 'family' shapes the kinds of intimate relationships we pursue, as well as the legitimization and de-legitimization of particular kinds of intimate relationships (such as same-sex intimacies). Family policy and families in the law tend to be defined institutionally and in accordance with marriage, legal, biological or kinship connections. If, however, we take instead a more 'family practices' approach (Morgan, 1996), family becomes something that is *done* rather than *given*: family is defined

(Continued)

by practices and customs. By recognizing family practices rather than structures, a range of relationships can have equal legitimacy.

Studying intimacy also entails an overlap with the sociology of emotions, in particular with scholars who examine love. There are many different forms of love, such as between parents and children, siblings and friends. Romantic love has dominated scholarly research, however, probably because it is thought to be less stable across time and place. Typically *romantic* love has been assumed to be limited to, or a product of, 'Western' culture. Most historians pinpoint the industrial revolution as a pivotal moment. Variously, it has been argued that falling mortality rates and better health in the 18th century meant that people had longer to form attachments with their partners and children (Ariès, 1962), or that as young people became more economically independent, they were freer to choose their own spouse (Engels, 1972). But there is evidence of romantic love and attachment in marriage or non-marital relationships throughout history and from all over the world (e.g. Coontz, 2006). Nonetheless, what intimacy means and looks like now is likely to be very different from how it was experienced 1000 years ago, 100 years ago, or even for our grandparents. And how it is experienced in different cultures is also likely to vary. This approach to understanding intimacy and emotions draws on social constructionism. That is, meanings and understandings of intimacy are variable and reflect our wider social conditions and cultural and historical milieu. For some sociologists, the very emotions we experience will vary depending on our culture, time, and geographical location. As Hochschild (2003b: 122) states: 'People in different eras and places do not just feel the same old emotion and express it differently. They feel it differently.'

Given the socially constructed nature of love and intimacy, many scholars examine how intimate relationships are shaped by social change and vice versa. A recent focus has been on how and whether individualization has shaped intimate relationships. Two main debates emerge from this literature – whether there is a breakdown of institutions such as marriage, and whether and how relationships are becoming more egalitarian. This debate often emerges from a difference in perspective with large-scale statistics and a focus on cultural studies leading to conclusions of fragile families and temporary liaisons, while smaller-scale qualitative studies aimed at understanding experiences of and values towards relating lead to the opposite conclusions. Newer literature attempts to reconcile these viewpoints.

Increasingly, these debates are moving beyond the borders of the Global North (i.e. higher-income countries), and, as such, sociologists interrogate whether and how changing ideals about love and intimate relationships circulate across the globe, and to what effect. Much of this literature has focused on the relationship between love and marriage and changes in family authority and structure. Broadly speaking, there emerge localized forms of intimate relationships, reacting both to globalized messages about appropriate and desirable intimate relationships, and local culture and histories associated with understandings of love and family (see Pause for Thought below).

The bulk of these studies focus on (heterosexual) couples, but an increasing body of research is looking at alternative or queer intimacies, such as polygamy, asexuality and friendships. These studies decentre the (hetero)sexual couple from studies of intimate life, pointing towards the problematic hegemonic norm that social theory reproduces by focusing only on the romantic couple (Budgeon and Roseneil, 2004). We will be focusing on some of these key themes in the remainder of this chapter, including intimacy and social change, inequalities and globalization. In the next section, you will learn more about the current debates in the sociology of intimacy and the most important explanations used to understand changes in intimacy.

 Pause for Thought

In Nepal, Laura Ahearn (2001) found that literacy rates amongst young people had transformative effects on how people met and chose their future partner. Once young men and women were able to read and write, they could send love letters to one another, arranging courtship independently of their parents, leading to a demise of parentally arranged marriages.

- What other social changes can you think of that might impact on intimate life?

Intimacy and Social Change

An important strand in studies of **intimacy** has been the ways in which intimacy has changed over time, and its relation to broader shifts in society. An influential group of scholars argue that there has been an accelerated **detraditionalization** of intimacy since the 1980s and 1990s. These scholars argue that relationships and intimacy in the past were characterized by their embeddedness in the moral frameworks of families and local communities. Marriage decisions were heavily guided by **family** and social expectations around status-matching, heritage and courtship rules. In these structured relationships, intimacy was secured and grounded in community approval of the match. Scholars such as Bauman (2003) and Beck and Beck-Gernsheim (1995) argue that a political and social restructuring of **ideology** towards individualism and away from collectivism resulted in traditional forms of personal relationships being undermined by values of **autonomy** and the market-driven logic of consumption and individual attainment. They are largely pessimistic about the impacts on intimate relationships.

Giddens (1991), on the other hand, suggests that the dissolution of traditional family and gender roles has provided an opportunity for the **pure relationship** to flourish – an intense couple connection noted for its gender equality – but which is also confluent, existing solely while the couple are satisfied by it. This form of intimacy is dependent upon two individuals, disembedded from family and community and freed from the constraints of class and gender, coming together and opening out, each to the other. This 'disclosing intimacy' relies on two individuals (whether friends or romantic partners) trusting each other enough to expose their private thoughts and feelings. For Giddens, the old and traditional constraints of kin obligations, gender and class inequalities and social mores regarding mate selection have declined to the extent that intimacy can be freely chosen and freely exited at will.

Feminist and scholars of social class have highlighted significant problems with Giddens's transformation of intimacy thesis. Lynn Jamieson (2011), for example, points out that this specific form of disclosing intimacy is not found globally and intimate relations tend to be characterized by a much wider repertoire of practices. These practices are set within ongoing constraining structures and stratification systems such as gendered care work, inequalities in income and wealth, race and **racism**, class-related inequalities, parental disapproval and unequal power relations in intimate and family relations (such as between parent and child). For Jamieson, intimacy is more than revealing the self through mutual disclosure; relationships frequently involve care work, non-verbal communication, sacrifice, physical labour in the form of unpaid housework, gifts (material or of labour) and so on, that are considered essential to relationships. This conceptualization of intimacy works in conjunction with complementary concepts of love, family and kinship. Practices of intimacy can be defined as: 'practices which cumulatively and in combination enable, create and sustain a sense of a close and special quality of a relationship between people' (Jamieson, 2011: 2:1).

Similarly to Bauman and Beck and Beck-Gernsheim, Eva Illouz (2012) argues that contemporary forms of intimacy are 'cold': intimacy now operates through the **rational** logics of economic reasoning and calculated emotions. Illouz (2012) argues that our intimate lives are risky and insecure – leading to relationship breakdown, temporary connections and romantic suffering – because the moral communities of the past no longer guide romantic decision-making, and individuals are left to rely solely upon their own reflexive and rational thought processes in choosing a partner. This choice is justified through a regime of 'emotional authenticity' which 'demands that actors [...] make decisions about relationships and commit themselves based on these feelings' (2012: 31). Illouz notes an ongoing gender inequality in intimacy since 'men can follow the imperative for autonomy more consistently and for a longer part of their lives and, as a result, they can exert emotional domination over women's desire for attachment, compelling them to mute their longing for attachment and to imitate men's detachment and drive for autonomy' (2012: 138).

Arlie Hochschild, like Illouz, points to the deep penetration of economic logics into **personal life** to explain modern conditions of intimacy, which has become increasingly regulated by the market and transactional interactions. This is evidenced by the reliance of couples upon outsourced help (or experts) such as carers for the elderly, nannies, dating websites or relationship counsellors. In these cases, decisions are made based upon an economic rationale, leading to the illusory idea that intimacy and happiness can be fulfilled through consuming the correct market product. Furthermore, Hochschild, along with Illouz, argues that feminism, 'abducted' by a commercial spirit, encourages women to disengage from warm, intimate bonds and to prioritize their own personal fulfilment and parity in care and housework. While leading to a rather pessimistic conclusion, it should be noted that the basis of the arguments put forward by Hochschild (and Illouz) rely on a homogeneous picture of 'Western' society which assumes both universal access to resources (such as money, institutions, geographical mobility) and the absence of constraining traditions and structures. You will read more about these issues in the next section.

16.1 Key Case

Does Gender Equality Lead to 'Cold' Intimacy?

Drawing on qualitative studies with parents in the UK who shared parental leave and those who did not, Twamley demonstrates that seeking equality in intimate relationships – which may be interpreted as motivated by rational, transactional logics – does not inevitably lead to cold intimacy among couples. On the contrary, drawing on both 'individualized' and family-oriented rationales when making decisions about parenting, care work, housework and coupling can lead to a relationship that is both equal and 'warm'. (Twamley, 2019)

— Pause for Thought —

- What kinds of assumptions are inherent in the idea that gender equality might lead to cold intimacy?
- What might happen to intimacy in intergenerational relationships (i.e. between parents and children) with greater parity in care work?

Connectedness and Continuity

Many sociologists have questioned to what degree an emphasis on individualization is a key factor in changes in personal life. They point to evidence of continuity in intimate relations, rather than great change. Recent literature has attempted to provide alternative explanations for ongoing desires for commitment and closeness that are not captured by the previous theories of social change. This recent reframing of intimacy starts with a broader interpretation of intimacy, an emphasis on connectedness, and uses a **family practices** approach (see Morgan, 1996, above). You will learn about these developments in this section.

Among others, Jennifer Mason has noted that the idea that the individual is a reflexive author of his own biography, able to exercise his own rights and responsibilities, is only a lived reality for a small and privileged group of white, middle-class men who are 'apparently unencumbered by kinship or other interpersonal commitments' (2004: 163). Mason contends that intimate decision-making is not free-floating or disembedded but is rather relational, connected and embedded. She illustrates this argument using the stories told to her by interviewees about how they made decisions about where they lived; the majority of these stories involved a consideration of intimate others in choosing where to reside. The pervasive presence of others in the narratives of individuals contests the dominance of the individual as the prime decision-maker in individual projects of the self. This is not to overstate the positive aspects of relating, for while some relational practices may be warm and supportive, others may equally be conflictual, oppressive and exclusionary. Overall, Mason suggests that individuals seek a balance between agency (promoting self-worth and economic progression) and interdependence and familial support.

Love and commitment are often considered to be key components of intimacy. While for the **individualization** theorists discussed above, these have become transient in the late modern era (e.g. Giddens, 1991; Illouz, 2012), other sociologists have highlighted their intransigency and permanence, both in terms of experiences and aspirations. One research project which highlighted this focused on living apart together (LAT) relationships in Britain. Simon Duncan et al. found that the reasons for living apart from a partner varied considerably and included the constraining impact of children from previous relationships, institutional barriers such as being in education or working abroad, as well as a preference for continuing to live apart (Duncan et al., 2013). For those expressing the latter sentiment, they found that LAT offered a 'both/and' solution that allowed them both autonomy and intimacy. However, the research also demonstrated that even when a preference for LAT was stated, this was often combined with a statement of love and commitment to the relationship and a desire for relationship longevity, stability and security that was belied by their living apart status. Thus, despite the appearance of impermanence, LAT relationships can often be as committed and secure as co-residential (including married) couple relationships. (This topic is also covered in Chapter 15.)

As can be seen from the example from Twamley (2019) above and in the work of numerous other researchers, care work and obligations continue to have a significant impact on practices of intimacy. This research demonstrates the importance of structures and constraints of care on agency, as well as the impact of gender inequalities that continue within intimate and wider familial relationships. It is equally important to consider that care and work obligations are structured through **social systems** and institutions so that women are already placed in a disadvantaged position, as are the working classes and people of colour. Taking this into account, it is clear that we need to understand intimacy and the workings of intimate practices within their social and material context. Taking a pragmatic approach to understanding intimacy, Julia Carter and Simon Duncan (2018) suggest that continuities in family life, such as gendered divisions of labour, marriage, and marital name-change for women, are coupled with aspects of **modernity**, such as the emphasis on choice in making these decisions. By choosing traditional intimate practices, individuals are reinventing family life by piecing together aspects of **tradition** with elements of modernity (**bricolage**) to produce a supposedly new and unique approach (also called 'individualized conformity'). These reinvented intimate practices look much like traditional ones but key elements such as aspirations to equality, agency and autonomy are assumed. The authors call this approach extended intimacy since intimacy is extended through time (i.e. includes traditional practices), while being extended beyond the disclosing intimacy of Giddens to include wider contexts and relationships.

16.2 Key Case

Why Do People Still Get Married?

While marriage rates have been in decline in Britain since their peak in the 1970s, many young people continue to express a desire to marry and most people will marry in their lifetime. Through conducting qualitative interviews with men and women in the UK, some of whom were planning their wedding, Julia Carter found that the idea of 'tradition' was still very important in guiding people's choices: both the decision to marry ('it's traditional') and as a resource for weddings (e.g. the traditional white wedding). Carter argues that tradition is used both as a means to re-embed individuals into a history and community and as a tool to navigate a supposedly individualistic and self-centred society. (Carter, 2017)

Pause for Thought

- Why do you think marriage is still a popular option for couples?
- What happens when same-sex couples have traditional white weddings? What purpose does 'tradition' serve here?
- Why might someone choose a civil partnership over marriage (available to both mixed and same-sex couples in the UK since 2019)?

Intimacies and Inequalities

Although intimacy is typically associated with equality, at least in its idealized forms, in reality intimate relationships may intersect with inequalities in many different ways, such as:

INTIMACIES AND RELATIONSHIPS

- parent–child relationships;
- intimate relationship violence;
- prostitution/sex work;
- power and labour differentials within couples, friends and so on;
- **state** regulation of intimacies;
- unequal migration possibilities structuring marriage migration and family reunification;
- taboos around certain kinds of relationships or practices;
- racism, classism, sexism, **ageism**, homophobia.

Some of these, such as the prohibition of **same-sex relationships** or marriage, may be enshrined in state law. Most develop out of long-standing prejudice and historical inequalities of power. In this section, you will read about two major themes in this research: gender and intimacy, and **intersectionality** (intersections of inequalities such as gender, disability, race, **age**, sexuality and so on) and intimacy.

Gender and Intimacy

Sexuality and intimacy, involving relationships between gendered bodies, are difficult to study without reference to gender. Gender stereotypes and expectations shape sexual behaviour and intimate relationships, perhaps especially heterosexual relationships. In studies on sexuality and gender, much research has centred on the gendered cultural scripts which men and women draw on when entering relationships (Gagnon, 1990). As discussed further in the section on mediated intimacy, understandings of appropriate sexual practices often prioritize men's pleasure (Gill, 2009). Scripts associated with romantic love are considered particularly (hetero)gendered. By scripts we mean commonly held and recurring understandings of how romantic love ought to be performed. A script may teach you the proper object of romantic love, how to assess its authenticity and how to perform it. Ellen Lamont (2014) examines how women in the US continue to expect romantic courtship practices that are inherently sexist, positioning women as passive and dependent, and men as active breadwinners – such as the idea that men should pay for dinner or hold the door open for a woman. Like Carter's young women in the UK who expect traditional weddings, these women understand these practices as a means to demonstrate and recognize romance, even if they also recognize that they are highly gendered.

Second-wave feminists were highly critical of romantic love, arguing that it acted as a kind of 'dupe', enticing women into unequal relationships with men. They argued that the association of romantic love with passion and monogamy entrapped women into relationships which historically were seen as a means through which men gain exclusive access to women and their heirs. The idea of love as a dupe has been critiqued as being overly simplified, while also failing to take into account the material conditions of women's lives which may leave them dependent on marriage for financial security (Jackson, 1995). Nonetheless, there remains the question of why women (and men) enter into relationships of inequality where they have financial independence. For Paul Johnson (2005), heteronormativity is a key means through which unequal relationships are forged. He argues that sexuality works together with love, creating a normative ideal which draws on ideas of opposite characteristics as natural, thereby affirming gendered differences. Even same-sex couples may draw on these ideas in their relationship practices, situating one as oppositional to the other, if not in sex/gender, then in their **role** within the relationship or family.

As seen above, Giddens (1991) and other theorists have posited that the more egalitarian pure relationship has replaced romantic love relationships. Overall, the **empirical** evidence suggests that relationship equality is more of an ideal than a necessary condition of contemporary intimate relationships. In fact, women in opposite-sex relationships have been shown to accept loving acts in place of egalitarian relations as a demonstration of a good relationship (Twamley, 2012). Furthermore, research in South Asia demonstrates that the idea that the pure relationship would necessarily entail more equal gender relations is a **Eurocentric** assumption, rooted in 'contemporary neoliberal visions of person and society' (Osella and Osella, 2006: 3). In fact, the trend in India towards the couple as central to intimate life has led to *increased* gendering, since there is more emphasis on the heteronormative ideal, loosening homosocial bonds which offer less gendered social spaces for men and women (Osella and Osella, 2006). This is an important corrective to remind us to situate theories within the context and positioning of the participants.

Intersectionality and Intimacy

Many studies conducted in the UK and the US tend to focus on white, middle-class couples. Sometimes there is a very good **theoretical** reason for doing so, but research amongst more diverse groups to understand the multiple layers of inequalities that may intersect with intimate practices, is lacking. As seen in the following section on intimacy and globalization, unequal access to different forms of capital can shape the abilities of families and couples to maintain intimate relationships. A very poignant example of how poverty can shape intimacy comes from Nancy Scheper-Hughes's (1992) ethnographic research in the favelas of northeast Brazil. She showed how mothers' love for their newborn babies was delayed or withheld in response to the high mortality rate of young babies. These studies can be considered as part of a body of research which examines the 'political economy of love', exploring how material conditions 'constitute certain kinds of subjects and enable particular kinds of relationships' (Thomas and Cole, 2009: 4).

Material conditions may also shape with whom you will enter into a relationship. A large body of research has shown how **endogamous** couple relationships tend to be. That is, people tend to marry or partner those of a similar class and educational background to themselves. In part, this relates to the social circle within which individuals mix. However, as Paul Johnson and Steph Lawler (2005) reported in their research with heterosexual men and women in the North East of England, people may also *prefer* to go out with someone from a similar class background, because they feel that they are more likely to 'fit together' (2005: 1.6). Such processes, they argue, are facilitated by notions that class is defined by personal characteristics rather than systems of inequality (though class prejudice is likely to inform these notions of who can fit together). (For more information on this topic, see Chapter 11.)

In addition to class and material inequalities, other forms of prejudice can interact with intimacies in various ways. Race is one very important axis of prejudice that can intersect with intimacy. Historically in various contexts, such as in the US and South Africa, marriage between black and white men and women was illegal. Mixed-race (and mixed-caste in the context of South Asia) couples continue to face discrimination, and research has shown how they may experience isolation from family members and friends who do not accept their relationship. Historical inequalities between racialized groups can also shape the relationship dynamics within mixed-race couples. Chinyere Osuji (2019) studied the experience of interracial couples in the US and Brazil. She found that the couples could at times reproduce racial hierarchies within their relationships, and at others challenge notions of black inferiority and white superiority.

Intersectional inequalities will exacerbate the forms of inequalities which occur within couple relationships – that is, a black woman from a poor background is more likely to be positioned as inferior or lacking than a black man from a wealthier background. These studies show the pervasiveness of prejudice even in the most intimate of contexts. (For more on this topic, see Chapter 12.)

Expand Your Knowledge

- Do children's friendships replicate the social divisions of ethnicity and class?

Friends, and in particular children's friendships, are often lauded as the archetypal egalitarian relationship. But research conducted by Vincent et al. (2017) in the UK found that opportunities for children to develop friendships across certain divisions were inhibited by parents. Read this study to find out more about how children's friendships were shaped by parents' class and 'race' prejudice.

Mediated Intimacy

How often do you interact with family and friends online? Most people now have multiple and frequent interactions with intimate others through various forms of social media. An aunt sees regular updates of her nieces and nephews, interacting with them online, even as her family is dispersed across the world. Men and women peruse the dating profiles of potential partners on their mobiles, 'liking', ignoring or swiping to arrange a series of face-to-face dates. Intimate pictures of celebrities are shared across Instagram and analysed in multiple newspaper articles and blogs. Such quotidian examples demonstrate how, in an increasingly digital world, social and mainstream media *mediate* our intimate relationships. That is, how we practise our relationships, what we consider to be right or appropriate, are influenced by and in turn influence various forms of technology and the public stories circulated through the media. The study of mediated intimacy focuses attention on the ways in which discourses of intimacy enter and influence our lives through various forms of media and technology, as well as attending to what stories are highlighted and those that are silenced.

While stories of relationships have always circulated, Tyler and Gill (2013) argue that this current level of mediation is unique for the following reasons:

1. Images and stories of intimacy are ubiquitous, 'from stories about politicians' affairs, celebrity pregnancies and experiences of heartbreak, to reality shows preoccupied with "making over" intimate life' (2013: 80).
2. A new kind of intimate gaze has come to characterize the media, such that 'all mediated life becomes refracted through a lens of intimacy' (2013: 80). That is, we are invited in media stories to share in and unpick the personal lives of distant intimates, through personalized accounts, reality TV, and other such intimate formats.
3. New media **technologies** have become increasingly implicated in the ways that people practise their intimate relationships, whether through initiating a new relationship or maintaining current ones.

A good example of mediated intimacy lies in the advice columns of magazines and other texts, which directly call upon (usually) women to behave in specific ways with their (normally male) partner. Rosalind Gill (2009) analysed how relationship advice offered in women's magazines between 2005 and 2008 reflects and shapes particular understandings of intimate relationships, which are then taken up as an idealized or 'proper' standard. The repertoires she uncovered in the magazines drew on neoliberal rationalities, exhorting women to work on their sexual selves and invest in their intimate skills. The advice emphasized women's choice and empowerment in these activities, while ironically exhorting women to focus their energies on pleasing men. This, Gill argues, reflects and reinforces the dominant discourses of postfeminism in the UK. This research reflects the two-way dynamic of mediated intimacy – it both draws on cultural understandings of appropriate behaviour and reinforces such behaviour through, in this case, the advice or rules that are set out for readers.

A related strand of research focuses on how relationships are mediated through technology, such as via social media applications such as Instagram and Facebook. Deborah Chambers (2013) has been at the forefront of this research. She argues that such technology offers new opportunities for individuals in how they manage and construct their identities, as well as generating new modes of self-presentation, interaction and 'etiquette'. The informal and networked modes of these social sites, Chambers argues, challenge conventional boundaries between 'private' and 'public', intimate and non-intimate. Even casual acquaintances are now 'friends'. But the public exposure can be fraught with community and self-disciplining processes, as individuals monitor their online presentation and those of others. (See Chapter 23 for more information.)

How technology influences intimate relationships is a contentious topic, with many fearing that technology inhibits personal connection and social skills. However, the research is not clear-cut (see Key Case 16.3). Focusing on media representations and interpellations allows an interrogation of how new technologies and media platforms *constrain and enable particular kinds of intimacies*, and how these reinforce or work against social and cultural rationalities.

16.3 Key Case

Does Social Media Enhance or Inhibit Personal Connections?

Wang's research with young Chinese rural-to-urban migrant workers in China shows how access to social media can create new forms of relating, and that these forms take on localized meanings. For these migrants, social media is less a means to stay in touch with the families they left behind and more a means to gain autonomy from family. These migrants make friends online, where previously 'friendship' was a concept largely unknown to them. In this context, then, social media enables what they perceive as 'purer' (*geng chun*) relationships, beyond the practicalities of offline life. (Wang, 2016)

Pause for Thought

- What kinds of digital technologies did you use to stay in touch with family and friends during the global COVID-19 pandemic?
- Did they shape the kinds of conversations you were having, and with whom?
- Were all your family and friends equally able to participate? If not, why not?

Love and Globalization

Globalization is 'the intensification of worldwide social relations which link distant localities in such a way that local happenings are shaped by events occurring many miles away and vice versa' (Giddens, 1990: 64). Following on from the previous section, flows of ideas through social and other forms of media are a key means through which this intensification occurs. For example, the novel *Fifty Shades of Grey* by E.L. James has topped best-seller lists around the world, sold over 125 million copies and been translated into 52 languages. Later, it was made into a film, which grossed US $404.8 million at the box office outside of North America. There has been much controversy around the portrayal of intimate relationships in this book as being unhealthy and unequal, but largely speaking, it follows a common formula of heterosexual romance books: the couple overcome obstacles (usually the man's reluctance to commit), culminating in a traditional white wedding. Such relationship 'scripts' are not universal. In some contexts, for example, romantic love is not associated with marriage. As sociologists, we are interested in how stories and ideals of intimacy are 'read' in different contexts and by different people. It is not assumed that relationship stories are straightforwardly taken on board by all in similar ways, nor that everyone is equally placed to do so. As noted by DeVault (1990), reading is a socially-located activity shaped by history, by the social-organizational context and by the social background of the reader.

For example, research conducted in the last 20 years in various settings around the world has suggested that processes of globalization have contributed to changing understandings of marriage and the role of love and intimacy within it (Padilla et al., 2007). These scholars argue that young people are placing more emphasis on love as a basis for marriage than their parents did before them. In part, this is attributed to globalized forms of media circulating like never before. But other processes are also at work. As you read above, in Nepal, Laura Ahearn (2001) found that increased literacy rates amongst young people contributed to a transformation of intimate practices. This was combined with globalized discourses of **'development'** in Nepali school textbooks which encouraged young people to turn away from family-arranged marriages to self-selected marriages as a sign of 'modernity'. As Ahearn (and other scholars, e.g. Povenelli, 2006) notes, there is a valorisation of notionally 'Western' forms of intimate relationships, which operate symbolically through associations with modernity and development. However, we must be careful not to assume that practices that are most common in the Global North are superior to those found elsewhere, or that modernization will inevitably lead to cultural **homogenization**.

Indeed, despite these globalized discourses of appropriate marriage and intimacy, a homogenization of intimate relationships is not emerging. Diverse relationship forms develop across different locations, even when individuals draw on similar ideals of love within marriage. In India, for example, researchers have pointed to pervasive 'traditional' understandings of marriage amongst young Indian couples, together with discourses of intimacy. Fuller and Narasimhan (2007) conducted research amongst Hindu Brahmans in Tamil Nadu, south India. They observed that young people valued 'personal compatibility' along with education and employment when choosing a future spouse, blurring the lines between arranged and love marriage.

Another aspect of globalization is the increased movement of people across the globe. A central interest for sociologists has been the impact of migration and other forms of intensive mobility (long-distance commuting, frequent business trips) on family and intimate relationships. Such mobilities may open up new possibilities in relating, opportunities to form new relationships or freedom from familial or cultural constraints. But equally, they may create tensions and heartache as families and couples struggle to maintain contact, or when emigrants fail to make intimate connections in their new home. While much scholarly focus has been on new relationship opportunities, research also demonstrates how mobility may re-entrench traditional relationship practices. For example, Kathryn Charsley (2018) has examined **transnational** British Pakistani marriage practices. Her research indicates that the distance afforded by marriages between UK-born and Pakistan-born individuals enables and incentivises traditional cousin-marriage practices. The geographical distance between the potential couple ameliorates the perceived proximity of kin as being too close for marriage, while marrying someone from within the same family assuages worries about cultural differences being too big.

Hear from the Expert

Rhacel Salazar Parreñas

An important aspect of research around mobilities and relationships is to attend to how local and transnational inequalities may shape experiences of intimacy. For example, Rhacel Salazar Parreñas (2005) has studied the experiences of Filipino migrant women and their families. Many of these women emigrate to the Global North to work as nannies and housemaids. The remittances they send home may be used to pay for a nanny or housemaid, usually from poorer families or women who live in rural areas, to look after their home and children. These women in turn leave their children, usually to the care of female relatives. This sequence of employment for care is referred to as a 'global care chain', recognizing the links which traverse the world as women are employed to care for other women's children. While this is not a new phenomenon, it is exacerbated by new possibilities in migration and growing global inequalities. Such a chain highlights the inequalities across countries and regions, resulting in a 'care drain' (Hochschild, 2003a) for families left behind in the global and rural south. This research highlights how globalization can create both opportunities and benefits for intimate relationships, but may also exacerbate and build on existing inequalities.

Adapted from Rhacel Salazar Parreñas, *Children of Global Migration: Transnational Families and Gendered Woes*. Copyright © 2005 by the Board of Trustees of the Leland Stanford Junior University. All rights reserved.

 **Pause for Thought**

- Can technology help overcome the limitations of distance in maintaining intimacy?

In order to sustain intimate connections with their children left at home, migrant women, such as those studied by Parreñas, draw on technologies like Skype and WhatsApp. But the access to and quality of these technologies are not evenly distributed:

- A nurse has more flexibility and economic resources to call home than a housemaid.
- Depending on the country of work, some women may have no day off; coupled with earning disparities across countries, this can affect their ability to maintain contact.
- Many rural areas have poor phone coverage.

INTIMACIES AND RELATIONSHIPS

However, even when migrant women manage to keep regular contact through video calls and texts, children describe the nurturing provided by transnational mothers as 'not enough'. Parreñas (2005) argues that an ideological belief that mothers should be the main nurturers increases this perception, leaving the migrant women in a difficult bind.

CHAPTER SUMMARY

- Some theories of intimacy overemphasize the impact of social change. More recent theories highlight the importance of continuity of social practices within wider changes in structures of intimacy ('living apart together' relationships are a good example).
- Couple relationships, while more equal than in the past, remain a site of inequality, particularly in terms of gender and race but also with regard to sexuality, age, disability and class.
- Intimacy is increasingly mediated through technologies, leading to a blurring of the boundaries of 'public' and 'private'. While for many this has the effect of constraining intimacy, others point to the enabling aspects of new technologies.
- Globalization likewise has a significant impact on intimacy and care. This may allow for more diversity in intimate life, but global movements may also exacerbate existing inequalities. For example, a care deficit in poorer countries is created by migrants moving to wealthier countries to care for families there.

REVIEW QUESTIONS

1. What are our contemporary understandings of intimacy and why do such meanings change over time?
2. What are the debates about changes in intimacy? Is intimacy more transitory now or are intimate relationships now even more important than in the past?
3. What is the impact of mediated intimacy? Has social media weakened intimate ties?
4. How are intimacy and love experienced across the globe? How is intimacy impacted when families are separated across borders?

Go Further

Books

- Gabb, J. and Fink, J. (2015) *Couple Relationships in the 21st Century*. Basingstoke: Palgrave Macmillan.

This book provides a comprehensive and up-to-date picture of contemporary relationships in Britain.

- May, V. and Nordqvist, P. (2019) *Sociology of Personal Life*, 2nd edition. London: Red Globe Press.

This book is important because it covers in more detail the important aspects of personal life, beyond couple relationships, for individuals in the 21st century.

(Continued)

- Padilla, M.B., Hirsch, J.S., Munoz-Laboy, M., Sember, R.E. and Parker, R.G. (2007) *Love and Globalization: Transformations of Intimacy in the Contemporary World*. Nashville, TN: Vanderbilt University Press.

This book provides a global overview of changes within intimacy and love in an increasingly interconnected world.

Journal Articles

- Dawson, M. (2012) Reviewing the critique of individualization: The disembedded and embedded theses. *Acta Sociologica* 55(4): 305–19.

This paper is useful in understanding individualization theory at a deeper level as well as its key critiques.

- Donner, H. and Santos, G. (2016) Love, marriage, and intimate citizenship in contemporary China and India: An introduction. *Modern Asian Studies* 50(4): 1123–46.

This paper is important because it unpacks the relevance of individualization theories beyond the Global North and considers alternative interpretations of change in contemporary forms of relating.

- Hobbs, M., Owen, S. and Gerber, L. (2016) Liquid love? Dating apps, sex, relationships and the digital transformation of intimacy. *Journal of Sociology* 53(2): 271–84.

This was one of the first papers to explore in-depth the dating app revolution and the potential of these to transform (or not) practices of intimacy.

Websites

- http://feministlovestudies.azc.uam.mx

The feminist love studies website brings together interdisciplinary research and researchers focused on studying love across the globe.

- www.britsoc.co.uk/groups/study-groups/families-relationships-study-group

This is the website of the British Sociological Association Families and Relationships study group.

- www.rewriting-the-rules.com/blog

This is the blog and website for Meg-John Barker, who has written extensively on sex, gender, and relationships.

REFERENCES

Ahearn, L. (2001) *Invitations to Love: Literacy, Love Letters, and Social Change in Nepal*. Ann Arbor, MI: University of Michigan Press.
Ariès, P. (1962) *Centuries of Childhood*. New York: Random House.
Bauman, Z. (2003) *Liquid Love*. Cambridge: Polity Press.
Beck, U. and Beck-Gernsheim, E. (1995) *The Normal Chaos of Love*. Cambridge: Blackwell.

Budgeon, S. and Roseneil, S. (2004) Editors' introduction: Beyond the conventional family. *Current Sociology* 52(2): 127–34.

Carter, J. (2017) Why marry? The role of tradition in women's marital aspirations. *Sociological Research Online* 22(1): 1–14.

Carter, J. and Duncan, S. (2018) *Reinventing Couples: Tradition, Agency and Bricolage*. London: Palgrave.

Chambers, D. (2013) *Social Media and Personal Relationships: Online Intimacies and Networked Friendship*. Basingstoke: Palgrave Macmillan.

Charsley, K. (2018) Closeness and distance in Pakistani transnational marriage. *Families, Relationships and Societies* 7(3): 521–6.

Coontz, S. (2006) *Marriage, A History: How Love Conquered Marriage*. London: Penguin.

DeVault, M.L. (1990) Novel readings: The social organization of interpretation. *American Journal of Sociology* 95(4) Jan.

Duncan, S., Carter, J., Phillips, M., Roseneil, S. and Stoilova, M. (2013) Why do people live apart together? *Families, Relationships and Societies* 2(3): 323–38.

Engels, F. (1972) *The Origin of the Family, Private Property and the State*. London: Lawrence and Wishart.

Fuller, C.J. and Narasimhan, H. (2007) Information technology professionals and the new-rich middle class in Chennai (Madras). *Modern Asian Studies* 41(1): 121–50.

Gagnon, J.H. (1990) The explicit and implicit use of the scripting perspective in sex research. In C.D. Bancroft and D. Weinstein (eds) *Annual Review of Sex Research*. Mt. Vernon, IA: Society for the Scientific Study of Sex, pp. 1–44.

Giddens, A. (1990) *The Consequences of Modernity*. Stanford, CA: Stanford University Press.

Giddens, A. (1991) *Modernity and Self-identity: Self and Society in the Late Modern Age*. Stanford, CA: Stanford University Press.

Gill, R. (2009) Mediated intimacy and postfeminism: A discourse analytic examination of sex and relationships advice in a women's magazine. *Discourse and Communication* 3(4): 345–69.

Hochschild, A. (2003a) Love and gold. In B. Ehrenreich and A. Hochschild (eds) *Global Woman*. London: Granta Books.

Hochschild, A.R. (2003b) *The Managed Heart: The Commercialization of Human Feeling*. Berkeley, CA: University of California Press.

Illouz, E. (2012) *Why Love Hurts: A Sociological Explanation*. Cambridge: Polity Press.

Jackson, S. (1995) Even sociologists fall in love: An exploration in the sociology of emotions. *Sociology* 27(2): 201–20.

Jamieson, L. (2011) Intimacy as a concept: Explaining social change in the context of globalisation or another form of ethnocentrism? *Sociological Research Online* 16(4): 151–63.

Johnson, P. (2005) *Love, Heterosexuality and Society*. London: Routledge.

Johnson, P. and Lawler, S. (2005) Coming home to love and class. *Sociological Research Online* 10(3).

Lamont, E. (2014) Negotiating courtship: Reconciling egalitarian ideals with traditional gender norms. *Gender & Society* 28(2): 189–211.

Mason, J. (2004) Personal narratives, relational selves: Residential histories in the living and telling. *The Sociological Review* 52(2): 162–79.

Morgan, D. (1996) *Family Connections: An Introduction to Family Studies*. Cambridge: Polity Press.

Osella, C. and Osella, F. (2006) *Men and Masculinities in South India*. London: Anthem Press.

Osuji, C.K. (2019) *Boundaries of Love: Interracial Marriage and the Meaning of Race*. New York: NYU Press.

Padilla, M.B., Hirsch, J.S., et al. (2007) *Love and Globalisation: Transformations of Intimacy in the Contemporary World*. Nashville, TN: Vanderbilt University Press.

Parreñas, R.S. (2005) *Children of Global Migration: Transnational Families and Gendered Woes*. Stanford, CA: Stanford University Press.

Povenelli, E. (2006) *The Empire of Love*. Durham, NC: Duke University Press.

Scheper-Hughes, N. (1992) *Death without Weeping: The Violence of Everyday Life in Brazil*. Berkeley, CA: University of California Press.

Smart, C. (2007) *Personal Life*. Cambridge: Polity Press.

Thomas, L.M. and Cole, J. (2009) Thinking through love in Africa. In J. Cole and L.M. Thomas (eds) *Love in Africa*. Chicago: University of Chicago Press.

Twamley, K. (2012) Gender relations among Indian couples in the UK and India: Ideals of equality and realities of inequalities. *Sociological Research Online* 17(4): 103–13.

Twamley, K. (2019) 'Cold intimacies' in parents' negotiations of work-family practices and parental leave? *The Sociological Review* 67(5): 1137–53.

Tyler, I. and Gill, R. (2013) Postcolonial girl: Mediated intimacy and migrant audibility interventions. *International Journal of Postcolonial Studies* 15: 78–94.

Vincent, C., Neal, S. and Iqbal, H. (2017) Encounters with diversity: Children's friendships and parental responses. *Urban Studies* 54(8): 1974–89.

Wang, X. (2016) *Social Media in Industrial China*. London: UCL Press.

WORK
Lynne Pettinger

LEARNING OBJECTIVES

- To understand what we talk about when we talk about work, what counts as work and what kinds of work have social status.
- To understand how class, race, gender and age affect how work is organized, who does it and how it is valued.
- To understand how different kinds of paid and unpaid work are interconnected, and how they contribute to global capitalism.
- To understand how work has changed in recent years and to consider how it might change in the near future.

 Framing Questions

1. Is factory work the archetypal form of work?
2. How is work in one setting (place, industrial sector) affected by work elsewhere?
3. What does doing work demand of an individual? What elements of a self are 'for sale' in the employment relationship?
4. How are social inequalities manifested in work, and how does work contribute to maintaining inequalities?

PART 4 CONNECTING THE PERSONAL AND THE SOCIAL

Introduction

The aim of this chapter is to introduce you to key ideas in the study of work by exploring how work has been studied in the past, and how work is changing in the present. You will learn about important concepts that help us to understand how workers are treated and what it's like to do work. Sociology makes it possible to draw connections between personal and intimate questions about how people live, feel and work, and the social and economic structures and institutions through which everyday life is organized. We will see this relationship at play when we look at how work is affected by global social inequalities, and how people's sense of themselves is made through work.

The chapter starts with a discussion of how the sociology of work changed at three key moments in the past, in order for you to see the origins of our current understanding of work. We then ask a naïve but important question: what is work? This involves us exploring paid and unpaid work. We follow a pair of jeans as they are made and sold, in order to understand the complexity of work in global capitalism. We see how work is exploitative, what skills and knowledge workers need, how people are treated at work, how technologies affect work and how people's sense of themselves is part of work. After that, we will look at work right now, and explore important debates about precarious work and the future of work.

Mapping the Terrain

When sociology was a new discipline in the 19th century, its practitioners were concerned to understand the changing world around them. One of the most significant changes in the late 19th century was the growth of factory production through an 'industrial revolution' that took place in Europe, especially in Britain. Towns and cities grew around new 'manufactories'. The immediate interest of many of those early sociologists was to understand life for those workers displaced from established rural communities, who sold their labour power in return for a wage. They were less interested in issues that concern us now, including the lives of those working elsewhere in the world, including the enslaved workers growing cotton and sugar on plantations, or the vast numbers doing domestic service work.

The origins of sociology as a discipline lie in this attempt to understand industrial society: its exploitative and alienating effects, and the crises it caused for people's sense of who they are in the world (this topic is also covered in Chapter 7). Marx's ideas about the difference between those who sell their labour power (proletariat) and those who own the means of production (bourgeoisie), for example, provided a compelling starting point for understanding how doing paid work creates divisions and hierarchies between people. Key themes that emerged are the division of labour and differences between workers.

Sociologists writing in Europe and the US after the Second World War retained this earlier interest in the relationship between paid work and social class. By this time, factory work had been further rationalized with the use of Fordist production lines. Fordism is a shorthand term for the mass production of consumer goods using standardized processes, so that individual workers made just one small contribution to the manufacture of a standard product. The rationalization of production was part of the reason why factory work was alienating. Alienation refers to the ways that workers in capitalist systems come to feel disconnected from other humans, with whom they compete for work; from the products they make, which are sold for the benefit of capitalists; and from their daily work, because they have no control over it. Fordist production and 'scientific management' that advocated the separation of the mental work of the manager from the manual work of the low-skilled worker made clerical, service and factory work especially alienating as complex tasks were broken down into the smallest possible units to become routine, repetitive, unskilled and unrewarding. The key sociological themes of alienation and skill emerged from this analysis, and workers' resistance to managerial control was widely studied.

In the late 1960s, the stories told by the 'sociology of industrial societies' were challenged by researchers inspired by – and actively contributing to – political movements for gender and racial equality. These researchers read accounts of the factory work done by men, of apparently homogeneously white workforces living and working in the white suburbs of Europe and the US. They asked: where was women's work? How did being black or Asian affect how people were treated at work? What work did people do beyond Europe and North America? The invisibility of some workers, and the work that they did, was challenged and questioned. Key themes emerged about the interdependencies of work, about the gendering and racialization of occupations, skill and technology.

A further significant shift in the concerns of sociologists of work emerged in the 1980s. This involved thinking more deeply about what was for sale when labour is bought and sold for a wage. What features of a person's selfhood have to be brought into play if they are to do their work? If you've ever seen a job advert that asks for a 'bubbly personality' or been told to smile and be polite when you're serving even the rudest customers, you'll have an idea about this. Arlie Hochschild (1983: 7) described emotional labour as 'the management of feeling to create a publicly observable facial and bodily display'. Since then, many researchers have found ways that a person's selfhood, identity or lifestyle is part of what they bring to an employment relationship. Women socialized to be caring, the different form that 'professionalism' takes for a brand ambassador than for a lawyer, the training a manager gets (and does or doesn't apply) in how to get the best from their staff – these are other instances of emotional labour. Key themes were the importance of recognizing previously invisible elements of work, and of the role of customers, clients and patients in managing workers.

Sociologists of work have located work within the social and economic system of the time and studied how work is organized and how different kinds of workers are treated. They have considered: who does what kind of work, what skills are demanded of workers, how do workers use technologies, and how is work managed?

What is 'Work'?

We use 'work' in everyday conversation quite a lot. 'I'm going to do a work-out', 'you have to work hard to pass this module', 'that was hard work'; you will come up with other examples as well, I'm sure. Work is a powerful phrase we use to describe effort and drudgery; it is also used to describe the outcomes of effort, as in 'works of art', or some process of transition between states (the production of 'fruits of labour', 'working out the problem' with a therapist). These everyday uses are indicators of the cultural importance of work as a part of everyday life, and although we won't talk more about these uses in the rest of the chapter, you might bear in mind that when we do the **sociology** of work, we do so in societies that already have complicated understandings of what work is. For me, thinking about work as a set of activities that changes the world, and that is organized and experienced differently according to the social and economic relations around, is the way to go. That quite simple definition leaves space for two things that matter. One is that 'work' is not one simple kind of activity; it's geographically and historically contingent, and we need to then think about the specificity of what we mean when we say something is work. The other, more abstract thing is that something is done in the world when we describe an activity as 'work' or 'not work'. That is, the words we use have a power and an effect and contribute to the creation of worlds.

And yet you might be thinking: isn't it obvious what work is? It is what you get paid for. It is all the stuff you don't want to do but your boss makes you do. It is the reason you're at university – to get a good job. It gives you a sense of who you are, of purpose in your life. It is (simultaneously) often demanding and unpleasant. And to some extent, it is indeed that obvious. Work, more precisely paid work – a job, employment, an occupation, a profession – can involve all these features. But it is worth interrogating common-sense around 'work', starting with the big assumption: work is what you're paid to do. Often that is true. Many of us go to work, do what we are told, get paid for it and come home. But three very common kinds of work complicate the idea that work can be defined by whether or not it is paid for and contains an element of compulsion. The first is voluntary work, which is work-like, in that it contains tasks that have to be done that require sustained effort. But it isn't paid. And sometimes the tasks done by voluntary workers are identical to those done by paid workers. A referee at a football match imposes the same rules on players but in some instances is paid and others not (Taylor, 2004, discusses this extensively). The second is slavery, where compulsion and control are excessive and wages are low or absent (we will discuss that in the section 'From Cotton to Denim'). The third is domestic work. Domestic work is perhaps the most common form of work in the world, and it provides the most significant challenge to the idea that work means paid work, and that the work that matters (and that should be studied) is paid work. After all, many domestic labour tasks you do yourself could be done by someone you pay (when it becomes '**domestic service**'). The task doesn't change when something is paid for rather than done for free, but the social relations, the motivation and the power relationships involved in it do.

Domestic Labour, Care and Domestic Service

What we mean when we say 'work' was a question much discussed in the 1970s as part of the 'domestic labour debates', where feminists argued that unpaid work, especially that done in the home, was work (Weeks, 2011). Domestic labour debates were crucial in countering how women's domestic labour was marginalized 'through the recognition that housework, the "labour of love" performed by women, was a form of work' (Beechey, 1987: 126). An important theme in these discussions is feelings that care work and domestic work involve and produce, and we can think with the concept of **emotional labour** to understand that more fully. Caring for someone is often associated with caring about them, and one marker of the quality of paid or unpaid care is whether it comes with kindness and other good feelings. Emotional labour reminds us that providing care kindly might come at a cost to the care-worker. Care is work, but it overlaps with other, complicated human experiences.

Domestic service is often highly gendered; women are likely to do both domestic labour and provide paid-for domestic services like cooking, cleaning and care. It is also often racialized and done by **migrant** women. It has a class dynamic too as low-status and low-skilled work that wealthier and more privileged people pay for. Care work, including domestic work, is often made invisible. **Invisible work** is that which is 'economically devalued' through cultural, legal and spatial mechanisms (Hatton, 2017: 337). It is the work that makes production possible. And it is the work needed to look after those not able to look after themselves. It is the everyday work of provisioning, tidying, and recycling. It is invisible when it is not noticed; but sometimes it is hidden from view deliberately. It raises many of the sociological questions that paid work raises: who does it, under what conditions, with what reward, what **skill** does it require, how has technology changed it, what personhood is involved?

WORK

Expand Your Knowledge

The Dimensions of Care Work

- Cottingham, M.D., Johnson, A.H. and Erickson, R.J. (2018) 'I can never be too comfortable': Race, gender, and emotion at the hospital bedside. *Qualitative Health Research* 28(1): 145–58. DOI: 10.1177/1049732317737980.

These American researchers analyse audio diaries made by professional black nurses in US hospitals and use vignettes to discuss the emotional labour of doing care work.

- Hansen, A.M. and Grosen, S.L. (2019) Transforming bodywork in eldercare with wash-and-dry toilets. *Nordic Journal of Working Life Studies* 9(S5). DOI: 10.18291/njwls.v9iS5.112689.

Denmark has introduced an array of 'welfare technologies', intended to improve the dignity of patients and care-workers. The researchers discuss how professional carers and the work they do with patients is affected by these kinds of technologies.

Work in a Globalized World: Follow the Denim

In this section, we will follow the production of one commodity all the way to the lifeworld of the end-consumer. This is called **Global Value Chain** analysis, a form of analysis used to understand the complexities of global **post-Fordist** production. Jeans may be the most popular clothing item in the world and make the ideal commodity to use for this exercise. Let's imagine we are talking about your jeans, assuming they are mid-priced, fashionable, and bought new from a well-known brand. Many different workers were involved in making the jeans: cotton pickers, brand managers, warehouse staff, and sales assistants, to name just a few. We can learn a lot about contemporary divisions of labour, and conditions of work, about skilled and unskilled work of many kinds, about the relationships between technology and working bodies, about hidden work, and about emotion and aesthetics. We do this by comparing occupations and sectors, and by thinking about the **intersectionality** of gender, race and class.

Designing Denim: Creative Work and Knowledge Work

A whole array of professional workers are involved in making a global value chain possible, including lawyers and accountants who set up and manage contracts with factories to produce the products, software engineers, and managers. What do these jobs share? They all involve handling information, and so we call these kinds of workers **knowledge workers**. Some knowledge workers are actively involved in doing creative work. The designers who decided on the cut, colour and trim of your jeans are the obvious occupation of interest, but marketing and brand managers also have a say in deciding what their imagined customer (you!) might want, given what they know about customers and what they think will be fashionable. The concept of **'cultural intermediary'** is a good way to understand this kind of creative work. Cultural intermediaries are taste-makers; they contribute to social understandings of what consumer goods are and are not desirable. Keith Negus describes them as 'continually engaged in forming a point of connection or articulation between production and consumption' (Negus, 2002: 503–4). That is, they contribute to how your jeans are produced by thinking about what consumers want. This is work that relies on creativity, but also an understanding of consumer markets. Lise Skov (2002) describes the tensions between Hong Kong fashion designers' ideas about creative design and business managers from the same company's preference for safe, proven ideas. Cultural intermediary workers are often employed on specific projects and can struggle to find security in a competitive labour market. They talk about their work as meaningful as it enables them to express their creativity, but always within constraints.

From Cotton to Denim

Quite different to creative workers are the cotton growers and pickers who produce the raw materials for your jeans. In studies of raw material production, questions of the exploitation of workers and of poor employment conditions are right at the forefront of sociological research. Cotton is grown in many places around the world. It is grown on plantations and harvested by machines operated by workers, often under conditions of '**adverse incorporation**' in the labour market, and sometimes under conditions of slavery. The Global Slavery Index (2018) estimates (conservatively – it's very hard to measure **forced labour** accurately, because it is hidden labour) that 40.3 million people live in modern slavery, of whom 15 million are in forced marriages, doing domestic and sex work, and others are in **indentures**, **debt bondage** or **false contracts**. Very few are now in **chattel slavery**.

Of the 16 million in private sector slavery, electronics production has the highest number, followed by garment production. How is this possible? After all, labour markets are regulated by nation-states, and governed by global agencies who have spoken out against forced labour. Forced labour persists because the pressure for cost-cutting in production to maximize profits is taken for granted. Nation-states even facilitate forced labour, for example when migrant workers can only get a visa if they are sponsored by an employer and so they dare not complain about how the employer treats them. In Uzbekistan, the **state** organizes forced labour, compelling private sector organizations to get their own employees to pick cotton (McGuire and Laaser, 2018).

Despite anti-slavery laws and the condemnation of global institutions like the **ILO**, the UN and the World Bank, deeply exploitative working conditions persist.

Not all exploitative work can be called forced labour. Adverse incorporation (Philips and Mieres, 2015) is a term used to explain how workers are trapped in exploitative working conditions. Adverse incorporation exists where work is organized in ways that keep people in poverty so that they find themselves trapped in lives where they have few options but to do that kind of exploitative work. Working with cotton is seasonal work, and that adds a layer of uncertainty as demand for labour varies. Further, the work can damage the people who do it. Once cotton is harvested, it is woven into textiles and dyed (and perhaps bleached or stonewashed). The chemicals used in fabric dyeing affect the worker's health. In our study of cotton production, we can see the links between how employment is organized and the effects of the work on human bodies. Raw material production is 'dangerous, demanding and dirty' (Pajnik, 2016: 160).

Factories and Sweatshops

Many sociologists of work consider factory work as the exemplary form of work. In factories, workers do repetitive activities according to a clear **division of labour**. Factory work, including garment production, raises sociological questions about relationships between working bodies and the technologies they use.

WORK

New technologies (which of course have to be designed, manufactured and maintained) change how work is done. The biggest revolution in garment production came in the 1850s, with the invention of the sewing machine, central to the growth of garment factories. Later inventions that affected how jeans production is now organized include fabric-cutting machines and new fabric types.

Sewing machines need a lot of human labour to operate: put on the reel of thread, arrange the fabric, push the foot pedal whilst pushing the fabric through, hear the whirr of the machine, keep it steady, turn, finish, snip. It is a complex process. But it is poorly paid. Why is that? One explanation that carries weight is that the skill it takes to sew jeans well is not recognized as a skill, because this work has historically been done by women, especially poor women, and often in small factories or sweatshops. A description of something as 'high skilled' or 'low skilled' is not a neutral description that relates to an established set of criteria for assessing skill. It is a specific, culturally inflected claim about what a society thinks counts as a skill. This social shaping of skill is also affected by intersections of race, class and gender. Garment production is often done by poor women living in poor countries, or by minority groups working in city-centre sweatshops in rich countries. Aihwa Ong, writing about Malaysian women working for Japanese companies, reports how managers described female factory workers as having 'nimble fingers, slow wit' (Ong, 2010: 151): they are deemed capable by dint of biology, and adjudged to be malleable because of racist interpretations of cultural difference. Several issues in the sociology of work combine in this case: judgements about the nature of work affect who gets recruited to which job, how skilled they are seen to be, and how they are treated. **Gender**, **ethnicity** and migration status are all relevant.

17.1 Key Case

The Rana Plaza Fire

What Happened?

In 2013, the Rana Plaza building in Dhaka collapsed. The collapse led to the death of 1,134 Bangladeshi garment workers. Around 2,500 were injured. Lower levels of the building were evacuated the day before, but the garment factories in the upper floors still operated. Rana Plaza is the garment production sector's worst industrial accident. It brought to light the dreadful employment conditions of garment production and the lack of concern with protecting workers.

Important Ideas

It's unlikely you'll have heard of the Rana Plaza factories. But I am sure you will have heard of the brands whose clothes were being made at Rana Plaza. Brands negotiate with a potentially large number of 'labour intermediaries' (Barrientos, 2013), more commonly called 'middlemen', whether or not they are men, to determine which organization(s) get the contract to sew them. That is, they outsource the work.

Now Do Your Research

You can look into campaigns for greater transparency and fairness for garment workers (*War on Want* and *Who Made your Clothes* are two examples). You can look into the response of the ILO. [www.ilo.org/global/topics/geip/WCMS_614394/lang--en/index.htm]. You can look into the responses by brands, which varied from pledging not to use these factories or donating to victims to denial of responsibility for what outsourcing organizations do. You can look into how Bangladesh's legal system responded. You can look into other, subsequent accidents in garment production.

Discussion Questions

- What does studying Rana Plaza and its aftermath tell us about work in global capitalism?
- Factory owners, branded garment retailers, nation-states, consumers: what responsibility does each of these have for incidents like Rana Plaza?

Logistics and Transportation

How did your jeans arrive at the shopping centre where you bought them? They were packed in plastic wrap, boxed and then sent on a container ship. Modern container ships do not require a lot of human labour, and their introduction resulted in the loss of jobs in shipping and on dockyards. Still, the transportation of component parts and finished goods relies on workers: drivers, ship crew, distribution warehouse staff, and the like. Post-Fordist production makes use of an array of **'just-in-time' (JIT)** technologies to manage this process, determining what goes where, via what route. And technologies re-shape work. When we think about logistics, we see some more invisible work, work that is taken for granted: the work of the IT programmer, the software engineer who designs the technologies, as well as the operators of the hand-held scanners that keep track of inventory and enable managers to assess how fast a worker completes their tasks. The development of IT has made a big contribution to reshaping logistics and transportation work. We see this in how **gig economy** services are provided: when you order pizza on an app and a cyclist brings it round to your house, you are making use of this kind of logistics management technology. The technology also enables surveillance of the worker (how happy are her customers, how quick did she deliver) and gathers knowledge about customers. Customers on self-service tills, internet shoppers inputting their own payment details and so on are further examples of how IT enables changes to who does the work, and how. In this case, customers do the work that paid workers used to do.

Promotion, Sales and Service

Why did you buy your jeans? You might have been influenced by one of the following promotional activities: photos of Instagram influencers, print adverts or online pop-ups that follow you round the internet after you did a search, the aesthetics and atmosphere of the store where you bought the jeans, the reputation of the brand, the discount on offer because your jeans are in the sale. None of this happens by accident. To put it another way, a lot of work goes into making us buy what we buy, including the work of gathering knowledge about customers, of persuasion and seduction, technical, abstract 'mental' labour. In this kind of work, we can see the presence of technologies developed and used by knowledge workers in order to do cultural intermediary work.

If you tried on your jeans in an actual shop, then it is likely you encountered one or two sales assistants. Sales assistants create the shop spaces – arranging displays and tidying racks. They work the till. And often

WORK

they do 'emotional labour'. They smile, they offer to bring you other sizes, they complement you, they encourage you to buy. Perhaps in the shop you went into, they seemed a bit like you: similar in **age**, dressed a bit like you. This is an example of a feature of some forms of contemporary work: that workers are recruited because of how they look, their background and their consumer preferences. They embody a brand, or an ideal about service – and other workers, with different bodies, might be excluded from that work. We call that **aesthetic labour**. Both emotional labour and aesthetic labour are ways of thinking about how work is embodied, both through what working bodies look like and must do, and how workers feel and think.

 —— Pause for Thought ——

- Here we are applying concepts introduced to explain one kind of work to understand another. Take another of the concepts and think about using it to explain a different kind of work. For example, consider the idea of the social shaping of skill and consider whether it helps to explain the status of nurses in comparison to doctors.

Understanding Work Now

In the previous section, we looked at many themes in the study of work that mattered to previous researchers. These themes, and the concepts that we have used to understand them, are relevant to thinking about two big questions about work for current society: what is happening to working conditions? (are they worsening?), and what will happen to work in the future?

Understanding Precarious Work

How can we explain how and why paid work is **flexible** and more **precarious?** What kinds of jobs are affected, and what kinds of workers? Paid jobs that could once be relied on to provide a life's commitment (and perhaps a life's meaning), that brought the sense of security that knowing you have the money to live on provides, or that were a rung on a career ladder, are fewer in number and harder to rely on. Instead, labour markets have become more flexible, with 'portfolio careers', contract-to-contract working, and flatter career ladders amongst the ever-more-common kinds of flexibility for professional workers. For others, **zero hours contracts**, gig economy work, seasonal flexibility, and underemployment (where people work fewer hours than they would like to) are more prevalent. Recent research tells us that work has become more precarious, although it is easy to overstate the idea that a 'job for life' is in decline: for many workers, work has long been informally organized or contingent and unstable.

The first explanation for that change is the idea of **job polarization**, discussed by Arne Kalleberg (2011) in the US. Job polarization means that there are fewer 'middle range' jobs. Instead, there are more low-skilled, low-status jobs, and a smaller number of high-skilled, high-status jobs. Kalleberg argues that this shift to more flexible employment relations is a result of changes to the economic system towards globalization and deregulation: these changes remove protections for workers. When corporations move production to another country where wages are cheaper, they benefit from globalization and deregulation. Kalleberg also says that this is because returns to shareholders (dividends) are seen as more important than wages to workers. Workers' wages are kept low in order for a corporation to be 'competitive'. Lee and Kofman (2012) are amongst those who consider Kalleberg's argument too blunt. They argue that concepts developed to understand the US case (polarization) can't be applied elsewhere very easily, where different kinds of non-standard contracts are the norm, or where trade unions play a different **role** in politics.

A second line of explanation is presented in *The Precariat: The New Dangerous Class* (Standing, 2011). Standing's thesis is that precariousness has increased everywhere, and this has created a new class identity for precarious workers, who in other respects live in quite different circumstances. The **precariat** live insecure lives, having to move between jobs that offer little reward or meaning. A woman working in garment production in a **SEZ** is a precarious worker, vulnerable to losing her job if the 'footloose' corporation decides to move production elsewhere, but so too is the marketing executive, or designer in London, Paris or Milan, who is only as good as their last contract. Both are precarious in the face of constantly shifting markets. Both are vulnerable, anxious and insecure. Standing's ideas have been criticized for reducing the complexity of global inequalities to the idea of precariousness. It might also be argued that labour market insecurity has been longstanding and normal for some groups of often invisible workers: piece workers, home workers, day labourers, and others who face conditions of adverse incorporation.

A third explanation relies on a more nuanced conceptualization of precariousness. Andrew Herod and Rob Lambert (2016) say that precariousness has several elements: low earnings, a minimal social safety net (e.g. few state benefits for those who can't work), little regulatory protection and limited **autonomy** for workers to shape their work. Herod and Lambert are economic geographers, but they think like sociologists when they draw our attention to the interplay between intimate **personal life** and feeling, and the social and economic structures and institutions within which life is lived. They argue that social relations can 'amplify' or 'cushion' (2016: 17) the effects of precarious work on an individual. For example, a student with a zero hours contract does precarious work, but if they have parental support and the prospect of a better job on graduating, they are not necessarily precarious workers. It gets more complicated, though, as many with ostensibly good jobs may live in 'conditions of precarity', knowing that they have it good, but worrying about what could happen when they look around them and see how others are living. A group of workers with good pay and conditions negotiate with the fear in mind that they too could end up with precarious work, living in conditions of precarity.

 Pause for Thought

- What do you think about contemporary precarity?
- Who amongst your acquaintances counts as precarious, and for what reasons?
- Is your generation more precarious than your parents' or grandparents' generation?

WORK

Debating the Future of Work

At the time of writing, there is a lot of discussion about the future of work. There is fear and anxiety but also optimism, as many feel that now is a time to make work better, and do less of it. One of the key features of new precariousness is the sense that it is not just jobs for life that are disappearing but that all jobs may soon be at risk due to the increasing ability to automate certain tasks in the workplace. And then how will we live? Stories in the media and popular non-fiction books can focus on – and fearmonger about – **automation** in work. We see in these accounts different versions of a concern about what happens to jobs as technological development means human labour can be done 'more efficiently' (more cheaply) by machines. Whether robots in factories, or artificial intelligence that can make apparently better decisions than trained and skilled human professionals, it can be made to sound as though the future for the human worker who wants a (fulfilling) job is bleak.

This dream – or nightmare – of a 'post-work' society is gaining increasing amounts of attention. The optimistic standpoint posits that people will be released from drudgery and exploitation. Productive work in factories is routinized, unrewarding and physically demanding: is it not desirable to save people from this and free them to do better things? It might also address the environmental damage caused by the production and consumption of so many goods and services in the quest for a better life. Those less in favour of technology replacing human labour ask how people will find a way to live that does not replicate or enhance existing inequalities. They also raise the question of the meaning people find in work, and how losing that meaning could affect people.

A sociological response to automation and post-work debates might ask: what kinds of jobs might (or might not) be affected by automation, and how? What happened in the past when work was automated, and what can be learned from that? What kind of effects does discussing automation and post-work have in the world? In so doing, sociology helps to pose ethical and political questions, as well as providing some answers.

What kinds of work count? A common but narrow assumption is that factory work is the work that will be substituted by machines, and some of the worry about automation is the loss of production jobs. The common work of changing dirty nappies or clearing tables is rarely under consideration (although in fast food joints, the work of clearing tables has already been moved away from paid workers to paying customers). Previous evidence of the effects of machines on human work often suggests that technological change produces new kinds of jobs. For example, tasks that machines are unable to do such as programming software, or mending and repairing, might become more important, and so these skills will be needed.

New technologies reshape relations between humans and machines. For example, aeroplanes need far less human input to fly than they used to, and pilots are needed in case of unexpected problems. That might seem okay. But pilots risk losing the tacit knowledge that comes from handling planes every day, and can struggle to reach the right decisions when under pressure. This is an example of a broader societal question: what is lost when human labour is reorganized by technologies? Does automation bring problems?

Conversations about new technologies often assume that change is inevitable and indicative of progress. That's a kind of **technological determinism**. The effect of that sense of inevitability is to hide the socio-economic dynamics that affect the adoption of technologies: nation-states and corporations actively make decisions about new technology. And remember the idea of 'conditions of precarity': living with the fear that your job will disappear because of new technology might well contribute to feeling precarious. By questioning the assumption of the inevitability of change, we can start to see some of the politics of technologies to replace workers.

PART 4 CONNECTING THE PERSONAL AND THE SOCIAL

Environmental Crisis and the Future of Work

Technological change is only a small part of the future of work; environmental change may be of more fundamental importance. Growing awareness of the catastrophic environmental effects of consumer behaviour might push people towards living differently, and that might mean less paid work, as fewer new goods are manufactured and sold, or more likely, the rise of different kinds of work, including repair and recycling work. Since 2010, with ideas like the 'Green New Deal', 'green jobs' have been developed by nation-states and by big non-state organizations like the UN and the EU. These are attempts to address the current environmental crisis, and more often, to anticipate future environmental changes by making some alterations to how economies (and therefore jobs) are organized. '**Sustainable**' economies involve 'green jobs' which do not cause (and sometimes redress) environmental damage.

The potential difficulty is that 'green jobs' may not always be skilled jobs, done under good employment conditions. Think back to our story of jeans. We saw how production and consumption were resource-intensive, and how greening that system would mean producing and consuming differently. A more radical change, stressing re-use and repair, has quite different implications for formal and informal work. The evidence is that green jobs are not always good jobs. Researchers who have looked at recycling, for example, have come up with a similar finding: recycling work might be important to reduce the use of scarce resources, but it is rarely decent work. It is in fact dirty, dangerous and demanding.

CHAPTER SUMMARY

- Work can be paid and unpaid, and not all work is equally visible and valorised in society.
- Both within households and across the globe, work in one area relies on and contributes to work elsewhere.
- People's working conditions are often damaging. Exploitation, including modern slavery, is still part of people's lives, and many people's work is precarious.
- Technological change has had and will continue to have an impact on work and workers. It's not always clear who benefits from new technologies.
- What work will look like in the future is unclear. Sociology plays a role in thinking about why work changes, and what effects those changes have on social inequality.

REVIEW QUESTIONS

1. Is 'skill' a neutral concept?
2. How would you describe the work of cleaning a home?
3. Give two examples of 'knowledge work' and consider how they are similar and how they are different.
4. What concepts can we use to understand poor quality work in contemporary societies?
5. What is 'emotional labour'?

Go Further

Books

- Aneesh, A. (2006) *Virtual Migration: The Programming of Globalization*. Durham, NC: Duke University Press.

A detailed empirical study of the work of computer programmers that explores how globalization works.

- Pettinger, L. (2019) *What's Wrong with Work?* Bristol: Policy Press.

This book contains a lively discussion of how work has changed in recent times, and how we as sociologists should understand that change.

- Strangleman, T. and Warren, T. (2008) *Work and Society: Sociological Approaches, Themes and Methods*. London: Routledge.

This is one of several textbooks that do a great job of informing undergraduates about key ideas in the sociology of work.

Journal Articles

- Kang, M. (2003) The managed hand: The commercialization of bodies and emotions in Korean immigrant-owned nail salons. *Gender & Society* 17(6): 820–39.

An interesting study of gender and race in service work in the US that develops the idea of emotional labour.

- Kothari, U. (2013) Geographies and histories of unfreedom: Indentured labourers and contract workers in Mauritius. *The Journal of Development Studies* 49(8): 1042–57.

Studies the history of colonialism in order to understand contemporary slavery.

- Roy, D. (1959) 'Banana time': Job satisfaction and informal interaction. *Human Organization* 18: 158–68.

A 'classic' in the sociology of work: great on how boring work is, but notice the absence of gender and race from the analysis.

Websites

- https://futuresofwork.co.uk

Up-to-date blog posts on important questions about work today.

- www.ilo.org/global/lang--en/index.htm

The website of the International Labour Office, the main non-governmental organization concerned with working lives.

REFERENCES

Barrientos, S.W. (2013) 'Labour chains': Analysing the role of labour contractors in global production networks. *Journal of Development Studies* 49(8): 1058–71.

Beechey, V. (1987) *Unequal Work*. London: Verso.

Global Slavery Index (2018) Minderoo Foundation. Available at: www.globalslaveryindex.org/resources/downloads (last accessed May 2021).

Hatton, E. (2017) Mechanisms of invisibility: Rethinking the concept of invisible work. *Work, Employment and Society* 31(2): 336–51.

Herod, A. and Lambert, R. (2016) Neoliberalism, precarious work and remaking the geography of global capitalism. In R. Lambert and A. Herod (eds) *Neoliberal Capitalism and Precarious Work: Ethnographies of Accommodation and Resistance*. Cheltenham: Edward Elgar Publishing, pp. 1–42.

Hochschild, A.R. (2003 [1983]) *The Managed Heart: Commercialization of Human Feeling*. Berkeley, CA: University of California Press.

Kalleberg, A. (2011) *Good Jobs, Bad Jobs: The Rise of Polarized and Precarious Employment Systems in the United States, 1970s to 2000s*. New York: Russell Sage.

Lee, C.K. and Kofman, Y. (2012) The politics of precarity: Views beyond the United States. *Work and Occupations* 39(4): 388–408.

McGuire, D. and Laaser, K. (2018) 'You have to pick': Cotton and state-organized forced labour in Uzbekistan. *Economic and Industrial Democracy*. 0143831X1878978.

Negus, K. (2002) The work of cultural intermediaries and the enduring distance between production and consumption. *Cultural Studies* 16(2): 501–15.

Ong, A. (2010) *Spirits of Resistance and Capitalist Discipline: Factory Women in Malaysia*, 2nd edition. New York: SUNY Press.

Pajnik, M. (2016) 'Wasted precariat': Migrant work in European societies. *Progress in Development Studies* 16(2): 159–72. DOI: 10.1177/1464993415623130.

Phillips, N. and Mieres, F. (2015) The governance of forced labour in the global economy. *Globalizations* 12(2): 244–60. DOI: 10.1080/14747731.2014.932507.

Skov, L. (2002) Hong Kong fashion designers as cultural intermediaries: Out of global garment production. *Cultural Studies* 16(4): 553–69.

Standing, G. (2011) *The Precariat: The New Dangerous Class*. London: Bloomsbury Academic.

Taylor, R.F. (2004) Extending conceptual boundaries: Work, voluntary work and employment. *Work, Employment and Society* 18(1): 29–49.

Weeks, K. (2011) *The Problem with Work: Feminist, Marxist, Antiwork Politics, and Postwork Imaginaries*. Durham, NC: Duke University Press.

HEALTH

Sarah Cant

LEARNING OBJECTIVES

- To understand the social patterning of health outcomes, and the extent of health inequality.
- To appreciate that all knowledge about health, including medicine, is socially constructed.
- To recognize the breadth and value of sociology for understanding health.

Framing Questions

1. What do we mean by biomedicine, and what wider role does it play in society?
2. What are the relative strengths and weaknesses of social causation and social constructionist perspectives in medical sociology, and how can we reconcile their insights?
3. Why do inequalities in health persist?
4. In what ways do complementary and alternative medicines, new health technologies, and processes of globalization influence health care?

PART 4 CONNECTING THE PERSONAL AND THE SOCIAL

Introduction

Understanding the factors that contribute to good health, and serve to compromise it, is deeply complicated, and of central concern to sociologists. Defined by the World Health Organization (2019) as a 'state of complete physical, mental and social wellbeing and not merely the absence of disease and infirmity', health is shaped by our biological makeup, social relationships, access to economic resources, cultural values, attitudes and lifestyle choices, the ecological and physical environment, and politics. Ostensibly, in the Global North, people's health has never been so good: they can hope to live long into old age, a privilege not enjoyed by all global citizens. However, socio-economic inequalities in life expectancy are seemingly impervious to change. Disabling conditions such as arthritis, diabetes, dementia, coronary heart failure, and so on, reduce our *healthy* life expectancy and, at present, palliative, rather than curative, interventions prevail. In addition, rates of mental illness are on a steep upward trajectory, suggesting that human wellbeing across the life-course is under considerable stress.

In this chapter, you will learn how sociology can make a valuable contribution to understanding health by identifying the social causes of illness and disease, and through its examination of how people access health care and make health choices. You will also be introduced to some of the ways that sociology has critiqued the biomedical model. Sociology teaches us that all conceptions of health and illness are socially constructed, and that health care choices and outcomes are shaped by, for instance, ideologies of individualism, capitalist economics, patriarchal social structures, and the legacies of colonialism. To illustrate some contemporary concerns within the sociology of health, we explore the rise in mental health disorders, the renewed popularity of complementary and alternative medicines, and the impact of new technologies and globalization on health. Inevitably, this will be both a partial and whistle-stop tour that can only signpost some of the key sociological questions about health.

Mapping the Terrain

All societies have mechanisms for dealing with health and illness and access to a range of healing systems, treatments and knowledge. However, across the globe, biomedicine dominates our understanding of health. The journey from antiseptics and anaesthetics to vaccines, antibiotics, the contraceptive pill, in vitro fertilization (IVF) and organ transplants, and then to antivirals, personalized cancer treatments, artificial organs, cosmetic surgery and gender realignment, has been rapid. Our understandings of genomic difference now provide ways to alter embryonic humans and allow us to tailor medical interventions. Such advances are, of course, associated with undeniable successes, but also tend to reinforce essentialist, biological understandings of human health differences, and minimize the attention given to sociological factors. Biomedicine's corporeal paradigm has conceptualized and researched the mechanical body, and in doing so has tended to bracket out connections between the body and the mind, and its wider social, economic and cultural location.

Despite the global reach and power of biomedicine, public distrust of this complex monolith now abounds. In this context, self-responsibility for health and lifestyle 'choices' take on new importance for tackling contemporary health risks. Thus, the sociology of health or, more accurately, the sociology of health, illness, healing, disease and medicine, has never been more important, and for this reason constitutes the largest sub-discipline within sociology.

Dating back to the 1950s, the original sociological contributions provided an appreciation of the social distribution and social causation of ill-health, making connections between health outcomes and poverty, income and class position. Ill-health was viewed as a form of deviance, with biomedicine regarded as central to the restoration of economic productivity through returning citizens to optimal health. Specifically, Parsons' (1951) conception of the sick role described a mutual and consensual relationship between the doctor and the patient and inaugurated what has been described as 'sociology *in* medicine' – with sociology supporting the needs and interests of biomedicine.

The critical capacity of sociology soon was turned onto biomedicine itself, however. By the 1970s, sociology began to challenge the power and authority of biomedicine, gave voice to lay perspectives on health, and showed that the doctor–patient relationship was often far from consensual. This new 'sociology *of* medicine' had many iterations. Understanding the persistence of health inequalities was central: Thomas McKeown's (1976) vivid depiction of falling death rates from infectious diseases established that these were correlated with improved sanitation, decent housing, food and income, rather than the introduction of biomedical vaccines. This work championed the role of sociology for understanding differential health outcomes and this has been further showcased during the COVID-19 pandemic.

In other analyses, the professional project of medicine and its powerful position was critically explored rather than taken as read and had several dimensions. Marxist writers explored the role medicine played within capitalism: in keeping workers healthy, and directing attention for ill-health away from class inequality, towards lifestyle and biology. Marxist and neo-Weberian writers showed that the power of biomedicine was rooted not simply in its claims to knowledge but was linked to its occupational and professional success in securing an autonomous and monopolistic position in the health care market, and its ability to create social distance between doctors and patients (see reviews in Barry and Yuill, 2016; White, 2017).

Scholars questioned biomedicine's therapeutic role, pointing to the existence of iatrogenic effects – not just the side-effects of medicines but also the way that patients were increasingly rendered dependent on doctors' expertise. Feminist writers described the patriarchal structures that underpinned biomedicine and recounted women's societal responsibility for health, as mothers, wives and lower-status health workers, as well as the disproportionate medicalization of women's bodies and lives. Viewing medicine as having a role in the reproduction of social divisions was not simply confined to the investigation of gender and class. Important critical analyses also revealed the significance of race, ethnicity and racism for understanding health care outcomes and experiences (see Chapters 11, 12 and 13).

Concurrently, Foucauldian analyses spawned multiple strands of enquiry within the broad church of social constructionism and asked radical questions about the history, form and status of medical knowledge claims and diagnosis (see Chapter 8). This work contributed to a broader questioning of medical power and expertise, suggesting that biomedicine was implicated in the surveillance, ordering and disciplining of populations.

These developments have, in turn, raised several complicated questions and challenges for a future sociology of health. For example, how can sociology reconcile the insights of both social constructionist and social causation perspectives? How does sociology balance an understanding of the impact on health of lifestyle choices on the one hand, and material social structures on the other? How must medical sociology adapt to account for the social changes brought about by globalization and new technologies? This chapter explores, in a preliminary way, these areas of enquiry. As such, the chapter inevitably omits more than it includes: it cannot do justice to the wide-ranging concerns within the sociology of health or comprehensively review the many and intersecting axes of stratification that shape health experiences and outcomes.

PART 4 CONNECTING THE PERSONAL AND THE SOCIAL

Health Inequalities: The Enduring Importance of Social Position

It is important that we turn your attention first to the question of health inequality. Differences in life expectancy (morality rates) and illness prevalence (morbidity rates), both within the UK and between countries, endure and continue to deepen, shaped by broader economic trends such as recession and austerity. In this section, we explore health inequalities in the UK, a country where everyone has access to the **National Health Service** (NHS), and yet where socio-economic, gender and ethnic inequalities continue to prevail. The value of **sociology** for both describing and explaining these differences remains imperative.

In the 19th century, the impact of poverty on health was increasingly palpable and subject to scrutiny and condemnation (Engels, 1997 [1845]). Yet, health inequalities endure. In 2012, the vivid mapping of life expectancy in London against the underground tube-line (subway) revealed continuous and shocking station-by-station differences. For instance, the Office for National Statistics (ONS) data exposed a 20-year difference in life expectancy between people living near Oxford Circus compared to those that resided close to Docklands Light Railway, a 5.4 mile (8.6 km) tube journey that takes just 19 minutes (Cheshire, 2012). In 2020 in the UK, rates of infection with, and survival rates from, coronavirus varied dramatically by region, **ethnicity**, deprivation, **age** and occupation (Public Health England, 2020), and also demand sociological study.

Official data thus requires us to interrogate the relationship between health, place and other socio-demographic factors. If we examine 2017 health outcomes in England by indices of deprivation (ONS, 2019), we find that men living in the most deprived (MD) areas can expect to live until the age of 74, compared to 83.3 years for those living in the least deprived (LD) areas – an almost 10-year difference. For women, life expectancy is greater across all groups (78.7 [MD] years versus 86.2 years [LD]), but the impact of deprivation is still evident, with men in LD areas expecting to live longer than the MD women – that is, deprivation has an impact on health outcomes that **intersects** with gender.

In turn, the impact of social class (see also Chapter 11), as measured by the proxy measure of occupation, has long been documented as having a significant influence on health outcomes. The landmark Black Report (1982), followed by the Whitehead Report (1987), the Acheson Enquiry (1988) and the important Whitehall studies, which charted health differences within the Civil Service and showed fine-grained inequality across all grades, have collectively tracked the persistence and deepening of class inequities (see Barry and Yuill, 2016, for a review of these reports). The most recent data from the ONS examined life expectancy for the years 2007–11, using the Registrar General's Classification of class by occupation. This shows that people from Social Class I (e.g. doctors, accountants) can expect to live for 5.9 years longer than those from Social Class XII (e.g. cleaners, refuse collectors) – an increase from the 4.9-year difference observed in 1982–6.

So how can we account for these differences? Access to, and use of, health services can explain some of the gap, but it is material and structural inequalities (poverty, income, housing, pollution and working conditions) and lifestyle choices (diet, exercise, alcohol consumption and smoking) that sociologists recognize to be critical. In turn, sociologists are often concerned that disproportionate policy attention is given to lifestyle choices, diverting attention away from the prevailing social and economic conditions. Indeed, understanding the mutually reinforcing relationship between **social structure** and agency is central to sociology and, more recently, drawing on the work of Pierre Bourdieu, writers have preferred to talk of *structured lifestyle choices*.

HEALTH

Expand Your Knowledge

- Read the work of Pinxten and Lievens (2014) and Kandt (2018) to gain a deeper and more nuanced understanding of the relationship between lifestyle and social position.

Another, more radical way of understanding the relationship between health choices and social structures is simply to suggest that the latter underscores the former.

 **Pause for Thought**

Phelen, Link and Tehranifar (2010) suggest that lower socio-economic status is directly linked to higher rates of smoking and obesity, less exercise and restricted access to health resources, and thus stands as the 'fundamental cause' of ill-health. They question the current policy attention that is given to changing individual risk factors and to improving medical interventions. Instead, they propose that we need broader societal interventions to redistribute socio-economic resources.

- What changes to state health policy does such a view lend support for?

A popular adage, drawn from health statistics, is that 'men die and women get sick'. Certainly, women have always lived longer than men, and appear to use the health service more extensively. This idea is worth unpacking and challenging however, not least because focusing on gender alone might miss the intersectional impact of other socio-demographic factors such as class (as we saw above) and directs attention disproportionately to women rather than men (see also Chapter 12). Whilst women do still live longer than men, the gap is beginning to narrow, especially when the greater number of deaths of young men (through accidents and suicide) are controlled for, and the effects of women's changing lifestyle (engagement in paid work, greater levels of alcohol consumption, etc.) begin to impact negatively on their life expectancy gains. Moreover, when general life expectancy is compared to healthy life expectancy, the additional years that women currently enjoy are revealed to be characterized by poor health. Data from 2016 (Public Health England, 2017) shows that, on average, men can expect to live to 79.5 and women to 83.1, a difference of 3.6 years compared to a six-year difference in 1981. Yet, healthy life expectancy is 63.4 for men and 64.1 for women, giving the proportion of one's lifetime in poor health as 20% and 23% respectively.

The idea that women are sicker than men is then rather simplistic: if women are living longer with compromised health, we would expect their use of the health services to be greater. The available data also suggests that usage differences are actually marginal, with any disparity being accounted for by the fact that many women have more challenging social roles, visit the doctor more often (especially during pregnancy – not in itself an illness), and are more likely to seek help. Indeed, feminist scholars suggest that women's health has been more consistently medicalized – with their reproduction cycle, menstruation, pregnancy, infertility, and the menopause subject to medical diagnosis and intervention. If **medicalization** accounts for the greater levels of attention *given* to women, rather than absolute differences in illness, it also points to the relative lack of attention given to men, another manifestation of gender inequality. More recent work in this area has shown how men are more likely to engage in risky behaviours, as a demonstration of their masculinity (see White, 2017, for a review). This also means that men are less likely to seek medical help, which may account for their earlier deaths. These contributions teach us that inequalities in health by gender are important and are underscored by cultural expectations about appropriate gender roles, but also by access to economic resources.

— Pause for Thought —

- Think about the ways in which gender roles and expectations might impact on the experience and diagnosis of heart disease.
- A quick Google search of images of heart attacks shows that pictures of men predominate. This contributes to lay health conceptions that coronary heart disease (CHD) is a male disease, but the relative risk in women is actually higher. Overall women are often diagnosed later than men and are given fewer intensive treatments. Why do you think this might be the case?

— Expand Your Knowledge —

- You might want to read the research conducted by Adams et al. (2008). This identified significant differences in doctors' treatment of men and women and suggested that stereotypically-gendered thinking affected the medical diagnosis, treatment and management of CHD.

Finally, in this section, we turn to health outcomes by ethnicity (see also Chapter 13), a comparatively more nascent area of enquiry, thwarted in the past by incomplete data and less research interest, but nevertheless another central axis of stratification. Data suggests that there are significant differences in health outcomes across ethnic groups: the poorest health outcomes are experienced by British Bangladeshi and Pakistani people, followed by British Caribbean and Indian people, with the best outcomes associated with British Chinese and white people. Such groupings point immediately to some problems of measurement: these broad categories, derived from self-reported classifications, are based on proxy measures of regional heritage rather than ethnicity, and therefore can mask heterogeneous experiences. Despite these problems, some persistent patterns emerge. For example, diabetes is almost four times more prevalent among British Bangladeshi men and almost three times more prevalent among British Pakistani and Indian men than among men in the general **population**.

Karlson (2007) argues that understanding these differences in terms of biology or behaviour alone is flawed. Instead, ethnicity intersects, first, with socio-economic factors. Nazroo (2003) meticulously explored these correlations and suggested that differentials in income, housing and employment play a strong independent **role** in accounting for health outcomes. However, he notes that socio-economic explanations are not sufficient, and the impacts of racial harassment and discrimination on health outcomes are also critical. Collating evidence from a range of studies, Karlson (2007: 1) situates **racism** as the underlying cause of health differences: 'Racist victimisation makes people ill. It can explain the health impact of (perceived) "cultural" or "biological" differences (which are used as a justification for unfair treatment) and the concentration of people from minority ethnic groups in socioeconomic and other forms of disadvantage'. Racism then stands as another 'fundamental' cause of health inequality, underscoring differences in opportunities, access to health services, and the levels of stress endured.

HEALTH

Inevitably, this has been a cursory examination: other axes of stratification, such as age, disability and sexuality, are also central to discussions of health inequality. We have established the importance of sociology to make sense of the intersecting socio-economic factors that shape health chances and have explored the impact of class, gender roles, **patriarchy** and racism on health experiences and outcomes.

 Pause for Thought

- Construct a list of the social factors that shape health outcomes and think about the priority you would give to each one.

The Social Construction of Health

In the section on health inequalities, you learned that our ideas about heart disease are gendered, and how these ideas impact on health care delivery and practice. In this section, we introduce you more fully to the insights of **social constructionism**: a perspective in sociology which argues that knowledge is always the outcome of social processes through which we make the world meaningful. To say that ideas of health and illness are **socially constructed** is not to suggest that health concerns are not real, or that they are not associated with genuine pain and suffering. Rather, it is to open up the possibility of interrogating the social circumstances that shape our ideas about health and illness. It requires us to think about what it is we are able to know about health at any point in time and explore how categories of thought about health shape our experiences and identities.

Let's illustrate this perspective by considering the history of medicine. It is usual in medical history books to chart the **rational** and progressive **development** of medical knowledge, a story that reveals the foolhardiness of once having viewed the body as being made up of four humours or vital energies, and instead celebrates the putatively objective and self-evident truth of the body as a corporeal entity consisting of organs, DNA, and genes. This is not to deny that there is a biological reality to the body, which can be observed and studied. However, historically and culturally there has been considerable variation in the ways that this biological reality has been thought about. Therefore, sociology asks questions that focus on the social, cultural and economic conditions that made specific ways of knowing and seeing the body, health and illness *possible*, and to show that these 'ways' reflect prevailing world views. When you follow this line of thinking, the idea of scientific objectivity becomes problematic as science is also revealed to be shaped by its social context. The influential work of Foucault (1976) showed that the development of biomedical knowledge was underpinned by a decline in religious thought and the development of **capitalism**: the belief that the body was a machine that operated separately from the mind, and a conceptualization that disease was located in the body rather than the environment began to dominate. Such thinking, he argued, underpinned the development of a new '**medical gaze**' that, in turn, altered the relationship between the doctor and the patient: the former accruing power and status, and the latter becoming a passive recipient of medical expertise and intervention.

Social constructionist analysis then invites consideration of the power relations that inform, and are reproduced and mediated through, biomedical knowledge. These are seen to reflect wider social divisions, for instance along the lines of class, gender, ethnicity and sexuality. Important work has shown, for instance, that biomedical emphasis on individual bodies and behaviours fits with late modern capitalism and diverts attention away from structural causes and collective solutions to health concerns, and thus justifies and reproduces class inequality. In relation to gender, it has been argued that **biomedicine**, shaped by patriarchal conditions, constructed the female body as inherently pathological due to its reproductive functions and its difference from the 'normal' male body. Similarly, it has been observed that biomedicine first developed in the Global North and was thus implicated in European **colonialism**. In turn, non-white bodies, behaviours and populations have often been constructed as mentally, culturally and sexually pathological. This understanding can help explain the differential treatment of certain groups of people by biomedicine and we can see the value of social constructionism for thinking differently about the health inequalities discussed in the section above.

The perspective has developed into a sociology of diagnosis to explore how diagnostic categories impact on the illness experience, validate and judge certain medical conditions, and shore up medical power (Jutel and Nettleton, 2011). Getting a diagnosis of a condition can, of course, be reassuring: it can help us make sense of our illness experience. It can, though, in the case of **chronic illnesses**, also lead to a loss of identity, requiring '**biographical adjustments**' to rebuild a sense of self, in line with biomedical categories.

Expand Your Knowledge

- In a qualitative study that explored young people's adjustment to life with a stoma (an opening on the abdomen that can be connected to either the digestive or urinary system to allow waste (urine or faeces) to be collected outside the body), Polidano et al. (2019) describe how their respondents had to adjust their conception of self and adapt to new ways of living with this life-changing medical intervention.

More than this, medical diagnoses can lead to processes of **labelling**, sometimes with profound and negative impacts. That homosexuality was diagnosed as a mental illness until 1973 stands as an example of how social conditions shaped diagnostic categories and helped frame sexuality as pathology. In the present day, diagnoses of Attention Deficit Hyperactive Disorder certainly enable families and children to achieve support and legitimacy but can also contribute to feelings of victimization and **stigmatization** (Singh, 2011). Indeed, stigma has been an important concept for sociologists of health, shown to have direct and indirect health consequences through its 'felt' impact on self-esteem and its 'enacted' impact on access to health care.

 Pause for Thought
---

Lian and Bondevik (2015) chart the historical changes in the medical understanding of long-term exhaustion to reveal a cultural bias in diagnosis. Specifically, they chart the shift from seeing exhaustion as a male condition, manifest through physical symptoms, and the result of high-level intellectual demands, to a female and self-inflicted psychiatric ailment.

- Think about what the implications of this discursive shift might be for the way that exhaustion is viewed and treated.

HEALTH

Diagnoses are also an important foundation for medicalization, an idea that we use to draw this section to a close. You have already been introduced to the idea that medicine distinguishes the normal from the pathological. However, the purview of biomedicine has become ever more extensive: all people are increasingly subject to scrutiny by doctors, as we are all 'potentially' ill. The development of health promotion, for example, gave permission for biomedical practitioners to interrogate the homes and lifestyles of the healthy: their alcohol consumption, sunbathing practices, diet, choice of sexual partners, and so on. Indeed, arguably, all aspects of life are increasingly subject to medical judgement, as illustrated through the example of shyness.

 ——— Pause for Thought ———

Medicalization of Shyness

Susie Scott's (2006) article charts how shyness became increasingly defined as a treatable problem. First appearing in the statistical manual of Mental Disorders under the category of Social Phobia in 1980, we see the emergence of a medical category used to define a previously social category of 'shyness', and the role medicine played in diagnosing this as a health 'problem', with an associated development of pharmacological interventions, psychological treatments, and self-help manuals. Scott (2006: 140) describes it thus: 'as shyness becomes less and less socially acceptable, the "shyest" people are finding that their erstwhile deviant identities are being recast in biomedical terms and subjected to psychiatric treatment'.

- Think about other areas of social life that might be increasingly subject to processes of medicalization – Insomnia? Impotence? Alcoholism? Gambling?

A Spotlight on the Mental Health Crisis: Combining Insights from the Sociologies of Causation and Construction

Thus far, you have learned in broad terms about the value of social causation and the social constructionist perspectives within the sociology of health. In this section, we explore the merits of both for understanding the distribution of mental health conditions. In 2014, it was estimated that one in four people in the UK would experience a mental health problem every year, constituting a 20% increase on data for 1993 (Baker, 2018). Children, university students and the general population are all described as at increasing 'risk' of experiencing mental disorders, with the suggestion that we are in the throes of an **epidemic**. Again, there are socio-demographic patterns, as revealed by statistics: women are diagnosed more vulnerable than men to depression, although more men commit suicide; British Caribbean people are around six times more likely to be diagnosed with a severe psychotic mental illness than other ethnic groups; and socio-economic disadvantage and unemployment can also be mapped against mental instability (see Rogers and Pilgrim, 2014, for a review).

This socio-demographic profile has supported social causation theories, with attention given to the impact of changing social structures and the constraints of particular societal roles. Greenfeld's (2013) application of Durkheim's concept of **anomie** (see Chapter 7) is particularly instructive, and explains why rates of mental ill health might be on the rise. She posits a causal relationship between nationalism (characterized by open systems of stratification, an impersonal **state** and an economy organized on the principle of sustained growth) and schizophrenia, manic depression and unipolar depression. Mental disease, she argues, emerges when a highly individualized society is organized around ambition and aspiration.

--- Expand Your Knowledge ---

- Read the research paper by Prins et al. (2015): they suggest that people who exhibit anxiety and depression are actually 'suffering from capitalism', with the class gradient in prevalence revealing the impact that relative material disadvantage and work stress have on wellbeing.

It is not just changes to the economy that explain why mental illness might be on the rise. Research evidence reveals the impact that stress and female oppression have on women's mental wellbeing, suggesting that women's labour in the domestic sphere and motherhood can be 'maddening' (see Barry and Yuill, 2016, for a review); and Nazroo et al. (2019) importantly point to how institutional racism, as well as deprivation, cause differential mental health impacts for some ethnic groups.

At the same time, social constructionist analyses have revealed the historical and cultural relativity of diagnosis, to show how meanings, responses and manifestations of distress are socially shaped, as we saw in the example of long-term exhaustion in the previous section. Thus, is it that men with Afro-Caribbean heritage are more likely to come to the notice of the police and psychiatric professionals and are, in turn, seen, labelled and misdiagnosed as mentally disordered? Feminist scholars too question the **validity** of official statistics, seeing women as similarly labelled as deviant and given disproportionate attention by the medical profession. Historical examples of both *drapetomania* (the mental illness that allegedly afflicted slaves and explained why they tried to run away from their owners) and *hysteria* (a common 19th-century female mental illness) are thus better explained as social diagnoses used to categorize troublesome slaves and difficult women, and justify treatments designed to keep them in their place. More broadly, this perspective requires us to ask whether the recent mental health crisis is as much a product of new vocabularies and burgeoning mental health diagnoses as it is of a factual rise.

Both perspectives are independently valuable and, because they come from different **epistemological** positions, they ask different questions and produce different insights. However, a deeper question is whether they are contradictory or whether their insights can be reconciled. There is a danger that social constructionist work, by directing our attention to the relativity of diagnosis, might unintentionally marginalize **empirical** work on social causes. Here, a critical **realist** perspective can help us: this recognizes that social and cultural factors shape our understandings, and that official data and psychological measures are problematically construed and time-bound, but shows that we can still use them as a way to identify real distress and propose solutions. This requires us to remember that we are concerned with the *social construction* of a *reality*: of course, mental illness is real in its expression and experience, but we can still examine the social conditions that make it possible to be known, diagnosed and treated, and which are correlated with prevalence rates.

An example of this approach is given by Cant (2018). She explored the fivefold rise in the number of undergraduate students exhibiting psycho-pathological symptoms during the last ten years, and whilst recognizing that the language of mental distress is now more readily used by students to describe what might be seen as a 'normal' university experience, she argues that this should not deny the experience of real distress or divert our attention away from the impact of sociological risk factors such as: student debt; adaptation to university life; and worries about future employment.

From Patient to Proactive Consumer: Lay Health 'Expertise' and Self-responsibility

In the section on the social construction of health, we showed how biomedicine has gained a central role and the authority to define health and make decisions about medical interventions. Alongside efficacy, this power base was built during the 20th century through eliminating, limiting and subordinating competitor health care modalities and practitioners, by securing a monopoly in state-sponsored health care and **autonomy** in decision-making, and by rendering the patient as the passive recipient of medical expertise, rather than an active participant in their own healing (see Barry and Yuill, 2016). This position of authority has been questioned more recently, and here we explore three factors linked to these challenges. First, the emergence of a critical sociology of medicine revealed that forms of lay expertise exist and are widely used by patients to navigate their understandings of, and conduct in relation to, their health. Second, the lay public has become increasingly sceptical of medical authority, as the limitations and risks of biomedical intervention have become more visible. This can be illustrated by the turn to **complementary and alternative medicines** (CAM). Third, new **technologies** – in particular the internet and more recently health apps – have equipped the lay public with opportunities to educate, test, diagnose and medicate themselves in line with biomedical knowledge, but without recourse to a practitioner. All of these factors intersect with wider trends to an increasingly individualized and consumerist society, in which responsibility for health becomes fundamentally personal (rather than social or professional), and linked to market choices.

The focus on **lay health beliefs** and **lay 'expertise'** has been important for understanding health care. A large body of work has established that lay people have their own valid explanations and accounts for their health, in turn shaped by socio-cultural factors. Such work has helped explain why people seek medical care, or choose to ignore it, as well as pointing to how the experience of health care for patients might be improved. Particularly insightful has been the study of people with chronic illnesses, who amass both medical and biographical expertise, often build self-help groups (outside the medical arena), and develop their own treatment regimes (see Barry and Yuill (2016) for a review).

Whilst biomedicine can adapt to patient needs and alter its practice, with the support of sociology, it is also the case that broader social and technological changes have unsettled the relationship between doctors and their patients. One way of exploring these changes is by turning our attention to the deliberate decision taken by some people to choose to pay for alternatives to biomedicine. Despite the fact that biomedicine is free at the point of delivery in the UK, from the 1980s onwards significant numbers of the population turned to CAM – with estimates varying between 6 to 27% of the population. It should be noted that these users constitute a discrete subsection of the population – those in a position to afford such decisions – predominantly middle-class women. Their motivations have been shown to include: the desire to have a more holistic understanding of health; wanting to protect themselves from the perceived side-effects of biomedical interventions; the search for a more dialogic and equal relationship with their practitioner; support for conditions where biomedicine could only offer palliative care; and wanting to have their views taken seriously. Taken together, these motivations reveal many current dissatisfactions with biomedicine and a desire to reinstate the patient more centrally in the healing process.

It is tempting to see the turn to CAM as a radical change in health practices. However, this form of resistance also reproduces many aspects of biomedicine. In the first place, global capitalistic and neoliberal imperatives, those that emphasize choice, individuality and profit, underscore the expansion of CAM. Second, it is debatable whether consultations in CAM are more equal: they are certainly lengthier, but practitioners maintain control of the consultation, and the development of training programmes has meant that CAM practitioners have become more professionalized, more like medical doctors, and thereby more socially distant. More than this, CAM has been shown to be implicated, like biomedicine, in processes of surveillance, demanding greater self-responsibility for health (Cant, 2021). This case study reveals not only the changing levels of support for biomedicine, but also indicates that all health practices are shaped by the wider socio-economic context and play a role that extends beyond simple health delivery.

Our third example serves to further illustrate these ideas. The launch of the internet immediately had widespread implications and opportunities for the sharing of health knowledge, including biomedical research papers, and unsettled our understanding of who could call themselves an expert. Social media has had the similar effect of providing more, differently communicated, information. Facebook, for instance, provides an opportunity to share biomedical knowledge, learn from other users' experiential expertise and garner mutual support.

Expand Your Knowledge

- Read Maslen and Lupton's (2019) study of women's use of Facebook through a feminist lens. This reveals how online communities validate lay health experiences and provide an intimate and empathetic space to share health stories.

Moreover, a huge array of health technologies is now available – smartphone and apps or specialist fitness devices – for people to track and manage their own health. We can record the amount of exercise we engage in, the calories we consume, and we can log our personal readings of blood pressure, cholesterol and blood sugar. We can contact medical practitioners via teleconsultation rather than being physically present, and the elderly can be monitored at home by sensors and alarms so that caregivers can be alerted to falls or lack of movement. Smart textile medical devices can now monitor heart rate, oedema and respiration rates, woven into clothing so that they are 'invisible, mundane and familiar' (Joyce, 2019: 158).

Pause for Thought

Think about how often, and the ways in which, you and your family use the internet, health apps and wearable health technologies:

- Do you use the information to frame your consultations with doctors?
- Does accessing health information serve to reassure you, or does it make you feel more anxious?

There is much discussion in the popular media about the privacy risks associated with health apps. Why not read some of these articles and debate with others the pros and cons of new health technologies.

HEALTH

Whilst such technologies stand as examples of medical advance, they also raise questions for sociologists. We can see that they pose new challenges to medical authority as consumers can self-diagnose and can challenge medical advice. But alongside the empowerment of users, we are also witnessing the intrusion of medical technology further into our everyday lives, which produces a blurring of the boundary between home and clinic. Using social constructionist insights, we can see that these new technologies engender ever more pervasive and self-directed surveillance of the (already diagnosed) unwell, and also the (currently still) healthy. Considering that the mass of information generated by these apps can be fed into big data about our bodies and lives, which in turn can support the creation of marketing profiles for pharmaceutical and biotech companies, these 'big brother' potentials require sociological scrutiny.

Hear from the Expert

Deborah Lupton, an eminent medical and digital sociologist, has conducted extensive work looking at the internet and health apps which support the self-tracking of health. She draws our attention to the ways that these technologies can simultaneously reassure and terrify; empower and surveill. Why not follow her blog: *This Sociological Life*, which contains podcasts, interviews and publications (https://simplysociology.wordpress.com).

Globalization and Global Inequalities

The sociology of health can be critiqued for its Global Northern focus and, thus far, our discussion has been predominantly centred on the UK. To conclude this chapter, we turn our attention to the impact of **globalization** on health and global inequalities, and the effect of biomedicine on global health. Globalization has served to establish and strengthen biomedicine's structural dominance across the globe, and major biomedical drug companies have coalesced into global firms with global markets. This expansion of biomedicine has had the impact of both reducing the reach and status of local health traditions (except where the poor cannot afford biomedical care) while, at the same time, fostering opportunities for exchanges between traditional, non-orthodox and biomedical health knowledges.

However, the globalization of biomedicine has not signalled absolute improvements to global health: on the contrary, the divergence between the increasingly wealthy and the desperately poor has been concretized (Marmot, 2016). These differences do not simply reflect local environmental conditions, cultural differences and varying levels of GDP, but emanate from global decisions such as: permits on life-saving drugs; low incentives for pharmaceutical companies to invest in the development of drugs for the poor; and the impact of recruitment and migration of health workers from 'developing' countries.

In the same way that national inequalities are underscored by social and economic factors, global inequalities reflect differences in income. The WHO (2017) document how 16,000 children die every day before their fifth birthday, from preventable diseases such as malaria, tuberculosis and diarrhoea. And maternal mortality, a key indicator of health inequity, is a risk factor that characterizes 'developing' countries. Life expectancy varies from 50 in Sierra Leone to 84 in Japan. These figures, whilst shocking, also draw attention to the importance of sociological factors for understanding health outcomes: the conditions into which people are born and live, as well as their access to medical care, shape life expectancy.

The sociology of health requires that we give our attention to a number of global concerns. First, climate change and global warming threaten the health of all people but are likely to have a disproportionate effect on the poorest people living in poorly resourced countries in the Global South. Second, new infectious diseases, such as Ebola and Coronavirus, cannot be contained to the area of initial outbreak, and with COVID-19 we have seen the rapid development of a modern-day **pandemic**. It is not simply that these diseases threaten the 'rest' of the word that is our concern: they importantly cause devastation – global inequalities, economic decisions and colonial histories have rendered certain areas vulnerable to outbreaks of disease and explain why they have fewer resources to respond (Brisbois and Plamondon, 2018). Third, migration patterns unsettle the balance of health workers: in English-speaking, high-income countries, 20 to 35% of all practising doctors are foreign trained (OECD, 2010) and, in the UK, the number of foreign-trained nurses grew from 12 to 55% between 2004 and 2014. Fourth, there is a mismatch between pharmaceutical research and development and the global burden of disease. A lack of profit incentive impacts on business decisions, with more money spent, for instance, on surgical procedures for hair loss than malaria. Finally, sociologists have examined the exchange of medicinal treatments and practices across the globe; this not only includes health tourism for surgery and abortions and biopiracy, but also international birth markets and the use of surrogates. Taking all these factors into account reveals how imperative it is that sociology studies the global interconnections in health and contributes to our understanding of global health differences and colonial, biomedical power relations.

CHAPTER SUMMARY

- The sociology of health covers the human journey from birth to death, and encompasses a rich array of research topics, informed by the whole breadth of sociological theory and through employing the full range of sociological research methodologies.
- Social class, gender and ethnicity (as well as other axes of stratification) impact on physical and mental health outcomes.
- Material inequality intersects with lifestyle choices, stress, societal norms and prejudice to shape health outcomes both within the UK and across the globe.
- Sociology reveals how all knowledge, including biomedicine, is a social product, implicated in both the improvement of medical outcomes as well as the medicalization and ordering of populations.
- Biomedicine can be resisted and challenged by taking account of lay understandings of health, by the turn to alternative healing systems, and through access to new health technologies.

REVIEW QUESTIONS

1. How can sociology contribute to an understanding of health inequalities?

Think about the value of extending our understanding of health outcomes beyond biology and disease, to focus on material inequality and its link to lifestyle choices. Sociology draws our attention to the differential treatment of certain groups – how does capitalism, colonialism, patriarchy and racism impact on health outcomes?

HEALTH

2. Explore the ways in which sociology has critiqued the biomedical model.

While sociology recognizes the undeniable successes of biomedicine, think about the ways it also questions the power of the medical profession, and its role in ordering and surveilling populations. You might also want to think about which health knowledge and health providers have been marginalized as biomedicine has been accorded both status and a monopoly in the delivery of state-funded health care in the UK.

3. Compare and contrast social causation and social constructionist approaches for understanding health.

In this question, you should outline the two approaches and think about their relative merits and limitations, but also explore the ways in which we might reconcile their insights.

4. Explore how sociology can enhance our understanding of coronavirus and COVID-19.

In this question, you could examine the social patterning of the disease, the social factors linked to contagion, and the social consequences – for example, long-term chronic health and biographical disruption, social isolation, unemployment and mental health.

Go Further

Books

- Bartley, M. (2017) *Health Inequality: An Introduction to Theories, Concepts and Methods,* 2nd edition. Cambridge: Polity Press.

This book offers a comprehensive and nuanced review of health inequalities and why they remain persistent.

- Gabe, J. and Monoghan, L.F. (2022) *Key Concepts in Medical Sociology,* 4th edition. London: Sage.

Medical sociology comprises many concepts that are explained in this compendium. To extend your understanding and find out more about the breadth and scope of health sociology, there are many textbooks. Two excellent choices are:

- Nettleton, S. (2013) *The Sociology of Health and Illness,* 3rd edition. Cambridge: Polity Press.
- White, K. (2017) *An Introduction to the Sociology of Health and Illness,* 3rd edition. London: Sage.

REFERENCES

Adams, A., Buckingham, C.D., Lindenmeyer, A., McKinlay, J.B., Link, C., Marceau, L. and Arber, S. (2008) The influence of patient and doctor gender on diagnosing coronary heart disease. *Sociology of Health and Illness* 30(1): 1–18.

Baker, C. (2018) *Mental Health Statistics for England: Prevalence, Services and Funding.* Available at: https://researchbriefings.parliament.uk/ResearchBriefing/Summary/SN06988 (last accessed 14 October 2019).

Barry, A-M. and Yuill, C. (2016) *Understanding the Sociology of Health: An Introduction.* London: Sage.

Brisbois, B. and Plamondon, K. (2018) The possible worlds of global health research: An ethics-focused discourse analysis. *Social Science and Medicine* 196: 142–9.
Cant, S. (2018) Hysteresis, social congestion and debt: Towards a sociology of mental health disorders in undergraduates. *Social Theory and Health* 16(4): 311–25.
Cant, S. (2021) Complementary and alternative medicine. In J. Gabe and L. Monaghan (eds) *Key Concepts in Medical Sociology*, 4th edition. London: Sage.
Cheshire, J. (2012) Lives on the line: Mapping life expectancy along the London Tube network. *Environment and Planning A* 44(7). DOI: 10.1068/a45341.
Engels, F. (1997 [1845]) *The Condition of the Working Class in England*. Harmondsworth: Penguin.
Foucault, M. (1976) *The Birth of the Clinic: An Archaeology of Medical Perception*. London: Tavistock.
Greenfeld, L. (2013) *Mind, Modernity, Madness*. Cambridge, MA: Harvard University Press.
Joyce, K. (2019) Smart textiles: Transforming the practice of medicalisation and health care. *Sociology of Health and Illness* 41(S1): 147–61.
Jutel, A. and Nettleton, S. (2011) Towards a sociology of diagnosis: Reflections and opportunities. *Social Science and Medicine* 73(6): 793–800.
Kandt, J. (2018) Social practice, plural lifestyles and health inequalities in the United Kingdom. *Sociology of Health and Illness* 40(8): 1294–1311.
Karlson, S. (2007) *Ethnic Inequalities in Health: The Impact of Racism*. Available at https://raceequalityfoundation.org.uk/wp-content/uploads/2018/03/health-brief3.pdf (last accessed 23 October 2019).
Lian, O.S. and Bondevik, H. (2015) Medical constructions of long-term exhaustion, past and present. *Sociology of Health and Illness* 37(6): 920–35.
Marmot, M. (2016) *The Health Gap: The Challenge of an Unequal World*. London: Bloomsbury.
Maslen, S. and Lupton, D. (2019) 'Keeping it real': Women's enactments of lay health knowledges and expertise on Facebook. *Sociology of Health and Illness* 41(8): 1637–51.
McKeown, T. (1976) *The Role of Medicine: Dream, Mirage or Nemesis?* London: Nuffield Provincial Hospitals Trust.
Nazroo, J.Y. (2003) The structuring of ethnic inequalities in health: Economic position, racial discrimination, and racism. *American Journal of Public Health* 93(2): 277–84.
Nazroo, J., Rhodes, J. and Bhui, K. (2019) Where next for understanding race/ethnic inequalities in severe mental illness? Structural, interpersonal and institutional racism. *Sociology of Health and Illness* 42(2): 262–76.
OECD (Organization for Economic Cooperation and Development) (2010) *International Migration of Health Workers*. Available at: www.who.int/hrh/resources/oecd-who_policy_brief_en.pdf. (last accessed 30 October 2019).
ONS (Office for National Statistics) (2019) *Health State Life Expectancies by National Deprivation Deciles, England and Wales: 2015 to 2017*. Available at: www.ons.gov.uk/peoplepopulationandcommunity/healthandsocialcare/healthinequalities/bulletins/healthstatelifeexpectanciesbyindexofmultipledeprivationimd/2015to2017 (last accessed 24 October 2019).
Parsons, T. (1951) Illness and the role of the physician: A sociological perspective. *American Journal of Orthopsychiatry* 21(3): 452–60.
Phelan, J.C., Link, B.G. and Tehranifar, P. (2010) Social conditions as fundamental causes of health inequalities: Theory, evidence, and policy implications. *Journal of Health and Social Behavior* 51(1_suppl): S28–S40.
Pinxten, W. and Lievens, J. (2014) The importance of economic, social and cultural capital in understanding health inequalities: Using a Bourdieu-based approach in research on physical and mental health perceptions. *Sociology of Health and Illness* 36(7): 1095–1110.

Polidano, K., Chew-Graham, C.A., Bartlam, B., Farmer, A.D. and Saunders, B. (2019) Embracing a 'new normal': The construction of biographical renewal in young adults' narratives of living with a stoma. *Sociology of Health & Illness* 42(2): 342–58.

Prins, S.J., Bates, L.M., Keyes, K.M. and Muntaner, C. (2015) Anxious? Depressed? You might be suffering from capitalism: Contradictory class locations and the prevalence of depression and anxiety in the USA. *Sociology of Health and Illness* 37(8): 1352–72.

Public Health England (PHE) (2017) *Life Expectancy and Healthy Life Expectancy*. Available at: www.gov.uk/government/publications/health-profile-for-england/chapter-1-life-expectancy-and-healthy-life-expectancy (last accessed 24 October 2019).

Public Health England (PHE) (2020) *Disparities in the Risk and Outcomes of COVID 19*. Available at: https://assets.publishing.service.gov.uk/government/uploads/system/uploads/attachment_data/file/892085/disparities_review.pdf (last accessed 10 July 2020).

Rogers, A. and Pilgrim, D. (2014) *A Sociology of Mental Health and Illness*. Maidenhead: Open University Press.

Scott, S. (2006) The medicalisation of shyness: From social misfits to social fitness. *Sociology of Health and Illness* 28(2): 133–53.

Singh, I. (2011) A disorder of anger and aggression: Children's perspectives on attention deficit/hyperactivity disorder in the UK. *Social Science and Medicine* 73: 889–96.

White, K. (2017) *An Introduction to the Sociology of Health and Illness*. London: Sage.

World Health Organization (WHO) (2017) *10 Facts on Health Inequalities and their Causes*. Available at: www.who.int/features/factfiles/health_inequities/en (last accessed 30 October 2019).

World Health Organization (2019) *Constitution*. Available at: www.who.int/about/who-we-are/constitution (last accessed 24 October 2019).

EDUCATION

Nasima Hassan

LEARNING OBJECTIVES

- To connect voices from the geographical South with critical reflections on education.
- To introduce sociological theories to world views on education, exploring how sociology informs and shapes current educational policy and practice.
- To explore the origins and impact of colourism on educational attainment and society.
- To explore critical pedagogy and its transformative ideologies.
- To consider the role of race in shaping the experiences of black and minority ethnic (BME) students.

 Framing Questions

1. How is sociology of education informed by history, philosophy and politics?
2. In which ways do inequalities shape educational experiences?
3. How can education be transformative for all students?

EDUCATION

Introduction

The sociology of education is a significant branch in the discipline of sociology which explores how public institutions and experiences of the individual impact on education and its outcomes. Education is of acute importance in the study of sociology for many complex and interconnected reasons, including the study of inequalities such as educational attainment patterns, the contested nature of politics on policy and practice, the myth of meritocracy, social and cultural capital, debates around intelligence that draw on eugenics and immigration, inclusion and special needs provision, multiculturalism and the impact of race, gender and social class on pupil outcomes at all levels.

A primary area of focus is the compulsory schooling sector which consists of primary and secondary education provision; however, sociology of education is also concerned with early years provision, further education and higher education, as well as adult and continuing education, reflecting a cradle-to-the-grave, holistic educational landscape. Reflect back on your own early schooling experiences and think about how your personal experiences have made an impact on your educational outcomes.

In this chapter, you will learn about voices that have traditionally been absent or excluded from the study of sociology of education and which explore inequality in education from a social and cultural perspective. The main body of the chapter will encourage you to think sociologically by unpacking theoretical positions, namely Grand Theory and labelling theory. (The issue of theoretical positions in sociology is also discussed further in Chapters 6, 7, 8 and 9.) In addition, in this chapter you will be introduced to the notion of colourism as racism and critical pedagogy, which includes punk learning and hip-hop pedagogy. The chapter will conclude with a summary of research into the experiences of BME students at an institute of higher education in London and the author's personal experiences of microaggressions and invisibility.

Mapping the Terrain

In mapping the terrain of sociology of education, we need to be mindful of influences from disciplines such as history, philosophy and psychology as important elements that inform and shape a theoretical foundation for a vast array of careers including teaching, academic research, work in human relations, social work and journalism. Additionally, we need to be mindful of the endemic nature of Eurocentric influences understood as the 'geographical North' (Connell, 1997) which have not embraced the sociological advances and imagination of the South, which encompasses Africa and all its vast diversity, Latin America and Asia. To illustrate, textbooks from Key Stage 4 to further education and into higher education on sociology consistently speak of Plato, Aristotle, Marx, Weber and Durkheim, referring to them as the 'classics' and as the forefathers of ideologies that inform the place and value of schooling and education in the wider context. Marginalized voices from minority groups, such as Paulo Friere (Brazilian educator and philosopher) and Ibn Khaldun (Arab historian/economist), are rendered almost invisible in the curriculum. Our task as students of sociology requires us to address this Eurocentric imbalance so that the works produced by the examples cited here, and indeed the

(Continued)

works of their country men and women, have become fully integrated and embedded into our curricular so that we can engage fully, in a holistic way, with the many voices that contribute to the discourses. This will not only offer us a richer and deeper understanding of the issues but also help to dismantle endemic and institutionalized exclusionary practices. (The topic of Eurocentrism is also discussed in Chapters 3 and 6.) A key distinction we as students of sociology of education are encouraged to make in this chapter is to actively seek balance in representation from the Global South, not just about the South but from the South. This will allow us to frame narratives in a thoughtful context, to learn about the key thinkers behind the theory and the context of their writing and, in time, to dismantle the limiting nature of the Eurocentric curriculum which we continue to be exposed to in the West.

A key theme in this chapter is an exploration of critical education which seeks to expose inequality from a social, cultural and economic perspective. Furthermore, critical education is engaged in a reconstruction of the purpose of education, how formal education should be delivered, how teachers are trained and how the empowerment of pupils can be a focal and intended aim. As the reader, you are guided to understand that critical education is therefore concerned with transformation that can lead to justice. To illustrate, you can apply the literature we encounter and interrogate your own practice. This process will support you to make constructive use of your privilege to open up spaces (like universities) for those who are not represented and to hear from voices that are not included in that space. As the author, I aim to deliver on my commitment to critical education by introducing readers to a broad and global scope of academia that will deliver on a dual aim: first, to inform a deeper understanding of the issues explored in this chapter and, second, to act as an impetus for further reading and research.

Additionally, it is important to understand the intersectionality of race, gender and class in terms of educational experiences when exploring inequality. The term intersectionality refers to the lens through which various forms of inequality operate. First coined by Professor Kimberlé Crenshaw in 1989, intersectionality is a framework that takes into account people's overlapping identities and experiences in order to understand the complexity of prejudices they face. In this chapter, I will consider the impact of race in the form of colourism; however, it is important to reflect on the fact that some people are affected by multiple disadvantages. To illustrate, the debate around funding for free school meals during the global pandemic was not a singular debate about social class but one that demonstrated how class and race 'intersect', particularly in the lived experience of Marcus Rashford, who leads the campaign.

Similarly, the role of class and gender occupy an important space in the sociological interrogation of education when we consider access and engagement at higher education in elitist institutions and in STEM (science, engineering, technology and maths) subjects. In the secondary schooling context, discourses around closing the gender gap of attainment take account of the different ways in which girls and boys learn, but if we look carefully at why white, working-class boys occupy the lowest levels of attainment, we can learn a great deal about the impact of intersectionality.

The chapter will now explore the work of C. Wright Mills, specifically Grand Theory.

C. Wright Mills: Grand Theory

Wright Mills was an influential American sociologist who believed that knowledge, correctly applied, could bring about change and the good society. In his book ***The Sociological Imagination*** (1959), Mills offers a critique of established sociological research, arguing that the 'promise' of **sociology** was accessible if people were liberated from their private troubles. Mills was interested in the **role** of intellectuals, power and

EDUCATION

social stratification. Mindful that the structure of society involved both macro (large scale) and micro (specific relationship between individuals) interactions, Mills argued that private troubles were best understood in the context of wider societal issues. This is an example of Grand Theory, a term coined by Mills to reflect an abstract theory based on an understanding of how society functions. It is grand because it attempts to explain all **social structures** in society. Theories with broad perspectives like this are referred to as paradigms. Paradigms are philosophical and **theoretical** in their makeup but link to sociological thinking due to the dominance of the following three paradigms:

1. **Structural functionalism**, which explains the way society functions as a whole, e.g. Durkheim.
2. **Conflict theory**, which explains how inequalities contribute to social differences and perpetuate differences in power, e.g. Marx.
3. **Symbolic interactionism**, which explains one-to-one interactions, e.g. George Herbert Mead.

To explore this further, functionalists view education as a very important social **institution** which contributes in two ways. First, manifest or primary functions are the visible and intended functions of education. Examples include socialization in the work of Durkheim, who explored how schools teach children how to get along with each other and prepare them for adult economic roles.

Hear from the Expert

Tom Boronski on the Importance of Education in Durkheim's Theory

Tom Boronski is a former teacher and now an academic and writer on a range of subject matter, including critical pedagogy and how sociology informs and shapes current educational policy and practice. His publications are concerned with the social construction of reality and ideology, concentrating on the main areas of sociology that relate in particular to knowledge production, such as religion, education and science. He is the co-author of *Sociology of Education* (2020). Here, he explains how classical (Western) thinkers, in this case Durkheim, inform current classroom practice.

Emile Durkheim (1858–1917) is regarded as the forefather of modern European sociology and is particularly renowned for his theoretical understanding of education, which could provide the foundations for a new industrial society. Durkheim believed that social solidarity should be established and maintained through social institutions in which individuals voluntarily submit to something morally superior to themselves. This is where Durkheim felt that schools can play a crucial role in the teaching of moral education which included self-disciple, attachment and individual autonomy. Durkheim's primary intention was to create a new secular curriculum that prepared young people for wider society in the modern era, marking a shift from the onus placed on the Church or the family to lead on this important aspect. Self-discipline has the intention of promoting a sense of dignity, as Durkheim did not approve of any use of corporal punishment, which was the practice of the time. Attachment had the aim of developing schools as mini societies with respect for the rules, and autonomy nurtured an appreciation of meaning making so that rules were valued

(Continued)

> over time and social solidarity was the end result. We can see the contemporary manifestation of Durkheim's theory of education in the popularity of character education across all sectors of education. The language used in mission statements, the inclusion of pupil/student voice, the values-driven enrichment curriculum, sustainability education, volunteering, supporting social justice campaigns and leadership initiatives such as the Duke of Edinburgh Award are just a few examples of how schools, colleges and universities aim to achieve social solidarity in the wider context of a global, inclusive, equal and pupil-centred educational philosophy. (The work of Durkheim and other classical sociologists is discussed further in Chapters 5, 7 and 8.)
>
> Tomas Boronski & Nasima Hassan, *Sociology of Education*,
> SAGE Publishing. Copyright © Tomas Boronski and Nasima Hassan, 2020

Having considered Grand Theory and Durkheim's thoughts on the importance of education, the discussion will now focus on **labelling** theory, which continues to preoccupy educational discourses to the present day.

Howard Becker: Labelling Theory

Becker's (1963) book entitled *Outsiders* introduced labelling theory, which explored the use of language to shape the perceptions we have of others in order to influence their behaviour. Though originally linked to **deviance** and the study of criminal behaviour, labelling theory has long-established associations with schooling in Britain, particularly in relation to teaching black pupils and pupils with special educational needs. To illustrate, Coard's (1971) publication *How the West Indian Child Became Educationally Sub-Normal in the British Schooling System* is a compelling and disturbing example as it consists of quantitative and qualitative evidence of the widespread mistreatment of West Indian children, including cultural and class bias in assessments. The book also questions the fundamental aims of education which challenges policy-makers and argues for a system that promotes self-improvement and emancipation against a dilemma-riddled balancing act of the interests of the **state**, its varied communities and the individual. The global relevance of labelling theory is evident in Samkange's (2015a, b) research from the Zimbabwean schooling context, which links labelling to teacher behaviours and discriminatory practices, leading to the notion of the self-fulfilling prophecy. **Symbolic interactionism** is a lens via which labelling theory is seen in action. From this theoretical standpoint, labelling is conducted by those in power to those who become labelled, resulting in a self-fulfilling prophecy.

 Pause for Thought

Labelling theory is associated with studies in criminology where mainstream culture has attached specific and negative images to labels of deviance. To illustrate, individuals labelled as delinquent or criminal are connected to a wide range of character traits including immorality, violence and lacking empathy. The identity of the individual is consequently attached to stigma. The labelling process gives rise to the notion of the self-fulfilling prophecy and a likelihood of continuing deviant behaviour referred to as secondary deviance. If labelling had not taken place, the deviant behaviour would remain as primary deviance.

EDUCATION

Consider the following questions:

- How have some young people been criminalized in the schooling system?
- What does it mean to be excluded in a wider societal context?
- What are the sociological links with educational failure and crime?

This section of the chapter has reflected on the importance of accessing voices of authority from the Global South in literature on sociology of education. Important theoretical positions and paradigms have been introduced in a wider consideration of the role and purpose of education.

Colourism and Educational Experience

Colourism (also known as skin-tone bias), like all forms of **racism**, rationalizes colourism inequities with racist ideas, by claiming the inequities between dark and light-skinned people are not due to discriminatory notions against dark-skinned people, but the assumed inferiorities of dark-skinned people. (For further discussion of the sociology of race, see Chapter 13.) Abrams et al. (2020) is a timely body of work that delves deeper into racist notions about colourism by associations with skin tone and educational attainment, attractiveness and personality traits with a sample of African American young women. In relation to educational attainment, this paper makes reference to social and behavioural outcomes such as low self-esteem and negative self-perceptions that impact on progress made in schooling. This research, therefore, is an educational tool to address the social conditions that limit African American young women from achieving their full potential in an educational context. Their findings suggest that colourism is an interracial (across groups) and intrarracial (within groups) system of inequality based on skin tone, texture of hair and facial features. The socio-historic origins of colourism are noted in the traumatic experiences of enslaved African women and their children by white slave owners, as noted in Reuter's (1918) publication entitled *The Mulatto in the United States*, in which he argued that anything black people achieved was in fact the achievement of biracial, light-skinned people. His theory placed biracial, light-skinned people in a sort of racial middle-class strata, below superior whites but importantly above inferior 'full blacks'.

A contemporary exemplar of colourism is evident in an autobiographical blog by Shamihah Mudabbir, submitted as part of a wider study into identity and heritage and published by Our Shared Cultural Heritage (OSCH), which is a British Council project funded by the Heritage Lottery Fund and supported by Manchester Museum. Mudabbir's (2020) blog is a raw and honest account of her experiences of colourism from early childhood where she had a sense that dark skin equated to being ugly. Writing about her teenage years, a **family** trip to attend a wedding in Bangladesh captures a keystone moment when the pre-wedding trip to the beauty parlour drives home the deeply rooted notions of beauty equated to whiteness in Bangladeshi culture when the beautician applies the whitest shade of foundation to Mudabbir's skin. Writing reflectively, Mudabbir can connect the consequences of **colonialism** in Bangladesh as a visible need for a closer proximity to whiteness which carries associations of privilege and power that are much sought after to this day. Mudabbir's personal account in the context of a wider study about identity is compelling because of the impact on her own self-image and self-confidence as a young woman growing up in multicultural Britain. Family, global communities, fashion, media representation and even comedy all contributed to her experience of being othered. The blog concludes with Mudabbir's resistance, informed by her rejection of the fact that her skin is the problem.

― Pause for Thought ―

Mudabbir's personal experience paints an inspirational and positive mindset in comparison to the sample in Abrams et al.'s (2020) study, which speaks of low self-esteem, bullying, depression, suicidal thoughts, ostracism, marginalization and mockery as well as a gap in black psychology as a consequence of the lived experiences of colourism. Consider the following questions in relation to education:

- How can schools acknowledge and address colourism?
- What can universities do to support students who are affected by colourism?

― Expand Your Knowledge ―

- A progressive example of the wider discourses on colourism is noted in: Abrams, J., Belgave, F., Williams, C. and Maxwell, M. (2020) African American adolescent girls' beliefs about skin tone and colourism. *Journal of Black Psychology* 46(2–3): 169–94.

This section of the chapter has explored colourism linked to literature which makes associations with important sub-themes, including racism and educational attainment. Moving forward, the chapter will invite you to reflect deeply on the work of key thinkers and how their ideas have shaped education linked to critical **pedagogy**.

Critical Pedagogy

Critical theory, which is a source for critical pedagogy, finds its roots in the work of many Western thinkers including Hegel, Kant, Marx, Engels and supporters of Fabian **socialism**, which started in Britain in 1884. Rooted in Marxist socialist thought, Fabian society brought a critical perspective to educational issues. Critical theory is heavily linked to the Frankfurt School (Institute for Social Research at the University of Frankfurt), which reflects the work of a range of progressive thinkers on education including Michael Apple, Henry Giroux and Peter McLaren.

Critical pedagogy is concerned with transforming the interconnectedness of teaching, knowledge production, schooling and the state. It is a transformative **ideology** concerned with relationships, **social action** and self-consciousness. When we consider relationships, this can include the power dynamic of the teacher/pupil relationship and pupils as agents of change who will go on to transform society. Therefore, critical pedagogy has the aim of resulting in critical action. Reflection on social action and self-consciousness incorporates critical thinking about practices that have been oppressive and challenging them as the status quo. The role of the teacher in the context of critical pedagogy is not simple a transfer of knowledge and/or skills, which is a passive role, but a conceptualization of the role of the teacher as an intellectual with a vast range of experiences that can only benefit their pupils.

In addition, the teacher fully understands the political and social consequences of schooling, for example how classroom cultures are constructed, how curricula can limit and the importance of creating space for research. Teachers work in cooperation with their pupils in a process of knowledge production linked to their reality. Through this process, the critical pedagogic perspective frames and informs classroom practice and becomes a stepping stone in the process of pupils transforming themselves and their society.

A distinguishing feature of critical pedagogy is that it is both a form of practice and a form of action. It does not specify how to teach or indeed what to teach, rather it challenges us to use the process of teaching to action social change. In terms of practical applications, critical pedagogy would include debate and dialogue activities which invite students to embrace co-ownership of the learning process as well as building respect for the learning process and for each other. Here the goal is for students to have a voice in curriculum design and implementation. It is important to introduce you, at this point, to the influential Brazilian educationalist and philosopher Paulo Freire (1921–97). Freire lived and worked in the slums of Recife as a teacher with a focus on addressing the issue of adult literacy. His strong belief in social justice and working with rather than for the community supported his progression to lead the Brazilian National Literacy Programme following his doctoral studies. Freire's seminal work, *Pedagogy of the Oppressed* (1970), challenged traditional education systems, which he called 'banking systems', where students were passive recipients of deposits from an all-knowing teacher. His radical pedagogy, in contrast, proposed an education based on dialogue with the community of learners, thereby generating a permanent process of reflection and action.

To apply a Frierian perspective, the process of teaching is not to transfer knowledge but to share in the construction of knowledge production. Understanding who students are and learning about their lives are steps in constructing a classroom environment that legitimizes their voices and develops in them a self-awareness that they are agents of social change. Critical pedagogy champions a liberatory and transformative mission that embraces equality and social justice. Students are guided to look deeply into systems of privilege and to work towards changing society as an ultimate aim. At the core of Frierian pedagogy is a critique of the banking method of education whose information (curriculum context) is deposited in the minds of students who are later required to regurgitate it in informal assessments.

In this classroom context, students are the subjects, not the objects, of social transformation. Culture, **hegemony** and ideology are key concepts, particularly relevant in applying critical pedagogy. Culture is understood as knowledge, beliefs and values that recognize diversity in terms of identity. School leaders have a responsibility and a duty to research and deliver a culturally relevant pedagogy that incorporates the characteristics and perspectives of the ethnically diverse (wider) school community. By designing a culturally relevant curriculum, teachers transmit a message to students and to their communities that they are invited to invest at a deeper level in the learning process. This investment then becomes, it is hoped, the catalyst for social and political change. Hegemony is understood as the dominance and authority of a specific group or society over other specific groups or nations, typically through cultural, economic or political mechanisms. Developed by the Italian philosopher Gramsci to explain why working-class people did not rise up and revolt against the capitalist state in Western countries, hegemony is fundamentally understood as dominance. The term cultural hegemony therefore refers to dominance through a cultural standpoint. It is achieved when institutions, such as schools, allow a particular cultural position with its associated **norms** to strongly influence the values, ideas, expectations and world view of the entire institution. Inherent in a deeper understanding of cultural hegemony is the power dynamic which results in socialization and ways in which cultural narratives reflect the beliefs and values of the ruling class. A contemporary example is opposition to the wearing of the hijab in the school setting, as it is loaded with a broader narrative of subjugation, oppression and **force** as reflected in the geo-political events of the last 20 years. Finally, ideology is understood as a set of ideas or beliefs of a group or an individual that can be characterized by particular political influences. These beliefs influence how a person acts and views the world holistically. Some examples of ideology are **Marxism**, socialism, **fascism** and **imperialism**.

PART 4 CONNECTING THE PERSONAL AND THE SOCIAL

> **Student Voices**
>
> 'Sociology of education plays an integral role in my writing as it presents ideas from outside the psychological field and allows a deeper understanding of the perspectives I write about. Sociology of education allows me to think about the ideas behind psychological concepts such as behaviourism and social learning. In an essay on traditional versus alternative education I looked at the sociological debates within education; from functionalism and Marxism to social interactionism, my writing took advantage of the many works from these educational sociologists to discuss the successes of both educational formats. Links between education and the models of Biesta and Bourdieu were considered; Biesta's model on educational function and Bourdieu's forms of capital, focusing on social capital and its contribution to education, delved into the purpose and practical applications of these formats.'
>
> Salma Rehman
> BSc (Hons) Educational Psychology
> Manchester Metropolitan University

The Role of Race in Higher Education

Attainment differentials are complex at all levels of education and higher education is no exception. Current scholarship on race in UK higher education (Bhopal and Henderson, 2019; Boliver, 2016; Stockfelt, 2018) highlights the endemic nature of institutional racism which endures despite the presence of compelling mission statements about inclusion alongside equality and diversity policies and the 2010 Equalities Act. A report commissioned by the National Union of Students (2019) on BME attainment in UK universities speaks of the matrix of discrimination as well as the need to interrogate the data through the lens of the factors that contribute to the gap in the first place. There are multiple complex layers to a discussion of the role of race in higher education, including:

- an absence of BME professors and senior leaders
- the attainment gap in degree outcomes
- a curriculum that does not represent diverse groups
- structural inequality within universities
- inequalities in higher education that mirror inequalities in wider society, e.g. in housing
- pressure by the Office for Students in setting targets for recruitment and closing the attainment gap as a data exercise.

The Office for Students is the independent regulator for higher education in England that aims to ensure that all students have a fulfilling experience. The setting of key performance measures on addressing the attainment gap of BME students includes eliminating the unexplained gap in degree outcomes (1sts or 2:1s) between white students and black students by 2024–5 and also eliminating the absolute gap (the gap caused by both structural and unexplained factors) by 2030–1. Furthermore, through the Race Disparity Unit who collect and analyse data on the experiences of people from different backgrounds, the government seeks to hold universities to account on progress in this crucial area. Combined, these collective elements aim to address the inequalities experienced by BME students whilst at university. The case study (Akel, 2019) in this chapter meticulously demonstrates how the issues discussed here play out in practice.

19.1 Key Case

Akel's (2019) 'Insider-Outsider: The Role of Race in Shaping the Experiences of Black and Minority Ethnic Students'

'Insider-Outsider' is a study which started in Goldsmiths Students' Union but was completed and published by the main university. The study revealed that BME students face racism on a daily basis in halls of residence, in social meeting spaces and in lecture theatres and seminar rooms. The study analysed responses from 195 students to the following key questions:

- What are BME students' experiences of decolourisation and representation in academic settings and staff structures? This question explored staff diversity and how this might impact on the participants' engagement with their studies as well as experiences of tokenism.
- What are BME students' experiences of racism and microaggressions in both social and academic spaces and how does it impact them? This question looks at how racism can impact on the experience of being at university such as contributing in lectures/seminars and completion of degree courses.
- What are BME students' views on the role of race in affecting academic attainment? This question explores how participants experience teacher expectations and grading.

In terms of findings, the following key points are of significance:

- 74% of respondents found that their course content was rooted in Eurocentrism.
- 51% of respondents felt they needed to support the position expressed by their lecturer in order to get good grades.
- 26% of respondents shared that they had experienced racism whilst at university (racist name calling).
- 43% of respondents reported experiences of a more subtle form of racism, namely microaggression (hostility, insults or behaviour that excludes on a daily basis).
- 50% of respondents felt they must work twice as hard to achieve academic success when compared to non-BME students.
- 37% of respondents felt excluded from participating in social aspects of university life due to their experiences of racial discrimination.
- 34% of respondents described having to modify their ethnic or cultural identity in order to fit in with the mainstream culture of the university.

In conclusion, the study made a series of recommendations, including:

- curriculum audits that implement global representation with the aim of raising BME attainment
- curriculum co-creation: invite students to participate in curriculum planning and design with the aim of enhancing representation and natural learning
- review of governance: this key area aims to address the imbalance of the white, male senior leadership of the university.

Building on the recommendations of Akel (2019), the work of Suhaiymah Manzoor-Khan, captured in the Hear from the Expert section, further explores the central importance of global representations in the curriculum. Suhaiymah Manzoor-Khan is an author, writer and spoken-word poet born in Bradford to second-generation British-Pakistani parents. She was educated at the University of Cambridge (History) and SOAS (**Post-Colonial** Studies). A video of Manzoor-Khan performing 'This Is Not a Humanising Poem' at

The Last Word Festival in 2017 launched her social media presence, which has evolved into a career as an activist. She blogs under the name The Brown Hijabi (www.thebrownhijabi.com) and is the author of a poetry collection entitled *Postcolonial Banter* (2019a) and co-author of an anthology about the experiences of women of colour at Cambridge entitled *A Fly Girl's Guide to University: Being a Woman of Colour at Cambridge and Other Institutions of Power and Elitism* (2019b).

Hear from the Expert

Suhaiymah Manzoor-Khan: Decolonize the Curriculum

In 2017 Suhaiymah was a post-graduate student at SOAS, University of London. During this time, she blogged about her experience of being unchallenged in her course (MA in Postcolonial Studies), leading to her (re)writing the decolonized curriculum, full details of which are noted here: https://thebrownhijabi.com/2017/11/01/the-lessons-i-learnt-from-writing-my-own-decolonised-syllabus.

Manzoor-Khan reflects on the limitations of her studies, specifically that the reading lists were confined to publications in the English language only, arguing that a course of study in postcolonial writing needed to extend beyond the English-speaking world. She labels this experience as 'double erasure' and asks key questions including:

- How do you centre colonial subjects in a language their memories can't be spoken in?
- How can we access the tools and the language to address the double erasure of the current curriculum?

The double erasure she wrote about was the acknowledgement that her formal education in an elitist institute of higher education hindered access to a more diverse curriculum, and the fact that she was studying only in the English language meant that even if she could access a more diverse canon of literature, language was a secondary barrier. Erasure also encapsulates the notion that literature from global sources is de-valued, lost, violently destroyed, written over, denied, hidden or accredited to others. The decolonizing project is therefore a painful one of self-reflection that embraces the deep complexities of access and inclusion. Manzoor-Khan refers to this as 'out of reach', which taps into the frustration and angst of the critical thinker limited by their own language barrier. Decolonizing the curriculum is an activist movement, a social media campaign, a mandate of student politics and a topical contemporary discourse. To illustrate, in June 2020 activists toppled a statue of the slave trader Edward Colston from its plinth and pushed it into the harbour. The statue had occupied a central position in Colston Square since 1895, a commemoration of Colston's philanthropy to the city of Bristol. However, historical archives reveal that most of Colston's fortune was made by selling slaves from west Africa. Sharing this example illustrates the gap in the social, economic and political history of Britain in the national curriculum. It also illustrates the momentum of the current geo-political climate in relation to race.

In her work as a poet, Manzoor-Khan argues that decolonizing the curriculum is a disruption, a rallying cry, a provocation. It requires commitment to invest in a long-term vision to dismantle and unsettle in order to reconstruct, and it is not something that can be reduced to a sensationalized moment in time.

EDUCATION

---- **Expand Your Knowledge** ----

- Landrieu, M. (2018) *In the Shadows of Statues: A White Southerner Confronts History.* New York: Penguin.

Mitch Landrieu was the Mayor of New Orleans from 2010–18, during which time he commissioned the removal of four Confederate monuments across the city. This action received national recognition and praise, but at a local level it led to violent protests as an assault on the southern American identity. In this book, Landrieu reflects on race and the legacy of slavery that endures to this day in America, and offers a manifesto that embraces the notion that as Americans 'we are not as we once were', thereby justifying the removal of the monuments. This book is written in a very inclusive autobiographical style which allows the reader to understand the macro and micro of some contemporary discourses at a personal level.

Akel's study is supported in the wider context of racism in higher education, and the under-representation of BME academies in positions of senior leadership. The work of Arday (2018a, b) and Bhopal (2019) explores race and inequality in higher education. Their research is conducted in a wider context of six high-profile cases of racism in UK universities (Warwick, Lancaster, Sheffield Hallam, Kent, Nottingham and Exeter) and 996 formal complaints about racist incidents made over a five-year period across 131 universities (Batty, 2019). Additionally, the Equality and Human Rights Commission launched an inquiry into racial harassment in higher education which found that:

- University staff often lack the understanding, skills and confidence to manage conversations about race effectively.
- Staff did not report racial harassment due to a lack of **transparency**.
- A culture of intolerance by leaders prevented positive action and change.

In terms of recommendations, the following key areas are noted:

- Transparency – how to address racist incidents, actions taken and work to ensure that the university is a safe space for all students.
- Data – to capture improvements and demonstrate that progress has been made.
- Culture – where leaders set clear expectations and implement training that embeds a more tolerant culture.

My own experiences as a British Muslim woman in a leadership role in higher education reflect the patterns exposed in the range of evidence cited above. I share my personal experiences of microaggressions and othering at this point to illustrate the importance of the personal narrative and sense-making. My writing has been informed and shaped by critical race theory (CRT) as this theoretical framework embraces the importance of storytelling as a means by which transformations can take place. (For more discussion of critical race theory, see Chapter 13.) The following incidents are therefore part of my story of transformation:

- At a social gathering following a research seminar for staff, I was asked about progress I was making in my doctoral thesis when I referred to W.E.B. Du Bois and Edward Said as key thinkers in my writing. A member of staff commented: 'it's great that you are introducing us to new writers from your worldview'. I am a working-class British Muslim with South Asian heritage; Du Bois is an African American academic from an elitist background; and Said is a Palestinian-Egyptian academic with a **refugee** background.

- During a discussion on language acquisition theory, I shared that I came from a large extended family where many different languages were spoken. A staff member commented during a follow-up discussion on multilingualism: 'Most Asian families have lots of children, don't they?'

This section of the chapter has explored the role of race in shaping the experiences of BME students with reference to a key case which has introduced dominant themes including teacher expectations, the **decolonized** curriculum and the concept of erasure.

CHAPTER SUMMARY

- This chapter has introduced key thinkers from diverse backgrounds in order to gain a deeper and fuller understanding of how education impacts on the individual.
- A consideration of the impact of theory (Grand Theory, labelling) on educational outcomes informs a deeper understanding of sociology of education.
- An exploration of critical pedagogy from the British (punk learning) and American (hip hop) contexts has supported reflections on the potential for students to take control of their learning in a participatory, culturally relevant and empowering way.
- The chapter concludes with a consideration of the role of race in shaping the experiences of BME students, including recommendations that make concrete links to the principles of critical pedagogy.

REVIEW QUESTIONS

The following review questions require you to refer to information in this chapter. In your answers, it will be helpful to use and define key vocabulary (see Glossary) and provide concrete examples as evidence.

1. What is your understanding of critical education?
2. Explain conflict theory linked to an example.
3. How is labelling theory linked to the notion of the self-fulfilling prophecy?
4. Evaluate hip-hop education as a teaching and learning strategy.
5. Explain erasure in relation to the Eurocentric curriculum.

Go Further

Books

- Arday, J. (2018) *Dismantling Race in Higher Education*. London: Springer International.

This edited collection explores the roots of structural racism that limit social mobility for black and ethnicized students and academics in higher education.

- Boronski, T. and Hassan, N. (2020) *Sociology of Education*, 2nd edition. London: Sage.

This book offers a critical overview of theories and ideas about education from a global perspective.

EDUCATION

- Downes, G. and Simon, C. (2020) *Sociology for Education Studies*. London: Routledge Education.

This book helps students to apply sociological theory to their own educational experiences.

Journal Articles

- Bradbury, A. (2019) Making little neo-liberals: The production of ideal child/learner subjectivities in primary school through choice, self-improvement and 'growth mindsets'. *Power and Education* 11(3): 309–26.

This paper explores the idea of the individual child as a self-improving learner and the impact of neoliberal policy on early educational inequalities.

- Chadderton, C. (2020) School-to-work transitions support: 'Cruel optimism' for young people in 'the state of insecurity'. *Power and Education* 12(2): 173–88.

A critique of the DfE's careers education strategy which concludes that the labour market is likely to remain unequal, creating a relationship of cruel optimism between young people and the fantasy of a good life, a good job and an equal society.

- McCoy-Wilson, S. (2020) 'We have a black professor?' Rejecting African Americans as disseminators of knowledge. *Journal of Black Studies* 51(6): 545–64.

This essay considers the racialized lens through which black students view black faculty staff in the wider context of racism in higher education in America.

Websites

- https://soundcloud.com/britishacademy/sets/identities-belonging

The British Academy podcast on identity politics by journalist and author Gary Younge.

- http://classonline.org.uk/blog/item/universities-in-crisis

Dr Sol Gamsu's blog for CLASS (Centre for Labour and Social Studies) on how we need to think creatively about new models of organizing higher education.

- www.ted.com/talks/anindya_kundu_the_opportunity_gap_in_us_public_education_and_how_to_close_it

Sociologist Anindya Kundu takes a deeper look at the personal, social and institutional challenges that keep students from thriving in the United States.

REFERENCES

Abrams, J., Belgave, F., Williams, C. and Maxwell, M. (2020) African American adolescent girls' beliefs about skin tone and colourism. *Journal of Black Psychology* 46(2–3): 169–94.

Akel, S. (2019) *Insider-outsider: The role of race in shaping the experiences of black and minority ethnic students*. Goldsmiths, University of London, UK. Available at: www.gold.ac.uk/racial-justice/insider-outsider (last accessed 30 May 2021).

Arday, J. (2018a) *Dismantling Race in Higher Education*. London: Springer International.

Arday, J. (2018b) Understanding race and educational leadership in higher education: Exploring the black and ethnic minority (BME) experience. *Management in Education* 32(4): 192–200.

Batty, D (2019) 'Universities Failing to Address Thousands of Racist Incidents', *The Guardian*, Available at: www.theguardian.com/world/2019/oct/23/universities-failing-to-address-thousands-of-racist-incidents

Becker, H. (1963) *Outsiders*. New York: The Free Press.

Bhopal, K. (2019) 'Same old story, just a different policy': Race and policy making in higher education in the UK. *Race, Ethnicity and Education* 23(4): 530–47.

Bhopal, K. and Henderson, H. (2019) *Advancing Equality in Higher Education: An exploratory study of the Athena SWAN and Race Equality Charters. British Academy Research Report*. Centre for Research in Race and Education, University of Birmingham, UK.

Boliver, V. (2016) Exploring ethnic inequalities in admission to Russell Group universities. *Sociology* 50(2): 247–66.

Boronski, T. and Hassan, N. (2020) *Sociology of Education*, 2nd edition. London: Sage.

Coard, B. (1971) *How the West Indian Child is Made Educationally Sub-normal in the British School System*. London: New Beacon Books.

Connell, R. (1997) Why is classical theory classical? *American Journal of Sociology* 102(6): 1511–57.

Freire, P. (2017 [1970]) *Pedagogy of the Oppressed*. New York: Penguin.

Manzoor-Khan, S. (2019a) *Post-colonial Banter*. Birmingham: Verve Poetry Press.

Manzoor-Khan, S. (2019b) *A Fly Girl's Guide to University*. Birmingham: Verve Poetry Press.

Mills, C.W. (1959) *The Sociological Imagination*. New York: Oxford University Press.

Mudabbir, S. (2020) Colourism: Community racism. *Education Researcher*, 24 April. Available at: https://sharedculturalheritage.wordpress.com/2020/04/24/colourism-community-racism (last accessed 30 May 2021).

National Union of Students (2019) *Black, Asian and Minority Ethnic Student Attainment at UK Universities: #closingthegap*. Available at: www.universitiesuk.ac.uk/policy-and-analysis/reports/Documents/2019/bame-student-attainment-uk-universities-closing-the-gap.pdf (last accessed September 2020).

Reuter, E.B. (1918) *The Mulatto in the United States: Including a Study of the Rôle of Mixed-blood Races throughout the World*. Windermere: Badger Press.

Samkange, W. (2015a) Causes of low student enrolment at the Zimbabwe Open University's Harare-Chitungwiza Region for the period 2008–2013. *Turkish Online Journal of Distance Education* 16(2): 94–100.

Samkange, W. (2015b) The role of labelling in education. *Global Journal of Advanced Research* 2: 1419–24. http://gjar.org/publishpaper/vol2issue9/d275r66.pdf

Stockfelt, S. (2018) 'We the minority-of-minorities': A narrative inquiry of black female academics in the United Kingdom. *British Journal of Sociology of Education* 39(7): 1012–29.

RELIGION

Adam Possamai and Kathleen Openshaw

LEARNING OBJECTIVES

- To provide a critical introduction to some of the major theorists and concepts in the sociology of religion.
- To learn how one can apply a sociological perspective to the study of religion.
- To critically evaluate the complexities of sociological understandings of religion in contemporary society.

Framing Questions

1. What is religion and how does the sociological understanding of it change through time?
2. In what ways can the sociology of religion help us to understand religion?
3. Is change a constant for religions?

Introduction

Would you consider yourself to be religious or spiritual? Perhaps, you believe yourself to be simultaneously both? Or instead, are you a hardline atheist who finds your sense of awe in the wonders of science? Do you think religiosity is a personal issue or one that should inform government policy? Are the religious practices of your grandparents outdated and incompatible with your contemporary social world? Are parts of the world becoming more or less religious? Certainly, these are some of the many questions that sociologists of religion set out to answer.

Today, we live in a rapidly changing world – one that is more consumer-driven and connected than ever before. This has affected all parts of human society – including our relationship with religion. In this chapter, you will learn about four broad themes, starting with 'Sociology of Religion and its Western Roots'. In this section, you will explore the European foundations of this sub-discipline. The second section, 'Religion Never Really Disappeared', details a change in disciplinary perspective that begins to acknowledge the behaviours of religiosity beyond what sociology initially understood to be 'religion'. As you will see, there are two major shifts that have influenced how we understand religion today. In 'Global Religions and the Globalization of Religion', you will be introduced to the relationship between global religions and local religious practices in the contemporary globalized age. In the final section, on 'Lived Religion and Pop Culture', you will see how different religion can appear when it is codified by religious professionals than when it is lived by people in their everyday lives. However, before going through the heart of the matter, let's have a small detour and provide a general background to the sub-discipline.

Mapping the Terrain

The discipline of sociology does not provide adequate tools to study **otherworldly** phenomena (that which is beyond the boundaries of this physical world, e.g. heaven and hell, reincarnation, curses) associated with religion, as these are not always measurable, interviewable, or observable. It must be noted that some do indeed study otherworldly phenomena (such as near-death and out-of-body experiences) but mostly rely on self-reporting measures, that is, their interlocutors' explanations of their experiences. Sociologists of religion, generally, understand religion to be a human social construct, created by humans for humans. Sociologists are not theologians seeking the truth of whether god(s) or other supernatural entities exist. Instead, they are interested in understanding how and why people believe (or not), how and why people in society interpret certain texts as sacred, what they do with their interpretations, and how these beliefs and practices impact on society. Sociologists study how religion interacts with both macro levels (for example, government, law, and 'national security') and micro levels (for instance, families and small communities) of society.

By gathering data (e.g. using methodological tools such as interviews, audio and video records, surveys, and participant observation), and then applying analytical frameworks, sociologists research how believers and non-believers understand, live and express the otherworldly in the **innerworldly** (that is, inside of this world, e.g. someone commenting on a religious text in front of a congregation). In summary, sociologists of religion research the very mundane lived expression of what people interpret to be the extramundane.

If sociology is renowned for its jargon (or what we call our 'tools of analysis'), the sociology of religion is a 'double tap' sub-discipline, as it also uses concepts from theology and religious studies. Although this discipline emerged out of a European, and rather Christian-centric context, today in our globalized and post-colonial period, it is now expanding its already vast specific vocabulary to contexts from diverse and often overlooked parts of the world (e.g. the concept of 'Pancasila' in Indonesia or of 'Assabiyah' from the medieval Arabic world). The sociology of religion aims to provide clarity and understanding of religious phenomena in the world, and if this sub-discipline can sometimes be seen as complex, it is nothing compared to the lived realities of any of the plethora of religions in the world. (The idea of different sub-disciplines of sociology is explored further in Chapters 2, 4, 7, 8 and 16.)

Sociologists can be religious, atheist or undecided, and can be part of the community with whom they are doing research. However, whatever their faith, they often use a methodological approach to religion, called

RELIGION

> methodological agnosticism. This is an approach in which the researcher suspends (or brackets out) whether they personally believe or disbelieve in the more-than-human entities (such as God or ghosts) or happenings referred to by their interlocutors. Sociologists largely understand religion within two broad definitions. These are the **functionalist** approach, that is, what religion does for the individual or society (e.g. religion holds people's values together), and the **substantive** approach, that is, how religion is understood and defined by people (e.g. 'I am spiritual but not religious'). Sociologists can also study religion through different types of association.

Pause for Thought

Imagine that you are a sociologist of religion and have been awarded a grant of enough money to cover your research expenses for a year abroad or in your home country:

- What would your ideal research project be about?
- What research methods are best to collect data in this project, and why?
- What are the ethical implications of doing research with this religious group?
- As a sociologist of religion, how do you do research with people who believe something different to you?
- *Or* As a sociologist of religion, how do you do research with your own community? And does this have implications for the type of data you gather and your responsibilities to your community and to the academy?
- How would you use the research that you gathered?

Ernst Troeltsch (1865–1923) was one of the first to sociologically consider different types of religious organisations – these can often be useful for sociologists to think with. For Troeltsch (1950), a church is a large organization that usually professes to embrace all members of a society. Members of a church are usually so by birth or marriage and few demands are made on them. They tend to come from the middle and upper levels of society and are led by a formal organization with a strong hierarchy of paid professionals. Churches are usually ideologically conservative and tend to support the status quo. Sects, according to Troeltsch, on the other hand, are smaller and have the most power over their members compared to any other type of religious organization. Contrary to churches, they tend to be against the status quo and are world rejecting. Whereas churches are in communication with the power of the state, sects are antagonistic and sometimes even refuse to cooperate with it. Their members tend to come from a lower class or from people who are opposed to the state. Members can be expected to withdraw from the outside world and devote their entire time to the beliefs and activities of their group. Sometimes, sects have a 'charismatic' leader rather than a hierarchy of paid officials. Troeltsch also created another ideal-type of religious organization, which he called, from a sociological perspective, 'mysticism' (1950). They are small, loosely-knit groups organized around some common spiritual and religious interests but are lacking a well-contained belief system. These groups tend to be more tolerant and leave to each of its members their own authority in religious and spiritual matters. Mystic groups/networks often have divergent opinions and may be short-lived. Later, the American sociologist H.R. Nieburh added a fourth type to Troeltsch's typology to cover the middle ground between church and sect. He called this type 'denomination' (e.g. the Christian Methodists in their current form). Many people are born into this type of religious organization and some also join them. Like churches, they have a professional ministry and are large. These groups are not exclusive and are relatively undemanding of their members.

At this point, it is important to draw your attention to the fact that Troeltsch was a German, Protestant theologian who was writing from a very particular historical and scholarly position (1950) which, during the late 19th and early 20th centuries, was very much concerned with classifying the social world. Since then, much sociological work has been done to further unpack the complicated ways people understand their religiosity and how these religious communities negotiate their presence within their societies. These do not always neatly fit into boxes, nor are their 'labels' agreed by all. For instance, a loose collection of people who have formed a community with their own spiritual ideas and practices distinct from other established religious institutions in their society may be considered by their neighbours to be in a 'cult'. But contemporary sociologists would prefer the less value-laden term 'new religious movement' (NRM) to describe the emergence of this community and its new ideas. Furthermore, the people within the NRM may refer to themselves as something else entirely (perhaps a commune or community, perhaps even a family). As budding sociologists, we must be wary of essentializing religious groups into neat categories given the very fluid nature of human relationships with the supernatural.

The term *religion*, it must be pointed out, is a Western construct (Debray, 2005). It emerged in Latin with the birth of Christianity. This word, as we understand it in the Western world, is not found in Sanskrit, Hebrew, Greek or Arabic. Christianity was not born a religion but rather emerged as a movement within Judaism. Christianity did not become a religion – in the sense of the word as we know it today – until the third century. This is mostly because during the first two centuries of the Christian era, Christian theologians had their thoughts formulated within a Greek language which ignored this Latin category. This concept of 'religion', then, developed in Western theological and philosophical thinking in the Middle Ages, influencing the thinking of sociologists of religion. Talad Asad (1993) points out that scholars of a predominantly Western academy have studied religions across the world as if the definition of 'religion' were a universal. Religion as understood by the academe is firmly embedded within a Christian etymology and is not a native term but rather one created by scholars for their intellectual purposes. This understanding was mainly about religion as an institution (that is, **official religion**) and not the way it is lived by people (that is, **popular religion**). Thus, because of the diversity of human existence, there is no 'one size fits all' understanding of how people experience and understand that which is beyond the profane.

20.1 Key Case

No Religion

What does it mean when people claim to be non-religious? Are they atheist? And if yes, what type of atheist are they? Perhaps, they actively campaign against the public existence of religions, or maybe they simply do not believe in the existence of anything which cannot be proved by science but have no issue with people who do practise/have a faith. Some 'non-religious' people identify as being spiritual and interpret religion to be an institution they don't want to be part of. Indeed, being spiritual can mean you are not religious but still believe in a god(s), or do not believe in a god at all. And don't forget the people who claim to be both spiritual and religious!

Grace Davie (2015), in her research on religion in the UK, has claimed quite famously that there is a type of 'people who believe but do not belong'. They believe but they are not religious. When Jim Cox and Adam Possamai

RELIGION

(2016) did some fieldwork trying to understand why a high proportion of Australian Aboriginal peoples claimed to be non-religious in the Australian 2011 census, they found one person who claimed to be non-religious *because* he is Christian. For him, religion is man-made, and Christianity is his close connection to God. For him, Christianity has nothing to do with religion. If it's hard to understand what non-religion is from a substantive perspective, imagine how much more difficult it is with religion.

Sociology of Religion and its Western Roots

The sociology of religion has had a strong presence in the development of sociology as a discipline. In its infancy, the Frenchman Emile Durkheim (1858–1917), an atheist and son of a rabbi, was a product of the Third Republic, a society that was building itself as a social entity away from aristocracy and away from its second emperor, Napoleon III (in case you are wondering about the maths, the figures are correct as Napoleon II never ruled). Durkheim's aim was to build a strong and organic society (i.e. a type of society that started with industrialization in which everyone's labour and expertise are dependent on those of others) that will be held together by common values. He acknowledged how religion can play a strong role in creating this cohesiveness. Durkheim called this social glue 'collective consciousness'. However, for Durkheim (2001) religion was under threat from societal changes brought about by modernity, namely the development of science, urbanism and mass education. For Durkheim, religion had no place in a modern world. Instead, he believed that religion could be replaced by the norms and values of his nation, thereby becoming the religion of his time, or what he called 'civil religion'. (More discussion of Durkheim can be found in Chapters 5 and 7.)

While Durkheim wanted to design theoretical tools to develop modernity, his German counterpart, Max Weber (1864–1920), was interested in the root of modernity, asking himself what started it. Both sociologists were living in a time of profound change that saw how previous ways of living were being radically altered by intense industrialization. According to Weber and his 'Protestant Ethic and Spirit of Capitalism' thesis, this industrial progress was sparked not by science but religion, more specifically Calvinism. Calvinism is a sectarian Protestant group that emerged from the theology of John Calvin. A 16th-century French theologian from Geneva, Calvin led the Reformation (that is, the move away from Catholicism by Protestant groups who were protesting against the Popes of their time). The Calvinists were frugal, not indulging in any excess or ostentatiousness and remaining puritanical. They had a new belief system that demarcated them from the Catholics (the dominant religion of the time in Europe) that focused on the notion of predestination. Within Catholicism, one goes to paradise in the afterlife based on his or her actions during their lives. If one has sinned, one can be forgiven through confession and atonement. One way to secure a place in heaven was to pay the church for forgiveness (known as the 'regime of the indulgence'). This could take many forms – perhaps financial offerings at a series of masses dedicated to the swift delivery of a recently departed to heaven, or procuring an artist to paint or sculpt for the church. This is one of the reasons that the Italian Renaissance produced so many beautiful pieces of art – there were many wealthy sinners seeking forgiveness through art (Lee, 2014). Rejecting the lavishness of these indulgent practices, Calvin proposed instead his theological understanding of predestination: one has already been determined by God (even before birth) as to whether they will access heaven or go to hell. For Weber (1930), this new approach led to an unintended consequence. As the Calvinists believed they were given a job on earth for a reason (a vocation), they endeavoured to work hard at fulfilling their role as decided by God. Even though they could not influence God's decision with regard to going to heaven, by being saint-like, they looked for signs of their eternal destiny. If Calvinists were successful at their vocation, they interpreted this to be a sign that God had predestined them to go to heaven. For Calvinists, this meant making a substantial profit. Moreover, given that they were frugal and only used the money they needed, Calvinists would simply re-invest their profits into their businesses, thereby making more money, which in turn would be re-invested to make yet more money, slowly developing a new trend in world history – that of making money for the sake of money. Weber argues that this change in religious belief is at the root of modern capitalism. This practice, for the German sociologist, has been what he called 'routinized' (that is, turned into a routine that no one questions anymore). From the 18th century onwards, this new practice of making money simply for the sake of money caught on beyond Calvinist circles. This, however, to be clear, was no longer in line with a desire for frugality.

A generation before Durkheim and Weber were studying the development and advancement of modernity in light of religion, Karl Marx (1818–83) raised damning critiques of modernity. For Marx, capitalism led to the oppression and exploitation of the proletariat (the disenfranchised labouring class). Religion was not neutral in this class struggle as it helped the upper class (or the bourgeoisie) to maintain their hold on the lower classes. Marx is famous for associating religion with opium, a drug that dulls the senses and thus does not make people cognisant of the reality of their lives, and of their exploitation. He contended that if someone believes that he or she has been put on earth to work long hours for little pay in a factory, that person is not going to contest this state. If someone believes that the earth is about to end (as found in many apocalyptic theologies) or that a place in heaven will be secured if one does not revolt, that person is not going to try to change the world order. Thus, religion was a means to suppress proletariat revolt to benefit the bank balances of the bourgeoisie. For Marx, religion posed an obstacle in the creation of an egalitarian society, and so needed to disappear.

All three theorists saw religion slowly disappearing from the world due to the advancement of scientific knowledge and industrial discoveries. This led to the theory of **secularism**, that is, religion is disappearing from society.

 Pause for Thought

- Although these theorists were writing about religion and society about 100 years ago, can you think of how their ideas may *still* be useful for understanding our world today?

Religion Never Really Disappeared

Sociology was so influenced by the predictions of these scholars that many sociologists took for granted that religions would disappear (Martin, 2005). Certainly, fewer and fewer people were attending religious services, but yet somehow religion was still present in people's lives. From the secularist thesis that predicted that religion would vanish, sociologists moved to another perspective, that of the **privatization of religion**. This perspective holds that religion still exists in modern life but has shifted to the private sphere and is no longer involved in governance and in particular politics. However, social theories are products of their context and so only draw from their own frame of reference; thus, this is not universally true. For instance, some people started to use religion for political purposes. The 1980s saw the revolution in Poland against the Communist Party led by Solidarity, a union movement strongly influenced by Catholicism; the rise of Catholic movements (called Liberation Theology) that were questioning why the poor were poor and pushing back against the corruption of certain Latin American governments; the overthrowing of a secular government and replacement by a theocratic one in Iran by the Ayatollah Khomeini; and the influence of the New Christian Right on American politics. While some sociologists could see the place of religion in the world changing, it was the events of 9/11 (when, on 11 September 2001, the Islamist terrorist group al-Qaeda coordinated four attacks which included the destruction of the Twin Towers in New York) that prominently marked a greater shift by sociologists towards reconsidering the perception that religion will disappear or become an entirely private matter (Casanova, 2006).

Who is the Exception?

For a long time, sociologists were studying the decline of religion in Europe and the rest of the Western world. As the advancement of industrialization, science, urbanization and education was going at full steam in the European industrial towns, religion – as in Europe – was expected to disappear from the rest of the world. Somehow, the United States appeared at that time to be an exception, in that although it is a very modern nation, religion was (and still is) prominent in its public sphere. Grace Davie (2002), whom we met earlier, began to question this exception. What if the United States were not the exception but the norm? Indeed, although Western ideas of what it means to be modern are spreading across the world, religion has not disappeared. On the contrary, religious adherence is actually growing everywhere in the world, except in Europe. The birthplace of the Industrial Revolution, Europe is, in fact, the exception. The theorists who were influenced by the disappearance of 'official' religion in front of their eyes simply assumed that *they* were the norm and the rest of the world was about to follow *their* lead. It is a good thing that sociologists of religion are reflexive, not only about religion but also about their own sub-discipline.

 Pause for Thought

Have you reflected on your own understanding of religion since reading this chapter? Has your view changed? Are you more mindful now of the multifarious ways people engage with belief systems?

The evidence against the secularization thesis was so great that the German social philosopher Jürgen Habermas (2006) moved away from his previous secularist approach and created the theory of '**post-secularism**' to describe what was really taking place in contemporary society. Sociologists began to acknowledge that religion was once again back in the public sphere, where, as many outside of the West knew, it never left.

20.2 Key Case

Are We Expecting a Growth of Religions in the Near Future?

The Pew Research Center (2015) is based in the US and studies religious change and its impact around the globe. In 2015, it released a report on the projected growth of major religious groups. In 2010, the world had around 6.9 billion people, and almost a third (31%) were Christian. Islam was second with 23%. In 2050, demographers are expecting the population to be 9.3 billion, which equates to a 35% increase. The numbers of Christians are estimated to increase but at the same rate as the world population. They should still represent a third of the population. However, the number of Muslims, who are now, overall, younger than Christians and have a higher fertility rate, is likely to grow and, for the first time in history, reach parity with Christianity (and therefore make up a third of the global population). All other major religions are expected to grow, except Buddhism, which will remain stable. This is because of the low fertility rate and the ageing population in countries such as China, Thailand and Japan. Europe is the only region in the world which will see its population shrink. Christianity will remain the largest religion in Europe in 2050 but nearly a quarter is expected to have no religion. Muslims will represent 10% of the European population and the number of Hindus and Buddhists will increase with the former close to doubling.

In multicultural societies, it can be challenging to manage diverse (and at times conflicting) attitudes towards the presence of religion in the public sphere. Religions, if they are able to speak to each other, including atheism, can offer a discourse from civil society that is not about bureaucratic or instrumental rationalization but about the quality of life (e.g. welcoming refugees instead of debating about political and instrumental interest). However, the German theorist believed governments should remain secular as only a secular perspective can remain independent and not take the side of one religion over another, and that the language of 'reason' should be the lingua franca used in public debates. This has been contested by other social scientists such as the Catholic philosopher Charles Taylor (2007). He claimed that post-secularism remains secular as religions are not able to express themselves with their theological language (e.g. quoting the Bible) in the public sphere. The American sociologist Craig Calhoun (2011) also argues along these lines by stating that post-secularism is still a process set by secularists, which limits the presence of religion in the public sphere and prevents them from understanding religious discourse. By creating a basis for equal inclusion based on reason, it provokes what he calls an 'ironic exclusion'. This, as he claims, is a privilege usurped by the secular middle class in many Western countries, and, in the US, by white elites at the expense of the more religious African Americans, Latinos, and migrant groups. (The issue of multiculturalism is also discussed in Chapters 13 and 19.)

Some recent research has pointed out the difficulties of managing the consideration of debates in the public sphere between religious groups when it comes to issues of legislation and governance: for example, the passing of same-sex marriage legislation in some Western countries where some religious groups vocally oppose same-sex union in the public sphere, invoking both theological and rational languages (Possamai-Inesedy and Turner, 2016). Or discussions in the West about allowing *Shari'a* courts alongside common law have often become heated (Possamai et al., 2015). *Shari'a* is in fact more a way of life than a law and is practised as part of a Muslim's daily adherence. In Western countries, many populist politicians and journalists have used this as a claim that Muslim people are changing 'their' country. These debates are often sensationalist and overlook the fact that Muslims are obliged to follow the laws of their host country (for the first generation) and country of birth (for subsequent generations). These debates are used to racialize and 'other' Muslims. In practice, *Shari'a* law is often used adjacent to local laws: for instance, finding a *Shari'a* compliant financial system that does not invest in alcohol and pornography, or having a *Shari'a* court acknowledging that a Muslim woman is divorced in the eyes of her religion, even if already legally divorced, so she can remarry someone else from her community. As another example, Bano (2012) surveyed 22 *Shari'a* councils in England and found that they tend to be part of the whole gamut of services offered by the mosque in which they are based. Their focus is on reconciliation and mediation services; they do not operate as distinct or unofficial legal bodies and are not about introducing Islamic law into English law.

Global Religions and the Globalization of Religion

Religion has always had the capacity to 'go global', with migrants, merchants and missionaries spreading its 'one truth' ideology across the world. These flows make it difficult for the nation-states to contain religions within their borders. Religions may have sacred homelands but they are deterritorialized, constantly crossing global borders. Modernity, with its ever-advancing technology, compresses time and space (Harvey, 1989) and has only made religions able to expand both faster and more efficiently. However, world religions were initially left out of discussions concerning globalization. It is only in recent times that scholars have begun to pay attention to the relationship between religion and globalization. Scholars tended to focus on the global flows of people, information, technology, capital and worldviews, or what Appadurai (1996) termed ethnoscapes, mediascapes, technoscapes, finanscapes and ideoscapes, respectively. Filling the gap, Thomas Tweed (2006) coined the term 'sacroscapes' to illustrate the multidimensional, often transformative, flows of religion across the world. It has become increasingly apparent that sociologists cannot study religion without paying attention to the global forces around it.

Through the processes of globalization, religions are shaped and shape people's way of being. For Altglas (2010: 11), religion has contradictory and complex responses to globalization, which offers it great expansion opportunities but also alters its influence and authority. As religions are permeable, they adapt to and incorporate the practices and beliefs of local communities as they move across the world. This blending of both local and global religious practice (or 'glocalization') is evidence that globalization is not a homogenizing phenomenon.

Religions can simultaneously speak to the needs of a local community as well as disrupt its dynamics, creating tensions and conflict between adherents of different religious communities. These tensions are often perpetuated between and within different communities as religion can play an important role in how people define themselves (for example, socially, ethnically and politically) in an ever-shifting modern context where people are able to pick, mix and change their identities. Outward signs of religious observance (or a rejection thereof) can provoke already existing tensions. For instance, wearing Muslim religious items of dress in a post-9/11 climate, such as the thobe, hijab or even the Sikh turban, often (ignorantly) associated with the practice of Islam, has meant many adherents of the Islamic faith in the West have been victims of Islamophobia. This holds true too for popular religions (to be discussed in the next section), such as the wearing of the colander on the head in the Church of the Flying Spaghetti Monster (a **hyper-real** religion; see below) by way of parodying religious dress, invoking rage by those who see this mocking of religion as blasphemous. Globalization can also elicit religious responses to modern circumstances across the world: for example, the effects of climate change being interpreted as the fulfilment of Christian 'end of days' prophecies or the rise of religious fundamentalism as a result of foreign occupation and exploitation. Like all processes of globalization, religions flow not only from the powerful West to the Rest but are involved in ever-shifting global centres and peripheries: for instance, the spread of Zen Buddhism from countries in the East to affluent countries such as the United States.

If there was one example that illustrates well the complicated relationship between modernity, globalization and religion, it is that of Pentecostalism, a form of Protestantism that emphasizes a direct and personal relationship with God through the baptism of the Holy Spirit. Many sociologists of religion who study Pentecostalism speak of Pentecostalism*s*, in the plural, given the diversity of churches and practices that self-identify as Pentecostal or focus on the manifestation of the Holy Spirit. Pentecostalism is among the most diverse of all Christian denominations as its different forms of expression are rooted in the local. Pentecostals are known for their expansionist goals, often planting churches across the world. Indeed, Michael Wilkinson (2008: 6) has argued that Pentecostals are 'globalizers'. Pentecostalism has an ability to replicate itself in canonical form and simultaneously adapt to the context within which it finds itself. This is often accompanied by ruptures in the local context as followers are encouraged to reject aspects of their existing culture. For instance, Pentecostal churches in many African countries dissuade congregants from engaging in traditional rituals to honour ancestors as these practices are deemed evil. This often results in fractures between congregants and their kin.

Pentecostals are not merely passive products of globalization but also agents in transmitting and moulding globalization. Although there are many examples of Pentecostal churches expanding from the Global North, both historically along colonial routes and right up to today (such as the American Assemblies of God or the Australian Hillsong Church), there is also a bountiful geographical distribution of Pentecostal denominations originating from the Global South (Africa, Latin America and Asia), thereby illustrating that globalization should not be confused with westernization. Two of the most successful Pentecostal churches from the Global South are the Nigerian Redeemed Christian Church of God (RCCG) and the Brazilian Universal Church of the Kingdom of God (UCKG). Both came from humble beginnings and now have extensive transnational networks and global adherents that number in the millions. They have not only amassed huge global congregations but also great wealth and political sway, both in their homelands and in some of the countries to which they have expanded. Certainly, the global flows of Christianity no longer reflect that of Western world power and wealth.

Expand Your Knowledge

- To learn more about how belief and religious materiality (such as sacred objects, places, infrastructures and digital media) are entangled in the processes of globalization, read: Rocha, C. (2020) Materiality and global spiritual networks: Old and new sacred places and objects. *Australian Journal of Anthropology* 31: 210–23. https://doi.org/10.1111/taja.12357
- Are you interested in finding out some of the ways that Pentecostal churches are 'globalizers'? Check out the article by Kathleen Openshaw (one of this chapter's authors) on how Pentecostal churches can facilitate the movement of ideas, people, material culture and spirits across the globe: Openshaw, K. (2019) The Universal Church of the Kingdom of God in Australia: Local congregants and a global spiritual network. *Journal for the Academic Study of Religion* 32(1): 27–48.

Lived Religion and Pop Culture

With this revitalized spread of religion around the globe, religion can be understood differently in the way it is lived at the grassroots. To understand this, sociologists make reference to the term **lived religion** (McGuire, 2008) or popular religion (Possamai, 2015) and acknowledge that religion is context-dependent. For example, in a location where there is a sharp contrast between an urban and a rural setting, the official religion is often dominant in cities whereas popular religion (e.g. syncretic aspects of Catholicism with nature religion or animism) tends to be more practised in villages and among marginalized peoples. However, this does not stop urbanites from tapping into popular religion and seeking the help of, for example, a spiritual healer who will perform alternative rituals to those performed within institutionalized religion. Another context is that of a colonized country in which the official religion is the one brought by the new dominant ethnic group (e.g. Catholicism in Latin America), and popular religion is the one practised by the dominated ethnic group (e.g. Indigenous religion). This can also happen when a non-dominant group moves to another country and brings with it its own religion. For example, the Afro-Brazilian religious tradition of Candomblé is a syncretic blend of African religious traditions and Roman Catholicism formed when enslaved peoples were brought from Africa to Brazil (Cohen, 2007). Although popular religion comprises a multitude of informal elements, often in contradiction, some theorists define popular religion not in terms of an urban/rural divide or a colonial context but specifically with regard to class divide and power, with the upper class belonging to official religion and the lower class and marginal people to popular religion.

During the perceived secularization phase, many influential Western social scientists saw these practices of popular religion as being antiquated and believed that they were bound to disappear far quicker than official religions. Weber wrote about this as the 'disenchantment of the world' which started with Judaism – a religion that emerged amidst pagan religions and which completely broke with magic. Indeed, Weber made a clear distinction between religion with an irrational aim (e.g. going to paradise, being reincarnated) but providing a rational process (e.g. clear conduct in life, a rigorous lifestyle in a monastery) as opposed to magic, which has a rational goal (e.g. making someone fall in love or recover from an unknown illness) but irrational means (e.g. rituals and incantations). Jewish prophets distanced themselves from previous polytheist religious traditions as they became the tools of one and only one God. Pagan gods, on the other hand, could help people in their everyday life. In this new worldview, nothing magical was allowed to exist as there was no point in expecting God to help people in their everyday life. Later, in contrast to Judaism, Catholicism re-enchanted parts of the world with, for example, the introduction of saints who could intercede on people's behalf through prayer. The worship through saints' relics and some forms of pilgrimage can also be viewed sociologically as magical actions rather than religious ones. Again, later, Protestantism moved away from what Weber saw as a magical practice and put in place another disenchantment process which would lead to modernity, as seen above with Weber's 'Protestant Ethic and Spirit of Capitalism' thesis.

Expand Your Knowledge

How the Social Construction of Religion in the West Can Socially Construct Religion in the East

According to Goossaert (2003), in China around 1900 there were approximately one million temples openly dedicated to the veneration of ancestors and deities. Today, only a few thousand are still open as religious sites, and a few more thousand as museums. Some of the others (that were not destroyed) have been transformed into factories, depots or dwellings. The functions of these local deities vary from protecting households from evil spirits and curing illness to controlling the weather. These communities were neither directly from Confucianism, Buddhism nor Taoism but had strong links with all three. Some of these popular religious beliefs were even recognized by the emperor of the time and were considered part of the state religion. In the early 20th century, many Chinese thinkers (e.g. Kang Youwei, 1858–1927) became so influenced by Western reason that they wanted to 'modernize' their country, which meant creating a totally new religious project for the whole country. To build the new China, the country needed new schools, post offices, police stations and local government buildings, and the local temples were confiscated so that they could be turned into these spaces. The local belief systems came to be seen by the new intelligentsia as superstitious and in need of being removed. First Confucianism, followed by Buddhism and Taoism, became state religions because the Chinese reformers believed that the strength of a country was dependent upon having a state religion, as was the case in most, if not all, countries in Europe. Each of these three religions was required to re-invent itself as an institutionalized religion. To do this, they had to get rid of all their relations with Chinese popular religion and become official religions. By bringing the Western model into their country, Chinese officials had to distinguish religion (a term which appeared only in Chinese as *zongjiao* in the 20th century) from the so-called superstitions of its local belief systems. Because these local adherents could not organize themselves as an institution (such as a type of church) and because they did not follow any 'noble' written tradition, they could not be recognized as an official religion.

Popular religions do not have to be based within an established church; they can be lived outside of them, while others can nevertheless remain in these structures, often at the margins. Because of this impasse, with regard to defining and pinpointing exactly what popular religion is, some theorists moved away from this notion and started thinking about religion as it is lived in people's daily lives. Meredith McGuire (2008) is one of the best-known scholars for highlighting the everydayness of 'lived religion'. For McGuire (2008), scholars must study religion not as it is defined by religious organizations but as it is actually lived in people's everyday lives. Indeed, the increase of consumerism, instant communication technologies, and hyper-globalization have created a type of free religious market in which people can pick-and-choose how they wish to worship, thereby individualizing their religion. McGuire (2008) moved away from studying religion at the institutional level and concentrated her research at the individual level. She was concerned with the amalgam of beliefs that are often ever-changing, multifaceted and can be contradictory – aspects of religion that religious institutions do not often consider of importance. Lived religion reflects the fact that not only do religions and the messages from official spokespersons change, but what ordinary people understand by those changes and how they practise their daily religiosity is important too.

Hear from the Expert

Scholars of religion, especially sociologists, must re-examine their assumptions about individuals' religious lives. What might we discover if, instead of looking at affiliation or organizational participation, we focused first on individuals, the experiences they consider most important, and the concrete practices that make up their personal religious experience and expression? What if we think of religion, at the individual level, as an ever-changing, multifaceted, often messy – even

> contradictory – combination of beliefs and practices that are not necessarily those religious institutions consider important?
>
> McGuire, M. *Lived Religion: Faith and Practice in Everyday Life*. New York: Oxford University Press (2008: 4). Reproduced with permission of the Licensor through PLSclear.

Another example of popular religion is hyper-real religion (Possamai, 2012). It refers to the simulacrum (i.e. the representation or imitation) of a religion created out of, or in symbiosis with, commodified popular culture which provides inspiration at a metaphorical level and/or is a source of beliefs for everyday life. It is constructed as a mix of religions, philosophies, and commodified popular culture. In our globalized world, commodified popular culture offers a library of narratives to be borrowed and used by anyone ready to consume them for their religious bricolage. The most commonly known 21st-century example is Jediism (from the *Star Wars* films): a group mainly active on the internet that has created a popular religion out of inspiration from the *Star Wars* narratives, especially its Jedi Knights' spirituality, and the syncretic assemblage between various religions and philosophies through the *Star Wars* narrative.

This hyper-real religious phenomenon is not limited to full-blown cases such as Jediism but can also involve people being religiously inspired by popular culture. For example, this could include watching *The Da Vinci Code* or *Avatar*, playing a game such as *World of Warcraft*, or being influenced by conspiracy theories.

The influence of popular culture on young minds is such an issue that some Christian groups have attempted to prevent their children from reading and watching *Harry Potter*. The fear is often that these young minds could be desensitized from the reality of the world of magic and the occult and join a pagan coven in later years. By the way, we are sure the reader would be interested to note that there is an actual school of wizardry inspired by the stories of Harry Potter available on the internet. There are more than 400 classes that budding wizards and witches can do online.

And how about you? Have you been inspired by popular culture and has it influenced the way you see the world? Has your addiction to fantasy novels made you more spiritual? Perhaps the 'gods as aliens' argument in those sci-fi Space Opera stories you have read have made you move away from religion? Or perhaps both, and you are somewhere in between, sometimes moving in a direction depending on your life experience and your circumstances? Certainly, it is worth considering how society has shaped you and the degree to which pop culture has shaped your generation and what they believe and practise when it comes to the supernatural.

CHAPTER SUMMARY

- Attempts to define religion have largely come from a Western scholarship tradition that has led to some deficiencies in understanding the true complexities of how humans live their religions.
- Human religiosity across the world does not only exist within institutions but can be informal and dynamic.
- Religions absorb and discard elements of practice and theology through acting and reacting to global and local influences.

PART 4 CONNECTING THE PERSONAL AND THE SOCIAL

REVIEW QUESTIONS

1. How has the study of religion by sociologists been influenced by the history of sociology?

Consider how the roots of sociology in Western industrialization and colonial expansion have influenced what sociologists understood to be religion, and how religion has influenced and is influenced by society.

2. What are some of the complexities involved in studying religion sociologically?

Look to consider the methods employed by sociologists to the study of religion or how the personal belief system of the sociologists may or may not influence their research.

3. How can Meredith McGuire's 'lived religion' or Adam Possamai's 'popular religion' explain what is happening today in contemporary society?

Think about how these concepts might explain how people are religious. Are they useful to understand how religion is actually practised by people? Can we use these concepts to illustrate how people are influenced by technology and easy access to ideas when 'doing' their religion?

Go Further

Books

- Davie, G. (2013) *The Sociology of Religion: A Critical Agenda*. London: Sage.

A key reading on the overview of this sub-discipline by one of the leading UK sociologists.

- Pew Research Center (2015) *The Future of World Religions: Population Growth Projections, 2010–2050: Why Muslims are Rising Fastest and the Unaffiliated Are Shrinking as a Share of the World's Population*, 2 April. Available at: www.pewforum.org/2015/04/02/religious-projections-2010-2050

A comprehensive report on religion in the world and the projected growth in the near future.

- Possamai, A. and Blasi, A. (eds) (2020) *The SAGE Encyclopaedia of the Sociology of Religion (Two Volumes)*. London: Sage.

With more than 500 entries on key concepts in the sociology of religion and key groups, and more than 200 contributors from around the world.

Journal Articles

These articles focus on the critical and very contemporary discussions taking place among sociologists of religion around how the discipline now understands 'everyday religion', how it can be far more inclusive of the cosmovisions, works and scholars beyond the West, and what this means for how the sociology of religion may look in the future:

- Ammerman, N.T. (2016) Lived religion as an emerging field: An assessment of its contours and frontiers. *Nordic Journal of Religion and Society* 1(2): 83–99.

- Day, A. (2020) Towards increasing diversity in the study of religion. *Religion* 50(1): 46–52. DOI: 10.1080/0048721X.2019.1681086.
- Spickard, J.V. (2019) The sociology of religion in a post-colonial era: Towards theoretical reflexivity. *Religions* 10(1): 18. DOI: 10.3390/rel10010018.

Websites

- *The Religious Studies Project Podcast*: www.religiousstudiesproject.com
- *Oxford Research Encyclopaedia of Religion*: https://oxfordre.com/religion
- University of Victoria (n.d.) *Religion in Society: Sociology of Religion Blogging Noosphere*. https://onlineacademiccommunity.uvic.ca/sociologyofreligion/home

REFERENCES

Altglas, V. (2010) Religion and globalization: Introduction. In V. Altglas (ed.) *Religion and Globalization: Critical Concepts in Social Studies*. London: Routledge, pp. 1–22.

Appadurai, A. (1996) *Modernity at Large: Cultural Dimensions of Globalization*. Minneapolis, MN: University of Minnesota Press.

Asad, T. (1993) *Genealogies of Religion: Discipline and Reasons of Power in Christianity and Islam*. Baltimore, MD: Johns Hopkins University Press.

Bano, S. (2012) *An Exploratory Study of Shariah Councils in England with Respect to Family Law*. Reading: University of Reading.

Calhoun, C. (2011) Secularism, citizenship, and the public sphere. In C. Calhoun, M. Juergensmeyer and J. Vanantwerpen (eds) *Rethinking Secularism*. New York: Oxford University Press, pp. 75–91.

Casanova, J. (2006) Rethinking secularization: A global comparative perspective. *The Hedgehog Review* 8(1–2): 7–22.

Cohen, E. (2007) *The Mind Possessed: The Cognition of Spirit Possession in an Afro-Brazilian Religious Tradition*. New York: Oxford University Press.

Cox, J. and Possamai, A. (eds) (2016) *Religion and Non-Religion among Australian Aboriginal Peoples*. London: Routledge.

Davie, G. (2002) *Europe: The Exceptional Case. Parameters of Faith in the Modern World*. London: Darton, Longman and Todd.

Davie, G. (2015) *Religion in Britain: A Persistent Paradox*. Oxford: Wiley Blackwell.

Debray, R. (2005) *Les communions humaines. Pour en finir avec la 'religion'*. Paris: Fayard.

Durkheim, E. (2001) *The Elementary Forms of Religious Life*. Oxford: Oxford University Press.

Goossaert, V. (2003) Le destin de la religion chinoise au 20ème siècle. *Social Compass* 50(4): 429–40.

Habermas, J. (2006) Religion in the public sphere. *European Journal of Philosophy* 14(1): 1–25.

Harvey, D. (1989) *The Condition of Postmodernity: An Enquiry into the Origins of Cultural Change*. Cambridge: Blackwell.

Lee, A. (2014) *The Ugly Renaissance: Sex, Disease and Excess in an Age of Beauty*. London: Arrow Books.

Martin, D. (2005) *On Secularization: Towards a Revised General Theory*. Aldershot: Ashgate.

McGuire, M. (2008) *Lived Religion: Faith and Practice in Everyday Life*. New York: Oxford University Press.

Pew Research Center (2015) *The Future of World Religions: Population Growth Projections, 2010–2050*. Washington, DC: Pew Research Center.

Possamai, A. (ed.) (2012) *Handbook of Hyper-Real Religions*. Leiden: Brill.

Possamai, A. (2015) Popular and lived religions. *Current Sociology* 63(6): 781–99.

Possamai, A., Richardson, J. and Turner, B. (eds) (2015) *The Sociology of Shari'a: Case Studies from Around the World*. Leiden: Springer.

Possamai-Inesedy, A. and Turner, B. (2016) Same sex marriage and the Christian conservative reaction. In J.G. Goulet (ed.) *Understanding and Experiencing Religious Diversity in Today's World*. Santa Barbara, CA: Praeger.

Taylor, C. (2007) *A Secular Age*. Cambridge, MA: The Belknap Press of Harvard University Press.

Troeltsch, E. (1950) *The Social Teaching of the Christian Churches*. London: George Allen & Unwin.

Tweed, T. (2006) *Crossings and Dwellings: A Theory of Religion*. Cambridge, MA: Harvard University Press.

Weber, M. (1930) *The Protestant Ethic and the Spirit of Capitalism*, trans. Talcott Parsons. New York: Scribner's.

Wilkinson, M. (2008) What's 'global' about global Pentecostalism? *Journal of Pentecostal Theology* 17: 1–13.

PART 5

SOCIOLOGICAL FRONTIERS

PART 5 SOCIOLOGICAL FRONTIERS

Introduction to Part 5

This part of *An Introduction to Sociology* contains five chapters that engage with some prominent contemporary and global challenges for sociology in the 21st century – consumption, violence, science, migration and social movements. As you will see in the chapters, these are not 'new' topics in or to sociology as they were discussed by or can be connected to some of the key figures in sociology from previous centuries. However, contemporary issues in the world make them important public and global concerns that apply in some way to almost every person in the world. As we hope you might by now expect, the analyses of each of these is informed by the ways that sociology has made sense of them and how it can be used to understand them now; in this way, we think these chapters underline the ways the dynamism of sociology as a discipline that is engaged with the present day, reflects on its own histories but is not bound by them or by previous conceptual frames.

In Chapter 21, David Wright examines consumption. The idea that we live in 'a consumer society' is commonplace; shopping and taste are closely tied to issues of identities (providing a link to the chapters in Section 4 of this book). Moreover, as Wright shows, the consumption and circulation of goods are ways in which sociologists understand how social life is made and re-made. We have, or we think we have, freedom to consume as we wish, but this choice also connects us to other people and places across the world that may remind you of the point about interconnectedness raised in Chapter 6, as well as having some environmental cost, which should remind you of Chapter 4.

In Chapter 22, Christian Olsson focuses on what sociology can contribute to analysing violence and war. Violence, as Olsson explains, can be defined narrowly or broadly, and the implications of taking one or the other perspective impacts on how we 'see' what violence is, and how it is framed in terms of dichotomies such as nature/nurture and modern/primitive. While violence is sometimes treated as a 'pre-social' phenomenon, Olsson shows the extent to which it is embedded in gender and politics, as well as the role of the state.

In Chapter 23, Ros Williams starts by noting that you may be surprised to see the topic of science and technology in a sociology book, even though technology is part of our everyday life in many ways, from music and entertainment to our engagement with, say, health services. Rather than being remote, science and technology are part of society, including shaping identities and their impact on the environment. Williams introduces you to the ways that sociologists understand how science is organized (and this is picked up again in Chapter 27 by William Outhwaite), suggesting that it is intrinsically social and political. For example, Williams highlights how the idea of race (this links to Chapter 13), as well as how internet algorithms work in a racist way, reveal the ways in which science and technology are not free of values and bias.

In Chapter 24, Anna Gawlewicz discusses migrations, showing that it is a social and global policy issue as well as one that interests sociologists and geographers in the social sciences. The topic of migration is in the news regularly and has been linked to crises in Europe and beyond. Race has been a common theme in that, and a key factor in policy and politics, including Brexit and the UK government's hostile environment approach. Gawlewicz presents you with a number of different meanings of migration as well as what the drivers of migration are, and its impacts on patterns of urban and rural settlement. She introduces the important concept of transnationalism as a way that sociologists explain the social relations of migrants and migrations across the world.

In Chapter 25, Nick Crossley looks at the sociology of social movements. As he notes, these are visible and active in many movements across the world, including ones such as Black Lives Matter (also discussed by

PART 5 SOCIOLOGICAL FRONTIERS

Olsson in Chapter 22) and the #MeToo movement. Yet focusing on what is visible and on protest movements can be limiting in terms of what is not seen as a social movement, as Crossley shows. Taking you through debates around two key questions – what is a social movement, and how do they form? – Crossley introduces the main theorists in this area.

The five chapters in this section are just some of the topics that show how sociology engages with the contemporary. There are more social and political issues that you might consider and, looking in a library or online, you will not find it hard to identify sociologists analysing and writing about almost any topic you can think of. Some of the concepts and names used differ as this reflects the wide span of sociological work, but these chapters show you how a rigorous sociology aims to define and clarify key terms and combine theory and evidence.

Key Questions

- How do classical and contemporary debates in sociology contribute to your understanding of consumption?
- What does sociology bring to or add to understanding violence?
- In what ways is it useful to view and understand science and technology in social terms?
- How would you draw on and apply the concept of transnationalism to study migration?
- How do sociological analyses of social movements highlight their diversity?
- Identify two or three contemporary topics or issues that interest you (and which are not covered in this section or elsewhere in this book) and that you think are global challenges for sociology. How would you go about addressing them using the approach of one or more of the chapters in this section?

CULTURES AND CONSUMPTION

David Wright

LEARNING OBJECTIVES

- To introduce and elaborate on sociological approaches to consumption.
- To understand consumption and consumerism as social processes.
- To appreciate how consumer goods have come to be meaningful in making contemporary identities.
- To use the concept of 'taste' to explore the sociological tension between the individual and the social.

Framing Questions

1. What is *sociological* about consumption?
2. How have sociologists contributed to understanding the consumer society?
3. What are the relationships between consumer goods and 'identity'?
4. How can *individual* tastes and preferences shape and reflect *social* patterns?

PART 5 SOCIOLOGICAL FRONTIERS

Introduction

In this chapter, you will consider contemporary consumption as a social and cultural phenomenon and think about the ways in which sociologists have refined and contributed to our understanding of this topic within the social sciences. You will reflect on how the sociological approach to consumption has emerged in relation to other social scientific stories. On the one hand, sociology has been concerned with critiquing a still dominant *economics-led* model of consumption focused on the exchange of goods between rational agents within a capitalist marketplace. On the other, sociological study has also been informed by anthropological accounts of material culture and the ways in which human beings relate to and make use of the objects that they live with. This combination of emphases has allowed elements of a sociological understanding of contemporary consumption to become central to everyday understandings of social life in what has come to be known as a consumer society. The chapter proceeds by reflecting on two stories about this kind of society – first, about consumer society as a 'trap' and, second, about consumer society as a 'symbolic resource' to which sociologists have contributed.

 Pause for Thought

- Think about and list the last five things you have 'consumed'. These could be things you have bought, eaten, used, watched, or read – perhaps including this chapter. It would be useful to reflect on the processes you went through in acquiring and consuming these things as you proceed through the chapter.

Mapping the Terrain

Although a specific sub-specialism concerning the sociology of consumption has been formulated in the last 30 years or so, questions of consumption can be seen to underpin sociological accounts of the world since the discipline emerged as a distinct voice in the social sciences in the mid to late 19th century. This is perhaps partly attributable to the fact that the early voices in these foundational accounts were concerned with explaining different elements of what appeared to be a new social world in Western Europe and North America, characterized by urban, industrial **capitalism**. Consumption, or at least the satisfaction of needs through the exchange of money for goods and services – one of the characteristics Max Weber (1920) uses to describe a mature capitalist society – was clearly a key mechanism in this order. Strands from these early thinkers inform a range of sociological stories about consumption – and some, such as the concept of **conspicuous consumption** which emerges from a sociological analysis of the American upper classes (Veblen, 1899), have entered everyday speech and retain considerable explanatory power. As we'll see in the following section, a Marxist critique of **commodity fetishism** can be read into critical accounts of **consumer society** as a trap, as can Durkheimian anxieties about the tension between the individual and the social in relation to the pursuit of material wealth and personal, spiritual happiness (Durkheim, 1893) in late 19th-century France. (More discussion of Marx and Durkheim can be found in Chapters 5, 7, 8 and 26.)

A final significant intervention from early sociological theorizing comes from Georg Simmel's reflections on how life in the still growing cities of the late 19th century was characterized by a tension engendered by the need to fit into an increasing blurring of established feudal orders and statuses. One needed to live with, to integrate into, to adapt to social life but also try to maintain a sense of distance from it to preserve a sense of individual, personal identity. One mechanism to do this was 'the fashion system' (Simmel, 1997). The 'double function' of fashion was to signal one's membership of certain groups or strata in society but also to distinguish oneself from others. This tension between the individual and the social is a recurring one in sociology in general and in the sociology of consumption in particular, and you'll return to it throughout this chapter.

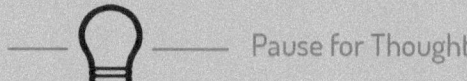 Pause for Thought

What is a Consumer?

In contemporary discussion, the term 'consumer' is often used as a kind of synonym for a 'person'. But what specific characteristics does a consumer have, in comparison to other general words for 'people'?

- How might a consumer be different from, for example, a 'subject' or a 'citizen'?
- What qualities, abilities, rights, or duties does a *consumer* have which these other labels might not imply?
- What is a consumer expected to *do* and for whom?

The development of a more focused interest in consumption in British sociology was part of a re-alignment of the discipline away from its founding concerns with questions of work and labour (or *production*) and the changed status of the worker as the central concern of sociological analysis. This was a response to the apparent social and political re-alignments of class and political affiliation which post-war British sociology had partly attributed to the increased affluence of society across classes. One element of this affluence was the availability of new consumer goods, the pursuit of which had appeared to displace the struggles for better pay and working conditions, at least in the minds of some study participants (Goldthorpe et al., 1968). An increased focus on the significance of consumption to social life was a feature of post-war society, arguably across the Global North. By the end of the century, this had crystallized into a powerful story in which manufacturing industries were 'in decline' (although, more accurately, 'exported' south and eastwards) and the service industries, including retail, were gaining in importance in driving economic growth – the principal measure of national success. The quick circulation of consumer goods, and the accompanying growth of advertising and marketing industries to promote these goods, as well as the increased availability of personal credit to buy them, underpinned the emergence of what was labelled 'the consumer society' (Baudrillard, 1970).

Claims for this apparently novel, post-industrial sociological experience, initially in Europe, North America, and Japan, but eventually as an exemplar of globalization, are complicated by interventions from social history (McCracken, 1988). These trace the emergence of modern consumption right back to the Industrial Revolution of the 18th and 19th centuries, re-imagining this as much as a revolution in *consumption* as it was a transformation in working life or a driver of urbanization. The success of **capitalism** in this formative period not only required people to move from fields to factories, but it also required people to buy and to have reasons to buy the things that factories produced. The more recent intensification of interest in the

(Continued)

sociology of consumption, then, reflects a story explaining the emergence of contemporary social life and a longer history. It emerges from both identifiable changes in the mode of production and shifts within the **sociological imagination** itself.

A principal contribution of a sociological account of consumption is to complicate notions of choice and preference as phenomena which emerge from *individuals*, and to foreground the *social* processes which inform and shape the choices we make. In this, the sociological approach to consumption shares much with those approaches that emerge from economics, specifically in the case of those accounts which focus on what we might identify as the *moments* of consumption, i.e. when a choice is made and a good or service is purchased. What sociology has consistently attempted to preserve is that these moments – in the shop or supermarket or even in the disembodied online encounter – are not reducible to the facts of price, money and the exchange of goods, or even the more abstracted forces of supply and demand. Instead, they are also *social* encounters, overlain with meanings about appropriate forms of conduct and behaviour, informed by cultural norms and shaped by relationships of power. Sociological accounts might even maintain that issues of cost, price or value for money, which are the preserve of a crude economic analysis of the exchange of goods in a capitalist marketplace, are *less* significant to these moments than their role in performing or cementing social roles or rituals. Consider a mother shopping for a family meal. Her skilled bargain-hunting in relation to the responsible management of a domestic budget might be within the remit of economic analysis. Her performance of gender, caring and parenting roles, all of which, together with the rituals and meanings of the family meal itself, are *socially* produced and understood, or not.

Shops and Shopping

Thinking about shops and shopping is useful for revealing the complexities of consumption. Consider the management of the service interaction itself. The supermarket checkout has its own culturally specific scripts and roles which might differ from those of a smaller greengrocer and might differ still from the forms of behaviour in a bookshop – and even further from an online store so distant from the messy, fleshy elements of social exchange. Each of these institutions (the variety of shops) and practices (the ways shopping is organized and conducted) has a history, and their rules and rituals can be revealed through a sociological eye. While freedom to *choose* is one of the characteristics of a consumer society, the rise of the fixed-price shop creates the consumer as a rather *passive* part of the economic process, restricted to choosing or not. It also represents the end of explicit bargaining over price between buyers and sellers – except, perhaps, in the encounter of the Western tourist in North Africa or Asia where the *performance* of haggling over price becomes part of the *experience* of a holiday.

Practices of shopping are also fundamental to understanding urban space and how it is designed and experienced. A key sociological figure in this is the flâneur, the name given to the strolling dandy of the emerging 19th-century city – normally a man of relative privilege and affluence – who remade urban space as a site of leisure and contemplation (Tester, 1994). Shopping as a pleasurable leisure experience in itself is further enhanced by the development of the department store in the late 19th century – 'cathedrals of consumption' as the novelist Emile Zola termed them. The late 20th century out-of-town shopping mall had different resonances (reflecting a mobile consumer moving through privatized space – a 'non-place' as Augé (1995) describes it), while the early 21st century return of the artisan or small shop spaces reflects an apparent appeal of more 'authentic' experiences that are, paradoxically, resistant to the narratives of consumerism. In all these different arrangements, how we *shop* can be used by sociologists to understand how we live.

 — Pause for Thought

- Thinking about your own recent experiences of shopping, what kinds of shop did you visit?
- What, if any, interaction did you have with other people?

From a sociological perspective, then, not only are issues of price and value not necessarily the most interesting part of what I have identified as the moments of consumption, but also these moments might themselves not be the only interesting thing about consumption. Whilst an economist's interest might wane once money for the goods has been exchanged in a discrete market transaction at least until it is time for the goods to be replaced – sociologists also concern themselves with how goods are *used* and lived with and how their use and life make processes of consumption an active process of the creation and re-creation of social life.

Consuming: Trap or Symbolic Resource?

Given **sociology**'s abiding concerns with tensions between the individual and society, and the specific **methodological** and **theoretical** tools it draws on to explore these tensions, accounts of the consumer society which are *critical* of its values, however these are defined, have been central. We might see early manifestations of this in Marx's (1867) account of commodity fetishism. Marx describes the powerful 'trick' of capitalism in shifting value from the bodies of workers who make things onto the things themselves. The capitalist producer sells the things back to the workers, extracting excess value as profit. This is a modern analytic manifestation of older anxieties, implicit in many religions, about the risks of valuing things and money above other spiritual concerns. As the labelling of the societies of the Global North as consumer societies became more widespread from the middle of the 20th century, a more general anxiety about the *values* of such a society pervaded cultural life – and sociology. As Sassatelli describes it, a significant amount of sociological reflection in the post-war period was 'aimed at unmasking the manipulative character of the symbolic dimension of goods and, in this way, tended to conceptualise consumption as the ultimate domain of deceitful domination' (Sassatelli, 2007: 64). Consumer culture, in this vision, was associated with a kind of inevitable spiritual impoverishment or corruption in which the very selves of people, re-labelled as consumers, are built not on the apparently solid foundations of nation, **family** or class but on the ephemeral, shifting sands of consumer goods.

For some analysts in this critical tradition, informed by Marxist perspectives, re-casting all processes of human exchange as processes of consumerism can be understood as a reflection of the iniquitous and exploitative relations of capitalism. Consumer culture, in this sense, becomes an **ideology** to manipulate consumers into desires for ever more novel goods to satisfy quests for self-actualization which are ultimately illusory.

The mis-recognition of these desires as a search for self-fulfilment blinds consumers to their **role** in the reproduction of the capitalist order, including, from feminist perspectives (Bordo, 2000), the patriarchal order, and extends the **alienation** of the labour process to the family, to leisure time and to the very constitution of identities. Consumers are unable, in this story, to genuinely and authentically craft their selves, if this crafting depends solely upon repeated trips to the marketplace. Instead, as Marcuse has it, they 'find their soul in their automobile, hi-fi set, split level home' (Marcuse, 1968: 24). It is a sense of the inevitable disappointment in consumer culture, and the accompanying implication that consumers themselves seem incapable of seeing through its illusory qualities, that pervades these critical accounts – a sense that is nicely captured by Baudrillard's analogy linking consumer society with the Melanesian cargo cults that were observed by anthropologists attempting to lure down passing planes through the creation of models of planes from branches and vines. 'The beneficiary of the consumer miracle', he suggests, 'also sets in place a whole array of sham objects, of characteristic signs of happiness, and then waits … for happiness to alight' (Baudrillard, 1970: 31).

The rise and establishment of the consumer society in this story was about broader changes than those involved in the buying and selling of goods. Instead, it was implicated in the re-imagining of people, their capacities, and motivations. The sociologist Zygmunt Bauman captures this well in reflecting on the status of poverty in a consumer society. In the 'pre-consumer' society ordered around production, or work, poverty could be alleviated through the practices of the welfare **state** and collectivization of the risks of the labour market or cycles of economic growth or recession. In the consumer society though, in which individual agency is framed through the exercise of consumer choices, poverty itself becomes understood as a choice. As he describes it:

In a consumer society, a 'normal life' is the life of consumers, preoccupied with making their choices among the panoply of publicly displayed opportunities for pleasurable sensations and lively experiences. … As in all other kinds of society, the poor of a consumer society are people with no access to a normal life, let alone to a happy one. In a consumer society however, having no access to a happy or merely a normal life means to be consumers manquées, or flawed consumers. (Bauman, 2004: 38)

21.1 Key Case

Always a Consumer

Applying the denomination of *consumer* to a whole range of institutional relationships beyond the immediate exchange of consumer goods was a feature of **new public management** approaches to public services that emerged towards the end of the 20th century in the UK – such that citizens became *consumers* of welfare, public transport, health or higher education. Critical sociological voices emphasized how this changed the nature of these relationships (Clarke et al., 2007). On the one hand, being treated as a consumer implies being treated as an *individual*, and as one with freedom and agency over one's life and choices, in contrast to the kinds of treatment apparently available from the grand public service bureaucracies of the mid-to-late 20th century. On the other hand, the notion of consumer freedom rings hollow when the meaning of 'choice' is less clear. If there is one hospital in your town, or one train line to where you wish to travel, the reality of being a *consumer*, rather than a patient or passenger, in these institutions might amount to not much more than the opportunity to enjoy branded waiting rooms and cafes.

CULTURES AND CONSUMPTION

Sociologists of various stripes have been central to the perpetuation of this critical story of consumerism as a kind of trap – and it remains a powerful one within and beyond the academy. Indeed, somewhat paradoxically several influential accounts in this tradition (Packard's *The Hidden Persuaders* (1958) and Lasch's *The Culture of Narcissism* (1979)) have themselves become bestsellers.

In the second story, consumer society is characterized by new forms of freedom to shape one's self, in contrast to a differently imagined recent past in which grand **social structure**s such as class, nation, gender, family and the workplace *constrained* our identities and determined our place in the world. In the consumer society, according to this story, these structures are weakened and replaced by the ability of individuals to take responsibility for crafting themselves. The weakening of tradition opens up the possibility of a wider range of possible selves, which can be chosen 'off the peg', with consumer goods becoming resources from which the uncertainty that accompanies the decline of these structures can be at least partly countered.

Pause for Thought

'I shop therefore I am'

The practices of consumption are so ingrained in everyday life, it can be difficult to see them as a product of social processes:

- Think about what you have bought this week or month.
- Which of your purchases were necessities (for food, clothing, shelter)?
- What kinds of reflection informed your choices?
- To what extent were you influenced by the choices of your peers, or by the messages from advertisers or marketers in choosing between products, or between different brands of the same product?

This element of a relationship with objects draws from anthropological traditions, which reveal that Western consumer societies are not the only ones to be organized around a central role for the accumulation and exchange of goods. Indeed, the denomination *consumer culture* might well be better understood as a specific form of a more general and longer-lived **material culture** in which people's identities and relationships are mediated through the circulation of meaningful symbolic objects. Sociological analysis has revealed how processes of consumption can transform the meaning of objects, removing them from their position in commodity circuits and placing them in the realm of everyday life experience, where the meanings of things are not determined by the objects themselves but in their relations with their owners. In a key contribution to this tradition of analysis, Dant (2000) describes a knife he had owned for 27 years. Whether it was bought – acquired through the 'cash-nexus' as Dant terms it – or, instead, borrowed or found is rather insignificant to its story. Nor, as a functional object, does its significance stem from any aesthetic or stylistic quality (albeit that, over the period, the particular brand of knife became a fashionable one). Instead, the knife narrates the different stages of Dant's life and relationships (with parents as he leaves home, with flatmates, with partners, with children) which the object accompanies him on. The systems of accumulation and circulation of objects, then, extend far beyond the moment of consumption which represents, in most cases but not all, only the beginning of the kinds of social relationships of consumption to which sociologists have paid attention.

This story about the symbolic resources of consumption has antecedents but it came into particular prominence towards the end of the 20th century, being critiqued as part of what Warde (1994) describes as the 'reflexive modernisation' thesis which exemplified the **social theory** of the late 20th century and in which 'commodities became the principal channels for the communication of self-identity' (Warde, 1994: 878). It also, though, requires something of a cultural shift, which Sassatelli conceives of as a process of de-*commoditization*. Things might be made into commodities by producers operating within the marketplace, but the process of consumption can also be understood, if we assume the *agency* of consumers in the process, as the 're-translation of the meanings and uses of commodities through daily life, on the basis of needs that are not reducible to those of production, retail or promotion' (Sassatelli, 2007: 115). Consumers in this vision might be constrained by the injunction to choose, but they are relatively free in how to use the things they choose in the shaping of their immediate symbolic environment. Producers can feed off this creativity in the re-shaping of their products – but the desires of consumers are only ever dimly known. It is always the process of consumption that determines what things *mean*.

Expand Your Knowledge

The British Cultural Studies Approach: 'Style' and 'Resistant' Consumers

A strand of work in which this agency of consumers is examined is provided by the British Cultural Studies tradition, which combined sociological methods and approaches with those of literary studies and critical theory. Through small-scale ethnographic studies, or through the analysis of texts, advertisements, and representations mostly from within the popular commercial cultures of the mid-20th century (e.g. pop music or teen magazines), researchers from this tradition revealed that consumer goods themselves and the processes of consumption are more complex than simply reflecting the creation and manipulation of consumers' desires by producers or advertisers. Instead, consumers themselves can manipulate and shape the meaning of consumer goods – often in ways which are unexpected or unintended by producers. As Hebdige (1998) describes, for example, the Italian Vespa motorcycle which was initially conceived of by its manufacturers as an elegant, feminine transport solution, was transformed, in British culture, to one associated with aspirational forms of working-class masculinity, particularly within 'mod' culture. Such sub-cultures, and especially the spectacular sub-cultures associated with young people and popular culture (Hall and Jefferson, 1975), reveal how 'mass' forms of production do not lead, necessarily, to 'mass' forms of consumption but can provide instead the resources for symbolic meaning making for individuals and groups, including that which might be resistant to dominant ideologies.

This notion of consumption as a dialogue or **semiotic** struggle between producers and consumers serves to *create* the consumer as an object of analysis and a particular problem to be solved. Those of us schooled in the rhetoric of consumer society might tell ourselves that our choices are symbolically significant to the forging of our individual identities and communicative of meaning – and that we are not subject to the trends and whims of the fashion industry. Those who produce the things consumers choose might also try, through branding and marketing, to inscribe the products that are being chosen with meaning and indeed may draw from sociological insights into the symbolic nature of consumption and sociological techniques for gathering information about how consumers respond to or interpret these intended meanings. Such **methods**, including the focus group, the qualitative interview and ethnography (Gladwell, 2000), migrate into applied fields to become part of the toolkits of marketing, branding and business as firms seek to understand their consumers better, so as to better inspire and meet their desires. While the tools of social scientific analysis have been incorporated into the practice of these industries, sociology has also subjected these industries to critical analysis in generating explanations about their significance for contemporary life. The sociology of branding (Arvidsson, 2005; Moor, 2007) reveals the centrality of meaning-making to contemporary economies – in which, for example, the *brand*-value of global firms such as Apple exceeds the value of its plants and machinery. This influence extends to the transformation of even the most mundane and everyday goods, required for the re-production of day-to-day life in contemporary societies: food, washing powder or detergents, even water (Wilk, 2006), through the techniques and **technologies** of branding and advertising, into repositories of meaning which can be co-opted by consumers in the satisfaction of their own desires.

This more empowered and reflective version of the consumer, implicated in the collaborative making of meaning rather than the passive experience of consumption, sets the scene for the emergence of what has been termed **the prosumer** (Ritzer and Jurgenson, 2010), a late 20th/early 21st century figure whose practices collapse distinctions between production and consumption. This figure builds on the earlier insights from George Ritzer in his book *The McDonaldization of Society* (2008). This work reflects on the relations between the **rational**, calculative, efficient organization of the fast-food restaurant and the general ordering of social life, principally in the US and Global North but with an increasing presence elsewhere. The production and consumption of food in this context is tightly ordered, but the consumer is an essential part of how the system operates efficiently. The consumer is effectively put to work, learning the permitted combinations of products within menus, carrying their tray and clearing away when they are done. In the business models of fast-food restaurants – and also supermarkets and airlines where self-service counters replace till or check-in counter operators – such innovations allow producers to extract more surplus value through savings on wages for workers while rhetorically focusing on convenience and efficiency for consumers.

Hear from the Expert

George Ritzer

George Ritzer, Professor of Sociology at the University of Maryland, has done much to establish the terms of the sociological study of consumption. His classic work *The McDonaldization of Society* relates the organizational techniques of the 20th-century fast-food outlet back to Max Weber's 'iron cage of rationality'. His more recent work on the 'prosumer' places more emphasis on the complexities and contradictions of a technologically enabled blurring of distinctions between production and consumption.

George Ritzer has a blog which curates his published writing and includes reflective pieces on current debates in the sociology of consumption (https://georgeritzer.wordpress.com). You can hear him discussing the importance of the study of consumption to contemporary sociology here (https://sk.sagepub.com/video/george-ritzer-discusses-consumption).

Distinctions between production and consumption become more blurred with the development of new technologies. Within these, typified by the interactive 'Web 2.0' digital technologies of the noughties, Ritzer and Jurgenson argued that there is the possibility of less obviously exploitative, more apparently collaborative relations between producers and consumers. On social media or video-sharing sites, for example, producers provide the platform, while consumers themselves provide the content and other consumers can access this, even without directly exchanging money for the service. Further, the ubiquity of requests for rating and reviewing within online retail allows consumers to display expertise and connoisseurship in sharing information about their choices with producers and one another. For Ritzer and Jurgenson, such developments trouble assumptions that consumers are simply exploited. Such a notion 'is contradicted, by among other things, the fact that prosumers seem to enjoy, even love, what they are doing and are willing to devote long hours to it for no pay' (Ritzer and Jurgenson, 2010: 22). This enjoyment means the prosumer can be imagined as a harbinger of a new mode of capitalism itself.

Expand Your Knowledge

- To learn more about how digital data-collecting technologies have re-shaped advertising and marketing, read: Ruckenstein, M. and Granroth, J. (2020) Algorithms, advertising and the intimacy of surveillance. *Journal of Cultural Economy* 13(1): 12–24.
- To consider how emerging forms of music distribution might revise and recreate social patterns of consumption, read: Webster, J. (2019) Music on-demand: A commentary on the changing relationship between music taste, consumption, and class in the streaming age. *Big Data & Society* 6(2): 1–5.

The establishment of business models in which tech giants profit from the collection of vast and more complex modes of data through highly centralized platforms (Van Dijck et al., 2018) and in which knowledge of the ever more intimate and intricate behaviours of the consumer of apparently free services becomes the product sold on to advertisers and other producers (Zuboff, 2019), suggests that the early optimism associated with the prosumer may be dissipating. Or it suggests that this is the latest manifestation of the ongoing dance between the two stories of consumption as a trap or symbolic resource. Sociologists are, then, implicated in making and critiquing both these stories about consumer culture and in the construction of the consumer as a category of person, be it one who is a passive dupe, subject to the whims of capital, or a creative agent forging their identity despite them.

Taste: Back to the Personal and the Social

To end our discussion of the significance of the sociological approach to consumption, we'll turn to the question of taste because it is a useful concept through which to reveal and explore key sociological paradoxes. The first of these concerns is its relation to the body – the container of the individual. As one of the five primary senses, taste is understood as one of the ways in which the body interacts with and perceives the world, and there are dedicated organs – the tongue, the taste buds – which do this work. Individual human bodies *taste* things and respond to them in various ways, including pleasure or revulsion, making taste a *biological* concept as well as a sociological one. As with other senses, though, this biological meaning of taste has been overlaid through the operation of human culture (Wright, 2015). Taste may be a reaction of cells to stimuli, but it is experienced and understood by and through social mechanisms. One way to illustrate this is through reflection on our own changing experiences of tasting. As a child I well recall, for example, being repulsed by the bitterness of the taste of an offered sip of my grandfather's Boxing Day afternoon beer. By the time I was 18, though, the taste of beer had become a more pleasurable and sought-after experience, indicating membership of a largely masculine pub drinking culture. No doubt my own tastebuds had changed or developed over time, and the techniques of brewing may have changed too – but this changing experience of the taste of beer cannot be accounted for solely through these considerations. Taste here becomes more than a sensory biological response to a stimulus and a social process central, in this case, to the shift from an infant to an adult social world.

Expand Your Knowledge

- To think about the shifting social meanings of beer in contemporary consumer culture, read: Wallace, A. (2019) 'Brewing the truth': Craft beer, class and place in contemporary London. *Sociology* 53(5): 951–66.
- To learn more about how taste is related to regimes of expertise, read: Maguire, J.S. (2018) The taste for the particular: A logic of discernment in an age of omnivorousness. *Journal of Consumer Culture* 18(1): 3–20.

Like other sensory experiences, taste has become a rich source of metaphorical language. It is also a thing which people *do* and a quality which people possess (as in, 'she is a woman of refined tastes'). It is these elements of the concept of taste that allow us to move further away from the question of individual bodies and their responses to stimuli and towards the kinds of concerns that sociologists have about the relationship between taste and the kinds of wants, desires and preferences which have been the primary concern of the sociology of consumption. Just as the experience of taste can be understood in light of the social context of the taster, the meanings of tastes are inscribed with the influence of the social. In my beer example, whilst bitterness was initially what repelled my younger palate, for my older self the bitterness was an important element of the experience of beer, signifying an association with *northernness*. Warmer, flatter, browner beers were preferable in the attempt to cement these associations than the colder, fizzier, paler lager beers that, we thought, other kinds of people, from other places, drank. Taste here becomes part of a **mechanism** for placing things and people in their place in the structure of the social world – it evokes a whole range of meanings about the kind of person I was – or at least the kind of person I saw myself as or aspired to be – and the kind of person I was not.

Categories of taste have social meanings too, then, and these are shaped through social processes. Sidney Mintz's (1986) study of the social history of sugar, for example, reveals that, when sugar was scarce in pre-colonial Europe, 'sweetness' was a taste more readily associated with the higher echelons of society in a manner that reflected its rare, luxury status. The increased presence of sugar as an exotic commodity brought back to European markets from colonial outposts, through the exploitation of slave labour, cements this position – but the increased volume of production and circulation meant sugar also became more accessible to broader echelons of imperial society. Eventually, the abundant circulation of sugar meant that sweetness no longer had its distinguishing potential as a marker of status, becoming instead a taste associated with less refined palates.

Taste might occur as a sensation on the tongue here, but it also has a geography and a history and the choices, preferences and experiences of individuals caught up in this geography and history become inflected with complex power structures beyond our individual mouths and nervous systems.

Most prominent in bringing questions of taste under the modern sociological lens was the French sociologist Pierre Bourdieu. His work *Distinction* (1984) is an **empirical** and theoretical exploration of the ways in which taste was socially patterned in France in the 1960s and 1970s, and an explicit attempt to reveal that judgements of taste were not merely neutral or benign expressions of personal preference but the culmination of a complex range of experiences, including those of family and the education system. Our preferences are shaped by these experiences, making expressions of taste – whether it is what we consider pleasing, pleasurable or beautiful, on the one hand, or disgusting, repellent, or repulsive, on the other – into sensory manifestations of the social structures of which we are a part.

Bourdieu discovered this through deployment of some established, exemplary sociological methods. He used survey analysis to gather demographic data about **age**, gender, occupation, and educational experiences. These were combined with questions about how people decorated their homes, their preferred styles of clothing, their preferences in preparing food for guests and questions about their general leisure activities, reading, listening and viewing habits and preferences for art and music. The survey was complemented by interviews conducted with Parisians about similar topics, and the analysis is based upon both the statistical patterns and the narratives which emerge from the answers from both strands of the empirical work, attempting to capture both objective relationships between categories of people and things as well as their lived experiences.

From this evidence, Bourdieu was able to identify relationships between the preferences of people for items in cultural hierarchies and their position in social or class hierarchies. Central to this analysis was the concept of **cultural capital**, which served as a metaphor for understanding how certain types of experience (of family or education), certain types of behaviour (how one speaks, dresses or manages one's body) and certain types of choice (of objects to own and display) crystallize as resources which, like economic capital, can be accumulated, used to the owner's advantage, traded and passed on to future generations. Having the right tastes, then, is more than a matter of personal preference – it is an expression of one's inherited and accumulated cultural capital and a resource to draw on in distinguishing oneself from others. For Bourdieu, art and culture are especially significant to this process, with tastes for legitimated or consecrated forms of art and access to the codes through which art is understood and discussed, being powerful indicators of cultural capital. This is an especially interesting and provocative insight precisely because the appreciation of such things is often imagined as something of a refuge from or antidote to consumer society. For Bourdieu, possession of different volumes of cultural capital gives the owner different access to what constitutes the 'right' kinds of taste and provides them with access to the tacit rules of the game for what is the appropriate kind of behaviour for the social context in which they find themselves. At the level of society, these forms of knowledge and their operation help to explain the different practices and lifestyles of different social classes. Here, the things we like and choose are strongly influenced by a range of social experiences, including our class position, and help to place us in social space.

The focus on taste indicates how, even at the level of sensory experience of the world, the social is always present and how the questions of personal preference which underpin the study become implicated in social organization. *Distinction* continues to be a significant benchmark for the empirical study of taste, with subsequent studies (e.g. Bennett et al., 2009) including **ethnicity** (which French regulations prohibited Bourdieu asking questions about) as an additional variant in understanding how tastes are socially patterned.

CULTURES AND CONSUMPTION

It has been especially influential in the study of class, with contemporary sociological understanding of that concept (notably *The Great British Class Survey* of 2011) giving prominence to leisure and consumption choices, alongside position in the hierarchies of production, in revealing how contemporary class structures are experienced (see Savage et al., 2015). The example of Bourdieu's work further reveals how taste is significantly loaded, sociologically, and how consumer choices and preferences shape social division. Importantly, it also demonstrates how the tools and methods of the sociologist – the empirical study of people's lives, choices, and activities – help in challenging assumptions that tastes are simply a matter of personal preference.

CHAPTER SUMMARY

- Consumption is a key concept in the aim of sociology to explain and understand the contemporary world.
- Sociological approaches to consumption complicate and contextualize the market exchange of money for goods and services and claims for the rational consumer.
- Sociologists have revealed the histories and power relations that underpin the emergence of the 'consumer society'.
- The approaches and techniques of sociological research have been important in understanding the relations between consumer goods and identity.
- Individual tastes and preferences are shaped by social forces.

REVIEW QUESTIONS

1. How might a sociologist's approach to consumption be different from an economist's?

In approaching this question, it would be useful to review and reflect on the different concepts that these social sciences work with and their different objects of analysis. It might also be worthwhile considering their origins and the kinds of problems early thinkers were trying to resolve.

2. Is consumer society a trap or liberation?

The chapter has outlined these two aspects to the story of the development of the consumer society. In thinking about this question, which of these stories are you more persuaded by? Which is more useful for explaining the contemporary experience of consumption?

3. What methods might a sociologist use to understand consumer behaviours?

This question invites you to reflect on the basis of the claims for knowledge that sociologists make. What kinds of evidence, gathered through what kinds of techniques, would you need to get to know 'the consumer'?

4. To what extent might tastes and preferences be shaped by gender, ethnicity, or class?

An answer to this question would include reflection on the paradox outlined towards the end of the chapter – that taste is both felt and experienced personally/individually but socially patterned. How might different facets of our identities shape the things we like or dislike?

> ## Go Further
>
> ### Books
>
> - Lury, C. (2011) *Consumer Culture*. Cambridge: Polity Press.
>
> An accessible but authoritative theoretical contribution to the breadth and complexities of consumer culture, especially strong on the relations between identities and a symbolic material cultural economy.
>
> - Sassatelli, R. (2007) *Consumer Culture: History, Theory, Politics*. London: Sage.
>
> A comprehensive and wide-ranging introduction to the field which places both consumer culture and the sociological study of it in their historical contexts.
>
> - Warde, A. (2017) *Consumption: A Sociological Analysis*. London: Palgrave.
>
> A leading British scholar in the field reviews and re-appraises the debates and theories which have shaped it, with an eye on contemporary and future challenges.
>
> ### Journal Articles
>
> - Karademir-Hazir, I. (2014) How bodies are classed: An analysis of clothing and bodily tastes in Turkey. *Poetics* 44: 1–21.
>
> A study of the social meanings of clothing in Turkey that draws off and develops insight and methods from Bourdieu about cultural capital, embodiment, and social patterns.
>
> - Pettinger, L. (2010) Brand culture and branded workers: Service work and aesthetic labour in fashion retail. *Consumption, Markets and Culture* 7(2): 165–74.
>
> An empirical study of how shops and their workers help to create meaning in consumer societies.
>
> - Ritzer, G. and Miles, S. (2018) The changing nature of consumption and the intensification of McDonaldization in the digital age. *Journal of Consumer Culture* 19(1): 3–20.
>
> Two significant scholars in the field reflect on how a key concept might be re-imagined and applied in explaining the apparent liberations of digital forms of consumerism.

REFERENCES

Arvidsson, A. (2005) Brands: A critical perspective. *Journal of Consumer Culture* 5(2): 235–58.
Augé, M. (1995) *Non-places: An Introduction to the Anthropology of Super-modernity*. London: Verso.
Baudrillard, J. (1998 [1970]) *The Consumer Society: Myths and Structures*. London: Sage.
Bauman, Z. (2004) *Work, Consumerism and the New Poor*. Maidenhead: Open University Press.
Bennett, T., Savage, M., Silva, E., Warde, A., Gayo, M. and Wright, D. (2009) *Culture, Class, Distinction*. London: Routledge.
Bordo, S. (2000) Hunger as ideology. In J.B. Schor and D.B. Holt (eds) *The Consumer Society Reader*. New York: The New Press.
Bourdieu, P. (1984) *Distinction: A Social Critique of the Judgement of Taste*. London: Routledge.

Clarke, J., Newman, J., Smith, N., Vidler, E. and Westmarland, L. (2007) *Creating Citizen-Consumers: Changing Publics and Changing Public Services*. London: Sage.

Dant, T. (2000) Consumption caught in the cash nexus. *Sociology* 34(4): 655–70.

Durkheim, E. (1893) *The Division of Labour in Society*. New York: The Free Press.

Gladwell, M. (2000) The coolhunt. In J.B. Schor and D.B. Holt (eds) *The Consumer Society Reader*. New York: The New Press.

Goldthorpe, J.H., Lockwood, D., Bechhofer, F. and Platt, J. (1968) *The Affluent Worker: Industrial Attitudes and Behaviour*. Cambridge: Cambridge University Press.

Hall, S. and Jefferson, T. (eds) (1975) *Resistance through Rituals: Youth Subcultures in Post-war Britain*. London: Hutchinson.

Hebdige, D. (1998) *Hiding in the Light: On Images and Things*. London: Routledge.

Lasch, C. (1979) *The Culture of Narcissism*. New York: Norton.

Marcuse, H. (1968) *One Dimensional Man*. London: Sphere.

Marx, K. (1990 [1867]) *Capital: A Critique of Political Economy*, Vol. 1. London: Penguin.

McCracken, G. (1988) *Culture and Consumption*. Indianapolis, IN: Indiana University Press.

Mintz, S.W. (1986) *Sweetness and Power: The Place of Sugar in Modern History*. London: Penguin.

Moor, L. (2007) *The Rise of Brands*. New York: Berg.

Packard, V. (1958) *The Hidden Persuaders*. New York: McKay.

Ritzer, G. (2008) *The McDonaldization of Society*, 5th edition. Los Angeles: Pine Forge Press.

Ritzer, G. and Jurgenson, N. (2010) Production, consumption, presumption: The nature of capitalism in the age of the digital 'prosumer'. *Journal of Consumer Culture* 10(1): 13–36.

Sassatelli, R. (2007) *Consumer Culture: History, Theory, Politics*. London: Sage.

Savage, M., Cunningham, N., Devine, F., Friedman, S., Laurison, D., McKenzie, L., Miles, A., Snee, H. and Wakeling, P. (2015) *Social Class in the 21st Century*. London: Penguin.

Simmel, G. (1997) The philosophy of fashion. In D. Frisby and M. Featherstone (eds) *Simmel on Culture*. London: Sage, pp. 187–205.

Tester, K. (ed.) (1994) *The Flâneur*. London: Routledge.

Van Dijck, J., Poell, T. and de Waal, M. (2018) *The Platform Society: Public Values in a Connective World*. Oxford: Oxford University Press.

Veblen, T. (1970 [1899]) *Theory of the Leisure Class: An Economic Study of Institutions*, rev. ed. London: Allen and Unwin.

Warde, A. (1994) Consumption, identity-formation and uncertainty. *Sociology* 28(4): 877–98.

Weber, M. (1980 [1920]) *General Economic History*. New Brunswick, NJ: Transaction Books.

Wilk, R. (2006) Bottled water: The pure commodity in the age of branding. *Journal of Consumer Culture* 6(3): 303–25.

Wright, D. (2015) *Understanding Cultural Taste*. London: Palgrave.

Zuboff, S. (2019) *The Age of Surveillance Capitalism*. London: Profile Books.

WAR AND VIOLENCE
Christian Olsson

LEARNING OBJECTIVES

- To understand what is at stake in the debates about narrow or broad definitions of violence.
- To understand how the social character of humans accounts both for non-violent and violent behaviour, irrespective of their aggressiveness or fear of violence.
- To understand the link between political power and violence.

 Framing Questions

1. What is violence and what are its main forms and manifestations?
2. Why and when do people resort to violence?
3. How has war shaped modernity and its institutions?

Introduction

Forms of violence vary greatly depending on level and scale considered: interpersonal, collective, intergroup, inter-state. Their level of intensity, organization and institutionalization varies to such an extent that it might sometimes be difficult to see any commonality. What has domestic violence in common with war or genocide? To this heterogeneity

WAR AND VIOLENCE

of the object 'violence', one has to add the contested nature of the concept 'violence': widely divergent definitions of 'violence' inform academic debates on violent crime, domestic violence or political violence.

Given this diversity of the objects and concepts of violence, it would be relatively vain to search for a general theory of violence in sociology. Just think of aggressivity (as a human faculty or individual tendency). You will surely recognize that it might play a part in some violent crimes and might even shed light on the comparatively higher propensity for violence of young males in comparison to young females in most societies. However, it hardly explains why two world wars happened in the first half of the 20th century, and none in the second half.

Accordingly, most sociological studies try to account for diversity, singularity and heterogeneity rather than aiming for overarching explanations. This may be one of the hallmarks of sociological approaches to violence (Walby, 2013): they generally focus on one type of violent behaviour or consider multiple forms of violence in order to highlight specificities and differences. However, even so, authors and books focusing on forms of violence are rare in sociology. Reflections on violence and war tend to be dispersed throughout the literature, with few authors connecting the different threads (Joas and Knöbl, 2012; Malešević, 2010). It is worth noticing that, traditionally, sociology has focused on criminal and interpersonal interactions when dealing with violence (Rule, 1989), leaving other types of violence to other disciplines. It is only with the rise of historical sociology in the 1980s, especially in the US, that sociologists have reclaimed war as an object of study rather than leaving it to political scientists as previously often was the case.

Mapping the Terrain

General and Sociological Debates on Violence and War

Substantial sociological debates pertaining to war and violence often oppose different sociological schools of thought. Their underlying questions are, however, often quite common: is violent behaviour learnt or does it come naturally to people who have not been taught to behave non-violently? Is violence a primitive phenomenon that was pervasive during the 'dark ages' of humanity or is it compatible with, or even emblematic of, civilization and modernity? Is violence a purely destructive force or can it sometimes be seen as a necessary evil in the defence of fundamental values, of law and order? Do you always recognize violence when you see it or is it sometimes a matter of perception and of personal sensitivities?

Nature or Nurture?

A question that preoccupies philosophers and social scientists is whether the propensity to use violence comes 'naturally' to humans when they are not prevented from doing so by social institutions (Hobbes, 2002 [1657]), or if 'naturally' non-violent humans are turned into potential killers under the effect of social institutions and constraints (Rousseau, 1761). In sociology, Norbert Elias leans towards the first point of view and argues that the level of interpersonal violence decreases with the development of social interdependencies and the individual self-control that comes with the advent of the modern state (Elias, 1994 [1938]). Other sociologists, however, lean towards the second stance. For Randall Collins, for instance, humans are neither very competent at nor very easily drawn towards violent behaviour. It is only in the context of specific 'social interaction rituals' and emotional group dynamics that collective violence is likely to appear (Collins, 2009; Tilly, 2003).

(Continued)

Modern or Primitive?

Another debate concerns the relation between violence and modernity. According to some, history is a long process of decline of violence, humanity's 'dark ages' being long past (Mueller, 2004). For others, on the contrary, the lethality of organized violence culminates with the 20th century (Bauman, 1989; Malešević, 2010). Just think of the Holocaust during the Second World War. In fact, everything depends on the timescale as well as on the type of violence one considers. In the long run, the advent of the modern state and urbanization has led to a decline of interpersonal violence in most Western states since the 13th century (Muchembled, 2012). At the same time, interstate wars, state-organized massacres and mass repression have increased over the same period, culminating in the Second World War (Mann, 2005). One of the questions here is what it is in modernity that has pushed organized violence towards its extremes. Most sociologists agree that the cumulative expansion of the bureaucratic state has played a central role by increasing organizational capacity (Bauman, 1989; Malešević, 2017; Mann, 2005). The question of the decline or increase in violence can also be raised with regard to the advent of spectacular 'terrorist' attacks. Are they the expression of an increasingly violent 'late modernity'? Is it not rather the case that the rarer violence becomes, the more the residual forms of violence become intolerable and thus rewarding for those who seek to instil a climate of fear for political purposes?

Constitution or Destruction of Society?

War and violence have provoked numerous crises, famines and epidemics throughout history. Accordingly, they are analysed by some as a wasteful outcome of societal dysfunctions, as a potentially dehumanizing force threatening society with dissolution (Girard, 2013). Others, on the contrary, highlight that violence and war can be a factor of social development, intercultural exchange, societal dynamism and technological innovation (Barkawi, 2006; Coser, 1957, 1966; Mann, 1986). Cannot our contemporary institutions be said to have been shaped by the history of war and organized violence (Giddens, 1985; Malešević, 2017; Tilly, 1993)? Has war not been an important although contradictory driving force behind our historical heritage, be it through its role in the definition of traditional gender roles as well as in the emancipation of women in the 20th century (Goldstein, 2003; Grayzel and Proctor, 2017), in the emergence of social stratification as well as in the equalization of conditions in modern democratic states (Malešević, 2010)?

Is Violence in the Eye of the Beholder?

Finally, there is a discussion on the role of subjective perceptions of violence in relation to its materiality (Wieviorka, 2009). Would you qualify situations as violent in which violence is subjectively felt, yet unrelated to any use of physical violence, as when a believer feels violated by the claim that 'God does not exist'? Another question is whether violence can be analysed independently of the cultural meanings attached to it as rational choice theoreticians typically do. For example, during 2020, several statues and monuments emblematic of slavery and colonization were attacked, dismounted or destroyed by demonstrators throughout the world. Are these acts of violence? Is it not rather the glorification of a racist past by monuments that is violent? To use violence against a person is to inflict something one would in principle not want to be inflicted upon oneself. In societies governed by law, it is to refuse to the other a right one generally claims for oneself. In this sense, violence is intrinsically linked to questions of personal worth, but also to socially conditioned privilege and status (Malešević, 2013). This explains why violence commonly causes outrage and undermines the self-esteem of victims. This is also why violence is likely to be used by the self-same victims if they find no legal redress or recognition of their plight. Finally, it is the reason for which the use of organized violence against vulnerable groups generally is preceded by narratives depreciating these groups (Malešević, 2010). Ultimately, can the use of violence be analysed independently of the values and meanings attached to it by a variety of audiences?

 ── Pause for Thought ──

- How would you position yourself in the context of these four debates and why?
- What views do you generally hear on the questions raised by these four debates: in the news, in movies, when talking with family and friends?
- What are the specificities of the patterns of violence you observe in the country you live in, or come from, compared to other places?

The Difficulty of Defining Violence: Narrow or Broad Definitions?

Wars, revolutions, genocide and terrorism are some of the phenomena that figure prominently in the study of violence. The range of topics and practices involving violence is, however, much larger: domestic violence, law enforcement, violent crime, child abuse, slavery, **state** repression, and so on. An important question is, accordingly, what qualifies as violence and how much diversity the concept can tolerate without losing its internal coherence.

Violence is a problematic concept in **sociology** for different reasons.

A first problem is that its **empirical** criteria are unclear: is violence necessarily physical, direct and intentional or can it not also be symbolic (that is, non-physical), structural (that is, indirect), non-intentional and hence ultimately insidious? Can the victims consent to the violence without it ceasing to be violence, as in medical surgery? Can violence only be done to humans or also to matter or nature? And what if the effect of an act is physical – for example, temporary incapacitation or immobility – without it intending to cause permanent injuries, as with some 'non-lethal weapons', or even imprisonment? Depending on one's definition of violence, the answer to these questions will vary (Baron et al., 2019).

Among the broad concepts of violence, one finds the notion of 'structural violence'. The idea is that violence can be built into, and hence exerted by, structures of inequality and oppression (Galtung, 1971). It is both a powerful and a problematic concept. On the one hand, it correctly identifies that the probability of falling prey to mass shooting, labour-related deaths or injuries, domestic violence or even the risk of being killed at times of war is not randomly distributed through a **population**, irrespective of 'race', class or gender (Nussbaum, 2005; Walby, 2013). On the other hand, it is confusing since it often goes so far as to imply that 'violence is present when human beings are being influenced so that their actual somatic and mental realizations are below their potential realizations' (Galtung, 1969: 168). Any constraint can accordingly be portrayed as violence. Such a definition makes it very difficult to imagine a situation in which violence would not be present in some form: are not our realizations always below what they could have been in an ideal situation? Moreover, it implies that many forms of violence are consented to by their 'willing victims'. If a student in medicine decides to become a nurse rather than a doctor in order to be able to start earning money sooner, does this necessarily mean this student is subjected to (economic) violence?

A second reason for which the concept of violence is problematic is that violence increasingly is so morally reviled that it often becomes a synonym of everything that is unrighteous, unfair or alienating in the world. Accordingly, depersonalizing bureaucratic processes or cultural beliefs justifying seemingly arbitrary hierarchies are often described as violent/violence (Galtung, 1969). Conversely, the violence that is deemed justified or legitimate is often described euphemistically as not being violence at all: the legal violence used by the police is generally called 'law enforcement' and the expression 'police violence' is in principle reserved for the illegal and excessive 'use of **force**' on the part of law-enforcement agents. Reversely, Wacquant highlights how media narratives on 'urban violence' might lead to the criminalization of whole populations, rather than incriminating the neoliberal policies at the source of 'urban delinquency' (Wacquant, 2009).

As a dominant belief, the quasi-universal condemnation of violence is, however, quite recent (Joas and Knöbl, 2012). Until the beginning of the 1970s, especially on the far left, the point of view that violence can be emancipatory was well represented in academia. Following this Marxist or radical line of reasoning, violence is the 'midwife of every old society pregnant with a new one' (Marx, 2018 [1867]), the only means for politically and culturally dominated groups to overturn their domination (Fanon, 2007 [1961]; Sorel, 1999 [1908]). The contemporary conflation of violence with what is morally reprehensible is problematic because it implies that the claim, for example, that 'economic exploitation' or 'extreme ideologies' are 'not violence per se' (although they might be conducive to violence), could be interpreted as an attempt to justify them. This, however, by no means needs to be the case.

Violence will here refer both to acts pursuing the physical destruction of bodies and matter – provided this destruction is unwanted by those that are thus 'targeted' – or to acts seeking to inflict physical or psychological suffering on humans. Our definition of violence is purposely quite narrow, focusing on direct violence. Our view is indeed that the broader the definition, the less useful it might be in the precise analysis of social phenomena.

Key Question: Narrow or Broad Definitions of Violence? The Example of Gender-Based Violence

According to a broad definition of gender-based violence, it is:

the denial of the needs or capacity to achieve one's potential […]. Hence, if a woman is restricted in her movements by her husband, the restriction in itself is a form of violence, and it denies her capacity to form affiliations […] – thus resulting in further violence. (Scriver et al., 2015)

This definition sees denials of a woman's needs and full potential as violence along with wife battering, male-on-female rape and other forms of physical violence (Merry, 2009). When asked why restrictions on movement and self-realization constitute violence, obvious answers would be: because they create a climate that furthers domestic violence, because they 'weaponize masculinity' by assigning to men the role of 'protector' of women, or because they might serve to justify sexual assault in the case of a woman not respecting these restrictions.

Such answers highlight that physical violence very often remains the implicit benchmark by which structural factors – such as unequal constraints – are deemed violent. They indirectly endorse a restrictive definition of violence but at the same time attribute to causes the characteristics of their effects: that which might favour (or threaten) violence is seen as violence itself. This is precisely the kind of confusion we want to avoid. It leads to a potentially endless extension of the concept of violence. While there is a rationale in saying that what favours (or threatens) violence is violence itself, it at the same time invalidates the notion of threatening someone with violence (since the threat then is violence and not a threat of it). (This topic is also dealt with in Chapter 12.)

 **Pause for Thought**

- Can you give two reasons to prefer broad definitions of violence over narrow ones, two that might lead one to opt for narrow definitions?
- Can words or symbols be violent (please give examples)?
- What do you think of the claim that 'words can kill'? Can you give examples of non-physical direct violence, physical indirect violence, non-physical indirect violence, and physical direct violence?
- What exactly is meant by 'systemic violence' as used in the context of the Black Lives Matter movement? How does it relate to seemingly similar concepts such as 'structural violence' or 'cultural violence'?

Violence and Political Order: An Ambiguous Relation

While violence is generally seen to wreak havoc, there is the diffuse sense that in the last resort it also upholds political societies, or even allows them to improve. **Functionalist** accounts of violence are illustrative in this regard. Violent crime, revolts or riots are, on the one hand, seen as the consequence of societal dysfunction and/or pathologies: Durkheimian **anomie**, social exclusion (Coser, 1966), or contradictory injunctions (Merton, 1938) lead people to use violence to contest a society that does not recognize them and/or to take forcefully what is denied to them. On the other hand, as a material manifestation of societal crises, violence forces **social structure**s to adapt and become more responsive to social demands (Coser, 1966). Violence thus both reveals the existence of societal problems and pressures authorities into addressing the underlying issues. Just as an inflammatory reaction may reveal the presence of an infectious agent inside a body, the irruption of violence might highlight the existence of deep-seated dysfunctions in a society. Just as an inflammatory reaction leads the body's wider immune system to fight back, violence may bring society to address the causes of its internal tensions.

22.1 Key Case

The 'Black Lives Matter' Movement

Recent examples of police brutality against black people in the US, epitomized in the second half of 2020 by the killing of George Floyd, reinvigorated the previously created Black Lives Matter movement. The latter denounces racist violence on the part of the police, calls upon authorities to take systemic racism seriously, and highlights continuities between slavery and the violence of contemporary race relations in the US. Non-violent resistance and peaceful demonstrations lie at the heart of the movement, but there is no denying that anti-police violence, robberies and riots have accompanied its demonstrations. While some defenders of Black Lives Matter claim these acts to be committed by infiltrated 'extremists' (from the extreme left or extreme right), the staunchest opponents of the movement denounce this violence as proof that the movement is out to undermine law and order. A functionalist would, however, typically highlight that this violence is the direct consequence of the very inequalities, injustice and anti-black violence denounced by the Black Lives Matter movement. By resorting to violence, the rioters affirm themselves in a society that denies and excludes them. By looting, a small minority among them highlight (be it intentionally or unintentionally) the contradictions of a society that values material wealth yet excludes large sectors of the population from it. Perhaps even more importantly, a functionalist would argue that, were it not for the societal disruption caused by this violence, it is unlikely the authorities and the wider public would have taken the movement seriously. In this sense, the violence accompanying the demonstrations highlights the importance of the political system to address the issues raised by Black Lives Matter rather than considering the latter movement as the problem.

Functionalism is, however, not alone in highlighting the ambivalence of violence with regard to society. Many authors, including outside of sociology, have highlighted that violence symbolizes both the foundation of political orders and the transgression of their rules (Benjamin, 2009). The Weberian **tradition** in sociology seems to confirm this ambivalence: while social violence might undermine the ordering principles of a given society, political authorities in the last resort uphold these selfsame principles through violence (Mann, 1984).

For Weber, physical violence provides a form of power that, contrary to wealth or legitimacy, is not dependent on consent, cognition or recognition to be effective. It is therefore the means of last resort through which political decisions can be enforced by the powers that be, if necessary, against the will of wielders of other forms of power (economic, social, cultural…). In this sense, the capacity to use armed force is the most basic way of making a 'sovereign' claim, provided this capacity is exclusive to the 'sovereign'.

The modern state, as famously argued by Weber in *Politics as Vocation*, is a 'compulsory association which organizes domination. It has been successful in seeking to monopolize the legitimate use of physical force as a means of domination within a territory' (Weber, 1965 [1919]). The state is ultimately created and maintained through the monopolistic use of legitimate violence on a given territory. By so doing, it also establishes the political sphere as being partially autonomous from the social sphere.

For Weberian historical sociologists, the monopolization of the 'legitimate use of physical force' by the state creates relatively pacified societies. Indeed, if state agents are the only ones to be effectively able to use violence and the other social actors have been deprived of this capacity, this most likely leads to a decline in violence amongst these actors. Empirical studies partially confirm this stance: historian Robert Muchembled notes that the advent of the modern state has played an important **role** in stemming interpersonal killings since the Middle Ages until today in most Western societies (Muchembled, 2012). At the same time, political authorities continue to use violence both to forcefully 'maintain law and order' and to wage war externally (Elias, 1994 [1938]; Giddens, 1985; Tilly, 1993; Weber, 1978 [1921]). While outlawing interpersonal violence (except for strictly defined conditions), the state does not fully exorcise violence from society: it turns societal violence between persons into war between rival states (Aron, 2003 [1962]). Violent **conflict** between political communities does not contradict 'social pacification' domestically. On the contrary, international armed conflict might strengthen intra-national ties (Simmel, 2010 [1922]).

Yet, Weber did not see state power to be necessarily dependent on the routine use of violence (Weber, 1965 [1919]). Indeed, once force is monopolized by the state, the violent manifestations of the latter become partially redundant: if the state is virtually uncontested, it does not need to use violence to enforce its order. State violence becomes a last resort. Monopolization, at least in theory, hence transforms 'pure' violence into force and **coercion**. For example, penal systems have become relatively less violent since the end of the Middle Ages in most democratic societies (Foucault, 2012 [1975]). To put it in stark terms, one could say that the ideal-typical 'legitimate violence' of Weber is not actualized violence at all, or rather the more it is, the less it is legitimate (Olsson, 2013). It is in this respect that force and coercion make state power effective, not the actual use of physical violence (except as a last resort) that instead signals its weakening and might even spur violent resistance (Goodwin, 2001; della Porta, 2013 [2001]).

In this sense, the fact that many governments use incredible levels of violence against their own and other populations (Mann, 1995; Rummel, 2011) must be considered as a sign of the unachieved character of their state monopoly (Cohen et al., 1981). At the same time, it is often the ideal of the state, as monopoly, that fuels extreme violence by inducing struggles between would-be monopolists, possibly accompanied by

WAR AND VIOLENCE

genocidal attempts to homogenize populations (Bauman, 1989; Mann, 1995). It is therefore not astonishing that societies in which monopolization is possible, yet unachieved, tend to be the ones in which levels of violence are the highest.

Anthropologist Michael Taussig has highlighted the fundamentally ambiguous relation between the state and violence when highlighting how the Colombian state's incapacity to deal with violent crime in the 1990s led its agents to adopt the same **methods** as those of the 'gangs' they are meant to police, the distinction between law enforcement and the extrajudicial killing of suspected criminals becoming increasingly blurred (Taussig, 2003).

> ### Hear from the Expert
>
> From murder to traffic accidents, kidnapping or being mugged for your tennis shoes, the state is powerless whether you are rich or poor [...]. But that is only the beginning of the betrayal. Much worse is to come, for the very authority you might want to turn to for protection is likely to make things worse [...]. And this corruption is what both the guerrilla and then the paramilitaries largely grew out of, in my opinion. In a sense, people have only themselves to blame, because they actually welcome the police acting unlawfully when they secretly or semi-secretly kill petty criminals. Glancing at my previous diaries I see that all through the 1990s I am being told about this; as when in October 1998, an all-knowing friend tells me the not-so-hidden reason the previous mayor was dismissed was because he was adamantly against a *limpieza* [an extrajudicial killing of presumed petty criminals by para-military death squads]. [...] Even more surprising for me was the way she talked about this, as if instead of being a putrid criminal activity, the *limpieza* is a legal, even natural, state of affairs; a matter, if you like, of routine local government policy, much the same as waste disposal, street cleaning or education. (Taussig, 2003: 30–1)

 —— Pause for Thought ——

- Does Weber's definition of the state necessarily entail that states are violent?
- If violence is a last resort against violence, is it possible to conceive of a society in which there would be absolutely no place for violence?
- Why would a government based on popular consent still need to be able to use violence to enforce its decisions? Is violence anti-democratic?

'Symbolic Violence': Muddling or Clarifying the Concept?

Bourdieu defines symbolic violence as: 'the violence which is exercised upon a social agent with his or her complicity' (Bourdieu and Wacquant, 1992: 167). Symbolic violence, according to Bourdieu, is that which pushes a social agent to do willingly what one would have expected him to do only under the threat of violence, unwillingly. It is the power to create an incorporated sense of obligation that leads social agents to obey willingly against their best interests. What Bourdieu has in mind is, for example, the former slave's consent to the political domination of his former master, the colonized subject's consent to the cultural domination of the colonizer, a woman's acceptance of co-responsibility for the sexual harassment she has been victim of on the part of a male co-worker, and so on. We are here dealing with a very broad definition of violence in which it is tightly linked, just as with Galtung's above-mentioned 'structural violence', to structural inequalities.

According to Bourdieu, symbolic violence appears when physical violence or coercion on the part of the dominant is sufficiently internalized as an impending possibility by the dominated for its effect to continue even when violence or coercion is not (or cannot be) resorted to. While the use of physical violence might erode the legitimacy of its user by highlighting the arbitrariness of his power, this is not the case for symbolic violence (Bourdieu, 2000) since it is 'misrecognized as arbitrary' (Bourdieu, 1991: 170) by those upon whom it is exercised. The dominant party might not even be conscious that they are exerting symbolic violence.

Let us try to explain this through an example. Walter Benjamin has noted that peace ceremonies transform military territorial conquests into 'new law', by dissimulating their foundation on pure violence (Benjamin, 2009). Bourdieu claims that it is a similar process that leads military parades during national holidays to produce power. These solemn parades convey the same message of might as the Roman victory marches through conquered 'enemy land' during classical antiquity, the idea being to 'show force in order not to have to use it'. The power produced by contemporary ceremonial parades during national holidays is, however, more efficient than 'victory marches' as it is misrecognized as coercive by most of those who attend. Nobody imagines that the military could use these weapons against the members of the public, mostly fellow countrymen, that attend these parades (Bourdieu, 2000: 196). The potentiality of violence is hence totally transmuted into a symbolic rather than coercive form. Symbolic violence is hence not simply potential violence, as is coercion. It has undergone a trans-substantiation.

Many sociologists of violence are critical of the concept of symbolic violence (Collins, 2009; Malešević, 2017), seen as too broad. While potentially misleading, the concept has essentially two merits. First, it highlights that the mere possession of material means of coercion (weapons, armies, military hardware, money, etc.) produces power even when (and especially when) those upon whom this power is exercised do not realize that their domination is indirectly rooted in these means. Their domination on the part of the dominant is incorporated into the bodily dispositions of the dominated. As such, the resulting behaviour on the part of the under-dogs might remain even when the resources of violence of the dominant decline. The concept of symbolic violence highlights that the resources of violence participate in the maintenance of a given social order by operating at different levels of realization: that of the actual (violence), the potential (coercion) and the virtual (symbolic violence).

Second, physical and symbolic violence often work hand in hand. Bourdieu notes that 'domination, even when based on naked force, that of arms or money, always has a symbolical dimension' (Bourdieu, 2000: 172). What he means is that the use of physical violence might, under certain conditions, command respect and seemingly voluntary obedience. Many kings or dictators have sought to portray themselves as ruthless, arguably not only to deter opponents, but also to highlight their unwavering resolve, strength of will and ultimately arouse an admiration, or even veneration, based on a cult of force. The ambiguity of the term 'respect' as used in the 'street code' of urban gangs, combining fear and admiration, bears testimony to this potential effect of violence: it might lead some to cower in fear and others to hold those who wield this violence in high esteem.

WAR AND VIOLENCE

From Social to Violent Conflict: Between Instrumental and Expressive Violence

Violence and conflict are often analysed in tandem. Conflicts can be violent, and violence can be both a source and expression of a conflict. There are, however, good reasons to consider them separately. Conflicts are pervasive and many are non-violent: labour conflicts, **family** conflicts, conflicts between neighbours... Moreover, violence might occur independently of any initial conflict, as in random drive-by shootings. In fact, somewhat paradoxically, the recognition and institutionalization of (non-violent) conflicts may contribute to the prevention of violence (Coser, 1957; Oberschall, 1973).

For example, pluralist democracies are based on the institutionalization of political conflicts through multi-party systems, rather than on their violent repression (that in itself might foster anti-government violence) as in many authoritarian regimes. In the same way, the institutionalization of the relations between trade unions and employers' unions in many countries has contributed to the limitation of social violence. Inversely, while violent riots have taken place in the impoverished areas of major cities over the last few decades (Los Angeles in 1992, Paris in 2005, London in 2011), this must be analysed against the backdrop of the absence of organizations capable of channelling the underlying economic, social and political demands into the political system. These forms of violence are generally expressive: they both express emotions (frustration, hate, despair) and provide immediate 'consummatory rewards' (Rule, 1989) to those who experience these emotions. Charles Tilly and Doug McAdam, however, have shown that this type of violence might also be instrumentally and purposefully used by organized social movements (provided they exist) to impose themselves as legitimate contenders in struggles over the definition of governmental policies (McAdam, 2010; Tilly, 1989).

How can violence be instrumental in the context of social conflicts? In spite of its many drawbacks, violence has one important advantage: among the many ways in which scarce resources (material or symbolic) can be allocated, violence is the only means that does not require a minimum of trust and a minimal agreement on the rules of the game between the parties involved. Rolling a dice, having a third person settling the conflict, playing Russian roulette, bilateral negotiations ... all suppose a minimum of cooperation between the parties to the conflict. They suppose the latter to stick to their commitments, to abide by the rules and to trust that the adversary also will do so. Violence or coercion, on the contrary, allows allocating these resources through imposition or violent extortion (Vasquez, 2009). If there is a lack of trust between the parties, or the institutional context is not conducive to firm commitments, violence can still be a way to adjudicate the conflict. As a physiological sensation, pain, and the fear of pain, injury and death, are unanimously considered as negative experiences. Violence can hence be used, as **rational** choice theorists typically would insist upon, as a bargaining chip in the context of a conflict strategy over the allocation of resources (Schelling, 1980). In this sense, violence can sometimes be considered as a way of solving a conflict when all forms of cooperation have broken down. As such, one can see it as a particularly destructive mode of conflict resolution. The problem is, however, that a deal imposed through violence is likely to depend on the continuous use of coercion, and the maintenance of asymmetric power relations, in order to remain in place.

Moreover, if lethal violence is resorted to by a party to a conflict, the other parties are likely to respond in kind. At this point, the nature of the conflict is likely to change: from a conflict over scarce resources, it becomes a struggle for survival. Although violence might be used to signal determination and resolve in the context of a non-armed conflict, these signalling strategies often entail significant risks of violent escalation spiralling out of control. Violence then becomes entrenched in the conflict relation. Indeed, violence furthers hostility and escalates the stakes of the conflict. Many sociologists accordingly have highlighted the propensity of violence to beget violence, although the precise causal mechanisms involved might vary: state repression might further clandestine political violence (della Porta, 2013 [2001]) or outright revolution (Goodwin, 2001), blood crimes generate cycles of vengeance (Girard, 2013), previous (civil or interstate) war increase the risk of war recurrence (Vasquez, 2009), and so on.

The shift from the limited use of violence to the entrenchment of violence in the conflict relation implies that the causal pathways towards violent conflict and the factors that maintain and prolong violent conflicts are often distinct. More broadly, violent conflicts create a context in which violence not directly related to the conflict might unfold. If civil war causes civil authority to crumble, people locked in family feuds, economic disputes or other interpersonal conflicts might seize the opportunity to 'settle scores' that could not have been settled previously, if not for any other reason than to prevent their adversaries from doing the same.

 Pause for Thought

- Do you think that strategies of non-violent resistance can be efficient in the conflict between violence-prone governments and a democratic oppositional movement?
- Why is it so tempting to fight violence with violence rather than to employ non-violent means?
- Fear is often seen as a central driver of violence. Why is this the case? Do you agree?

From Organized Violence to War

War is best described as a simultaneously institutionalized, organized and armed conflict between political organizations (Olsson and Malešević, 2017). War involves large-scale, sustained and high-intensity violence between organizations interacting in a more or less institutionalized way (Vasquez, 2009). Wars are often conceived of as a duel between political entities. Just as duels have rules of the game and allow settling a dispute between individuals, war is often seen as an institutionalized means of settling a conflict between political units. This has especially been the case for interstate wars. For example, following the Law of Nations of early modern Europe, wars needed to be declared, to discriminate between civilians and combatants, and they could only be fought by internationally recognized sovereigns. Clausewitz has, however, shown that wars, by furthering the resort to the utmost force on the part of the protagonists, have an irresistible tendency to emancipate themselves from these institutionalized rules if left unchecked by political authorities (Clausewitz, 2010 [1832]). Wars are hence permeated by a dialectical movement by which rules of the game tend to be stated, yet in which attempts to circumvent those rules are part of the game itself.

The ability to wage war does not come naturally or spontaneously to individuals or political groups (Collins, 2009). It is essentially a social and hence a learnt activity. It implies for the political units involved to order their social activities in a way allowing for significant resources to be diverted to this activity. In other words, it implies a high degree of social organization (Malešević, 2017). Three types of organizational processes are involved in wars between polities.

The first one is military in nature. It seeks to coerce, incentivize and/or condition combatants to stand and fight, rather than to cower or flee in the face of extreme violence, as they would spontaneously do. Such coercion can be exercised by repression, disciplinary measures, legal institutions prosecuting desertion or indiscipline, and so on. These measures seek to deter combatants from eschewing battle. Incentives to fight have historically been provided by the right to take war booty, the prospect of social promotion, economic and symbolic retributions, ideological exhortations, exploitation of the solidarity between fellow fighters within military units, and so on. Conditioning might involve diverse training techniques to develop a habituation to act in competent ways in the heat of the battle, as well as disciplining techniques (marching drills, target practice) (King, 2013). Since war implies patterned activities, both sequenced in time and ordered in space, combatants are required to play an active part in maintaining collectively coordinated behaviour and group discipline.

The second type of organizational process is political. War, as traditionally defined, is not an aim in itself but a purposive activity on the part of those who hold what Michael Man calls **despotic power** (Mann, 1984). Military and political organizations might very well be perfectly overlapping. This is especially so in complex chiefdoms in which military and political elites might be indistinguishable. In most polities, there is, however, some level of specialization of functions between political and military elites.

The third organizational process concerns society as a whole. Social structures play an important role in disposing societies to war: for example, only societies producing economic surplus have the resources allowing them to engage in sustained wars (Malešević, 2010). Indeed, wars need to be prepared by storing weapons, saving money, stockpiling goods, etc. Furthermore, they suppose the ability of the combatants to live off the wealth produced by others, at least during the time of active combat. Inversely, the experience of war transforms societies by favouring social stratification, social inequalities and the emergence of extractive bureaucracies. With the advent of the total wars of the 20th century, the participation of women in the national war effort has become indispensable and the proportion of women in this traditionally male-dominated professional activity has accordingly grown. The intimate link between war and social structure implies that different modes of social organization produce different types of war. Clausewitz in this regard compares war to a chameleon that constantly changes appearance yet remains essentially the same (Clausewitz, 2010 [1832]; Shaw, 2005).

When combined, the three above-mentioned organizational processes shed light on the frequent claim by historical sociologists that war and state-building have historically been linked (Elias, 1994 [1938]; Giddens, 1985; Tilly, 1993). Indeed, military competition between territorially delimited polities favours the competitive centralization of their respective bureaucracies. As extractive administrations grow stronger, they progressively envelop and penetrate society. At the same time, these administrations might need to co-opt societal interests and groups into the process to avert resistance. In this sense, the emergence of parliamentary and other representative political institutions is historically an indirect consequence of the necessities of war-making between increasingly centralized and extractive states (Tarrow, 2015). More generally, it is not a coincidence that polities that regularly wage war with each other tend to become increasingly alike, each one trying to appropriate the competitive advantage of the other. Wars are hence complex phenomena that do not only entail the exchange of blows but also the circulation of practices, the diffusion of **technologies** and the encounter of otherwise enclaved societies (Barkawi, 2006).

The link between war-making and state-making is, however, not a universal phenomenon (Olsson, 2015). It supposes the coexistence of territorialized political units of relatively equal military strength and hence unable to engage in elimination struggles. War can otherwise lead to imperial extension and/or internal fragmentation rather than to the type of territorial monopolies of violence that define states (Weber, 1965 [1919]). It is important in this context to remember that many wars occur *within* rather than *between* polities. Alternatively, they can occur between states so unequal that they inevitably lead to the invasion of one by the other. Even in civil wars, state-making might, however, play a role: the warring forces generally inherit the material and organizational capacities of the previous polity and carry them through into the post-war political structures. In some cases, civil war is the result of state-making rather than of state-breaking, for example when it is triggered by the increasingly extractive nature of state bureaucracies (Cohen et al., 1981). The link between the two activities, state-making and war-making, is hence essentially contingent and dependent on a multiplicity of contextual factors.

Expand Your Knowledge

- To learn more about the increasingly central role played by women in most Western armed forces, read: King, A.C. (2015) Women warriors: Female accession to ground combat. *Armed Forces & Society* 41(2): 379–87.
- On the ways in which war affects state–society relations, see: Tarrow, S. (2020) War and social movements. In R. Scott and S. Kosslyn (eds) *Emerging Trends in the Social and Behavioral Sciences*. https://onlinelibrary.wiley.com/doi/full/10.1002/9781118900772.etrds0381

CHAPTER SUMMARY

- Sociologists disagree on the defining elements and typologies of violence.
- In particular, they disagree on the comparative advantages of broad and narrow definitions of violence.
- The wide diversity of forms of violence makes it difficult to generalize or to approach violence as a single phenomenon.
- There are, however, links between different forms of violence: one form might trigger or lead to another, one form might be used to counter another.
- Sustained high-intensity violence often occurs as the result of conflicts between organizations, especially when no alternative mechanisms of conflict resolution exist.

REVIEW QUESTIONS

1. In Shakespeare's *Macbeth*, the main character claims that 'blood will have blood', a phrase that has become an English proverb. What does it mean? Is it always apposite?
2. Is violent behaviour necessarily asocial/antisocial behaviour? When is it and when is it not?
3. In situations of endemic violence, the social behaviour of people is reputed to become rational and predictable. At the same time, violence is often seen as unpredictable and irrational. How might one explain this disparity?

Go Further

Books

- Collins, R. (2009) *Violence: A Micro-Sociological Theory*. Westport, CT: Greenwood Publishing.

This is one of the rare books in sociology trying to give a comprehensive account of very diverse forms of violence through a theoretical framework rooted in symbolic interactionism.

- Malešević, S. (2010) *The Sociology of War and Violence*. Cambridge: Cambridge University Press.

This manual gives an excellent overview of the literature on collective violence and armed conflict while also introducing innovative ideas.

- della Porta, D. (2013) *Clandestine Political Violence*. Cambridge: Cambridge University Press.

In this book, the author sheds light on what generally is called terrorism through a framework rooted in the sociology of social movements and collective action.

Journal Articles

- Baron, I.V., Havercroft, J., Kamola, I., Koomen, J., Murphy, J. and Prichard, A. (2019) Liberal pacification and the phenomenology of violence. *International Studies Quarterly* 63(1): 199–212.

This article offers a good illustration of what is at stake in broad and restrictive definitions of violence from a point of view that favours the first option.

- Mann, M. (2018) Have war and violence declined? *Theory & Society* 47(1): 37–60.

In this article, leading sociologist Michael Mann debates the diverse arguments that have recently been advanced to claim that violent conflicts are globally on the decline.

- Walby, S. (2013) Violence and society: Introduction to an emerging field of sociology. *Current Sociology* 61(2): 95–111.

This introduction to a special issue on violence presents the state of the art of the sociology of violence and explores new avenues for research.

Websites

- www.ijcv.org/index.php/ijcv

International Journal of Conflict and Violence is an entirely online and interdisciplinary journal on violence and conflict broadly defined. Its website gives a good overview of the different levels of analysis, scales and perspectives from which violence can be considered in sociology and beyond.

(Continued)

- www.drrandallcollins.com

Randall Collins is a leading scholar in the sociology of conflict and violence. His personal website is a rich source of information on his very diverse publications. The blog in particular offers previously unpublished articles and posts on diverse topics, often related to violence.

- www.beyondintractability.org

This is the joint website of CRinfo and Moving Beyond Intractibility, both created by the Conflict Information Consortium (CIC) based at the University of Colorado at Boulder. It offers a rich knowledge base on conflicts and their consequences with contributions of more than 500 scholars.

REFERENCES

Aron, R. (2003 [1962]) *Peace and War: A Theory of International Relations*. Piscataway, NJ: Transaction.
Barkawi, T. (2006) *Globalization and War*. Lanham, MD: Rowman & Littlefield.
Baron, I.V., Havercroft, J., Kamola, I., Koomen, J., Murphy, J. and Prichard, A. (2019) Liberal pacification and the phenomenology of violence. *International Studies Quarterly* 63(1): 199–212.
Bauman, Z. (1989) *Modernity and the Holocaust*. Cambridge: Polity Press.
Benjamin, W. (2009) *One-Way Street and Other Writings*. London: Penguin.
Bourdieu, P. (1991) *Language and Symbolic Power*. Cambridge, MA: Harvard University Press.
Bourdieu, P. (2000) *Pascalian Meditations*. Stanford, CA: Stanford University Press.
Bourdieu, P. and Wacquant, L.J.D. (1992) *An Invitation to Reflexive Sociology*. Chicago: University of Chicago Press.
Clausewitz, C. von (2010 [1832]) *On War*. Auckland: The Floating Press.
Cohen, Y., Brown, B.R. and Organski, A.F.K. (1981) The paradoxical nature of state making: The violent creation of order. *American Political Science Review* 75(4): 901–10.
Collins, R. (2009) *Violence: A Micro-Sociological Theory*. Westport, CT: Greenwood Publishing.
Coser, L.A. (1957) Social conflict and the theory of social change. *The British Journal of Sociology* 8(3): 197.
Coser, L.A. (1966) Some social functions of violence. *The ANNALS of the American Academy of Political and Social Science* 364(1): 8–18.
della Porta, D. (2013 [2001]) *Clandestine Political Violence*. Cambridge: Cambridge University Press.
Elias, N. (1994 [1938]) *Civilizing Process*. Hoboken, NJ: Wiley.
Fanon, F. (2007 [1961]) *The Wretched of the Earth*. New York: Grove/Atlantic.
Foucault, M. (2012 [1975]) *Discipline and Punish: The Birth of the Prison*. New York: Knopf/Doubleday.
Galtung, J. (1969) Violence, peace, and peace research. *Journal of Peace Research* 6(3): 167–91.
Galtung, J. (1971) A structural theory of violence. *Journal of Peace Research* 8(2): 81–117.
Giddens, A. (1985) *The Nation-State and Violence*. Berkeley, CA: University of California Press.
Girard, R. (2013) *Violence and the Sacred*. London: Bloomsbury.
Goldstein, J.S. (2003) *War and Gender: How Gender Shapes the War System and Vice Versa*. Cambridge: Cambridge University Press.
Goodwin, J. (2001) *No Other Way Out: States and Revolutionary Movements, 1945–1991*. Cambridge: Cambridge University Press.

Grayzel, S.R. and Proctor, T.M. (2017) *Gender and the Great War*. Oxford: Oxford University Press.
Hobbes, T. (2002 [1657]) *Leviathan*. Peterborough (Canada): Broadview Press.
Joas, H. and Knöbl, W. (2012) *War in Social Thought: Hobbes to the Present*. Princeton, NJ: Princeton University Press.
King, A. (2013) *The Combat Soldier: Infantry Tactics and Cohesion in the Twentieth and Twenty-First Centuries*. Oxford: Oxford University Press.
King, A.C. (2015) Women warriors: Female accession to ground combat. *Armed Forces & Society* 41(2): 379–87.
Malešević, S. (2010) *The Sociology of War and Violence*. Cambridge: Cambridge University Press.
Malešević, S. (2013) Forms of brutality: Towards a historical sociology of violence. *European Journal of Social Theory* 16(3): 273–91.
Malešević, S. (2017) *The Rise of Organised Brutality*. Cambridge: Cambridge University Press.
Mann, M. (1984) The autonomous power of the state: Its origins, mechanisms and results. *European Journal of Sociology* 25(2): 185–213.
Mann, M. (1986) *The Sources of Social Power: Volume 1 – A History of Power from the Beginning to AD 1760*. Cambridge: Cambridge University Press.
Mann, M. (2005) *The Dark Side of Democracy: Explaining Ethnic Cleansing*. Cambridge: Cambridge University Press.
Marx, K. (2018 [1867]) *Capital, Volume 1*. Lulu.com.
McAdam, D. (2010) *Political Process and the Development of Black Insurgency, 1930–1970*. Chicago: University of Chicago Press.
Merry, S.E. (2009) *Gender Violence: A Cultural Perspective*. Hoboken, NJ: John Wiley & Sons.
Merton, R.K. (1938) Social structure and anomie. *American Sociological Review* 3(5): 672–82.
Muchembled, R. (2012) *A History of Violence: From the End of the Middle Ages to the Present*. Oxford: Polity.
Mueller, J. (2004) *The Remnants of War*. Ithaca, NY: Cornell University Press.
Nussbaum, M.C. (2005) Women's bodies: Violence, security, capabilities. *Journal of Human Development* 6(2): 167–83.
Oberschall, A. (1973) *Social Conflict and Social Movements*. Englewood Cliffs, NJ: Prentice Hall.
Olsson, C. (2013) 'Legitimate violence' in the prose of counterinsurgency: An impossible necessity? *Alternatives* 38(2): 155–71.
Olsson, C. (2015) Wars among nation-states: Patterns and causes. In J.D. Wright (ed.) *International Encyclopedia of the Social & Behavioral Sciences*, 2nd edition. Oxford: Elsevier, pp. 420–7.
Olsson, C. and Malešević, S. (2017) Chapter 43: War. In W. Outhwaite and S.P. Turner (eds) *The SAGE Handbook of Political Sociology, Vol. II*. London: Sage, pp. 715–33.
Rousseau, J-J. (1761) *A Discourse Upon the Origin and the Foundation of the Inequality Among Mankind*. Library of Alexandria.
Rule, J.B. (1989) *Theories of Civil Violence*. Berkeley, CA: University of California Press.
Rummel, R.J. (2011) *Death by Government*. Piscataway, NJ: Transaction Publishers.
Schelling, T.C. (1980) *The Strategy of Conflict*. Cambridge, MA: Harvard University Press.
Scriver, S., Duvvury, N., Ashe, S., Raghavendra, S. and O'Donovan, D. (2015) Conceptualising violence: A holistic approach to understanding violence against women and girls. Available at: www.whatworks.co.za/resources/evidence-reviews/item/85-conceptualising-violence-a-holistic-approach-to-understanding-violence-against-women-and-girls (accessed 30 May 2021).
Shaw, M. (2005) *The New Western Way of War: Risk-Transfer War and Its Crisis in Iraq*. Hoboken, NJ: Wiley.
Simmel, G. (2010 [1922]) *Conflict and the Web of Group Affiliations*. New York: Simon and Schuster.
Sorel, G. (1999 [1908]) *Reflections on Violence*. Cambridge: Cambridge University Press.
Tarrow, S. (2015) *War, States, and Contention: A Comparative Historical Study*. Ithaca, NY: Cornell University Press.

Taussig, M. (2003) *Law in a Lawless Land: Diary of a Limpieza in Colombia*. Chicago: University of Chicago Press.
Tilly, C. (1989) *The Contentious French*. Cambridge, MA: The Belknap Press of Harvard University Press.
Tilly, C. (1993) *Coercion, Capital and European States: AD 990–1992*. Hoboken, NJ: Wiley.
Tilly, C. (2003) *The Politics of Collective Violence*. Cambridge: Cambridge University Press.
Vasquez, J.A. (2009) *The War Puzzle Revisited*. Cambridge: Cambridge University Press.
Wacquant, L. (2009) *Prisons of Misery*. Minneapolis: Minnesota University Press.
Walby, S. (2013) Violence and society: Introduction to an emerging field of sociology. *Current Sociology* 61(2): 95–111.
Weber, M. (1965 [1919]) *Politics as a Vocation*. Philadelphia, PA: Fortress Press.
Weber, M. (1978 [1921]) *Economy and Society: An Outline of Interpretive Sociology*. Berkeley, CA: University of California Press.
Wieviorka, M. (2009) *Violence: A New Approach*. Thousand Oaks, CA: Sage.

SCIENCE AND TECHNOLOGY

Ros Williams

LEARNING OBJECTIVES

- To think critically about the role of science and technology in our social worlds.
- To understand the sociological importance of science and technology.
- To grasp some of the key ideas from important thinkers who have engaged in discussions about the social dimensions of science and technology.
- To develop a knowledge of some current sociologically relevant debates regarding the social implications of science and technology.

 Framing Questions

1. Why should sociologists concern themselves with topics like science and technology?
2. In what sense might we understand science as social?
3. What does it mean to suggest that technologies have politics?

PART 5 SOCIOLOGICAL FRONTIERS

Introduction

You may be surprised to see a chapter on science and technology in an introductory textbook to sociology. Perhaps some students thought they had left the world of biology, physics, chemistry, maths and so on far behind them by choosing to study sociology. Some might ask why sociologists – who are interested in things like social practices, identities, values and inequalities – would concern themselves with science and technology. But as this chapter is going to lay out, these issues sit at the very heart of science and technology. Through what kinds of social practices might science be accomplished? In what ways might science reproduce social identities like, for example, race? What does it mean to suggest that technologies can be imbued with particular values, or that technologies can produce or even reinforce social inequalities?

In this chapter, you are going to learn some of the different ways in which science and technology are intensely social and political. The literature and ideas drawn on in this chapter come from a range of academic researchers. Not all of the writers you will read about are sociologists, though most of them would describe their work as social science. Some of them might describe themselves as sociologists, historians or even philosophers of science and technology. Increasingly, the term Science and Technology Studies (STS) has also been used to capture the diversity of work exploring the social and political complexities of this area. Over the course of this chapter, however, you will develop a clearer understanding of some of the central threads of argument that make up this body of ideas.

Mapping the Terrain

Maybe one of your family members recently had a medical test. Perhaps you've just heard a podcast about a new government policy to tackle climate change. You might even be reading this via your phone screen as an electronic chapter provided to you by your university's library. Either way, and no matter who or where you are, science and technology are directly implicated in how you live. You may have a rather positive view of science and technology, too. Advances in chemistry mean your smartphone's battery can last all day without you needing to charge it. The availability of technologies like music streaming services mean you can use the phone to fill your spare time on the way to class by catching up on the latest release from your favourite musician. Yet not everybody is experiencing these developments in the same way.

First, let's go back to our phones. Controversy abounds about the production processes that bring them into being. There are significant concerns over workers' health in the (typically non-Western) countries in which these devices are built, given the potential exposure of many factory workers to various chemicals and materials during the phone's production. The Korean smartphone manufacturer Samsung, for example, has been held legally responsible for multiple cancers amongst its factory workers (Agence France-Press, 2018). It had been accused of blocking systematic scientific research that could produce the vital evidence needed to demonstrate the deleterious consequences of factory workers' chemical exposure (see Lee and Waitzkin, 2012). So whilst you might be enjoying the benefits of your smartphone, others have a very different relationship to the science and technology that mediate it.

In a different vein, let's think about the music you might have listened to on that phone today. Innovations in audio streaming have led to their own significant controversy. In a relatively short period of time, streaming services like Spotify have become a dominant means of listening to music. This has implications for how we might 'buy' music (when was the last time you bought a CD?). It has also been consequential in how artists are paid for their music, with independent artists and smaller record labels potentially negatively affected by

SCIENCE AND TECHNOLOGY

per-listen payment models that appear increasingly to benefit large record labels and their popular artists (Marshall, 2015). Again, whilst I might find it fantastic that I can switch between the songs of innumerable artists through such a service, other people are experiencing its consequences in a very different way. (The issue of digital platforms is explored further in Chapter 2.)

Sociologists interested in science and technology explore these complex interrelations, and try to map out their social, political and ethical implications. For much of the 20th century, social scientists and humanities scholars, including sociologists as well as historians, philosophers and others, have been busy trying to understand both how science and technological innovation are organized and accomplished in practice and what the consequences of this are for us and our world.

This work has partly been concerned with unpicking the organization of science. What constitutes 'good' science? Is there even such a thing? These questions are explored in the work of philosophers like Karl Popper and Thomas Kuhn, who were influential in legitimizing science as a focus for the social sciences and humanities. Their work, explored in this chapter, helped to prepare the ground for questions that would emerge more specifically about the actual 'doings' of science – how are scientific facts made through the work that scientists do? How do these facts then get mobilized in our social world? These are questions we will also unpick in reference to a range of scholarship from the past several decades – for example, the laboratory studies of scholars like Bruno Latour and Steve Woolgar who look at how the day-to-day work of people in a laboratory 'constructs' facts. We will also consider more recent work from academics exploring the role of science in the (re)constitution of social life. In particular, the chapter will focus on the contemporary role science plays for one of the most significant and salient social categories in our world – race.

Relatedly, scholars researching in this area have asked similar questions of the technologies that so often become embedded in our everyday lives. Is it fair, for example, to claim that technologies *affect* us? Can they make us smarter or more anxious? Much of the scholarship in this area has been busy challenging these claims, which arguably devolve responsibility from the social world to the material world (i.e. from the people who make and use technologies to the technologies themselves). Instead, as a range of different authors argue, technology is intensely social from the moment of its inception, in the sense that the social world is written or encoded into these technologies. Again, to bring these themes to sociological life, we will ponder them through the lens of race. For example, can you think of why a beauty contest judged not by a human being but by artificial intelligence invariably awards its top prizes for beauty to white contestants over contestants of colour?

At the heart of the literature, and the key claim of the chapter ahead, is that science and technology have intrinsically social, material and political qualities. What our societies deign to be scientific facts, as well as how these are made and mobilized, the machines and devices that surround us and the work that goes into making and maintaining them – all of these have massive implications to which we as sociologists should pay attention.

From Discovering Scientific Truths to Constructing Scientific Facts

What images does the word 'science' conjure in your mind? Perhaps your imagination travels to scientists wearing white laboratory coats, squinting into microscopes. Maybe your mind goes back to school – you are sat at a bench, fiddling with Petri dishes or Bunsen burners, and learning how to design an experiment to test a hypothesis. As well as a number of images, terms like science or its adjectival form 'scientific' might also conjure up a set of ideas and claims: science discovers objective truths, or scientific work tells us about the reality of the natural world around us.

This understanding of science, which many scholars argue has dominated our thinking for the past century or two, pitches science as a form of accumulating knowledge through, and of, the natural world in which we exist. This understanding frames scientists as those who collect and analyse evidence using a scientific method that other scientists should be able to repeat. Through this process, scientists are able to unearth facts that can then be verified. Scientists should then be able to discuss their findings and come to an agreement or consensus about the facts. Science's authority can be seen to rely on this claim that it seeks and propagates only facts, and this relies on the notion that science (and, by extension, scientists) are value-free and politically neutral.

A rich history of debate has problematized this claim in different ways. Some, like philosopher Karl Popper, sought to define science by the willingness of sciences to disprove their own hypotheses as opposed to '**pseudo-sciences**' that find ways of absorbing evidence that contradicts their theories, so that they may continue to propound them. Others, like his contemporary, the historian Thomas Kuhn, instead proposed that science is the ongoing result of working within a particular conceptual framework until enough anomalies compel a scientific revolution that transforms science from one **paradigm** to another.

The Structure of Science? Popper and Kuhn

For Austrian philosopher Karl Popper, the most important thing about science is that it should always be critical: scientists should start without any background theories that they hold as true. Rather, science ought to begin from a position of scientists actively trying to 'falsify' their own theories. A good scientist knows that another datum might yet be collected that could disprove their original theory so is necessarily open to their theories being falsified, in favour of newer theories. According to Popper, this approach distinguishes science from '*pseudo*-science'. From his perspective, sociological theories like **Marxism** were pseudo-scientific because they shielded themselves from falsifiability: Marx's writings, for example, forecast a violent proletarian revolution. Popper claims that this did not happen, but that Marxism's dialectic materialism is 'vague and elastic enough to interpret and explain ... the situation which is predicted and which happened not to come true' (Popper, 1963: 448).

Around the same time as Popper, the American historian Thomas Kuhn published his own, quite different, understanding of the workings of science. Whilst Popper felt that falsification was the way in which science ought to operate, Kuhn argued that in practice scientists actually *resist* efforts to falsify their theories. He elaborates his argument in a stage model. In the stage of what Kuhn called 'normal science', scientists are actually *not* very critical and do not seek to test the theories that guide them.

Within any phase of normal science, Kuhn argued, there is a range of **methods**, instruments, tools and theories that go unquestioned – for example, the concept that our bodies comprise many billions of cells; that those cells can be viewed through a measuring instrument like a microscope (itself perceived as a valid tool for scientific inquiry); and that they contain deoxyribonucleic acid (DNA) that to some extent determines our appearance and possibly our behaviour. None of these theories are themselves questioned and they underpin the hypotheses that scientists test. They also form the foundation of a scientific education – you can expect the body-cell-DNA account to appear in school textbooks (see the Key Case box below), which Kuhn describes as the 'pedagogic vehicles for the perpetuation of normal science' (1970: 136). These understandings constitute a '**scientific paradigm**', and normal science constitutes the stability of that paradigm.

23.1 Key Case

The Idea of Race and High School Textbooks

In a study into how students think and learn about the idea of 'race' in the USA, sociologist Ann Morning considers a sample of high school textbooks used in high school courses from biology to sociology. 'The impact of high-school textbooks is both wide and deep' (2011: 66), argues Morning, building on Kuhn's claim that textbooks play an important role in how we learn the accepted theories of a given scientific paradigm – be that biology or sociology.

Sociologists of race and ethnicity have long tended to agree that race is a 'social construct', an argument that suggests racial categories are established and reasserted through our social relations rather than seeing race as an *a priori* fact. As a student of sociology, you may already be familiar with this argument. In opposition to this constructivist viewpoint sits the discourse of biological essentialism, which asserts that categories of difference like race are not social but biologically innate.

Perhaps unsurprisingly, sociology textbooks in Morning's sample generally (though, interestingly, not always!) framed race through a constructivist lens, describing it as a category of difference produced through social life. Biology textbooks, however, tended to reassert race as an essential category of biological or even genetic difference (i.e. at the level of DNA) amongst humans. Morning suggests that the prominence of biological essentialism in many of the biology textbooks matters, because it perpetuates (to use Kuhn's language) this scientific knowledge to the young adults reading these books, and to the teachers educating them.

- Thinking through a Kuhnian lens, what impact might the dominance of a biological essentialist discourse in high school biology textbooks have on the contemporary biological sciences?

According to Kuhn, in a period of normal science, scientific pursuits become a kind of puzzle solving. Like a jigsaw puzzle, so long as all the pieces are in the box, there is a means of solving the puzzle. Within a period of normal science, scientists are inclined to choose problems for which they assume there is a solution: 'The man [sic] who succeeds proves himself an expert puzzle-solver, and the challenge of the puzzle is an important part of what usually drives him on' (1970: 36).

The inability to solve a particular puzzle need not be read by the scientist as a falsification (think back to Popper's claim that scientists are always ready for the evidence to falsify their theory). Rather, in Kuhn's understanding, evidence that challenges the theory is purely an anomaly in the operation of normal science. However, according to Kuhn, once enough anomalies started to stack up, the tools, methods and theories of a paradigm might come into question. A crisis stage, and potentially even a scientific revolution, might occur, transitioning those within the paradigm to a new set of theories with which a new articulation of normal science begins to stabilize.

The Construction of Scientific Facts?

Both Popper and Kuhn's arguments were very influential, and arguably helped to solidify science as a legitimate area for social scientists and humanities scholars to explore. The second half of the 20th century saw the instantiation of various sub-disciplines that counted amongst them a number of sociologists, like 'science studies', or studies of 'science, technology and society'. An increasingly all-encompassing moniker that, for some, has absorbed these other terms is 'science and technology studies' or, simply, STS.

For many within STS, there has been significant work done by scholars to try and understand how science is organized – like Popper's and Kuhn's influential contributions. But for others within STS, it was also important to think about how science was being accomplished in practice – i.e. what exactly were scientists *doing*? As such, over the last few decades of the 20th century, a number of important **empirical** studies were undertaken in laboratories, observing the work that scientists do in practice. Perhaps the most well-known of these studies was written by Bruno Latour and Steve Woolgar. Their book, *Laboratory Life* (1979), was based on observing scientists as they went about their daily working lives in the laboratory. Latour and Woolgar borrowed an ethnographic methodology that at the time was most commonly found not in **sociology** but in anthropology. The authors observed scientists working with scientific tools and materials, exploring the everyday practices that take place in the laboratory like informal discussions, often-intense note-keeping, and the relations between the people and materials within the laboratory setting.

The authors argue that much of the work taking place in that laboratory was essentially a process of *inscription*. By inscription, they refer to the ways that different pieces of apparatus are used to 'transform a material substance into a figure or diagram which is directly usable' (1979: 51) in, for example, conference presentations and scientific journal articles. They argue that much of this work of inscription involves scientists deciding what data ought to be kept or not, hence the subtitle to their book: *The Construction of Scientific Facts*. A fact (for example, the existence of a particular peptide) does not have an obvious history. A peptide just exists. But facts have histories that bring them into being. Consider the slow and methodical work of scientists and technicians bent over microscopes in the laboratory who undertake the work of inscription, or the conversations between two scientists who debate whether a third scientist's work should hold credence because of previous mistakes in their work. Social negotiations and machinations like these are the means through which facts take shape. This is not necessarily to say that what we understand as facts are somehow not real, but that our acknowledgement of them is contingent.

Such an account, you might notice, also acknowledges the importance of the materials: microscopes, the pens used to jot notes, research papers, diagrams, or even a telephone if the conversation between scientists happens at a distance. Latour is well known, along with Michel Callon and John Law, for theoretically elaborating these networks between humans and non-humans with the notion of **Actor-Network Theory** (ANT). ANT would become incredibly influential for its effort to explain how it is networks between **technologies**, objects and humans – rather than simply 'the social' – that validate knowledge claims. The importance of materiality is something we will discuss more generally later in the chapter.

The Social Implications of Scientific Knowledge

Sociologists of science and technology are interested in exploring how science is organized, and how **scientific knowledge** is 'constructed' or 'accomplished' – science is a highly social activity. So too are they interested in the social implications of that scientific knowledge. Take, for example, the biological sciences. Even if you are not a professional scientist, you have probably heard of terms like DNA and genes. You might even be able to give a basic explanation of your understanding. For example, if somebody asked me what DNA was, I might say 'DNA is made up of chemicals that combine into genes. These biological elements determine all kinds of things about us: our eye colour, whether we have freckles or maybe even our personality.'

Perhaps you learned about DNA and genes in school. Yet, outside of an educational setting, most of us regularly hear or engage in what Dorothy Nelkin and M. Susan Lindee call 'gene talk' (1995: 1), regular articulations across different domains of social life that use the concept of the gene to explain and describe things. In their important book *The DNA Mystique*, Nelkin and Lindee describe the gene as 'a cultural icon' invoked regularly in popular culture to explain everything from tastes to attitudes and behaviours (e.g. music is in my DNA!).

As technological developments have led to ever-finer ways of engaging with DNA and genes, argue Nelkin and Lindee, the power of the gene as a cultural icon has continued to grow. Genetic analysis can now be used to determine one's probability of developing a particular disease. Companies even sell tests that claim to determine somebody's 'ancestry'. The ability to know our bodies at the 'molecular' level has arguably led to a new politicization of medicine, human life, and biotechnology. There are potentially huge social implications for this kind of knowledge, not least the emergence of new concepts of kinship, community and responsibility – some scholars have named this **biosociality** (Rabinow, 1996).

These notions share an acknowledgement of the increasing **role** of biological knowledge in projects of **citizenship**, and of entering into and reasserting certain forms of sociality. For example, a group set up by parents whose children all have the same rare disease locate a mutual solidarity described by researchers as a kind of biosociality (Dimond et al., 2015). A genetic ancestry test might produce new feelings of kinship towards a distant community after the test results tell the customer that their ancestors come from a specific place that the individual may have otherwise never felt any connection to (Nelson, 2016).

Another example of this is the practice of bone marrow stem cell transplantation, a common treatment for blood cancers in which doctors search for donors on a bone marrow registry who will be a match for their patient. Scientists have established that donors and recipients who come from similar 'genetic populations' are most likely to match. As Williams (2015, 2018) argues, in this scientific context, notions of '**population**' often transmute into 'racial groups', so that black people are thought more likely to find their match in the pool of black volunteer donors. Because there are fewer black and minority **ethnicity** people registered as stem cell donors on the UK bone marrow registry, black and minority ethnicity patients are believed to be less likely to find their tissue match than white patients. In response, the UK's statutory health provider, the **National Health Service**, has been working with bone marrow registries and smaller charities to engage black and minority communities as stem cell donors. Through various techniques, like publicity campaigns and stem cell drives, this work aims to bring 'ethnic minorities to a realisation of the sharedness of their community and the mutuality of their responsibility toward one another' (Merz and Williams, 2018: 568) by asking them to do something for 'their' community, which potentially reasserts problematic essentialist claims of racial difference.

From Technologies with Effects to Technologies with Politics

So far, we have discussed science in some depth. But what about technology? It would probably go unquestioned simply to suggest that technology is essentially the product of applied science. A need is located, and scientific knowledge is perhaps creatively gathered together in an effort to meet that need. From this perspective, science may be the key determinant of technology. If this is the case, and we assume that science is politically and socially neutral and value-free, then we need not explore the process of technological development, or assume that there is anything sociologically or politically relevant about technology. Of course, there are some issues with this assumption. It is clear, through discussing the work above which forms part of a much larger set of literature, that science is not neutral and value-free. It is equally reductive to assume that either all technologies clearly emerge out of scientific development or that technologies' production and use are themselves not also heavily socially inflected.

Do Technologies Have Effects?

Nonetheless, let's take the simplistic relationship that science makes technology as a starting point. Rather than leading us to ask questions about how and why technologies do – and do not! – come to be, other questions seem more obvious to ask: what are technology's positive or negative effects? Such a question assumes that technology is external to, and has effects on, society. Nonetheless, it is quite straightforward and probably a little tempting to make claims that technology has an effect on us.

For example, if you want to find the answer to a question – say, what time does the bus leave this morning or how tall is the Eiffel Tower – where do you look? The first thing I would do now is pick up my phone (if it isn't already in my hand) and search on Google. Over ten years ago, American writer Nicholas Carr (2008) wrote a popular article in the magazine *The Atlantic*, describing his concern that Google was 'making him stupid'. As a writer, he noted that his research 'once required days in the stacks or periodical rooms of libraries [but could] now be done in minutes'. In writing this chapter, I had a few hard copies of books, but much of my reading was based on Google Scholar which helped me to find copies of articles, electronic versions of books and meant I did not have to travel to the library. So, did Google make me stupid, or lazy? What does it mean to say that this technology has changed us?

This claim can be understood as an example of the discourse of **technological determinism**: that technology determines things. This discourse implies that technologies can have a causal effect, or even have agency – can do things like make us stupid or make our lives easier. It also implies that we, as human actors, do not necessarily have any agency in the terms of our engagements with technologies. But is it simply enough, in arguing against this position, to put all the agency back onto people? Don't technologies have *some* determining effects?

Technologies with Politics

A lively debate over the past few decades has critically engaged with these ideas. A well-known example can be found in the influential article written 40 years ago by Langdon Winner: 'Do Artefacts Have Politics?' The piece was interested in the then rather controversial claim that, far from being neutral, technological objects (or, as he describes them, artifacts) themselves have politics. His paper was in response to the well-trodden claim at that time that it is not technologies themselves that have politics but the social and economic systems in which they are embedded. Winner disagreed with the claim 'that people have politics, not things'

(1980: 122). The argument, he noted, appears to make sense. After all, are we not giving artifacts – non-human objects – *agency* by saying they have power? Or falling into the trap of 'technological determinism' if we say that technologies themselves determine things (e.g. Google makes us stupid)?

Expand Your Knowledge

Engagement and Agency in Digital Technology Use

- Ditchfield, H. (2019) Behind the screen of Facebook: Identity construction in the rehearsal stage of online interaction. *New Media & Society* 22(6): 927–43. DOI: 10.1177/1461444819873644. Ditchfield's paper explores how people edit their communications via Facebook Messenger before posting messages. She demonstrates that people often undertake large amounts of editing to 'perfect' their posts before sending them. Importantly, this reveals how significant work goes into the presentation of self online.
- Weiner, K., Will, C., Henwood, F. and Williams, R. (2020) Everyday curation? Attending to data, records and record-keeping in the practices of self-monitoring. *Big Data and Society* 7(1): 1–15. Weiner et al. explore the different ways that people engage with health self-monitoring (through objects like weighing scales, blood pressure monitors and smart fitness devices). They argue that people 'curate' the data they generate through using their devices, rather than having no agency in relation to technology.

Both of these pieces of research help to push against the idea that we are passively affected by technologies. Rather, we are constantly engaging with them in various ways and for various purposes in our everyday lives.

Winner uses the example of New York overpasses, the bridges spanning key city roads. Some of these bridges were 'deliberately designed to achieve a particular social effect' (1980: 123). The urban planner who designed them, argues Winner, wanted to discourage certain demographics from travel to particular areas of the city. Building the overpasses to a limited height had the effect of excluding certain vehicles from travelling beneath them towards the public park – notably, the public transport buses carrying those who could not afford a car, many of whom were black. Winner's point here is that the bridge was not neutral but purposefully designed to produce specific consequences through its use.

But we need not, as Winner himself noted, look only for cases in which technologies have been wilfully designed to exclude. Winner's is an example of some of the earlier scholarship that analysed how socio-economic patterns were embedded in technologies, often at the point of design. Over the course of the late 20th century, various STS scholars would explore the **social construction of technology**. This is not to say that technologies aren't materially real, but that society is implicated in their construction. Users, designers, funders, states and so on all play a foundational role in which technologies are imagined, designed, created, marketed and used. For some, like ANT scholars, even the notion of 'the social' was problematic because it gave undue primacy to human actors. A comprehensive analytic approach would require us to acknowledge and incorporate non-human actors into our analyses as well. Though there remains some contestation about the appropriate weight to give to non-human elements in our analyses, increasingly it has been acknowledged that sociologists have to take the material world (like technologies, and the other 'stuff' of our environments) seriously, as they constitute an important and constitutive part of our world.

A Racist Algorithm?

In this spirit, scholars interested in contemporary articulations of **racism** wisely focus their analysis not just on how we as members of society treat one another, but how the material world enfolds into this issue too. Take, for example, STS scholar Safiya Noble's (2018) sociological consideration of how contemporary technologies might be designed with very particular worldviews in mind. She explores how Google's search engine function, which relies on a set of proprietary algorithms, generates what can be perceived as racist and sexist search results. For example, Noble's Google image search for 'beautiful' returned a set of images dominated by results of white women with normatively attractive features. A search for 'professor style' generated a set of images almost completely comprising white men dressed in suits and sweaters. These, along with other results, allow Noble to make the argument that Google's algorithms reproduce culturally dominant **norms**. For Noble, these search results represented 'Google's algorithmic conceptualizations of a variety of people and ideas' (2018: 24) which reflect dominant narratives in popular culture.

Another STS author, Ruha Benjamin, explores how forms of social oppression like racism are embedded in, and reproduced by, technologies. She discusses Noble's work, arguing that an apparently racist Google search result is not a 'symptom or outcome, but a precondition for the fabrication of such technologies' (2019: 44). Via this logic, Benjamin suggests that it is not only possible but probable that newer technologies like artificial intelligence (AI) software can produce biased results. Benjamin introduces us to Beauty AI to exemplify her argument. Beauty AI is a 'beauty contest' judged by artificial intelligence. 'What', Benjamin despairs, 'could possibly go wrong?' (2019: 50), as she maps out how the designers' personal preferences inevitably work their way into the AI system through – if nothing else – the collation of a reference library of what are deemed by those in charge to be beautiful faces. It is these human-selected faces against which contestants will be compared. There is, of course, no one kind of beautiful, because our ideas of beauty are necessarily culturally situated. As such, the AI judge takes on the designers' eye. Sure enough, the finalists were nearly all white. (Further discussion of race and racism can be found in Chapters 2 and 13.)

Since Noble's research, the Google search results that she based her study on have changed. Whether or not this was in response to Noble's research is perhaps less important than the fact that the results need never have been so problematic in the first place. As Benjamin writes, gesturing to the ability of Google's results to be more inclusive than Noble found them to be, 'the technical capacity was always there, but social awareness and incentives to ensure fair representation online were lacking' (2019: 94). In short, then, where there is a will, perhaps there is a way to make technologies more inclusive.

 Pause for Thought

Open up an image search engine app or website on your tablet, phone or computer. Search for the word 'beautiful', then the word 'handsome'. What images come up in your search results? Are they images of people? If so, what are the common body shapes, skin colours, hair colours, ages, and genders of those people?

- What might these results be able to tell us above normative social ideas about what constitutes the beautiful or the handsome?
- Could the results be more inclusive? Should they be? Why? Why not?

SCIENCE AND TECHNOLOGY

Pushing Back Against Technologies

Thinking back to the idea that technologies can have politics just as we can, then the very idea of a divide between technology and everything else begins to break down too. Materials need not be electronically powered or sold in stores to be technologies. If traffic lights are technologies, then so are speed bumps. If smartphones are technologies, then so are pens and paper! These material technologies that help make up the worlds in which we live can have politics. (If you doubt that pens have politics, the recent design of the Bic pen 'For Her' is a good critical starting point for thinking about why a stationery designer thought women needed their own, separate pens (O'Meara, 2012).)

But if technologies can have politics, does that mean we are beholden to those politics? To some extent, we surely are. An interesting idea that has emerged out of this discussion is the argument that artefacts do not simply have politics but have what some scholars have termed a **script** or a **program** inscribed within them. STS scholar Madeleine Akrich (1992) has been an influential voice in this discussion. She notes that the designers of technologies must necessarily define users' tastes, abilities, aspirations and political leanings and design this vision or 'script' into the object itself. In the use of the technology, a user essentially reads this script as if it were a movie script.

Latour, who was mentioned earlier in the chapter, has similarly proposed the idea of a 'programme' to describe how imperatives and instructions become embedded in technologies. He uses the example of a hotel key: a hotelier has been losing many of his room keys. He decides he wants his guests to hand in their keys each day before they head out to enjoy the city. Initially, he asks guests to do this verbally, but they do not follow his instruction. He then places a sign in the hotel requesting that people return their key each day. They don't heed the request, so he attaches a large keyring to each key that is so cumbersome that guests prefer to hand the key in before leaving for the day. The programme which was initially verbal, then written on a sign, became materially embedded in the technology, and strongly directed a certain course of action for its users. But must we always engage with technologies on their terms? Both Akrich and Latour acknowledge that users might read or respond to these scripts in unexpected ways.

For example, a doctor might prescribe some medication for a patient, instructing them to take a specific number of tablets each day for two weeks. The drug packaging might repeat this guidance to the patient. STS scholars Kate Weiner and Catherine Will (2016) undertook qualitative interviews with people who had been prescribed drugs. They found that, even with a specific script for use in the form of a doctor's instructions and written guidance, people might not always consume these drugs in line with the script or programme laid out – some people resisted using drugs at all, or adapted their consumption of the drugs.

Take a very different example: the 'Me Too' movement that has emerged to highlight sexual harassment and assault. Though the 'Me Too' concept began some years ago by activist Tarana Burke, the term was drawn to popular attention by actor Alyssa Milano, whose post on social media platform Twitter invited other victims of sexual assault to write 'me too'. The post was responded to, retweeted and liked in massive numbers. Soon, the term would become a recognizable hashtag – #MeToo – used on various platforms to pinpoint debate and conversation around the topic as hashtags are scripted to do. In this sense, MeToo can be read as a range of users following the technical scripting of Twitter – Milano posted a tweet, and tens of thousands of people pressed like buttons, retweeted the post, or even responded using the platform's reply function.

Yet an interesting story of resistance, or of pushing against a technical script, can be found in the same movement. A number of users on Weibo, the popular Chinese microblogging site, sought to gain traction for the hashtag: #我也是 (#WoYeShi, or Me Too in Mandarin). However, in compliance with Chinese internet censorship rules, censors deleted content related to such hashtags (Lim, 2018). In response, and pushing against the platform's script or programme, users have found interesting ways to resist, most prominently using the term 米兔(Mi Tu, a homonym for Me Too, which literally translates to rice bunny) and rice and bunny emojis to articulate otherwise censorable wording. The use of a homonym to circumvent the platform's censorship infrastructure (see Zeng, 2019) offers a particularly powerful example of how people can resist the scripts of technologies.

These examples demonstrate how technologies from prescription drugs to microblogging platforms can be the site of inventive diversions from intended use. Keeping this and the other insights outlined in this chapter – about how scientific knowledge and technological developments come to be, and our variegated roles and associations in relation to these – is key to how we as sociologists enquire into the relationships we have with science, technology and, more broadly, our social and material worlds.

CHAPTER SUMMARY

- Both science and technology are fundamental facets of our societies, and are themselves social phenomena, produced through and in reference to our social world.
- Facts constructed in the laboratory circulate through our everyday lives, reasserting or challenging our ideas of who we are and the communities to which we belong.
- The technologies that we use may appear to be neutral. They may also appear to have an effect on us in some way or another. Importantly, though, they are suffused with values and politics from their inception, scripted with particular expectations of how they will be used.
- Overall, we can understand science and technology not as separate to the issues that sociologists should be concerned with, but as integral to the very things that sociologists are interested in and committed to researching.

REVIEW QUESTIONS

1. To what extent can we understand science as 'neutral'? Why does it matter?
2. Using examples from beyond the chapter, can you think of how scientific 'facts' and knowledge can have social consequences?
3. What exactly is meant by the term 'technological determinism', and why might this discourse be problematic?
4. Drawing on examples from your own life and the environment around you, in what ways might technologies have politics?

> ## Go Further
>
> ### Books
>
> - Felt, U., Fouché, R., Miller, C.A. and Smith-Doerr, L. (eds) (2017) *The Handbook of Science and Technology Studies*. Cambridge, MA: MIT Press. https://mitpress.mit.edu/books/handbook-science-and-technology-studies-fourth-edition
>
> This is a useful collection of essays on a range of topics from leading scholars in the field of STS.
>
> - Kleinman, D.L. and Moore, K. (eds) (2014) *Routledge Handbook of Science, Technology, and Society*. Oxford: Routledge. www.routledgehandbooks.com/doi/10.4324/9780203101827
>
> This is an edited volume of contributions for STS scholars, exploring different areas of science and technology.
>
> - Sismondo, S. (2011) *An Introduction to Science and Technology Studies*. London: John Wiley & Sons. www.wiley.com/en-gb/An+Introduction+to+Science+and+Technology+Studies%2C+2nd+Edition-p-9781405187657
>
> Sismondo's introductory book offers a helpful overview of key concepts within the field of STS.
>
> ### Websites
>
> - EASST. https://easst.net
>
> This is the website for the European Association for the Study of Science and Technology (EASST), which includes various resources and access to open-access research articles from the association's journal.
>
> - *How to think about science* (podcast). www.cbc.ca/radio/ideas/how-to-think-about-science-part-1-24-1.2953274
>
> *How to Think about Science* is a podcast series featuring interviews with important figures whose research explores society's intersection with science and technology.
>
> - Somatosphere. http://somatosphere.net
>
> This is a collaborative website offering a regularly updated selection of original and accessible academic content covering the intersections of science and technology studies, medical anthropology, cultural psychiatry, psychology and bioethics.

REFERENCES

Agence France-Press (2018) Samsung apologizes for cancer cases in semiconductor factories. *Al Jazeera*, 23 November. Available at: www.aljazeera.com/news/2018/11/samsung-electronics-apologises-factory-worker-cancer-cases-181123024347676.html (last accessed 7 October 2019).

Akrich, M. (1992) The description of technical objects. In W. Bijker and J. Law (eds) *Shaping Technology/Building Society: Studies in Sociotechnical Change*. Cambridge, MA: MIT Press, pp. 205–24.

Benjamin, R. (2019) *Race After Technology: Abolitionist Tools for the New Jim Code*. Cambridge: Polity Press.

Carr, N. (2008) Is Google making us stupid? Why you can't read the way you used to. *Atlantic Monthly* 302(1): 56. Available at: www.theatlantic.com/magazine/archive/2008/07/is-google-making-us-stupid/306868 (last accessed 7 October 2019).

Dimond, R., Bartlett, A. and Lewis, J. (2015) What binds biosociality? The collective effervescence of the parent-led conference. *Social Science & Medicine* 126: 1–8.

Kuhn, T.S. (1970) *The Structure of Scientific Revolutions*. Chicago: University of Chicago Press.

Latour, B. and Woolgar, S. (1979) *Laboratory Life: The Construction of Scientific Facts*. Princeton, NJ: Princeton University Press.

Lee, M. and Waitzkin, H. (2012) A heroic struggle to understand the risk of cancers among workers in the electronics industry: The case of Samsung. *International Journal of Occupational and Environmental Health* 18: 89–91.

Lim, L. (2018) China's #MeToo censorship bypassed through netizens' creative use of language. *South China Morning Post Magazine*, 2 March. Available at: www.scmp.com/magazines/post-magazine/short-reads/article/2134847/chinas-metoo-censorship-bypassed-through (last accessed 7 October 2019).

Marshall, L. (2015) 'Let's keep music special. F— Spotify': On-demand streaming and the controversy over artist royalties. *Creative Industries Journal* 8(2): 177–89.

Merz, S. and Williams, R. (2018) 'We all have a responsibility to each other': Valuing racialised bodies in the neoliberal bioeconomy. *New Political Economy* 23(5): 560–73.

Morning, A. (2011) *The Nature of Race: How Scientists Think and Teach about Human Difference*. Oakland, CA: University of California Press.

Nelkin, D. and Lindee, M.S. (1995) *The DNA Mystique: The Gene as a Cultural Icon*. New York: WH Freeman & Co.

Nelson, A. (2016) *The Social Life of DNA: Race, Reparations, and Reconciliation after the Genome*. New York: Beacon Press.

Noble, S.U. (2018) *Algorithms of Oppression: How Search Engines Reinforce Racism*. New York: New York University Press.

O'Meara, S. (2012) BIC for her: Sexist biros cause review storm on Amazon. *Huffington Post*, 28 August. Available at: www.huffingtonpost.co.uk/2012/08/28/bic-for-her-sexist-biros-review-storm-amazon_n_1835952.html (last accessed 7 October 2019).

Popper, K. (1963) *Conjectures and Refutations: The Growth of Scientific Knowledge*. Oxford: Routledge.

Rabinow, P. (1996) Artificiality and enlightenment: From sociobiology to biosociality. In *Essays on the Anthropology of Reason*. Princeton, NJ: Princeton University Press.

Weiner, K. and Will, C. (2016) Users, non-users and 'resistance' to pharmaceuticals. In *The New Production of Users*. Oxford: Routledge, pp. 273–96.

Williams, R. (2015) Cords of collaboration: Interests and ethnicity in the UK's public stem cell inventory. *New Genetics and Society* 34(3): 319–37.

Williams, R. (2018) Enactments of race in the UK's blood stem cell inventory. *Science as Culture* 27(1): 24–43.

Winner, L. (1980) Do artefacts have politics? *Daedalus* 109: 121–36.

Zeng, J. (2019) You say #MeToo, I say #MiTu: China's online campaigns against sexual abuse. In B. Fileborn and R. Loney-Howes (eds) *#MeToo and the Politics of Social Change*. London: Palgrave Macmillan, pp. 71–83.

MIGRATIONS

Anna Gawlewicz

LEARNING OBJECTIVES

- To understand human migration in its various forms, and what gets and keeps it going.
- To explore key sociological perspectives on why, how and where people migrate.
- To understand how migrations are shaping contemporary societies and the lives of migrants.
- To enable critical engagement with key sociological concepts and debates concerning migration.

 Framing Questions

1. What is migration?
2. Why do people migrate?
3. How is migration shaping places, societies and individual lives?
4. How can migration be governed globally?

Introduction

In this chapter, you will be able to develop your sociological understanding of human migration in its various forms and guises. We will look at key sociological debates concerning migration, in particular: types of migration, ideas about drivers of migration and motivations to migrate, explanations for why migration is predominantly an urban

PART 5 SOCIOLOGICAL FRONTIERS

issue despite a long history of migration to rural areas, perspectives on 'lived' experience of migration, key concepts and approaches that have shaped how we understand migrations, and migration as a global policy issue.

> ### Mapping the Terrain
>
> ### Developments in the Sociological Study of Migrations
>
> Sociological interest in migration often revolves around:
>
> - Who is a migrant given the variety of personal motivations to migrate and migration experiences on the one hand and legal and political implications of migration on the other. The questions that have been particularly debated are: What is the difference between voluntary and forced migration? Are people who are forced to move against their wish migrants (e.g. refugees, displaced people, victims of trafficking)?
> - Drivers of migration, essentially the underlying structural factors that get migration going and keep it going, and how they interplay with more personal or individual desires and motivations to migrate.
> - Why certain places have attracted more migrants than others, in particular urban locations vis-à-vis small town and rural locations, and how these places have been shaped by historical and contemporary migrations.
> - How the experience of migration is affecting who we are as individuals, especially how moving between places and societies is affecting our values and attitudes, lifestyle, and a sense of identity, belonging and home.
> - The relationship between migration and race, and how the everyday experience of migration may differ fundamentally depending on the ethnicity, religion, class, age, gender and sexuality of each migrant.
> - Migration as a global policy issue given the planetary scale of contemporary migrations. The question that has attracted particular attention is: How might migration be governed collectively?
>
> Human migration is a phenomenon that has been debated and researched across a range of academic disciplines, including anthropology, history, economics, law, sociology, geography and political sciences, among others. Overall, this interdisciplinary scholarship is referred to as migration studies. While in this chapter we will prioritize sociological perspectives on migration, we will also draw upon wider insights in migration studies.

Understanding Contemporary Migration

As of 2020, over 270 million people do not live in the country where they were born, which accounts for around 3.5% of the world's population. This equals the population of Indonesia, the fourth largest country in terms of population size. If we include migrations that take place within single states, this number will be much higher.

While people have always been *on the move*, the pace of migration has accelerated since the 18th century because of industrialization, the slave trade, **colonialism** and political conflicts. The total number of international migrants has grown significantly in the last five decades: from 82 million in the 1970s to 150 million in 2000 to 270 million in 2019, although as a proportion of the world's population it has remained fairly stable (3% in the early 2000s to 3.5% in 2020).

MIGRATIONS

Describing theories, concepts and approaches that can be applied to understanding these migrations could easily form a separate textbook. Given the breadth of this knowledge, in this chapter we focus on the most prevalent, debated or 'new' sociological approaches that relate to migration. These cover different types of migration, the underlying drivers of migration and more personal reasons to migrate, migration to predominantly urban locations vis-à-vis rural migrations, concepts that we can use to theorize how migration is shaping people's lives and everyday experiences, and emerging **migration governance** structures.

What is Migration?

Most of us have a sense of what migration is: we often know somebody who has migrated from 'elsewhere', have a history of migration in our **family** or hear of 'migrants'. In many societies, migration has become one of the hottest and most divisive topics, in particular in relation to policy and politics (e.g. see 'Brexit in the UK'; 'Migration, Brexit and Hostile Environment'; 'European Migration Crisis'). As a result, many people develop 'opinions' about migration or take it for granted, which may lead to myth-making and misconceptions (see Key Case below).

24.1 Key Case

Immigration in the British Media

Media play an important role in shaping and reinforcing opinions about immigration. Recent sociological research (Crawley et al., 2016) shows that in the British media immigrants are often presented as victims (e.g. of inequality, discrimination, political turbulence), villains or a threat to the political and economic security of the UK (e.g. in terms of the availability of jobs, education or health services) as well as those who contribute to UK society. These portrayals differ substantially across UK media outlets, with some being far from accurate and substantiated. In tabloid media, in particular, international migrants tend to be othered (i.e. constructed as inherently different), racialized (i.e. given an imposed racial or ethnic identity) and wrongfully presented as a homogeneous group of people.

Have a look at the tabloid headlines below. How is immigration portrayed? How are migrants othered, racialized and homogenized here? What role does the choice of wording play in this process? (The links between race and immigration are discussed further in Chapter 13.)

'Asylum: You're right to worry' (*Daily Mail*, 7 February 2005)

'Immigrants bring more crime' (*Daily Express*, 17 April 2008)

'Migrants rob young Britons of jobs' (*Daily Express*, 18 August 2011)

'Migrant influx fuels new crisis in schools' (*Daily Mail*, 7 September 2013)

'The "swarm" on our streets' (*Daily Mail*, 31 July 2015)

'Send an army to halt migrant invasion' (*Daily Express*, 30 July 2015)

'7 migrants an hour try to sneak into Britain' (*Daily Express*, 23 March 2016)

Given the contested nature of the political, media and public debate about migration, it is important to start this chapter by defining migration and exploring what it entails. The International Organization for Migration (IOM), a key intergovernmental organization in the field of migration, defines migration as 'the movement of persons away from their place of usual residence, either across an international border or within a **state**' (IOM, 2019: 137). This definition reflects the broadest understanding of migration and is often quoted in sociological research. However, it is worth noting that there are narrower definitions that refer to either different types of migration or differences in disciplinary approaches (e.g. anthropological, economic, legal). Therefore, in attempting to understand migration it is worthwhile exploring its basic types.

Types of Migration

There are three basic typologies that allow greater understanding of the variety of contemporary migrations. They are structured around key questions regarding migration: *why people migrate; where to and from they migrate;* and *how long they intend to stay in the place of destination.*

1. Distinction between voluntary migration and **forced migration** with voluntary migration referring to a movement that is enacted by the persons involved, and forced migration referring to a movement that takes places against people's will, often under the threat of danger, persecution or death. The boundary between voluntary and forced migration is sometimes blurred because people may subjectively feel that they are 'forced' to leave their place of residence for a range of reasons, including severe poverty or lack of job opportunities. What usually falls into the category of forced migration, though, is escaping or being displaced because of an armed **conflict**, persecution, violation of human rights, natural or human-made disaster or **human trafficking**. However, there are ongoing, largely legal, debates as to whether or not people undertaking some of these forms of movement should be considered migrants. The IOM and most contemporary sociologists are of the position that '**migrant**' is an umbrella term inclusive of all forms of movement. It covers **asylum seeker**s, **refugee**s, displaced persons, victims of human trafficking, children separated from guardians, documented and undocumented migrants and students, among others.

24.2 Key Case

Child Refugees: Rifat's Story

'But then [the military] came to my home and said, "You are going to join us to fight" and that time I was hiding myself for one month at home and then my father told me that they had got our neighbour's child, he was 15, he was my age, and then I run away from home. That is what they were telling me. Don't get out of the country until like they didn't have any choice any more. They didn't want me to go but it was for my safety. They take any young children … They force them to join the military to fight with them.' (Rifat, 17, child refugee from Syria)

In 2016, Rifat was 15 and living in the war-ravaged city of Aleppo in Syria with his parents, three sisters (aged 9, 15 and 16) and a younger brother (13). He was targeted for recruitment into an armed group and his parents feared for his life. Many other boys of Rifat's age in the neighbourhood had already been taken from their homes and forced to fight for armed groups.

Rifat said that his family insisted that he would not leave the country and that they would stay together. He spent some time in hiding before his parents decided that he had to leave Syria. Rifat said this was the 'last choice' his family could make to save his life. Rifat's uncle took responsibility for getting him safely out of Aleppo and across the Turkish border.

Rifat, aged 17 when he was interviewed, lives in the UK with a foster family. He has not seen his parents or siblings for about 16 months and has been unable to contact them by phone or text for some time. He does not know whether they are alive or dead; he is waiting to hear from the Red Cross. Every day Rifat moves between grief and hope as he lives with this terrible uncertainty. (Connolly, 2019: 11–12)

This is a true story collected as part of research on child refugees in the UK, commissioned to Dr Helen Connolly by Amnesty International UK, the Refugee Council and Save the Children (2017–18) in support of the aims of the Families Together campaign to expand refugee family reunion rules in the UK. The text in this box has been copied in full from: Connolly, H. (2019) *Without My Family: The Impact of Family Separation on Child Refugees in the UK*. Amnesty International UK, the Refugee Council and Save the Children. Available at: https://resourcecentre.savethechildren.net/library/without-my-family-impact-family-separation-child-refugees-uk

© Amnesty International UK, the Refugee Council and Save the Children. Permission granted by Dr. Helen Connolly.

2. Distinction between international migration and internal migration with international migration referring to a movement of people across state borders, and internal migration referring to a movement within a single state. In both cases, we can further distinguish rural and urban migration, where people move between a rural and an urban location (e.g. large-scale migrations from rural to urban China: Keung Wong et al., 2007), urban to rural migration (e.g. 'urbanites' settling in remote rural Scotland in the UK: Stockdale, 2010) as well as urban to urban and rural to rural migrations.

3. Distinction between permanent/long-term migration and temporary/fixed-term migration. Permanent or long-term migration indicates movement that is intended to last for a long period of time or even the lifetime of the migrant. Temporary or fixed-term migration covers movement that is intended for a limited period of time, a few months or years, usually with an intention to return to the place of origin or move elsewhere. Temporary migrants are, for instance, students, migrant workers or highly-skilled migrants who come to a different city, rural region or country for the duration of their degree or contract. The boundary between these types of migration is often blurred: what starts as fixed-term migration sometimes turns into a permanent one because of changing personal, family or professional circumstances. Likewise, what is intended as long-term migration may be interrupted due to unexpected developments.

A somewhat separate form of migration is **circular migration**, in which people repeatedly move back and forth between two or more places or countries. This often involves seasonal workers, usually agricultural, who come to a rural location repeatedly across a period of time. But it may also involve other groups (e.g. professionals, retirees) or people repeatedly migrating to urban locations.

 Pause for Thought

- Who is a 'migrant'?

According to the IOM, migrant is: 'an umbrella term, *not defined under international law*, reflecting the common lay understanding of a person who moves away from his or her place of usual residence, whether within a country or across an international border, temporarily or permanently, and for a variety of reasons. The term includes a number of well-defined legal categories of people, such as migrant

(Continued)

workers; persons whose particular types of movements are legally defined, such as smuggled migrants; as well as those whose status or means of movement are not specifically defined under international law, such as international students.' (IOM, 2019: 132)

However, note that there is yet no universally accepted definition for 'migrant'. Different state administrations, institutions or organizations may have their own definitions of the term which may not overlap with that of the IOM.

- Why do you think there is no universally accepted definition for 'migrant'? Do we need one?

Why Do People Migrate?

Why people migrate is a central question in **sociology** of migration and one that has been extensively debated. Contemporary sociologists largely agree that decisions to migrate are the outcome of an interplay of structural conditions (external drivers) and individual agency (personal motivations) (Van Hear et al., 2018). Neither structural conditions nor individual agency can explain migration on its own because individual agency is always exercised in the wider context of structural conditions (Bakewell, 2010). Structural conditions can *enable* and *constrain* individual agency. Agency, in turn, is often exercised *in response* to these structural conditions.

Drivers of Migration

Drivers of migration are the structural conditions or 'the factors that get migration going and keep it going once begun' (Van Hear et al., 2018: 928). Historically, poverty was argued to be the key driver of migration. However, since the 1990s, sociologists have increasingly recognized that the poorest usually do not have the resources to migrate (UNDP, 2009). This led to a scholarly debate about the relationship between migration and **development** – referred to as the migration-development nexus (Faist, 2008) – which stipulates that migration is intricately connected to development. Development can both stimulate and discourage migration as well as create inequalities between people and places (De Haas, 2010).

Globalization, environmental change, urbanization and **demographic transformation** are usually mentioned as key global forces that create a context for migration. These processes are likely to lead to economic, political or environmental disparities between societies and places, which may encourage population movements. More direct structural triggers of migration may involve, among others, economic decline (e.g. growing unemployment), worsening socio-political security or disrespect of human rights (e.g. outbreak of war, persecution of ethnic or religious minorities) as well as environmental degeneration (e.g. natural or human-induced disaster). It is also important to mention mediating drivers of migration (Van Hear et al., 2018), essentially the factors that facilitate or constrain population movement such as transportation infrastructure (e.g. low-cost carriers), information and communications **technologies** (e.g. the internet and social media), governmental policies (e.g. **immigration** regime) or pre-existing migrant networks (e.g. the presence of a strong **diaspora** comprising migrants and their descendants whose origin lies elsewhere; see Glossary). (The historical context of migration and mobility is also discussed in Chapter 6.)

MIGRATIONS

Motivations to Migrate

Personal motivations to migrate are individual, subjective reasons for people to move – sometimes intimate, emotional or irrational, at other times aspirational or opportunistic (Carling and Collins, 2018). They are profoundly 'human' motivations and may be complicated, reflecting the many aspects of human nature. These motivations may be economic (e.g. job opportunities), education-related (e.g. an overseas degree) or family-related (e.g. joining a family member) (King and Ruiz-Gelices, 2003; Ryan, 2010). They may be linked to falling in love, a desire to experience an adventure in a different cultural context or an aspiration to start a 'new life' elsewhere (Mai and King, 2009; Suter, 2019). They may also be related to different attitudes and norms in the **country of origin** and destination – for example, in relation to **ethnicity**, religion, gender or sexuality. Finally, they may include a more inclusive legal framework in the **country of destination** (e.g. marriage, childcare and/or adoption rights for same-sex couples) (Akin, 2017).

Importantly, sociologists stress that people may have more than one reason to migrate or many interconnected reasons. For instance, by focusing on lesbian, gay and bisexual migrants to Scotland from Central and Eastern Europe and the former Soviet Union, Stella et al. (2018a, b) show that economic or family motivations may overlap with those regarding sexual identity, public attitudes towards non-normative sexualities and legal solutions regarding same-sex marriage (see Key Cases).

24.3 Key Case

Motivations to Migrate (Sexual Identity and Legal Status): Nadya and Marta's Story

'Marta and I have been together since 2000 after meeting at university in Poland. We decided to move to Scotland in 2005 after finishing our studies. We weren't prepared to hide our sexuality any longer, and so couldn't continue to live in Poland where we often had to pretend we were just friends, where only our close group of friends knew that we were actually in a relationship.

We knew very little about Scotland before moving here. We packed whatever we could and travelled by bus for 45 hours. We didn't decide to move to Scotland for money or jobs – issues to do with sexuality were the main motivation. We heard that in 2005 civil partnership was legalized in Scotland and that's why we chose Scotland. We got our civil partnership in 2009. One of the main reasons we wanted to register our civil partnership was that we were planning to have children at some point, and we wanted our family to be secure in terms of our legal status. We knew that we wanted to have a child and that it would be impossible in Poland. So, we came here. To be honest, we moved to Scotland to be able to start a family, to be together, without having to hide.

Following our son's birth, we were happy to find out that we had the same rights as any other new parents. Both our names are listed on the birth certificate, and we both got parental leave from work to look after our new baby.'

This is a true story collected from research participants of a project about lesbian, gay and bisexual migrants to Scotland led by Dr Francesca Stella (2015–17). The text above has been adapted from interview material and comes from: Stella, F., Campbell, M., Williams, B., MacDougall, J., Liinpää, M. and Speirs, J. (2018) *Engaging with LGBT and Migrant Equalities: A Youth and Community Practitioner Toolkit.* University of Glasgow. Available at: http://eprints.gla.ac.uk/160957

 **Pause for Thought**

- What other personal motivations to migrate can you think of?
- Have you ever thought of migrating to a different place or society?
- What would be the reason(s) for you to migrate?

Migrant Destinations

Migration is a planetary phenomenon and there is no exaggeration in saying that it affects nearly all habitable places on the globe (although in different ways and to a different extent). Statistical data show that some places attract way more migrants than others. Countries with a long-standing history of attracting migrant populations are routinely referred to as countries of **immigration** while countries with a history of people leaving are countries of **emigration**. Countries where migrant populations stop for a period of time before moving further are referred to as **countries of transit**.

Some countries can play two or all of these roles at the same time or at different times. Morocco, for example, has a long history of emigration (people leaving their country of residence) to European destinations, in particular Spain and France, and a more recent history of immigration (settlement of foreign-born population) and transit from sub-Saharan Africa (Baldwin-Edwards, 2006). Poland, historically a country of westward emigration to the United States, the UK or Germany, among others, has recently become a country of immigration with over one million Ukrainian migrants as of 2015 and smaller numbers of Vietnamese and other nationals (White et al., 2018).

Large urban locations with strong economies are also places that have always attracted considerable migrant populations, both international and internal. Let's look at why migration is predominantly an urban issue and what we know about contemporary rural migrations.

Migration as an Urban Issue

You may have guessed that cities attract the majority of migrants. Around 50% of international migrants concentrate in the cities of 10 highly urbanized and high-income countries: Australia, Canada, the US, France, Germany, Spain, the UK, the Russian Federation, Saudi Arabia and the United Arab Emirates (IOM, 2015b). The city with the largest foreign-born population share as of 2015 is Dubai (83%), the second largest – Brussels (62%) and the third – Toronto (46%).

Cities have always attracted 'new' populations and, as such, have intrigued scholars. In sociological research, the relationship between migration and the city is understood to be reciprocal: migration and the city are mutually constitutive and *construct* each other. This means that cities are profoundly impacted by migrants, and migrant lives are profoundly impacted by cities. Sociologists agree that beyond significantly contributing to the city workforce and economy, migrants introduce 'new' cultures, identities and economies and actively take part in urban transformation (Sandercock, 1998; Sassen, 1991). They also make cities more diverse, creative and productive, and contribute to the increase of urbanization (Portes, 2000). Conversely, the cities, their specific histories, cultures, economies, organizations and people, impact on

MIGRATIONS

migrant populations: they not only offer economic, livelihood and development opportunities, but shape migrant settlement, the formation of diaspora as well as migrant identities and sense of belonging (Fong and Berry, 2017) (see 'Migration and the City').

Sociologists also draw attention to challenges that migration to cities brings. While migrants are builders of resilience, city-makers and agents of change, their settlement contributes to population growth, which puts pressure on infrastructure, the local environment and the social fabric of the city (IOM, 2015b). The IOM also emphasizes that migrants are overrepresented among the urban poor. With oftentimes limited resources, they are more likely to settle in urban areas with less access to the job market, suitable accommodation, and health and social services, particularly at an early stage of migration (Zulu et al., 2011).

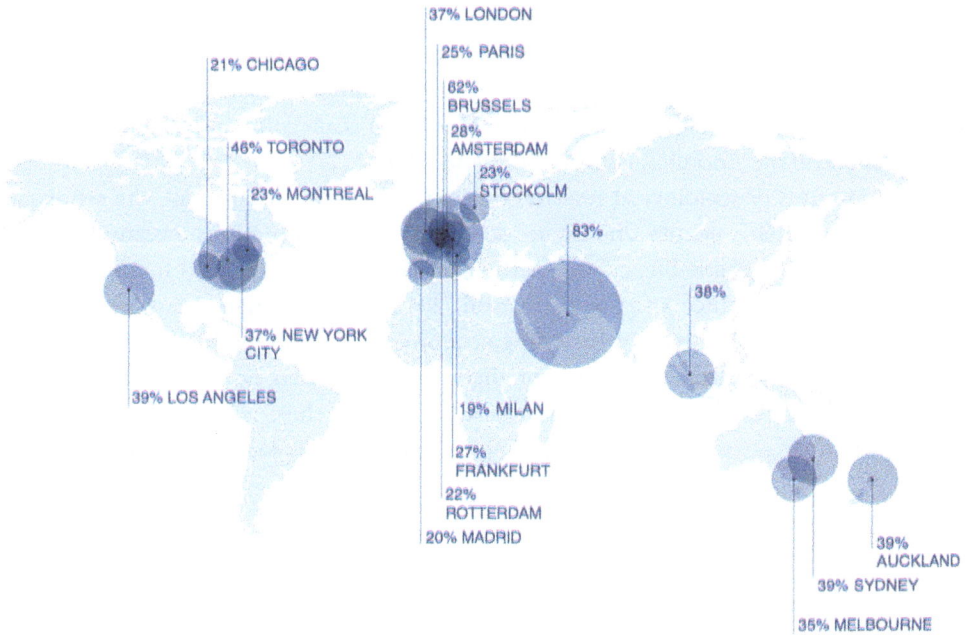

Figure 24.1 Cities with the Largest Foreign-born Population Share

Compiled by IOM from various sources, 2015

Credit: Compiled by IOM from various sources, 2015. IOM's GMDAC 2019 www.migrationdataportal.org

---

Hear from the Expert

Migration and the City

'The urban experiences of new migrants, their struggle to redefine the conditions of belonging to "their" new society are reshaping cities.' (Leonie Sandercock, 1998: 14)

'Migration and the city can be viewed as two sides of the same coin, having built and accompanied each other's development over the centuries leading to the contemporary global system.' (Alejandro Portes, 2000: 154)

Pause for Thought

- Why do you think cities matter to migrants?
- Why do you think migrants matter to cities?
- What challenges and opportunities do you see for migrants in the city, and for the city in the age of migration?

Migration as a Rural Issue

While the majority of migrants settle in urban areas, sociological research shows that rural migrations are not rare. Despite being sometimes constructed as places of imminent departure, rural areas do have a long history of in-migration. These migrations are much smaller in scale compared to urban ones, but may be equally impactful on rural economies, communities and change.

There are a few strands of sociological research on rural migrations. First of all, the scholarship on **lifestyle migration**, whereby people choose to settle in rural destinations because of their arguably slower-paced and more affordable life, as well as their proximity to nature. This includes, for example, the work on British retirees in France and Spain (Benson, 2013). Second, there is a sizable body of work on international migrations to rural regions including economic migration, both seasonal or longer-term (e.g. agricultural workers). An illustrative example of this work is research on Central and Eastern European migrants in rural areas in Scotland (Flynn and Kay, 2017). Finally, there is work related to rural settlement policies, in particular refugee settlement or dispersal, for example the work on Afghan refugees in Australia (Radford, 2016).

Place, Identity, Border and Race: Key Concepts and Approaches in Migration Experience

Over the past few decades, sociologists and migration scholars have developed a number of conceptual frameworks that have challenged how we think about and study migration. Overall, these frameworks conceptualize migration as everyday 'lived' experience: complicated, messy, changeable, embodied and emotional. They put *people* at the centre of migration research: their identities, feelings, values and desires as well as how their experience is shaped by their position in terms of ethnicity, religion, class, sexuality, gender, **age** or disability.

One of the most important concepts in sociological work on migration is **transnationalism**. The term transnationalism is used to describe 'processes by which immigrants forge and sustain multi-stranded social relations that link together their societies of origin and settlement' (Basch et al., 1994: 7). Theoretically progressed in the 1990s, transnationalism is underpinned by an understanding that migrants create 'social fields' that span their country of origin and destination (Levitt and Glick Schiller, 2004). Rather than operating in one of these places at a time, they build their lives, develop ties and social networks *across* or *in-between* them. As an approach, transnationalism allows us to move away from thinking about migration in simplistic terms as a linear, complete move from one geographical location to the other. Transnationalism disrupts this assumption and re-conceptualizes migration as a process that stretches in space and time. An interesting recent example of transnationalism is a study of Sri Lankan migrants in Australia providing care for their **aging** parents in Sri Lanka 'from abroad' (De Silva, 2018).

— Pause for Thought —

- What other examples of transnationalism can you think of?
- In what other ways do migrants maintain ties with the country of origin and the destination at the same time?

Another conceptual framework that has attracted a lot of sociological attention is **integration**. In sociological research, integration implies mutual adaptation by migrants and the long-settled residents (Ager and Strang, 2008). The term integration is contested and has been critiqued for its exclusionary potential and analytical vagueness (Grzymala-Kazlowska and Phillimore, 2018). In particular, sociologists have shown how exclusionary divisions between migrants and the long-settled population can be created under the umbrella frame of integration, and how migrants are those usually assumed to 'adjust'. They have also pointed out that it is unclear what people are supposed to integrate into: local community or wider society – what society specifically? However, critical debates *around* integration have been very productive in better understanding everyday encounters and relationships between migrants and the long-settled populations. They have drawn attention to the complexities of these processes, their profoundly human nature as well as the role of the institutions in facilitating or inhibiting them.

In discussing how the understanding of migration has been shaped in sociological research, it is also crucial to mention the work of **feminist scholars**. Until the 1990s, migration research implicitly put men at the centre of inquiry (Silvey, 2004). Women were largely invisible in this work or treated superficially despite a long history and significance of women's migrations. Feminist scholars have challenged this problematic assumption and focused on gendered dimensions of migration, and diverse migrant subjectivities and identities (Kofman and Raghuram, 2015). They have shown how the experience of migration differs in terms of gender as well as through the intersections of gender with ethnicity, religion, class, sexuality, age and disability (e.g. the experience of young, black, Somali women on the move may be fundamentally different from the experience of white, Norwegian, middle-aged, male migrants). This has revolutionized how sociologists think of migration: as a subjective and bodily experience that is constantly re-negotiated against societal norms and expectations as well as political developments both in the place of origin and the destination (see 'Migration, Brexit and Hostile Environment'). This work has been further nuanced by researchers of queer migrations who have challenged the assumptions of heteronormativity in migration research and focused on the distinctive experiences of LGBT+ migrants (Stella et al., 2018a, b).

Migration, Brexit and Hostile Environment

There is a complex relationship between migration and the UK's withdrawal from the European Union (i.e. Brexit). Immigration was used as one of the key elements in the pro-Brexit campaign unfolded by the right-wing and populist political parties in the run-up to the Brexit referendum (23 June 2016). Immigration was presented as a 'threat' to the British economy and society, and migrants were made scapegoats by being wrongly portrayed as being responsible for the rising unemployment levels. This influenced public attitudes towards immigration and led to a spike in racist and xenophobic violence towards migrants. Both migration and Brexit remain highly divisive topics in British public debates, with strong voices of support and opposition on each side.

The use of immigration in the pro-Brexit campaign and the consequences of Brexit for migrants are also intricately tied to the hostile environment policy. The aim of this policy, introduced in the early 2010s, is to make the UK inhospitable and unwelcoming for migrants in order to reduce overall immigration levels. The hostile environment policy involves dehumanizing practices of surveillance, hostility and discipline (e.g. regular checks of legal status in everyday spaces such as workplaces, schools or hospitals, greater risk of deportation), and has been shown by sociologists to contribute to inequality, injustice and racialization of migrants. (The issue of immigration is also discussed further in Chapter 13.)

Expand Your Knowledge

- To explore the complex relationship between migration and Brexit, watch six bite-sized videos as part of the short online course 'Six Impossible Ideas (After Brexit)' via Migration Matters: http://migrationmatters.me
- To learn more about the hostile environment policy in the UK and what it means for migrants, read: Yuval-Davis, N., Wemyss, G. and Cassidy, K. (2018) Everyday bordering, belonging and the reorientation of British immigration legislation. *Sociology* 52(2): 228–44.

Pause for Thought

- How do you think Brexit is affecting migrants in the UK?
- What are the impacts of hostile environment policies on migrants' everyday lives?

Importantly, alongside these developments, we have seen growing sociological interest in the relationship between migration and race. Sociologists have increasingly called for a rigorous debate about the links between evolving patterns of migration and racial, ethnic and religious diversity, on the one hand, and contemporary forms of **racism** and anti-immigration sentiment, on the other (Erel et al., 2016; Solomos, 2020). These calls have intensified in the first two decades of the 21st century in the context of the global rise of populist ideologies and fear-mongering discourses about minorities and migrants, in particular Muslim communities and asylum seekers following the European migration crisis (see below). Key research in this area has been preoccupied with how migrant populations are being racialized and othered, and how this affects individual migrants, the construction of diaspora and relations between the long-settled and migrant populations. It has shown that the experience of migration is deeply differentiated, hierarchically structured and profoundly unequal along racial and ethnic lines, with white migrants clearly capitalizing on their putative whiteness. A reflection of these hierarchies and racialization of migration more broadly is also an imbalance in debating migration in 'mainstream' academic research in favour of North–North and South–North migration patterns. Less attention has been paid to South–South migrations, despite their significance not least from the purely quantitative point of view (see Hear from the Expert below).

European Migration Crisis

The European migration crisis is a humanitarian crisis involving unprecedented numbers of people arriving in Europe from across the Mediterranean Sea in what is a critically dangerous boat journey. More than a million migrants crossed into Europe in 2015 to seek refuge. This sparked a Europe-wide crisis as countries experienced difficulties in dealing with the volume of in-migration and in finding a common ground about how best to resettle people. Since 2015 nearly 2 million people have arrived and nearly 16,000 are reported to have died while crossing the sea, with many more dying elsewhere (e.g. in detention centres, asylum units, camps) (UNHCR, 2020). Most people who took the journey were escaping armed conflict and/or persecution in Syria, Afghanistan and Iraq, with smaller proportions coming from other countries.

Expand Your Knowledge

- To learn more about the European migration crisis and personal experiences of the newly arrived migrants, read: McMahon, S. and Sigona, N. (2018) Navigating the central Mediterranean in a time of 'crisis': Disentangling migration governance and migrant journeys. *Sociology* 52(3): 497–514.

Hear from the Expert

South–South Migrations

'In 2015, South–South migration exceeded South–North migration by two percentage points, representing 37 per cent of the total international migrant stock. 90.2 million international migrants born in developing countries resided in developing countries in 2015, compared to 82.2 million in 2013.' (IOM, 2015a)

'We observe new patterns in south–south migration that are in need of new analysis ... [which] is also made possible by the very recent availability of new bilateral migration data at a global scale. ... There are good reasons to argue that south–south migration has (still) a number of specific features, to some extent differentiating it from north–north or north–south migration including the role of borders, the migration-conflict nexus, and the issue of regional migration governance.' (De Lombaerde et al., 2014)

Migration as a Global Policy Issue

As a planetary phenomenon which affects many people, countries, institutions and organizations at the same time, international migration is an important global policy issue. There is growing agreement among migration scholars that states and trans-boundary organizations (e.g. the United Nations) should work collectively to govern migration to some degree, for example offer legal protection to people *on the move* who are not yet protected. The sub-field of **migration studies** which looks at this issue in detail is called **migration governance**. Migration governance entails legal norms, laws, policies, organizational structures and processes that regulate state responses to international migration. It is a relatively new area of study and is likely to expand in the future.

In contrast to other global policy fields such as international trade or finance, international migration does not have a coherent governance framework (Betts, 2011). There are many reasons for that, including concerns about state sovereignty, different interests between individual states in relation to migration, the fact that migration may be a contested issue in state politics or that it involves people (as opposed to money or goods). All this makes decision-making in relation to international migration very difficult and time-consuming.

The current migration governance framework is fragmented and complex, with many overlapping and parallel institutions that are spread across different policy fields (e.g. human rights, labour) and levels of governance (Betts, 2011). Different policy categories (e.g. asylum and refugee protection, human trafficking and smuggling, labour migration) are also regulated legally and institutionally to different degrees or not at all. For example, asylum and refugee protection is strongly regulated, but voluntary migration is largely unregulated. So, even though asylum seekers and refugees are usually among the most vulnerable migrants, from the migration governance perspective their rights are better defined than those of voluntary migrants.

The leading global body in the field of migration is the already mentioned International Organisation for Migration (IOM), which promotes humane and orderly migration and international cooperation on migration. But there are other organisations, such as the UN Refugee Agency (UNHCR), the International Labour Organisation (ILO), the World Health Organisation (WHO) and the Global Forum on Migration and Development (GFMD), among others, that also have some responsibility and power.

── Pause for Thought ──

- What should a sustainable migration governance framework look like?
- Why do you think it may be difficult to implement it globally?

CHAPTER SUMMARY

- Migration assumes various forms depending on why people migrate, where to and from, and how long they intend to stay in the place of destination.
- Migration may mean different things to different people, societies and places, and may be experienced in many different ways.

- While migration is predominantly an urban issue, rural migrations are not rare.
- Sociological perspectives on migration help us to think critically about the nature of human mobility, everyday experiences of those *on the move*, their relationships with those who are not, and the role of states and institutions in shaping these experiences and relationships. They allow us to take a look at our own assumptions and taken-for-granted 'myths' about migration.
- Sociology equips us with a set of critical analytical lenses through which to understand and debate migration in its various forms and guises as well as its impacts on people, societies and places.

REVIEW QUESTIONS

1. What are the key forms of migration?
2. What are the underlying drivers of migration and key personal motivations to migrate?
3. Why is migration predominantly an urban issue?
4. What are the key concepts and approaches to understand migration experience?
5. What is migration governance?

Go Further

Books

- De Haas, H., Castels, S. and Miller, M. (2019) *The Age of Migration: International Population Movements in the Modern World*. London: Red Globe Press.

A solid introduction to migration and a great revamp of the Stephen Castels' classic: a must-read.

- Inglis, C., Li, W. and Khadria, B. (2020) *The SAGE Handbook of International Migration*. London: Sage.

A timely go-to handbook with strong disciplinary, theoretical and policy insights from a range of migration experts across the globe.

- Jones, H., Gunaratnam, Y., Bhattacharyya, G., Davies, W., Dhaliwal, S., Forkert, K., Jackson, E. and Saltus, R. (2017) *Go Home? The Politics of Immigration Controversies*. Manchester: Manchester University Press.

An eye-opening intervention asking uncomfortable questions about immigration to the UK: you will not be able to put it down.

Journal Articles

- Castles, S. (2007) Twenty-first century migration as a challenge to sociology. *Journal of Ethnic and Migration Studies* 33(3): 351–71.

(Continued)

A strong disciplinary reading: it will tell you why and how sociology can contribute to the development of migration research.

- McMahon, S. and Sigona, N. (2018) Navigating the central Mediterranean in a time of 'crisis': Disentangling migration governance and migrant journeys. *Sociology* 52(3): 497–514.

A powerful reading on the European migration crisis, drawing upon personal experiences of the newly arrived migrants.

- Yuval-Davis, N., Wemyss, G. and Cassidy, K. (2018) Everyday bordering, belonging and the reorientation of British immigration legislation. *Sociology* 52(2): 228–44.

A thought-provoking reading on the 'hostile environment' policy in the UK and what it means for migrants.

Websites

- Migration: The COMPAS Anthology: http://compasanthology.co.uk

An eclectic collection of how migration is 'touching' people in different ways, encompassing personal reflections, short expert overviews, questions, images and poetry.

- Migration Matters: http://migrationmatters.me

An award-winning educational resource on contemporary migrations and their impacts, including videos, bite-sized courses and commentaries from some of the most renowned migration scholars.

- World Migration Report: www.iom.int/wmr

A free, comprehensive and state-of-the-art report on contemporary migrations published regularly by the International Organization for Migration (IOM). Fully downloadable.

REFERENCES

Ager, A. and Strang, A. (2008) Understanding integration: A conceptual framework. *Journal of Refugee Studies* 21(2): 166–91. DOI: 10.1093/jrs/fen016.

Akin, D. (2017) Queer asylum seekers: Translating sexuality in Norway. *Journal of Ethnic and Migration Studies* 43(3): 458–74. DOI: 10.1080/1369183x.2016.1243050.

Bakewell, O. (2010) Some reflections on structure and agency in migration theory. *Journal of Ethnic and Migration Studies* 36(10): 1689–1708. DOI: 10.1080/1369183x.2010.489382.

Baldwin-Edwards, M. (2006) 'Between a rock and a hard place': North Africa as a region of emigration, immigration & transit migration. *Review of African Political Economy* 33(108): 311–24. DOI: 10.1080/03056240600843089.

Basch, L., Glick Schiller, N. and Szanton Blanc, C. (1994) *Nations Unbound: Transnational Projects, Postcolonial Predicaments and Deterritorialized Nation-States*. Amsterdam: Gordon and Breach.

Benson, M. (2013) *The British in Rural France: Lifestyle Migration and the Ongoing Quest for a Better Way of Life*. Manchester: Manchester University Press.

Betts, A. (2011) Introduction: Global migration governance. In A. Betts (ed.) *Global Migration Governance*. Oxford: Oxford University Press, pp. 1–33.

Carling, J. and Collins, F. (2018) Aspiration, desire and drivers of migration. *Journal of Ethnic and Migration Studies* 44(6): 909–26. DOI: 10.1080/1369183x.2017.1384134.

Connolly, H. (2019) *Without My Family: The Impact of Family Separation on Child Refugees in the UK*. Amnesty International UK, the Refugee Council and Save the Children.

Crawley, H., McMahon, S. and Jones, K. (2016) *Victims and Villains: Migrant Voices in the British Media*. Coventry: Centre for Trust, Peace and Social Relations, Coventry University.

De Haas, H. (2010) Migration and development: A theoretical perspective. *International Migration Review* 44(1): 227–64. DOI: 10.1111/j.1747-7379.2009.00804.x.

De Lombaerde, P., Guo, F. and Neto, H.P. (2014) Introduction to the Special Collection: South–South migrations – What is (still) on the research agenda? *International Migration Review* 48(1): 103–12. DOI: 10.1111/imre.12083.

De Silva, M. (2018) Making the emotional connection: Transnational eldercare circulation within Sri Lankan-Australian transnational families. *Gender, Place & Culture* 25(1): 88–103. DOI: 10.1080/0966369x.2017.1339018.

Erel, U., Murji, K. and Nahaboo, Z. (2016) Understanding the contemporary race–migration nexus. *Ethnic and Racial Studies* 39(8): 1339–60. DOI: 10.1080/01419870.2016.1161808.

Faist, T. (2008) Migrants as transnational development agents: An inquiry into the newest round of the migration–development nexus. *Population, Space and Place* 14(1): 21–42. DOI: 10.1002/psp.471.

Flynn, M. and Kay, R. (2017) Migrants' experiences of material and emotional security in rural Scotland: Implications for longer-term settlement. *Journal of Rural Studies* 52: 56–65. DOI: 10.1016/j.jrurstud.2017.03.010.

Fong, E. and Berry, B. (2017) *Immigration and the City*. London: John Wiley & Sons.

Grzymala-Kazlowska, A. and Phillimore, J. (2018) Introduction: Rethinking integration. New perspectives on adaptation and settlement in the era of super-diversity. *Journal of Ethnic and Migration Studies* 44(2): 179–96. DOI: 10.1080/1369183x.2017.1341706.

International Organization for Migration (IOM) (2015a) *2015 Global Migration Trends: Factsheet*. Geneva: IOM/Global Migration Data Analysis Centre.

IOM (2015b) *World Migration Report 2015: Migrants and Cities, New Partnerships to Manage Mobility*. Geneva: IOM.

IOM (2019) *Glossary on Migration*. Geneva: IOM.

Keung Wong, D.F., Li, C.Y. and Song, H.X. (2007) Rural migrant workers in urban China: Living a marginalised life. *International Journal of Social Welfare* 16(1): 32–40. DOI: 10.1111/j.1468-2397.2007.00475.x.

King, R. and Ruiz-Gelices, E. (2003) International student migration and the European 'Year Abroad': Effects on European identity and subsequent migration behaviour. *International Journal of Population Geography* 9(3): 229–52. DOI: 10.1002/ijpg.280.

Kofman, E. and Raghuram, P. (2015) *Gendered Migrations and Global Social Reproduction*. London: Springer.

Levitt, P. and Glick Schiller, N. (2004) Conceptualizing simultaneity: A transnational social field perspective on society. *International Migration Review* 38(3): 1002–39.

Mai, N. and King, R. (2009) Love, sexuality and migration: Mapping the issue(s). *Mobilities* 4(3): 295–307. DOI: 10.1080/17450100903195318.

Portes, A. (2000) Immigration and the metropolis: Reflections on urban history. *Journal of International Migration and Integration/Revue de l'integration et de la migration internationale* 1(2): 153–75.

Radford, D. (2016) 'Everyday otherness': Intercultural refugee encounters and everyday multiculturalism in a South Australian rural town. *Journal of Ethnic and Migration Studies* 42(13): 2128–45. DOI: 10.1080/1369183x.2016.1179107.

Ryan, L. (2010) Transnational relations: Family migration among recent Polish migrants in London. *International Migration* 49(2): 80–103. DOI: 10.1111/j.1468-2435.2010.00618.x.

Sandercock, L. (1998) *Towards Cosmopolis: Planning for Multicultural Cities*. London: John Wiley & Sons.

Sassen, S. (1991) *The Global City: New York, London, Tokyo*. Princeton: Princeton University Press.

Silvey, R. (2004) Power, difference and mobility: Feminist advances in migration studies. *Progress in Human Geography* 28(4): 490–506. DOI: 10.1191/0309132504ph490oa.

Solomos, J. (2020) Racism and the age of super-diversity. In C. Inglis, W. Li and B. Khadria (eds) *The SAGE Handbook of International Migration*. London: Sage, pp. 538–51.

Stella, F., Campbell, M., Williams, B., MacDougall, J., Liinpää, M. and Speirs, J. (2018a) *Engaging with LGBT and Migrant Equalities: A Youth and Community Practitioner Toolkit*. Glasgow: University of Glasgow.

Stella, F., Flynn, M. and Gawlewicz, A. (2018b) Unpacking the meanings of a 'normal life' among lesbian, gay, bisexual and transgender Eastern European migrants in Scotland. *Central and Eastern European Migration Review* 7(1): 55–72.

Stockdale, A. (2010) The diverse geographies of rural gentrification in Scotland. *Journal of Rural Studies* 26(1): 31–40. DOI: 10.1016/j.jrurstud.2009.04.001.

Suter, B. (2019) Migration as adventure: Swedish corporate migrant families' experiences of liminality in Shanghai. *Transitions: Journal of Transient Migration* 3(1): 45–58. DOI: 10.1386/tjtm.3.1.45_1.

United Nations Development Programme (UNDP) (2009) *Human Development Report. Overcoming Barriers: Human Mobility and Development*. New York: UNDP.

United Nations High Commissioner for Refugees (UNHCR) (2020) *Mediterranean Situation*. Refugee situations: Operational Portal. Geneva: UNHCR. Available at: http://data2.unhcr.org/en/situations (last accessed 30 May 2021).

Van Hear, N., Bakewell, O. and Long, K. (2018) Push-pull plus: Reconsidering the drivers of migration. *Journal of Ethnic and Migration Studies* 44(6): 927–44. DOI: 10.1080/1369183x.2017.1384135.

White, A., Grabowska, I., Kaczmarczyk, P. and Slany, K. (2018) *The Impact of Migration on Poland: EU Mobility and Social Change*. London: UCL Press.

Zulu, E.M., Beguy, D., Ezeh, A.C., Bocquier, P., Madise, N.J., Cleland, J. and Falkingham, J. (2011) Overview of migration, poverty and health dynamics in Nairobi City's slum settlements. *Journal of Urban Health* 88(2): 185–99. DOI: 10.1007/s11524-011-9595-0.

SOCIAL MOVEMENTS

Nick Crossley

LEARNING OBJECTIVES

- To develop a rich and nuanced understanding of what social movements are.
- To acquire an understanding of their sociological importance and dynamics.
- To explore some of the factors which sociological research has shown to be important to their mobilization.

 Framing Questions

1. What are social movements?
2. Why do they form when and where they do?
3. What are the most influential movements today?
4. What might prominent movements reveal about the structure of society?

Introduction

Social movements are an important and often very visible part of most societies across the world today. At the time of writing, the pro-democracy movement in Hong Kong is several months into a campaign against encroaching Chinese involvement in the region's affairs. The TV news in Britain has featured almost nightly updates about their demonstrations and the increasingly violent clashes with police they have attracted. Here in Manchester, meanwhile, the environmental group, Extinction Rebellion, has just begun a projected four-day occupation and blockade of a central trunk road in the city. The people involved in the group are protesting about what they claim is a failure of political leaders, including Manchester's local MPs and councillors, to take sufficient action to tackle our climate emergency. (The role of the environment in sociology is discussed further in Chapter 3.)

Sociology has both studied and been shaped by social movements since its inception. Marx's writings were inspired by and sympathetic to the growing labour movement of his day, for example, and his reflections on revolution and class consciousness were an attempt to explain and make sense of it. Later, as the Western world staggered victorious but wounded from the defeat of fascism in the mid-20th century, sociologists were more inclined to perceive danger in social movements, but this once again generated enthusiasm for their study. It was important to understand 'the crowd' and its tendencies, lest they become gripped by another destructive ideology, akin to fascism.

At this same time, however, a movement was emerging that would have a profound effect on social movement studies: the black civil rights movements in the USA. Several key studies focus upon this movement and it served to shift perceptions of social movements from 'danger' to 'progressive force'. Moreover, it was succeeded in the political limelight, during 'the sixties', by a succession of movements which many sociologists, if not directly involved in, were at least sympathetic to: for example, feminism, environmentalism and pacifism. Some of these movements, most obviously feminism, impacted directly on the practice of sociology. In addition, along with the civil rights movements, they prompted a paradigm shift in the sociological approach to movements.

Ideas have continued to evolve, of course. New theories have been proposed and fresh questions raised. However, for all of its internal tensions and debates, social movement studies remains a relatively cohesive (and very big) area of sociological study, centred upon that thread of debate instigated in the wake of 'the sixties' and the preceding civil rights struggle. For this reason, and because I find it both interesting and a useful device for explaining important ideas, I will structure much of my discussion around this paradigm shift.

I will focus upon two key questions: *(1) What are social movements? (2) How do they form?* Social movement scholars address other questions besides these in their work, but these two questions have been very important and the answers to them that we will consider often provide the basis upon which further questions are raised and addressed.

 — Pause for Thought

- What movements are hitting the headlines at your time of reading this chapter?
- What are these movements campaigning about and doing?
- Have you ever been involved in a social movement?
- What did your involvement entail?

Mapping the Terrain

What is a Social Movement?

As with most key concepts in sociology, the definition of social movements is subject to debate and disagreement. However, major protest events, such as the afore-mentioned Manchester protest, provide a useful starting point. A single event probably wouldn't qualify as a movement for most people. However, this is one of several such actions organized by Extinction Rebellion, and Extinction Rebellion are just one of several groups, past and present, campaigning on environmental issues. A network of successive and sometimes simultaneous protests probably would constitute a social movement for most sociologists.

To talk of a 'network' here is to suggest that the protests in question are connected. A succession of protests in itself does not constitute a movement if there is no connection between them. How might protests be connected? Minimally, their connection might involve a flow of influence. Later protests might be inspired by earlier ones, for example borrowing claims, techniques (of protesting and organizing) and rhetoric from them, such that they are about the same thing, adopt a similar perspective upon it and such that particular slogans, chants, banners and symbols recur across them. We would expect to find a shared, collective identity, moreover, with participants identifying themselves as participants in a common movement and classifying themselves in the same way (as environmentalists, feminists, etc.).

--- Expand Your Knowledge ---

- To learn more about social movement networks, read: Krinsky, J. and Crossley, N. (2015) Social networks and social movements: An introduction. *Social Movement Studies* 13(1): 1–21.
- To learn more about collective identity, read: Fominaya, C. (2010) Collective identity in social movements. *Sociology Compass* 4(6): 393–404.

In many cases, moreover, we would expect to find a stronger connection. Participants in simultaneous protests are usually in communication, for example agreeing to coordinate their efforts, as the participants in any single protest do. Marchers do not just happen to turn up at the same place on the same day. Their actions are coordinated within communication networks. Likewise, a succession of protests is usually connected by the common involvement of a core of protestors who participate in most, if not all, of them. Communication links and serial participants are most often the reason why we find similar elements across different protest events (Edwards, 2014). They facilitate a flow of ideas, information, instructions, and so on, which combine individual protests into a single, (loosely) coordinated and organized whole: a movement.

Parallel to our network of protest events, the above discussion suggests, we have a network of protestors involved in, and in some cases organizing, those events. The protestors are linked by their common participation in many of the same events but, in addition, key participants will often know one another from planning meetings, debating fora (on-and off-line) and, as I will discuss further below, various less formal contexts of interaction. Embedded within these networks, moreover, we typically find 'social movement organizations' (SMOs), such as Extinction Rebellion. Definitions of SMOs vary. Some define them narrowly, as formal organizations with bureaucratic structures, but I prefer a broader definition which encompasses a variety of organizational forms, including some which are loose and informal. Some might be very large membership and subscription organizations which millions of people join, usually for a fee. Others might be small informal cells of activists who decide upon what they will do and do it without involving anybody else. And there are many variations between. Even the big subscription SMOs tend to centre upon a relatively small core of activists, however, who either engage in high-profile actions on behalf of the larger group, funded by their subscription fees, and/or undertake the organizational work required for mass demonstrations. Hundreds of thousands of people can march through a big city and size is important for such protests. The bigger the better. However, hundreds of thousands of people cannot attend a planning meeting, collectively deciding how the march will

(Continued)

go and allocating organizational roles between themselves. This is better left to a smaller team who make the decisions and then try to mobilize as many people as they can for the march.

There may be several SMOs within the same movement and they are often linked within a network too. For example, they often share members and may cooperate and coordinate their efforts in common campaigns. However, as I discuss further below, they must often compete for the available support and other resources, and they typically disagree about such matters as the exact causes of the problems they are addressing and the tactics and strategies they deem appropriate to tackling them.

 Pause for Thought

- What are the main SMOs that you are aware of?
- Are they membership organizations that you can join and pay a subscription to?
- What movements do they belong to?

The discussion so far has focused upon protest. However, an influential movement theorist, Alberto Melucci (1989), was famously very critical of what he perceived to be the exclusive focus of social movement scholars upon protest. Whilst agreeing that protest is an important part of what most movements do, Melucci argued that it is only one of the things that they do and that much of the time activists, as activists, are involved in other activities: for example, debating ideas, planning and organizing events, fundraising but also socializing (and thereby strengthening the bonds between them), forging a collective identity and often carving out alternative spaces where they can experiment with social practices and lifestyles in ways which prefigure the social changes they would like to see in wider society. Feminists might be involved in consciousness raising, for example, or running shelters for victims of domestic abuse; animal rights activists might run vegan food shops and cafes; and many activists are involved in 'social centres', which in various ways support individuals wishing to live an alternative lifestyle. Protests are spikes in movement activity, for Melucci, which bring them into the public eye, but much of the time movements are 'submerged networks' centred around much less dramatic and less visible activity. The social movements Melucci studied were alternative communities, often based in squats, which they fashioned in accordance with their political ideals.

Expand Your Knowledge

Alberto Melucci (1943–2001)

- Influential Italian social movement analyst.
- A 'new social movement' theorist (see below).
- Interested in the underground networks that activists often belong to, which sustain their commitment and shape their identity between protest events.
- Suggests that the frameworks of meaning and identity generated by such networks are integral to the importance and effect of movements.

Further reading: Melucci, A. (1989) *Nomads of the Present*. London: Radius.

SOCIAL MOVEMENTS

Submerged networks and their activities are no less important than the more dramatic protests, according to Melucci. Indeed, they are a precondition of them. In part, this is for reasons we have already covered. Submerged networks, in the form of SMOs, plan and organize protest. No less importantly, however, they form the context in which movement-related identities and outlooks are formed and maintained, alongside commitment to the cause. Participants politicize one another, support one another when the going gets tough and dissuade 'defection' back to the status quo. They help to maintain what, in the context of wider society, might be regarded and negatively sanctioned as a deviant perspective on the world. Such activities are seldom planned in the way that a protest is planned. They evolve as a consequence of interaction between activists. However, they are no less important for that.

Pause for Thought

- Are you aware of any alternative movement communities existing close to where you live?
- Is their collective identity expressed by way of visible markers, such as clothing, which makes them stand out?
- In what ways does their lifestyle differ from yours?

Few sociologists would disagree with Melucci but his work raises a further question: is protest necessary to the definition of a social movement? Would a network involved only in the kinds of alternative activity identified by Melucci and never engaging in explicit protest count as a social movement? The work of another leading movement thinker, Charles Tilly, suggests not (see Tilly and Wood, 2012). Tilly puts social movements in historical perspective, arguing that though political contention is ubiquitous across human societies, it began to take on a specific form, adopting a specific repertoire of activities, in Western Europe during the 19th century, in response to wider social and political changes in those societies. It is this form, which centres on protest activities directed at political elites and which subsequently spread to other societies outside of Western Europe, which he identifies with social movements. The social movement is a historical invention, for Tilly, a particular way of organizing to achieve political influence and air grievances, and protest is integral to it. 'Repertoires of contention', as Tilly calls them, have continued to evolve since the 19th century – the advent of 'hacktivism' and other online forms of protest being an obvious recent example – but within parameters established at that time which maintain the basic form of what we know as social movements. Collectives which do not protest fall outside of these parameters and are therefore not social movements.

Hear From the Expert

Charles Tilly (1929–2008)

- Influential US movement analyst.
- Pioneered historical-sociological research on movements.
- Devised numerous important analytic concepts, including 'repertoires of contention'.
- Argued that the social movement is a historically specific means of pursuing collective grievances.

Further reading: Tilly, C. and Wood, L. (2012) *Social Movements 1768–2012*. London: Routledge.

I do not have the space to fully debate this issue but I will make three arguments, two directly in support of Tilly and one which considers a downside before coming round to his position. First, pragmatically, if the concept of social movements is to have any meaning and the field of social movement studies any coherence then we need a relatively clear and tight definition. Tilly gives us that. This doesn't detract from Melucci's observations or preclude analysis of submerged networks and their practices. It simply suggests that such networks only count as social movements if their participants *also* engage in protest. This begs the further question of how we should define protest, but I will dodge that one for present purposes. Second, Tilly's claim that social movements are historical inventions demands historical and cross-cultural sensitivity from us, warning us against unwarranted universalization. It suggests, in an almost Durkheimian fashion (for more detailed discussion about Durkheim, see Chapters 5, 7, 8 and 26), that social movements are phenomena found in some societies but not others (they are 'social facts'), such that social movement theory is appropriate to the analysis of some societies but perhaps not others. These are important demands and suggestions which keep our reflections and analyses disciplined and sociological.

My hesitation with respect to the criteria that Tilly suggests is that so much in social life seems amenable to the concepts and forms of analysis which social movement scholars have forged. I borrowed from social movement studies in a study of the birth of punk music in the UK, for example, and in subsequent work on wider 'music worlds' (Crossley, 2015). Social movements are forms of collective action but so too is art, as Howard Becker (1982) has argued. Indeed, I would suggest that society itself, and everything in it, is collective action. This makes social movement studies an extremely fertile area for sociology. There is plenty which specialists in other areas may wish to borrow. It also underlines my first point, above, however. It would be easy to embrace large parts of the social world under the heading 'social movements' but not very helpful. It is better to define social movements narrowly, following Tilly, whilst acknowledging parallels in other domains and the consequent potential for mutual learning between social movement studies and other sociological specialisms.

As a postscript to this discussion, it is important to acknowledge that whilst all social movements involve 'submerged networks' of some description, they do not necessarily involve the alternative communities to which Melucci refers, and even where such communities do exist there are usually much larger networks of ordinary participants in a social movement who do not belong to them. Like major protests, alternative communities are amongst the more visible aspects of social movements – the tip of a much bigger and generally less colourful iceberg.

What then are social movements? They are networks of individuals, SMOs and their activities, including (necessarily) but not restricted to protest activities, which coalesce around a set of shared concerns and issues, are distinguished by a shared collective identity and repertoire, and which seek to influence social and political life.

How and Why Do Social Movements Form?

An interesting way into these questions is by way of the aforementioned **paradigm** shift in social movement studies. In the 1970s, a new wave of young sociologists, many of whom had been involved in the movements of the 1960s, sought to challenge the then prevailing 'collective behaviour' approach. Their portrayal of this approach, which comprised three key points, was a caricature in my view which masked variety and many insights, but it provides a useful way of structuring our discussion. I will take each of their points in turn.

Strain

The collective behaviour approach, as its critics portrayed it, understood movement formation and mobilization as a direct response to '**structural strains**' in society and the hardships particular groups experience as a result of them. This is problematic in the view of some critics because historical studies find no correlation between worsening socio-economic conditions and movement mobilization, as one would expect if strain were the cause of mobilization. The amount and scale of protest in a society often remain the same during periods of economic decline and sometimes rise as economic conditions improve. Other critics have argued that strain and hardship cannot explain protest and mobilization because they are ever present whilst protest and movement formation are sporadic. A **variable**, it was argued, cannot be explained by reference to a constant.

Expand Your Knowledge

The Collective Behaviour Approach

- Retrospectively defined (and caricatured) by later critics.
- According to the caricature, advocates explained the rise of social movements as an irrational response to increased social strain on behalf of a mass of poorly socially integrated individuals.
- Whilst there is no smoke without fire, thinkers associated with this theoretical camp were often much more subtle and sophisticated in their thinking than the caricature suggests, and many of the analytic themes they raised have been resurrected by the critics of their critics.

Further reading: Smelser, N. (2011) *The Theory of Collective Behaviour*. New Orleans, LA: Quid Pro Books.

This criticism is itself problematic for three reasons. First, researchers in the collective behaviour tradition did not typically focus upon objective strain and hardship, such as might be captured by the economic indicators used by their critics, but rather subjective or intersubjective strain and hardship caused by a mismatch between expectations and reality. People will often accept extreme hardship if they are used to it and have come to expect it. However, even quite comfortable conditions can provoke protest if they fall short of what is expected. From this point of view, rising expectations are as likely a cause of movement mobilization as declining living conditions, and improving living conditions can trigger protest if they fail to keep pace with such expectations. This may be why we sometimes see a spike in protest during economic upturns: because expectations rise more quickly than tangible benefits and well-being.

E.P. Thompson's (2010) notion of 'moral economy', which has been revisited in a number of recent studies, builds upon this idea by suggesting that it is not hardship per se that mobilizes protest but rather the perception that it is unjust and a consequence of the choices of others. Jasper's (2018) notion of 'moral shock' makes a similar point. It is not so much hardship which provokes mobilization as affronts to normative and ethical convictions. Relatedly, some scholars focus upon blame attribution. In a classic study, McAdam (1999) argues that the black civil rights movement in the US was mobilized, amongst other things, by a cultural shift away from self-blame and perceived helplessness within the black community, towards a critical focus upon the structures of a white-dominated society.

Expand Your Knowledge

- To learn more about 'moral economy', read: Ibrahim, J. (2014) The moral economy of the UK student protest movement 2010-2011. *Contemporary Social Science* 9(1): 79-91.
- To learn more about moral shocks and emotion in movements, read: Jasper, J. (2014) Constructing indignation: Anger dynamics in protest movements. *Emotion Review* 6(3): 208-13.

A further nuance which the critics of the collective behaviour approach failed to appreciate was the distinction which some made between 'strains' and 'triggers'. Longstanding hardships and strains often fail to result in mobilization, according to Neil Smelser (2011), a key figure in the collective behaviour tradition, because they can be diffuse and even abstract within people's experience. It is difficult for people to point to the problem and therefore mobilize against it. Mobilization often requires a shocking event which crystallizes and symbolizes underlying strains. A death in police custody, for example, might symbolize a more general tension in relations between the police and a particular community, whilst the misbehaviour of an individual politician may symbolize the corruption of a whole regime. Strain and trigger work together in this account. Trigger events serve to make underlying strains concrete, such that people are able to mobilize against them, but those events take on the significance that they do because they are symbols of underlying strains. Responses to a trigger may seem disproportionate to outside observers but that is because people are not only responding to the event but also expressing their wider frustration and anger at the underlying strain that it symbolizes.

 Pause for Thought

- Can you recall any events in recent history which have triggered protest and/or movement formation?
- Might these events have symbolized underlying strains?
- What underlying strains?

Trigger events have made their way back into the vocabulary of social movement researchers. However, reflecting the positive work of the critics of the collective behaviour approach, there is greater recognition of their mediation by SMOs. In the extreme, this may be a matter of staging. Perhaps the most famous trigger event in recent Western movement history is Rosa Parks' refusal to give up her seat to a white person on a bus, which triggered the Montgomery Bus Boycott, galvanizing the black civil rights movement in the US during the 1950s. The events of that day and the **racism** it revealed were real. Parks did refuse to give up her seat. The driver did notify the police and she was arrested. However, the situation was not quite as spontaneous as it might at first seem. Parks had refused to give up her seat before and there is some evidence that on this occasion her refusal was intended to give the key civil rights SMO, the National Association for the Advancement of Coloured People (NAACP), of which she was the local secretary, occasion to mobilize a boycott. Moreover, there is at least some evidence that other NAACP members had advance notice of this and were ready to respond.

Short of staging, SMOs may also play a role in bestowing meaning and symbolic value on events. We may need a little help from environmental SMOs, for example, if we are to experience extreme weather events as signs of global warming and feel moved to respond by lending them our support. There has been a great deal of work on the 'meaning work' that SMOs do in recent years, much of which draws upon Goffman's (1986) concept of '**framing**'. SMOs strive to win our support and other resources, not least donations, by attempting to frame the way in which we perceive events and actions, including their own.

Expand Your Knowledge

- To learn more about framing, read: Benford, R. and Snow, D. (2000) Framing processes and social movements. *Annual Review of Sociology* 26: 611–39.
- To learn more about trigger events, read: Cheng, E. and Chan, W-Y. (2017) Explaining spontaneous occupation. *Social Movement Studies* 16(2): 222–39.

The final problem with criticizing collective behaviour theory for its strain-response model is that many collective behaviour theorists have identified strains and hardship as only one amongst a number of factors leading to mobilization. Collective behaviour theorists were no more persuaded than their critics that strain or hardship alone suffices to mobilize social movements. Many other factors have been identified over the years. Here I will briefly discuss three.

The first is resources. 'Resource mobilization' theorists in particular have argued that protests and campaigns require resources. Most protests require some resources, including placards, banners, transport to and from demonstrations, legal support, not to forget the expertise and a great deal of time and effort on behalf of organizers, who may need to be paid. This can make levels of protest dependent upon levels of affluence in a society (explaining why protest sometimes increases as economic conditions improve). It also means that strains and hardship are more likely to generate protest when they attract resources, either via donations or the patronage of elites. Disadvantaged groups who fail to attract the sympathy and therefore resources of more affluent others may struggle to mount effective protests and campaigns.

Expand Your Knowledge

Resource Mobilization Theory

- An early challenger to the collective behaviour approach.
- Suggested that grievances are ubiquitous but only give rise to protest and social movements when their proponents have the necessary resources to mount a challenge.
- Suggested that SMOs (even within the same movement) often compete for resources.
- Some advocates highlighted the importance of (political) entrepreneurs who can 'make things happen' in return for the rewards this brings them.
- Most advocates subscribe to a form of 'rational choice theory'.

Further reading: Zald, M. and McCarthy, J. (2017) *Social Movements in an Organisational Society*. London: Routledge.

Given that the resources available for protest within a society at any point in time are finite and usually scarce, this tends to result in competition between SMOs. Zald and McCarthy (2017) argue that competition manifests at three levels: (1) individual SMOs within a movement, such as environmentalism, feminism or pacifism, compete with one another for resources and support; for example, Extinction Rebellion must compete with other environmental SMOs for the support and resources of the general public; (2) movements themselves are in competition, such that feminism's gain might be environmentalism's loss, and so on; and (3) the 'social movement sector' itself is in competition with the public, private and voluntary sectors; for example, high taxation may dissuade people from donating any more of their money to a good cause, to the detriment of social movement activity, whilst the lure of consumer items might reduce their willingness and capacity to donate. Everybody has limited time, effort, money etc. to invest in activities and a range of options for where to invest. If they are to succeed then SMOs need to ensure that a good proportion of these resources flow their way.

 Pause for Thought

- Can you think of a movement which involves competing SMOs?
- How do these SMOs differ?
- Do any of these SMOs appeal to you more than the others?
- If so, why?

Another much discussed precipitating factor for protest is '**political opportunity structure**'. In a nutshell, the argument is that activists and other potential participants are much more likely to protest and campaign when they believe they are likely to succeed, which is in turn more likely when they perceive weakness in the power structure of their society. This argument tends to work best in relation to the toppling of repressive regimes. The uprisings which bring down such regimes sometimes seem to be triggered by gestures towards liberalization on behalf of the regime and the argument is that these gestures signal to campaigners that the regime is vulnerable, encouraging them to risk overt protest.

Opportunity structures may also be involved in '**cycles of contention**'. The idea here is that we periodically observe phases in a society's history where various movements mobilize in quick succession and general levels of protest rise. One explanation for such cycles is that 'early risers', at least if they achieve any degree of success, signal to others that protest can be effective, thereby encouraging those others to pursue their own grievances by these means. The Arab Spring of 2011 provides an international example of this. An apparently successful uprising in Tunisia triggered similar uprisings across a number of countries in North Africa and the Middle East, and it is reasonable to assume that one factor behind this spread was the perception that it could be done; that protest was possible in an authoritarian context and could make a difference. Within a national society, there may also be an element of competition in these inter-movement dynamics. Participants in one movement may feel pressed to pursue their own grievances more forcefully if they perceive other movements to be achieving advantages by doing so. They don't want to be left behind and may fear that the available opportunities are being 'used up' by others.

The political opportunities argument is that perceived 'softness' on behalf of governments and other elites can precipitate **conflict**. However, some have also argued the contrary case; that responses to protest and political dissent which are perceived to be too harsh can amplify that protest and dissent and become an object of protest in their own right. We are back to trigger events to some extent but they are worth raising again both because they illuminate another side to the political opportunity argument and because they introduce a further important theme in relation to movements and protest: temporality and process (see also Gillan, 2020). Movements and SMOs each evolve through time as an effect of interaction both internally and with external actors. What happens at one point in time affects what happens at the next. The Hong Kong protests mentioned at the start of this chapter illustrate these points. Aggressive policing of early protests became an issue in its own right, for example causing a shock which drew more people into the protests. In addition, the hostilities that ensued apparently persuaded the protesters of the dangers of Chinese control such that the protests continued even after the government had backed down with respect to the proposed law which provoked the original protests. The focus of the protest changed as a consequence of events as they unfolded – although of course it is probably also true to say that the specific law which provoked the early protests was only a trigger event and that the threat of Chinese control was the strain underlying the protests all along.

One final point about strain: it is interesting because it links social movements to broader conceptions of society and more general social theories. Classical **Marxism**, for example, argued that capitalist societies are characterized by a tension in social relations (a strain) between the bourgeoisie and the proletariat, which has generated a workers movement and will lead to revolutionary transformation of society. Marxism characterizes the whole of society in terms of this divide, predicting social change and explaining many further aspects of **social structure** by reference to it. Writing in the aftermath of the 1960s, theorists of so-called 'new social movements' argued that **capitalism** had adapted to contain and defuse the strains identified by Marx, incorporating the labour movement, but that all 'advanced' societies (which they characterized in a variety of ways) were now beset with further strains highlighted by the environmental, feminist and peace movements, amongst others. Society had changed, they argued, but it was still founded upon problematic fault lines which provoked social movement mobilization, making social movements, again, a key to deciphering the nature of society. Things have moved on again since these debates but there is still a tendency amongst some social movement scholars, particularly when protest levels are high, to track movements back to strains and to use these strains as a starting point for thinking about the type of society we live in.

──────────── Expand Your Knowledge ────────────

New Social Movements

- Marx famously suggested that the labour movement sprung from a central tension within society and would bring about a revolutionary transformation of it.
- However, the apparent political incorporation of the labour movement and the simultaneous growth of such movements as feminism, pacifism and environmentalism during the latter part of the 20th century persuaded some that society, its central tensions and key social movements had all changed.
- Key advocates of this approach included Alain Touraine, Jürgen Habermas and Alberto Melucci.
- Initially, this was a distinctly European interest which contrasted with the more analytic approach to social movement studies favoured in the US, but over time the two camps converged.

- Critics of the approach have often argued that there was little new about the movements of the late 20th century and the 21st has seen a resurgence of labour-related movements, but the theories of new social movements remain a rich reservoir of ideas all the same.

Further reading: Edwards, G. (2014) *Social Movements and Protest.* Cambridge: Cambridge University Press (see Chapter 5, 'From Old to New Social Movements').

Reason, Emotion and Identity

The second claim which the critics of the collective behaviour approach made against it was that it portrayed mobilization as an irrational outburst of emotion which, because irrational, oversimplifies both problems and solutions. Against this, the critics argued that protest and mobilization are **rational**. Interestingly, however, many adopted a definition of rationality which made their task more difficult than it might at first sound: a rational choice model which defines rationality as the capacity to select efficient and effective means for realizing one's goals and, importantly, which assumes those goals to be narrowly self-interested. Explaining protest and other forms of collective action is not straightforward with this model because of what Mancur Olson (1971) called 'the **free-rider problem**'.

Protest, Olson argues, typically pursues '**public goods**'; that is, goods which everybody within a community or social group benefits from, whether or not they contribute to securing them. All women got the vote as a consequence of suffragist and suffragette campaigning, for example, whether or not they took part in the campaigning. Likewise, we all stand to benefit from measures intended to halt global warming, whether or not we campaign for those measures. Given that the benefit is the same whether or not one incurs the costs (e.g. time and effort) of participation, Olson continues, the rational individual will sit back and let others do the work, taking a 'free ride' on their efforts. As everybody is assumed to be rational, however, the result of this will be that nobody protests.

The idea sounds implausible because we know that people, sometimes in significant numbers, do protest. The point, however, is to encourage the researcher to look for the conditions which make participation beneficial and therefore rational. I return to one key suggestion, concerning **network**s, later. Presently, however, note that much of the early work on SMOs engages with this question. Crudely put, the argument is that a small number of people might be motivated to do the lion's share of the work involved in protest if sufficiently rewarded, both symbolically and materially, by everyone else. And everyone else might be incentivized to make a small (usually financial) contribution if rewarded in ways only available to those who contribute. The promise of a button badge demonstrating my commitment to a good cause and thereby raising my esteem amongst friends and colleagues might just be enough to persuade me to make a small donation, for example, and if enough people make a small donation that might be sufficient to fund a team of relatively well-paid professional campaigners, who will also benefit from an elevated status as high-profile campaigners.

The free-rider problem has also generated some interest in the intrinsic rewards of activism. The sense of solidarity often generated on a protest can be both exciting and fulfilling; for example, involvement in submerged networks can be a source of friendship and **social capital**, and 'doing good' can bestow a sense of purpose and satisfaction. Note that these are 'selective benefits', only available to those who participate directly and additional to the public goods enjoyed by all. Participation in protests and movements might just be 'rational' after all!

 —— Pause for Thought ——

- Is the free-rider problem genuine in your view?
- Do you believe that political participation is shaped by (non-political) considerations of personal cost and benefit?
- Why do some people participate in movements rather than free riding on the efforts of others?

Rational choice models have generated some interesting and fruitful questions and it would be difficult to dismiss the free-rider problem altogether. Few movement theorists adhere exclusively to rational choice models these days, however, and there has been a resurgence of interest in emotion (decoupled from the idea that it is necessarily irrational) in recent years (Jasper, 2018). This overlaps in some part with the interest in moral sensibilities, such as a sense of injustice, referred to above. The sense that something is unjust is as much felt as thought and political passions may override rational self-interest, or at least the opportunity to exercise political passions may be a further intrinsic reward of participation.

This brings us to another key theme in much contemporary movement thinking: identity. Identity has figured in a number of ways in recent debates on social movements. It is important at the individual level, for example, as a motivating factor in involvement. Diehard activists campaign because doing so has become central to their sense of who they are and to their sense of purpose and worth. It has important collective dimensions too, however. For Melucci (1989), who I mentioned earlier, the creation of a **collective identity** (e.g. 'feminist', 'pacifist' or 'anarchist') is a central aspect of the mobilization process and many researchers inspired by his work have explored the trials and tribulations which it entails. Who 'we' are, where our boundaries lie and what we are about are sometimes central issues of internal debate within a movement.

Isolates and Networks

The final charge levelled against the collective behaviour approach by its critics was that it portrays participants in movements as outsiders who are poorly integrated into society and, as a consequence, vulnerable to manipulative recruiters and ideologies. Against this the critics, taking the black civil rights movement in the US in the mid-20th century as their paradigm, argued that mobilization is much more likely where aggrieved parties are connected in relatively dense networks, and that participants are typically well-connected both within such networks and thereby wider society. It has been observed, for example, that much mobilization within the black civil rights movement occurred within churches and colleges, drawing upon the pre-existing connections within such communities and involving 'block recruitment' of their membership as a whole (McAdam, 1999).

Given that a social movement is a social network, it is perhaps obvious that social movement formation and mobilization will be easier and more likely where social networks already exist. Existing channels and relations are repurposed for protest. It would be useful at this point to consider why networks are so important (see also Crossley, 2007; Crossley and Krinsky, 2015). Before I do, however, two qualifications are necessary.

First, when movement scholars discuss the importance of social networks they usually mean either *dense* or *centralized* network *components*; that is, networks or parts of networks in which everyone is at least indirectly connected to everybody else (a network component); in which a high proportion of people are connected to one another (dense networks); or in which a small number of leaders have relatively direct and quick access to all other network members (centralized). Social networks have variable properties and it is particular network properties that increase the likelihood of mobilization rather than the presence of a network per se.

Second, networks are not inherently radical. They can be conservative and/or serve elites ('old boy' networks are an obvious example) and they can inhibit protest and movement mobilization. Biggs (2006), for example, notes that church attendance actually reduced the likelihood of participation in the civil rights movement in many cases. Where a pastor was politicized, their flock often became politicized and the church network became a vehicle of recruitment and mobilization, but many pastors were not politicized and the networks formed around their churches tended to serve, rather, as a social control mechanism reducing participation. Similarly, McAdam (1999) notes that where blacks and whites were better integrated, this tended to inhibit protest. Mobilization was most likely where the black population was densely networked within itself but segregated from the white population. Networks within the black community facilitated protest but networks across the black and white communities served as a social control mechanism, constraining it.

With these qualifications noted, we can consider some of the reasons why dense or centralized network components can increase the likelihood of mobilization. Communication and coordination constitute one very obvious reason. If members of a population are to act collectively then they must communicate and coordinate their efforts. This can only happen when they are in contact with one another and when their channels of communication are fast and effective; similarly, when resources have to be pooled and exchanged. On another level, some writers have argued that dense networks help to overcome the free rider problem because everybody observes and is observed by everybody else, so that free riders are easily detected and punished. It is rational for members of a dense network to act in the collective interest of that network because failure to do so is more costly than participation itself. James Coleman (1990) uses a similar argument to explain the 'social capital' which, in his view, is more common in dense networks; that is, the tendency for dense networks to cultivate trust, mutual support and cooperation amongst their members. This social capital is itself conducive to protest, according to Coleman, particularly where risk is involved. Participants need to know that they can trust others and may need the support (material, symbolic and emotional) of those others in order to see a campaign through.

I could cite other potential effects of network properties. Presently, however, I will conclude by noting the well-documented effect of networks upon recruitment to activism. There has been a lot of research in this area, with three findings tending to recur: (1) SMOs typically and most effectively recruit via the personal networks of their members; (2) from the other side, a large number of activists report having been recruited in this way; and (3) more specifically, personal connections appear to be important for converting interest into participation, particularly where participation involves risk. There is another side to these points, however. As noted above, studies also indicate that personal connections, where they link an individual to more conservatively inclined others, may serve as a social control mechanism, dissuading the individual from involvement. Moreover, there is some work suggesting that activists are more likely to drop out of a movement when their close friends within it do so. Social networks are very important but they can work both for and against movement mobilization.

SOCIAL MOVEMENTS

CHAPTER SUMMARY

- Social movements are networks of individuals, SMOs and their activities, including (necessarily) but not restricted to protest activities.
- They coalesce around a set of shared concerns and issues, are distinguished by a shared collective identity and repertoire, and seek to influence social and political life.
- However, there is a great deal of variation both within and between them.
- And they are dynamic. They wax and wane.
- The formation of movements and also the peaks and troughs in their levels of activity are affected by many factors.
- Triggers and strains, understood in moral rather than simply material terms, play an important role but mobilization can also be an effect of political opportunities, of the way in which events, activities and issues are framed, of resource mobilization and of wider social networks, to name only some.
- Social movements are central to sociology because they draw our attention to key fault lines within social structure and because the study of social movements highlights the processes and dynamics of collective action which are fundamental to all aspects of social life.

REVIEW QUESTIONS

Select an example of a social movement, past or present, with which you are familiar and consider:

1. Why do you consider this to be a social movement? Which of its features make it a movement?
2. How might sociologists try to explain its formation?
3. Does the existence of this movement tell us anything about wider society, its structure and divisions?

Go Further

Books

- Crossley, N. (2002) *Making Sense of Social Movements*. Maidenhead: Open University Press.
- Della Porta, D. and Diani, M. (eds) (2017) *The Oxford Handbook of Social Movements*. Oxford: Oxford University Press.
- Edwards, G. (2014) *Social Movements and Protest*. Cambridge: Cambridge University Press.

Journal Articles

- Fadaee, S. (2019) The permaculture movement in India: A social movement with southern characteristics. *Social Movement Studies* 18(6): 720–34.
- Gillan, K. (2020) Temporality in social movement theory. *Social Movement Studies* 19(5–6): 516–36.

(Continued)

- Vasi, I. and Suh, C. (2016) Online activities, spatial proximity and the diffusion of the Occupy Wall Street movement in the United States. *Mobilisation* 21(2): 139–54.

Social movements are a frequent topic in many general sociology journals, particularly in the USA, but the specialist journals, *Social Movement Studies* and *Mobilisation*, are essential reference points for an understanding of the contemporary state of play in this area.

Websites

- Hong Kong Protests Explained (a YouTube video explaining the Hong Kong protests referred to in this chapter and showing footage of them): www.youtube.com/watch?v=6_RdnVtfZPY (last accessed 16 March 2021).
- Social Movement Studies Twitter (linked to the Social Movement Studies journal, providing both activist reports on ongoing protests and information about new research): https://twitter.com/SocMovStudies (last accessed 16 March 2021).
- Wikipedia List of Social Movements (gives links to sources on a wide range of movements, past and present): https://en.wikipedia.org/wiki/List_of_social_movements (last accessed 16 March 2021).

REFERENCES

Becker, H. (1982) *Art Worlds*. Berkeley, CA: University of California Press.
Biggs, M. (2006) Who joined the sit ins and why. *Mobilisation* 3: 241–56.
Coleman, J. (1990) *Foundations of Social Theory*. Cambridge, MA: The Belknap Press of Harvard University.
Crossley, N. (2007) Social networks and extra-parliamentary politics. *Sociology Compass* 1(1): 222–36.
Crossley, N. (2015) *Networks of Sound, Style and Subversion*. Manchester: Manchester University Press.
Crossley, N. and Krinsky, J. (eds) (2015) *Social Networks and Social Movements*. London: Routledge.
Edwards, G. (2014) Infectious innovations? The diffusion of innovation in social movement networks: The case of suffragette militancy. *Social Movement Studies* 13(1): 48–69.
Gillan, K. (2020) Temporality in social movement theory: Vectors and events in the neoliberal timescape. *Social Movement Studies*, 19(5–6): 516–36. DOI: 10.1080/14742837.2018.1548965.
Goffman, E. (1986) *Frame Analysis*. Boston, MA: Northeastern University Press.
Jasper, J. (2018) *The Emotions of Protest*. Chicago: University of Chicago Press.
McAdam, D. (1999) *Political Process and the Development of Black Insurgency 1930–1970*. Chicago: University of Chicago Press.
Melucci, A. (1989) *Nomads of the Present*. London: Radius.
Olson, M. (1971) *The Logic of Collective Action*. Cambridge, MA: Harvard University Press.
Smelser, N. (2011) *Theory of Collective Behaviour*. New Orleans, LA: Quid Pro Books.
Thompson, E.P. (2010) *Customs in Common*. New York: The New Press.
Tilly, C. and Wood, L. (2012) *Social Movements 1768–2012*. London: Routledge.
Zald, M. and McCarthy, J. (2017) *Social Movements in an Organisational Society*. London: Routledge.

PART 6
WHAT IS SOCIOLOGY USEFUL FOR?

PART 6 WHAT IS SOCIOLOGY USEFUL FOR?

Introduction to Part 6

This final part of *An Introduction to Sociology* is headed 'What is sociology useful for?'. At this stage, as you have worked through several or all of the preceding chapters, we hope you have your own answer to this question. Sociology clearly is useful for analysing a wide range of social phenomena, from what seem to be very 'big' issues like climate change or wars, to what seem to be 'smaller' ones, like personal identity issues, as discussed in the chapters in Part 4 of this book. But what is big or small, or near or far in time and space, are what sociology brings together or connects. Another version of this idea is captured in the sense of sociology as linking personal troubles and public issues, which is one of the best-known sayings in Mills' *The Sociological Imagination* (there is more about this in the concluding Using Sociology chapter).

Debates within and beyond sociology about its 'uses' are as old as sociology itself, as are those questioning the value of sociological knowledge and understanding. As set out in Chapter 1 of this book, we have deliberately chosen not to start with sociology's origin story or stories; instead, this book closes by bringing together two chapters that provide different insights into those issues.

In Chapter 26, William Outhwaite takes the discussion of sociology back to its 19th-century origins and debates about whether it is *a* or *the* 'science of society'. In taking you back to some of the key names in early sociology – such as Weber and Durkheim – Outhwaite provides you with ways of making connections between what you have learnt across the book, including Chapters 7 and 8 on classical and contemporary social theories. As to whether sociology is a science, Outhwaite introduces a distinction about whether this means it shares the same kind of content or is organized in the same way as science. While sociology does not produce knowledge like the discovery of subatomic particles in physics, it does provide new and detailed knowledge that is both descriptive and explanatory of the social world. As Outhwaite shows, whether sociology is a science or not depends to an extent on what is meant by science, although sociology is undoubtedly a systematic field for the study of the full range of social relations.

In Chapter 27, Paul Jones takes up a different and more recent discussion about how sociology can be useful – the idea of 'public sociology'. As Jones shows, this was given a major spur in an American Sociological Association presidential lecture. This identified four different 'types' of sociology, and while the lecture argued that they all need to exist alongside each other, it made the case for a more public sociology to address the social conditions of the time. As always, the internal debate among sociologists about this asked questions about the meaning and value of the idea of public sociology. As well as taking you through that debate, Jones looks at the ways in which sociologists have made their work more 'public'. While the internet and social media have opened up new avenues, Jones shows that a kind of public sociology was being practised over a century ago by W.E.B. Du Bois. Indeed, issues of ethnicity/race, as well as gender, are prominent in examples of public sociology historically, and the names Jones mentions also take you back to some themes suggested in Chapter 1 of this book about sociology's stories of its emergence and what that sometimes overlooks.

In Chapter 28, the editors provide an overview of some of the key themes that run through the book as a whole. Drawing on examples from the experience of studying sociology, sociological responses to the Covid-19 pandemic from 2020 onwards and links between theory and method, they explore the issue of the uses of sociology in the contemporary environment. In doing so, they suggest that part of the challenge of studying sociology in the contemporary environment lies in making sense of the ever changing boundaries of sociology as a field of teaching and research.

PART 6 WHAT IS SOCIOLOGY USEFUL FOR?

Taken together, these three chapters provide you with an overview of some of the key debates about the uses of sociology. As you will see, these are informed by both historical and contemporary issues; they are debated by sociologists themselves, and they produce a variety of answers. In this way, they underline the model of 'unity in diversity' that Outhwaite puts forward.

Key Questions

- Why has sociology been more concerned about its status as a science than other disciplines?
- In what ways does sociology provide and combine descriptive and explanatory accounts of social phenomena?
- What are some examples of public sociology you can find on the internet today? How effective do you think they are, and how would you try to make them available to a wider audience?
- How can public sociology make the case for the value and uses of sociology to government, to the public, to students, and to your peers and friends?

SOCIOLOGY AS A SCIENCE

William Outhwaite

LEARNING OBJECTIVES

- To understand the ways in which the social sciences, and in particular sociology, relate to philosophy.
- To understand the historical and contemporary controversies over the status of sociology as a science.
- To see how the sociology of science may contribute to critical engagement with this issue.

 Framing Questions

1. What is science? Is it basically one thing or several?
2. How do the intellectual objectives of science relate to its nature as a social practice?
3. What is sociology *about*?

Introduction

Before you look at this chapter, you should read Chapter 23 (Ros Williams' chapter on Science and Technology) for a critical account of the sciences, for example biology, as a form of social practice. In this chapter, I am focusing more on the *image* of science as it relates to sociology. If you are studying sociology at a university or college, you may find that it is located in a school or faculty of 'social science'. But what do we mean by science and by social science?

The question of whether sociology should be called a science can be asked in basically two ways. One is whether the *intellectual* content of sociology is wholly or partly scientific; the other is whether sociology is *socially* organized like the other sciences. These are related, since social science disciplines which see themselves as scientific and orient themselves towards a natural science model will tend to be more tightly organized, with more agreement on their subject matter and the appropriate ways to study it.

Since the publication in 1962 of Thomas Kuhn's *Structure of Scientific Revolutions*, the idea has become accepted that the natural sciences typically converge on what he called 'paradigms', or generally agreed theoretical frameworks within which scientists work until a new paradigm overthrows the old one. In the social sciences, economics tends to follow this model; sociology tends to be more diverse.

This chapter explores some of these issues, beginning with the question of the scientific status of sociological knowledge as discussed both by philosophers and sociologists. The sociology of scientific knowledge is not just a specialism like the sociology of sport or sex but an important resource in helping sociology to understand itself. The middle section of the chapter draws on this area of sociology for some ideas about how to think sociologically about sociology itself ('reflexivity') – the third of the 'learning objectives' listed at the beginning – and the chapter ends with some final thoughts about the question I began with.

Mapping the Terrain

For the moment, I shall give sociology the benefit of the doubt and include it in a broad conception of science as systematic study of the kind pursued in universities, as in the German term *Wissenschaft* (which includes, for example, the study of literature). One way of approaching sociological knowledge is to ask whether it tells us things we did not know already. The natural sciences typically do this. Chemistry, for example, tells us that water, which we already know is wet and can freeze or evaporate, is made up of two gases: hydrogen and oxygen. Oxygen itself was discovered by Lavoisier in 1778 and this enabled him to explain the chemical basis of combustion.

What about sociology? My teacher, colleague and friend, the sociologist Tom Bottomore (1920–92), reflected after watching a TV programme about the discovery of DNA in 1951 that his own work on Marx, on elites and classes and in sociological theory had not discovered much by comparison. I once hosted a meeting of the sociology section of the British Association for the Advancement of Science at its annual conference. In a year when the experimental physicists had discovered a new elementary particle, we could only offer some new research about the experience of unemployment.

I shall suggest in this chapter that, although sociology does not have the revelatory power of the natural sciences, it does provide new and valuable knowledge. Later in the chapter we will see that sociology, like other scientific disciplines, typically offers explanations or more detailed understandings of processes or states, whether combustion (for chemistry) or unemployment (for sociology), which we already know something about. (For more discussion of the differences between sociology and the natural sciences, see Chapters 5, 7, 8 and 23.)

What (and How) Do We Know?

Any form of systematic study will typically involve some reflection on the status of the knowledge obtained. Sometimes this comes from others, as when your essay is returned with a grade and comments or my latest book is reviewed in a journal. But we also do this ourselves, even if we do not anticipate external feedback.

SOCIOLOGY AS A SCIENCE

Philosophy, a term which used to cover any systematic knowledge (as in the old term 'natural philosophy'), has come to mean reflection on our knowledge and our other practices (for example, our moral behaviour).

The philosopher Michel de Montaigne (1533–92) is famous for asking the question 'What do I know?'. We often question the status of our beliefs. Can I be *sure* that gods do not exist or that 'Brexit' is a disaster? Philosophers are sometimes mocked for continually asking if the table they are writing on is real, but there are in fact interesting questions to be asked about how the common-sense solid table relates to the table as analysed by a physicist, made up mostly of empty space between the particles of which it is composed.

Whereas physicists and other natural scientists may or may not be concerned with science as a social **institution**, thinking as a sociologist necessarily also requires you to focus on the question of the social organization of **sociology**. This is where Max Weber began his 1917 lecture on 'science as a vocation', in which he referred to one of his other disciplinary identities as an economist in addressing the 'material conditions' of the academic profession. Over a century ago, Weber (1946) sketched out the precarious prospects for an academic career in terms which are very familiar today.

I shall return to this question of social organization later, after examining the first question, that of sociology's intellectual content. Within the broad conception of science as *Wissenschaft* or scholarship, there is the question of what is sometimes called the 'classification of the sciences' or, in more sociological terms, the division of scientific labour between different specialisms.

Auguste Comte (1798–1857) described a hierarchy of sciences, with mathematics as the most basic and sociology (the term which he popularized) as the topmost science, based on biology, chemistry and physics and ultimately astronomy and mathematics. These sciences become properly scientific or 'positive' in a historical sequence, as, for example, when astronomy breaks with astrology and chemistry with alchemy. When sociology finally reaches the positive stage, as it was doing, he modestly suggested, in *his own* work, the system of human knowledge becomes complete.

Just under a century later, in the 1920s and 1930s, the 'logical empiricists' (sometimes also called logical positivists) of the 'Vienna Circle' of philosophers of science developed a model of 'unified science' in which the laws discovered by the individual sciences could ultimately be 'reduced' to the laws of physics or to **empirical** 'observation sentences': sociology is based on, successively, psychology, biology, chemistry and physics.

These **positivist** models can be contrasted with one in which the 'moral', 'cultural' or 'social' sciences are distinguished from the sciences of nature by their subject matter and/or their **methods**. John Stuart Mill (1806–73), who introduced the term 'moral sciences', shared Comte's desire to pursue law-like knowledge but argued that the complexity of social phenomena meant that what he called the 'historical method' of inquiry would most often be all that was possible, augmented by laws of human nature (which he called 'ethology').

The term 'cultural sciences' (*Kulturwissenschaften*) is found in Weber and the philosophers on whom he drew, notably Wilhelm Windelband and Heinrich Rickert. On this model, history is an *individualizing* science, focused on particular events, such as the French Revolution, rather than generalizations in which this is just one example of a revolution. Weber applied this individualizing approach in *The Protestant Ethic*, asking about the specific circumstances in which, he believed, a variant of Protestant Christianity gave a decisive impetus to the development of **capitalism** in early modern Europe. But he also broadened this approach in his famous essay on 'The Economic Ethic of the World Religions' and the comparative sociology of religion of which it was a part. Weber compared Hinduism, Buddhism, Judaism, Christianity and Islam, with some reference also to Chinese religion (for a more detailed discussion of the sociology of religion, see Chapter 20). A more recent example of what is sometimes called 'small-N' comparison is Theda Skocpol's classic book on revolutions, focused on the French, Russian and Chinese revolutions (Skocpol, 1979).

 Pause for Thought

- If you studied comparative religion at school, think back to those comparisons and what you might now say about them in the light of your sociological studies so far.

Sociology and Its 'Object'

As he moved from law and economic history towards sociology around 1910, Weber retained the idea that the social sciences, including economics, differed from the natural sciences in that their explanations typically referred to an understanding of the ideas, intentions and motives of human beings. As he put it in the opening sentence of what was published after his death as *Economy and Society*, 'sociology … is a science which attempts the interpretive understanding of human action and thereby an explanation of its course and effects'. A sociological explanation must be both 'causally adequate', in that it accounts for what actually happened, and 'meaningfully adequate', in that it refers to patterns of action which 'make sense'. Weber gives the example of 'Gresham's Law', in which 'bad money' (coins adulterated with cheaper metal) 'drives out good'. The operation of this law is confirmed by experience and it also makes sense in terms of motivation: you obviously want to offload your junk currency and hold on to the better one.

This model of sociology contrasts with that of his contemporary Emile Durkheim, who argued that '**social facts**' should be studied from the outside, 'as things'. Human intentions were inaccessible, and not just in the case of suicide. What he called the 'collective consciousness' was best studied *indirectly*, through its expression in, for example, legal codes, as in his book on the **division of labour**.

Sociology, then, does not have a distinct object on which all sociologists would agree. Some, like Durkheim, are happy to use the term 'society', while others, like Max Weber, avoid it as much as possible. (In Weber's *Economy and Society*, the term appears only two or three times – as well as in the title of the book which was given it after his death.) These two models of sociology run through the rest of the 20th century and into the present. Durkheim has certain affinities with the more individualistic approach of **behaviourism** in psychology and behaviouralism in political science, and with the use of statistical methods in explanations. A more Weberian approach was radicalized in the work of Alfred Schütz, who drew on **phenomenology** in philosophy to explore the meanings of things as they *appear* to us, and the linguistic approach of the British philosopher Peter Winch, who argued that learning to understand a society was like learning a language; anthropologists frequently have to do both as they encounter a new society (along with its language) without the aid of dictionaries or grammar books. In the US, Harold Garfinkel's '**ethnomethodology**' similarly studied the ways in which people make sense of social reality through language and other means. The emphasis on language meant that ethnomethodology has also moved into more formalized and **scientific** versions of sociolinguistics.

SOCIOLOGY AS A SCIENCE

 — Pause for Thought

Even if you have not studied these two strands of sociological theory in much detail, think about the types of knowledge they aim for and which seem most attractive to you.

Two influential ways of reworking something like Weber's dualistic model of sociology can be found in the critical theory of Jürgen Habermas (1929–) and Karl-Otto Apel (1922–2017) and in the **critical realism** of Roy Bhaskar (1944–2014) and others. Habermas, in 1971 [1968] (*Knowledge & Human Interests*), suggested a model in which a natural-scientific and a **hermeneutic** or **interpretative** approach were combined in what he called 'critical' sciences which uncovered causal obstacles to understanding. Thus in Freudian psychoanalysis, the analyst may help me to understand the cause of my fear of spiders by helping me to relive a traumatic childhood experience; once I remember this, I may be able to develop a more **rational** attitude which distinguishes between harmless and poisonous spiders. Habermas's other, more sociological example is Marx's theory of **ideology**, in which exploitative social relations are systematically obscured, for example by ideas of 'a fair wage'.

In his later work, Habermas developed a rather different model of what he calls 'reconstructive sciences'. These explain *how* we do the things we do, such as speak one or more languages or coordinate our interaction with other people; his own theory of communicative action is an example. The theory of communicative action reconstructs what is presupposed by other sociological action theories (rational action theory, **functionalism**, dramaturgical theories in Goffman and **symbolic interactionism**). More fundamentally, it reconstructs the underlying notion of action aimed at, and oriented by, mutual understanding. This is a feature of everyday interaction, says Habermas, but it occurs most systematically in 'discourses', when assumptions made by one speaker are challenged by another.

Another approach is that of **realism**, as presented by Russell Keat and John Urry in their *Social Theory as Science* (1975). Realists claim that natural science has been misunderstood by positivists, focusing on appearances and observations rather than the underlying structures and forces which explain those events. As I write this sentence I am sitting still, but I am subject to the gravitational force of the earth which prevents me from spinning off into space as the earth rotates. There is no event and nothing to be observed, except the movement of my fingers and the slow growth of the text on the screen, so theories which confine themselves to observable events will not be much use. The interaction of gravity and the centrifugal force from the earth's rotation mean that I can jump a metre or so into the air and land without hurting myself. This is a human-centred perspective; a fuller story would include the way in which the universe developed and humans and other animals evolved on the earth's surface. Humans, like natural objects, have both powers and liabilities: ice can cool my drink or it can break if I walk on it; I can walk or write but also trip or mistype a wrod [*sic*]. A theory of causality framed in terms of powers and tendencies is better able to handle the uncertainties in what are called 'open systems' in which a number of causal factors interact, leading to outcomes which may not be predictable. The warning on a cigarette packet points to dangers, rather than *guaranteeing* illness and premature death.

This approach sheds light on Weber's conception of explanatory 'adequacy' and the relation between description and explanation in sociology. To describe an action as an action of a certain type, say 'praying', is to give a partial explanation of it. There may however be a further layer of explanation, as when we ask why a convinced atheist has turned to prayer and are told s/he has a terminal illness; then we can go further and ask just *why* they think prayer might help and how they reconcile this with their previous beliefs.

A realist approach may suggest a better way of thinking about the scientific status of sociology and the other social sciences. Some realists use **social structure**s of 'class' or 'gender' to explain social outcomes such as differences in educational opportunities; others, such as **ethnomethodologists**, frame their explanations in terms of structures of interpersonal interaction. A social structure may be claimed to be real even if it cannot be precisely described, like the structure of a molecule or a bridge (where the internal and external forces acting on the bridge can be calculated). There is an element of *choice* between alternative explanations of an outcome: I may like to explain my educational successes by ability and hard work, but the sociologist will tend to point to structures of advantage and privilege. Sometimes structural explanations are accused of 'reifying' structures and ignoring our capacity to change things.

In the social sciences, there is an element of feedback, since humans can, with luck, understand the explanations offered for their behaviour. In some cases, they may adopt these explanations for themselves, as expected in Marxist theories of **class consciousness** or the idea of the self-fulfilling prophecy. Other explanations are less easy to internalize. If I was a religious believer, I'm not sure what I could make of Marx's or Durkheim's explanations of religion as a comforting illusion (Marx) or the way societies celebrate *themselves* (Durkheim). Some capitalists have read about Marx's theory of capitalism, but they tend not to find it congenial, even if they make use of Marxist accounts of innovation and capitalist cycles ('Kondratiev waves') in their forward planning or speculation.

In the social sciences, realists argue that without abandoning the ideal of science they can incorporate social actors' perceptions, the understanding of meaning and even the 'social construction of reality'. To understand the *point* of a social process and the actors' purposes is part at least of its explanation. Realism, they claim, also accounts for the reconstructive aspect of scientific theories, which typically ask how something is possible: what would explain a process which we know to exist, such as combustion, language use or warfare? The elements of the explanation will vary in each of these cases, and in research approaches to them: a neuroscientist or a phoneticist will be interested in different aspects of language than those which concern a sociolinguist. Experimentation may or may not be an appropriate approach; it would be unethical, as well as difficult and probably pointless, for me to start a war to test my theory. Despite all these differences, sociology has as strong a claim as any other academic discipline to be counted as a science – broadly understood.

Whether it should exist as a separate discipline is another question altogether, which I discuss in more detail below. Sociologists study political and economic processes, language use, gender, law and a host of other things, as do social anthropologists (often in a more informal and interactive way). So far as there is a single common feature to the work of sociologists and anthropologists, as distinct from people working in these other disciplines, it is that they will tend to be focused on the broader social context of these practices, rather than the details of, for example, electoral behaviour (politics) or profitability (economics).

 Pause for Thought

- Compare the different ways sociologists have conceived the 'object' of sociology.

Expand Your Knowledge

- The term 'behavioural science' has come to prominence with the response to the COVID-19 pandemic. Take a look at some uses of it on sites such as www.weforum.org/agenda/2020/06/behavioral-science-social-distancing, and think about how its public image compares with that of more natural-scientific branches of epidemiology. Have people 'had enough of experts' (Michael Gove, UK politician) or have 'the geeks come out on top' (John Crace, columnist on *The Guardian*)?

Is Sociology Organized like a Science?

Having raised the question of the classification of the sciences, I need to ask whether sociology is *socially* organized like other sciences. Here we can draw on a rich vein of work in the sociology of science. This sub-discipline of sociology began, arguably, with Comte, and was one aspect of the work of the early 20th-century US sociologist Robert Merton, but it was fundamentally reshaped in the second half of the century by the historian of science Thomas Kuhn (1922–96). Kuhn, whose background was in physics, was struck by the *differences* in the social organization of the social and natural sciences.

> ### Hear from the Expert
>
> If you're studying sociology, you will learn quite a bit about the history of the subject – far more, probably, than if you were studying physics or even economics or psychology. As Kuhn wrote in the Preface to *The Structure of Scientific Revolutions* (Kuhn, 1962):
>
> I was struck by the number and extent of the overt disagreements between social scientists about the nature of legitimate scientific problems and methods. Both history and acquaintance made me doubt that practitioners of the natural sciences possess firmer or more permanent answers to such questions than their colleagues in social science. Yet, somehow, the practice of astronomy, physics, chemistry, or biology normally fails to evoke the controversies over fundamentals that today often seem endemic among, say, psychologists or sociologists. Attempting to discover the source of that difference led me to recognize the role in scientific research of what I have since called 'paradigms.' These I take to be universally recognized scientific achievements that for a time provide model problems and solutions to a community of practitioners.

Kuhn had already seen through the simplistic idea that natural science was simply a matter of the replacement of bad theories by better ones. But nor were natural scientists, as the philosopher Karl Popper had argued they should be, constantly questioning their assumptions and looking to refute established knowledge. Was this because they were conformist or conservative? Only up to a point, and often for good reasons: you don't want to drop a theory until there's another one to replace it. The adoption of a new theory, Kuhn suggested, is more like religious conversion, where the accumulation of doubts may finally tip you over into the new system of belief after a period of hesitation. Scientific change, when it finally occurs, tends to be revolutionary rather than a matter of gradual evolution. In Kuhn's controversial phrase, referring to his example of Lavoisier's discovery of oxygen, 'after a revolution scientists work in a different world' (1970: 135).

Are there anything like paradigms in sociology? No, said the Portuguese sociologist Hermínio Martins, in a classic article of 1972: 'the same piece of work may conjoin the Marxist theory of **alienation**, the Durkheimian theory of **anomie**, the Parsonian pattern variables … etc.' Alternatively, however, sociologists, like nationalists, can use this weaker conception of **paradigm** as a protection against criticism from outside: 'my paradigm right or wrong' (Outhwaite, 2018).

Student Voices

A Sussex student once wittily wrote:

All my tutors

Know a lot

Some are Marxists

Some are not.

26.1 Key Case

Whitley

Does a look at the social organization of other scientific disciplines lead you to think differently about sociology?

Richard Whitley, a sociologist working in management science, published in 1984 a comprehensive study of *The Intellectual and Social Organization of the Sciences*, in which he analysed scientific disciplines as 'work organizations' of a particular kind, substantially self-organizing (though increasingly open to state and market pressures) and defining their own tasks. To simplify his seven-fold typology of scientific fields, these can be 'fragmented', 'polycentric' or 'bureaucratically integrated'. These patterns apply across all the sciences including sociology and the emergent field of management science. Sociology, especially British sociology, is located here at the fragmented end of a continuum; elsewhere, notably in Italy or Germany, there is a stronger polycentric pattern, with sociology departments, like others, typically dominated by one or more senior figures and those who follow their approach to the subject.

A striking feature of British sociology, as compared to that in Germany or the US, was and remains, despite the managerialization of universities and the casualization or even 'uberization' of teaching in recent years (Holmwood, 2011), that if you are lucky enough to secure a permanent post you can become tenured and relatively independent at an early career stage. Senior colleagues may help or hinder your promotion but are unlikely to demand your loyalty to their preferred **theoretical** approach or to block your tenure.

Another element more specific to sociology is that we typically study inequalities and processes of hierarchization, professionalization, bureaucratization and managerialism; with luck, we may therefore take a more critical view of them in our own environments. (This topic of what sociologists study is addressed in more detail in Chapters 9, 10 and 27.) Sociology has a debunking tendency, not least in its approach to the study of science. The recent rise of 'public sociology' explicitly urges sociology not to pursue disciplinary science behind closed doors but to address issues in ways which are accessible to a wide readership. The online and open access *Discover Society* is a good example, prefigured in Britain by magazines like *New Society* (1962–88).

Some scientific disciplines, then, are more tightly organized than others. As Holmwood (2010) puts it: 'Sociology ... is a subject that has resisted formation as a discipline based around a fixed frame of reference or "core"'. International Relations, established (for obvious reasons) just after the First World War, is another interesting example. Despite its relatively short history and wide global range, it has developed its own set of leading texts, theorists and codified approaches. It tends not, however, to present itself as a *science*, and this is perhaps a more defensible path for sociology to take. Social anthropology, too, is less hung up on the question of science, though this question is always in the background, for example in its relation to sociology. In the mid-20th century, A.R. Radcliffe-Brown and Raymond Firth presented anthropology as a science, while E.E. Evans-Pritchard located it in the humanities.

This brings us back to the question of the status of sociological knowledge, which was a central concern in sociological theory from the 1970s onwards and also reflected the rise of the sociology of **scientific knowledge**. The Kuhnian revolution had demonstrated the limitations of an approach which treated science as a 'black box' (Woolgar, 1988) and 'concentrated on the analysis of scientists' actions and patterns of their social organization in isolation from the knowledge they produced and changes in it' (Whitley, 1984: 1).

The bottom line for sociology is that science is a human practice which produces science (scientific knowledge) as its product. This knowledge may be true or false, built on in later work or superseded and abandoned. Once we abandon the simple idea of a linear advance of scientific knowledge, which social processes can only speed up or delay, we are brought up against the question of the status of scientific knowledge. Is it based on anything more than consensus, or is that all we need or can expect? Sociologists of scientific knowledge have been particularly inclined to flirt with **relativism**, since they were sociologically suspicious of the prestige of natural science and the linear advance model, which looked like a self-serving professional ideology and a justification for government funding.

Sociologists of science were not surprised to discover that scientists were more 'social' (unpredictable, informal, prejudiced, etc.) than their public image. There were also **methodological** reasons for taking a distance from scientific knowledge, just as sociologists of religion, even if they have religious beliefs of their own, can hardly include these as part of their explanations of religious developments. (A sequence in which Christianity superseded Judaism and was in turn superseded by Islam could not be taken seriously.) As David Bloor (1976: 4) put it, his 'strong programme' and its insistence that 'true' and 'false' beliefs should be explained in the same way 'embody the values which are taken for granted in other scientific disciplines'. On the other hand, it seems odd to exclude from an explanation of the growing popularity of the belief that the earth goes round the sun (rather than the other way round) the fact that it is actually true (and therefore more likely eventually to be accepted as true). The strong programme found itself in the paradoxical position of making stronger claims for *itself* than it allowed for the sciences it examined.

Overall, then, the sociology of scientific knowledge made it easier for sociology to 'stop worrying and live with science' (Woolgar, 1988: 107). Along with the impact of the sociology of science, the other element in a possible rapprochement is that post-positivist philosophies of science, whether realist or **conventionalist**, have been largely welcomed in sociology, whereas other disciplines such as political science and International Relations often retain a rather formulaic model of hypothesis testing and other positivist elements. (Social anthropology, of course, is also far away from using this sort of language.)

So is it a Science?

The theme of interdisciplinarity brings together the two aspects of the question of the scientificity of sociology. Once again, I shall begin with the intellectual content of the subject and then discuss its social organization. Sociology and its practitioners emerged from other areas of inquiry in its early years. Max Weber's career is a good illustration. Having studied law and legal and economic history, he held chairs in economics, coming to define himself as a sociologist only around the time that he was one of the founders of the German Sociological Association in 1909. His friend and co-founder of the Association, Georg Simmel, had a background in philosophy, and the third co-founder, Ferdinand Tönnies, had studied classical philology before teaching philosophy, economics, statistics and sociology. Durkheim, perhaps the most emphatic supporter of sociology as a distinct science, held posts for some time which combined it with education, and his journal, the *Année Sociologique*, was thoroughly interdisciplinary in its focus, especially in the books it reviewed. In a later generation, Norbert Elias (1897–1990) studied medicine before moving into philosophy and then sociology.

Intellectually, sociology drew massively on history, law, economics and philosophy, bringing together elements from these and other sources into classic works such as Durkheim's *Division of Labour* and his and Marcel Mauss's work on religion, Simmel's *Philosophy of Money*, and Weber's *Protestant Ethic* and his posthumously published *Economy and Society*. Alfred Schütz (1932) drew on Husserl's phenomenological philosophy in his distinctive approach to sociology. Sociology can hardly avoid doing this, for the simple reason that legal, political or economic processes, religion, war or pandemics are *also* social processes. In explaining revolutions, for example, historians and historical sociologists often have to decide between 'society-centred' and 'politics-centred' explanations, between political blunders by the former rulers and longer-term processes of social, economic and ideological change.

Sociology is therefore necessarily wide-ranging, drawing on more specialized disciplines and incorporating their contributions into its explanations. And unlike economics, which tends to produce grotesquely one-sided accounts when it tries to provide an economic explanation of, say, prayer, sociology can do justice to the complexity of these phenomena. The downside of this is that sociology's disciplinary identity is less easily grasped. A law textbook will often have a cover image of scales or the statue of justice; one in politics will typically have a picture of Washington or Westminster; economics can have pictures of banknotes, whereas a sociology textbook may have to make do with a picture of some *people*.

To put it more systematically: sociology is an 'importing' subject, though it also 'exports' its approaches into new fields like media and cultural studies or management studies, which then take off on their own. And like a country which imports more than it exports or whose key industries move offshore, its market image may suffer in the minds of academic managers in universities and governments (Holmwood, 2010). Interdisciplinary work, though perhaps better off in the UK than in the highly departmentalist US, is threatened, for example, by the UK's 'Research Excellence Framework', despite the lip service paid to interdisciplinarity, and also in other ways (Garforth and Kerr, 2011). Sociology also has a reputation, partly deserved (and for good reasons), for affinities with social democratic social policy initiatives such as the development of welfare states, and this may also render it suspect, along with the other social sciences. In the early 1980s, the new British prime minister Margaret Thatcher came close to abolishing the Social Science Research Council, the main UK funding body, on the grounds that there was no such thing as social science. She was eventually persuaded just to have the SSRC renamed the Economic and Social Research Council; meanwhile, the SSRC in the even more neoliberal USA has retained the name.

Thatcher suffered the usual fate of recent Conservative prime ministers, her career ended by party controversies over the UK's relations with the rest of Europe, but sociology's problem remains. It can respond by trying to reconstruct a strong disciplinary identity, but this might be at the cost of losing much of the diversity which has made the subject so much more stimulating in recent decades. John Holmwood (2010: 645) quotes a study of the US which also applies more generally. In the early 1970s:

sociology had a well-defined core consisting of quantitatively oriented fields, such as **social mobility**, methodology, demography, and the **family**. In 1987, the study of social classes and class mobility was no longer linked to methodology and formal theory. Instead, it was linked to Marxian economics, studies of political ideology, and the role of the **state**, and, more distantly, to European theorizing, in one direction, and the study of revolution, historical sociology, and economics in the other direction. (Crane and Small, 1992: 226)

Turner and Turner (1990) provide a similar analysis of 'the impossible science'. Stephen Turner (2014: 100) argues that 'the campaign to make sociology a science ... has essentially disappeared as a focus of effort'. To turn this clock back is hardly an attractive proposition, even if there are signs of it happening, especially in the US. A more attractive approach, in my view, is to strengthen the focus on 'public sociology', addressing a wider public outside the academy (Burawoy, 2005), and the long-standing links between sociology and social criticism (see, for example, Bottomore, 1975). Social criticism can come from the political right as well as the left: there is a historical link between finding something politically problematic and finding it intellectually problematic. Karl Mannheim (1986) had suggested in 1927 that both Marxism and conservative thought share a critique of the insubstantial character of liberalism: that it neglects the social and economic roots of political processes. Robert Nisbet (1966) had argued for the conservative origins of many of sociology's key concepts or 'unit ideas': community, authority, status, the sacred and alienation.

More often, the challenges come from the left: the sociology of the late 19th century was massively shaped by the 'social question' and the rise of labour movements; that of the later 20th century by feminist and environmentalist movements and those contesting racial inequalities and the persecution of sexual minorities. More broadly, Peter Wagner (1994) has argued that sociology in its beginnings was essentially an attempt to explain the limits of political action – to paraphrase a beer advertisement, to reach the parts politics can't reach.

This brings me back to a feature of scientific explanation stressed by realists. Just as Kant asked how our experiences of space and time are possible, science typically asks how it is possible that a familiar process such as combustion is possible. In this case, it offered what turned out to be a bad answer, phlogiston, and later (what we believe to be) a good one, oxygen. Similarly, Marx asked how it is possible that a (usually free) exchange of labour for a wage produces exploitation and inequality; Durkheim asked how the division of labour could, in normal circumstances, produce social solidarity and how religious belief and practice could be so prevalent in human societies, in the absence (he assumed) of any real **supernatural** objects of that belief. Weber asked why early modern European regions practising extreme versions of Protestantism seemed to have been more economically innovative than others.

Does sociology display the same progress as natural science? There is nothing comparable to astronomy's detection of more and more remote stars and planets, or that of subatomic particles by experimental physics. Often, sociologists return to recognizably Marxist, Durkheimian or Weberian questions, though hopefully in more developed ways. But this is surely because of fundamental continuities in the ways human societies organize themselves. Aristotle's model of political self-rule, that we should be both objects and subjects of politics, is still a fundamental principle, even if women are now included and slavery is largely abolished.

The tension between a sociology oriented to an ideal of science and one which stresses its similarities to other aspects of 'literary culture' (MacInnes, 2019) is likely to persist. But let's not, as Thatcher did, get hung up on the word science. The systematic study of social relations remains a central concern for human societies and for those of us fortunate enough to spend a few years, or a lifetime, specializing in it.

CHAPTER SUMMARY

- Philosophers and sociologists have disagreed among themselves on the scientific status of sociology. Some have seen no difference of principle between the social and the natural sciences, while others have stressed their difference – either because we can 'understand' social processes 'from the inside' because we are human beings ourselves, or because we are interested in them in a different way.
- The chapter approaches this question of the scientific status of sociology through the lens of the sociology of scientific knowledge, asking whether sociology is socially organized similarly to, or differently from, the other sciences.

REVIEW QUESTIONS

- Compare the various models of sociology discussed in this chapter. How many do you think there are?
- 'Between literature and science': do sociologists have to choose?

Acknowledgements

My thanks to Peter Phillimore for invaluable advice on the debates over this question in social anthropology, the not-quite-identical twin of sociology. Also to John Holmwood and Ken Smith for helpful comments on an earlier version.

Go Further

Books

- Bishop, R.C. (2007) *The Philosophy of the Social Sciences: An Introduction*. London: Bloomsbury Academic.

Excellent readable introduction.

- Fuller, S. (1997) *Science*. Buckingham: Open University Press.

Critical overview of science.

- Woolgar, S. (1993 [1988]) *Science: The Very Idea*. London: Routledge.

Critical discussion of the image of science.

Book Chapters and Journal Articles

- Manicas, P. (2007) The social sciences since World War II: The rise and fall of scientism. In W. Outhwaite and S.P. Turner (eds) *The SAGE Handbook of Social Science Methodology*. London: Sage, pp. 7–31.

Presents a realist approach in a broader historical context.

- Kincaid, H. (2012) Introduction: Doing philosophy of social science. In H. Kincaid (ed.) *The Oxford Handbook of Philosophy of Social Science*. New York: Oxford University Press, pp. 3–17.

Kincaid (p. 3) 'denies that there is something special about the social world that makes it unamenable to scientific investigation'.

- Outhwaite, W. (2014) Hermeneutics and the social sciences. In J. Malpas and H.-H. Gander (eds) *The Routledge Companion to Hermeneutics*. London: Routledge, pp. 486–97.

- Fuller, S. (2020) What does it mean to hear the call of science? Listening to Max Weber now. *Social Epistemology* 34(2): 105–16.

Discusses Weber in terms of two varieties of protestant Christianity.

Websites

- https://discoversociety.org

Useful short articles on topical issues.

- www.bruno-latour.fr

Latour, inventor of actor-network theory, has an interesting model of the sciences in their relation to the natural and social world.

REFERENCES

Bloor, D. (1976) *Knowledge and Social Imagery*. Chicago: University of Chicago Press.
Bottomore, T. (2010 [1975]) *Sociology as Social Criticism*. Abingdon: Routledge.
Burawoy, M. (2005) For public sociology. *American Sociological Review* 70 (Feb.): 4–28.
Crane, D. and Small, H. (1992) American sociology since the seventies: The emerging identity crisis in the discipline. In T.C. Halliday and M. Janowitz (eds) *Sociology and Its Publics: The Forms and Fates of Disciplinary Organization*. Chicago: University of Chicago Press.
Garforth, L. and Kerr, A. (2011) Interdisciplinarity and the social sciences: Capital, institutions and autonomy. *British Journal of Sociology* 62(4): 657–78.
Holmwood, J. (2010) Sociology's misfortune: Disciplines, interdisciplinarity and the impact of audit culture. *British Journal of Sociology* 61(4): 639–58.
Holmwood, J. (ed.) (2011) *A Manifesto for the Public University*. London: Bloomsbury Academic.
Keat, R. and Urry, J. (1975) *Social Theory as Science*. London: Routledge.
Kuhn, T. (1962) *The Structure of Scientific Revolutions*. Chicago: University of Chicago Press.
Kuhn, T. (1970) *The Structure of Scientific Revolutions*, 2nd edition, enlarged. Chicago: University of Chicago Press.
MacInnes, J. (2019) What kind of 'ology'? Two cultures and the success of British sociology. In P. Panayotova (ed.) *The History of Sociology in Britain*. London: Palgrave Macmillan, pp. 389–414.
Mannheim, K. (1986) *Conservatism. A Contribution to the Sociology of Knowledge*. London: Routledge and Kegan Paul.
Nisbet, R. (1966) *The Sociological Tradition*. New York: Basic Books.
Outhwaite, W. (2018) Kuhn and social science. In J.E. Castro, B. Fowler and L. Gomes (eds) *Time, Science and the Critique of Technological Reason: Essays in Honour of Hermínio Martins*. Basingstoke: Palgrave Macmillan, pp. 81–98.
Schütz, A. (1967 [1932]) *The Phenomenology of the Social World*. Evanston, IL: Northwestern University Press.
Skocpol, T. (1979) *States and Social Revolutions: A Comparative Analysis of France, Russia and China*. Cambridge: Cambridge University Press.
Turner, S.P. (2014) *American Sociology: From Pre-disciplinary to Post-normal*. Basingstoke: Palgrave Macmillan.
Turner, S.P. and Turner, J.H. (1990) *The Impossible Science: An Institutional Analysis of American Sociology*. Newbury Park, CA: Sage.
Wagner, P. (1998 [1994]) *A Sociology of Modernity: Liberty and Discipline*. London: Routledge.
Weber, M. (1946) *Science as Vocation*. In H.H. Gerth and C.W. Mills (eds) *From Max Weber*. New York: Free Press.
Whitley, R. (2000 [1984]) *The Intellectual and Social Organization of the Sciences*. Oxford: Clarendon Press.
Woolgar, S. (1993 [1988]) *Science: The Very Idea*, 2nd edition. London: Routledge.

PUBLIC SOCIOLOGY?
Paul Jones

LEARNING OBJECTIVES

- To learn about some of the central questions that emerge from the debate on public sociology.
- To appreciate how and why some sociological research can be considered to be public.
- To gain an understanding of where in public that sociology can happen.

 Framing Questions

- What does public sociology mean?
- Why is public sociology not straightforward to define?
- What are some examples of sociology that has been made public?

Introduction

Fundamental questions seem to haunt every corner of sociology: who does it, how, why, and for whose benefit? Most often, these issues sit quietly in the background of the discipline, but when it comes to public sociology, they become noisy and get lots of people thinking and talking and writing.

PART 6 WHAT IS SOCIOLOGY USEFUL FOR?

Trying to resolve the central concerns of sociology in one book chapter is just not possible. Instead, in what follows I want us to think about public sociology in a way that keeps these questions in view, using them to open up some ways of helping our understanding of sociology's publicness.

So, this chapter is a discussion of some of the ways in which sociologists have made their sociology public. The overall aim here is not so much to come to a clear, once-and-for-all definition of public sociology, but to think through – via examples – some of the ways that sociology can be seen to interact with publics. Let's see where that takes us …

Mapping the Terrain

Here is a misleadingly simple version of the story of public sociology: in 2004 the then American Sociological Association President Michael Burawoy (who is a Professor of Sociology at the University of California, Berkeley) made a high-profile speech calling for more public sociology. He wrote up a version of the talk for an important journal. The combination of the article and the lecture prompted lots of sociologists to think seriously about what sociology is, and what it's for. Ta-dah! The end!

This wasn't the end of the public sociology story of course. As we'll see, it wasn't even really the beginning. For now though, it's enough to note that Burawoy definitely *did* get lots of other sociologists thinking and talking and writing about what public sociology is. Yes, I think Burawoy's talk and his publications served to shake up the discipline in some revealing ways. But what did he actually say? What was all the fuss about?

27.1 Key Case

Michael Burawoy

Watching Michael Burawoy's presidential address will perhaps give you a sense of why his talk interested so many sociologists across the world. Please, do yourself a favour: put an hour aside, and listen to what Burawoy says in his own words – there's a lot to learn about public sociology in his talk, and it's also pretty crucial for what follows in this chapter. Here it is in its entirety:

www.youtube.com/watch?v=jDDnBr9bUlw

Personally, I find Burawoy an extremely engaging and persuasive speaker. One of the things that becomes apparent from listening to Burawoy's lecture is that he is very positive about the potential of sociological thinking to bring about better-informed, fairer societies. (On the link between sociology and issues of justice, see the discussion in Chapters 3, 4, 18 and 25.) In my opinion, in the lecture he makes a powerful argument for the importance of public sociology; in fact, it's so persuasive that it can be difficult to disagree with what he's saying (although over the next few pages, you'll hear about why some sociologists were highly critical of his views!).

In addition to the video footage of his talk, you can also read a written version (Burawoy, 2005). As is usually the case, the written paper is more precise than the spoken word, and as a result it is perhaps more difficult to stick with, and to understand. Do try though. Reading sociology and figuring out what the key arguments of books and articles are is tough, but trying is the main way to get better at doing it.

From the video and the article, Burawoy is suggesting the existence of four different 'types' of sociology:

- Professional sociology: which is directed towards other academic sociologists, and is to be found in academic journals, books like this one, or talks delivered at sociology conferences. The main form of communication here is 'sociologist to sociologist'; it's sociology aimed towards others with a professional interest in the discipline and its findings.
- Critical sociology: Burawoy tells us that this type of sociology has close connections with projects of social change and transformations that aim to bring about a fairer world; critical sociology has links with activist movements such as, for example, the Occupy Movement, The Morcambe Bay Poverty Truth Commission, or Black Lives Matter. In this type of sociology, sociologists are communicating with/perhaps even on behalf of social movements and activist networks, helping them by using sociological research to bring to light findings that will be useful in support of the causes the movements are campaigning for.
- Policy sociology: this type of sociology provides data and research in support of the production of social policy. Analysis is directed towards government arrangements and legislation; even when attempting to bring about change in that sphere, which could mean research that illuminates the strengths and weaknesses of welfare policies and their impacts on service users, this type of sociology is based on sociologists finding ways to communicate their research to policy makers and government officials.
- Public sociology: this is the type of sociology that this chapter deals with. It is based on bringing 'sociology into a conversation with publics, understood as people who are themselves involved in conversation' (Burawoy, 2005: 7). In other words, public sociology involves taking sociological knowledge into spaces where it can be used to open up and inform debates with non-sociological groups, and assist in the framing – and perhaps even the solution – of practical sets of social problems. Here the communication is between sociologists and publics.

The four main types of sociology are interconnected in Burawoy's account. 'Professional sociology is not the enemy of policy and public sociology, but the *sine qua non* of their existence' (Burawoy, 2005: 10); if your Latin is a bit rusty – mine is, so I looked up the meaning of that phrase on the internet – it means that there is no public or policy sociology without professional sociology. The same is true for critical sociology too; there's none of that without professional sociology.

Even though they are intertwined, Burawoy suggests that there is a hierarchy between these four different types in practice. He identifies 'a ruling coalition of professional sociology and policy sociology and a subaltern mutuality of critical and public sociology' (2005: 18). Put differently, professional sociology is so popular because it provides sociologists with career progression, promotions, jobs, invitations to go to nice places to speak, citations, and general esteem from colleagues within sociology (so from some of the people that sociologists look up to). Policy sociology can be attractive as it provides the opportunity for funding for research and for influence to change the ways in which governments work.

But public sociology seems like a really good idea: who could *not* want to want more of it? Why is public sociology not already the most popular way to do sociology? Here's the contradiction: public sociology, regrettably for Burawoy, gets squeezed out by the combination of professional and policy sociology, as does critical sociology for that matter. Burawoy seems to be arguing that lots of sociologists have turned 'inwards', addressing their sociology towards other sociologists, rather than thinking about the broader benefits of their work.

To reiterate then, Burawoy is *definitely not* suggesting that what he calls 'professional sociology' – what we can think of as dialogues between sociologists at conferences, in books, journals, and so on – is problematic or to be avoided. In fact, according to Burawoy the relationship between these professional and public types of sociology benefits both, stimulating ideas and helping to sharpen our understanding of the world. When you listen to or read Burawoy, it becomes clear that for him professional sociology is a key foundation to the whole sociological discipline; it is the foundation on which everything else is built.

As a way of going beyond sociologists only talking to other sociologists, Burawoy tells us that public sociology should be valued and supported and given higher status within universities and colleges like the ones that you and I are at now. Public sociology is an index of how strong sociology is in general. Putting this the other way around, Burawoy is suggesting that we should remember that sociologists have very valuable contributions to make to public understandings of the world – to social knowledge – and that we should, on more occasions than we typically do, look to share it.

So far, so clear (I hope)...

Pause for Thought

Before moving on to discuss why Burawoy's vision came in for some friendly – and some not-so-friendly – criticism, let's revisit his general argument:

- Burawoy suggests four general types of sociology. What are they?
- Why would sociologists – the people whose ideas you've read and heard about in your course – do sociology at all? What's the point of sociology? List as many reasons as you can.
- Can you name one sociological study that would fit into each of Burawoy's four types?
- Apart from in your classroom and in books like this, where could you learn about sociology?

Criticisms of Burawoy's Vision of Public Sociology

Burawoy's argument has a kind of 'feel-good', positive character; why would anyone be against public **sociology**? However, the more you dig into the nuances of the arguments from a sociological perspective, the more problems pop up.

In an excellent article, the British sociologist John Holmwood – a Professor of Sociology at the University of Nottingham – takes issue with Burawoy's central claims, arguing that his version of public sociology is 'dogmatic' (2007: 47) – in other words, that it is based around strict sets of rules (that in this case are themselves on rather shaky ground).

One key criticism Holmwood (2007) makes of Burawoy's position on public sociology concerns his projection of sociology as a 'partisan profession'; that is, the assumption that sociologists are generally in a kind of moral-political agreement about how the world should work. As you will have seen from this book, and heard in your sociology classes, different sociologists have very different versions of what a better society would look like, or what's right or wrong with today's social world. (This issue of the **role** of sociology in society is addressed from a range of angles in Chapters 2, 4, 15 and 23.) If Burawoy is suggesting that public sociology should help to improve societies, how does that work exactly, and are sociologists all supposed to take sides? If so, whose side are we to be on (Becker, 1967)?

More questions for Burawoy fall out of Holmwood's critique: if we do take sides, then on what does our authority rest? Does the fact that we are sociologists make our position more important and than those of non-sociologists?' Are sociologists just like other citizens in democracies, or does their special sociological insight mean that they should somehow have more power? Is our 'partisan' position the result of objective sociological analysis, or one reading of evidence amongst others? Tough questions!

Another key element of Holmwood's critique is that Burawoy asserts the stable existence not only of a coherent discipline of sociology itself, but also of some structures within society, including the **state**. Simply put, for Burawoy's vision of public sociology to make sense, a separate and identifiable sphere of democratic government must exist. As we'll see later on in this chapter, government and politics are often very entangled with other types of organization, and just not altogether always easy or obvious to find and work with/against (Jones and Mair, 2016); this makes public (and professional) sociology difficult to clarify in practice, as without a clear space for government, where does independent sociology happen, and who does it communicate with?

Professor Charles Tittle focuses on Burawoy's fuzzy definition of public sociology itself, which he suggests contains lots of elements. Reassembling Burawoy's own ideas, Tittle suggests that the definition of public sociology he uses is very messy, and includes: '(1) engagement in political activities to promote [somebody's conception ... of] social justice, (2) actively revealing to nonprofessional audiences the knowledge that sociologists think they have or the truths they think they know, (3) orienting our research and writing around moral issues, (4) engaging the public in debate about moral questions based on sociological insights, and (5) helping various "publics" solve problems or gather information relevant to their concerns, or helping to create such publics' (2004: 1639). Tittle is arguing that if the definition of public sociology is so elastic, and it can be stretched over lots of different things, then it's not precise enough, and we can't really answer the fundamental question: 'what is public sociology?'. To put it bluntly then, Tittle argues that 'Burawoy's position is not entirely clear' (2004: 1639).

Taking aim at – to quote the title of his article – 'the arrogance of public sociology', Tittle (2004) strikes at the heart of Burawoy's arguments in support of public sociology by suggesting that if it cannot be clearly defined, and no one really knows exactly what it is, then a real danger is that it is only of interest to sociologists as a way of representing themselves. Public sociology is more of an aspiration than a real practice. Similarly, in a critical blog piece, Lambros Fatsis argues that without a tight, clear definition, public sociology can become a 'mere rhetorical gesture or a self-righteous posture, rather than a defining feature of our daily scholarly lives' (Fatsis, 2019).

Another of Tittle's central arguments about public sociology is very important. He argues that sociologists' 'supposed knowledge is quite shaky ... [and] as likely to be wrong as right and in the process they can easily cause damage' (2004: 1641). I don't think that Tittle is being dismissive of sociological knowledge here, but rather is pointing out that understanding of societies is always based on interpretation, and as such is always contested from another perspective. For example, I research about architecture, and I can tell you – for absolutely certain – that some other sociologists who work on this topic completely disagree with the claims I make in my articles, books, and talks. This isn't personal or a problem, because as sociologists we are constantly in disagreement with other sociologists (Burawoy called this professional sociology); this is a way that our knowledge of the world is sharpened. Tittle's critique is not that sociological knowledge is weak, just that it is partial and that this means that we must be extremely cautious if proposing we have correct answers to very complicated questions, in situations where lots of other potential answers exist.

All of this being said, it is possible – and as Holmwood suggests – to 'believe[s] strongly that a public role is central to the sociological undertaking' (2007: 46), and also to criticize Burawoy's arguments. Let's hold this in mind as we dig deeper into some questions that emerge from the debate on public sociology we've covered so far; we'll see where we end up…

Who Does Public Sociology?

The temptation in a chapter like this one is to make a kind of a list, with public sociology starting with the work of Sociologist A, who was followed by Sociologist B, who wrote a book with Sociologist C, who was a big influence on Sociologist D, who disagreed with Sociologist A, who worked with Sociologist E, and on, on and on through to Sociologist Z. Whatever, and whoever, is included in these types of accounts, or narratives, the influence of some is overlooked and the influence of some others is overstated. Crucially then, not only do alternative lists exist, but some groups are typically favoured by this type of exercise at the expense of others.

A very important book called *Decolonizing Methodologies*, written by Professor Linda Tuhiwai Smith (2012 [1999]), addresses why certain ideas, certain ways of making and sharing knowledge, are celebrated while others are undermined and problematized. The implications of these processes are massive; Smith shows how indigenous peoples and other marginalised groups face structural and often violent exclusions that are underpinned and legitimated in part by colonial and racist bodies of 'scientific' knowledge. From this, a particular issue for sociology, and public sociology in particular, lies with more powerful groups of people doing research 'on' – but not with – less powerful groups.

Smith asks a series of questions that have profound questions concerning whom knowledge is for, whom it benefits, and whose voices are heard and whose are made silent. Significantly for our discussion here, Smith's analysis poses a series of very important questions for public sociology: who does it, why, and for whom? Thinking carefully about whose perspectives are heard, and about who is absent from debates, is crucial to the project of decolonization.

One further thing that makes the story of public sociology less straightforward than I suggested at the start of this chapter is that Burawoy's writings and talks were not the start of the debate. As you may remember from his talk and/or his article, Burawoy suggests W.E.B Du Bois – a sociological pioneer writing over 100 years ago – was 'perhaps the greatest public sociologist of the twentieth century' (2005: 17). (For more discussion of Du Bois, see Chapter 13.)

Although a sophisticated theorist, who carried out numerous city-level and national studies that set an intellectual agenda for sociologists in revealing and challenging 'the problem of the color line', Du Bois has been '[u]njustly neglected … the explicit and implicit **racism** of sociology has positioned Du Bois as a peripheral figure' (Davidson, 2021: 382). By evidencing, challenging, and drawing attention to the workings of the racist arrangements of his day, Du Bois' sociology was a 'vehicle of a public discussion about the nature of U.S. society – the nature of its values, the gap between its promise and its reality, its malaise, its tendencies' (Burawoy, 2005: 7). The very sets of racist policies and practices that Du Bois drew attention to in his work excluded him from academic status both in his day and long after his death.

However, despite his often being overlooked in sociology classes, books and debates, it is clear when looking at Du Bois' groundbreaking sociology that it was 'public' in a number of key respects (Davidson, 2021; Gilroy, 1993). As well as his directly political public interventions – such as his activism against lynching, and discrimination in education and employment, for example – Du Bois sought to make his sociological analysis understood widely, as the beautiful sets of infographics reflect (The Public Domain Review, n.d.).

There are other traditions of thought that are frequently overlooked and/or undervalued in the ways disciplines and contributions to them are arranged. As Joan Acker (2005) points out, a version of public sociology was happening within feminist sociology a long time ago too; questions regarding which groups were being represented and how, and which issues were being analysed and how, were fundamental to the very ways in which feminism has been organized. The gendered history of sociology (Acker, 2005: 328) means that the important contributions of key feminist voices and perspectives have been overlooked. As well as pointing out the antecedents, the founding mothers of these ways of thinking, such as Jane Addams, Beatrice Webb and Eleanor Rathbone (to take some names for you to look up), in unpacking public sociology, Ackers shows the practical importance of the point made by Smith (2012 [1999]). As we try to understand the effects of patriarchal assumptions within sociology itself, we have our attention drawn to particular sets of ideas and thinkers, and away from others. A potential within public sociology is to keep these sets of key issues at the forefront, to not let them slip into the background: who does sociology, with whom or on whom, and how?

Where is Public Sociology?

Burawoy's fourfold distinction of different 'types' of sociology is suggestive of four distinct audiences: professional (other sociologists); activist (erm, activists); policy (policy makers); and public (members of the public). Herbert Gans – a bit confusingly, also in an ASA Presidential Address in 1988 – suggested public sociology as a kind of a 'bridge' between the world of the university and broader society. Calling for sociologists to have a bigger public profile, Gans argued for sociologists to be more prominent in media debates, to have a more influential voice in advising governments, to be 'out there' supporting community organizations, trades' unions, charities and other organizations, armed with sociological insight and knowledge, and the skills that sociologists develop when they're doing sociology. In as clear a definition as can be found, Gans tells us that a 'public sociologist ... applies sociological ideas and findings to social (defined broadly) issues about which sociology (also defined broadly) has something to say' (Gans, 2002). Arguably this is a little 'flatter' idea of public sociology than is Burawoy's; it's certainly less detailed in terms of identifying different 'types' of sociology and their relationship to publicness.

Anyway, I mention Gans here as his version of public sociology involves sociologists using media platforms to get sociology involved in as many debates as possible, and in places you might not expect to find it. But what is the best way to get sociology 'out there', outside of universities and into the wider world? Following are a couple of recent examples from the UK of sociologists getting 'out there', outside of universities and colleges, and sharing widely the sociological knowledge that they have generated through their research.

PART 6 WHAT IS SOCIOLOGY USEFUL FOR?

27.2 Key Case

Gurminder K. Bhambra

Here's Gurminder K. Bhambra, Professor of Postcolonial and Decolonial Studies at University of Sussex, delivering a lecture: 'Everything You Know About Brexit is Wrong' (www.youtube.com/watch?v=dkBnkBT_x-M).

This lecture – which is a TED Talk, pretty-slickly produced – has been viewed 129,888 times at the time I'm writing this (for context, it's worth noting that 129,888 is a lot for views/reads of sociology). This makes us think about the audience for Bhambra's talk: who is watching? How do they find out about it? How is it accessed?

In her lecture, Bhambra situates Brexit alongside a long history of the political organization of communities that has led to the 'arbitrary exclusion of peoples in the present'. In challenging some of the ways that taken-for-granted ideas about Brexit have become normal, on a platform that reaches far outside the university space, Bhambra is a sociologist doing sociology in public, adding to our understanding of the social forces that have shaped Brexit, and its implications.

Bhambra's argument is a distinctly sociological one that analyses the available evidence in a way that doesn't take for granted the thing that is being discussed and that develops some innovative lines of inquiry that invite us to think differently about Brexit.

- How can Professor Bhambra's talk be considered public sociology? In your answer, think about the topic she addresses in her talk, the format of the presentation, and its audience.
- What are some of the limits to the 'publicness' of Professor Bhambra's intervention here? List three reasons why certain groups may be unable to access this presentation.

27.3 Key Case

Professor Robert Dingwall

Another recent example of a slightly different kind of sociology in public – that is, generally outside of the university – can be found in the work of Professor Robert Dingwall, a sociologist at Nottingham Trent University. Dingwall has been a prominent voice, often critic, of the UK Government's responses to the COVID-19 pandemic, in a series of radio interviews, opinion pieces in newspapers, and other media appearances. His Twitter account is @rwjdingwall, and there is a great deal of information linked through to his research.

Dingwall has added thoughtful commentary and critique that are grounded in analysis of the ways that social interaction – between people and things – is crucial for understanding the transmission of COVID-19. One morning, in early summer 2020 I think, I heard Dingwall was being interviewed on Radio 4's *Today* programme about the pandemic. The interviewer asked a question along the lines of 'with all due respect Professor Dingwall, you're a sociologist, not a medical professional, so what would you know about the transmission of the virus?' Dingwall responded that the transmission of the virus was in part a social issue, bound up with social interaction, collective gatherings in spaces that mattered to people. Dingwall advocated strongly for the benefit of sociological analysis in helping illuminate this crucial public health issue of our time.

PUBLIC SOCIOLOGY?

- In Burawoy's formulation, Dingwall is perhaps a professional sociologist doing both policy sociology and public sociology. Look at his Twitter feed for some of his commentary on COVID; can you explain why he straddles these categories?
- Professor Dingwall gives lots of interviews and comment on his research relevant to the pandemic. This engagement includes with some right-wing tabloid newspapers – amongst many other media platforms – and this can draw criticism from some other sociologists. List reasons why:
    o certain groups may be unable or unwilling to access his sociology in these newspapers
    o you think sociologists should or should not agree to interviews in media outlets that express problematic social views.

When sociologists try to connect large numbers of people to their sociology, they often use channels that are owned and/or controlled by major corporations and governments; in this case it can be difficult to retain one's own independence and sociological research can get tangled up with editorial lines and other agendas, or misrepresented or partially represented, or read by some and automatically passed over by others. Fundamentally, who gets to have access to the sociological knowledge that sociologists share?

To take an example: the chapter that you are reading now is in a book. Not a bestselling book like the *Twilight* ones for example, but a book written specifically for people like you and me who are interested in sociological ideas. How did you get access to this book? Someone – perhaps you, or your college lecturer, a librarian – somewhere, probably paid so that you could read it. Even if you got it from the library, in effect you borrowed it from an organization who bought it. Anyway, in all of these cases, money has changed hands before you got access to this chapter and the rest of the book (I'm very glad that you did and that you're reading this!). If a book is private, it is only open to those who have paid to access it, or public if a library has paid for its members to read it, for example.

Without wanting to start off another very complicated question as this chapter draws to a close, a public is something more than a collection of individuals, or simply an audience: it exists with respect to those within the public having a sense of their connection to each other and debating sets of issues that affect *them* (not equally). As John Dewey argued over a hundred years ago, what is in the 'public interest' is itself a matter for publics themselves to decide upon (1952 [1927]). This means that in a democracy one should be wary of those speaking for the public interest. In Dewey's terms, the public is outside of the state or the market and exists in civil society, in a space that should not be dominated by particular interests, or contributions to which limited by social background.

Think for a moment about the current political landscape – for instance, as is reflected by Donald Trump in the US, Boris Johnson in the UK, Jair Bolsonaro in Brazil, or Vladimir Putin in Russia – there are many who are willing to assert what the public interest is (and align such with their own actions). As we have already seen, interrogating who gets to represent whom, and on what basis, can be the starting point for sharp sociology.

Reducing audiences to numbers of online clicks, or numbers of readers, fundamentally misunderstands the nature of public sociology (which is not always broadcast – sometimes it is narrow cast) and of publics. Sometimes, sociologists address issues of public importance in places and/or in ways that limit the size of the audience. Or sometimes the issue at stake is a pretty niche one that is primarily of interest to other sociologists who are working in that area (typically a far smaller group, but with specialist knowledge).

27.4 Key Case

Supermarkets in the UK

Myself and my friend and colleague at the University of Liverpool, Michael Mair did a sociological study about supermarkets. In general, we are both interested in the political organization of UK society, and the ways in which local settings – cities, neighbourhoods, the streets where you live, and places that you go to shop – can be tangled up with important questions involving work, accountability, and how large corporations make their profits.

We did sociological analysis of the 'Big Four' supermarkets in the UK (ASDA, Morrisons, Tesco, Sainsbury's) and found out lots about the ways that these big stores get products on their shelves, provide certain types of jobs, and have certain types of relationships with governments, other smaller shops, and the communities in which they exist. Our conclusion was that we must understand the political and economic contexts that allow supermarkets to flourish if we are to make full sense of why there are so many of them in the places that many of us live.

After doing this sociological research, we wrote a chapter – in a book a bit like this one – and did some talks at universities and conferences about our findings. Hopefully some other sociologists listened to what we had to say, read the chapter that we wrote, and it helped them to think about how contemporary UK societies are organized. Although relatively small numbers of people came to our talks or read the chapter, and they were mainly other sociologists, our reason for doing this was to try to contribute to a discussion about the importance of political and economic contexts for sociological explanation of things that seem on the surface so strange, or so natural ('why are there so many supermarkets?'). Basically, we wanted to communicate with other sociologists; this group is a profession, yes, but it's also a public!

Our research was public in another way, as it addressed an issue of public significance, one that wasn't solely of importance to Michael and me, but rather that was key to the shape and organization of jobs, food availability, our communities and cities in general.

To end then, one crucial way in which sociology can be understood to be public is in its dealing with **public issues** (Mills, 1959). Public issues, as defined by C. Wright Mills in his classic book *The Sociological Imagination*, are those structuring elements of social life that lie beyond our personal control or interpretations of them. Sociology is 'public' inasmuch as it addresses things that have a public reality; of course, specific things that happen in our lives are unique, but they may be unique manifestations of more general things that are happening in similar ways to other people.

So, from Mills (1959), the things that happen in our life feel to us to be personal; they are *social*, that is, the outcome of widely existing patterns and processes. And, as you will have seen from other chapters in this book, not all sociologists study the same topic. In fact, no element of social life at all is off limits to sociological explanation. There can be 'sociologies of' anything: families, music, architecture, online gaming, love, **capitalism**, food, care, money, time, art, pubs, sexuality, death, maths, racism, art, supermarkets, etc., etc. When dealt with sociologically, these are all *public issues* in Mills' (1959) sense of the term. Sociologists do not automatically use the official or commonsense ways in which such public issues are framed though; *doing* sociology on these issues means disrupting taken-for-granted explanations, and looking at them from creative and new perspectives (Becker, 1967; Mills, 1959).

Conclusion

Putting the word 'public' in front of 'sociology' risks making what is already very difficult to define even more so. If we can't definitely definitively define sociology, then what chance do we have with 'public sociology'? Here, I have left the big argument concerning precise definitions of public sociology in the background of our discussion, and instead have focused on some of the ways in which different types of sociology can be said to have a public character. My argument has been that, in one way or another, good sociology involves questioning things that matter to publics (which are the very sets of things that matter to sociology itself).

As we saw, one of the most fundamental criticisms of Burawoy's four types is that they do not bear relationship to the ways in which sociology *actually* happens (Holmwood, 2007: 60); the absence of any really satisfactory evidence for the existence of public sociology. But, even with this being the case – and I think it is – the debate about public sociology that Burawoy reanimated in 2004 (but that has a very long history) was a very good thing for the discipline. It re-started discussion about some fundamental questions in sociology, allowed for those involved to read new ideas, and to think seriously about who was at sociology's 'table' (Tuhiwai Smith, 2012 [1999]). Far from being complacent and self-absorbed, the discussion about public sociology – in large part thanks to the critiques of people working in the field (Acker, 2005; Holmwood, 2007; Tittle, 2004) – can help us to broaden and refresh the discipline, helping to keep sociology relevant and illuminating. As a key part of this process, we must all 'be alert to changes in the society that may be bringing new publics into being' (Acker, 2005: 331), and work to ensure that public sociology questions the basis of sociology itself, which is a valuable and important thing to do.

CHAPTER SUMMARY

- Thinking sociologically is a brilliant way to understand the world. It helps us illuminate things about social life that otherwise remain unexplained or unexplored.
- The debate around public sociology encourages us to reflect on the sociological knowledge that is being made, the way it's produced, for what, and for whom. The relationship between sociology and its various publics underpins these key questions.
- Those who try to nail down a tight definition of public sociology tend to struggle (as was the case with Michael Burawoy's very detailed and ostensibly comprehensive definition).
- The complicated starting points and very diverse nature of sociology itself make public sociology difficult to understand and explain, and it also produces the temptation to try to organize it. But at the core of the debate concerning public sociology is a commitment to widening the benefits of sociology itself, a profoundly important way of interrogating social life.
- Although the definition remains imprecise, public sociology points to an important tendency within the discipline: its publicness (understood in different ways).
- Who gets to speak for publics, how and on what basis? In a democratic society, these are key issues and ones that sociologists must approach carefully.

REVIEW QUESTIONS

- If you had to, how would you go about attacking sociology? How would you defend sociology from these attacks? What evidence would you use?
- Do sociologists '[ignore] the public and the role it plays in the realization of public sociology' (Gans, 2016: 3)?
- Think of a topic, any topic, that you would like to understand sociologically. How would you go about explaining it – and what could we perhaps find out about it using sociology – in a TV interview? Or in a blog? A Tweet? A newspaper? Or to a friend who doesn't study sociology?
- What was Burawoy's central argument with respect to public sociology, and what evidence did he use to back this up?
- Burawoy's version of public sociology was subject to many criticisms. Can you describe three of them?
- Think of a topic in the media today. What might a sociological perspective on it seek to explore, and think of three ways a sociologist who researches in the area might intervene in the debate? Think of (i) where this intervention might happen, and (ii) who might benefit from it and how.

Go Further

Books

- Du Bois, W.E.B. (2008 [1903]) *The Souls of Black Folk*. At www.gutenberg.org/files/408/408-h/408-h.htm

You can read Du Bois' classic book online for free; it 'defies easy summary … [and] ranges across Du Bois's own life in the North and the South [US], and includes detailed analyses of the social and economic conditions in the post-Reconstruction South' (Gilroy, 1993: 125), as well as reflections on particular political movements of the day, music, education in apartheid societies, and short pieces of fiction. A key point here is that this wide-ranging sociological work that connects historical structures with personal circumstances is often, or at least until now has often been, excluded from mainstream scholarship.

- Mills, C.W. (1959) *The Sociological Imagination*. London: Pelican.

This book, I guess, has been responsible for getting lots of us into sociology. Full of the excitement of *doing* sociology, of actually applying ideas and perspectives to the world around us, Mills advocates for understanding 'the relationship between personal experience and the wider society' (1959: 6). Mills famously tells us that imaginative, sociological thought can help explain things about the way the world is that are most usually not explained. It is in part by reading sociology – this book, this chapter and the resources discussed here – that you will develop your own sociological imagination.

- Smith, L.T. (2012 [1999]) *Decolonizing Methodologies: Research and Indigenous Peoples*. London: Zed Books.

This is a wonderful, inspirational book, in which Professor Linda Tuhiwai Smith draws out ways in which scientific knowledge – including social scientific and sociological knowledge – maps onto patterns of geo-political power and colonialism. Questions of truth, and how we think we know facts about particular groups (but not others), are crucial throughout this book, in which Smith shows how certain ways of knowing that emerge from indigenous peoples are overlooked and/or appropriated in scientific discourse. Smith also delivered a talk based on the book at *The Sociological Review*'s Annual Lecture 2019, which can be viewed here: www.thesociologicalreview.com/decolonising-methodologies-20-years-on-the-sociological-review-annual-lecture-by-professor-linda-tuhiwai-smith.

Journal Articles

- Becker, H. (1967) Whose side are we on?' *Social Problems* 14(3): 239–47.

A great, provocative article, which argues that sociologists always do research in a way that is shaped by our 'personal and political sympathies' (p. 239), and that as such we always take sides in our research. A lively and thought-provoking piece, Becker's point concerning values was extremely controversial when he made it in 1967, and re-reading it for this chapter I was surprised at how fresh it seemed. While the language is often problematic to the contemporary reader, it was written in the midst of a world-changing moment for many, and in my opinion Becker's argument chimes with our discussion of public sociology. What do you think?

- Bhambra, G.K. (2017) Brexit, Trump, and 'methodological whiteness': On the misrecognition of race and class. *British Journal of Sociology* 68(1): 214–32.

This article connects extremely well with the lecture by Professor Bhambra that features above. It also brings together a number of the threads from this chapter, as well as reflecting – I think – a particular take on public sociology. The article looks at the ways in which social class is deployed in politics as a racialized category – it becomes a way of people like outgoing US President Donald Trump signalling a 'whiteness' without explicitly doing so, or Brexit campaigners doing similar when seeking to position this move without discussing the 'methodological whiteness' implied. The article deals with public issues (Mills, 1959) while drawing attention to the importance of sociologists not taking for granted the ways in which such issues are framed within political discourse.

Websites

- Global Social Theory (www.GlobalSocialTheory.org)

An absolutely super resource for learning about: (i) sociologists from across the world; (ii) concepts that tend to not appear so much in the sociological mainstream; and (iii) important topics of inquiry. The site is organized by Professor Gurminda Bhambra, whose research you heard about above. Here's a way I often use this site: pick one concept, at random or one that sounds interesting to you, read it and answer the questions. Then, do the same for a thinker – follow all the links before answering the questions – and do the same for a topic. In an hour or two, you can learn a *lot* about public sociology the world over.

- The Sociological Review (www.TheSociologicalReview.com)

I should say I am one of the editors of *The Sociological Review*, so in effect I'm marking my own homework here. But, but … this website is an absolutely awesome resource that contains a great deal of free-to-view sociology and is full of different things to engage with: short blogs, interviews, book reviews, sociological fiction, linked social media sites (Instagram and Twitter amongst them), recorded lectures, and lots

(Continued)

more. I am biased, but I think that it really is a go-to place to read 'public sociology' in the sense (i) of the issues being addressed, and (ii) that all of this material is open and free to access, assuming you have an internet connection.

- Personal website of Michael Burawoy (http://burawoy.berkeley.edu)

Here you will find a great deal about Professor Burawoy's research as well as a number of important resources with specific respect to his work on public sociology. A great deal of the material on this site is open access, free for you to view and read and watch; there's a lot of thoughtful and thought-provoking sociology to look at here.

REFERENCES

Acker, J. (2005) Comments on Burawoy on public sociology. *Critical Sociology* 31(3): 327–31.
Becker, H. (1967) Whose side are we on? *Social Problems* 14(3): 239–47.
Bhambra, G.K. (2017) Brexit, Trump, and 'methodological whiteness': On the misrecognition of race and class. *British Journal of Sociology* 68(1): S214–S232.
Burawoy, M. (2005) For public sociology. *American Sociological Review* 70(1): 4–28.
Davidson, J.P.L. (2021) Ugly progress: W.E.B. Du Bois's sociology of the future. *The Sociological Review* 69(2): 382–95.
Dewey, J. (1952 [1927]) *The Public and Its Problems: An Essay in Political Inquiry*. Athens, GA: Swallow Press/Ohio University Press.
Du Bois, W.E.B. (2018 [1903]) *The Souls of Black Folk*. London: CreateSpace.
Fatsis, L. (2019) The practice of public sociology: Common practice or wishful thinking? *The Sociological Review*. Available at: www.thesociologicalreview.com/the-practice-of-public-sociology-common-practice-or-wishful-thinking (last accessed 30 May 2021).
Gans, H. (2002) More of us should become public sociologists. *Footnotes: American Sociological Association*. Available at: www.asanet.org/sites/default/files/savvy/footnotes/julyaugust02/fn10.html (last accessed 30 May 2021).
Gans, H. (2016) Public sociology and its publics. *American Sociologist* 47(1): 3–11.
Gilroy, P. (1993) *The Black Atlantic: Modernity and Double Consciousness*. Cambridge, MA: Harvard University Press.
Holmwood, J. (2007) Sociology as public discourse and professional practice: A critique of Michael Burawoy. *Sociological Theory* 25(1): 46–66.
Jones, P. and Mair, M. (2016) Genealogy, parasitism and moral economy: The case of UK supermarket growth. In D. Whyte and J. Wiegratz (eds) *Neo-liberalism and the Moral Economy of Fraud*. London: Routledge.
Mills, C.W. (2000 [1959]) *The Sociological Imagination*. Oxford: Oxford University Press.
Smith, L.T. (2012 [1999]) *Decolonizing Methodologies: Research and Indigenous People*. London: Zed Books.
The Public Domain Review (n.d.) W.E.B. Du Bois' hand-drawn infographics of African-American life (1900). Available at: https://publicdomainreview.org/collection/w-e-b-du-bois-hand-drawn-infographics-of-african-american-life-1900 (last accessed 30 May 2021).
Tittle, C.R. (2004) The arrogance of public sociology. *Social Forces* 82(4): 1639–43.

USING SOCIOLOGY

Karim Murji, Sarah Neal and John Solomos

LEARNING OBJECTIVES

- To appreciate the multiplicity of sociological theories, concerns and perspectives.
- To apply sociology to the social world and events.
- To consider what it means to be a reflexive sociologist.

 Framing Questions

1. Why do we need to be critical of sociology?
2. How and in what ways does sociology provide distinctive insights into social relationships, social processes and social emergencies?

Studying Sociology

As you reach the final chapter of this volume, we very much hope that this book has provided you with a broad and engaging introduction to **sociology**, and that it will encourage you to explore sociology more deeply. This is the start of a journey that has taken you through a broad range of theories, a wide variety of topics and some **empirical** studies. The chapters in this book reflect the efforts by various sociologists to combine theories and **methods** to address key aspects of the social relations that help to shape contemporary societies. They also show how to *communicate* sociological ideas and perspectives, to reveal the kinds of questions and data that sociologists are concerned with, and to explain these things in a way that is clear. As the range of topics and issues covered indicate, sociology is a rich and engaged discipline and field of study. You will see that the book includes chapters that focus on many of the issues that you will cover both in the first year of your studies and in subsequent years, and so we hope that you will see that it can be a useful resource for you to continue to consult alongside the other books, articles and resources that you will encounter.

The chapters in the six parts of the book have moved from more traditional areas of sociological concern (for example, social class in Chapter 11 and work in Chapter 17) to much more recent ones (for example, digital society in Chapter 2, the interconnected world in Chapter 6 and science and technology in Chapter 23). As we suggested in Chapter 1, this capacity to develop fresh insight into older areas of ongoing concern and curiosity, while also addressing new social phenomena, is a core strength of sociology: its concern to make sense of social life as it is while we live in it, and a world that every person both makes in some way and is also made or formed by. As his classic text *The Sociological Imagination* (Mills, 1959) suggests, what C. Wright Mills calls the 'first fruit' of a **sociological imagination** is that this imagination 'is the idea that the individual can understand her own experience and gauge her own fate only by locating herself within her period, that she can know her own chances in life only by becoming aware of those of all individuals in her circumstances'. And 'the task and promise' of sociology is to enable 'us to grasp history and biography and the relations between the two within society' (Mills, 1959: 5–6).

All the chapters in this book are framed in such a way as to encourage you to use your sociological imagination by suggesting ways to think about the social relationships that make up what we think of as society and the social world, and the patterns and causes of its social arrangements, as well as the multi-scalar ways in which these are experienced, constituted and understood. The book therefore provides you with a kind of touchstone that will help to guide you through your sociological studies. As you progressed through the various parts of this volume, you will have seen the inspiring scope and scale of sociology. It is important to remember that, as a discipline, sociology is a profoundly inquisitive field of study, and that sociologists do not offer simple, one-dimensional accounts of social relations, since what often intrigues us is the complexity of processes and actions that help to shape social life, and ways of making sense of them.

The authors whose chapters make up this book have used ideas and methods from sociology, as well as other disciplines and interdisciplinary approaches, to develop a better understanding of how particular aspects of social life are organized. In introducing you to their specific areas of scholarly research, they have outlined some of the key approaches that have helped to shape particular fields of sociological research, mentioned some of the key authors that have framed research agendas, and suggested some issues in need of further research and analysis. So, rather than seeing individual chapters as a kind of end point, use them as a way to frame your curiosity to find out more about the key social issues that interest and intrigue you, to explore and dig further.

While this book seeks to promote the importance, capacity and reach of sociology, both we as editors and the authors have also highlighted the limits, absences, marginalizations and even the harms of sociology. As we noted in Chapter 1, postcolonial, feminist and decolonizing scholarship, as well as related social protest movements, have shown the necessity to question sociology, the importance of being critical of sociology and of reflecting on sociology 'sociologically'. Whether this relates to the Western-centric focus of sociology (Go, 2016), academic inequalities within universities and sexism and **racism** on campus (Warikoo, 2016) or global inequalities of academic knowledge production (Collyer, 2018), what this means is that sociological concerns about power, exclusion, representation and voice are not simply 'out there' for sociologists to study but rather that these profoundly shape and impact on sociology too.

Recognizing this means that the study of sociology also needs to involve a disposition and willingness to be reflexive. While being reflexive is itself a significant area of interdisciplinary study, theorizing and practice (Archer, 2003, 2007; Beck et al., 1995), we define it for the purposes here as the process of critically questioning our own assumptions and approaches to the social world and, in light of this, being open to reconsidering and challenging the partiality of **theoretical** and empirical arguments that you come across as your studies develop. And all the chapters here have been presented in ways to encourage you to get a feel for what it means to begin to unpick and interrogate our more taken-for-granted understandings of the 'why and how is it that' of sociology (Bourdieu, 2001) and become a more reflexive sociologist. As Boström et al. (2016) remind us, '**reflexivity** is a point of departure rather than an end in itself [...] it is an opening for dialogue and action rather than a point of closure' (2016: 13). It is important then that you use your studies to be both critical of what you are being taught and reflexive about what facets of sociology appeal to and interest you.

You will have also seen from the various **substantive** chapters that make up the various parts of this book that sociology is always characterized by a plurality of both theoretical and **methodological** frames. This is by no means an accident, since from its very origins sociology has been characterized by curiosity about how social relations have evolved over time and what processes and actions help to shape contemporary forms of these social relationships. It is this curiosity to better understand the world around us that has driven different generations of sociologists to rethink their conceptual and methodological tools and the ways they carry out research. It has helped to drive sociology forward, both as a specific field of research and inquiry and as part of the broader group of social sciences that it helps to inform and to collaborate with.

Given the challenges that societies across the globe face today, it is also important for you to think about how the sociological ideas and methods you are studying have been used to explore and make sense of new phenomena and social issues. Indeed, it is important to see sociology not as a discipline with fixed **boundaries** but as a field that is always evolving in order to make sense of new issues. As the authors who have contributed to this book have argued, it is best to see sociology as constantly evolving and changing in order to respond to new conceptual and empirical challenges. The focus of sociology is on engaging with contemporary issues but placing them in context. It is particularly alive to the need to address new issues through theoretical reflection and empirically focused research. The dynamic nature of the discipline makes it highly attuned to rethinking more established areas of sociological work as well as addressing contemporary issues and challenges. The chapters in Parts 1 and 5 highlight the importance of remembering that sociology has much to say about some of the most pressing social issues and to come back to the concept of 'wicked problems' (Rittel and Webber, 1973) that was discussed in Chapter 1, which include cultures and consumption, war and violence, environment, migrations and social movements. These issues are not necessarily new to sociology but what makes them new frontiers are the ways in which the contemporary form of each forces sociology to expand its field of vision to include emerging challenges within its conceptual frame and empirical research agendas.

However, sociology is not journalism or current affairs, since its analytical scope and conceptual frame and depth are altogether different. Sociology's engagement with the social world is always contextual; it is also always informed by theories and usually by data and evidence too. The contextual nature of sociology refers to placing issues, debates and problems in society within a frame. That frame can be historical, asking questions such as: how, why and in what form have such issues arisen before? Or this might be seen as identifying the historical basis or historicity of the present. In making connections between past and present, sociologists make decisions as they select what and which aspects of the past matter, and to what extent. As well as this temporal dimension, there is also a spatial one. This entails questions such as: in what places or locations have some issues appeared before? Making connections or identifying the relations between 'here' and 'there' is thus also part of the sociological imagination. But just as sociology is not history, it is not geography either, but rather draws on other times and spaces in ways that are significant to understanding things – relationships, practices, and social and systemically disruptive events, as well as longer term cultural and political shifts – that are both part of and active in the making of the contemporary social world.

As a way of encouraging you to explore the 'live' or evolving nature of sociological research and analysis, we want to focus the next part of this chapter on an issue that speaks directly to social disruption in our time – namely, the COVID-19 **pandemic**, which in 2020/21 had an estimated global death toll running into the millions, as well as over 100 million people infected. In reflecting on this event, we aim to suggest the ways in which you can use sociology as a way of making sense of it. As a specific example, we highlight the ways in which crisis events like this link up with core sociological questions and topics like those explored in this book. While this example is focused on how sociologists have drawn on theories and analytical frames to make sense of COVID-19 as a social phenomenon, it also highlights the potential of sociology to interrogate and explain.

Pause for Thought

Before we move on, take a little pause and have a look back at the Table of Contents of this book:

- In each of the six parts, can you identify one chapter whose topic could be linked to the COVID-19 global health crisis?
- Try to write a bullet point for each of the topics you can think of and what the connection may be. This does not mean that the chapter itself discusses COVID-19. But ask yourself where or how it could be extended or applied to making sense of the pandemic.

Sociology and the COVID-19 Pandemic

We raised the question of how sociology will respond to the global health pandemic in Chapter 1 to this book, and we return to it here. There can be little doubt that the COVID-19 pandemic has provided a major challenge to many nations and regions of the world. It has been global in a way that underscores a meaning of global as something that occurs in and touches every part of the world. It also touched every part of humanity in a way that emphasizes our fragility as a species whatever other characteristics are used to define us as social beings. While there had been long-standing predictions of a global pandemic for which the world was not prepared, the hugely uneven infection and death rates and the varying responses of government and international bodies signalled how COVID-19 presented many policy and political challenges. This challenge can also be extended to other academic disciplines, across the natural and social sciences, and the humanities. Although all of these fields had had some discussions about the historical and contemporary

USING SOCIOLOGY

impact of epidemics and pandemics, particularly in relation to AIDS from the 1980s onwards and SARS and Ebola in the 2000s, COVID-19 posed a new and different kind of challenge around what academic research and disciplines had to say about the social and political impact of a real-world global health crisis.

Writing about sociology's response to the pandemic, the Australian sociologist Raewyn Connell argued forcefully that 'sociology as we know it is not very good in handling a historical moment, unpacking a conjuncture, let alone grasping a radically new situation like this' (Connell, 2020: 749). This may or may not be the case – and one of the core features of sociology is that sociologists take a variety of stances on almost all issues and they can disagree about the scale and extent to which sociology is (or is not) capable of addressing new or radically new situations. But in thinking about Connell's argument, the various chapters in this book offer insights into the ways in which sociology has sought to provide a timely response to new challenges and trends in society.

Some of the ways that sociology can be seen as relevant to and useful in thinking about COVID-19 are to be found in the chapters of this book. In the Pause for Thought activity, it is likely that you thought of some of these connections yourself. Perhaps the most immediate one would be with Chapter 18 on health, where you saw how sociology understands and analyses the social determinants of health and illness, and how those things are not equally spread throughout the **population** but structured along lines of social and economic inequalities. Various inequalities are examined in Part 3 of this book, but the social changes that COVID-19 highlighted are also connected to issues such as the **role** of science and technology in society and the nature of international migration.

As it is widely established that vulnerability to COVID-19 varies across a range of social and demographic factors, the mention of inequalities may have made you think about the ways in which social differences such as **age**, race/**ethnicity** and gender are significant in framing the pandemic (Islam et al., 2020). A sociological viewpoint or sensibility would draw attention to the pandemic's **variable** or uneven effects (Murji and Picker, 2020).

28.1 Key Case

Pandemic Inequalities

One study of structurally vulnerable neighbourhoods and racial-ethnic inequalities noted that:

The consequences of the pandemic reach far beyond COVID-19 morbidity and mortality. The effects of social and economic insecurity and the trauma of massive loss of life will continue to impact societies around the world for generations. Just as we are seeing during the pandemic, residents of colour in structurally vulnerable neighbourhoods are at risk of bearing the brunt of these long-term consequences if nothing is done. (Berkowitz et al., 2020: 3)

Indeed, what became evident from the start of 2020 was that one of the features of COVID-19 was that although it impacted on all nations at a global level it was also experienced differently by black and minority communities, by migrants, by refugees and other vulnerable groups (The New Yorker, 2020). The mention of 'structurally vulnerable neighbourhoods' above also raises important questions about the role that living in deprived localities played in making people more vulnerable to the pandemic. Such neighbourhoods typically have less access to good health services and other mechanisms for dealing with a crisis such as the one represented by the COVID-19 pandemic.

PART 6 WHAT IS SOCIOLOGY USEFUL FOR?

28.2 Key Case

COVID-19 and Race

As one study notes about the situation in the US:

In the United States, race-ethnic disparities in COVID-19 cases emerged rapidly. Although data remain woefully incomplete, the proportion of cases and deaths among Black, Latino, and Indigenous Americans ranges from twofold to fourfold higher than the presence of those groups in the population. And deaths for people of color are occurring at younger ages. (Bassett, 2020: 230)

The linkages between COVID-19 and race have also been highlighted by the impact of the pandemic on workers and workplaces and you may have made a link to Chapter 17 and work. For example, it is important to note that many frontline health professionals and support workers in the **National Health Service** are from minority or **migrant** backgrounds. A similar, if more gendered, pattern can be traced in the context of care homes for elderly people. The theme of age and the **life course** was the focus of Anna Wanka's chapter in Part 3, and the ways in which the pandemic differentially impacts on older populations has been a powerful driver in exposing how age shapes not only health and social inequalities but also the nature of personal lives and how the social world is experienced.

The pandemic was at once global and differentiated across national and more localized contexts. That is, identifying it as a 'global' phenomenon does not mean it was the same across the world as there were huge variations in infections and deaths, as well as responses by national governments. The fact that Europe and the USA were among the epicentres of the pandemic establishes that this is more than a North/South matter but also highlights the ways in which all societies had to deal with its health and broader social and economic consequences.

There are other connections that you might have made drawing on the contents of this book. COVID-19 generated a great deal of debate around track and trace apps and health monitoring systems, as well as data sharing and accuracy. As a novel virus – although history has seen many viruses and the likelihood of a pandemic had been predicted – COVID-19 also shed light on the emergent and changing nature of biomedical knowledge. Thus, the chapters on the digital society as well as on science and technology can also be related to and drawn upon in thinking about sociology's ability to explain COVID-19 and its effects.

- The connections between COVID-19 and this book point to contents in Parts 1, 3, 4 and 5. What about Parts 2 and 6 though? Look again at the title and summary of the chapters in those parts – what connections can you see from those?

Links Between Theory and Method

Perhaps at first sight you thought theories and methods look somewhat dry and abstract. You may have asked: How can they be related to 'real world' issues like COVID-19? Theory can indeed seem rather abstract and even rarefied, sometimes more like speculation than grounded thinking. However, theory, as it has been presented in this book, is both distinctive and generic. In the latter sense, you have been seeing and using theories throughout the book. All of the chapters draw on one or more theories of the social world in order to understand and explain a particular topic or theme in society. In this sense, theory is not an abstraction but a vital and central tool of sociological thinking. While the discussion of theories in Chapters 7 and 8 may seem different, they are also key resources in thinking about how societies respond to issues like a pandemic, with some classical theories perhaps laying more stress on order and cooperation, while others highlight the role of **conflict**. As you saw in Chapters 7 and 26, the rise of sociology was linked to its claim to offer a new science of society, as a way of understanding rapid and sometimes confusing periods of social change. But it is also important to remember that the study of society using theoretical and methodological tools from sociology is not an abstract approach, since human beings are active agents who make and re-make social life all the time. Sociology therefore always necessarily involves a process of trying to make sense of the everyday processes that help to shape the complex patterns of social life.

Modern or contemporary theories deal with the complex and interconnected nature of social worlds to highlight the ways in which risk and uncertainty about what is knowledge, or the ways in which identities are freer floating than once seemed to be the case, might be used. The use of theory in this respect may take multiple forms. At one level, it may be used to develop an argument or a case that is in itself theoretical. Or theory might be used to frame or shape questions for further and empirical investigation – such as, is there more uncertainty about scientific and expert knowledge due to the pandemic?

The question of the uses of sociology frames the final section of the book and returns us to some of the questions we raised in Chapter 1 about what makes sociology valuable, reflecting the debate that was revived in the early 21st century about what sociology is for and what it can do. There is no simple answer to these questions, as you saw in Chapter 1 and in many of the chapters in this book. For example, in Chapter 27, one of the key figures in this debate identified a number of different types of purpose for sociology, ranging from sociology as a rather technical discipline aimed at solving social problems through government and policy, to a more active and outward facing discipline seeking to critically examine social relationships and interactions and engage publics in the widest sense about pressing social issues such as migration and mobility, local and global inequalities, and power differentials, as well as exploring the nature of social ties, **family** forms, identities and identification, solidarity and the significance of micro, everyday and personal lives. The chapters in Parts 3 and 4 examined these themes as well as particular sites of sociological inquiry such as work and education, which both have long associations with social divisions and exclusion.

Finally, in this journey connecting sociology and the contents of this book to COVID-19, there is also a link to research methods. At its widest, there was throughout the COVID-19 pandemic an issue about data accuracy, quality and **reliability**, and this stretches far beyond the social sciences into fields such as **epidemiology**. The numbers reported were subjected to many questions such as why some countries had relatively low rates and whether these were 'real' or not. At the same time, the numbers and data were subject to revision and recalculation, such as when the official agency in the UK changed the way in which the number of deaths linked to COVID-19 was measured from any mention of it on a death certificate to only including individuals who had died in the 28 days after diagnosis. As you have seen in many of the chapters in this book and specifically in Chapters 9 and 10, sociology is driven by a range of very different research methods. We noted in Chapter 1 that sociology has become increasingly inclusive and creative in relation to the research methods it uses and in terms of the quantitative and qualitative ways in which it collects and generates data about social life. Through in-depth **mixed methods** and qualitative work, sociological methods can add rich material on the experiences and practices of people, for example in lockdown, including mental health and personal and family relationships.

Drawing on the experience of COVID-19 to take a journey through sociology has been attempted by other sociologists. For instance, Matthewman and Huppatz (2020) saw COVID-19 'as a living laboratory ... ripe for sociological analysis'. They suggest links such as the theory of risk society, the extent of social solidarity following Durkheim, and the uneven pattern of who did or did not become victims of the virus, drawing on theories of social inequalities as well as criminology, and connections to gender inequalities, statistical and focal data, and the impact of COVID-19 on work and family life. In a similar way, Lupton (2020) draws attention to the effect of the pandemic on the Global South and internal and international relations with and between nations, while social class and gender inequalities are a strong feature in both the Global North and South.

Using Sociology and the Uses of Sociology

Interrogating the case of COVID-19 provides a means of showing the range and types of connections that sociology can be utilized for. But doing so also raises fundamental questions about the value of sociology, like those identified in Chapter 26, drawing on Burawoy (2005), who posed them as follows: Useful for what? And useful to whom?

As you will have seen in Part 6 of this volume, a recurring concern in sociology is its role in wider society. While related disciplines, such as geography, economics and politics, are often seen as having something more direct or immediate to say about particular social issues, sociology has sometimes been seen as having become preoccupied with its own theoretical conversations and as having less and less to say about the wider social issues that helped to frame its emergence as a field of research and scholarship in earlier times. Although many well-known sociologists have pushed back against this image of sociology as remote by highlighting a key role for public sociology (Burawoy, 2005; Calhoun, 2005), there remains a notion that sociologists have not always lived up to the promise of addressing the key challenges societies face in the contemporary global environment (Romero, 2020). As the preceding discussion has shown, however, this image of sociology as remote and abstract is misleading. As we have noted here and in this chapter, sociology has sought to examine and explain the social world and contribute insights for understanding social phenomena, the relationalities of the macro and the micro and social transformations as well as 'social shock' events like Brexit and COVID-19. The relevance and currency of sociology is a theme that runs through each of the chapters included in the book. For example, as Part 3 demonstrates, sociology has driven debates about social identities. As you saw in Chapters 11, 12 and 13, sociology has led on rethinking the meanings and social consequences of ideas of social class, gender, sexuality and race. More recently, the significance of age-stage and the life-course has preoccupied sociology, as Chapter 14 shows. In Part 5 of this book, you encountered a range of topics – war and violence, science and technology, consumption, migration and social movement – that are among the challenges facing societies across the world. The opening chapters on the digital society, the environment and crime explore both new and longer standing challenges in what Chapter 6 defines as interconnected worlds. The discussions of science and the environment raise profound questions for sociology and the social sciences as a whole about the impact of human societies on the planet and the arrival of the **Anthropocene**, where humans have created a new age or epoch in time. As Chapter 3 explores, these areas also raise bigger questions about the relationship between human and non-human worlds and the ways in which some early sociologies from the 19th and 20th centuries overstated the separation of social from natural worlds. While that may have made sense in a time when sociology was seeking to establish itself as a unique or distinctive field of study, it has become more questionable as **scientific knowledge** has developed.

Another example of the ways in which you can begin to use specific chapters of the book to think about specific social phenomena can be found if you look at Chapter 2 on Digital Society and Chapter 25 on Social Movements. In 2013 a group of activists used the hashtag *#BlackLivesMatter* to launch a discussion about issues such as violence against African Americans by the police and by white vigilantes. The killings of Trayvon Martin, Michael Brown and a number of others in 2013, 2014 and subsequent years created a space for mobilization on this issue, and eventually the Black Lives Matter movement evolved into a range of mobilizations that took place both on social media and in specific cities and towns, as activists sought to create alliances in order to challenge police violence and to raise consciousness about wider issues such as racial inequalities in employment, health, housing and education (Chatelain, 2019). Subsequently, the deaths of Breonna Taylor and George Floyd in early 2020 led to ever wider and broader mobilizations under the banner of Black Lives Matter that attracted support, and opposition, both within the United States and globally (Smith and King, 2021).

We hope you can see from examples such as this that although each chapter can be read independently it is also helpful for you to seek to think across the various chapters, and indeed parts, and to ask questions about what you can learn by trying to develop some links between them. Other disciplines also have a perspective on personal lives, migration, wars, digital societies, the environment and so on. Sociological knowledge is distinct as well as complementary to those, and the chapters in this book on those show how sociology develops a perspective on topics that is distinct from any other discipline while also interacting productively with them. Sociology is comfortable in its openness to engaging with other disciplines in this way. This *interdisciplinarity* has been part of why sociology can be thought of as a dynamic and sustainable discipline.

Its capacity to reflect on its own history, modes of knowledge production, its place in and impact on society is what makes sociology a reflective and critical discipline. This is something that sociologists like Pierre Bourdieu and Michele Lamont have sought to emphasize in their discussions of sociology as 'reflexive' (Bourdieu and Wacquant, 1992; Lamont, 2009). Hence, one answer to Burawoy's questions is that sociology is useful to *publics*, which in its widest sense includes you, students of sociology, plus all of us who are working as sociologists in the academy, as well as the general public that seeks to be informed by knowledge and science. Sociological research is informed by the need to think beyond taken-for-granted preconceptions in order to understand the ways in which people think about society and their own social positionings.

Staying with Sociology

If you continue to study sociology, as you go through the various stages of your sociological education try to ask yourself questions about how the ideas and methods that you are studying can help you to make sense of the social, cultural and political world around you. For example, if you are studying sociologies of digital society, families, crime, health, the environment, race or gender, try to think about how these different areas of research can help you to engage with questions about these issues in wider society. It is also important that you try to think through possible links and connections between the various fields of sociology that you are studying in specific modules. As we saw with the earlier discussion of the COVID-19 pandemic, social issues and wicked problems are rarely experienced as 'social silos' but rather as overlapping, colliding and intersecting phenomena.

As you have seen, sociology is a discipline that is home to a wide range of theories, ideas, methods and tools for research. While some may see this plurality of theories and methods as confusing, it is also part of the excitement of studying a subject that is constantly asking new and innovative questions about how social relations are organized and how they have evolved and changed. Rather than seeing this diversity of approaches as a problem, it is best to embrace it and to ask yourself how you can learn to think sociologically through a range of perspectives.

It is also important to remember that as one of the core social sciences sociology makes important methodological and theoretical contributions across a wide range of disciplines. Indeed, it has become even more evident at this juncture that as a global discipline sociology has been able to make important contributions to knowledge both through discipline-specific and interdisciplinary research, as well as public engagement and using our research to create impact, addressing major cross-cutting challenges – societal inequality, **ecological** crises, and technological transformations – facing contemporary societies and cultures.

REVIEW QUESTIONS

1. How does sociology respond to new challenges and situations?
2. Using examples from this chapter and other chapters in this book, discuss what the distinctive contributions are that sociology can make to analysing contemporary societies.
3. Again, reflecting on the issues that we have addressed in this chapter, ask yourself what some of the key contemporary challenges are that sociology faces.

Go Further

Finally, in thinking through the key issues that are addressed in this concluding chapter, we suggest that you look at the following two issues and reflect on them.

Some sociologists argue that sociology needs to align itself with struggles to change society as well as to understand how society works. In an article entitled 'Sociology Engaged in Social Justice', Mary Romero (2020), for example, argues that sociology needs to support and engage with struggles for social justice. In considering Romero's argument, ask yourself the following questions:

- What are the advantages of seeing sociology through the lens of struggles for social justice?
- Is this too limiting a conception of the normative values of sociology?

You will also find it useful here to look at the arguments developed by Nick Crossley in Chapter 25 and by Paul Jones in Chapter 27.

USING SOCIOLOGY

Thinking back to specific chapters in this volume, explore how sociology can help us to better understand and to act upon issues of social justice and the conditions for bringing about social change. Ask yourself whether a normative commitment to social justice may limit our ability as sociologists to critically research social phenomena and construct explanations about the processes that have helped to shape them.

For other sociologists, a key challenge that we face is how to use our theoretical tools and methods to make sense of the major challenges faced by humanity, such as climate change and environmental change. This is something explored fully in Chapter 3 by Kate Burningham and you will find it useful to look at the arguments developed there. You can also look at the article on 'Sociology and the Climate Crisis' by Eric Klinenberg, Malcolm Araos and Liz Koslov (2020). This article argues that the climate crisis represents a major challenge for sociology. In thinking about the arguments developed by both Burningham and Klinenberg, Araos and Koslov, ask yourself the following questions:

- How can sociology shed light on the core issues that underlie the climate crisis?
- How can sociological research help to address the social and cultural transformations that are necessary to deal with the climate crisis?

In thinking through the range of issues that are raised by these two articles, try to make some notes about the key arguments they offer and ask yourself how sociologists can critically engage with questions such as social justice and the climate crisis. You may also find it useful to make some notes about any problems that you see as arising from your efforts to read and understand the core arguments presented in the two articles.

REFERENCES

Archer, M.S. (2003) *Structure, Agency and the Internal Conversation*. Cambridge: Cambridge University Press.

Archer, M.S. (2007) *Making Our Way through the World: Human Reflexivity and Social Mobility*. Cambridge: Cambridge University Press.

Bassett, M.T. (2020) First AIDS, now COVID-19: Another plague shows us who we are. *Social Research: An International Quarterly* 87(2): 229–32.

Beck, U., Giddens, A. and Lash, S. (eds) (1995) *Reflexive Modernization: Politics, Tradition and Aesthetics in the Modern Social Order*. Cambridge: Polity Press.

Berkowitz, R.L., Gao, X., Michaels, E.K. and Mujahid, M.S. (2020) Structurally vulnerable neighbourhood environments and racial/ethnic COVID-19 inequities. *Cities & Health*. DOI: 10.1080/23748834.2020.1792069.

Boström, M., Lidskog, R. and Uggla, Y. (2016) A reflexive look at reflexivity in environmental sociology. *Environmental Sociology* 3(1): 6–16.

Bourdieu, P. (2001) *Masculine Domination*. Stanford: Stanford University Press.

Bourdieu, P. and Wacquant, L.J.D. (1992) *An Invitation to Reflexive Sociology*. Chicago: University of Chicago Press.

Burawoy, M. (2005) For public sociology. *American Sociological Review* 70(1): 4–28.

Calhoun, C.J. (2005) The promise of public sociology. *British Journal of Sociology* 56(3): 355–63; discussion 417–32.

Chatelain, M. (2019) Five years after Ferguson. *Dissent* 66(4): 127–32.

Collyer, F.M. (2018) Global patterns in the publishing of academic knowledge: Global North, Global South. *Current Sociology* 66(1): 56–73.

Connell, R. (2020) COVID-19/Sociology. *Journal of Sociology* 56(4): 745–51.

Go, J. (2016) *Postcolonial Thought and Social Theory*. New York: Oxford University Press.

Islam, N., Khunti, K., Dambha-Miller, H., Kawachi, I. and Marmot, M. (2020) COVID-19 mortality: A complex interplay of sex, gender and ethnicity. *European Journal of Public Health* 30(5): 847–8.

Klinenberg, E., Araos, M. and Koslov, L. (2020) Sociology and the climate crisis. *Annual Review of Sociology* 46(1): 649–69.

Lamont, M. (2009) *How Professors Think: Inside the Curious World of Academic Judgement*. Cambridge, MA: Harvard University Press.

Lupton, D. (2020) Special Section on 'Sociology and the Coronavirus (COVID-19) Pandemic'. *Health Sociology Review* 29(2): 111–12.

Matthewman, S. and Huppatz, K. (2020) A sociology of COVID-19. *Journal of Sociology* 56(4): 675–83.

Mills, C.W. (1959) *The Sociological Imagination*. New York: Oxford University Press.

Murji, K. and Picker. G. (2020) Racist morbidities: A conjunctural analysis of the COVID-19 pandemic. *European Societies*, DOI: 10.1080/14616696.2020.1825767.

Rittel, H.W.J. and Webber, M.M. (1973) Dilemmas in a general theory of planning. *Policy Sciences* 4(2): 155–69.

Romero, M. (2020) Sociology engaged in social justice. *American Sociological Review* 85(1): 1–30.

Smith, R.M. and King, D. (2021) Racial reparations against white protectionism: America's new racial politics. *Journal of Race, Ethnicity, and Politics*. DOI: 10.1017/rep.2020.38.

The New Yorker (2020) Dispatches from a pandemic. *The New Yorker*, 13 April: 34–50.

Warikoo, N.K. (2016) *The Diversity Bargain: And Other Dilemmas of Race, Admissions, and Meritocracy at Elite Universities*. Chicago: University of Chicago Press.

GLOSSARY

Actor-network theory A theory emerging from **STS** which posits that both human and non-human 'actants' comprise networks of association through which new scientific claims and innovations take shape and become stabilized.

Adverse incorporation Workers whose poor economic situation forces them to take work with low pay and poor working conditions.

Aesthetic labour The work of 'looking good and sounding right' for a specific job.

Age A category of difference that can be quantified in a number. From a sociological perspective, it is a social construct.

Age as a social construct Means that (social) age is not naturally, but rather socially and culturally, given and results in historically, socially and culturally contingent and dynamic practices and processes.

Ageism A concept that comprises age-based stereotypes, attitudes and age-discriminatory behaviour.

Age-segregated society A society in which different age groups are assigned specific roles, corresponding institutions and places, and are hence separated from one another.

Aging (or sometimes **Ageing**) The process of growing older. It refers to the social mobility between age categories.

Alienation A concept used by Karl Marx in his *Economic and Philosophical Manuscripts* (1844). Taken from the philosopher G.W.F. Hegel, Marx used it to describe how the modern wage labourer is estranged from his or her labour, which in turn reduces the individual to the level of a thing.

Anomie A term used by Émile Durkheim in his book *Suicide* (1897) to describe a conflict in belief systems that causes the breakdown of social bonds between the individual and the community.

Anthropocene A new geological time period in which significant human impacts on the planet's climate and ecosystems are apparent.

Anthropocentric A perspective that sees humans as separate from, and more important than, the rest of nature.

Asylum seeker A person who is seeking protection in a different country, but whose claim has not yet been decided on by the country's relevant authorities.

Automation The process by which human labour is replaced by machines.

Autonomy Freedom from external control or influence; independence.

GLOSSARY

Behaviourism   Approach to the study of humans and other animals which observes visible behaviour rather than speculating about the cognitive processes which may accompany it. Relatedly, **Behaviouralism** in political science concentrates, for example, on actual votes rather than intentions or the motives of voters.

Biographical adjustment   The questioning and reordering of identity after the onset and diagnosis of a chronic illness.

Biological essentialism   This term describes claims that specific qualities – e.g. race, gender or intelligence – are biologically innate. This counters arguments that these qualities are socially constituted.

Biomedicine   Scientifically informed medicine which views the body as a machine, separate from the mind, and seeks causes of ill-health within biological and chemical processes.

Biosociality   A form of sociality created through biological knowledge, such as an understanding that people share similar genes or a genetic risk factor.

Boundaries   A concept denoting symbolic, material and relational separations between people who are inside a category from those who are outside of it.

Bricolage   Something that is created from a diverse number of other (sometimes unrelated) components.

Capitalism   A social and economic system based on private (rather than state) ownership of the means of production, in which the production and distribution of goods and services is organized through market competition and the pursuit of profit.

Carbon footprint   The amount of carbon dioxide released into the atmosphere as a result of the activities of a particular individual, organization or community.

Center-periphery structure   The organization of the division of labour between interdependent world regions in the capitalist world economy according to the degree of profitability of economic production.

Chattel slavery   The ownership and control of a human being as a means to extract forced labour.

Chronic illness   A persistent health condition that lasts longer than three months and is distinguished from acute conditions.

Chrononormativity   Refers to the temporal normativity of age-appropriate behaviours, such as the notion of a 'right' time to have children or retire.

Circular migration   A form of migration in which people repeatedly move back and forth between two or more countries.

Citizenship   A legal bond between a person and a state recognizing that the person is a member of or belongs to the state.

Class consciousness   Deriving from Marxist class analysis, 'class consciousness' refers to a developing process in which those sharing common objective economic relations (a 'class in itself') become aware of their shared class interests and work together to achieve common class aims, acting as a self-conscious social grouping (a 'class for itself').

GLOSSARY

Classical social theories   Influential social theories developed in the 19th and early 20th centuries.

Coding   The process of transforming data into a set of analytically meaningful categories.

Coercion   A reference to the use of explicit or implicit threats of violence (and the use of violence itself in as far as it can be seen as conveying a threat), i.e. the manipulation of fear of violence, in order to compel someone to do something and/or to deter someone from doing something.

Collective efficacy   The extent to which a community exerts informal social control over a locality through cohesion and mutual trust.

Collective identity   A sense of group belonging often symbolized by a label (e.g. 'working-class') and cultivated and maintained through shared activities and rituals.

Colonialism   The practice of domination of various peoples (in African, Asia and the Americas) by European countries that led to resistance on the part of the colonized. Frantz Fanon and W.E.B. Du Bois speak eloquently on the effects of colonialism.

Coloniality   The counterpart of the modernity that emerged with Europe's colonial expansion in the 16th century; the racial, economic, political and cultural hierarchies persisting after formal decolonization.

Colourism   The practice, typically within the same racial group, of attaching meaning to skin tone. Colourism often results in discrimination against dark-skinned people.

Commodity fetishism   The belief – erroneous in Marx's view – that objects have intrinsic value beyond the labour power that goes into producing them.

Complementary and alternative medicine   (CAM) A shorthand to cover the huge array of knowledges and practices that range from herbalism, homeopathy, acupuncture and ayurvedic medicine to reflexology, iridology, faith healing, etc.

Conflict   The relation of reciprocal opposition between two or more interdependent entities. Conflict typically involves iterative interactions, and specific forms of exchange: of arguments, strategic moves, blows or bullets. As such, they establish more or less institutionalized social relations.

Conflict theory   A theory that society is in a state of perpetual conflict because of competition for limited resources.

Conspicuous consumerism   Another term for conspicuous consumption, where people buy expensive goods or services primarily to display their wealth and status, rather than from real need.

Conspicuous consumption   The practice – observed by Thorstein Veblen in the late 19th century – of consuming expensive goods for the purposes of displaying status and prestige.

Consumer society   A term used to describe a society where the market exchange of consumer goods is the primary mode of social organization.

Consumption-based emissions   A way of calculating carbon emissions associated with providing the goods and services consumed in a country – even if some of those emissions occur elsewhere.

GLOSSARY

Contemporary social theories Social theories developed from the mid-20th century onwards.

Control theory Maintains that delinquent acts arise when an individual's bonds to society are weak or broken.

Conventionalism An anti-positivist position in the philosophy of science which stresses the agreement of scientists as the ultimate foundation of scientific knowledge.

Cosmopolitanism The idea that all human beings are and should be treated as members of a single community.

Country of destination A country that is the destination of a person or a group of people who migrate internationally.

Country of origin A country of nationality or of former habitual residence of a person or group of people who have migrated internationally.

Country of transit A country through which a person or a group of people pass on a journey either to the country of destination or origin.

Critical gerontology A specialized field of gerontology that puts structural relationships of power at the centre of analysis.

Cultural capital The resources and advantages that accrue to an individual through their family and educational experiences, inclusive of art and culture.

Cultural gerontology A specialized field of gerontology that emphasizes culture and consumption as crucial factors in the making of later life.

Cultural intermediary A worker whose job involves them in encouraging others to consume goods, services and cultural products.

Cultural reproduction theory The method by which dominant classes within an unequal society replicate and legitimate aspects of their culture.

Cycles of contention A period of increased protest and social movement activity in a society in which earlier protests appear to encourage and trigger later protests, even on unrelated matters.

Data collection instruments The tools used to collect data in a research project.

Datafication The ideology of 'dataism', the belief that digital infrastructures today enable the transformation of social action into online quantified data. Sociologists have shown that this ideology creates blindspots, not least blindness to the ways in which digital systems shape the very 'social' phenomena that they presume to measure.

Debt bondage Forced labour extracted as repayment of a debt; the most common form of modern slavery.

Decolonization The process in which countries, largely in Africa and Asia, became independent of the colonizing country.

Decolonizing sociology A process that involves understanding and problematizing the ways in which power relationships have shaped assumptions with respect to how knowledge is generated.

GLOSSARY

Decolourization   To remove the colour from; in this context to ignore the difference in race or colour.

Deindustrialization   A process of social and economic change in which there is a decline of manufacturing and heavy industry in the economic sector within a region or country.

Democratization   Family forms and relationships holding out the possibility of democratic autonomy, equality and new forms of openness and mutuality.

Demographic transformation   The change in population that results from decreased fertility and mortality and increased longevity.

Dependency   An external condition imposed on colonized countries by colonial powers that maintains the flow of economic surplus from the former to the latter after independence.

Despotic power   An expression coined by Michael Mann to refer to the repressive capacities of the state, conceived of as a hierarchical organization dominated by a political and military elite. A power that allows eliminating opponents and coercing populations. Contrary to infrastructural power, it does not involve influencing the everyday life of individuals or transforming society in any significant way.

Detraditionalization   Where individuals are 'disembedded' from traditional roles, enabling them actively to seek out new life experiments in intimate and family living.

Development/Underdevelopment   Interdependent outcomes of the historical process through which natural and labour resources extracted from one world region fuel economic growth in the extracting region.

Deviance   Behaviour, conduct, beliefs and styles which depart from group rules, norms and expectations.

Diaspora   Migrants and/or their descendants whose origin lies elsewhere and whose identity and sense of belonging have been shaped by migration experience, whether recent or historical.

Differential association   How criminal behaviour is acquired through interactions with others.

Digital re-mediation of social life   As digital technologies increasingly serve as media of social life, everyday activities – from receiving a message to giving a present or paying a bill – increasingly occur through digital infrastructures. As such activities become mediated by digital devices, they are re-composed and re-formatted in the process, meaning that different actors, things, concepts and forms now play a part in organizing that activity.

Digital sociology   A broad term capturing different ways in which sociologists both study the digital world and make use of digital media and technologies to undertake sociological enquiry.

Digitalization of society   A multi-faceted process by which diverse digital technologies from search engines to computational navigation systems come to play a role in the restructuring of social life and wider societal arrangements.

Displacement   A movement of people who have been forced to leave their homes or places of habitual residence either for protection or because of a disaster.

Display   A concept highlighting how family members need to convey that they are a family to each other in a contemporary context where it is not immediately apparent what and who is 'my family'.

Division of labour How tasks within a manufacturing process or social system are separated and allocated.

Domestic service Paid work done within homes to maintain everyday life.

Ecological A perspective that emphasizes interconnections between living things and their environment.

Ecological limits The idea that the natural world has finite resources and limits to the emissions and pollution it is able to absorb.

Emigration The act of moving from the country of origin to another country or the process of international outward migration more broadly.

Emotional labour The work of managing feelings in order to create feelings in others.

Empirical Verifiable or provable by means of (sensory) experience, observation and/or experiment.

Empiricism A philosophical approach which stresses experience as the sole or principal source of knowledge. In sociology, empirical research (which may be quantitative or qualitative) is often conducted to test theories but also contrasted with more speculative theoretical models such as Marxism or psychoanalytic theory, where it is not clear what would be a crucial test of the theory.

Endogamous Marrying within a defined kin-group such as village or social class.

Entanglement Another term for interconnection; used here to point to the common origin and mutual influences between structures that developed and should therefore be analysed jointly.

Environmental justice A social movement and a policy principle which challenges socially disproportionate exposure to environmental risks and hazards and pursues the fair distribution of environmental benefits.

Epidemic Widespread occurrence of a disease; usually refers to infectious diseases but used here to describe extensive prevalence.

Epidemiology The study of the incidence and pattern of disease and ill-health.

Epistemological Related to the understanding, study and/or theory of knowledge – especially with regard to its nature, origin and scope as well as its construction through processes of justification.

Epistemology The theory of knowledge with regard to its methods and validity, and the distinction between justified belief and opinion.

Equal opportunities The principle of fair competition, which holds that everyone should have the same chance to compete for opportunities within education, the labour market or society more generally, and in which people should not be treated differently by characteristics such as their race, gender or social class background.

Ethnicity A collective that shares common cultural characteristics, such as religion, language or nationality. A term that is sometimes used as a euphemism for race.

Ethnomethodology A term invented by Harold Garfinkel, on the model of social anthropologists' term 'ethnobotany', to describe his study of the way people made sense of everyday situations.

GLOSSARY

Eurocentric   Focusing on European culture or history to the exclusion of a wider view of the world.

Eurocentrism   A term of criticism, suggesting that someone focuses solely on European, sometimes Western, phenomena and processes and their explanation while ignoring other contexts.

European Enlightenment   An intellectual and philosophical movement, in various European countries which, during the 17th to 19th centuries, was concerned with replacing tradition and superstition by the power of reason.

Exceptionalism   The view that an individual, community, country, or time period is extraordinary in terms of its (often self-imposed) superiority.

External validity   The extent to which the results of a study can be generalized in different contexts.

False contracts   A means to disguise slavery. Forced labourers may be made to sign contracts that enslave them; or forced labourers sign employment contracts that are not honoured.

Families of choice   People creating their own families made up of chosen friends and (ex)lovers as well as selected kin.

Family   Bonds of blood, legal or intimate relationships that endure over time and across generations.

Family practices   A concept that focuses on the 'doing' of family as an activity, in contrast to fixed ideas about family being a form or an institution to which individuals belong.

Fascism   A form of far-right, authoritarian ultranationalism characterized by dictatorial power.

Feminist scholar   A scholar who consciously brings to research the values of feminist approaches and challenges the 'traditional' understandings and approaches to research.

Financialization   A process of the increasing importance of financial services and shareholder value in the economy, with increasing monetization of social institutions which previously were not primarily run for profit (such as education).

Flexible work   Paid work that is not organized to a set schedule.

Force   The socially recognized (in the sense of cognition rather than 'acceptance') capacity to use violence. It is hence a function of (1) the possession of the resources necessary to do so (weapons, organizational assets, money, etc.); and (2) cognition of this capacity by other agents in a given context.

Forced labour   Work that is not entered into freely; this may include chattel slavery (ownership of one human by another); debt bondage (workers' 'wages' are used to pay off debts and interest incurred); false contract slavery (where workers sign contracts that are not honoured by employers); and forced marriage (where people are forced to provide domestic and sexual services).

Forced migration   A form of migration involving escaping or being displaced because of an armed conflict, persecution, violation of human rights, disaster or human trafficking.

Fordism/Post-Fordism   A form of economic organization involving mass production and mass consumption (Fordism) that shifted in the 1970s towards greater differentiation in production and consumption.

Fourth age   Refers to an 'old old' age (75+ years) characterized by frailty, loss of autonomy, and social isolation. Cultural gerontologists instead argue that the fourth age is a negative, more imaginary stage than an actual stage of life.

Frame/Framing   The way in which issues and campaigns are presented so as to encourage particular meanings, interpretations and judgements.

Free labour   The kind of work relations that characterize capitalism (i.e. as structured by the legal 'freedom' to choose what occupation one is engaged in), in contrast to the characteristic work relations of feudal and slave societies (where work was not freely chosen, in a legal sense, but subject to coercion and duty). Marx spoke of this freedom under capitalism as merely a 'formal freedom', by which he meant that the freedom existed more in theory than in practice.

Free-rider problem   If everybody is affected by a problem then we all have an incentive to sit back and let others sort it out. The fact that many of us do this is a practical problem for activists. The fact that activists don't do this poses an intellectual question (why not?) for sociologists.

Function   The contribution, positive or negative, that one part of a society makes to the continuation of another part. Often misunderstood as referring only to positive contributions and so to consensus and social stability; negative or contradictory functions (dysfunctions) are equally important.

Functionalism   The belief that each aspect of society is interdependent and contributes to society's stability and functioning as a whole.

Functionalist   A definition of religion that takes into account what religion *does* for people or for a community. Durkheim sees religion as holding the values of a community together whereas, for Marx, religion is used by the upper classes to control the lower classes.

Gender   A term used to refer to the learnt and normative social and cultural aspects of differences and hierarchies, for example between men and women, non-binary or gender queer people. Gender is social and fluid. It is culturally formed and may or may not correlate with the gender that a person is assigned at birth.

Gendered moral rationalities   A concept identifying that people make a moral choice about what is 'the right thing to do', where choices about care and employment are gendered according to their role or relationship.

Gig economy   A flexible form of service work facilitated by the use of apps, characterized by short-term contracts/work.

Global North and Global South   A socio-economic and political (rather than primarily geographic) division between blocs of countries grouped by their differing levels of wealth, global power or economic development. Many countries included in the category Global South experienced colonial domination by the countries of the Global North, and their different global positioning is seen as a continuing post-colonial legacy of the unequal relations enforced during the colonial period.

Global value chain   All the activities that are involved in producing goods and services.

GLOSSARY

Globalization The increased connectivity and independence between peoples and places: an interconnectedness in flows of trade, finance, migration and culture; the diffusion of ideas, goods, capital and people.

Grand Theory The formal organization and arrangement of concepts that takes priority over understanding the social reality.

Hawthorne effect The alteration of behaviour by the subjects of the study due to the awareness that they are being observed.

Hegemony Leadership or dominance, especially by one state or social group over others.

Hermeneutics The theory of interpretation of written texts, later extended to human actions (see also Interpretivism).

Homogenization To make different things similar.

Household A physical structure that houses or provides shelter for an individual or a group of people.

Human trafficking The recruitment, transfer or receipt of people by means of threat, force, coercion, abduction or deception for the purpose of exploitation.

Hyper-real religion A religion that mixes elements of commodified popular culture with philosophies and religion. Examples are Jeddiism from the *Star Wars* movies or Dudeism from the movie *The Big Lebowski*.

Iatrogenesis Derived from the Greek for physician; describes the damage that results from medical interventions.

Ideology A system of ideas and ideals, especially one which forms the basis of economic or political theory and policy.

ILO International Labour Organization; an agency of the UN with a mandate to set standards for the treatment of workers.

Immigration The act of moving into a country other than the country of origin or the process of international inward migration more broadly.

Imperialism An ideology of extending the rule or authority of a country over other countries, often by military force or by gaining political and economic control.

Individualization A social theory which claims that increasing affluence and consumption choice have permitted more choice and more individualized 'self-fashioned' lifestyles. It posits that this social process has weakened the influence of social class on identities and lifestyle, along with a rejection of hierarchical gender and generational relations. Modern couple and family relations are said to seek and be contingent on emotional satisfaction.

Indenture A form of forced labour; a contract to work without pay for an agreed period of time.

Industrial Revolution The process of transition to new manufacturing processes (characteristically led by machines and other developments in capacity in the production process) primarily in Europe and the United States, from the late-18th century to the mid-19th century.

GLOSSARY

Infrastructuralization Denotes the process by which internet-based systems are becoming **critical** to the functioning of society, as they increasingly becoming indispensable to accessing essential services like health care, community services and education.

Innerworldly Of this world and that which can be studied by sociologists.

Institution A cluster of norms concerned with a specific area or aspect of social life.

Integration Although there is no single definition, it usually implies a process of mutual adaptation by migrants and long-settled residents.

International Division of Labour The distribution of economic and political functions to core, semiperipheral and peripheral regions of the world economy that ensures capital accumulation.

Interpretivism An epistemological tradition that recognizes the existence of multiple realities and the contribution of the researcher's values in the production of meaning during the research process.

Intersectionality A term coined by scholars such as Kimberlé Crenshaw that refers to the interrelationship between different social forces and processes such as race, ethnicity, class, gender and sexuality in creating connected and disconnected systems of inequality, disadvantage and discrimination. Intersectionality offers explanations for how social worlds and institutions impact upon groups and individuals and shape life experience.

Intimacy Closeness between two or more people, often associated with romantic couple relationships but not exclusively.

Invisible work Paid and unpaid work that is not recognized as work.

Islamophobia A term used to understand anti-Muslim discrimination.

Job polarization The hypothesis that there are fewer 'middle' level jobs available so that more people work in low-status, low-paid work.

Just-in-time/Logistics A feature of post-Fordism, whereby goods and services are produced in response to consumer demand.

Knowledge work Work of comparatively high status and high pay that relies on education and training and that involves the use of abstract reasoning to do complicated tasks.

Labelling Emphasizes social reaction and suggests that norm violations have to be publicly exposed in order for deviance to exist.

LAT (living apart together) People who are in a long-term partner relationship, and who they and other people regard as a couple, but who live separately for most of the time.

Lay expertise A seeming oxymoron involving an appreciation and focus on the skills, knowledge and understanding that non-medically trained people draw on to make sense of health, illness and disease.

Lay health beliefs Beliefs held by non-health professionals and drawn upon to make sense of illness and to direct help-seeking behaviour.

GLOSSARY

Life stages   Categories of difference that consolidate a sequence of ages into one category. **Life course** is the sequence of life stages. It is the societal equivalent to the aging process.

Lifestyle migration   A type of migration whereby people choose to settle in a specific destination for 'lifestyle' reasons, e.g. they find the way of life there more appealing.

Live sociology   A sociological approach to understanding and researching the social world that is attentive to things as they are happening in everyday life and in real time.

Lived religion   The religion as it is lived and experienced by people in their everyday life.

Magic   Acts (often practised ritualistically) that attempt to compel supernatural entities or forces to realize the desires of the practitioner, or those on whose behalf the practitioner is working.

Marxism   A term used to describe bodies of thought influenced by the work of Karl Marx.

Mask of aging   The phenomenon of older adults feeling as if their 'true', youthful inner self is 'masked' by an aging body, which leads to one's subjective age differing from calendric age.

Material culture   A term that emerges from anthropology to describe the way in which human societies produce and use objects in their activities and practices.

Mechanism   The process through which an outcome comes into being.

Medical gaze   The term used by Foucault to describe the way that biomedical practitioners see/observe the patient, focusing on the body and physical signs that are regarded as separate from the patient.

Medicalization   The process whereby conditions come to be defined and treated by biomedicine.

Meritocratic   The principle that everyone should have the same chance to succeed by their ability and talent, regardless of their social background. However, the principle of meritocracy (society *should be* meritocratic) is sometimes conflated with meritocracy as a social outcome (society *is* meritocratic). Seeing society as meritocratic suggests that what you get out of the system is what you put into it, an idea that often justifies inequality in social outcomes, since it implies that people get what they deserve.

Metanarrative   A set of more or less logically interconnected assumptions made in order to provide a coherent and comprehensive account of the underlying mechanisms that shape, or are supposed to shape, both the constitution and the development of human existence in a fundamental way.

Methodological   Relating to the means of inquiry used in a particular area of study or activity.

Methodological agnosticism   A methodological approach in which the researcher suspends (or brackets out) whether they personally believe or disbelieve in the religious or more than human entities or happenings referred to by their interlocutors.

Methods   Systematic tools used to collect and analyse information for research purposes.

Microaggression   Everyday subtle intentional or unintentional insults or words that express prejudice.

Migrant   Although there is no single definition, generally any person who moves away from their place of usual residence, either within a country or internationally.

Migration Any movement of people from their place of usual residence, either within a state or across state borders.

Migration governance A framework of legal norms, laws and policies as well as organizational structures and processes that shape and regulate state approaches to international migration.

Migration studies Interdisciplinary scholarship across anthropology, history, economics, law, sociology, geography and political sciences that explores the forms, patterns, experiences and impacts of migration.

Mixed methods A research approach that involves the collection and analysis of both qualitative and quantitative data within a single study.

Mixed race families Parents each from different racial/ethnic backgrounds and their 'mixed', 'bi-', 'inter-' or multi-racial children.

Modernity A concept which refers to a stage of societal development identified as taking part in Europe in the 17th and 18th centuries. 'Modern' society (distinguished from 'traditional' society) is characterized by scientific progress, industrial capitalism, individualism and bureaucratic rationality. The concept of modernity was central in early sociological thinking; however, critics point to its Eurocentric nature and colonial assumptions: by conflating the 'modern' world with Europe, the rest of the world is framed as external to modernity. This emphasizes European uniqueness and non-Western inferiority and ignores the role of colonialism and slavery in the development of modern societies.

Moral panic Moments of heightened public awareness of social problems that occur when a society is undergoing rapid change.

National Health Service The publicly-funded health care system for the UK, founded in 1948, providing health care free at the point of delivery.

Naturalism The view that there is no *essential* difference between natural and social science. Anti-naturalism, which claims that there *is* a fundamental difference in approach and/or subject matter, is sometimes called 'methodological dualism'.

Naturalization of inequality Where inequality is seen as the result of people's natural differences (unequal abilities or effort) which makes inequality seem inevitable or unalterable. For example, where advantage or disadvantage become individualized as a question of personal failure or success, rather than seeing the structural factors which prevent equal opportunity.

Negotiation A concept highlighting interactions between family members about how to understand a situation and the course of action that emerges from these understandings.

Neoliberalism A set of political policies promoting an economic system which prioritizes the 'free' market, with de-regulated commodity and labour markets, a reduction of international trade tariffs, restrictions on trade unions, and the privatization of public welfare as part of a drive to a 'smaller' state (with the state no longer providing public services but instead contracting out services to the private sector). Neoliberalism also extends market competition into areas of social life previously not governed by market principles (see also **Financialization**).

GLOSSARY

Network   A network involves 'nodes', which in sociology usually means social actors (either human beings or organizations), and various types of relationships between different pairs of those nodes. Networks have variable, measurable properties which generate opportunities and constraints for those enmeshed in them.

New public management   Emerged in the 1980s, informed by the belief that public services (e.g. health or welfare) would be more efficient if users were treated as customers.

Non-response bias   A threat to representativeness occurring when those who respond to a study significantly differ from those who do not respond.

Norms   Societal rules or expectations that are socially enforced.

Official religion   Religion as codified by an established institution.

Online platforms   'Programmable digital infrastructures controlled by platform operators [...] which curate the interactions of [...] a variety of users' (Grabher and Konig, 2020), and which enable new forms of value extraction from these interactions.

Operationalization   The process of transforming concepts into measures.

Ordinary knowledge   Epistemic forms generated and used by laypersons, allowing for a largely intuitive, implicit, practical and/or common-sense immersion in, engagement with and understanding of the world.

Orientalism   A term associated with Edward Said that identifies a tendency in Western thought to exaggerate and inaccurately portray the differences between the West and the 'Orient'. Said applied the term particularly to representations of the East and the Middle East.

Outsourcing   The process of one corporation contracting another to produce the whole of or a component of a good/service.

Outerworldly   Of the other world, which can only be studied through the interpretation of social actors.

Pan-Africanism   A global movement that aims to strengthen political solidarity and achieve successful outcomes for all indigenous and diaspora ethnic groups of African descent.

Pandemic   An epidemic that spreads across large regions, across borders and sometimes worldwide.

Paradigm   As used by Kuhn, this term refers to an exemplary scientific achievement, such as Lavoisier's discovery of oxygen, which provides a framework for later work.

Patriarchy   The systematic institutional domination of men over women, of older men over younger men and over those who are considered deviant and don't conform to social norms, such as heterosexuality. Patriarchy operates in conjunction with other social institutions such as racism and heteronormativity.

Pauperization   A process predicted by Marxist theory in which workers' wages are forced down to the lowest possible level, creating poverty and hardship (i.e. paupers).

Pedagogy   The theory and practice of learning.

Personal life   A concept addressing personal connections to a range of significant others that shape the sense of self and relationships in different contexts.

Personal prejudice The positive or negative feelings toward someone based on perceptions of group membership, such as, but not confined to, race.

Phenomenology A philosophical approach to knowledge which suggests we should think about the way things *appear* to us, rather than speculate about how 'real' they are. Linked with sociology in the English title of Alfred Schütz's *Phenomenology of the Social World* (1967).

Photo-diary A form of data generated by taking photographs at intervals, either instead of or alongside text, in order to keep a record.

Photo-elicitation A research method which uses photographs, produced by either researchers or participants, to elicit memories and stories as data.

Photo-journalism A form of journalism reporting news stories through the use of photographic images.

Political opportunity structure The way in which the political arrangements of a society dis/encourage either particular types of protest or protest per se.

Politics of labelling The process by which placing people into certain categories affects these people in their self-understanding, and the courses of action open to them. With the digitalization of society, these dynamics of labelling do not only unfold between people and ideas, but notably involve technological agents of categorization.

Popular religion A religion that is practised by the popular classes outside of official religion. With the ever increasing blurring between the popular and the established, what the term means today is harder to pinpoint.

Population The broader group of subjects that a study seeks to generalize its findings to.

Populism Political movements which reject 'politics as usual', by making a binary division between the corrupt elites and the will of 'the people'. In attacking the rule of elites, populists' appeal to represent the 'people' are often framed in exclusionary, homogeneous and sometimes racist terms.

Positivism An epistemological tradition that argues that social phenomena can only be understood by the application of objective scientific methods.

Post-colonial The aftermath and continuing legacy of imperialism and colonialism on nations and global relations.

Post-industrial society A society which has gone through a process of **de-industrialization**, in which services rather than manufacturing dominate the economy and the labour market.

Postmodernism An intellectual movement in sociology and other disciplines that argues that we live in societies where the search for one grand truth and narrative is over.

Post-race A position wherein society has moved to a point with racism that it no longer is a significant problem or requires specialist intervention measures.

GLOSSARY

Post-secularism   A philosophy that engages with religions in the public sphere.

Precariousness/Precariat   Having paid work that does not enable a person to live comfortably and plan for the future/a class identity that emerges from the experience of having precarious work.

Primary sources   Texts produced by major scholars, whose contributions are typically examined and discussed by commentators in the secondary literature.

Privatization of religion   A perspective that acknowledges the existence of religion but outside of the public sphere.

Professional project   The analysis of the strategic ways in which medicine was able to carve out an authoritative position in the medical **division of labour**.

Program/Script   Words that convey how technologies are embedded with particular expectations for use. Users may follow the script or resist the expected program.

Prosumer   A consumer, often enabled and facilitated by technology, who is also involved in the production or customization of the goods/services they consume.

Pseudo-science   According to Popper, pseudo-science is a sham science because it resists attempts at falsification, contrary to good science, which is open to efforts to falsify.

Public issues   From C. Wright Mills' ground-breaking book *The Sociological Imagination*, public issues are those sets of things outside of our individual control but that shape our social experience.

Pure relationship   A term created by Anthony Giddens to characterize modern relationships which are based on principles of democracy, confluent love and satisfaction.

Qualitative methods   Methods that collect and analyse in-depth, non-numerical information.

Quantitative methods   Methods that collect and analyse information that can be numerically represented in the form of variables.

Queer families   A term capturing a broad set of families and family lifestyles that are outside of and challenge the boundaries of traditional and heteronormative binaries.

Race   A term used to describe the attribution of social meaning to physical and cultural differences in humanity. Although it is generally agreed that race is a social construct and not an essential characteristic of humanity, it is a term through which difference is represented and otherness produced.

Racialization   A term used to describe processes where racial meanings are applied to a social relationship, social or political practice, or to a social group.

Racism   A term used to refer to the belief that different groups of human beings possess distinct characteristics, abilities or qualities. Racist ideas are used to characterise different groups of human beings as superior or inferior to one another, and to justify the unequal treatment of population group(s) on the basis of perceived features that are usually biologically, psychologically, culturally and/or socially based.

Rational   In the context of consumption, referring to an individual's ability to make informed choices, weighing costs and benefits in relation to price, income and their own interests.

Rational choice theory A social theory that explains behaviour as the result of individuals weighing up costs and benefits and deciding on the course of action that maximizes benefits for them and/or the family household.

Rationalization A concept primarily developed by Max Weber that describes the replacement of traditions, values and emotions as the main motivators of behaviour in society with ideas based on instrumental rationality.

Realism/Critical realism In later 20th century and contemporary philosophy, an anti-positivist approach which stresses the underlying structures and mechanisms in the natural and social world which may or may not produce observable data.

Realist A perspective which emphasizes the independent reality of nature and environmental phenomena and their power to influence and impact aspects of society.

Redistributive taxation A policy in which richer people pay more tax than poorer people as a percentage of their income or wealth (as opposed to a flat tax, where everybody pays the same) as a means of redistributing income and wealth from rich to poor (through the rich paying more for publicly-funded services).

Reference group effects A distorting effect on people's understanding of class inequality when people base their sense of inequality on their immediate social environment and social connections. The distortion occurs because inequality structures social arrangements, with friends, neighbours and family sharing similar class backgrounds, so the limited nature of people's 'reference-group' comparisons restricts perceptions of the scale of inequality.

Reflexivity Reflection by members of human societies on their practice, as opposed to a more automatic observance of custom and belief, that has been seen as a defining feature of modernity by Anthony Giddens, Margaret Archer and others. Pierre Bourdieu in particular stressed the need to do the sociology *of sociology* as a preliminary to sociological investigation and he also wrote his own 'self-analysis'.

Refugee A person who migrates internationally because they are unable to secure the protection of their country of origin and whose asylum claim has been accepted.

Relativism The claim that there is no rational basis for choosing between alternative views. The 'strong programme' in the sociology of scientific knowledge argues that explanations of 'true' and 'false' beliefs should take the same form (as, for example, in the sociology of religion).

Reliability The extent to which a property or a concept is measured consistently.

Repertoires of contention The set of protest practices characteristic of a society at a particular point in time, which activists typically select from.

Replication The process of reproducing an existing study.

Representativeness How well a sample represents the composition of the population of interest.

Research A way of developing new knowledge; within sociology good research is systematic and follows certain sets of methods and/or theories.

GLOSSARY

Research design   The methodological framework a study adopts to answer its research questions.

Research question   An answerable inquiry around which researchers plan a research design.

Role   The behavioural expectations involved in a social category or position. Roles are learned through socialization but are creatively performed in interactional encounters.

Role theory   A social theory that explains patterns of people's behaviour as linked to the social expectations and prescriptions (social scripts) that are connected to their particular social position.

Same-sex relationships   Relationships between two persons of the same sex, whether marital, civic partnership, cohabiting or LAT.

Sampling   The procedure of selecting a sub-group from the population of interest as the focus of a research study.

Saturation   A criterion used to determine sample size in qualitative research, referring to the point where no new information is obtained by further data collection.

Science and technology studies (STS)   A term often used to describe a body of historical and contemporary academic literature exploring the diverse and complex intersections of science, technology and society.

Scientific knowledge   Epistemic forms produced and employed by researchers and experts, allowing for an analytic, logical, methodical, rational, explanatory, evidence-based and/or evaluative immersion in, engagement with and understanding of the world and/or the universe or multiverse.

Scientific paradigm   In the work of Kuhn, a scientific paradigm refers to a distinct collection of concepts, methods, theories and standards that comprise a specific scientific field.

Scientism   A term used to describe an excessive attempt to imitate science in inappropriate contexts.

Secondary data analysis   Analysis of data that have been previously collected for a different research purpose.

Secondary sources   Texts produced by commentators designed to offer systematic descriptions, analyses, interpretations, explanations and evaluations of primary sources.

Secularism   A philosophy that promotes the disappearance of religion from at least the public sphere.

Secularization   A process, common to the concerns of many classical sociological thinkers, of the transformation of a society from close identification with religious values and institutions towards non-religious values and secular institutions.

Selfhood   An individual's sense of who they are; their identity.

Semiotic   The study and interpretation of signs and symbols and their role in making social life meaningful.

Sensory methods   Techniques enabling researchers to account for a range of senses as well as vision, such as touch, sound and smell, so that their role in creating social meaning can be illustrated and understood.

GLOSSARY

SEZ Special Economic Zone; a feature of neoliberalism where some places pay less tax and dispense with labour rights in order to make production cheaper.

Sick role A concept coined by Talcott Parsons to define the rights and obligations of the sick person – that they should be exempt from social roles; not be held responsible for their condition; try to get well and seek help; and cooperate with the medical profession.

Simulacrum An imitation of something (which may or may not have an original). It essentially replaces reality with a copy. The sociologist Jean Baudrillard makes use of this term when considering how society has become 'hyper-real' in that it is one dominated by signs and symbols, full of copies of copies.

Skill The ability or expertise needed to do a specific task/set of tasks.

Social action A notion used by Max Weber to describe the acts of individuals which takes into account the actions and reactions of others.

Social capital The advantages (resources and opportunities) activists have in virtue of their contacts and networks.

Social cohesion The solidarity and connectedness of the members of a community or society, with higher levels of social cohesion argued to increase trust and people's willingness to cooperate for the shared public good.

Social construction of technology An STS approach exploring how social factors 'construct' technology. Users, designers, funders and so forth will determine whether and how technologies are produced and received.

Social constructionism An **epistemological** position that focuses on the ways that social processes inform the production and effects of knowledge.

Social desirability The tendency of social survey respondents to portray themselves in a socially desirable way.

Social differentiation The process by which groups or communities demarcate to form distinct or separate units.

Social disorganization An explanation of variations in criminal offending and delinquency, across both time and space, as a product of institutional disintegration in residential districts.

Social facts A notion developed by Émile Durkheim referring to the social aspects, whether value, cultural norm or social structure, that transcend and exert power over human individuals.

Social gerontology A specialized field of gerontology that focuses on the social aspects of age and aging.

Social mobility The movement (both upward and downward) that people make between unequal class positions. Social mobility can occur both intra-generationally (i.e. movement across classes during a person's life) or inter-generationally (i.e. movement across classes from one generation of a family to the next).

GLOSSARY

Social Movement Organizations (SMOs)   Organizational nuclei within social movement networks. Often formal organizations (e.g. Greenpeace) but potentially including informal activist cells, social centres and communes.

Social practices   Approaches that draw attention to shared ways of doing everyday activities, underpinned by social norms and understandings and social and technical infrastructures.

Social structure   The pattern of norms and social relations that is reproduced and transformed in social actions but which also constrains those actions.

Social system   Society understood as a collection of parts that are interdependent and exhibit varying degrees of autonomy, integration and antagonism.

Social theory   The attempt to provide a conceptually informed – and, in many cases, empirically substantiated – framework designed to (1) describe, (2) analyse, (3) interpret, (4) explain, and (5) assess the constitution, functioning and development of social reality, or particular aspects of social reality, in a more or less systematic fashion.

Socialism   An economic theory of social organization which advocates that the means of production should be owned by the community as a whole.

Socially constructed   The co-created methods and accepted meanings that members of society apply to something.

Sociation   A concept used by Georg Simmel to refer to the pattern or form that a particular social interaction assumes: from the interaction that takes places between two individuals to more complex levels, sociation is central to interactions between phenomena such as the family, clan, city or state.

Socio-cultural changes of aging   How the lifestyles, representations and values of the group of older adults are changing.

Sociological imagination   The professional sensibility of the sociologist to incorporate historical, theoretical and contextual perspectives in answering questions. The phrase was coined by C. Wright Mills.

Sociology   An academic discipline that involves theoretical and/or empirical investigation of the relation between social structures and meaningful practices.

Socio-structural changes of aging   How the socio-structural composition of the group of older adults is changing (i.e. increase in centenarians, feminization).

Socio-technical arrangement   A term used by sociologists to highlight that digital transformations are not 'caused' by either technology or society alone, but arise from interactions between technology and people, as well as organizations, data, practices and environments.

Specialization   The process in modern industrial work that characterizes the division of labour. Facilitated by developments in technology and machines, it has unleashed exponential increases in productive capacity but has also reduced the quality of work performed by humans to a single function.

State   An organized political community (or polity) acting under a government. Definitions of the state vary. Weber, for instance, understood the state as the 'monopoly of the legitimate use of physical force within a given territory'.

Statistical inference The statistical process of inferring properties of a population of interest using a sample with an underlying probability distribution.

Stigma Enduring discrimination against a person based on a perceivable social/medical characteristic.

Structural functionalism The belief that each of the institutions, roles and norms that together constitute a society serves a purpose, and each is indispensable for the continued existence of the others and of society as a whole.

Structural lag A mismatch between changes in people's lives and capabilities and the roles and responsibilities provided by social structures.

Structural strains Aspects of the social structure which create conflict or grievances amongst members of society; often cited as causes of protest and social movement formation – though only one amongst a number of causes according to social movement scholars.

Subculture A group of people within a culture that differentiates itself from the parent culture to which it belongs, while maintaining some of its founding principles. Often associated with the use of symbolic resources, such as clothes or music, to display their difference from the mainstream.

Supernatural Entities, manifestations or happenings that cannot be explained by the current human scientific laws of nature.

Sustainability The ability to meet the needs of the present without compromising the ability of future generations to meet their needs. The concept has environmental, economic and social elements.

Sustainable development An economic system that pays attention to the environmental effects of economic growth.

Symbolic interactionism Viewing society as composed of symbols that people use to establish meaning, develop views about the world and communicate with one another.

Technological determinism The widespread tendency to understand technology as the principal engine of social change, which may lead to an impoverished conception of society as a passive recipient of the 'impacts' or 'benefits' of technological innovation, without much agency of its own.

Technologies The materials, tools, machines and software used in carrying out tasks.

Terminological Referring to the vocabulary of technical terms, words or expressions used in a particular context, field, subject, science, art, institution, ideology or activity.

Theoretical Connected primarily with the systematic organization of ideas, concepts and principles on which a particular subject, belief system or epistemic framework is based.

Third age A 'young old' age (approximately 50 to 74), characterized by physical and cognitive functionality, social integration and high levels of activity.

Tradition An overarching, residual category defined in opposition to the modern as the condition to be overcome in the course of the process of modernization.

Transnational Extending beyond and across national boundaries and borders.

GLOSSARY

Transnationalism   A process which describes how international migrants forge and sustain multi-stranded social relations that link together their societies of origin and settlement.

Transparency   Making the decisions and procedures followed during data collection and analysis in a study publicly available.

Urban ecology   Insists that crime is linked to the (urban) environment in predictable ways.

Validity   The extent to which a measure employed in a study is a true reflection of the concept or property that it claims to capture.

Variable   A characteristic that varies across the population of interest.

Video-diaries   Similar to photo-diaries, but using moving rather than still images. Images in video diaries might be accompanied by sound and/or text.

World-systems analysis   An approach that argues that the unit of social reality which contains and constrains human relations is the capitalist world-economy, not individual nation-states.

Xeno-racism   A concept used to refer to a newer type of cultural racism that combines different types of discrimination, such as Islamophobia and xenophobia, to produce racialized zones of inclusion and exclusion.

Zero hours contract   An employment contract where workers have no fixed hours of work and are expected to be flexible in response to the employer's expectations.

INDEX

Page numbers in *italics* refer to figures, (KC) indicates Key Case.

Abrams, D. et al. 228, 229, 235
Abrams, J. et al. 315, 316
Acker, J. 449
activity theories of age 230, 231
actor-network theory 42, 133, 382
adverse incorporation 284
aesthetic labour 287
age 226–7
   as socio-cultural construct 228–9
   see also older adults
ageism 234–5
agency
   in consumer society 350, 352
   in digital technology use 384, 385
   structure and 79, 267–8, 296–7, 396
   see also autonomy
Agnew, R. 57, 63
Ahearn, L. 265, 273
Airbnb 24–5
Akel, S.: role of race in higher education (KC) 319
Akrich, M. 387
alienation 110, 350
Allen, L. 163
Alvaredo, F. et al. 183, 186
amplification, deviancy 61, 84
Andersson, R. 68
anomie 56–7, 63, 113
Anthropocene 43
anthropological approaches 434, 437, 438
   cargo cults 350
   material culture 351
   sex/gender diversity 199–200
   state violence 367
   subculture 59
   see also ethnography/ethnomethodology
Arab Spring 418
Ardévol, E. 164
Aristotle 8

Aronson, L. 235
artificial intelligence (AI) 386
asylum seekers *see* refugees/asylum seekers
Atlantic School 8–9
Australia
   Bosnian refugees 221
   indigenous population (Stolen Generations) 220
   schooling and photo-diaries 163
auto-ethnography 203
automation of work 289
autonomy
   age and ageism 233, 234
   family life and intimacy 250, 265, 266
   sociology 117
   see also agency; individualization

Baby Boomers 229, 233
Back, L. 166
   and Puwar, N. 166
Bangladesh
   colourism and colonialism 315
   Rana Plaza fire (KC) 285–6
Barker, N. 252
base and superstructure 85–6
Bassett, M.T.: COVID-19 pandemic inequalities, US (KC) 462
Baudrillard, J. 350
Bauman, Z. 6, 67, 86, 265, 266, 350
beauty norms and algorithms 386
Beck, U. 8, 43, 97
   and Beck-Gernsheim, E. 250–1, 265
   et al. 32
Becker, H. 314–15, 414
   and Cohen, S. 28
Beer, D. 26
behaviourism 432
benefits policy, UK 257
Benjamin, R. 386

INDEX

Benjamin, W. 368
Berger, J. 161
Berkowitz, R.L. et al.: COVID-19 pandemic inequalities (KC) 461
Betts, A. 404
Bhambra, G.K.: Brexit (KC) 450
Big Data *see* data
biological essentialism and race 381
biological sex and cultural gender distinction 199–201, 203–6
biological and social meanings of taste 354–7
biomedical knowledge and power relations 299–301
biosociality 383
Birmingham Centre for Contemporary Cultural Studies 61–2
black British population *see* British Caribbean/West Indian population
black civil rights movement 63, 415, 416, 421
black feminism 221–2
Black Lives Matter Movement (KC) 218, 365
black and minority ethnic (BAME) groups *see* race/ethnicity and racism
Black Power Movement 220
black women: community mothering 249, 251
Boatcă, M. 13
body
  embodiment 82–3, 203–4
  and society, analogy 83
border security industry, US–Mexico 68–9
Boronski, T. 313–14
boundaries
  classical and contemporary social theory 129
  disciplinary 39, 118, 134
  families and households 248–9
  gender differences 152
  race identity 217
Bourdieu, P. 7, 9, 83, 126, 181, 296
  symbolic violence 367–8
  taste 356–7
branding 353
Brayne, S. 22, 23
Brazil: mixed-race couples 270–1
Brexit 12, 220
  immigration policy 402
  public sociology approach (KC) 450
bricolage 268
British Caribbean/West Indian population
  health inequalities 298, 301, 302
  labelling in education system 314
British Cultural Studies: 'style' and 'resistant' consumers 352
British media, immigration in (KC) 393

British Sociological Association (BSA)
  definition of sociology 9
  race and ethnicity in curriculum 14
Buddhism, China 336
Burawoy, M. 439, 444–8
Burke, C. and Ribeiro de Castro, H. 159
Butler, J. 198–9, 200, 207
Butler, R.M. 234

Caballero, C. et al. 255
Calhoun, C. 332
Calvinism 329–30
capital
  cultural 181, 356
  social 181, 420–1, 422
  types of 181
capitalism
  and colonialism 92–4, 182
  and consumerism 349–50
  and environment 43–4
  and new social movements 419
  power relations and biomedical knowledge 299–300
  and Protestantism 110, 116, 329–30, 335, 431
  rise of 110–11
'Capitalocene' 43
carbon dioxide/greenhouse gas emissions 47–8, 185
carbon footprint 43–4, 47–8
care
  and domestic labour roles 151–2, 199, 255–8, 282–3
  'global care chain' 274
  of older adults 232
cargo cults 350
Caribbean 94, 97–8, 249
  see also British Caribbean/West Indian population
Carmichael, S. 220
Carter, J.
  and Duncan, S. 268
  marriage (KC) 268
Catholicism 331
  syncretic forms of 335
centre–periphery relationship 92–3, 94
Cevolini, A. and Esposito, E. 21–2
Chambers, D. 272
Chaplin, E. 163
Chicago School 57–60
child raising, gender-neutral 207
child refugees (KC) 394–5
children
  parenting and family transformations 249, 250–1, 256
  see also care
children and young people
  visual methods research 159–60, 162–3, 165, 167
  see also education

China
  global inequality 186
  religion 335–6
  WeChat 25
  Weibo 388
Chinese migrant workers: social media and personal connections (KC) 272
Christian European civilization 96
Christian Right 331
Christianity 328
  see also Catholicism; Protestantism
Christin, A. 28
chrononormativity 227, 228
Chun, W. 26
churches 327
circular migration 395
cities
  divided 64–7
  largest foreign-born population share *399*
  see also entries beginning urban
citizenship
  and biosociality 383
  and migration 98, 99–100
'citizenship premium' 99
'civilization racism' 220
Clarke, J. et al.: always a consumer (KC) 350
class 178–9
  and health inequalities 184–5, 296
  and intimacy 270
  persistence of inequalities 179–82
  and taste 356–7
  theorists 133
  and work 182, 280–1
  see also global inequalities; intersectionality; poverty
classical sociologies 108–9, 131–2
  and contemporary social theory, comparison 129–31, 136–7
  global perspective
    conceptual 114–15
    methodological 115–16
    normative 116
    vs Eurocentrism 114
  rapid historical social change 110–13
    modern science 112
    rise of capitalism 110–11
    rise of modern state 111
    social differentiation 112–13
  science and philosophy 117–18, 431–2, 438
Clausewitz, C. von 370, 371
climate change 45–6, 47–8, 185
  see also environment
Cohen, A.: delinquent boys (KC) 59
Cohen, S. 61, 62, 63
'cold' intimacy and gender equality (KC) 266

Colic-Peisker, V. 221
'the collective'/'the social' 113
collective behaviour theory of social movements and criticisms 414–20
'collective conscience' see 'conscience collective'
collective efficacy 63
collective identity and social movements 411, 412, 414, 421
Collins, R. 361, 370
Colombia: violence and political order 367
colonialism
  and biomedicine 300
  and Brexit 12
  and capitalism 92–4, 182
  Catholicism, syncretic forms of 335
  and colourism 315
  feminist theory 95
  and migration 90, 92
  and modernity/ies 95–7, 182
  see also decolonization
colourism 216, 221
  education 315–16
commodity fetishism 349
communicative action theory 433
Comte, A. 8, 112, 431, 435
conflict theories 132, 313
Confucianism, China 336
connectedness
  and continuity of intimacy 267–8
  see also interconnected world
Connell, R. 461
Connelly, L. 215–16
Connolly, H.: child refugees (KC) 394–5
Connolly, J. and Prothero, A. 48–9
'conscience collective'/'collective conscience' 56, 78, 80
Conservative governments: perspectives on society 76
consumerism
  and crime 57
  and cultures 346–8
    shops and shopping 348–9
    taste 354–7
    as trap vs symbolic resource 349–54
  and environment 43–4, 185
    fast fashion (KC) 46–7
    individual responsibility 47–50
  and stratification 67
contemporary social theory 122–4
  and classical social theory, comparison 129–31, 136–7
  key dimensions of 128–9
  knowledge-seeking spirit of 126–8
  relevance of 125–6
  trends and developments in 134–7

INDEX

control theory of crime 63
cosmopolitanism 133
cotton production 284
COVID-19 pandemic 12–13
  ageism 235
  behavioural science 435
  class inequalities 190–1
  criticism of government response (KC) 450–1
  limits of digitalization 25
  neighbourhoods and racial-ethnic inequalities 461–2
  racism 217
  uses of sociology 460–2, 463–4
Cox, J. and Possamai, A. 328–9
Crawley, H. et al.: immigration in British media (KC) 393
Crenshaw, K. 63, 203
crime 55
  Chicago School 57–60
  divided cities 64–7
  fault lines and theoretical reincarnations 62–4
  illicit mobilities and inequalities 67–9
  as normal 56–7
  radical directions 60–2
  see also violence and war
critical gerontology 230
critical pedagogy 316–17
critical race theory 218–20, 321–2
critical realism 433
critical self-reflection 13–14
critical sociology 444
critical theory 132, 433
critical whiteness studies 219, 221
cultural capital 181, 356
cultural class analysis 181–2
cultural comparison approach of classical sociology 115
cultural gerontology 230–1, 233
cultural hegemony 317
cultural homogenization 273
cultural intermediary workers 283–4, 286
cultural metanarratives 123
'cultural sciences' 431–2
culture
  and consumption *see* consumerism
  and social structure 80
'cycles of contention' in social movements 418

Daniels, J. and Gregory, K. 30
Dant, T. 350
data analytics
  discrimination in 21–2, 386
  methodological transformations 29–30
  technology and society interactions 22–3
dataveillance *see* surveillance technologies
Davie, G. 328, 331

De Lombaerde, P. et al. 403
de-commoditization 352
Dear, M. 65, *66*
decolonization 219
  of curriculum 320
  theorists 133
delinquency 58
  delinquent boys (KC) 59
Deliveroo 31–2
democratic government and public sociology 447
democratization of family life 250, 251
demographic change and aging 227
denim jeans: global value chain 283–7
'denomination' 327–8
dependency theory 92–3
detraditionalization of family life and intimacy 250, 251, 252–3, 265
developed and underdeveloped economies 92–4
deviance 56–7, 112, 314
  amplification 61, 84
  National Deviancy Conference (NDC) 60–1, 62, 63
Deville, J. and Van der Velden, L. 32
Dewey, J. 451
diaries
  photo- and video- 163–4
  time- 147, 149, 152
Dickens, P. 39–40, 42
differential association theory 58, 59
'digital divide' 25–6, 232
digital methods 31–3
digital sensors 25
digital society 19
  and digital methods 31–3
  forms of discrimination 19–23
  impacts of transformations 23–7
  and knowledge 27–31
digital visual methods 164–9
Dingwall, R.: government response to COVID-19 pandemic (KC) 450–1
Dirks, N.B. 96
discrimination, digital forms of 19–23
disengagement theories of age 230
display
  consumer expertise 354
  cultural capital 356
  of family relationships 254
division of labour 110, 432
  factories and sweatshops 284–5
  gender inequalities 151–2, 199, 255–8, 282–3
  international 92, 93, 96
DNA and genes 382–3
'double consciousness' 218–19
double erasure 320
Du Bois, W.E.B. 8–9, 214, 219, 321, 448–9

Duncan, S.
  Carter, J. and 268
  et al. 249, 267
Durkheim, E. 38, 39, 77, 109
  capitalism 110
  'conscience collective' 56, 78, 80
  deviance 56, 112
  education 313–14
  methodology 115
  normative order 81
  religion 329
  social facts 39, 78, 79, 80, 115, 432
  social reality 113
  social theory 131, 132
  sociology as science 432, 438, 440
  suicide (KC) 56

economic capital 181
economic factors in intimacy 265, 266, 270
economic growth
  and environment 43, 50
  and inequality 185
education 311–12
  colourism 315–16
  critical pedagogy 316–17
  grand theory 312–14
  labelling theory 314–15
  race and higher education 318–22
  school photographs 159–60
  as symbolic capital 181
Elias, N. 361, 438
embodiment 82–3, 203–4
emotion, reason and identity in social movement formation 420–2
emotional labour 281, 282, 286–7
empirical level of social-scientific research 125, 126
employment see work/employment
entanglements
  modernities 96–7
  technology and society 26
environment 38–9
  nature and society relationship 39–42
  social causes of problems 42–4
  sustainability and social change 47–50
  unequal distribution and experience of problems 44–7, 185
environmental crisis and future of work 290
environmental justice movement 44–5
'environmental sociology' 40
epidemiological research 182, 184–5
epistemological reflexivity 128
epistemological level of social-scientific research 125, 126
Equality Act (2010) 216–17, 318

Equality and Human Rights Commission 321
ethnicity see race/ethnicity and racism
ethno-conscious endeavour of social theory 135
ethnography/ethnomethodology 432, 434
  East London 66–7
  feminist research 203
  illegal migration 68
  visual methods 161, 162–3
Eurocentrism 114, 115, 182, 220, 270
European Enlightenment 112
European migration crisis 403
European Social Survey 229, 235
Evans, G. and Mellon, J. 181–2
everyday life 9–10, 132
explanation
  and description 433–4
  and understanding 132
expressive and instrumental violence 369–70
external validity see reliability/external validity
Extinction Rebellion 410–11

Facebook 26, 28, 272, 304, 385
falsification in science 380, 381
families of choice 249, 250–1
families and households 246–7
  definitions and types of 248–9
  meanings and actions in 253–5
  older adults 232
  roles vs rationalities in behaviour 255–8
  transformations 250–3, 265–7
  see also gender; intimacies and relationships
family background and class identity 182
'family practices' 254, 267
Fanon, F. 90, 219
fast fashion (KC) 46–7
feminism/feminist theory
  black 221–2
  colonization and housewifization 95
  criminology 62–3
  intimacy vs personal fulfilment 266
  medicalization and diagnosis 297, 302
  migration and gender 401
  public sociology 449
  romantic love 269
  sex/gender 199–201
  theorists 133
  unpaid work 282
  see also intersectionality
Ferrell, J. 67–8
Filipino migrant women: 'global care chain' 274
financialization 184
Finch, J. 254
flâneur 348
flexible and precarious work 287–8

flooding risks and impacts 45–6
flow of information and resources 84, 85–6
Floyd, George 218, 365
forced labour 284
forced migration
    vs voluntary migration 394, 404
    see also refugees/asylum seekers
Fordism 280–1
Foucault, M. 63, 299, 366
founding fathers of sociology 8, 56, 77, 129
fourth age 233
'framing' of social movements 417
Frankfurt School 132, 316
free labour 110
    and unfree forms 94
free-rider problem and social movements 420–1
Freeman, E. 228
Freire, P. 317
Friedman, S. and Laurison, D.: class advantage (KC) 180
Friends of the Earth 45
friendship and intimacy, digital mediation of 26, 271–2
functionalism 83, 84, 131
    age and aging 230
    education 313
    families and households 247, 250
    neo-functionalism 132
    structural 313
    violence 365–6

Galtung, J. 363, 368
Gane, N. and Back, L. 14
gangs 58, 59, 84, 368
    Colombia 367
Gans, P. 449
garment industry
    fast fashion (KC) 46–7
    global value chain 283–7
Garner, S. 216, 219
gender 197–9
    and biomedicine 300
    domestic labour and care roles 151–2, 199, 255–8, 282–3
    embodied selves 203–4
    equality and 'cold' intimacy (KC) 266
    gender-neutral child raising 207
    health and life expectancy 296, 297–8
    and intimacy 269–70
    measuring 201–3
    and sex 199–201
    sport, sex/gender classification in 204–6
    see also families and households; intersectionality
gender-based violence, broad vs narrow definition of 364

gendered moral rationality 256
gendered Orientalism 221
'general strain theory' 57, 63
generalizability of research 149–50
genes and 'gene talk' 382–3
German Sociological Association 93, 438
gerontology 229–30
Gherea, C.D. 92
Ghostery 32
Giddens, A. 8, 79, 84, 250, 265, 270, 273
gig economy 31–2, 286, 287
Gill, R. 271–2
Gilroy, P. 62, 218–19
'global care chain' 274
global inequalities 183–5
    and global power relations 185–91
    and national inequalities 97–100, 182
Global North–Global South 43, 46–7, 86, 334
Global South 13
    South–South migrations 403
global value chain analysis 283–7
global/world religions 333–4, 431–2
globalist view of classical sociology 114
globalization
    history of 92
    and love 273–5
    theorists 133
Google 146, 384, 386
Gramsci, A. 217
grand social theories 247, 313
    education 312–14
Granovetter, M. 144
'green jobs' 290
'green social theory' 40
greenhouse gas emissions/carbon dioxide emissions 47–8, 185
Greer, S. and Hagan, J. 55
Gregory, K.
    Daniels, J. and 30
    and Maldonado, M.P. 31–2

Habermas, J. 86, 331, 433
'habitus' 83
Hall, S. 61–2, 218, 219
    et al. 352
Hamilton, C. 220
Harlan, S.L. et al. 44, 45, 46
Harper, D. 157–8, 161, 164
Hawthorne effect 148
health 294–5
    inequalities 184–5, 296–9
    mental health crisis 301–3
    older adults 232
    social construction of 299–301

Heaphy, B. et al. 251
hegemony and critical pedagogy 317
Herod, A. and Lambert, R. 288
Hickel, J. 187
higher education *see* universities
historical constitution of social reality 130
historical photographic analysis 159–60
historical-materialism 131
history
   of globalization 92
   and practice of sociology 7–9
Hobbs, D. 66–7
Holmwood, J. 9, 436, 437, 439, 446, 447, 448
'homophily' 26
Hoschchild, A. 266, 281
   and Machung, A.: work and gender roles (KC) 151
housewifisation and colonization 95
housework and care roles 151–2, 199, 255–8, 282–3
human rights perspective on crime 55
human trafficking 394
hyper-real religion 337

identity
   collective, and social movements 411, 412, 414, 421
   and consumerism 48–9, 351–2
   race 215–18
      and racialization 218–20
   working-class 181–2
ideology
   consumerism 349–50
   critical pedagogy 316, 317
   individualism 265
   legitimacy of inequality 190
   race 216
   theory of 433
illicit mobilities 67–9
Illouz, E. 266
imperialism *see* colonialism
income inequality 98–9, 183
   and transnational migration 98–9
India
   colonialism 95, 96
   global inequality 186
   intimacy 270, 273
indigenous populations 219, 220
individual responsibility for sustainable future 48–50
individualization
   and class 180–1
   families and households 247, 250–1, 267–8
industrial production
   development of world-economy 92–4
   and environment 43

inequalities
   age 227
   environment 44–7, 185
   health 184–5, 296–9
   intimacies 268–9
   see also class; gender; global inequalities; race/ethnicity and racism
information and resources, flow of 84, 85–6
information technology (IT)
   logistics and transportation 286
   see also digital society
infrastructuralization, impacts of digital transformations 25–6
institutional approaches to age 228
'institutional racism' 220
institutionalization of political conflicts 269
institutions 81
   norms and roles 80–2
instrumental and expressive violence 369–70
insurance, discrimination and data analytics 21–2
integration and migration 401
inter-racial marriage *see* mixed-race couples/families
interconnected world 90–1
   emergence of sociology of 92–5
   history of globalization 92
   multiple modernities 95–7
   proper unit of analysis 97–100
interdisciplinarity 134, 438–9
internal migration 395
International Association of Athletic Federations (IAAF) 205
International Olympic Committee (IOC) 204–5
International Organization for Migration (IOM) 394, 395–6, 398, 399, 403
   and related organisations 404
internet *see* digital society; social media
interpretive sociology 131
intersectionality 81, 203, 220–2
   and global value chain 283–7
   and health inequalities 296–9
   and intimacy 270–1
   and migration 401
   and sport 205–6
intersex classification 205
intimacies and relationships 263–5
   connectedness and continuity 267–8
   inequalities 268–71
   love and globalization 273–5
   mediated 26, 271–2
   and social change 265–7
   transformations in families and households 250–1, 253
invisible work 282, 286, 287, 288

INDEX

Irwin, A. 42
Islam
   and Islamism 331
   Shari'a law in West 332–3
Islamophobia 214

Jackson, T. 43, 47–8, 50
Jamieson, L. 263, 265–6
Jediism 337
job polarization 287–8
Jones, P. and Mair, M.: supermarkets (KC) 452
Joseph-Salisbury, R. and Connelly, L. 215–16
Judaism 335
'just-in-time' (JIT) technologies 286

Kalleberg, A. 287–8
Karlson, S. 298
Keat, R. and Urry, J. 433
knowledge
   interactions between technology, society, and 27–31
   status of sociological 430–2, 437–8
   see also scientific knowledge
knowledge workers 283–4
knowledge-seeking spirit of social theory 126–8
Kochenov, D. 99–100
Kohli, M. 228
Korzeniwicz, R.P.
   and Albrecht, S.: wages across the world (KC) 99
   and Moran, T.P. 98
Kuhn, A. and McAllister, K.E. 160–1
Kuhn, T. 380–2, 435–6

labelling/labelling theory
   crime 55, 60
   education 314–15
   interactive dynamics of 28–9
   medical diagnosis 300
laboratories, empirical studies of 382
labour movement 419
Landrieu, M. 321
language 432
   analogy of social structure 78, 79, 80, 82–3
   communicative action 433
Latin America 92–3, 95–6, 97–8
   Brazil: mixed-race couples 270–1
   Buenos Aires: secondary schools and social inequality (KC) 162–3
   Colombia: violence and political order 367
Latour, B. 387
   and Woolgar, S. 382
law
   rise of modern state 111
   Shari'a 332–3

Lea, J. and Young, J. 62
Left 439
   idealist-realist polarity 62
   see also socialism
LGBTQ+ 200
   migrants 100, 397, 401
Lian, O.S. and Bondevik, H. 300
life expectancy
   global inequality 99–100
   health inequalities and 296–9
   increased 231
life stages/life course 228, 229
   older age 229–31
lifestyle choices and health 296
lifestyle migration 400
live sociological methods 166
lived religion and popular culture 335–7
living apart together (LAT) relationships 249, 267
Los Angeles, crime and policing in 22, 65
love
   and commitment 267
   and globalization 273–5
   romantic 269

McAdam, D. 144–5, 269, 415, 421
McBee, Thomas Page 205
McGuire, M. 335, 336–7
McLaren, D. et al. 45
Malešević, S. 362, 370, 371
Manzoor-Khan, S. 319–20
Marcuse, P. 64–5, 350
Margolis, E. 160
marriage 250, 265, 268
   and globalization 273–4
Martins, H. 436
Marx, K./Marxism 77, 109
   base and superstructure 85–6
   capitalism 110, 178
   consumerism 349–50
   and Engels, F. (*Communist Manifesto*) 91, 110
   methodology 115
   pseudo-scientific theories 380
   religion 330
   social movements 419
   social theory 131, 132
   sociology as science 433, 434, 440
   violence 364
Marxist feminists 199
masculinity 202, 204–5, 297–8, 364
'masking of aging' 229
Mason, J. 267
material conditions and intimacy 270
material culture 351
Me Too movement 387–8

Mead, G.H. 60
media
    British, immigration in (KC) 393
    newsroom metrics 28
    perception of inequalities 190
    see also social media
mediated/remediated friendship and intimacy 26, 271–2
'medical gaze' 299
medicalization 297
    and diagnosis 300–1, 302
Melucci, A. 412–13, 414, 421
mental health crisis 301–3
Meo, A.: photo-interviewing (KC) 162–3
meritocracy
    'myth' of 190
    and social mobility 57, 180
Merton, R. 56–7, 59, 63, 435
metanarratives 123–4
method and theory, links between 462–4
methodological individualism 132
methodological level of social-scientific research 125, 126
methodological pluralism 151–2
methodological transformations/shifts 29–30, 94, 95
methodology of classical sociologies 115–16, 117
Mexican-American women 221
Mexico–US border security industry 68–9
microaggressions 215–16, 321
Microsoft: Tay the Chatbot (KC) 29
Mies, M. 95
migrant: term 395–6
migration governance 404
migrations 391–2
    and colonialism 90, 92
    and crime control 67–8
    debate and definition of 393–4
    destinations 398
        rural 400
        urban 398–400
    developments in sociological study of 392
    drivers of 396
    family and intimate relationships 273–4
    global and national inequalities 98–100
    as global policy issue 404
    key concepts and approaches 400–3
    motivations 397–8
    statistics and pace of 392
    types of 394–6
Mijs, J. 190, 191
Milanovic, B. 99
military organizational processes 371
Mill, J.S. 431
Mills, C.W. 10, 14, 312–13, 452, 458
Mintz, S. 355
mixed-race couples/families 216, 255, 270–1

mixed-race/biracial individuals 315
mobile devices
    impact on daily life 153
    smartphones 165–6, 378–9
modern slavery 284
modern state, rise of 111
modernity
    classical social theory of 116
    and crime 58, 61
    family life and intimacy 268
    multiple modernities 95–7
    reflexive/'reflexive modernisation' thesis 132, 352
    and religion 329–30, 330, 333, 334
    theorists 132
    and violence 362
Modood, T. 214
money, role of 110
monopolization: state violence 366–7
Montaigne, M. de 431
monuments, removal of 320, 321
Moore, J.W. 43
'moral economy'/'moral shock' and social movements 415
moral panic 61, 84
'moral sciences' 431
Morgan, D. 254
Morning, A.: race and high school text books (KC) 381
Morocco, migration from 398
Mudabbir, S. 315, 316
multi-sensory methods 167
multiculture, urban 10
multiculural societies and religion 332–3
multimedia in visual sociology 164
multiple modernities 95–7
Musk, Elon 207
'mysticism' 327

narrative approach
    critical race theory 321–3
    feminist research 202–3
National Deviancy Conference (NDC) 60–1, 62, 63
National Health Service (NHS) 296, 462
national inequalities and global inequalities 97–100, 182
national societies 114
    and transnational/international societies 79, 86
nature and society relationship 39–42
nature vs nurture views of violence 361
Neal, S. et al. 10
negotiation in family life 253
Nelkin, D. and Lindee, M.S. 383
neoliberalism
    activity theories of aging 231
    individual responsibility and consumerism 49
    and inequality 184
Nepal: literacy rates and love 265, 273

INDEX

networks
    actor-network theory 42, 133, 382
    social movements 410–14, 421–2
'new aging populations' 233–4
'new religious movement' (NRM) 328
'new social movements' *see* social movements
Noble, S. 386
'non-religious' people (KC) 328–9
non-response bias 149
normative classical sociologies 116
norms
    age 228
    and deviance 56, 112
    gender 202, 204, 206, 207
    institutions and roles 80–2
nutritional labelling on food products (KC) 20

Oakley, A. 198, 199, 247
Office for National Statistics (ONS)
    definitions of family and household 248
    gender pay gap 201
    life expectancy differences 296
older adults
    ageism 234–5
    life stage 229–31
    as social group 231–4
        contrasting images of 232–3
        'new aging populations' 233–4
        socio-cultural changes 231
        socio-structural changes 231
Olson, M. 420, ?0
Organisation for Economic Cooperation and Development (OECD) 185
Orientalism, gendered 221
Orzech, K.M. et al.: taking and sharing digital photographs (KC) 165
Oxfam 183, 185

paradigms 132, 313
    scientific 380–1
Park, R. 58
Parks, Rosa 416
Parreñas, R.S. 274–5
Parsons, T. 84, 85, 86, 109
patriarchy 202
Pentecostalism 334
permanent migration and temporary migration 395
'personal life' vs family life/intimacy 252–3, 266
personality traits in older age 233
'personalization', algorithmic 23
Pew Research Center: projected growth in religions (KC) 332

phenomenology 432
    families and households 247, 253–5
philosophy
    metanarratives 123
    and science in classical sociologies 117–18, 431–2, 438
photo- and video-diaries 163–4
photo-interviewing (KC) 162–3
photography *see* visual sociology
Piketty, T. 183, 184
Plantin, J.C.
    and De Seta, G. 25, 27
    et al. 25
plastic waste problem (KC) 41
platform rankings and ratings 26–7, 354
platformization, impacts of 24–5
pluralism
    methodological 151–2
    social theory 136
Poland, migration from 397
policing
    and Black Lives Matter Movement (KC) 218, 365
    Los Angeles 22, 65
policy sociology 444
political metanarratives 123
'political opportunity structure' and social movements 418–19
political order: war and violence 365–7
political organizational processes in war 371
politics
    perception of inequalities 188–9, 190
    'personal is political' 199
    rise of modern state 111
    and technologies 20–1, 384–5, 387
Popper, K. 380, 381–2, 435
popular culture
    British Cultural Studies: 'style' and 'resistant' consumers 352
    hyper-real religion 337
population
    change and aging 227
    conscience collective 78, 80
    digital analytics 30
    genetic 383
populism and class inequality, USA (KC) 188–9
Portes, A. 399
positivism 115, 431
post-secularism 331, 332
'post-work' society 289
postcolonial societies 219
postcolonial theories 133
postmodern social theories 132–3
postmodern types: tourists and vagabonds 67
postmodern urbanism 66

poststructuralism 63, 228
poverty
    in consumer society 350
    environmental risks and hazards 44–7
power relations
    biomedical knowledge and 299–300
    classical and contemporary social theory 130
    digital technologies and 20–1
    global 185–91
    race and racialization 218–20
    stratification and 85–6
    theorists 133
pragmatism 132, 135
precariat 288
precarious work 287–8
primary sources 128
private and public spheres 199, 330–3
producer and consumers, blurred distinction between 352–4
professional sociology 444–5
promotion and sales workers 286–7
prosumers 353, 354
Protestantism
    and capitalism 110, 116, 329–30, 335, 431
    Pentecostalism 334
protests see social movements
'pseudo-sciences' 380
'public goods', free-rider problem and social movements 420–1
public issues 452
public and private spheres 199, 330–3
public sociology 443–4, 453
    Burawoy vision of 444–6
        criticisms of 446–8
    social theory as public endeavour 134–5
    voices and audiences 448–52
Puerto Rico and Germany, comparison 93
pure relationship 265, 270

qualitative research 147–8, 149–50, 152
    evidence of gender inequalities 202–3
    see also visual sociology
quantitative research 146–7, 149, 152
    evidence of gender inequalities 201–2
queer families 249

race/ethnicity and racism 212–14
    biosociality 383
    crime and policing 62
    digital technology/algorithms 29, 31, 386
    education
        high school text books (KC) 381
        higher 13–14, 318–22, 448–9
    environmental justice movement, US 44

health inequalities 298
    COVID-19 pandemic 461–2
    diagnosis of mental disorders 301, 302
identity 215–18
    racialization and power 218–20
migration 402–3
populism, US (KC) 188–9
public sociology 448–9
terminology 213
theorists 133
see also colonialism; colourism; intersectionality
Rana Plaza fire, Bangladesh (KC) 285–6
Randeria, S. 96–7
Ratelband, E.: age discrimination (KC) 234–5
rational choice theories 132
    gendered division of labour 256
    social movements 420–1
    violence 369
realism 433–4, 440
    nature and society relationship 39–40
'reconstructive sciences' 433
reference group comparisons 189–90
reflexive modernity/'reflexive modernisation' thesis 132, 352
reflexivity 459
    auto-ethnography 203
    in digital society 32
    epistemological 128
refugees/asylum seekers 67–8, 394, 404
    Bosnian, Australia 221
    child (KC) 394–5
    European migration crisis 403
relational perspective on global inequality 97–100
reliability/external validity of research
    qualitative research 147–8, 149–50
    quantitative research 146–7
religion 325–9
    European civilization 96
    global religions and globalization of 333–4
    lived religion and popular culture 335–7
    Protestantism 110, 116
    secularization thesis and persistence of 330–1
    Western sociology of 329–30
religious metanarratives 123
reputation: platform rankings and ratings 26–7
research methods 10–11, 143–5
    mobile devices, impact of 153
    principles of research design 145–51
    women's time (case study of methodological pluralism) 151–2
research problem 146
resistance
    consumers 352
    to technical scripts 387–8

resource mobilization and social movements 417–18
rich/super-rich 43–4, 69, 182, 183–4, 185–6
Riley, M.W. et al. 227
Ritzer, G. 353
  and Jurgenson, 353, 354
Robinson, J. and Godbey, G. 146, 147, 149, 151, 152
roles 81–2
  institutions and collectives 85
  institutions and norms 80–2
  vs rationalities in family and household behaviour 255–8
romantic love 269
Rousmaniere, K. 160
Rousseau, J.-J. 361

Said, E. 321
sales assistants 286–7
same-sex relationships/marriage 250, 251–2, 256
sampling
  and external validity 149–50
  and representativeness 149
Sandercock, L. 399
Sassatelli, R. 349, 352
saturation: qualitative research 150
Savage, M. 181, 182
  and Burrows, R. 29–30
Sayer, A. 43–4
Schnaiberg, A. 43
school photographs 159–60
Schor, J. 146, 151
science
  applied, technology as 383–4
  benefits of 112
  sociology as 429–30, 438–40
    classical sociologies 112, 117–18, 431–2, 438
    knowledge 430–2, 437–8
    models/approaches 432–5
    organization/structure 435–8
  structure of 380–1
science and technology studies (STS) 378–9, 381–2
  scientific truths and scientific facts 379–83
  technologies with effects and with politics 383–8, 387
  theorists 133
scientific facts, construction of 381–2
scientific knowledge
  biomedical knowledge and power relations 299–301
  social implications of 382–3
  vs 'ordinary knowledge' 126–7
Scotland, migration to 397, 400
Scott, S. 301
scripts, technical 387–8
Scriver, S. et al. 364
secondary data analysis 145
secondary sources 128

sects 327
secularization thesis 330–1
Seidman, S. 134–5, 136–7
Semenya, Caster 205
sex and gender 199–201
Shanbhag, Dr R. 216–17
Sharma, S.
  and Brooker, P. 31
  Tay the Chatbox (KC) 29
shops and shopping 348–9
Simmel, G. 346–7, 438
Sivanandan, A. 90, 220
skill, concept of 285
skin colour see colourism
slavery 8–9, 93, 94, 218–19
  modern 284
Smart, C. 62, 252–3
smartphones 165–6, 378–9
Smelser, N. 416
Smith, L.T. 448, 449
social and biological meanings of taste 354–7
social capital 181, 420–1, 422
social cohesion 25–6, 63, 185
social constructionism/social and cultural construction
  age 228–9
  gender 199–200
  health 299–301
    mental 302–3
  nature and society 40–2
  race and racism 217, 221
  religion 335–6
  technology 385
social differentiation 110, 112–13
social disorganization 58, 59, 63
social facts 39, 78, 79, 80, 115, 432
social gerontology 229–30
social housing 65, 66
social institutions see institutions; entries beginning institutional
social media 28, 304, 354, 385
  China 25, 388
    migrant workers and personal connections (KC) 272
  #MeToo movement 387
  mediated friendship and intimacy 26, 271, 272
  producers and consumers dialogue 354
  racism 29, 31
social mobility 57, 92, 180, 185
social movements (SMOs) 409–10
  definitions and concept of 410–14
  formation and mobilization 414
    networks 410–14, 421–2
    reason, emotion and identity 420–2
    strain and other factors 415–20

social policy 439
social practices 10–11
　classical sociologies 131–2
　and environment 43, 50
　post-structural perspectives 228
　and technology 29
Social Science Research Council (SSRC) 439
social shaping of technology 27–8
social structure/system
　and change 84
　and crime 56–7, 58
　and culture 80
　elements of 85
　and embodiment 82–3
　and environment 42
　and functions 83
　and individuals 78, 79
　integration 84–5
　norms, institutions, and roles 80–2
　organizational process of war 371
　stratification and power 85–6
social violence and violent conflict 369–70
socialism
　and critical pedagogy 316
　see also Left
socialization 82
sociation 114–15
society, study of 76–8
socio-conscious endeavour of social theory 136
socio-cultural approach to crime 55
socio-legal concept of crime 55
sociological imagination 10, 64, 458
sociology
　critical self-reflection 13–14
　definitions of 7, 9
　different scales 11–13
　divergent views and perspectives 9–11
　history and practice of 7–9
　as study of society 76–8
　using and uses of 457–66
South Asia see Bangladesh; India; Nepal
South–South migrations 403
specialization of economic functions 110, 113
Spencer, H. 83
sport, sex/gender classification in 204–6
Stafford, R. and Jones, P.J.: plastic waste problem (KC) 41
Standing, G. 288
Star, S.L. 28–9
　nutritional labelling on food products (KC) 20
state
　and public sociology 447
　rise of modern 111
　to world-economy perspective 92, 94, 95

state violence 366–7
state-building and war-making 371–2
statistical inferences 149
status anxiety 189
Stella, F.: motivations to migrate (sexual identity and legal status) (KC) 397
stigma/stigmatization 60, 300
storytelling see narrative approach
strain
　'general strain theory' 57, 63
　model of social movements 415–20
stratification and power 85–6
structural functionalism 313
'structural violence' 363, 368
structuralism, types of 132
structure and agency 79, 267–8, 296–7, 396
subcultural theory (KC) 59
submerged networks, social movements as 412–13, 414
subsystems 85–6
suicide (KC) 56
supermarkets (KC) 452
surveillance technologies 22, 63, 65
　Ghostery 32
　workers and customers 286
surveys 146–7
Susen, S. 122–4
sustainability and social change 47–50
Sutherland, E. 58, 59
sweatshops 284–5
symbolic capital 181
symbolic interactionism 60, 313, 314
symbolic resource vs trap, consumerism as 349–54
'symbolic violence' 367–8
system theory 84–5, 132
Sztompka, P. 10

Taoism, China 336
taste, cultures and consumption 354–7
Taussig, M. 367
taxation 183, 184
Tay the Chatbot (KC) 29
Taylor, C. 332
technical scripts, resistance to 387–8
technological determinism 28, 289, 384
'technology in use' studies 27–8
technology/ies
　as applied science 383–4
　automation of work 289
　garment industry 285, 286
　with effects 384
　older adults 232
　and politics 20–1, 384–5, 387
　see also digital society

INDEX

terminological level of social-scientific research 125, 126
testosterone 204, 205
Thatcher, M. 76, 439, 440
theoretical level social-scientific research 125, 126
theory and method, links between 462–4
Therborn, G. 97, 178
third age 233
Thomas, D. and Thomas, T. 28
Thompson, E.P. 415
Thrasher, F. 58
Tilly, C. 269, 413–14
time dimensions of work and leisure 145–52
Tinkler, P. 161, 165
Tittle, C. 447
transnational migration *see* migrations
transnational societies 79
transnationalism 400–1
transparency in research design 148, 149
triggers of social movements 416, 419
Troeltsch, E. 327–8
Trump, D. 188–9, 220
Twamley, K.: gender equality and 'cold' intimacy (KC) 266, 267–8, 270
Twitter 28, 29, 31, 387
Tyler, I. and Gill, R. 271

Uber 24
UK Government
  benefits policy 257
  Environmental Audit Committee (KC) 46–7
United Nations (UN)
  definition of aging societies 227
  Framework Convention on Climate Change (FCCC) 47–8
  measuring gender inequalities 201, 202
universalistic concept of humanity 116
universality vs spatiotemporal specificities of social theory 135
universities 112, 436–7
  and broader society, bridging 449–52
  race and racism 13–14, 318–22, 448–9
urban ecology 58
urban migration 398–400
urban multiculture 10
Urry, J. 69
  Keat, R. and 433
US
  black civil rights movement 63, 415, 416, 421
  class inequality and populism (KC) 188–9
  Los Angeles, crime and policing in 22, 65
  Mexican-American women 221
US–Mexico border security industry 68–9
utopian conflict approach to crime 55

validity of research 128
  and reliability
    qualitative research 147–8, 149–50
    quantitative research 146–7
Van Dijck, J. 25
  et al. 24, 354
Van Hear, N. et al. 396
Vasquez, J.M. 221, 369, 370
Vergragt, P.J. 50
video- and photo-diaries 163–4
video-sharing 164, 354
violence and war 360–3
  broad vs narrow definitions 363–5
  general and sociological debates 361–3
  organization processes 370–2
  and political order 365–7
  social violence and violent conflict 369–70
  'symbolic violence' 367–8
  see also refugees/asylum seekers
visual sociology 157–8
  digital visual methods 164–9
  methodological considerations 158
  visual methods 159–64
voluntary migration and forced migration 394
von Werlhof, C. et al. 95

Wacquant, L. 65
wages across the world (KC) 99
Wallerstein, I. 93–4
Wang, X.: social media and personal connections (KC) 272
war *see* violence and war
Warde, 352
'Web.2' *see* social media
Weber, M. 77, 79, 109
  capitalism and Protestantism 110, 116, 329–30, 335, 431–2
  class and status relations 86, 178–9
  methodology 115
  social theory 131, 132
  sociology as science 112, 431–2, 433–4, 440
  violence and war 366, 372
WeChat, China 25
West Indians *see* British Caribbean/West Indian population
'white collar crime' 58
whiteness 219
  'normative whiteness' 220
Whitley, R. 436, 437
'wicked problems' 11
Wilkinson, R. and Pickett, K. 184–5
Williams, Serena (KC) 206
Wilson, S. 167

Winner, L. 384–5
women
  black 249, 251
  and environment 45
  magazines 271–2
  migrants 100, 274, 401
  older 232
  and work
    domestic labour and care roles 151–2, 199, 255–8, 282–3
    garment factories/sweatshops 285
  see also feminism/feminist theory; gender
Wonga 21
Woolgar, S. 437, 438
  Latour, B. and 382
work/employment 280–1
  and class 182, 280–1, 296
  definitions and types of 281–2
  environmental crisis and future of 290
  flexible and precarious 287–8
  global value chain analysis 283–7
  paid and unpaid
    older adults 232
    see also women, and work
  technology and future of 289
working-class family life, post-war shift (KC) 247
working-class identity 181–2
working-class populism (KC) 188–9
world economy 92–4
world-systems perspective 93, 94
world/global religions 333–4, 431–2

xeno-racism 220

Yearley, S. 41
Young, I.M. 200
Young, J. 61, 84
Young, M. and Willmott, P.: post-war family studies (KC) 247

Zald, M. and McCarthy, J. 418
zero hours contracts 287